CONNECTED MATHEMATICS®3

CMP3

grade 7

Glenda Lappan, Elizabeth Difanis Phillips,
James T. Fey, Susan N. Friel

PEARSON

Boston, Massachusetts • Chandler, Arizona • Glenview, Illinois • Upper Saddle River, New Jersey

Connected Mathematics® was developed at Michigan State University with financial support from the Michigan State University Office of the Provost, Computing and Technology, and the College of Natural Science.

 This material is based upon work supported by the National Science Foundation under Grant No. MDR 9150217 and Grant No. ESI 9986372. Opinions expressed are those of the authors and not necessarily those of the Foundation.

As with prior editions of this work, the authors and administration of Michigan State University preserve a tradition of devoting royalties from this publication to support activities sponsored by the MSU Mathematics Education Enrichment Fund.

PEARSON

Authors

A Team of Experts

Glenda Lappan is a University Distinguished Professor in the Program in Mathematics Education (PRIME) and the Department of Mathematics at Michigan State University. Her research and development interests are in the connected areas of students' learning of mathematics and mathematics teachers' professional growth and change related to the development and enactment of K–12 curriculum materials.

Elizabeth Difanis Phillips is a Senior Academic Specialist in the Program in Mathematics Education (PRIME) and the Department of Mathematics at Michigan State University. She is interested in teaching and learning mathematics for both teachers and students. These interests have led to curriculum and professional development projects at the middle school and high school levels, as well as projects related to the teaching and learning of algebra across the grades.

James T. Fey is a Professor Emeritus at the University of Maryland. His consistent professional interest has been development and research focused on curriculum materials that engage middle and high school students in problem-based collaborative investigations of mathematical ideas and their applications.

Susan N. Friel is a Professor of Mathematics Education in the School of Education at the University of North Carolina at Chapel Hill. Her research interests focus on statistics education for middle-grade students and, more broadly, on teachers' professional development and growth in teaching mathematics K–8.

With... Yvonne Grant and Jacqueline Stewart

Yvonne Grant teaches mathematics at Portland Middle School in Portland, Michigan. Jacqueline Stewart is a recently retired high school teacher of mathematics at Okemos High School in Okemos, Michigan. Both Yvonne and Jacqueline have worked on a variety of activities related to the development, implementation, and professional development of the CMP curriculum since its beginning in 1991.

Development Team

CMP3 Authors

Glenda Lappan, University Distinguished Professor, Michigan State University

Elizabeth Difanis Phillips, Senior Academic Specialist, Michigan State University

James T. Fey, Professor Emeritus, University of Maryland

Susan N. Friel, Professor, University of North Carolina – Chapel Hill

With...

Yvonne Grant, Portland Middle School, Michigan

Jacqueline Stewart, Mathematics Consultant, Mason, Michigan

In Memory of... William M. Fitzgerald, Professor (Deceased), Michigan State University, who made substantial contributions to conceptualizing and creating CMP1.

Administrative Assistant

Michigan State University
Judith Martus Miller

Support Staff

Michigan State University
Undergraduate Assistants:
Bradley Robert Corlett, Carly Fleming,
Erin Lucian, Scooter Nowak

Development Assistants

Michigan State University
Graduate Research Assistants:
Richard "Abe" Edwards, Nic Gilbertson,
Funda Gonulates, Aladar Horvath,
Eun Mi Kim, Kevin Lawrence, Jennifer
Nimtz, Joanne Philhower, Sasha Wang

Assessment Team

Maine
Falmouth Public Schools
Falmouth Middle School: Shawn Towle

Michigan
Ann Arbor Public Schools
Tappan Middle School
Anne Marie Nicoll-Turner

Portland Public Schools
Portland Middle School
Holly DeRosia, Yvonne Grant

Traverse City Area Public Schools
Traverse City East Middle School
Jane Porath, Mary Beth Schmitt

Traverse City West Middle School
Jennifer Rundio, Karrie Tufts

Ohio
Clark-Shawnee Local Schools
Rockway Middle School: Jim Mamer

Content Consultants

Michigan State University
Peter Lappan, Professor Emeritus,
Department of Mathematics

Normandale Community College
Christopher Danielson, Instructor,
Department of Mathematics & Statistics

University of North Carolina – Wilmington
Dargan Frierson, Jr., Professor, Department
of Mathematics & Statistics

Student Activities
Michigan State University
Brin Keller, Associate Professor,
Department of Mathematics

Consultants

Indiana
Purdue University
Mary Bouck, Mathematics Consultant

Michigan
Oakland Schools
Valerie Mills, Mathematics Education Supervisor
Mathematics Education Consultants:
Geraldine Devine, Dana Gosen

Ellen Bacon, Independent Mathematics Consultant

New York
University of Rochester
Jeffrey Choppin, Associate Professor

Ohio
University of Toledo
Debra Johanning, Associate Professor

Pennsylvania
University of Pittsburgh
Margaret Smith, Professor

Texas
University of Texas at Austin
Emma Trevino, Supervisor of Mathematics Programs, The Dana Center

Mathematics for All Consulting
Carmen Whitman, Mathematics Consultant

. . . .

Reviewers

Michigan
Ionia Public Schools
Kathy Dole, Director of Curriculum and Instruction

Grand Valley State University
Lisa Kasmer, Assistant Professor

Portland Public Schools
Teri Keusch, Classroom Teacher

Minnesota
Hopkins School District 270
Michele Luke, Mathematics Coordinator

. . . .

Field Test Sites for CMP3

Michigan
Ann Arbor Public Schools
Tappan Middle School
Anne Marie Nicoll-Turner*

Portland Public Schools
Portland Middle School: Mark Braun, Angela Buckland, Holly DeRosia, Holly Feldpausch, Angela Foote, Yvonne Grant*, Kristin Roberts, Angie Stump, Tammi Wardwell

Traverse City Area Public Schools
Traverse City East Middle School
Ivanka Baic Berkshire, Brenda Dunscombe, Tracie Herzberg, Deb Larimer, Jan Palkowski, Rebecca Perreault, Jane Porath*, Robert Sagan, Mary Beth Schmitt*

Traverse City West Middle School
Pamela Alfieri, Jennifer Rundio, Maria Taplin, Karrie Tufts*

Maine
Falmouth Public Schools
Falmouth Middle School: Sally Bennett, Chris Driscoll, Sara Jones, Shawn Towle*

Minnesota
Minneapolis Public Schools
Jefferson Community School
Leif Carlson*,
Katrina Hayek Munsisoumang*

Ohio
Clark-Shawnee Local Schools
Reid School: Joanne Gilley
Rockway Middle School: Jim Mamer*
Possum School: Tami Thomas

*Indicates a Field Test Site Coordinator

CONNECTED MATHEMATICS 3

Shapes and Designs

Two-Dimensional Geometry

Lappan, Phillips, Fey, Friel

Two-Dimensional Geometry

Looking Ahead

How can mathematics be used to measure the difficulty of spins and flips by snow boarders and skate boarders?

What properties of a regular hexagon make it the shape of choice for the cells of a honeycomb?

Why are braces on towers, roofs, and bridges in the shapes of triangles and not rectangles or pentagons?

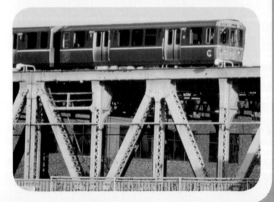

Objects in nature and designs are outlined and covered by an endless variety of geometric shapes. But some shapes have properties that make them especially important in science, engineering, construction, crafts, and arts. In your work on the Investigations of this Unit you will discover the special importance of *polygons*. Polygons are planar geometric shapes formed by linking points called *vertices* with line segments called *sides*.

Many of the Problems will focus on triangles and quadrilaterals. You will build models and use rulers and protractors to draw shapes meeting given conditions. These construction and drawing experiments will show why triangles are frequently used in engineering and construction.

You will also examine patterns in the measures of interior and exterior angles in regular and irregular polygons. You will develop formulas to find those angle measures without actually measuring. While working with interior and exterior angles of polygons, you will use facts about supplementary, adjacent, and vertical angles to find angle measures.

Mathematical Highlights

Shapes and Designs

The Problems of this Unit explore properties of polygons. Through work on tasks that require drawing, building, measuring, and reasoning about the size and shape of polygons, you will learn:

- How to sort polygons into classes according to the number, size, and relationships of their sides and angles

- How to find angle measures by estimation, by use of tools like protractors and angle rulers, and by reasoning with variables and equations

- Formulas for finding the sum of the interior and exterior angles in any polygon

- The relationships of complementary and supplementary pairs of angles, such as those formed by interior and exterior angles of polygons, and in figures where parallel lines are cut by transversals

- How to apply and design angle-side measurement conditions needed for drawing triangles and quadrilaterals with specific properties

- The symmetry, tiling, and rigidity or flexibility properties of polygons that make them useful in buildings, tools, art and craft designs, and natural objects

As you work on the Problems in this Unit, ask yourself these questions about situations that involve shapes.

What do these polygons have in common? **How** do they differ from each other?

When should I use estimation, freehand drawing, or special tools to measure and construct angles and polygons?

How do the side lengths and angles of polygons determine their shapes?

Why do certain polygons appear so often in buildings, artistic designs, and natural objects?

How can I give directions for constructing polygons that meet conditions of any given problem?

Mathematical Practices and Habits of Mind

In the *Connected Mathematics* curriculum you will develop an understanding of important mathematical ideas by solving problems and reflecting on the mathematics involved. Every day, you will use "habits of mind" to make sense of problems and apply what you learn to new situations. Some of these habits are described by the *Common Core State Standards for Mathematical Practices* (MP).

MP1 **Make sense of problems and persevere in solving them.**

When using mathematics to solve a problem, it helps to think carefully about

- data and other facts you are given and what additional information you need to solve the problem;
- strategies you have used to solve similar problems and whether you could solve a related simpler problem first;
- how you could express the problem with equations, diagrams, or graphs;
- whether your answer makes sense.

MP2 **Reason abstractly and quantitatively.**

When you are asked to solve a problem, it often helps to

- focus first on the key mathematical ideas;
- check that your answer makes sense in the problem setting;
- use what you know about the problem setting to guide your mathematical reasoning.

MP3 **Construct viable arguments and critique the reasoning of others.**

When you are asked to explain why a conjecture is correct, you can

- show some examples that fit the claim and explain why they fit;
- show how a new result follows logically from known facts and principles.

When you believe a mathematical claim is incorrect, you can

- show one or more counterexamples—cases that don't fit the claim;
- find steps in the argument that do not follow logically from prior claims.

MP4 Model with mathematics.

When you are asked to solve problems, it often helps to

- think carefully about the numbers or geometric shapes that are the most important factors in the problem, then ask yourself how those factors are related to each other;
- express data and relationships in the problem with tables, graphs, diagrams, or equations, and check your result to see if it makes sense.

MP5 Use appropriate tools strategically.

When working on mathematical questions, you should always

- decide which tools are most helpful for solving the problem and why;
- try a different tool when you get stuck.

MP6 Attend to precision.

In every mathematical exploration or problem-solving task, it is important to

- think carefully about the required accuracy of results; is a number estimate or geometric sketch good enough, or is a precise value or drawing needed?
- report your discoveries with clear and correct mathematical language that can be understood by those to whom you are speaking or writing.

MP7 Look for and make use of structure.

In mathematical explorations and problem solving, it is often helpful to

- look for patterns that show how data points, numbers, or geometric shapes are related to each other;
- use patterns to make predictions.

MP8 Look for and express regularity in repeated reasoning.

When results of a repeated calculation show a pattern, it helps to

- express that pattern as a general rule that can be used in similar cases;
- look for shortcuts that will make the calculation simpler in other cases.

You will use all of the Mathematical Practices in this Unit. Sometimes, when you look at a Problem, it is obvious which practice is most helpful. At other times, you will decide on a practice to use during class explorations and discussions. After completing each Problem, ask yourself:

- What mathematics have I learned by solving this Problem?
- What Mathematical Practices were helpful in learning this mathematics?

Unit Project

What I Know About Shapes and Designs

As you work in this Unit, you will be asked to think about the characteristics of different shapes. You will determine how unusual a shape can be and still be a triangle, quadrilateral, pentagon, or hexagon. You will also be asked to think about the relationships among these shapes. It is these characteristics of shapes and the relationships among them that affect the designs you see in your world.

One of the ways you will be asked to demonstrate your understanding of the mathematics in the Unit is through a final project. At the end of the Unit, you will use what you have learned to create a project. Your project can be a story, a book, a poster, a report, a mobile, a movie, or a slide show.

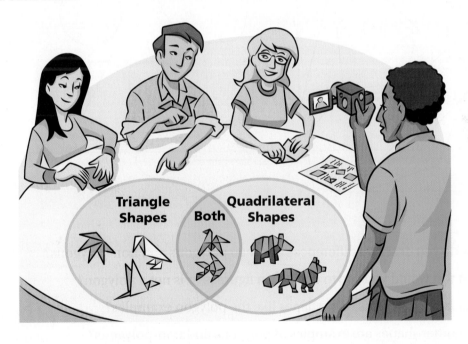

The Family of Polygons

This Unit is about the properties and uses of geometric figures called *polygons*. Some shapes below are polygons and some are not.

Polygons

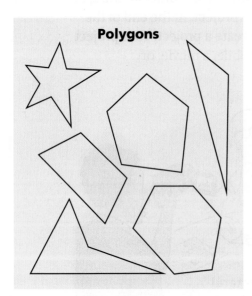

Not Polygons

- How do you describe differences between polygons and non-polygons?

- What test would you use to decide if a figure is or is not a polygon?

- What familiar objects have shapes like the polygon examples?

- What other shapes are examples of polygons and non-polygons?

Common Core State Standards

7.G.A.2 Draw (freehand, with ruler and protractor, and with technology) geometric shapes with given conditions . . .

1.1 Sorting and Sketching Polygons

Polygons come in many shapes and sizes. The set of 22 shapes shown here is only a sample of the infinite variety of polygons. Polygons are used in practical, artistic, and scientific shapes and designs.

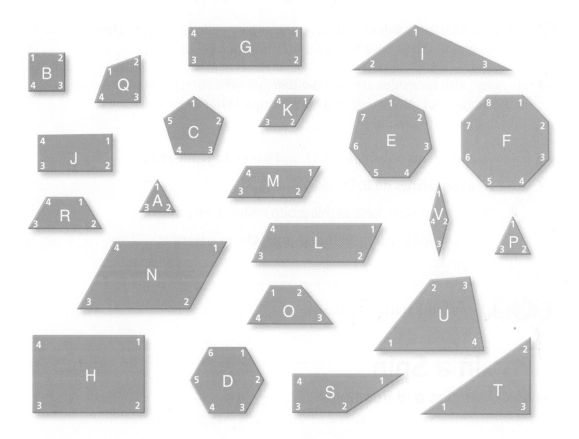

Mathematicians classify and name groups of polygons with similar properties.

Problem 1.1

(A) Sort the polygons in the Shapes Set into groups that have one or more properties in common.

    1. Describe the properties shared by the members of each group.

    2. Sketch another shape that belongs in each group.

(B) Polygons with three sides (and three angles) are called *triangles*. How are the triangles in the Shapes Set different from each other?

(C) Polygons with four sides are called *quadrilaterals*. Sort the quadrilaterals in the Shapes Set into two or more subgroups. What properties do the subgroup members share?

(D) A group of students put shapes R, O, and S into the same group.

    1. What properties do R, O, and S share?

    2. Would shape Q belong in this group? Why or why not?

    3. Would shape L belong in this group? Why or why not?

A C E Homework starts on page 24.

1.2 In a Spin
Angles and Rotations

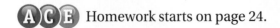

The shape of any polygon depends on the number and length of its sides. The shape also depends on the angles at which those sides meet. Here are two quadrilaterals with identical side lengths, but different shapes.

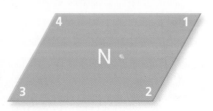

The term *polygon* is a Greek word that means "many angles." You will look at how the side lengths and angles affect the shape of a polygon. To begin, you will explore angles.

The *X-Games* are popular summer and winter sports events. Contestants perform spectacular jumps, flips, and spins on skateboards, snowboards, motorcycles, bicycles, and even snowmobiles. Judges, competitors, and fans describe the challenge of a flip or spin with numbers like 180, 360, 540, 720, 900, or 1080.

Snowboard Rotation

Measuring flips and spins involves thinking about an angle as a change in direction called a *rotation*. In mathematics, you measure an angle or a rotation with a unit called the **degree.** Rotation angles are measured from 0 degrees to 360 degrees or more to indicate turns from a small amount to one full turn (and more).

You measure rotation angles in a counterclockwise direction. A rotation angle has an *initial* and a *terminal side*. The initial side is the ray showing the starting direction while the terminal side is the ray showing the ending direction after the rotation.

A one-quarter rotation is 90°. A **right angle** measures 90°. Right angles are commonly marked with a small square. Suppose you draw a ray to divide a right angle into two angles of equal measure. Each angle would be a 45° acute angle.

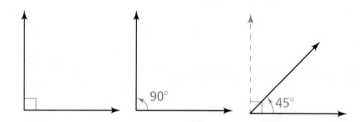

Suppose you draw 89 rays to divide a right angle into 90 angles of equal measure. Each angle would have a measure of 1°.

A rotation of one-half turn defines a *straight angle*. It measures 180°.

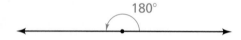

Recall that angles whose measures are less than 90° are called *acute angles*. Angles whose measures are between 90° and 180° are called *obtuse angles*.

- Can you jump and turn through angles of 90°, 180°, 270°, or even 360°?

Did You Know?

The ancient Babylonians measured angles in degrees. They set the measure of an angle that goes all the way around a point to 360°. They may have chosen 360° because their number system was based on the number 60. They may have also considered the fact that the number 360 has many factors. This makes it easy to measure many fractions of full turns.

Estimating and measuring rotation angles is easier if you know some *benchmark angles*. Playing the Four in a Row game will help you build your angle sense. The Four in a Row game is played on the circular grids shown below.

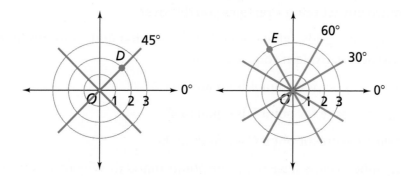

The grid on the left has lines at 45° intervals. The grid on the right has lines at 30° intervals. The circles are numbered 1, 2, and 3 as you move out from the center at 0. Point *D* has coordinates (2, 45°).

- What are the coordinates for the location of point *E*?

Four in a Row

Directions

Choose one of the circular grids. The grids have either 30° or 45° intervals.

- Player A chooses a point where a circle and grid line meet. Then Player A says the coordinates of the point.

- Player B checks that the coordinates Player A gave are correct. If they are, Player A marks the point with an X. If they are not, Player A does not mark the point.

- Player B chooses a point and says its coordinates. If the coordinates are correct, Player B marks the point with an O.

- Players continue to take turns, saying the coordinates of points and marking the points.

- The first player to get four marks in a row, either along a grid line or around a circle, wins the game.

Problem 1.2

A Play Four in a Row several times. Play games with the 30° grid and the 45° grid. Write down any winning strategies you discover.

On one of the circular grids, label points A, B, and C that fit the descriptions in parts (1)–(3) below. Explain your reasoning.

1. The angle measure for point A is greater than 120°.

2. The angle measure for point B is equal to 0°.

3. The angle measure for point C is less than 90°.

4. Will everyone in class have the same points marked? Why or why not?

B In the Four in a Row game, the circular grids have horizontal and vertical axes. They divide the playing area into four sectors called *quadrants*.

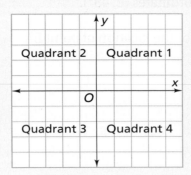

What can you say about measures of rotation angles with the first side on the positive *x*-axis (to the right) and second side in each quadrant below?

1. Quadrant 1

2. Quadrant 2

3. Quadrant 3

4. Quadrant 4

ACE Homework starts on page 24.

Did You Know?

The circular grids used to play Four in a Row are examples of polar coordinate systems. Sir Isaac Newton used polar coordinates in his contributions to mathematics and science.

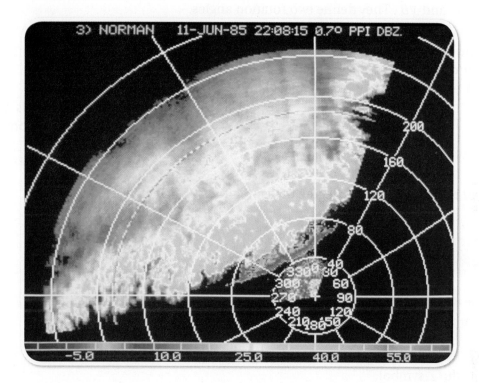

Polar coordinates are commonly used to locate ships at sea, planes in the air, or rain and snowstorms. An object appearing on a radar screen is a moving point or region. It has direction (in degrees) and distance from the radar site.

1.3 Estimating Measures of Rotations and Angles

The next sketch shows two rays with a common endpoint. The rays are named $\vec{VA}$ and $\vec{VB}$. They define two rotation angles.

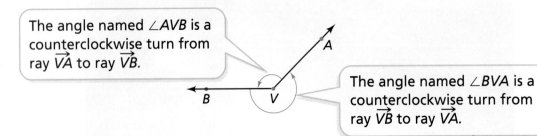

The angle named ∠AVB is a counterclockwise turn from ray $\vec{VA}$ to ray $\vec{VB}$.

The angle named ∠BVA is a counterclockwise turn from ray $\vec{VB}$ to ray $\vec{VA}$.

- What is the approximate degree measure of ∠AVB? Of ∠BVA?

Problem 1.3

Use what you know about measurement and naming of rotation angles to complete the Problem.

A Estimate the measure of each angle in degrees. Name each angle with the ∠ symbol.

1.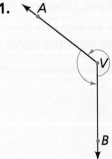

2.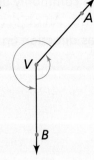

3.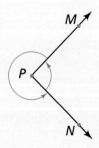

4.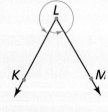

Problem 1.3 *continued*

B Sketch a rotation angle with approximately the given measure.

1. 220°

2. 270°

3. 150°

4. 300°

C Sketch each angle described. Find its measure in degrees.

1. one third of a right angle

2. one and a half times a right angle

3. three times a right angle

4. three and a half times a right angle

5. two thirds of a straight angle

6. one and two thirds times a right angle

7. one and a sixth times a straight angle

8. twice a straight angle

D For each rotation described, find its measure in degrees.

1. 1.5 turns

2. 2 turns

3. 1.25 turns

A C E Homework starts on page 24.

Did You Know?

Honeybees live in colonies. Each colony has a single queen and thousands of worker bees. The worker bees find flowers to get nectar. The nectar is used to make honey. Worker bees build the honeycomb and keep the beehive clean. They feed and groom the queen bee and take care of the young. They also guard the hive against intruders.

Scientific observation has shown that honeybees give each other directions to flowers by performing a lively dance!

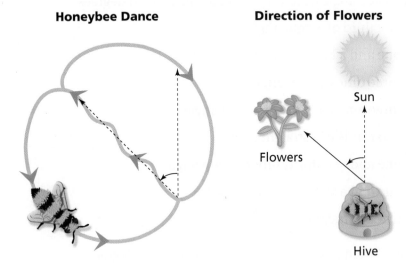

The messenger bee in the center shows the other bees the direction and distance from the hive to nectar. The bee does a dance called the figure-eight waggle. Worker bees watching the dance learn where to find nectar to make honey.

The dancing bee communicates the direction and distance to fly from the hive. The bee makes two semi-circles. He waggles along the straight run, the path through the center of his dance.

The angle in the dance made between the straight run and the direction of gravity is the direction. This is because the beehive is oriented vertically, not horizontally. The length of the straight run is proportional to the distance.

1.4 Measuring Angles

One common tool to use for measuring angles is the *angle ruler*. An angle ruler has two arms linked by a rivet. The rivet allows the arms to spread apart to form angles of various sizes. One arm is marked with a circular ruler showing degree measures from 0° to 360°.

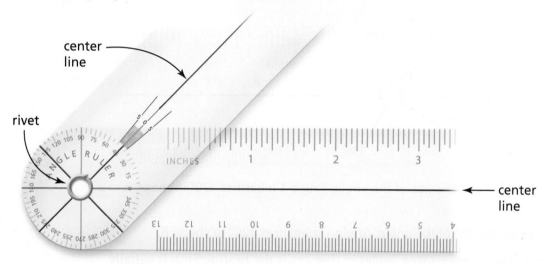

To measure an angle with an angle ruler:

- First place the rivet over the vertex.

- Set the *center line* of the arm marked as a ruler on the first side of the angle.

- Swing the other arm counterclockwise until its center line lies on the second side of the angle.

- Read the angle measure on the circular ruler.

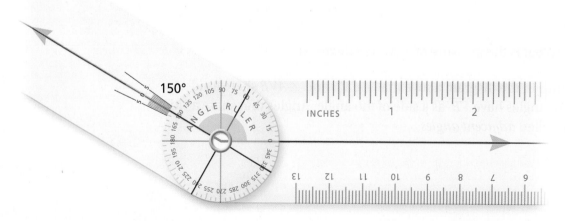

When you use an angle ruler to measure a polygon in the Shapes Set or another object, place the object between the two arms of the angle ruler.

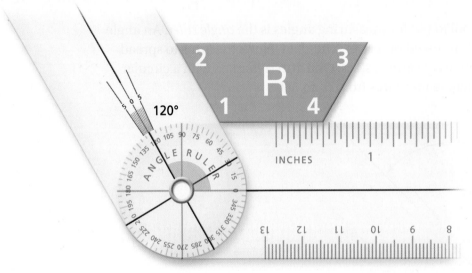

Read the size of the angle, Angle 1 measures 120° in shape R.

Then, read the size of the angle. Angle 1 measures 120° in shape R.

Another tool for measuring angles in degrees is the *protractor*. It is usually semi-circular and has a scale in degrees. The protractor below shows how to measure ∠AVB.

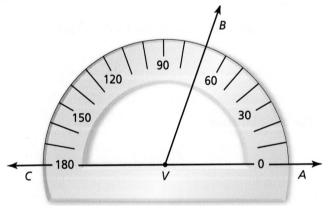

- What is the measure of ∠AVB in degrees?

Notice in the diagram above that ∠CVB and ∠AVB share a side. Both angles have $\overrightarrow{VB}$ as a side of the angle. Angles that share a side are called *adjacent angles*.

Problem 1.4

A For each polygon shape shown below, *estimate* the measure of each angle. Sketch each figure and label the angles with your estimates.

B **1.** Use an angle ruler to *measure* each of the angles from Question A.

2. Compare your estimates from Question A with your measurements. If your estimate and measurement differ by more than 10°, measure that angle again and check your work.

C Find measures of the angles shown in the diagram.

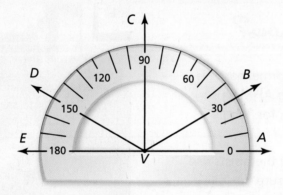

1. ∠AVB	**2.** ∠AVC	**3.** ∠AVD
4. ∠BVC	**5.** ∠BVD	**6.** ∠CVD

D If the measures of two angles add to 90°, they are called **complementary angles.** If the measures of two angles add to 180°, they are called **supplementary angles.**

1. Name the pairs of complementary angles in the diagram of Question C.

2. Name the pairs of supplementary angles in the diagram of Question C.

continued on the next page >

Problem 1.4 continued

E Find the measures of the angles. Use an angle ruler or a protractor.

1.

2.

3.

4.

A C E Homework starts on page 24.

Did You Know?

The **angle ruler's** formal name is *goniometer* (goh nee AHM uh tur). Goniometer is Greek for "angle measurer."

Doctors and physical therapists use goniometers to measure flexibility (range of motion) in knees, elbows, fingers, and other joints.

1.5 Design Challenge I
Drawing with Tools—Ruler and Protractor

Some problems challenge you to use tools to draw figures that are only described in words. For those problems, you can use line and angle rulers or protractors to accurately draw side lengths and angle measures.

Problem 1.5

A Draw an angle for each measure.

1. 25°

2. 175°

3. 200°

4. On the drawing for part (1), show a complement and a supplement of the angle.

B The symbol △ABC names a triangle with vertices A, B, and C. Draw each of the polygons, if possible.

1. △ABC with $\overline{AB}$ = 1 in., $\overline{BC}$ = 1.5 in., and ∠CBA = 35°

2. a rectangle with base 2 in. and height 1 in.

3. a triangle with angles 45° and 60° and one side of length 2 in.

4. a parallelogram with two sides of length 2 in., two sides of length 1 in., and angles of 60° and 120°

5. △KLM with side KL = 1 in., side LM = 1.5 in., ∠KLM = 135°, and side KM = 1 in.

6. a triangle with all sides of length 1.5 in. and all angles of 60°

C For each part below, and any polygon you choose, write one set of directions that are:

1. satisfied by only one unique shape.

2. satisfied by two or more different shapes.

3. not satisfied by any shape.

A C E Homework starts on page 24.

Applications

1. Tell whether each figure is a polygon. Explain how you know.

a.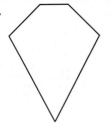

b.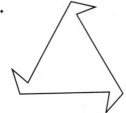

c.

d.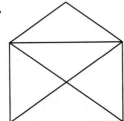

e.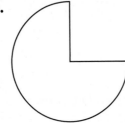

f.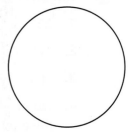

2. Copy and complete the table. Sort the Shapes Set into groups by polygon name.

Common Polygons

Number of Sides	Polygon Name	Examples in the Shapes Set
3	triangle	▪
4	quadrilateral	▪
5	pentagon	▪
6	hexagon	▪
7	heptagon	▪
8	octagon	▪
9	nonagon	▪
10	decagon	▪
12	dodecagon	▪

3. A figure is called a *regular polygon* if all sides are the same length and all angles are equal. List the members of the Shapes Set that are regular polygons.

4. Name the polygons used in these street and highway signs (ignore slightly rounded corners).

a.

b.

c.

d.

e.

f.

g.

h.

i.

5. An angle whose measure is less than 90° is called an *acute angle*. An angle whose measure is greater than 90° and less than 180° is called an *obtuse angle*. Which of these angles are acute, which are obtuse, and which are right?

a.

b.

c.

d.
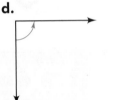

e.

f.

6. For two different angles, the angle with the greater turn from one side to the other is considered the larger angle. A test question asked to choose the larger angle.

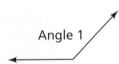

In one class, most students chose Angle 2. Do you agree? Why or why not?

7. List all polygons in the Shapes Set that have:

    a. only right angle corners.

    b. only obtuse angle corners.

    c. only acute angle corners.

    d. at least one angle of each type—acute, right, and obtuse.

8. Snowboarders use angle measures to describe their flips and spins. Explain what a snowboarder would mean by each statement.

   a. I did a 720.   **b.** I did a 540.   **c.** I did a 180.

9. Which benchmark angles (multiples of 30° or 45°) are closest to the rotation angles below?

   a. 40°   **b.** 140°   **c.** 175°

   d. 220°   **e.** 250°   **f.** 310°

10. In parts (a)–(h), decide whether each angle is closest to 30°, 60°, 90°, 120°, 150°, 180°, 270°, or 360° without measuring. Explain your reasoning.

   a.

   b.

   c.

   d.

   e.
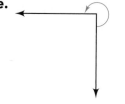

   f.
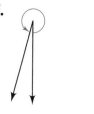

   g.
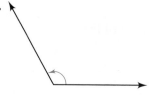

   h.

   i. For each angle in parts (a)–(h), classify them as right, acute, or obtuse.

11. Give the degree measure of each angle.

    a. one sixth of a right angle   **b.** three fourths of a right angle

    c. five fourths of a right angle   **d.** five thirds of a right angle

    e. two thirds of a full turn   **f.** one and a half full turns

12. For each pair of angles in parts (a)–(d), estimate the measure of each angle. Then, check your estimates by measuring with an angle ruler or a protractor.

a.

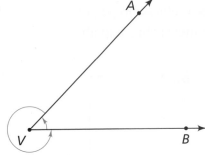

b.

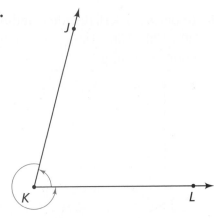

c.

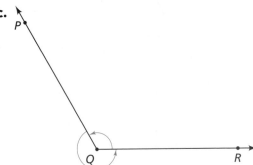

d.

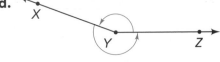

For Exercises 13–16, write an equation and find the measure of the angle labeled *x*, *without* measuring.

13.

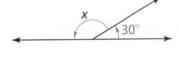

14.

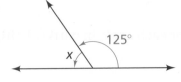

15.

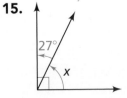

16.

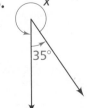

17. At the start of each hour, the minute hand points straight up at 12. In parts (a)–(f), determine the angle between the minute hand at the start of an hour and the minute hand after the given amount of time passes. For each situation, sketch the angle and indicate the rotation of the minute hand.

    a. 15 minutes   **b.** 30 minutes

    c. 20 minutes   **d.** one hour

    e. 5 minutes   **f.** one and one-half hours

18. One common definition of an angle is two rays with a common endpoint. There are many times when you are really interested in the region or area between the two rays. For example, when a pizza is cut into six or eight pieces, you are interested in the slice of pizza, not the cuts. Suppose a pizza is cut into equal size pieces. Calculate the measure of the angle for one slice given the number of pieces.

    a. 6 pieces   **b.** 8 pieces   **c.** 10 pieces

For Exercises 19–28, find the angle measures. Use the diagram of the protractor below. ∠JVK and ∠KVL are called adjacent angles because they have a common vertex and a common side.

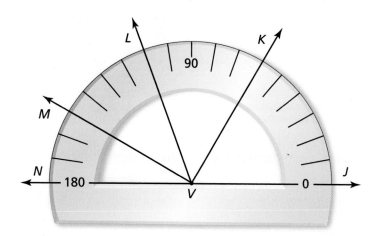

19. $m\angle JVK$ **20.** $m\angle JVL$

21. $m\angle JVM$ **22.** $m\angle KVL$

23. $m\angle KVM$ **24.** $m\angle LVM$

25. the complement of $\angle JVK$ **26.** the supplement of $\angle JVK$

27. the complement of $\angle MVL$ **28.** the supplement of $\angle JVL$

29. Without measuring, decide whether the angles in each pair have the same measure. If they do not, tell which angle has the greater measure. Then, find the measure of the angles with an angle ruler or protractor to check your work.

a.

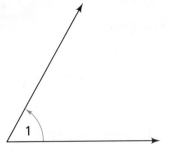 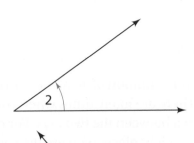

b.

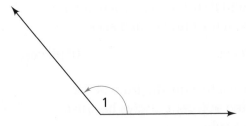

c.

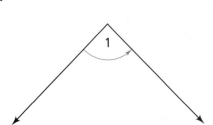 

30. For each polygon below, measure the angles with an angle ruler.

a. 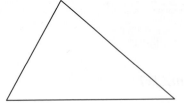   **b.**

31. Estimate the measure of each angle, then check your answers with an angle ruler or a protractor.

a.

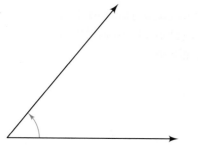

b.

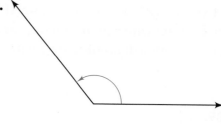

c.

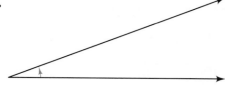

d.

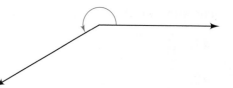

e.

32. Draw an angle for each measure. Include an arc indicating the turn.

    a. 45°

    b. 25°

    c. 180°

    d. 200°

In Exercises 33–36, draw the polygons described. If there is more than one (or no) shape that you can draw, explain how you know that.

33. Draw a rectangle. Perimeter = 24 cm and side of 8 cm.

34. Draw a triangle. Side $\overline{AB}$ = 2 in. Side $\overline{AC}$ = 1 in. $\angle BAC$ = 75°.

35. Draw a triangle. $\angle BAC$ = 75° and $\angle ACB$ = 75°.

36. Draw a trapezoid *PQRS*. $\angle QPS$ = 45°. $\angle RQP$ = 45°. Side $\overline{PS}$ = 1 in. Side $\overline{PQ}$ = 2 in.

Connections

In Exercises 37–40, find two equivalent fractions for each fraction. Find one fraction with a denominator less than the one given. Find another fraction with a denominator greater than the one given.

37. $\frac{4}{12}$

38. $\frac{9}{15}$

39. $\frac{15}{35}$

40. $\frac{20}{12}$

In Exercises 41–44, copy the fractions. Insert $<$, $>$, or $=$ to make a true statement.

41. $\frac{5}{12} \ \blacksquare \ \frac{9}{12}$

42. $\frac{15}{35} \ \blacksquare \ \frac{12}{20}$

43. $\frac{7}{13} \ \blacksquare \ \frac{20}{41}$

44. $\frac{45}{36} \ \blacksquare \ \frac{35}{28}$

45. Marissa takes a ride on a merry-go-round. It is shaped like the octagon shown. Marissa's starting point is also shown.

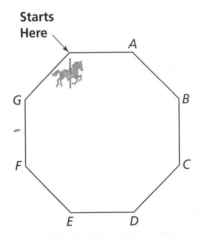

a. Multiple Choice Where will Marissa be after the ride completes $\frac{4}{8}$ of a full turn?

  A. point C   **B.** point D

  C. point E   **D.** point G

b. Multiple Choice Where will Marissa be after the ride completes $\frac{1}{2}$ of a full turn?

  F. point B   **G.** point C

  H. point D   **J.** point F

46. Multiple Choice Choose the correct statement.

A. $\frac{5}{6} = \frac{11}{360}$ **B.** $\frac{3}{4} = \frac{300}{360}$

C. $\frac{1}{4} = \frac{90}{360}$ **D.** $\frac{3}{36} = \frac{33}{360}$

47. The number 360 has many factors. This may be why it was chosen for the number of degrees in a full turn.

     a. List all of the factors of 360.

     b. Find the prime factorization of 360.

48. You can think of a right angle as one quarter of a complete rotation.

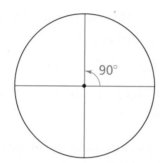

     a. How many degrees is $\frac{1}{3}$ of a quarter-rotation?

     b. How many degrees is two times a quarter-rotation?

     c. How many degrees is two and one third times a quarter-rotation?

For Exercises 49–52, replace the ▧ with a number that makes the sentence true.

49. $\frac{1}{2} = \frac{▧}{360}$ **50.** $\frac{1}{10} = \frac{36}{▧}$

51. $\frac{1}{▧} = \frac{40}{360}$ **52.** $\frac{▧}{3} = \frac{120}{360}$

53. A full turn is 360°. Find the fraction of a turn or number of turns for the given measurement.

     a. 90°

     b. 270°

     c. 720°

     d. How many degrees is $\frac{25}{360}$ of a full turn?

54. The minute hand on a watch makes a full rotation each hour. In 30 minutes, the minute hand makes half of a full rotation.

   a. In how many minutes does the hand make $\frac{1}{6}$ of a rotation?

   b. In how many minutes does the hand make $\frac{1}{6}$ of half a rotation?

   c. What fraction of an hour is $\frac{1}{6}$ of half a rotation?

   d. How many degrees has the minute hand moved in $\frac{1}{6}$ of half a rotation?

55. A ruler is used to measure the length of line segments. An angle ruler is used to measure the size of (or turn in) angles.

   a. What is the unit of measure for each kind of ruler?

   b. Compare the method for measuring angles to the method for measuring lines. Use a few sentences.

56. Use the diagram below. Write an equation using the angle measures shown. Then, find the measures of $\angle AVB$ and $\angle BVC$.

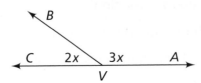

57. Ms. Cosgrove asked her students to estimate the measure of the angle shown.

Carly thought $150°$ would be a good estimate. Hannah said it should be $210°$. Who is closer to the exact measurement? Explain.

58. Find the area of the following polygons.

a.

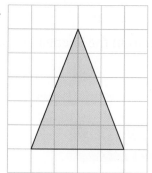

b.

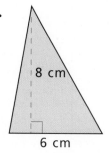

8 cm

6 cm

c.

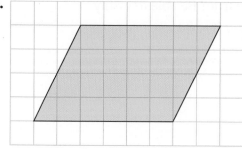

For Exercises 59–63, draw a polygon with the given properties (if possible). Decide if the polygon is unique. If not, design a different second polygon with the same properties.

59. a triangle with a height of 5 cm and a base of 10 cm

60. a triangle with a base of 6 cm and an area of 48 cm

61. a triangle with an area of 12 square centimeters

62. a parallelogram with an area of 24 square centimeters

63. a parallelogram with a height of 4 cm and a base of 8 cm

Extensions

64. Copy and complete the table. Sort the quadrilaterals from the Shapes Set into groups by name and description.

Common Quadrilaterals

Sides and Angles	Name	Examples in the Shapes Set
All sides are the same length.	rhombus	▪
All sides are the same length and all angles are right angles.	square	▪
All angles are right angles.	rectangle	▪
Opposite sides are parallel.	parallelogram	▪
Only one pair of opposite sides are parallel.	trapezoid	▪

65. Which of the following statements are true? Be able to justify your answers.

  a. All squares are rectangles.

  b. No squares are rhombuses.

  c. All rectangles are parallelograms.

  d. Some rectangles are squares.

  e. Some rectangles are trapezoids.

  f. No trapezoids are parallelograms.

  g. Every quadrilateral is a parallelogram, a trapezoid, a rectangle, a rhombus, or a square.

66. Design a new polar coordinate grid for Four in a Row in Problem 1.2. Play your game with a friend or family member. What ideas did you use to design your new grid? Explain. How does playing on your grid compare to playing on the original grids?

67. A *compass* is a tool used in wilderness navigation. On a compass, *North* is assigned the direction label 0°, *East* is 90°, *South* is 180°, and *West* is 270°. Directions that are between those labels are assigned degree labels such as NE at 45°, for example.

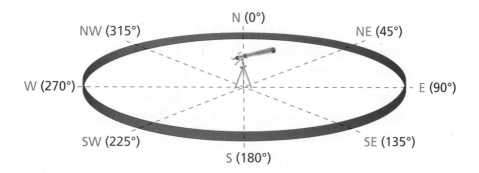

a. What degree measures would you expect for the direction south-southwest? For north-northwest?

b. A ship at sea is on a heading of 300°. Approximately what direction is it traveling?

68. Major airports label runways with the numbers by the compass heading. For example, a plane on runway 15 is on a compass heading of 150°. A plane on runway 9 is on a compass heading of 90°.

a. What is the runway number of a plane that is taking off on a heading due west? On a heading due east?

b. What is the compass heading of a plane landing on runway 6? On runway 12?

c. Each actual runway has two direction labels. The label depends on the direction in which a landing or taking off plane is headed. How are those labels related to each other?

69. When you and your classmates measure an angle, you have found that your measurements are slightly different. No measuring tool is absolutely precise, so there is a little error in every measurement. For example, when using angle measures to navigate an airplane, even small errors can lead a flight far astray.

In 1937, Amelia Earhart tried to become the first woman to fly around the world. On June 1, she left Miami, Florida. On July 2, she left Lae, New Guinea and headed towards Howland Island in the Pacific Ocean. She never arrived.

In 2012, 75 years later, investigators found evidence of the crash on the deserted island of Nikumaroro, far off her intended course. An error may have been made in plotting Earhart's course.

The map shows Lae, New Guinea; Howland Island (Earhart's intended destination); and Nikumaroro Island (the crash site).

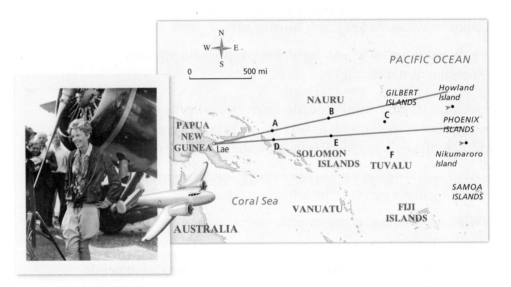

a. How many degrees off course was Earhart's crash site from her intended destination?

b. Suppose two planes fly along the paths formed by the rays of the angle indicated on the map. Both planes leave Lae, New Guinea, at the same time. They fly at the same speed. Use the scale in the upper left corner of the map. Find the distance between the planes at each pair of points labeled on the map (A and D, B and E, and C and F).

c. Amelia Earhart apparently flew several degrees south of her intended course. Suppose you start at New Guinea and are trying to reach Howland, but you fly 20° south. On which island might you land?

In this Investigation, you developed an understanding of the family of polygon shapes and angles that describe rotations or change of direction. You learned how to estimate angle measures and use tools to make more precise measurements. You also learned how to draw geometric shapes from a given list of properties. The following questions will help you summarize what you have learned.

Think about these questions. Discuss your ideas with other students and your teacher. Then write a summary of your findings in your notebook.

1. **What** are the common properties of all polygons?

2. **What** does the measure in degrees tell you about an angle? **What** are some common benchmark angles?

3. **What** strategies can be used to estimate angle measures? To deduce angle measures from given information? To find accurate measurements with tools?

Unit Project

At the end of this Unit, you will create a special report, a poster, a work of art, or a slide presentation. Your project will demonstrate what you learned about the properties and uses of polygons.

 What ideas from this Investigation seem important or attractive to include in your presentation?

Common Core Mathematical Practices

As you worked on the Problems in this Investigation, you used prior knowledge to make sense of them. You also applied Mathematical Practices to solve the Problems. Think back over your work, the ways you thought about the Problems, and how you used Mathematical Practices.

Ken described his thoughts in the following way:

> When working Problem 1.5, Sam thought that there was only one possible triangle that could have a base of 2 units and a height of 1 unit. Sam's example was a right triangle.
>
> But, Ali showed that the height does not have to be a side of the triangle. So, we could make a whole family of triangles that have a base of 2 units and a height of 1 unit.
>
> ....
>
> **Common Core Standards for Mathematical Practice**
>
> **MP3** Construct viable arguments and critique the reasoning of others.

 • What other Mathematical Practices can you identify in Ken's reasoning?

• Describe a Mathematical Practice that you and your classmates used to solve a different Problem in this Investigation.

Designing Polygons: The Angle Connection

This Investigation develops properties of polygons. These properties make polygons useful in many natural objects like the combs made by bees to store their honey.

2.1 Angle Sums of Regular Polygons

You have seen that polygons with the same number of sides can have different shapes. However, there is an important relationship between the number of sides and the angle sum of any polygon. You will develop a formula that relates the number of sides to angle measures.

A **regular polygon** is a polygon in which all of the sides are the same length and all of the angles have the same measure. In an **irregular polygon,** not all of the sides are the same length or not all of the angles have the same measure.

Polygons are named based on the number of sides and angles they have. For example, a polygon with six sides and six angles is called a *hexagon*.

Common Core State Standards

7.EE.A.2 Understand that rewriting an expression in different forms in a problem context can shed light on the problem and how the quantities in it are related.

7.EE.B.4 Use variables to represent quantities in a real world or mathematical problem, and construct simple equations . . . to solve problems by reasoning about the quantities.

Below are six examples of polygons from the Shapes Set. Study these examples to find a relationship between the number of sides and angles.

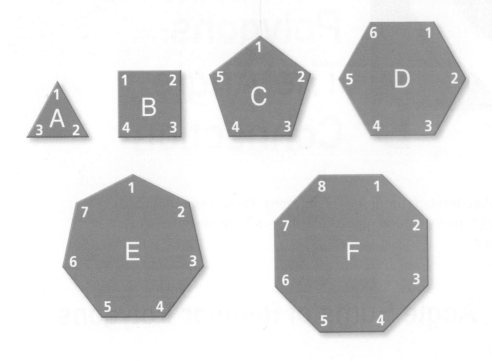

> **?** Is there a relationship between the size of the angles and the number of sides for regular polygons?

Problem 2.1

You can discover relationships between the number of sides and the angle measures of polygons. Measure some examples, organize the data, and then look for patterns.

A Use an angle ruler to measure the angles in the equilateral triangle, the square, the regular pentagon, and the regular hexagon from the Shapes Set.

1. Enter the results in a table like that begun here.

Polygon	Number of Sides	Measure of an Angle	Angle Sum
Triangle	▦	▦	▦
Square	▦	▦	▦
Pentagon	▦	▦	▦
Hexagon	▦	▦	▦
Heptagon	▦	▦	▦
Octagon	▦	▦	▦
Nonagon	▦	▦	▦
Decagon	▦	▦	▦

2. Find a pattern that suggests a way to fill in the table for regular polygons with seven, eight, nine, and ten sides. Then measure the angles of the Shapes Set heptagon and octagon. See if your pattern holds in those cases.

3. Describe a pattern relating angle sums to number of sides in regular polygons.

4. Describe a pattern relating measures of individual angles and number of sides in regular polygons.

continued on the next page >

Problem **2.1** *continued*

B The diagram below shows two sets of regular polygons of different sizes. Does the pattern relating number of sides, measures of angles, and angle sums apply to all of these shapes? Explain your reasoning.

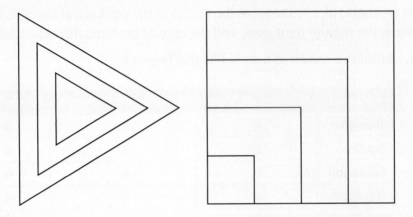

C Explain how you could find the angle sum of a regular polygon with *n* sides. Then, write your conjecture as a formula *S* = _____. The right side of the equation should give an expression for calculating the sum from the value of *n*.

D Explain how you could find the measure of each angle in a regular polygon with *n* sides. Then, write your conjecture as a formula *A* = _____. The right side of the equation should give an expression for calculating the measure of each angle from the value of *n*.

A C E Homework starts on page 52.

2.2 Angle Sums of Any Polygon

Does the pattern you observed in angle sums of regular polygons apply to irregular polygons? To tackle this question, you could draw many different polygons and measure all of the angles. But there are other strategies that provide answers with a little experimentation and some careful thinking.

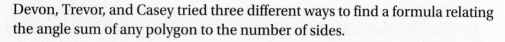

Devon, Trevor, and Casey tried three different ways to find a formula relating the angle sum of any polygon to the number of sides.

Ⓐ Devon began by drawing irregular triangles and quadrilaterals. Then he tore the corners off of those polygons and 'added' the angles by arranging them like this:

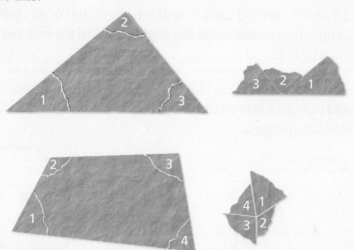

1. What angle sum does Devon's work suggest for the triangle? For the quadrilateral?

2. Test Devon's idea with triangles and quadrilaterals of your own design. See if you get the same result.

3. Draw irregular pentagons and hexagons. Use Devon's method to determine the angle sums for those figures.

4. Does this 'draw and tear' experimentation show the same angle sum pattern that you discovered with regular polygons? Why or why not?

continued on the next page >

Problem 2.2 continued

B Trevor examined Devon's results from his study of irregular triangles. This gave him a new idea to study polygons with more sides. He divided some polygons into smaller triangles by drawing diagonals from one vertex.

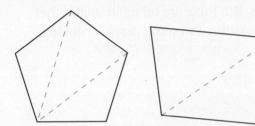 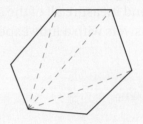

1. Describe the relationship between the number of sides of a polygon and the number of triangles formed.

2. Find the angle sum of each polygon. It might help to use Trevor's drawings and what you learned earlier about the angle sum of any triangle.

3. Will Trevor's method work to find the angle sum of any polygon? If so, what equation would relate the angle sum S to the number of sides n? If not, why not?

C Casey used Devon's discovery about triangles in a different way. She divided polygons into triangles by drawing line segments from a point within the polygon.

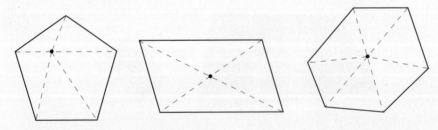

1. Study Casey's drawings to find the angle sum of each polygon.

2. Will Casey's method work to find the angle sum of any polygon? If so, what pattern would relate the angle sum S to the number of sides n? If not, why not?

D Think about your experimentation and reasoning about irregular polygons. Did you produce an angle sum pattern that agrees with what you found for regular polygons? Explain.

 Homework starts on page 52.

2.3 The Bees Do It
Polygons in Nature

Honeybees build nests called hives. A typical hive might be home for as many as 60,000 bees. Bees are small insects, but packing a hive with that many bees and the honey they make is tricky.

The honey is stored in a comb filled with tubes. The tops of those tubes cover the comb with a pattern of identical regular hexagons.

- Why do the bees form their honey storage tubes in the shape of hexagonal prisms?

- Why not some other shape?

The diagram below shows a pattern that uses regular hexagons to cover a flat surface without any gaps or overlaps.

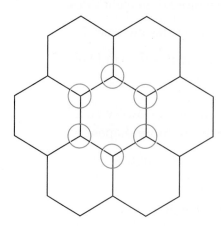

Notice that three angles fit together exactly around any point in the beehive pattern. These patterns are called **tilings** or **tessellations** of the surface.

 What other regular polygons do you think can be used to tile a surface?

Problem 2.3

Use regular polygons from the Shapes Set to explore possibilities for covering a flat surface with polygon tiles. Then, use what you know about the angles of regular polygons to explain your discoveries.

A Which regular polygons from the Shapes Set can be used to cover a flat surface without gaps or overlap like the hexagon pattern shown on the previous page?

- Sketch any tilings that you discover.

- Explain why copies of the shape fit neatly around the points where they meet.

B Which regular polygons from the Shapes Set cannot be used to cover a flat surface without gaps or overlap? Explain why.

C Think about tiling with regular polygons that have more than eight sides.

1. How do the angle sizes change as the number of sides increases?

2. Do you think any regular polygons of 9, 10, 11, or 12 sides could be used to tile a flat surface? Why or why not?

D Most regular polygons cannot be used to tile flat surfaces. However, it is often possible to include them in tilings that use two or more shapes.

1. Find and sketch tilings with two or more polygons from the Shapes Set.

2. What do you observe about angles that meet at a point in mixed tilings?

 Homework starts on page 52.

Did You Know?

A golf ball manufacturer developed a hexagon pattern for the cover of golf balls. They claim it is the first design to cover 100% of the surface area of a ball. This pattern of mostly hexagons almost eliminates flat spots that interfere with performance. The new design produces a longer, better flight for the golf ball.

2.4 The Ins and Outs of Polygons

Familiar figures like triangles, parallelograms, and trapezoids are called **convex polygons.** Figures like the star and the arrowhead pictured here are called **concave polygons.**

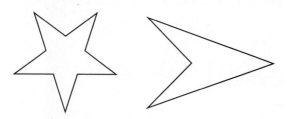

For convex polygons it is clear which points are on the inside and which are on the outside. It is also clear how to measure the **interior angles.**

By extending a side of a convex polygon, you can make an **exterior angle** that lies outside the polygon.

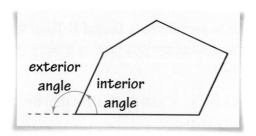

The figures below show two ways to form exterior angles. You can extend the sides as you move in either direction around the polygon.

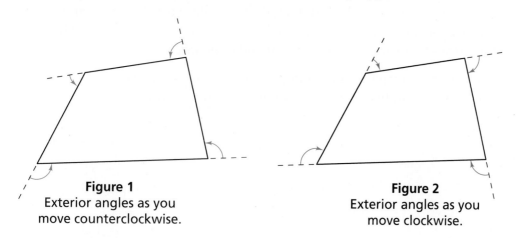

Figure 1
Exterior angles as you
move counterclockwise.

Figure 2
Exterior angles as you
move clockwise.

Measuring exterior angles provides useful information about the interior angles of a polygon.

Problem 2.4

Members of the Columbia Triathlon Club train by bicycling around the polygonal path shown.

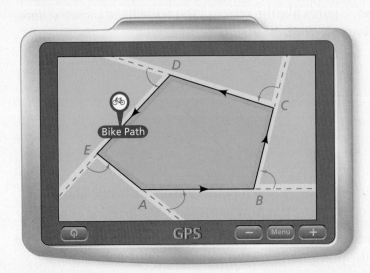

They start at vertex *A* and go on to vertices *B, C, D*, and *E*. Then they return to *A* and start another lap. At each vertex the cyclists have to make a left turn through an *exterior angle* of the polygon.

Ⓐ **1.** What is the sum of the left-turn exterior angles that the cyclists make on one full lap around this path?

  • Explain how you can arrive at an answer without measuring.

  • Then, measure the exterior angles to check your thinking.

2. Draw several other polygons. Include a triangle, a quadrilateral, and a hexagon. Find the sums of the turn angles if you cycle around each figure and return to your start point and direction.

3. Will the turning pattern you observed in cycling around several polygons occur in any other polygons? Why or why not?

Problem **2.4** *continued*

Each exterior angle and its adjacent interior angle are *supplementary angles*.

B 1. Consider the polygonal training track shown on the previous page. How many pairs of supplementary angles are there?

2. Amy says there are 5 straight angles in the diagram. They total $T = 5 \cdot 180°$. She thinks there is way to figure out the part of T that is the sum of the interior angles. She also wants the part of T that is the sum of the exterior angles. How can she find each part of T?

3. Becky says $T = n \times 180°$ should work for the total of exterior and interior angles for any polygon. So $n \times 180° - 360°$ should give her the sum of the interior angles of any polygon. But this does not look like the formula she found in Problem 2.2. Use the formula you developed in Problem 2.2. Explain to Becky why her formula is equivalent.

C Nic thought about exterior angles and 'walking around' a polygon. He came up with a new way to prove that the sum of the interior angles of any triangle is 180°. Answer Nic's questions that follow to complete his proof.

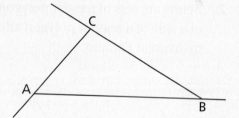

1. What is the sum of all of the interior and exterior angles in any triangle?

2. What is the sum of the exterior angles?

3. How much is left for the sum of the interior angles?

D For each of the following triangles write and solve an equation to find the value of x. Use the results to find the size of each angle. Find the supplement of each interior angle.

1.

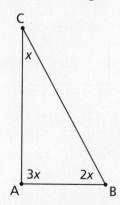

2.

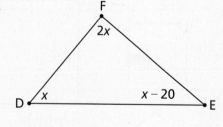

A C E Homework starts on page 52.

Applications

1. Without measuring, find the measure of the angle labeled x in each regular polygon.

a.

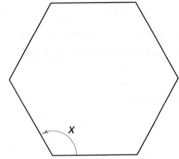

b.

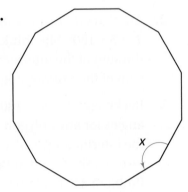

2. Below are sets of regular polygons of different sizes. Does the length of a side of a regular polygon affect the sum of the interior angle measures? Explain.

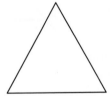

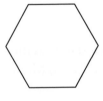

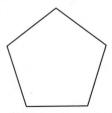

For Exercises 3–10, find the measure of each angle labeled *x*.

3.

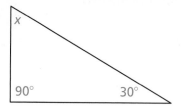

4.

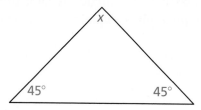

5.

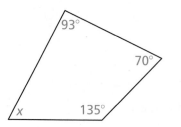

6.

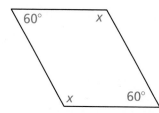

7.

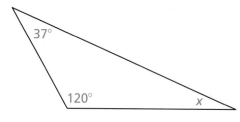

8. This figure is a regular hexagon.

9. This figure is a parallelogram.

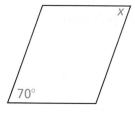

10. This figure is a trapezoid.

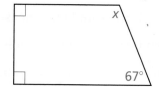

11. A right triangle has one right angle and two acute angles. Without measuring the angles, what is the sum of the measures of the two acute angles? Explain your reasoning.

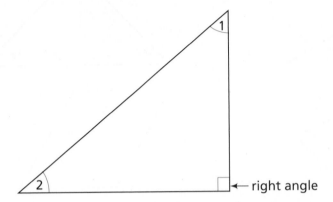

12. The figure below is a regular dodecagon. It has 12 sides.

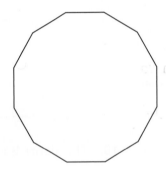

    a. What is the sum of the measures of the angles of this polygon?

    b. What is the measure of each angle?

    c. Can copies of this polygon be used to tile a flat surface? Explain.

13. Multiple Choice Which of the following combinations will tile a flat surface?

    A. regular heptagons and equilateral triangles

    B. squares and regular octagons

    C. regular pentagons and regular hexagons

    D. regular hexagons and squares

14. Suppose in-line skaters make one complete lap around a park shaped like the quadrilateral below.

What is the sum of the angles through which they turn?

15. Suppose the skaters complete one lap around a park that has the shape of a regular pentagon.

a. What is the sum of the angles through which they turn?

b. How many degrees will the skaters turn if they go once around a regular hexagon? A regular octagon? A regular polygon with *n* sides? Explain.

Connections

16. The regular decagon and star below are ten-sided polygons.

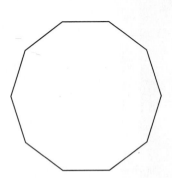 

a. Measure the angles inside the star to find the angle sum of the star.

b. Calculate the interior angle sum for a regular decagon and compare it to your measured sum for the star.

c. Use a strategy like that of Casey's to split the star into triangles. That is, draw lines from the center of rotation to each vertex of the star. Use that diagram to calculate the sum of angles for the star.

d. Explain why your result in part (c) does or does not match the measurements in part (a).

17. The diagram shows a line of symmetry for an equilateral triangle.

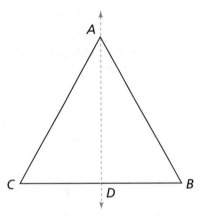

Examine the two smaller triangles that are formed using a part of the symmetry line. What do you know about the angles and the line segments of triangles *ABD* and *ACD*? Give reasons to support your answers.

18. **Multiple Choice** Figure QSTV is a rectangle. The lengths QR and QV are equal. What is the measure of angle x?

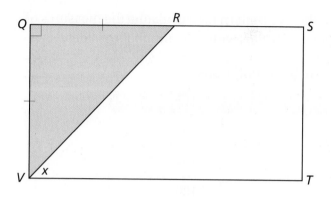

  F. $20°$ **G.** $45°$ **H.** $90°$ **J.** $120°$

19. Choose a non-rectangular parallelogram from the Shapes Set or draw one of your own. Using copies of your parallelogram, can you make a tiling pattern? Sketch a picture to help explain what you found.

20. Choose a scalene triangle (all three sides of different lengths) from your Shapes Set or draw one of your own. Using copies of your scalene triangle, can you make a tiling pattern? Sketch a picture to help explain what you found.

21. A class was asked what convinced them that the sum of exterior angles in any polygon is $360°$. Here are three different points of view.

> "We were convinced when we drew a bunch of different figures and used my angle ruler to measure the exterior angles. They all came out close to $360°$."

> "We were convinced when we thought about walking around the figure and realized that we made one complete turn or $360°$."

> "We used the results about sums of interior angles and the fact that the measure of each interior angle plus its adjacent exterior angle is $180°$ to deduce the formula using algebra."

What are the pros and cons of each argument?

Extensions

22. The table begun here shows a pattern for calculating the measures of interior angles in regular polygons with even numbers of sides.

Regular Polygons

Number of Sides	Measure of Interior Angle
4	$\frac{1}{2}$ of 180°
6	$\frac{2}{3}$ of 180°
8	$\frac{3}{4}$ of 180°
10	▦
12	▦

a. What entry would give the angle measures for decagons and dodecagons? Are those entries correct? How do you know?

b. Is there a similar pattern for regular polygons with odd numbers of sides? If so, what is the pattern?

23. Kele claims that the angle sum of a polygon he has drawn is 1660°. Can he be correct? Explain.

24. Look at the polygons below. Does Trevor's method of finding the angle sum (Problem 2.2) still work? Does Casey's method still work? Can you still find the angle sum of the interior angles without measuring? Explain.

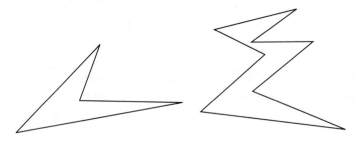

25. Below are a quadrilateral and a pentagon with the diagonals drawn from all of the vertices.

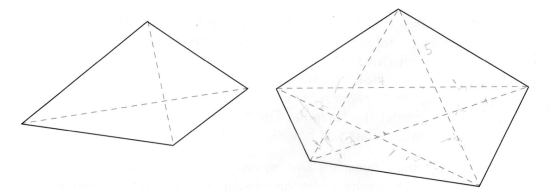

a. How many diagonals does the quadrilateral have? How many diagonals does the pentagon have?

b. Find the total number of diagonals for a hexagon and for a heptagon.

c. Copy the table below and record your results from parts (a) and (b).

Number of Sides	4	5	6	7	8	9	10	11	12
Number of Diagonals	▦	▦	▦	▦	▦	▦	▦	▦	▦

Look for a pattern relating the number of sides and the number of diagonals. Complete the table.

d. Write a rule for finding the number of diagonals for a polygon with *n* sides.

In this Investigation, you explored angle sums and tiling properties of polygons. You also used facts about supplementary angles to write and solve simple equations about angles in a polygon. In developing formulas for angle sums of polygons, you used variables to represent quantities in a mathematical problem and to construct the formula. The following questions will help you summarize what you have learned.

Think about these questions. Discuss your ideas with other students and your teacher. Then write a summary of your findings in your notebook.

1. **How** is the number of sides related to the sum of the interior angles in a polygon? **What** about the sum of the exterior angles?

2. **How** is the measure of each interior angle related to the number of sides in a regular polygon? **What** about the measure of each exterior angle?

3. **Which** polygons can be used to tile a flat surface without overlaps or gaps? **Why** are those the only figures that work as tiles?

Unit Project

Think about the discoveries from your work on the Problems in this Investigation.

 What seems worthy of including in a report, poster, or presentation about the *Shapes and Designs* Unit?

Common Core Mathematical Practices

As you worked on the Problems in this Investigation, you used prior knowledge to make sense of them. You also applied Mathematical Practices to solve the Problems. Think back over your work, the ways you thought about the Problems, and how you used Mathematical Practices.

Shawna described her thoughts in the following way:

When completing the table in Problem 2.1, we noticed there was a relationship between the number of sides of a regular polygon and the measure of each angle.

We recognized a pattern in our table and were able to use it to fill in the table for polygons with seven, eight, nine, and ten sides. Then, we wrote a formula to find the measure of each angle for any regular polygon with *n* sides.

Common Core Standards for Mathematical Practice

MP8 Look for and express regularity in repeated reasoning.

- What other Mathematical Practices can you identify in Shawna's reasoning?

- Describe a Mathematical Practice that you and your classmates used to solve a different Problem in this Investigation.

Designing Triangles and Quadrilaterals

Your work on Problems in Investigation 2 revealed properties of polygons that make them useful in natural objects like the honeycombs made by bees. In this Investigation you will discover properties of polygons that make them useful in buildings, mechanical devices, and crafts.

To explore the connections between shapes and their uses in construction, you will build some polygons using polystrips and fasteners like these.

 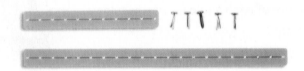

These tools will allow you to build and study polygons with various combinations of side lengths and angles.

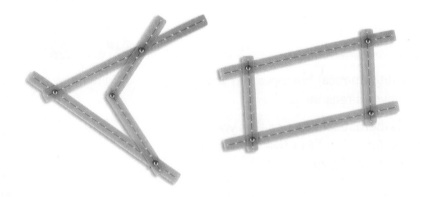

Common Core State Standards

7.G.A.2 Draw (freehand, with ruler and protractor, and with technology) geometric shapes with given conditions. Focus on constructing triangles from three measures of angles or sides, noticing when the conditions determine a unique triangle, more than one triangle, or no triangle.

7.G.B.5 Use facts about supplementary, complementary, vertical, and adjacent angles in a multi-step problem to write and solve simple equations for an unknown angle in a figure.

3.1 Building Triangles

Bridges, towers, and other structures contain many triangles in their design.

- What properties of these simple polygons could make them valuable in construction?

Problem 3.1

The best way to discover what is so special about triangles in construction is to build several models and study their reaction to pressure.

Ⓐ Make and study several test triangles using the steps below. Sketch and label your results.

Step 1 Pick three numbers between 2 and 20 for side lengths of a polystrip triangle.

Step 2 Try to make a triangle with the chosen side lengths. If you can build a triangle, try to build a different triangle with the same side lengths.

Repeat Steps 1 and 2 to make and study several other triangles. Record your results in a table with headings like this

Side Lengths	Triangle Possible?	Sketch	Different Shape?
▪	▪	▪	▪

1. List some sets of side lengths that did make a triangle.

2. List some sets of side lengths that did not make a triangle.

Ⓑ Study your results from Question A with different side length possibilities.

1. What pattern do you see that explains why some sets of numbers make a triangle and some do not?

2. For what side length relationships can you make more than one triangle from a given set of side lengths?

3. Find three other side lengths that make a triangle. Then, find three other side lengths that will not make a triangle.

 Homework starts on page 76.

3.2 Design Challenge II
Drawing Triangles

The drawing here shows a triangle with measures of all angles and sides.

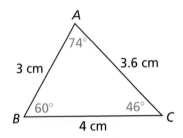

Suppose you want to text a friend to give directions for drawing an exact copy of the figure. What is the shortest message to do the job? How do you know?

Problem 3.2

To find an answer to the challenge of describing triangles in only a few words, work through this Problem.

A Which of these short messages give enough information to draw a triangle congruent to △ABC above?

1. $\overline{BC} = 4$ cm
   $\angle B = 60°$
   $\overline{AB} = 3$ cm

2. $\angle B = 60°$
   $\overline{BC} = 4$ cm
   $\angle C = 46°$

3. $\overline{AB} = 3$ cm
   $\overline{BC} = 4$ cm
   $\angle C = 46°$

4. $\angle B = 60°$
   $\angle A = 74°$
   $\angle C = 46°$

5. $\angle B = 60°$
   $\angle C = 46°$
   $\overline{AC} = 3.6$ cm

Problem **3.2** *continued*

B Write the shortest possible messages that tell how to draw triangles with the same size and shape as the ones below.

1.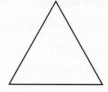

2.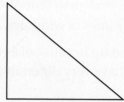

3.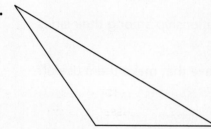

4.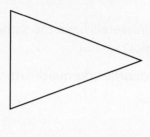

C What minimum information about a triangle allows you to draw exactly one triangle?

D Draw a triangle *ABC* in which angle *B* measures 90°. Then make a copy using the same three lengths of sides. Is your copy also a right triangle? Does it matter in what order you connect the sides?

 Homework starts on page 76.

3.3 Building Quadrilaterals

Quadrilaterals, especially rectangles, appear throughout buildings in which we live, work, and go to school. You see rectangles as the mortar around bricks, the frames of windows, and the outlines of large buildings.

Most buildings stand up because of a rectangular frame of studs and beams. Rectangles have very different physical properties from triangles.

- Do quadrilaterals have the same relationship among their sides as triangles?

- What properties do quadrilaterals have that make them useful?

Problem 3.3

Your study of triangle properties will help you understand quadrilaterals. You will use polystrips to build and test some sample quadrilaterals.

A Build polystrip quadrilaterals with each of the following sets of numbers as side lengths. If you are able to build one quadrilateral with a set of side lengths, try to build two or more different figures using those side lengths. Sketch and label your results.

1. 6, 10, 15, 15

2. 3, 5, 10, 20

3. 8, 8, 10, 10

4. 12, 20, 6, 9

B Choose your own set of four numbers. Use them as side lengths to try to build quadrilaterals. Record your results. Combine your results with your observations from Question A.

1. Is it possible to make a quadrilateral using any set of four side lengths? If not, how can you tell when you can make a quadrilateral from four side lengths?

2. Can you make two or more different quadrilaterals from the same four side lengths?

3. What combinations of side lengths are needed to build rectangles? Squares? Parallelograms?

Problem **3.3** *continued*

C Use several of your polystrip figures to study the reaction of triangles and quadrilaterals to stress.

1. Hold one of your triangles and push down on a vertex. What happens?

This stress test is similar to the way a bridge would act under the weight of a car or a train.

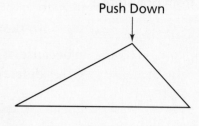
Push Down

2. What happens when you push down on a side or vertex of a quadrilateral?

3. How do the results from your stress tests in parts (1) and (2) explain the frequent use of triangles in building structures ike bridges and towers?

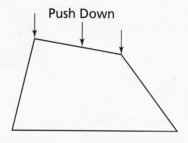
Push Down

D Use a polystrip to add a diagonal to a test quadrilateral from Question C, part (2).

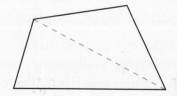

Repeat the same stress test from Question C, part (2). Does your quadrilateral respond differently? If so, why do you think there is a different response with an additional diagonal brace?

E Describe what you learned from experiments in building triangles and quadrilaterals. How are the two kinds of polygons similar and different? How do the differences explain the frequent use of triangles when building structures?

A C E Homework starts on page 76.

Did You Know?

Mechanical engineers use the fact that quadrilaterals are not rigid figures to design *linkages*. Here is an example of a quadrilateral linkage made from polystrips.

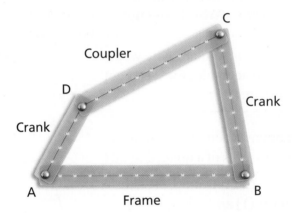

One of the sides is fixed. It is the *frame*. The two sides attached to the frame are the *cranks*. One of the cranks is the driver and the other the follower. The fourth side is called the *coupler*. Quadrilateral linkages are used for windshield wipers, automobile jacks, and reclining lawn chairs.

In 1883, the German mathematician Franz Grashof suggested an interesting principle for quadrilateral linkages. Sum the lengths of the shortest and longest sides. If that sum is less than or equal to the sum of the other two sides, then the shortest side can rotate 360°.

3.4 Parallel Lines and Transversals

Suppose you were asked to build a quadrilateral with side lengths 3, 8, 3, and 8. You might expect that the figure is a 3 × 8 rectangle. Your experiments in Problem 3.3 showed that when you push on a vertex of a polystrip rectangle, it loses its square-corner shape.

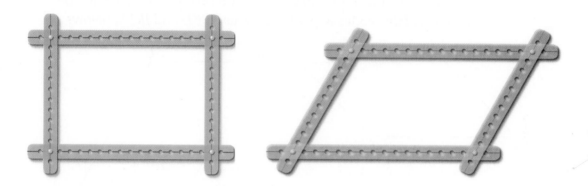

One thing that does not change about the polystrip figure is the relationship of the opposite sides. They remain equal in length and parallel to each other.

Parallel lines are lines in a plane that never meet. They are like railroad tracks, rows of a crop in a field, or lines on notebook paper. They remain the same distance apart and never meet, even if extended forever in both directions.

 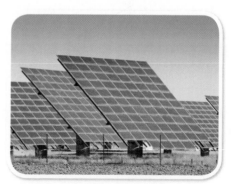

A **parallelogram** is a quadrilateral in which the pairs of opposite sides are parallel. The shape of a parallelogram is largely set by the angles at which those pairs of sides meet. A parallelogram with four right angles is a **rectangle.**

Problem 3.4

A There are nine parallelograms in the Shapes Set from Problem 1.1.

   1. What pattern seems to relate the measures of opposite angles in any parallelogram?

   2. What pattern seems to relate the measures of consecutive angles in any parallelogram?

   3. Suppose your conjectures in parts (1) and (2) are true. What are the measures of the angles in parallelograms *ABCD* and *JKLM* below?

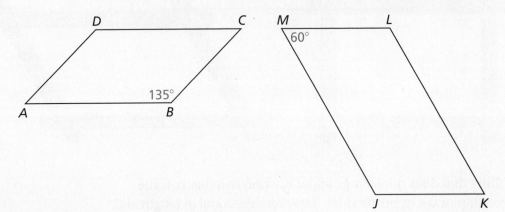

B Suppose your conjectures from Question A are true. The lines below form a parallelogram.

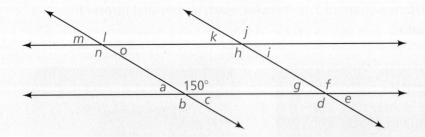

Find the measures of all labeled angles in this diagram. Be prepared to justify each answer.

Problem **3.4** *continued*

C A line that intersects two other lines is called a **transversal.**

1. From your work in Questions A and B, what can you say about the measures of the eight angles formed by a transversal and two parallel lines?

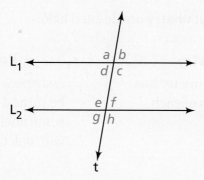

2. Suppose the measure of angle *f* is 80°. What are the measures of the other labeled angles?

D You probably noticed that when two lines intersect four angles are formed. The opposite pairs of angles are called **vertical angles.** For example, in Question C, angles *f* and *g* are vertical angles.

1. Name the other pairs of vertical angles in the figure of Question C.

2. Name the pairs of supplementary angles in that figure.

3. What is true about the measures of any vertical angle pair? Explain how you know.

E Use what you know about complementary, supplementary, and vertical angles. Write an equation and then find the value of *x* and the size of each angle in this figure.

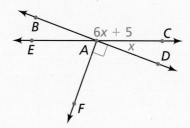

 Homework starts on page 76.

3.5 Design Challenge III
The Quadrilateral Game

Special properties of triangles and quadrilaterals make them useful in the design of buildings and mechanical objects. They also play an important role in the design of craft objects.

The two common forms of **symmetry** are defined below.

Reflectional Symmetry

A shape with reflectional symmetry has halves that are mirror images of each other.

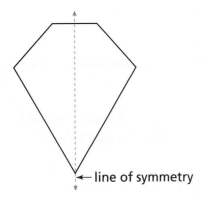

←line of symmetry

If you fold along the line of symmetry, the two halves of the figure match exactly. If you hold a mirror along the line of symmetry, the figure's reflection will match the half behind the mirror.

Rotational Symmetry

A shape with rotational symmetry can be turned about a center point through some angle between 0° and 360° and it will look the same.

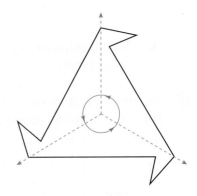

If you close your eyes as the figure above is rotated 120° or 240° and then open them, you won't notice any difference.

Problem 3.5

A Spotting symmetries in polygons is the first step in using those figures to make art and craft designs.

1. What kind of symmetries do the triangles in the Shapes Set have?

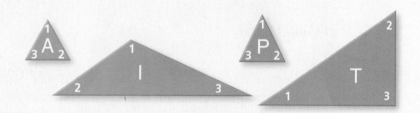

2. What kind of symmetries do the quadrilaterals in the Shapes Set have?

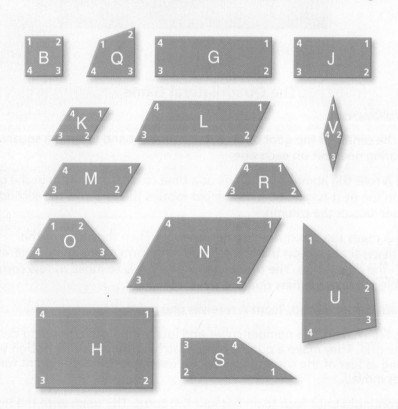

3. Look for objects in your classroom or in nature that have symmetries. What kind of symmetries do they have?

continued on the next page >

Problem 3.5 *continued*

The Quadrilateral Game challenges you to use all that you know about polygons, including symmetry. The game is played by two teams. To play, you need two number cubes, a game grid, a geoboard, and a rubber band.

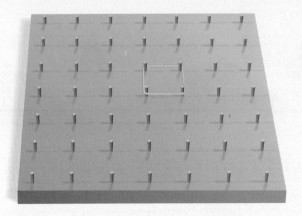

The Quadrilateral Game

Directions

- Near the center of the geoboard, put the rubber band around a square measuring one unit on each side.

- Team A rolls the number cubes one at a time to locate an entry in the game grid on the next page. The first number locates the row and the second number locates the column.

- Team A reads the description in that location. Then they look at the quadrilateral already on the game board, and form a new quadrilateral to match the description. The challenge for Team A is to move as few corners as possible to make the new quadrilateral.

- For each corner moved, Team A receives one point.

- Next, Team B rolls the number cubes and locates the corresponding description on the grid. They make a quadrilateral matching the new description by moving as few of the corners as possible. Team B receives one point for each corner moved.

- Play continues until each team has had five turns. The team with the lowest score at the end is the winner.

Problem **3.5** *continued*

B Play the Quadrilateral Game. Keep a record of interesting strategies and difficult situations.

1. When did you receive 0 points during a turn? Why didn't you need to move any corners on those turns?

2. Write two new descriptions of quadrilaterals that you could use in the game grid.

3. Make your own game board with descriptions for a Triangle Game.

Quadrilateral Game Grid

	Column 1	Column 2	Column 3	Column 4	Column 5	Column 6
Row 6	A quadrilateral that is a square	**Add 1 point to your score and skip your turn**	A rectangle that is not a square	A quadrilateral with two obtuse angles	A quadrilateral with exactly one pair of parallel sides	A quadrilateral with one pair of opposite side lengths equal
Row 5	**Subtract 2 points from your score and skip your turn**	A quadrilateral that is not a rectangle	A quadrilateral with two pairs of consecutive angles that are equal	A quadrilateral with all four angles the same size	A quadrilateral with four lines of symmetry	A quadrilateral that is a rectangle
Row 4	A quadrilateral with no reflectional or rotational symmetry	A quadrilateral with four right angles	**Skip a turn**	A quadrilateral with exactly one pair of consecutive side lengths that are equal	A quadrilateral with exactly one right angle	A quadrilateral with two 45° angles
Row 3	A quadrilateral with no angles equal	A quadrilateral with one pair of equal opposite angles	A quadrilateral with exactly one pair of opposite angles that are equal	**Add 2 points to your score and skip your turn**	A quadrilateral with no sides parallel	A quadrilateral with exactly two right angles
Row 2	A quadrilateral with both pairs of adjacent side lengths equal	A quadrilateral with two pairs of equal opposite angles	A quadrilateral with a diagonal that divides it into two identical shapes	A quadrilateral that is a rhombus	A quadrilateral with 180° rotational symmetry	**Subtract 1 point from your score and skip your turn**
Row 1	A quadrilateral with one diagonal that is a line of symmetry	A quadrilateral with no side lengths equal	A quadrilateral with exactly one angle greater than 180°	A parallelogram that is not a rectangle	**Add 3 points to your score and skip your turn**	A quadrilateral with two pairs of opposite side lengths equal

A C E Homework starts on page 76.

Applications

For Exercises 1–4, follow these directions. Use the given side lengths.

- If possible, build a triangle with the side lengths. Sketch your triangle.
- Tell whether your triangle is the only one that is possible. Explain.
- If a triangle is not possible, explain why.

1. 5, 5, 3

2. 8, 8, 8

3. 7, 8, 15

4. 5, 6, 10

5. From Exercises 1–4, which sets of side lengths can make each of the following shapes?

   a. an equilateral triangle (all three sides are equal length)

   b. an isosceles triangle (two sides are equal length)

   c. a scalene triangle (no two sides are equal length)

   d. a triangle with at least two angles of the same measure

For Exercises 6 and 7, draw the polygons described to help you answer the questions.

6. Suppose you want to build a triangle with three angles measuring 60°. What do you think must be true of the side lengths? What kind of triangle is this?

7. Suppose you want to build a triangle with only two angles the same size. What do you think must be true of the side lengths? What kind of triangle is this?

8. Giraldo is building a tent. He has two 3-foot poles. He also has a 5-foot pole, a 6-foot pole, and a 7-foot pole. He wants to make a triangular-shaped doorframe for the tent using the 3-foot poles and one other pole. Which of the other poles could be used for the base of the door?

9. Which of these descriptions of a triangle *ABC* are directions that can be followed to draw exactly one shape?

   a. $\overline{AB}$ = 2.5 in., $\overline{AC}$ = 2 in., $\angle B$ = 40°

   b. $\overline{AB}$ = 2.5 in., $\overline{AC}$ = 1 in., $\angle A$ = 40°

   c. $\overline{AB}$ = 2.5 in., $\angle B$ = 60°, $\angle A$ = 40°

   d. $\overline{AB}$ = 2.5 in., $\angle B$ = 60°, $\angle A$ = 130°

For Exercises 10–13, follow these directions. Use the given side lengths.

- If possible, build a quadrilateral with the side lengths. Sketch your quadrilateral.
- Tell whether your quadrilateral is the only one that is possible. Explain.
- If a quadrilateral is not possible, explain why.

10. 5, 5, 8, 8

11. 5, 5, 6, 14

12. 8, 8, 8, 8

13. 4, 3, 5, 14

14. From Exercises 10–13, which sets of side lengths can make each of the following shapes?

   a. a square

   b. a quadrilateral with all angles the same size

   c. a parallelogram

   d. a quadrilateral that is not a parallelogram

15. A quadrilateral with four equal sides is called a *rhombus*. Which set(s) of side lengths from Exercises 10–13 can make a rhombus?

16. A quadrilateral with just one pair of parallel sides is called a *trapezoid*. Which sets of side lengths from Exercises 10–13 can make a trapezoid?

17. In the diagram below, line T is a transversal to parallel lines L_1 and L_2.

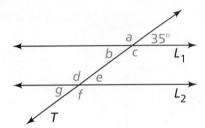

   a. Find the degree measures of angles labeled a–g.

   b. Name the pairs of opposite or vertical angles in the figure.

18. Which of these shapes have reflectional symmetry? Which of these shapes have rotational symmetry?

Multiple Choice For Exercises 19–22, choose the symmetry or symmetries of each shape.

19. rhombus (four equal sides)

   A. rotation   **B.** reflection   **C.** both A and B   **D.** none

20. regular pentagon

   F. rotation   **G.** reflection   **H.** both F and G   **J.** none

21. square

   A. rotation   **B.** reflection   **C.** both A and B   **D.** none

22. parallelogram (not a rhombus or a rectangle)

   F. rotation   **G.** reflection   **H.** both F and G   **J.** none

For Exercises 23 and 24, draw the polygons described to help you answer the questions.

23. To build a square, what must be true of the side lengths?

24. Suppose you want to build a rectangle that is not a square. What must be true of the side lengths?

25. Li Mei builds a quadrilateral with sides that are each five inches long. To help stabilize the quadrilateral, she wants to insert a ten-inch diagonal. Will that work? Explain.

26. You are playing the Quadrilateral Game. The shape currently on the geoboard is a square. Your team rolls the number cubes and gets the result to the right:

A parallelogram that is not a rectangle

Your team needs to match this description. What is the minimum number of corners your team needs to move?

27. Suppose you are playing the Quadrilateral Game. The shape currently on the geoboard is a parallelogram but not a rectangle. Your team rolls the number cubes and gets the result to the right. :

A quadrilateral with two obtuse angles

Your team needs to match this description. What is the minimum number of corners your team needs to move?

Connections

28. **Multiple Choice** Which of the following shaded regions is *not* a representation of $\frac{4}{12}$?

A.

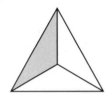

B.

C.

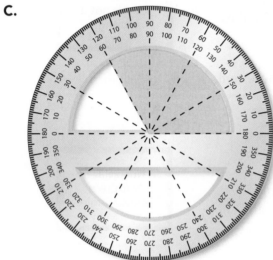

D.

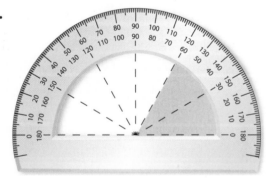

29. Compare the three quadrilaterals below.

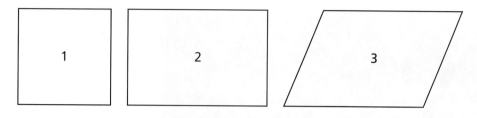

    a. How are all three quadrilaterals alike?

    b. How does each quadrilateral differ from the other two?

30. In the parallelogram, find the measure of each numbered angle.

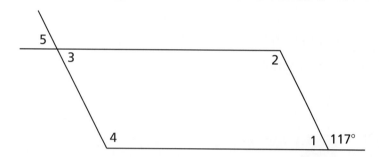

31. Think about your polystrip experiments with triangles and quadrilaterals. What explanations can you now give for the common use of triangular shapes in structures like bridges and towers for transmitting radio and television signals?

32. Below is a rug design from the Southwest United States.

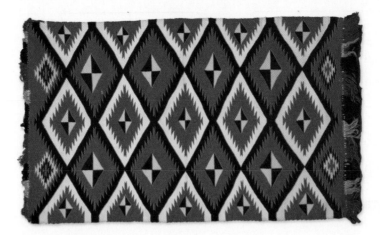

    a. Name some of the polygons in the rug.

    b. Describe the symmetries of the design.

33. Here are three state flags.

    a. Describe the lines of symmetry in each whole flag.

    b. Do any of the shapes or designs within the flags have rotational symmetry? If so, which ones?

    c. Design your own flag. Your flag should have at least one line of symmetry. Your flag should also include three shapes that have rotational symmetry. List the shapes in your flag that have rotational symmetry.

34. Multiple Choice A triangle has a base of 4 and an area of 72. Which of the following is true?

    F. These properties do not make a triangle.

    G. These properties make a unique triangle.

    H. There are at least two different triangles with these properties.

    J. The height of the triangle is 18.

35. Multiple Choice Which of the following could *not* be the dimensions of a parallelogram with an area of 18?

    A. base = 18, height = 1

    B. base = 9, height = 3

    C. base = 6, height = 3

    D. base = 2, height = 9

For Exercises 36–37, use these quilt patterns.

Pattern A

Pattern B

36. Name some of the polygons in each quilt pattern.

37. Describe the symmetries of each quilt pattern.

38. Half of the figure is hidden.

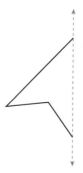

The vertical line is a line of symmetry for the complete figure. Copy the part of the figure shown. Then, draw the missing half.

Extensions

39. In the triangle *ABC*, a line has been drawn through vertex *A*, parallel to side *BC*.

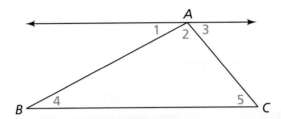

a. What is the sum of the measures of angles 1, 2, and 3?

b. Explain why angle 1 has the same measure as angle 4 and why angle 3 has the same measure as angle 5.

c. How can you use the results of parts (a) and (b) to show that the angle sum of a triangle is 180°?

40. In parts (a)–(c), explore properties of pentagons by using polystrips or making sketches. Use your results to answer the following questions.

a. If you choose five numbers as side lengths, can you always build a pentagon? Explain.

b. Can you make two or more different pentagons from the same set of side lengths?

c. Can you find side lengths for a pentagon that will tile a surface? Explain why or why not.

41. Refer to the *Did You Know?* after Problem 3.3.

a. Make a model that illustrates Grashof's principle using polystrips. Describe the motion of your model.

b. How can your model be used to make a stirring mechanism? A windshield wiper?

42. Build the figure below from polystrips. The vertical sides are all the same length. The distance from B to C equals the distance from E to D. The distance from B to C is twice the distance from A to B.

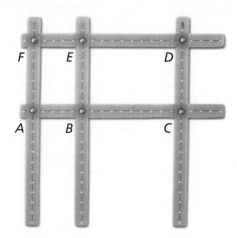

a. Experiment with holding various strips fixed (one at a time) and moving the other strips. In each case, tell which strip you held fixed, and describe the motion of the other strips.

b. Fix a strip between points F and B and then try to move strip CD. What happens? Explain why this occurs.

43. The drawing below shows a quadrilateral with measures of all angles and sides. Suppose you wanted to text a friend giving directions for drawing an exact copy of it.

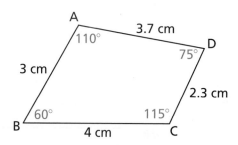

Which of the following short messages give enough information to draw a quadrilateral that has the same size and shape as *ABCD* above?

a. $\overline{AB} = 3$ cm, $\overline{BC} = 4$ cm, $\overline{CD} = 2.3$ cm

b. $\overline{AB} = 3$ cm, $\angle B = 60°$, $\overline{BC} = 4$ cm, $\angle C = 115°$, $\angle A = 110°$

c. $\overline{AB} = 3$ cm, $\angle B = 60°$, $\overline{BC} = 4$ cm, $\angle C = 115°$, $\overline{CD} = 2.3$ cm

44. In parts (a)–(d), write the shortest possible message that tells how to draw each quadrilateral so that it will have the same size and shape as those below.

a.

b.

c.
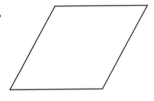

d.
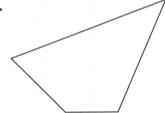

e. What is the minimum information about a quadrilateral that will allow you to draw an exact copy?

For Exercises 45–49, one diagonal of each quadrilateral has been drawn. Complete parts (a) and (b) for each quadrilateral.

a. Is the given diagonal a line of symmetry? Why or why not?

b. Does the figure have any other lines of symmetry? If so, copy the figure and sketch the symmetry lines.

45.
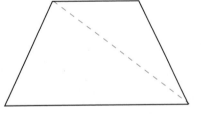

46.
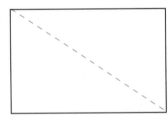

47.
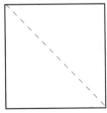

48.
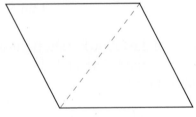

49.
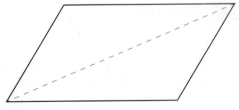

In this Investigation, you experimented with building polygons by choosing lengths for the sides and then connecting those sides to make a shape. You also studied ways to describe triangles and quadrilaterals accurately and efficiently. The following questions will help you summarize what you have learned.

Think about these questions. Discuss your ideas with other students and your teacher. Then write a summary of your findings in your notebook.

1. **What** information about combinations of angle sizes and side lengths provide enough information to copy a given triangle exactly? A quadrilateral?

2. **Why** are triangles so useful in building structures? **What** are the problems with quadrilaterals for building structures?

3. If two parallel lines are intersected by a transversal, **which** pairs of angles will have the same measure?

4. **What** does it mean to say a figure has symmetry? Provide examples with your explanation.

Unit Project

 What discoveries in this Investigation do you think should be included in your unit project?

Common Core Mathematical Practices

As you worked on the Problems in this Investigation, you used prior knowledge to make sense of them. You also applied Mathematical Practices to solve the Problems. Think back over your work, the ways you thought about the Problems, and how you used Mathematical Practices.

Sophie described her thoughts in the following way:

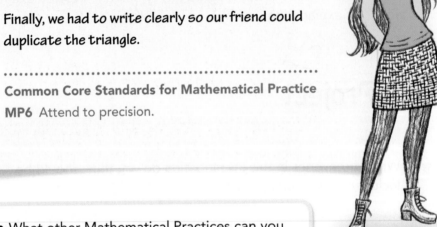

In Problem 3.2, we had to determine the shortest possible message we could send a friend so they could draw an exact copy of our triangle.

We noticed there were three pieces of information that we needed to include in our message. We also noticed that it was not just any three pieces. There were specific combinations of information that we needed and order mattered.

Finally, we had to write clearly so our friend could duplicate the triangle.

....

Common Core Standards for Mathematical Practice
MP6 Attend to precision.

- What other Mathematical Practices can you identify in Sophie's reasoning?

- Describe a Mathematical Practice that you and your classmates used to solve a different Problem in this Investigation.

Looking Back

As you worked on the Problems in this Unit, you extended your knowledge of two-dimensional geometry. Two-dimensional geometry is the study of shapes that fit on a flat surface. You learned:

- How side lengths and angle measures determine the shapes of triangles, rectangles, parallelograms, and other polygons

- Why some regular polygons can fit together to cover a flat surface while others cannot

- That polygon properties are important in design of natural and man-made objects

Use Your Understanding: Two-Dimensional Geometry

Test your understanding of shapes and designs by answering the following questions about angles and polygons.

1. This drawing of a building contains many angles and polygons.

a. Which labeled angles appear to be right angles? Which appear to be acute angles? Which appear to be obtuse angles?

b. List the labeled angles from smallest to largest. Estimate the degree measure of each angle. Then, use an angle ruler or protractor to measure each as accurately as possible.

c. Which polygon shapes can be found in the building plan?

d. What is the supplement of the measure of angle J? The measurement of angle H?

2. An interior decorator is considering regular pentagon and hexagon tiles for a floor design.

   a. What is the measure of each interior angle in a regular pentagon? Show or explain how you arrived at your answer.

   b. Is it possible to tile a floor with copies of a regular pentagon? Explain your reasoning.

   c. What is the measure of each interior angle in a regular hexagon? Show or explain how you arrived at your answer.

   d. What is the measure of each exterior angle in a regular hexagon? Show or explain how you arrived at your answer.

   e. Is it possible to tile a floor with copies of a regular hexagon? Explain your reasoning.

   f. Describe the symmetries of the two polygon tiles.

   g. Do either of these regular polygons have parallel sides? Explain your reasoning.

3. Complete the following for parts (a)–(d).

   • Tell whether it is possible to draw a shape meeting the given conditions. If it is, make a sketch of the shape.

   • If it is possible to make a shape meeting the given conditions, tell whether it is possible to make a different shape that also meets the conditions. If it is, make a sketch of one or more of these different shapes.

   a. a triangle with side lengths of 4 cm, 6 cm, and 9 cm

   b. a triangle with side lengths of 4 cm, 7 cm, and 2 cm

   c. a rectangle with one pair of opposite sides of length 8 cm

   d. a parallelogram with side lengths of 8 cm, 8 cm, 6 cm, and 6 cm

4. In your work on the Problems in this Unit, you discovered that triangles are especially useful polygons.

   a. Why are triangles so useful in building structures?

   b. Sketch a triangle that has both rotation and reflection symmetries.

   c. Sketch a triangle that has only one line of symmetry.

   d. Sketch a triangle that has no symmetries.

   e. What combinations of side and angle measurements can be used to decide if two given triangles are congruent?

adjacent angles Two angles in a plane that share a common vertex and common side but do not overlap are adjacent angles. In the parallelogram below, *a* and *b* are adjacent angles. Other pairs of adjacent angles are *a* and *c*, *b* and *d*, and *c* and *d*.

ángulos adyacentes Dos ángulos en un plano que comparten un lado común y el vértice común, pero no se superponen son ángulos adyacentes. En el paralelogramo a continuación, *a* y *b* son ángulos adyacentes. Otros pares de ángulos adyacentes son *a* y *c*, *b* y *d*, y *c* y *d*.

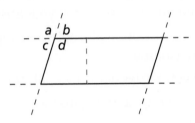

angle The figure formed by two rays or line segments that have a common vertex. Angles are measured in degrees. The sides of an angle are rays that have the vertex as a starting point. Each of the three angles below is formed by the joining of two rays. The angle at point *A* on the triangle below is identified as angle *BAC* or ∠*BAC*.

ángulo Figura que forman dos rayos o segmentos que se juntan en un vértice. Los ángulos se miden en grados. Los lados de un ángulo son rayos que tienen el vértice como punto de partida. Cada uno de los tres ángulos está formado por la unión de dos rayos. El ángulo del punto *A* del triángulo representado a continuación se identifica como el ángulo *BAC* o ∠*BAC*.

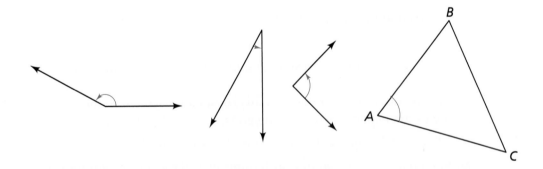

angle ruler An angle ruler is a tool with two transparent arms, linked by a rivet that allows them to swing apart to form angles of various sizes. One arm is marked with a circular ruler showing degree measures from 0° to 360°. A goniometer is one type of angle ruler.

regla de ángulo Una regla de ángulo ángulo es una herramienta con dos brazos transparentes, unidas por un remache que les permite pivotar aparte para formar ángulos de varios tamaños. Un brazo se marca con una regla circular que muestra las medidas de grado de 0° a 360°. Un goniómetro es un tipo de gobernante ángulo.

C

complementary angles Complementary angles are a pair of angles whose measures add to 90°.

angulos complementarios Los ángulos complementarios son un par de ángulos cuyas medidas suman 90°.

concave polygon A concave polygon is a polygon with at least one interior angle whose measure is greater than 180°. The concave polygon shown below has one interior angle that measures 258°.

polígono cóncavo Un polígono cóncavo es un polígono con al menos un ángulo interior, cuya medida es mayor que 180°. El polígono cóncavo muestra a continuación tiene un ángulo interior que mide 258°.

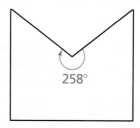

258°

convex polygon A convex polygon is a polygon with all interior angles measuring less than 180°.

polígono convexo Un polígono convexo es un polígono con todos los ángulos interiores miden menos de 180°.

135°   135°

D **degree** A unit of measure of angles is also equal to $\frac{1}{360}$ of a complete circle. The angle below measures about 1 degree (1°); 360 of these would just fit around a point and fill in a complete circle; 90 of them make a right angle.

grado Una unidad de medida de ángulos que equivale a $\frac{1}{360}$ de un círculo completo. El ángulo representado a continuación mide aproximadamente 1°; 360 de estos ángulos encajarían alrededor de un punto y llenarían completamente un círculo, mientras que 90 formarían un ángulo recto.

diagonal A line segment connecting two nonadjacent vertices of a polygon. All quadrilaterals have two diagonals as shown below. The two diagonals of a square are equal in length, and the two diagonals of a rectangle are equal in length. A pentagon has five diagonals. A hexagon has nine diagonals.

diagonal Un segmento de recta que conecta dos vértices no adyacentes de un polígono. Todos los cuadriláteros tienen dos diagonals, como se representa a continuación. Las dos diagonales de un cuadrado tienen longitudes iguales, y las dos diagonales de un rectángulo tienen longitudes iguales. Un pentágono tiene cinco diagonales y un hexágono tiene nueve diagonales.

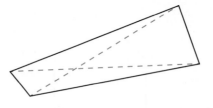

E **equilateral triangle** A triangle with all sides the same length.

triángulo equilátero Un triángulo que tiene tres lados de la misma longitud.

exterior angle An angle at a vertex of a polygon where the sides of the angle are one side of the polygon and the extension of the other side meeting at the vertex. In the pentagons below, angles *a, b, c, d, e, f, g, h, i,* and *j* are exterior angles.

ángulo exterior Ángulo en el vértice de un polígono donde los lados del ángulo son un lado del polígono y la extensión del otro lado se une en ese vértice.

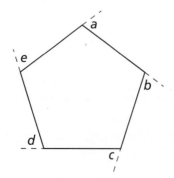
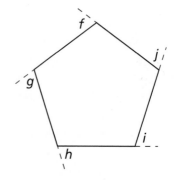

illustrate Academic Vocabulary

To show or present information usually as a drawing or a diagram. You can also illustrate a point using a written explanation.

related terms: *present, display*

sample The needle of a compass is pointing 90 degrees from North. In which direction can the needle be pointing? Make a sketch to illustrate this situation.

The needle could be pointing East, since a needle pointing east would form a 90° angle with North on the compass. The needle can also be pointing West because it also would form a 90° angle with North.

indicate Academic Vocabulary

To point out or show.

related terms: *demonstrate, show, identify*

sample Indicate which symbol is used to represent rotation.

The curved arrow is the symbol used to represent rotation. The small circle indicates the degrees of an angle. The dashed line is used to show symmetry.

ilustrar Vocabulario académico

Mostrar o presentar informacion por lo general como un dibujo o un diagrama. Tambien puedes ilustrar un punto usando una explicacion escrita.

Terminos relacionados: *presentar, exhibir*

ejemplo La aguja de una brujula apunta 90 grados desde el Norte. En que direccon puede estar apuntando la aguja? Haz un bosquejo para ilustrar esta situacion.

La aguja podría estar apuntando hacia el Este, puesto que una aguja que apunte al este formaría un ángulo de 90° con el Norte en la brújula. La aguja también puede estar apuntando al Oeste porque también formaría un ángulo de 90° con el Norte.

indicar Vocabulario académico

Apuntar o mostrar.

terminos relacionados: *demostrar, mostrar, identificar*

ejemplo Indica cual simbolo se usa para representar la rotacion.

La flecha curvada es el símbolo que se usa para representar la rotación. El círculo pequeño indica los grados de un ángulo. La línea punteada se usa para mostrar simetría.

interior angle The angle inside a polygon formed by two adjacent sides of the polygon. In the pentagon below, *a, b, c, d,* and *e* are interior angles.

ángulo interior Ángulo dentro de un polígono formado por los lados del polígono.

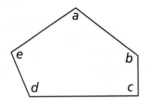

irregular polygon A polygon that has at least two sides with different lengths or two angles with different measures.

ipolígono irregular Polígono que tiene al menos dos lados de diferentes longitudes o dos ángulos con diferentes medidas.

J **justify** Academic Vocabulary
To support your answers with reasons or examples. A justification may include a written response, diagrams, charts, tables, or a combination of these.

justificar Vocabulario académico
Apoyer tus respuestas con rezones o ejemplos. Una justificacion puede incluir una respuesta escrita, diagramas, graficas, tables o una combinacion de estos.

related terms: *validate, explain, defend, reason*

terminos relacionados: *validar, explicar, defender, razonar*

sample Tell whether the following statement is true or false. Justify your answer.

ejemplo Di si la siguiente afirmacion es cierta o falsa. Justifica tu respuesta.

All squares are parallelograms.

Todos los cuadrados son paralelogramos.

> The statement is true. All squares are parallelograms because all squares have two pairs of parallel sides.

> El enunciado es cierto. Todos los cuadrados son paralelogramos porque todos los cuadrados tienen dos pares de lados paralelos.

parallel lines Lines in a plane that never meet. The opposite sides of a regular hexagon are parallel.

rectas paralelas Rectas en un plano, que nunca se encuentran. Los lados opuestos de un hexágono regular son paralelos. Los polígonos A y B tienen un par de lados opuestos que son paralelos. Cada uno de los polígonos C, D y E tienen dos pares de lados opuestos que son paralelos.

Polygons A and B each have one pair of opposite sides parallel.

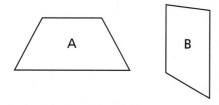

Polygons C, D, and E each have two pairs of opposite sides parallel.

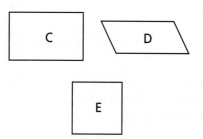

parallelogram A quadrilateral with opposite sides parallel. Both pairs of opposite angles are also equal. In the definition of parallel lines, figure D, rectangle C, and square E are all parallelograms.

paralelogramo Cuadrilátero cuyos lados opuestos son paralelos. Ambos pares de ángulos opuestos también son iguales. En la definición de rectas paralelas, la figura D, el rectángulo C y el cuadrado E son paralelogramos.

polygon A shape formed by line segments, called sides, so that each of the segments meets exactly two other segments, and all of the points where the segments meet are endpoints of the segments.

polígono Figura formada por segmentos de recta de modo que cada uno de los segmentos se junta exactamente con otros dos segmentos, y todos los puntos donde se encuentran los segmentos son extremos de los segmentos.

Polygons

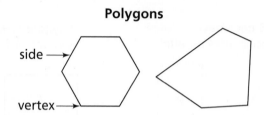

Special polygon names use Greek prefixes that tell the number of sides or the number of angles in a polygon.

- triangle: A polygon with 3 sides and angles
- quadrilateral: A polygon with 4 sides and angles
- pentagon: A polygon with 5 sides and angles
- hexagon: A polygon with 6 sides and angles
- heptagon: A polygon with 7 sides and angles
- octagon: A polygon with 8 sides and angles
- nonagon (also called enneagon): A polygon with 9 sides and angles
- decagon: A polygon with 10 sides and angles
- dodecagon: A polygon with 12 sides and angles

Los nombres especiales con que se designan los polígonos provienen de prefijos griegos que indican el numero de lados o el numero de ángulos del polígono.

- triangulo: polígono con 3 lados y ángulos
- cuadrilátero: polígono con 4 lados y ángulos
- pentágono: polígono con 5 lados y ángulos
- hexágono: polígono con 6 lados y ángulos
- heptágono: polígono con 7 lados y ángulos
- octágono: polígono con 8 lados y ángulos
- nonágono (también llamado eneágono): polígono con 9 lados y ángulos
- decágono: polígono con 10 lados y ángulos
- dodecágono: polígono con 12 lados y ángulos

protractor A protractor is a type of semi-circular ruler with scale measured in degrees. The degree measures on a protractor are listed both in ascending and descending order to measure angles regardless of their orientation.

transportador Un transportador es un tipo de semi-circular regla con escala mide en grados. Las medidas grados en un transportador de ángulos se muestran tanto en orden ascendente y descendente para medir ángulos con independencia de su orientación.

quadrants The four sections into which the coordinate plane is divided by the *x*- and *y*-axes. The quadrants are labeled as follows:

cuadrantes Las cuatro secciones en las que los ejes *x* y *y* dividen a un plano de coordendas. Los cuadrantes se identifican de la siguiente manera:

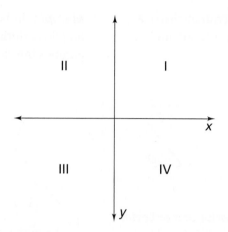

rectangle A parallelogram with all right angles. Squares are a special type of rectangle.

rectángulo Un paralelogramo con todos los ángulos rectos. Los cuadrados son un tipo especial de rectángulo.

Rectangles

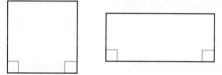

reflectional symmetry A shape with reflectional symmetry has two halves that are mirror images of each other.

simetría de reflexión Una figura con simetría de reflexión tiene dos mitades que son imágenes exactas una de la otra.

regular polygon A polygon that has all of its sides equal and all of its angles equal. The hexagon below is regular, but the pentagon is not regular, because its sides and its angles are not equal.

polígono regular Un polígono que tiene todos los lados y todos los ángulos iguales. El hexágono representado a continuación es regular pero el pentágono no lo es porque sus lados y sus ángulos no son iguales.

Regular   Not Regular

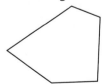

relate Academic Vocabulary
To find a connection between two different things.

related terms: *connect, match*

sample Tell how the exterior angles of a quadrilateral relate to the interior angles.

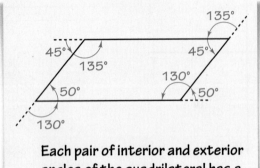

Each pair of interior and exterior angles of the quadrilateral has a sum of 180° because each pair of angles forms a straight angle.

relacionar Vocabulario académico
Hallar una conexion entre dos cosas diferentes.

terminos relacionados: *conectar, correspondar*

ejemplo Indica como se relacionan los angulos exteriones de un cuadrilatero con los angulos interiors.

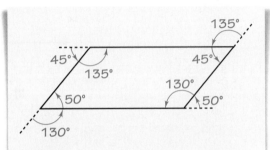

La suma de las medidas de cada par de ángulos interiores y exteriores es de 180° porque cada par de ángulos forma un ángulo recto.

---

rhombus A quadrilateral that has all sides the same length.

rombo Un cuadrilátero que tiene todos los lados de la misma longitud.

---

right angle An angle that measures 90°. A rectangle has four right angles.

ángulo recto Un ángulo que mide 90°. Un rectángulo tiene los cuatro ángulos rectos.

rotation A transformation that turns a figure counterclockwise about a point. Polygon $A'B'C'D'$ below is the image of polygon $ABCD$ under a 60° rotation about point P. If you drew a segment from a point on polygon ABCD to point P, the segments would be the same length and they would form a 60° angle.

rotacion Una transformación en la que una figura gira alrededor de un punto, en sentido contrario a las manecillas del reloj. El polígono $A'B'C'D'$ que se muestra es la imagen del polígono $ABCD$ después de una rotación de 60° alrededor el punto P. Si se dibujara un segmento de recta desde un punto en el polígono $ABCD$ hasta el punto P, los segmentos tendrían la misma longitud y formarían un ángulo de 60°.

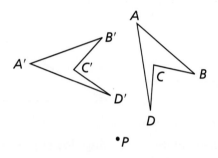

rotational symmetry A shape has rotational symmetry if it can be rotated less than a full turn about its center point to a position where it looks exactly as it did before it was rotated.

simetría de rotación Una figura tiene simetría de rotación si puede girarse menos de una vuelta completa sobre su centro hasta una posición en la que se vea exactamente igual que antes de girarse.

sketch Academic Vocabulary
To draw a rough outline of something. When a sketch is asked for, it means that a drawing needs to be included in your response.

related terms: *draw, illustrate*

sample Sketch a 30° angle.

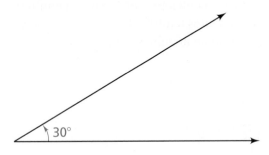

supplementary angles Supplementary angles are two angles that form a straight line. The sum of the angles is 180°.

T **tessellation** See *tiling*.

tiling Also called a tessellation. The covering of a plane surface with geometric shapes without gaps or overlaps. These shapes are usually regular polygons or other common polygons. The tiling below is made of triangles. You could remove some of the line segments to create a tiling of parallelograms, or remove still more to create a tiling of hexagons. In a tiling, a vertex is a point where the corners of the polygons fit together.

hacer un bosquejo Vocabulario académico
Dibujar un esbozo de algo. Cuando se pide un bosquejo, significa que necesitas incluir un dibujo en tu respuesta.

terminos relacionados: *dibujar, ilustrar*

ejemplo Haz un bosquejo de un angulo de 30°.

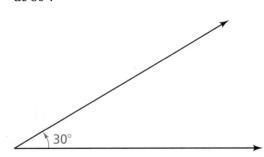

ángulos supplementarios Los ángulos suplementarios son dos ángulos que forman una recta. La suma de los ángulos es de 180°.

teselado Ver *embaldosamiento*.

embaldosamiento También llamado teselado. Embaldosar es llenar una superficie plana con figuras geométricas sin dejar espacios o superponer figuras. Estas figuras suelen ser polígonos regulares u otros polígonos comunes. El embaldosamiento representado a continuación está formado por triángulos. Se podrían quitar algunos de los segmentos de rectas para crear un teselado de paralelogramos y hasta eliminar otros más para crear un teselado de hexágonos. En un embaldosamiento, un vértice es un punto donde se unen las esquinas de los polígonos.

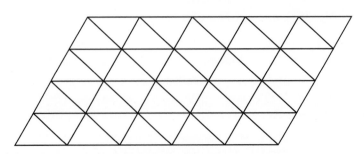

transversal A line that intersects two or more lines. Lines *s* and *t* are transversals.

transversal Recta que interseca dos o más rectas. Las rectas *s* y *t* son transversales.

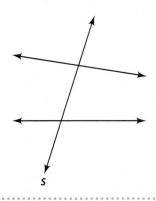

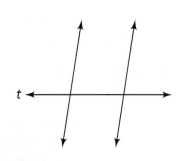

trapezoid A quadrilateral with exactly one pair of opposite sides parallel. This definition means that parallelograms are not trapezoids.

trapecio Un cuadrilátero que tiene exactamente uno par de lados paralelos opuestos. Esta definición significa que los paralelogramos no son trapecios.

Trapezoids

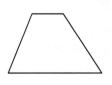
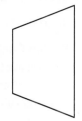

V

vertical angles Vertical angles are a pair of congruent nonadjacent angles formed by the intersection of two lines. In the figure below, angles *a* and *c* are vertical angles, and angles *b* and *d* are vertical angles.

ángulos verticales Los ángulos verticales son un par de congruentes no adyacentes ángulos formados por la intersección de dos líneas. En la siguiente figura, los ángulos *a* y *c* son ángulos verticales, y los ángulos *b* y *d* son ángulos verticales.

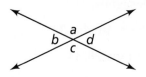

Index

Acknowledgments

Cover Design

Three Communication Design, Chicago

Photographs

Photo locators denoted as follows: Top (T), Center (C), Bottom (B), Left (L), Right (R), Background (Bkgd)

002 (CR) darios/Shutterstock; **002** (BR) Kelly-Mooney Photography/CORBIS; **003** Bizuayehu Tesfaye/Ap images; **015** OAR/ERL/National Severe Storms Laboratory (NSSL)/NOAA; **022** Spencer Grant/PhotoEdit; **038** Bettmann/Corbis; **047** darios/Shutterstock; **048** 3desc/Fotolia; **062** Pearson Education; **069** (BL) Dalibor Sevaljevic/Shutterstock, (BR) Ken Welsh/Design Pics/Corbis; **081** Kelly-Mooney Photography/CORBIS; **082** Christie's Images/Corbis; **083** (CL) Alex Melnick/Shutterstock, (CR) Bonnie Kamin/PhotoEdit, Inc.

CONNECTED MATHEMATICS® 3

Accentuate the Negative

Integers and Rational Numbers

Lappan, Phillips, Fey, Friel

Accentuate the Negative

Integers and Rational Numbers

Looking Ahead

A person goes from a sauna at 115°F to an outside temperature of ⁻30°F. **What** is the change in temperature?

A racetrack is marked by a number line measured in meters. Hahn runs from the 15-meter line to the ⁻15-meter line in 8 seconds. At **what** rate (meters per second), and in what direction, does he run?

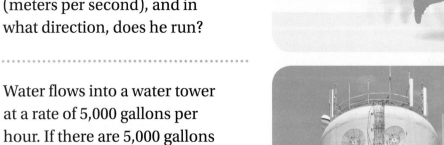

Water flows into a water tower at a rate of 5,000 gallons per hour. If there are 5,000 gallons of water at the start, **how much** is there after 4 hours?

Most of the numbers you have worked with in math class have been greater than or equal to zero. However, numbers less than zero can provide important information. Winter temperatures in many places fall below 0°F. Businesses that lose money have profits less than $0. Scores in games or sports can be less than zero.

Numbers greater than zero are called *positive numbers*. Numbers less than zero are called *negative numbers*. In *Accentuate the Negative*, you will work with both positive and negative numbers. You will study *integers* and *rational numbers,* two specific sets of numbers that include positive and negative numbers. You will explore models that help you think about adding, subtracting, multiplying, and dividing these numbers. You will also learn more about the properties of operations on positive and negative numbers.

In *Accentuate the Negative,* you will solve problems similar to those on the previous page that require understanding and skill in working with positive and negative numbers.

Mathematical Highlights

Integers and Rational Numbers

In *Accentuate the Negative,* you will extend your knowledge of negative numbers. You will use negative numbers to solve problems.

You will learn how to

- Use appropriate notation to indicate positive and negative numbers and zero

- Compare and order rational numbers and locate them on a number line

- Understand the relationship between a number and its opposite (additive inverse)

- Relate direction and distance to the number line

- Develop and use different models (number line, chip model) for representing addition, subtraction, multiplication, and division

- Develop algorithms for adding, subtracting, multiplying, and dividing positive and negative numbers

- Interpret and write mathematical sentences to show relationships and solve problems

- Write and use related fact families for addition/subtraction and multiplication/division to solve simple equations

- Use parentheses and the Order of Operations in computations

- Use the commutative properties of addition and multiplication

- Apply the Distributive Property to simplify expressions and solve problems

- Use models and rational numbers to represent and solve problems

When you encounter a new problem, it is a good idea to ask yourself questions. In this Unit, you might ask questions such as:

How do negative and positive numbers and zero help describe the situation?

What will addition, subtraction, multiplication, or division of rational numbers tell about the problem?

What model(s) for positive and negative numbers and zero help show relationships in the problem situation?

Mathematical Practices and Habits of Mind

In the *Connected Mathematics* curriculum you will develop an understanding of important mathematical ideas by solving problems and reflecting on the mathematics involved. Every day, you will use "habits of mind" to make sense of problems and apply what you learn to new situations. Some of these habits are described by the *Common Core State Standards for Mathematical Practices* (MP).

MP1 Make sense of problems and persevere in solving them.

When using mathematics to solve a problem, it helps to think carefully about

- data and other facts you are given and what additional information you need to solve the problem;
- strategies you have used to solve similar problems and whether you could solve a related simpler problem first;
- how you could express the problem with equations, diagrams, or graphs;
- whether your answer makes sense.

MP2 Reason abstractly and quantitatively.

When you are asked to solve a problem, it often helps to

- focus first on the key mathematical ideas;
- check that your answer makes sense in the problem setting;
- use what you know about the problem setting to guide your mathematical reasoning.

MP3 Construct viable arguments and critique the reasoning of others.

When you are asked to explain why a conjecture is correct, you can

- show some examples that fit the claim and explain why they fit;
- show how a new result follows logically from known facts and principles.

When you believe a mathematical claim is incorrect, you can

- show one or more counterexamples—cases that don't fit the claim;
- find steps in the argument that do not follow logically from prior claims.

MP4 Model with mathematics.

When you are asked to solve problems, it often helps to

- think carefully about the numbers or geometric shapes that are the most important factors in the problem, then ask yourself how those factors are related to each other;
- express data and relationships in the problem with tables, graphs, diagrams, or equations, and check your result to see if it makes sense.

MP5 Use appropriate tools strategically.

When working on mathematical questions, you should always

- decide which tools are most helpful for solving the problem and why;
- try a different tool when you get stuck.

MP6 Attend to precision.

In every mathematical exploration or problem-solving task, it is important to

- think carefully about the required accuracy of results: is a number estimate or geometric sketch good enough, or is a precise value or drawing needed?
- report your discoveries with clear and correct mathematical language that can be understood by those to whom you are speaking or writing.

MP7 Look for and make use of structure.

In mathematical explorations and problem solving, it is often helpful to

- look for patterns that show how data points, numbers, or geometric shapes are related to each other;
- use patterns to make predictions.

MP8 Look for and express regularity in repeated reasoning.

When results of a repeated calculation show a pattern, it helps to

- express that pattern as a general rule that can be used in similar cases;
- look for shortcuts that will make the calculation simpler in other cases.

You will use all of the Mathematical Practices in this Unit. Sometimes, when you look at a Problem, it is obvious which practice is most helpful. At other times, you will decide on a practice to use during class explorations and discussions. After completing each Problem, ask yourself:

- What mathematics have I learned by solving this Problem?
- What Mathematical Practices were helpful in learning this mathematics?

Investigation 1

Extending the Number System

One of the most useful representations of numbers is a number line. A number line displays numbers in order so that their relationship to each other is clear. You can determine whether numbers are less than or greater than other numbers by looking at their positions on a number line.

A number line also illustrates the relationships between signed numbers.

To avoid confusion with operation signs, you can use raised signs to show negative rational numbers, such as ⁻150. If a rational number does not have a sign, you can assume it is positive. For example, 150 is the same as ⁺150.

- What is the relationship between ⁻0.6 and 0.6?

- Which number is greater, ⁻2.3 or 1.2?

- How can you use a number line to help you list ⁻2.3, ⁻3.5, and 1.7 in order?

As you work on this Investigation, use number lines to help you think and reason about mathematical situations.

Common Core State Standards

7.NS.A.1 Apply and extend previous understandings of addition and subtraction to add and subtract rational numbers; represent addition and subtraction on a horizontal or vertical number line diagram.

7.NS.A.1a Describe situations in which opposite quantities combine to make 0.

7.NS.A.2b Understand that integers can be divided, provided that the divisor is not zero, and every quotient of integers (with non-zero divisor) is a rational number . . .

7.NS.A.3 Solve real-world and mathematical problems involving the four operations with rational numbers.

Also **7.NS.A.1b, 7.NS.A.1c, 7.EE.B.4, 7.EE.B.4b**

You have worked with whole numbers, fractions, and decimals in earlier units. In this Unit, you will work with integers. **Integers** are the set of whole numbers, their opposites, and zero. Integers and fractions, (and their equivalent decimals), are called *rational* numbers.

Problem 1.1 involves a game with positive and negative scores. As you work through the Problem, think about which operations you use to keep track of the scores. Notice how the score goes higher or lower depending on whether a team answers a question correctly or incorrectly.

1.1 Playing Math Fever
Using Positive and Negative Numbers

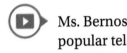 Ms. Bernoski's math classes often play Math Fever, a game similar to a popular television game show. The game board is shown. Below each category name are five cards. The front of each card shows a point value. The back of each card has a question related to the category. Cards with higher point values have more difficult questions.

Math Fever					
Operations With Fractions	Similarity	Probability	Area and Perimeter	Tiling the Plane	Factors and Multiples
50	50	50	50	50	50
100	100	100	100	100	100
150	150	150	150	150	150
200	200	200	200	200	200
250	250	250	250	250	250

Math Fever is played in teams. One team starts the game by choosing a card. The teacher asks the question on the back of the card. The first team to answer the question correctly gets the point value on the card. The card is then removed from the board. If a team answers the question incorrectly, the point value is subtracted from their score. The other teams may then try to answer the question. The team that answers correctly chooses the next card.

Problem 1.1

A At one point in a game, the scores are as follows:

Super Brains	Rocket Scientists	Know-It-Alls
⁻300	150	⁻500

1. Which team has the highest score? Which team has the lowest score? Explain how you decided.

2. Find the difference in points for each pair of teams.

3. Use *number sentences* to describe two possible ways that each team reached its score.

B The current scores are ⁻300 for Super Brains, 150 for Rocket Scientists, and ⁻500 for Know-It-Alls.

1. Write a number sentence to represent each sequence of points. Start with the current score for each team.

a. **Super Brains**

Point Value	Answer
200	Correct
150	Incorrect
50	Correct
50	Correct

b. **Rocket Scientists**

Point Value	Answer
50	Incorrect
200	Incorrect
100	Correct
150	Incorrect

c. **Know-It-Alls**

Point Value	Answer
100	Incorrect
200	Correct
150	Incorrect
50	Incorrect

2. At this point in the game, which team has the highest score? Which team has the lowest score?

3. Find the difference in points for each pair of teams.

continued on the next page >

Problem 1.1 continued

C The number sentences below describe what happens at a particular point during a game of Math Fever. For each number sentence:

- Find the missing number.

- Explain what the sentence tells about a team's performance and overall score.

1. BrainyActs: $^-200 + 150 - 100 = $ ■

2. Xtremes: $450 - 300 = $ ■

3. ExCells: $300 - 450 = $ ■

4. AmazingMs: $^-350 + $ ■ $= {}^-150$

D Sam forgot to record a score. Sam wrote this number sentence:

$$^-350 + ■ = {}^-450$$

What score goes in the box?

E 1. Find three different pairs of numbers that have a sum of $^-150$.

$$■ + ■ = {}^-150$$

2. Does the order of the addends matter? Explain your reasoning.

F Luisa answers a 300-point question correctly and a 400-point question incorrectly. Luisa and Sam use different methods to keep score:

Luisa's Method		**Sam's Method**
$300 - 400 = {}^-100$	OR	$300 + {}^-400 = {}^-100$

Who is correct? Which methods work for other pairs of scores? Explain your reasoning.

A C E Homework starts on page 20.

1.2 Extending the Number Line

Rational numbers are numbers that can be expressed as one integer a divided by another integer b, where b is not zero. You can write a rational number in the form $\frac{a}{b}$ or in decimal form.

For a rational number, $\frac{a}{b}$, why does b have to be nonzero?

- Are integers rational numbers? Explain.

- Is zero a rational number? Explain.

Each **negative number** can be paired with a **positive number.** These two numbers are called **opposites** because they are the same distance from zero on the number line, but in different directions.

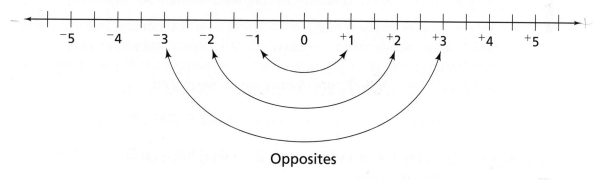

Opposites

- Where would the following pairs of numbers be located on the number line?

$$7 \text{ and } ^-7; \frac{21}{2} \text{ and } \frac{^-21}{2}; ^-3\frac{1}{2} \text{ and } 3\frac{1}{2}; ^-\frac{1}{2} \text{ and } \frac{1}{2}$$

- How would you graph the set of all numbers less than 4 on a number line? The numbers between 1 and $^-15\frac{1}{2}$?

Problem 1.2

A 1. Estimate values for points *A–E*.

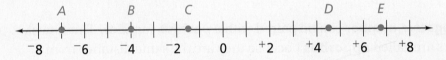

2. For each value you estimated in part (1), state the number's opposite.

3. A thermometer can be thought of as part of a vertical number line on which values above zero are positive. Sketch a thermometer (vertical number line), and place the following temperatures on it. Explain how you decided where each temperature should be placed.

$$0°F \quad ^+115°F \quad ^-15°F \quad ^-32.5°F \quad ^+40°F \quad ^+113.2°F \quad ^-32.7°F$$

4. How do the number lines from parts (1) and (3) help you find which of two numbers is greater?

B For each pair of temperatures, identify which temperature is further from $^-2°F$. Explain how you decided.

1. $^+6°F$ or $^-6°F$?

2. $^-7°F$ or $^+3°F$?

3. $^+2°F$ or $^-7°F$?

4. $^-10°F$ or $^+7°F$?

C Identify the temperature that is halfway between each pair of temperatures. Explain your reasoning.

1. $0°F$ and $^+10°F$

2. $^-5°F$ and $^+15°F$

3. $^+5°F$ and $^-15°F$

4. $^-8°F$ and $^+8°F$

Problem **1.2** *continued*

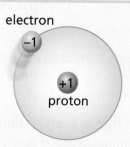

electron

−1

+1
proton

D Integers are also used in chemistry. For example, a hydrogen atom has one proton, which has a charge of ⁺1, and one electron, which has a charge of ⁻1. The total charge of a hydrogen atom is ⁺1 + ⁻1, or 0. Describe three more real-life situations in which opposite quantities combine to make 0.

E Recall that the graph of an inequality is a sketch on a number line on which possible answers are shaded. For each part, graph the possible solutions for x on a number line.

1. x is positive.

2. x is less than or equal to ⁻5.

3. $x < {}^-7$

4. $x \geq 5$

5. $6 < x$

6. ${}^-1 \leq x$

F Find the values of x that satisfy the inequality. Then graph the solutions.

1. $x + 5 > 0$

2. $x - 1 \leq 0$

3. $3x < 9$

G Describe how you drew your graphs for Questions E and F.

A C E Homework starts on page 20.

Did You Know?

In golf, scores can be negative. Each golf hole has a value called *par*. Par is the number of strokes a golfer usually needs to complete the hole. For example, a good golfer should be able to complete a par-4 hole in four strokes or less. If a golfer completes the hole in six strokes, then the score for that hole is "two over par" (⁺2). A player's score for a round of golf is the total number of strokes above or below par. A winning score at a golf tournament is often negative. The lower the score, the better!

Red Tee
Golf Club

HOLE	1	2	3	4	5	6	7	8	9	TOTAL
PAR	5	4	3	4	4	4	3	4	5	36
My Strokes	7	3	3	3	7	3	4	6	3	39
My Score	+2	−1	0	−1	+3	−1	+1	+2	−2	+3

1.3 From Sauna to Snowbank
Using a Number Line

In Finland, people sit for a short time in sauna houses that are heated up to temperatures as high as 120°F. Then they go outside, where the temperature may be as low as ⁻20°F, to cool off.

The two thermometers shown are similar to vertical number lines. On a thermometer, a move down shows a decrease in value. The temperatures get colder. A move up shows an increase in value. The temperatures get hotter.

Inside the Sauna

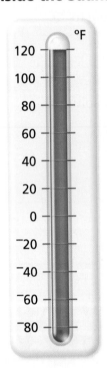

Outside in Snow

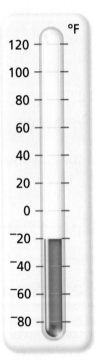

One horizontal number line can show the same information as the two thermometers.

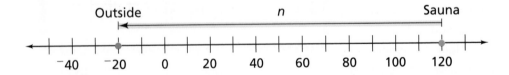

- What does *n* represent?

- What does the number sentence $120 + n = {}^-20$ tell you?

- What does the number sentence $^-20 + n = 120$ tell you?

On a number line, a move to the left is a move in a negative direction. The numbers decrease in value. A move to the right is a move in a positive direction. The numbers increase in value.

The National Weather Service keeps records of temperature changes. The world record for the fastest rise in outside air temperature occurred in Spearfish, South Dakota, on January 22, 1943. The temperature rose from $^-4°F$ to $45°F$ in two minutes.

- What was the temperature change over those two minutes?

- How could you show this change, n, on the number line?

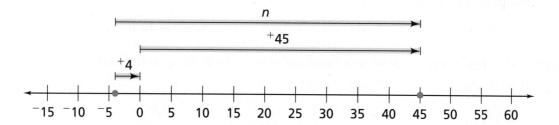

From $^-4°F$ to $0°F$ is a change of $^+4°F$. From $0°F$ to $45°F$ is a change of $^+45°F$. The total change is $^+49°F$. The following number sentences show this.

$$^-4 + n = {}^+45$$
$$^-4 + {}^+49 = {}^+45$$

The sign of the change in temperature shows the direction of the change. In this case, $^+49$ means the temperature increased $49°F$.

If the temperature had instead dropped $10°F$ from $^-4°F$, you would write the change as $^-10°F$. The final temperature would be $^-14°F$.

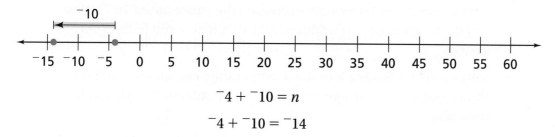

$$^-4 + {}^-10 = n$$
$$^-4 + {}^-10 = {}^-14$$

- If the current temperature is $5°F$, what change in temperature would result in a final temperature of $^-25°F$?

Problem 1.3

Sketch number lines for Questions A–D. Write number sentences for Questions A–E.

A A person goes from a sauna at 115°F to an outside temperature of ⁻30°F. What is the change in temperature?

B The temperature reading on a thermometer is 25°F at noon. During the afternoon, the temperature changes. What is the new reading for each temperature change?

   1. rises 10°F   **2.** falls 2°F   **3.** falls 30°F

C The temperature reading on a thermometer is ⁻15°F. What is the new reading for each temperature change?

   1. ⁺3°F   **2.** ⁻10°F   **3.** ⁺40°F

D What is the change in temperature when the thermometer reading moves from the first temperature to the second temperature?

   1. 20°F to ⁻10°F   **2.** ⁻20°F to ⁻10°F

   3. ⁻20°F to 10°F   **4.** ⁻10°F to ⁻20°F

   5. 20°F to 10°F   **6.** 10°F to 20°F

   7. Describe a strategy for finding the difference of two temperatures.

E **1.** The temperature was ⁻5°F when Sally went to school on Monday. The temperature rose 20°F during the day, but fell 25°F during the night. A heat wave increased the temperature 40°F on Tuesday, but then an arctic wind overnight decreased the temperature 70°F! What was the temperature on Wednesday? Explain how you found your answer.

   2. Sally's work for finding Monday's temperature changes in part (1) is shown below. Do you agree with Sally's computation? Explain your reasoning.

$$⁻5 + 20 + ⁻25 = ⁺15 + ⁻25$$
$$= ⁺15 - 25$$
$$= ⁻10$$

ACE Homework starts on page 20.

1.4 In the Chips
Using a Chip Model

When business records were kept by hand, accountants used red ink for expenses and black ink for income. If your income was greater than your expenses, you were "in the black." If your expenses were greater than your income, you were "in the red." You wanted to be "in the black."

Julia has this problem to solve:

> Tate owes his sister $6 for helping him cut the lawn. He earns $4 delivering papers. Is Tate "in the red" or "in the black"?

To solve this problem, Julia uses red and black chips to model income and expenses. Each black chip represents $^{+}1$ dollar of income. Each red chip represents $^{-}1$ dollar of income (expenses).

Julia puts chips on the board to represent the situation.

Julia's Chip Board

She decides that Tate is "in the red" 2 dollars, or has $^{-}2$ dollars. She writes

$$^{-}6 + {}^{+}4 = {}^{-}2$$

- Why do you think Julia concludes that $^{-}6 + {}^{+}4 = {}^{-}2$?

- What is another way to show a total value of $^{-}2$ on the chip board?

- What are some ways to show a total value of zero?

- Julia changes the board by adding one red chip and one black chip. By how much has Julia changed the total value?

- What groups of red and black chips can you add to the board that will not change the total value on the board?

Problem 1.4

A Use this chip board as the starting value for each part.

Write a number sentence to show the total value on the chip board for each move.

1. original chip board

2. add 5 black chips

3. remove 5 red chips

4. remove 3 black chips

5. add 3 red chips

6. What patterns do you see?

B Start with the original chip board from Question A.

1. Describe three ways to get a total value of $^-2$.

2. Describe three ways to get a total value of 0.

3. Describe three ways to get a total value of $^-4$.

C Give three combinations of red and black chips (using at least one of each color) that will equal each value.

1. 0

2. $^+12$

3. $^-7$

4. $^-125$

Problem 1.4 *continued*

D Find the missing part for each chip problem. Write a number sentence for each problem.

	Start With	Rule	End With	Number Sentence
1.	⚫⚫⚫	Add 5 ⚫	▪	▪
2.	⚫⚫⚫	Subtract 3 ⚫	▪	▪
3.	⚫⚫⚫ ⚫⚫⚫	▪	⚫⚫	▪
4.	▪	Subtract 3 ⚫	⚫⚫⚫⚫	▪

E Describe a chip board display that matches each number sentence. Find the missing value in each case.

1. $^+3 - {}^+2 = $ ▪
2. $^-4 - {}^+2 = $ ▪
3. $^-4 - {}^-2 = $ ▪
4. $^+7 + $ ▪ $ = {}^+1$
5. $^-3 - {}^+5 = $ ▪
6. ▪ $ - {}^-2 = {}^+6$

F Nadie has a chip board with 4 red chips. She needs to subtract 2 black chips, but there are no black chips on the board. Nadie says, "It is impossible to subtract 2 black chips. There are none on the board!" What can Nadie do to the chip board so that she can subtract 2 black chips? Explain your reasoning.

A C E Homework starts on page 20.

Applications

For Exercises 1–4, describe a sequence of five correct or incorrect answers that would produce each Math Fever score. Write a number sentence for each score.

1. Super Brains: 300

2. Rocket Scientists: ⁻200

3. Know-It-Alls: ⁻250

4. Teacher's Pets: 0

5. Multiple Choice Which numbers are listed from least to greatest?

    A. 300, 0, ⁻200, ⁻250

    B. ⁻250, ⁻200, 0, 300

    C. 0, ⁻200, ⁻250, 300

    D. ⁻200, ⁻250, 300, 0

For Exercises 6–8, find each Math Fever team's score. Write a number sentence for each team. Assume that each team starts with 0 points.

6.   **Protons**

Point Value	Answer
250	Correct
100	Correct
200	Correct
150	Incorrect
200	Incorrect

7.   **Neutrons**

Point Value	Answer
200	Incorrect
50	Correct
250	Correct
150	Incorrect
50	Incorrect

8.   **Electrons**

Point Value	Answer
50	Incorrect
200	Incorrect
100	Correct
200	Correct
150	Incorrect

For each set of rational numbers in Exercises 9 and 10, draw a number line and locate the points. Remember to choose an appropriate scale.

9. $\frac{-2}{8}, \frac{1}{4}, ⁻1.5, 1\frac{3}{4}$

10. ⁻1.25, $-\frac{1}{3}$, 1.5, $-\frac{1}{6}$

11. Order the numbers from least to greatest.

    23.6   ⁻45.2   50   ⁻0.5   0.3 $\frac{3}{5}$ $-\frac{4}{5}$

Copy each pair of numbers in Exercises 12–19. Then insert $<$, $>$, or $=$ to make each a true statement.

12. 3 ▮ 0

13. ⁻23.4 ▮ 23.4

14. 46 ▮ ⁻79

15. ⁻75 ▮ ⁻90

16. ⁻300 ▮ 100

17. ⁻1,000 ▮ ⁻999

18. ⁻1.73 ▮ ⁻1.730

19. ⁻4.3 ▮ ⁻4.03

20. a. Estimate values for points *A–E*.

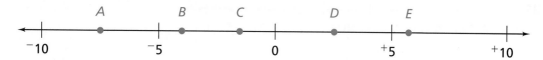

b. On a copy of the number line, graph the following numbers.

$$⁻9 \qquad 10.5 \qquad \frac{1}{2} \qquad -\frac{5}{2}$$

c. Describe the location of a number and its opposite on the number line.

21. For each pair of numbers, identify which number is farther from ⁺1. Explain your reasoning.

a. ⁻7 or ⁺3

b. ⁻10 or ⁺7

22. Identify the temperature that is halfway between each pair of temperatures.

a. ⁻23°F and ⁺23°F

b. ⁻20°F and ⁺10°F

c. ⁺20°F and ⁻10°F

Did You Know?

The record high and low temperatures in the United States are 134°F in Death Valley, California and ⁻80°F in Prospect Creek in the Endicott Mountains of Alaska. Imagine going from 134°F to ⁻80°F in an instant!

For Exercises 23–30, graph each statement on a number line.

23. x is less than 7.

24. x is greater than or equal to $^-7$.

25. $x < {}^-2$

26. $x \geq {}^-1$

27. $x \leq 8$

28. $x < 5$

29. $^-3 < x < 5$

30. $x > {}^-6$

For Exercises 31–34, write an inequality for each set of numbers on the number line.

31.

32.

33.

34.

35. The school cafeteria can hold at most 150 people.

a. Write a number sentence to represent the number of people that can be in the cafeteria at any time during the day.

b. Graph your answer to part (a) on a number line.

For Exercises 36–45, follow the steps using the number line. What is the final position?

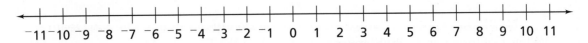

36. Start at 8. Add $^-7$.

37. Start at $^-8$. Add 10.

38. Start at $^-3$. Add $^-5$.

39. Start at 7. Add $^-7$.

40. Start at $^-2$. Add 12.

41. Start at 3. Subtract 5.

42. Start at $^-2$. Subtract 2.

43. Start at 4. Subtract 7.

44. Start at 0. Subtract 5.

45. Start at $^-8$. Subtract 3.

46. a. What are the opposites of 3, 7.5, and $^-2\frac{2}{3}$?

    b. For each number in part (a), find the sum of that number and its opposite.

47. The greatest recorded one-day temperature change occurred in Browning, Montana (bordering Glacier National Park), from January 23–24, 1916. The temperature fell from 44°F to $^-$56°F in less than 24 hours.

    a. What was the temperature change that day?

    b. Write a number sentence to represent the change.

    c. Show the temperature change on a number line.

48. Find the value for each labeled point on the number line. Then use the values to calculate each change.

    a. A to B **b.** A to C **c.** B to C

    d. C to A **e.** B to A **f.** C to B

For Exercises 49–52, find the missing part for each chip problem. Write a number sentence for each problem.

	Start With	Rule	End With	Number Sentence
49.	●●●	Add 5 ●	■	■
50.	●●●	Subtract 3 ●	■	■
51.	●●●●●	■	●●	■
52.	■	Subtract 3 ●	●●●●	■

53. Write a story problem for this situation. Find the value represented by the chips on the board.

For Exercises 54 and 55, use the chip board from Exercise 53.

54. What is the new overall value of the board when you

 a. remove 3 red chips?

 b. then add 3 black chips?

 c. then add 200 black chips and 195 red chips?

55. Describe three different ways to change the numbers of black and red chips on the original board, but leave the value of the board unchanged.

Connections

56. In a football game, one team makes seven plays in the first quarter. The results of those plays are (in order): gain of 7 yards, gain of 2 yards, loss of 5 yards, loss of 12 yards, gain of 16 yards, gain of 8 yards, loss of 8 yards.

    a. What is the overall gain (or loss) from all seven plays?

    b. What is the average gain (or loss) per play?

For Exercises 57 and 58, find the total number of strokes over or under par for each golf player. Write number sentences with positive and negative integers to show each result.

	Player	Round 1	Round 2	Round 3	Round 4
57.	Elijah Sparks	4 over par	6 under par	3 under par	1 over par
58.	Keiko Aida	2 under par	1 under par	5 over par	5 under par

For Exercises 59–64, draw a number line and label it with an appropriate scale. Graph and name the two numbers described on the number line.

59. two fractions between 0 and 1   **60.** two fractions between 2 and 3

61. two fractions between ⁻1 and 0   **62.** two decimals between ⁻3 and ⁻2

63. two decimals between 4 and 5   **64.** two decimals between ⁻4 and ⁻3

There is always a rational number between two other rational numbers. For Exercises 65–67, graph the two numbers on a number line. Then graph and label a point between the two numbers.

65. 1.4 and 1.5   **66.** ⁻1.42 and ⁻1.4   **67.** $^-5\frac{1}{2}$ and $^-5\frac{1}{4}$

For Exercises 68 and 69, copy the number line below.

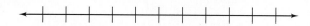

68. Label the first tick mark 28.36 and the last tick mark 28.37. Label the appropriate tick mark for 28.369. Then label the remaining tick marks.

69. Label the first tick mark ⁻7.7 and the last tick mark ⁻7.6. Label the appropriate tick mark for ⁻7.65. Then label the remaining tick marks.

For Exercises 70 and 71, label the tick marks on each number line.
Explain why you labeled them that way.

70.

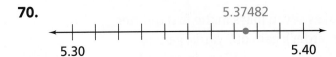

5.37482

5.30   5.40

71.

5.37482

5.370   5.380

For Exercises 72–75, order the numbers from least to greatest.

72. $\frac{2}{5}$, $\frac{3}{10}$, $\frac{5}{9}$, $\frac{9}{25}$
                           73. 20.33,   2.505,   23.30,   23

74. 1.52, $1\frac{4}{7}$,   2, $\frac{9}{6}$
                                75. 3, $\frac{19}{6}$, $2\frac{8}{9}$,   2.95

For Exercises 76 and 77, use the following. The highest point on earth
is the top of Mount Everest. It is 29,035 feet above sea level. The lowest
exposed land is the shore of the Dead Sea. It is 1,310 feet below sea level.

76. Multiple Choice What is the change in elevation from the top of
Everest to the shore of the Dead Sea?

     F. ⁻30,345 feet   **G.** ⁻27,725 feet

     H. 27,725 feet   **J.** 30,345 feet

77. Multiple Choice What is the change in elevation from the shore of
the Dead Sea to the top of Everest?

     A. ⁻30,345 feet   **B.** ⁻27,725 feet

     C. 27,725 feet   **D.** 30,345 feet

Dead Sea Shore   **Mount Everest**

Sea Level

Extensions

78. At the start of December, Kenji had a balance of $595.50 in his checking account. The following is a list of transactions he made during the month.

Date	Transaction	Balance
December 1		$595.50
December 5	Writes a check for $19.95	
December 12	Writes a check for $280.88	
December 15	Deposits $257.00	
December 17	Writes a check for $58.12	
December 21	Withdraws $50.00	
December 24	Writes checks for $17.50, $41.37, and $65.15	
December 26	Deposits $100.00	
December 31	Withdraws $50.00	

a. Copy and complete the table.

b. What was Kenji's balance at the end of December?

c. When was his balance the greatest? When was his balance the least?

For Exercises 79–84, find all the values of x that satisfy the statement. Then sketch the solution on a number line.

79. $x + 2$ is negative.　　**80.** $x - 5$ is greater than 0.　**81.** $x + 3 < 1$

82. $x + 3 \geq 2$　　　　　**83.** $3 - x < 0$　　　　　　**84.** $6 \leq x - 4$

For Exercises 85–87, find the missing temperature in each situation.

85. On Monday, the high temperature was 20°C. The low temperature was ⁻15°C. What temperature is halfway between the high and the low?

86. On Tuesday, the low temperature was ⁻8°C. The temperature halfway between the high and the low is 5°C. What was the high temperature?

87. On Wednesday, the high temperature was ⁻10°C. The low temperature was ⁻15°C. What temperature is halfway between the high and the low?

Find values for A and B that make each mathematical sentence true.

88. $^+A + {}^-B = {}^-1$　　　　**89.** $^-A + {}^+B = 0$　　　　**90.** $^-A - {}^-B = {}^-2$

In this Investigation, you learned ways to order and operate with positive and negative numbers. The following questions will help you summarize what you have learned.

Think about these questions. Discuss your ideas with other students and your teacher. Then write a summary of your findings in your notebook.

1. **How** do you decide which of two numbers is greater when

   a. both numbers are positive?

   b. both numbers are negative?

   c. one number is positive and one number is negative?

2. **How** does a number line help you compare numbers?

3. **When** you add a positive number and a negative number, how do you determine the sign of the answer?

4. If you are doing a subtraction problem on a chip board, and the board does not have enough chips of the color you wish to subtract, **what** can you do to make the subtraction possible?

Common Core Mathematical Practices

As you worked on the Problems in this Investigation, you used prior knowledge to make sense of them. You also applied Mathematical Practices to solve the Problems. Think back over your work, the ways you thought about the Problems, and how you used Mathematical Practices.

Nick described his thoughts in the following way:

We used the number line to determine the temperature in Problem 1.3, Question E. We started at ⁻5°F. Since the temperature rose 20°F during the day, we moved 20 tick marks to the right, which put us at 15°F. Since the temperature fell 25°F during the night, we moved 25 tick marks to the left and landed on ⁻10°F. Then we moved 40 tick marks to the right to 30°F because of the heat wave. The temperature fell 70°F, so we moved to the left 70 tick marks. We are now at ⁻40°F. We think it is unusual for the temperature to drop this much overnight and wonder where Sally lives.

Common Core Standards for Mathematical Practice

MP5 Use appropriate tools strategically.

- What other Mathematical Practices can you identify in Nick's reasoning?

- Describe a Mathematical Practice that you and your classmates used to solve a different Problem in this Investigation.

Investigation 2

Adding and Subtracting Rational Numbers

In Investigation 1 you used number lines and chip boards to model rational numbers. Now, you will develop algorithms for adding and subtracting rational numbers.

An **algorithm** is a plan, or a series of steps, for doing a computation. In an effective algorithm, the steps lead to a correct answer, no matter what numbers you use. Your class may develop more than one algorithm for each operation. Set a goal to understand and skillfully use at least one algorithm for adding rational numbers and one algorithm for subtracting rational numbers.

2.1 Extending Addition to Rational Numbers

There are two common ways that number problems lead to addition calculations like $8 + 5$. The first involves combining two similar sets of objects, as in this example:

> Linda has 8 video games, and her friend has 5.
> Together they have $8 + 5 = 13$ games.

You can represent this situation on a chip board.

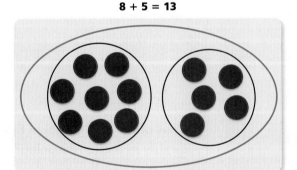

$8 + 5 = 13$

Common Core State Standards

7.NS.A.1b Understand $p + q$ as the number located a distance $|q|$ from p, in the positive or negative direction depending on whether q is positive or negative. Show that a number and its opposite have a sum of 0 (are additive inverses) . . .

7.NS.A.1c Understand subtraction of rational numbers as adding the additive inverse, $p - q = p + (-q)$. Show that the distance between two rational numbers on the number line is the absolute value of their difference, and apply this principle in real-world contexts.

Also 7.NS.A.1, 7.NS.A.1d, 7.NS.A.3, 7.EE.B.3

Number problems also lead to addition calculations when you add to a starting number. Here is an example:

> At a desert weather station, the temperature at sunrise was 10°C. It rose 25°C by mid-day. The temperature at noon was 10°C + 25°C = 35°C.

You can represent this situation on a number line. The starting point is $^+10$. The change in distance and direction is $^+25$. The sum ($^+35$) is the result of moving a distance of 25 to the right.

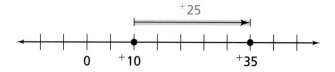

Suppose, instead of rising 25°C, the temperature fell 15°C. The next number line shows that $^+10°C + {}^-15°C = {}^-5°C$.

Suppose that the temperature change one day is $^-25°C$. What could the original temperature and the final temperature be for that day?

Use these ideas about addition as you develop an algorithm for addition of integers.

 How can you predict whether the sum of two integers is 0, positive, or negative? Explain.

Problem 2.1

Use chip boards or number line models to solve these problems.

A **1.** Find the sums in each group.

Group 1
$^+2 + {}^+8$
$^-2 + {}^-8$
$^+8 + {}^+12$
$^-8 + {}^-12$

Group 2
$^+2 + {}^-8$
$^-2 + {}^+8$
$^+8 + {}^-12$
$^-8 + {}^+12$

2. What do the examples in each group have in common?

3. Write two new problems that belong to each group.

4. Describe an algorithm for adding the integers in each group.

B You know that $^-5 + {}^-3 = {}^-8$. Use this information to help you solve the following related problems.

1. $^-5\frac{1}{4} + {}^-3$

2. $^-5\frac{1}{5} + {}^-3\frac{3}{5}$

3. $^-5\frac{1}{3} + {}^-3\frac{2}{3}$

C You know that $^-8 + {}^+5 = {}^-3$. Use this information to help you solve the following related problems.

1. $^-8.35 + {}^+5$

2. $^-8.55 + {}^+5.3$

3. $^-8.65 + {}^+5.25$

4. Does your algorithm for adding integers from Question A work with fractions and decimals? Explain.

Problem 2.1 continued

D For parts (1)–(3), decide whether or not the expressions are equal.

1. $^-4 + {}^+6$ and $^+6 + {}^-4$

2. $^+2\frac{2}{3} + {}^-5\frac{7}{8}$ and $^-5\frac{7}{8} + {}^+2\frac{2}{3}$

3. $^-7\frac{2}{3} + {}^-1\frac{1}{6}$ and $^-1\frac{1}{6} + {}^-7\frac{2}{3}$

4. The property of rational numbers that you have observed in these pairs of problems is called the **Commutative Property** of addition. Explain why addition is commutative. Give examples using number lines or chip boards.

E
1. Find the sums in Group 3.

2. What do the examples in Group 3 have in common?

3. Write three new problems that belong to Group 3.

Group 3
$^-5 + {}^+5$
$^+9.4 + {}^-9.4$
$^+2\frac{1}{4} + {}^-2\frac{1}{4}$

F Write a story to match each number sentence. Find the solutions.

1. $^+50 + {}^-50 = \blacksquare$

2. $^-15 + \blacksquare = {}^+25$

3. $^-300 + {}^+250 = \blacksquare$

G
1. Use properties of addition to find each value.

  a. $^+17 + {}^-17 + {}^-43$

  b. $^+47 + {}^+62 + {}^-47$

2. Luciana claims that if you add numbers with the same sign, the sum is always greater than each of the addends. Is she correct? Explain.

A C E Homework starts on page 44.

2.2 Extending Subtraction to Rational Numbers

In Problem 2.1, you explored some important properties of rational numbers. You found that the Commutative Property is true for addition of rational numbers.

You also found that the sum of an integer and its opposite is 0.

$$50 + {}^-50 = 0 \qquad {}^-17 + 17 = 0$$

Numbers such as 50 and −50 are **additive inverses** of each other. Their sum is 0. Zero is the **additive identity** for rational numbers. This means that zero added to a number does not change the value of the number.

$${}^-7 + 0 = {}^-7 \qquad \tfrac{1}{2} + 0 = \tfrac{1}{2}$$

These properties will be useful as you explore subtraction problems with rational numbers.

One way to think about subtraction problems is to take away objects from a set, as in this example:

> Kim had 9 DVDs. She sold 4 at a yard sale. She now has $9 - 4 = 5$ of those DVDs left.

 One way to represent this situation is to use a chip board

9 − 4 = 5

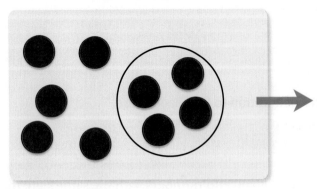

Here is another example:

> Otis earned $5 raking leaves. He wants to buy a used bike that costs $7. His older sister puts 5 black chips on the table to represent the money Otis has.

- What is the value of Otis's board?

Otis's sister asks, "How much more money do you need?" Otis replies, "I could find out by taking away $7. But I can't take away $7 because there aren't seven black chips on the board!" His sister adds two black chips and two red chips.

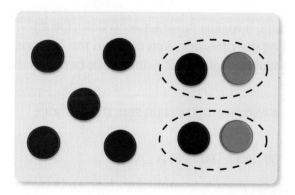

- Is the value of the board the same with the new chips added? Explain.
- How does this help Otis find how much more he needs?

You can also use subtraction to find the distance between two points:

> The Arroyo family just passed mile 25 on the highway. They need to get to the exit at mile 80.

- How many more miles do they have to drive?

You can use a number line to show this difference.

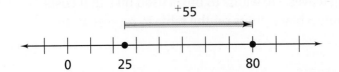

The number line above shows that they have to travel $80 - 25 = 55$ more miles. The arrow on the number line points in the direction that the Arroyos are traveling. They are traveling in a positive direction, from lesser values to greater values.

Suppose the Arroyos drive back from mile 80 to mile 25. They would travel the same distance as before. However, they would travel in the opposite direction.

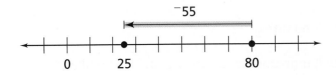

The number line above represents the Arroyos' distance as $25 - 80 = {}^-55$ miles. In this case, the arrow on the number line points to the left and has a label of $^-55$. Their distance is 55, but their direction is negative.

In some situations, such as driving, it makes more sense to describe an overall distance without including the direction. You can find the Arroyos' overall distance by taking the **absolute value** of the difference between the two points on the number line.

You can write two absolute value expressions to represent the distance between 25 and 80:

$$|25 - 80| \text{ and } |80 - 25|$$

You can evaluate these two expressions to show that the distance between the points 25 and 80 on a number line is 55.

$$|25 - 80| = |{}^-55| = 55 \text{ and } |80 - 25| = |55| = 55$$

 How can you predict whether the difference of two integers is 0, positive, or negative?

Problem **2.2**

Ⓐ Benjamin takes $75 from his savings. He goes shopping for school supplies and has $35 left when he is done. To figure out how much he has spent, he draws the following number line:

1. How much has he spent?

2. How should Benjamin label what he spent to show that this is money that he no longer has?

Ⓑ During a game of Math Fever the Super Brains have a score of ⁻500 points. Earlier in the game, they incorrectly answered a question for ⁻150 points. However, the moderator later determined that the question was unfair. So ⁻150 points are taken away from their score.

1. Will subtracting ⁻150 points increase or decrease the Super Brains' score? Explain your reasoning.

2. What is the Super Brains' score after ⁻150 points are removed?

3. Write a number sentence to represent this situation, and show it on a number line.

Ⓒ Use chip models or number line models to help solve the following.

1. Find the differences in each group given below.

Group 1
⁺12 − ⁺8
⁻5 − ⁻7
⁻4 − ⁻2
⁺2 − ⁺4

Group 2
⁺12 − ⁻8
⁻5 − ⁺7
⁻4 − ⁺2
⁺2 − ⁻4

2. What do the examples in each group have in common?

3. Write two new problems that belong to each group.

4. Describe an algorithm for subtracting integers in each group.

continued on the next page >

Problem **2.2** *continued*

D Apply the algorithm you developed on these rational number problems.

    1. $^-1 - {}^+3$
                2. $^-1 - {}^+\frac{3}{4}$

    3. $^-1\frac{1}{2} - {}^-2$
             4. $^-1\frac{1}{2} - {}^-\frac{3}{4}$

E **1.** Consider the points $^-10$ and 5 on a number line.

    a. Write two absolute value expressions to represent the distance between these two points.

    b. Evaluate both of your expressions. What is the distance between the points $^-10$ and 5 on a number line?

    c. Draw a number line to represent the distance you found in part (b).

  2. Write two absolute value expressions for the distance between the two points on the number line below. Then evaluate your expressions.

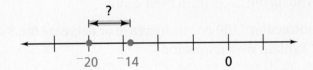

F For parts (1)–(4), decide whether or not the expressions are equal.

    1. $^-2 - {}^+3$ and $^+3 - {}^-2$

    2. $^+12 - {}^-4$ and $^-4 - {}^+12$

    3. $^-15 - {}^-20$ and $^-20 - {}^-15$

    4. $^+45 - {}^+21$ and $^+21 - {}^+45$

    5. Is there a Commutative Property of subtraction? Explain your answer.

A C E Homework starts on page 44.

2.3 The "+/ −" Connection

Addition and subtraction are related to each other in ways that can help you solve problems.

- If you know that $5 + {}^{-}8 = {}^{-}3$, how can this help you find the answer to $5 - 8$?

Examine these two expressions and think about how they are alike and how they are different.

$$A + {}^{-}B \text{ and } A - B$$

Substitute numbers for A and B and carry out the computations.

- What do your computations tell you about the two expressions: $A + {}^{-}B$ and $A - B$?

Think about points in a game like Math Fever. Write a story problem that could be represented by either expression.

As you work on Problem 2.3, look for ways that addition and subtraction are related.

Problem 2.3

Use your ideas about addition and subtraction of integers to explore the relationship between these two operations.

A The chip board in the picture below shows a value of ⁺5.

1. There are two possible moves, one addition and one subtraction, that would change the value on the board to ⁺2.

   a. How would you complete the number sentences to represent each move?

   $$^{+}5 + \blacksquare = {}^{+}2 \text{ and } {}^{+}5 - \blacksquare = {}^{+}2$$

   b. Describe how these moves are different on the chip board.

2. **a.** How would you complete the number sentences below to change the value on the board to ⁺8?

   $$^{+}5 + \blacksquare = {}^{+}8 \text{ and } {}^{+}5 - \blacksquare = {}^{+}8$$

   b. Describe how these moves are different on the chip board.

B 1. Complete each number sentence.

   a. $^{+}5 + {}^{-}4 = {}^{+}5 - \blacksquare$ **b.** $^{+}5 + {}^{+}4 = {}^{+}5 - \blacksquare$

   c. $^{-}7 + {}^{-}2 = {}^{-}7 - \blacksquare$ **d.** $^{-}7 + {}^{+}2 = {}^{-}7 - \blacksquare$

   2. What patterns do you see from part (1) that can help you restate any addition problem as an equivalent subtraction problem?

Problem **2.3** *continued*

C **1.** Think about how you can restate a subtraction problem as an addition problem. For example, how can you complete the number sentences below so that each subtraction problem is restated as an addition problem?

    a. $^+8 - {}^+5 = {}^+8 + \blacksquare$

    b. $^+8 - {}^-5 = {}^+8 + \blacksquare$

    c. $^-4 - {}^+6 = {}^-4 + \blacksquare$

    d. $^-4 - {}^-6 = {}^-4 + \blacksquare$

2. What patterns do you see from part (1) that can help you restate any subtraction problem as an equivalent addition problem?

D For parts (1)–(8), write an equivalent expression. Then choose one expression from each part, evaluate it, and explain why you chose to use that expression for the calculation.

    1. $^-5 + {}^-5$

    2. $^-5 - {}^-5$

    3. $^+396 - {}^-400$

    4. $^-75.8 - {}^-35.2$

    5. $^-25.6 + {}^-4.4$

    6. $^+\frac{3}{2} - {}^+\frac{1}{4}$

    7. $^+\frac{5}{8} + {}^-\frac{3}{4}$

    8. $^-3\frac{1}{2} - {}^+5$

A C E Homework starts on page 44.

Note on Notation You have been writing rational numbers with raised signs to avoid confusion with the symbols for addition and subtraction. However, most computer software and most writing in mathematics do not use raised signs. Positive numbers are usually written without a sign.

$$^{+}3 = 3 \text{ and } ^{+}7.5 = 7.5$$

Negative numbers are usually written with a dash like a subtraction sign.

$$^{-}3 = -3 \text{ and } ^{-}7.5 = -7.5$$

From now on, we will use this notation to indicate a negative number. This can be confusing if you don't read carefully. Parentheses can help.

$$^{-}5 - ^{-}8 = -5 - -8 = -5 - (-8)$$

The subtraction symbol also indicates the opposite of a number. For example, -8 represents the opposite of 8. The expression $-(-8)$ represents the opposite of -8.

$$-(-8) = 8$$

2.4 Fact Families

You have written fact families for whole numbers:

$$3 + 2 = 5$$
$$2 + 3 = 5$$
$$5 - 3 = 2$$
$$5 - 2 = 3$$

 Do the relationships below work for positive and negative numbers?

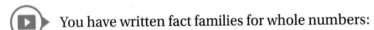

$$a + b = c \quad a = c - b \quad b = c - a$$

Problem 2.4

A For each part, choose values for *a* and *b*. Substitute those values into the three relationships below.

$$a + b = c \qquad a = c - b \qquad b = c - a$$

Then find the value of *c*.

1. *a* and *b* are positive rational numbers.

2. *a* and *b* are negative rational numbers.

3. *a* is a positive rational number, and *b* is a negative rational number.

4. *a* is a negative rational number, and *b* is a positive rational number.

For Questions B–E, use fact families to answer each question.

B Write a related subtraction sentence for each.

1. $-3 + (-2) = -5$

2. $25 + (-32) = -7$

C Write a related addition sentence for each.

1. $8 - (-2) = 10$

2. $-14 - (-20) = 6$

D **1.** Write a related sentence for each.

    a. $n - 5 = 35$ **b.** $n - (-5) = 35$ **c.** $n + 5 = 35$

  2. Do your related sentences make it easier to find the value of *n*? Why or why not?

E **1.** Write a related sentence for each.

    a. $4 + n = 43$ **b.** $-4 + n = 43$ **c.** $-4 + n = -43$

  2. Do your related sentences make it easier to find the value of *n*? Why or why not?

A C E Homework starts on page 44.

Applications

For Exercises 1–12, use your algorithms to find each sum without using a calculator.

1. $^+12 + {}^+4$

2. $^+12 + {}^-4$

3. $^-12 + {}^+4$

4. $^-7 + {}^-8$

5. $^+4.5 + {}^-3.8$

6. $^-4.5 + {}^+3.8$

7. $^-250 + {}^-750$

8. $^-6{,}200 + {}^+1{,}200$

9. $^+0.75 + {}^-0.25$

10. $^+\frac{2}{3} + {}^-\frac{1}{6}$

11. $^-\frac{5}{12} + {}^+\frac{2}{3}$

12. $^-\frac{8}{5} + {}^-\frac{3}{5}$

13. Find each sum.

    a. $^+3.8 + {}^+2.7$

    b. $^-3.8 + {}^-2.7$

    c. $^-3.8 + {}^+2.7$

    d. $^+3.8 + {}^-2.7$

14. Write an addition number sentence that matches each diagram.

    a.

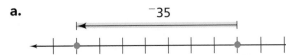

    b.

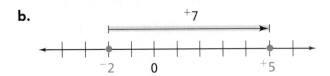

    c.

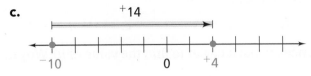

    d.

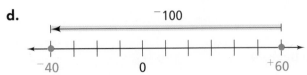

For Exercises 15 and 16, use the chip board below. The chip board has 10 black chips and 13 red chips.

15. What is the value shown on the board?

16. Write a number sentence to represent each situation. Then find the new value of the chip board.

   a. Remove 5 red chips from the original board.

   b. Then add 5 black chips.

   c. Then add 4 black chips and 4 red chips.

17. Use properties of addition to find each value.

   a. $^{+}43 + {}^{-}47 + {}^{-}43$ **b.** $^{+}5.2 + {}^{-}5.2 + {}^{-}\frac{4}{7}$ **c.** $^{+}5\frac{2}{5} + {}^{+}\frac{3}{7} + {}^{-}5\frac{2}{5}$

For Exercises 18–29, use your algorithms to find each difference without using a calculator. Show your work.

18. $^{+}12 - {}^{+}4$ **19.** $^{+}12 - {}^{+}12$ **20.** $^{-}12 - {}^{+}12$

21. $^{-}7 - {}^{+}8$ **22.** $^{+}45 - {}^{-}40$ **23.** $^{+}45 - {}^{-}50$

24. $^{-}25 - {}^{-}75$ **25.** $^{-}62 - {}^{-}12$ **26.** $^{+}0.8 - {}^{-}0.5$

27. $^{+}\frac{1}{2} - {}^{+}\frac{3}{4}$ **28.** $^{-}\frac{2}{5} - {}^{+}\frac{1}{5}$ **29.** $^{-}\frac{7}{10} - {}^{+}\frac{4}{5}$

30. Find each value without using a calculator.

   a. $^{+}12 + {}^{-}12$ **b.** $^{+}4 - {}^{+}12$ **c.** $^{-}12 - {}^{+}4$

   d. $^{-}12 - {}^{-}12$ **e.** $^{-}12 + {}^{-}12$ **f.** $^{-}12 + {}^{+}12$

For Exercises 31–36, find each value.

31. $^+50 + {}^-35$

32. $^+50 - {}^-20$

33. $^-19 - {}^+11$

34. $^-30 - {}^+50$

35. $^-35 + {}^-15$

36. $^+12 + {}^-18$

37. For each part below, write a problem about temperature, money, or game scores that can be represented by the number sentence.

    a. $^+7 - {}^-4 = {}^+11$

    b. $^-20 + n = {}^+30$

    c. $^-n + {}^-150 = {}^-450$

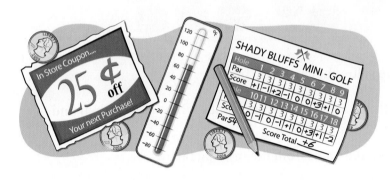

38. Without doing any calculations, decide which expression is greater. Explain your reasoning.

    a. $5{,}280 + {}^-768$ or $5{,}280 - {}^-768$

    b. $1{,}760 - {}^-880$ or $1{,}760 - 880$

    c. $1{,}500 + 3{,}141$ or $1{,}500 - {}^-3{,}141$

39. Without doing any calculations, determine which of the following results are positive and which are negative. Explain your reasoning.

    a. $^-23 + 19$

    b. $3.5 - {}^-2.7$

    c. $^-3.5 - {}^-2.04$

    d. $3.1 + {}^-6.2$

40. Find each missing part.

	Start With	Rule	End With
a.	●●	▪	●●●●●●●
b.	●●●	▪	●●●
c.	▪	Add 5 ●	●●●
d.	▪	Subtract 5 ●	●●

For Exercises 41–46, find each sum or difference. Show your work.

41. $15 + {}^-10$

42. ${}^-20 - 14$

43. $200 - {}^-125$

44. ${}^-20 - {}^-14$

45. ${}^-200 + 125$

46. $7 - 12$

47. Below is part of a time line with three years marked.

2003   2013   2023

   a. Write two sentences in words that refer to the year 2013. One should relate 2013 to 2003, and the other should relate 2013 to 2023.

   b. Write two number sentences that refer to the year 2013. One should relate 2013 to 2003, and the other should relate 2013 to 2023.

   c. Describe how these two number sentences are alike and different.

48. Compute each of the following.

   a. $3 + {}^-3 + {}^-7$

   b. $3 - 3 - 7$

   c. ${}^-10 + {}^-7 + {}^-28$

   d. ${}^-10 - 7 - 28$

   e. $7 - 8 + {}^-5$

   f. $7 + {}^-8 - 5$

   g. ${}^-97 + {}^-35 - 10$

   h. ${}^-97 - 35 + {}^-10$

   i. What can you conclude about the relationship between subtracting a positive number and adding a negative number with the same absolute value? In other words, what is the relationship between a $(-\ ^+)$ situation and a $(+\ ^-)$ situation?

49. Compute each of the following.

   a. $3 - {}^-3 - {}^-7$

   b. $3 + 3 + 7$

   c. ${}^-10 - {}^-7 - {}^-28$

   d. ${}^-10 + 7 + 28$

   e. $7 + 8 + 5$

   f. $7 - {}^-8 - {}^-5$

   g. ${}^-97 - {}^-35 - 10$

   h. ${}^-97 + 35 + {}^-10$

   i. What can you conclude about the relationship between subtracting a negative number and adding a positive number with the same absolute value? In other words, what is the relationship between a $(-\ ^-)$ situation and a $(+\ ^+)$ situation?

Multiple Choice In each set of calculations, one result is different from the others. Find the different result without doing any calculations.

50. **A.** $54 + {}^-25$ **B.** $54 - 25$

      C. $25 - 54$ **D.** ${}^-25 + 54$

51. **F.** ${}^-6.28 - {}^-3.14$ **G.** ${}^-6.28 + 3.14$

      H. $3.14 + {}^-6.28$ **J.** ${}^-3.14 - {}^-6.28$

52. **A.** $534 - 275$ **B.** $275 - 534$

      C. ${}^-534 + 275$ **D.** $275 + {}^-534$

53. **F.** $175 + {}^-225$ **G.** $225 - 175$

      H. $175 - 225$ **J.** ${}^-225 + 175$

54. Fill in the missing information for each problem.

     a. $5 + \frac{3}{4} = \blacksquare$ **b.** $\frac{4}{8} + (-6) = \blacksquare$ **c.** $-3\frac{3}{4} - \left(-\frac{3}{4}\right) = \blacksquare$

     d. $2\frac{2}{3} - \frac{1}{3} = \blacksquare$ **e.** $-2 + \blacksquare = -2\frac{1}{2}$ **f.** $-4.5 + \blacksquare = -5$

55. **Multiple Choice** Which is the correct addition and subtraction fact family for $-2 + 3 = 1$?

     A. $-2 + 3 = 1$ **B.** $-2 + 3 = 1$ **C.** $-2 + 3 = 1$ **D.** $1 - 3 = -2$

          $-2 + 1 = 3$ $3 - 2 = 1$ $1 - 3 = -2$ $1 - (-2) = 3$

          $3 - 1 = 2$ $3 - 1 = 2$ $1 - (-2) = 3$ $3 - 1 = 2$

56. For each of the following, write a related equation. Then find the value of n.

     a. $n - 7 = 10$ **b.** $-\frac{1}{2} + n = -\frac{5}{8}$ **c.** $\frac{2}{3} - n = -\frac{7}{9}$

57. Are ${}^+8 - {}^+8$ and $8 - 8$ equal? Explain.

58. Are ${}^+100 - {}^+99$ and $100 - 99$ equal? Explain.

59. Are the expressions in each group below equivalent? If so, which form makes the computation easiest?

     a. $8 + {}^-10$ **b.** $3 + {}^-8$

        $8 - {}^+10$ $3 - {}^+8$

        $8 - 10$ $3 - 8$

Connections

60. The Spartan Bike Shop keeps a record of their business transactions. They start their account at zero dollars. Write a number sentence to represent each transaction. Then find the new balance.

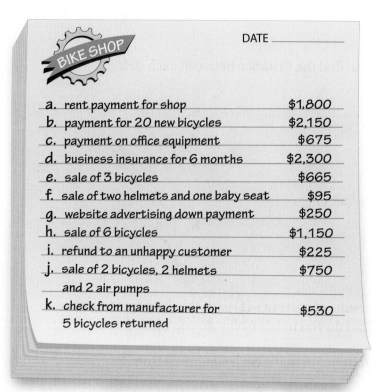

DATE _____

BIKE SHOP

a.	rent payment for shop	$1,800
b.	payment for 20 new bicycles	$2,150
c.	payment on office equipment	$675
d.	business insurance for 6 months	$2,300
e.	sale of 3 bicycles	$665
f.	sale of two helmets and one baby seat	$95
g.	website advertising down payment	$250
h.	sale of 6 bicycles	$1,150
i.	refund to an unhappy customer	$225
j.	sale of 2 bicycles, 2 helmets and 2 air pumps	$750
k.	check from manufacturer for 5 bicycles returned	$530

For Exercises 61 and 62, write a number sentence for each situation. Then answer the question.

61. The air temperature drops from 94°F to 72°F in 15 minutes. What is the change in temperature?

62. The Teacher's Pets team has 50 points in Math Fever. They miss a question worth 200 points. What is their new score?

63. Find four different numbers, in order from least to greatest, that lie between the two given numbers.

  a. ⁻4.5 and ⁻3.5

  b. ⁻0.5 and 0.5

Extensions

64. Which numbers, when added to $^-15$, give a sum

    a. greater than 0?

    b. less than 0?

    c. equal to 0?

65. Use a number line to find the distance between each pair of numbers.

    a. $^+8, ^+4$ **b.** $^-8, ^+4$

    c. $^+8, ^-4$ **d.** $^-8, ^-4$

    e. $^-3\frac{1}{2}, ^+\frac{3}{4}$ **f.** $^+5.4, ^-1.6$

66. Find each absolute value.

    a. $|^+8 - ^+4|$ **b.** $|^-8 - ^+4|$

    c. $|^+8 - ^-4|$ **d.** $|^-8 - ^-4|$

    e. $|^-3\frac{1}{2} + ^+\frac{3}{4}|$ **f.** $|^+5.4 - ^-1.6|$

    g. Compare the results of parts (a)–(f) with the distances found in Exercise 65. What do you notice? Why do you think this is so?

67. Replace n with a number to make each statement true.

    a. $n + ^-18 = 6$

    b. $^-24 - n = 12$

    c. $43 + n = ^-12$

    d. $^-20 - n = ^-50$

68. The table shows the profits or losses (in millions of dollars) earned by three companies from 2004 to 2013. Find the range of the annual results and the overall profit (or loss) for each company over that time period.

Top 3 Market Competitors

	Company	'04	'05	'06	'07	'08	'09	'10	'11	'12	'13
a.	Sands Motor	⁻5.3	⁻4.8	⁻7.2	⁻2.1	1.4	6.5	3.2	⁻3.5	10.2	2.4
b.	Daily Trans	6.0	3.4	⁻5.8	⁻12.3	⁻20.3	⁻1.5	2.5	9.8	19.4	32.1
c.	Sell to You	120	98	⁻20	⁻40	⁻5	85	130	76	5	⁻30

69. Starting from 0, write an addition sentence for the diagrams below.

a.

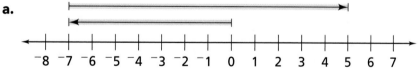

b.

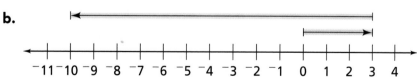

In this Investigation you applied your informal ideas about rational numbers to develop algorithms for calculating any sums and differences. The following questions will help you summarize what you have learned.

Think about these questions. Discuss your ideas with other students and your teacher. Then write a summary of your findings in your notebook.

1. **a. What** algorithm(s) will produce the correct result for the sum "$a + b$," where a and b each represent any rational number? Show, using a number line or chip board, why your algorithm works.

   b. What algorithm(s) will produce the correct result for the difference "$a - b$," where a and b each represent any rational number? Show, using a number line or chip board, why your algorithm works.

2. **How** can any difference "$a - b$" be restated as an equivalent addition statement, where a and b each represent any rational number?

3. **a. What** does it mean to say that an operation is *commutative*?

   b. Describe some ways that the additive inverse of a number is important.

Common Core Mathematical Practices

As you worked on the Problems in this Investigation, you used prior knowledge to make sense of them. You also applied Mathematical Practices to solve the Problems. Think back over your work, the ways you thought about the Problems, and how you used Mathematical Practices.

Sophie described her thoughts in the following way:

We noticed there was a relationship between addition and subtraction in Problem 2.4. If you know that $7 + {}^-8 = {}^-1$, then you can write two equivalent subtraction problems: ${}^-1 - 7 = {}^-8$ and ${}^-1 - {}^-8 = 7$. You can also write subtraction number sentences as addition problems. These patterns enabled us to rewrite number sentences to make it easier to find the missing number and complete the sentence.

Common Core Standards for Mathematical Practice

MP7 Look for and make use of structure.

- What other Mathematical Practices can you identify in Sophie's reasoning?

- Describe a Mathematical Practice that you and your classmates used to solve a different Problem in this Investigation.

3

Multiplying and Dividing Rational Numbers

In this Investigation, you will use time, distance, speed, and direction to think about multiplication and division of integers. You will also explore number patterns and develop algorithms for multiplying and dividing rational numbers.

You can use the times symbol, ×, the multiplication dot, •, or parentheses, ( ), to show multiplication.

$$3 \times 5 = 3 \bullet 5 = 3(5)$$

Did You Know?

Florence Griffith Joyner set an Olympic record when she ran 100 meters in 10.62 seconds in 1988.

How long would it take her to run 1,000 meters at her record speed?

Common Core State Standards

7.NS.A.2b Understand that integers can be divided, provided that the divisor is not zero, and every quotient of integers (with non-zero divisor) is a rational number. If p and q are integers, then $-(p/q) = (-p)/q = p/(-q) \ldots$

7.NS.A.2c Apply properties of operations as strategies to multiply and divide rational numbers.

7.NS.A.2d Convert a rational number to a decimal using long division; know that the decimal form of a rational number terminates in 0s or eventually repeats.

Also 7.NS.A.2, 7.NS.A.2a, 7.NS.A.3, 7.EE.B.3

3.1 Multiplication Patterns With Integers

The math department at Everett Middle School sponsors a contest called the Number Relay Race. A number line measured in meters is drawn on the school field. Each team has five runners. Runners 1, 3, and 5 stand at the −50-meter line. Runners 2 and 4 stand at the 50-meter line.

Team 1

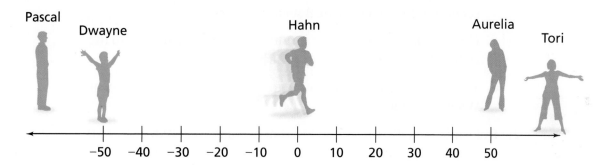

For Team 1:

- Hahn starts and runs from −50 to 50. He tags Aurelia.
- Aurelia runs back from 50 to −50. She tags Dwayne.
- Dwayne runs from −50 to 50. He tags Tori.
- Tori runs from 50 to −50. She tags Pascal.
- Pascal runs from −50 to the finish line at position 0.

Team 2 does the same with its 5 runners. Both teams line up on the same number line and start the race at the same time.

The team whose final runner reaches the 0 point first wins.

Problem 3.1

A **1.** Write and solve a number sentence for each situation. Use positive numbers for running speeds to the right, and use negative numbers for running speeds to the left. Use positive numbers for time in the future, and use negative numbers for time in the past. (Note: Each runner runs at a constant speed.)

   a. Hahn passes the 0 point running 5 meters per second to the right. Where will he be 6 seconds later?

   b. Aurelia passes the 0 point running to the left at 6 meters per second. Where will she be 8 seconds later?

   c. Dwayne passes the 0 point running 4 meters per second to the right. Where was he 6 seconds earlier?

   d. Tori passes the 0 point running to the left at 5 meters per second. Where was she 7 seconds earlier?

2. Determine whether the answer to each situation in part (1) is to the left or right of zero.

B Kalman wants to use red and black chips to model the relay race. He draws the following chip board to represent Aurelia's part of the race. How does this chip board relate to your work on Aurelia's part of the relay race? Explain.

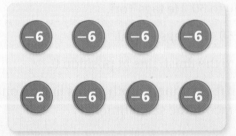

Problem 3.1 *continued*

C **1.** After studying the relay race problem, some students started looking for number patterns to see if what they found in the race made sense. How do the products change as the numbers multiplied by 5 decrease?

$$5 \cdot 3 = 15$$
$$5 \cdot 2 = 10$$
$$5 \cdot 1 = 5$$
$$5 \cdot 0 = 0$$

  2. Predict the following products. Explain your reasoning.

$$5 \cdot (-1) = \blacksquare$$
$$5 \cdot (-2) = \blacksquare$$
$$5 \cdot (-3) = \blacksquare$$

D **1.** Find each product. How do the products change as the numbers multiplied by -4 decrease?

$$-4 \cdot 3 = \blacksquare$$
$$-4 \cdot 2 = \blacksquare$$
$$-4 \cdot 1 = \blacksquare$$
$$-4 \cdot 0 = \blacksquare$$

  2. Predict the following products. Explain your reasoning.

$$-4 \cdot (-1) = \blacksquare$$
$$-4 \cdot (-2) = \blacksquare$$
$$-4 \cdot (-3) = \blacksquare$$

E **1.** The product $-4(-12)$ represents the location of a runner in the Number Relay. What question does the product answer? What location does it specify?

  2. The product $4(-12)$ represents the location of a runner in the Number Relay. What question does the product answer? What location does it specify?

  3. How do the locations in parts (1) and (2) relate to each other?

A C E Homework starts on page 66.

3.2 Multiplication of Rational Numbers

You have already examined patterns in multiplication of rational numbers that are integers. Now you will use patterns to develop algorithms for multiplication of rational numbers that include fractions and decimals.

Which of the following products will have the same value?

$$4 \cdot 5 \qquad 4 \cdot (-5) \qquad -4 \cdot 5 \qquad -4 \cdot (-5)$$

Problem 3.2

A   **1.** What do the examples in each group below have in common?

Group 1
$4 \cdot 3$
$5.1 \cdot 1$
$3 \cdot 4\frac{1}{2}$

Group 2
$4 \cdot (-3)$
$-5.1 \cdot 1$
$3 \cdot \left(-4\frac{1}{2}\right)$

Group 3
$-4 \cdot (-3)$
$-5.1 \cdot (-1)$
$-3 \cdot \left(-4\frac{1}{2}\right)$

   2. Find the products in each group above.

   3. Write and solve two additional problems for each group.

B   Find the products in each group below. Is multiplication commutative?

$$2 \times 3 \text{ and } 3 \times 2$$

$$-2 \times (-3) \text{ and } -3 \times (-2)$$

$$-2 \times 3 \text{ and } 3 \times (-2)$$

Problem 3.2 *continued*

C **1.** Describe an algorithm for multiplying two positive rational numbers.

2. Describe an algorithm for multiplying a positive rational number and a negative rational number.

3. Describe an algorithm for multiplying a negative rational number and a negative rational number.

D **1.** For each product, predict the sign. Then find the product.

  a. $7 \cdot (-8) \cdot (-3)$

  b. $-12 \cdot (-5) \cdot (-4)$

  c. $\frac{1}{2} \cdot \left(-\frac{2}{3}\right) \cdot 3$

2. Explain how you used what you know about multiplying two rational numbers to multiply three rational numbers.

E **1.** Predict whether the sign of each product is positive or negative. Explain your reasoning.

  a. $2 \cdot 3 \cdot 4 \cdot 5$

  b. $2 \cdot (-3) \cdot 4 \cdot 5$

  c. $2 \cdot (-3) \cdot 4 \cdot (-5)$

  d. $-2 \cdot (-3) \cdot 4 \cdot (-5)$

  e. $-2 \cdot (-3) \cdot (-4) \cdot (-5)$

2. Find each product in part (1). Check whether your predictions are correct.

3. Explain how to determine whether a product will be positive or negative.

A C E Homework starts on page 66.

3.3 Division of Rational Numbers

You know that there is a relationship between addition and subtraction facts. A similar relationship exists between multiplication and division. For any multiplication fact, you can write another multiplication fact and two different related division facts. Here are three examples of rational-number fact families.

Example 1
$5 \cdot 3 = 15$
$3 \cdot 5 = 15$
$15 \div 3 = 5$ or $\frac{15}{3} = 5$
$15 \div 5 = 3$ or $\frac{15}{5} = 3$

Example 2
$6 \cdot (-3) = -18$
$-3 \cdot 6 = -18$
$-18 \div (-3) = 6$ or $\frac{-18}{-3} = 6$
$-18 \div 6 = -3$ or $\frac{-18}{6} = -3$

Example 3
$4.5 \cdot (-2) = -9$
$-2 \cdot 4.5 = -9$
$-9 \div (-2) = 4.5$ or $\frac{-9}{-2} = 4.5$
$-9 \div 4.5 = -2$ or $\frac{-9}{4.5} = -2$

Recall that a rational number can be written as $\frac{a}{b}$ where a and b are integers and b is not zero. Fact families help to clarify why division by zero is impossible. If $\frac{15}{0} = a$, then $a \cdot 0 = 15$ and $\frac{15}{0} = a$ are in the same fact family.

- How does a fact family show that $\frac{15}{0} = a$ cannot be a true statement for any value of a?

Problem 3.3

A Use what you know about fact families and multiplication to rewrite, if necessary, and find the missing value. Then find the missing value.

    1. $-6 \times (-13) = \blacksquare$

    2. $6 \times (-13) = \blacksquare$

    3. $\blacksquare \times (-9) = 108$

    4. $8 \times \blacksquare = -48$

B The team in Problem 3.1 runs another relay. Write division sentences that express your answers to the questions below.

    1. Dwayne goes from 0 to 15 meters in 5 seconds. At what rate (meters per second) does he run?

    2. Pascal reaches -12 meters only 3 seconds after passing 0. At what rate does he run?

    3. Aurelia passes 0 running to the right at a rate of 5 meters per second. When did she leave the point -50? When did she leave the point -24?

    4. Tori wants to reach the point -40, running to the left at 8 meters per second. How long will it take her from the time she passes 0?

C **1.** What do the examples in each group have in common?

Group 1
$12 \div 3$
$4.5 \div 9$
$2\frac{1}{4} \div \frac{1}{2}$

Group 2
$12 \div (-3)$
$-4.5 \div 9$
$2\frac{1}{4} \div \left(-\frac{1}{2}\right)$

Group 3
$-12 \div (-3)$
$-4.5 \div (-9)$
$-2\frac{1}{4} \div \left(-\frac{1}{2}\right)$

    2. Find the quotients in each group above.

    3. Write and solve two additional problems for each group.

    4. Describe an algorithm for dividing rational numbers.

continued on the next page >

Problem 3.3 *continued*

D **1.** Find the quotients in each group below. Is division commutative?

$$-2 \div 3 \text{ and } 3 \div (-2)$$

$$-12 \div (-4) \text{ and } -4 \div (-12)$$

$$16 \div 8 \text{ and } 8 \div 16$$

2. Give two other examples to support your answer to part (1).

E **1.** Zero is the additive identity for addition. For example, $0 + a = a$, where a is a rational number. Explain in words what this means. Provide an example.

2. Is there a *multiplicative identity n* such that $a \cdot n = a$ for any rational number a? Explain.

F **1.** Each rational number has an additive inverse. For example, $a + (-a) = 0$, where a is a rational number. Explain in words what this means. Provide an example.

2. Is there a *multiplicative inverse b*, such that $a \times b = 1$, for each rational number a? Explain.

G Use properties of multiplication and division to find each value. State which properties you use.

1. $\dfrac{\frac{5}{4} \times 7}{\frac{5}{4}}$

2. $\dfrac{3}{5}\left(\dfrac{5}{3}\right)$

3. $0.2 \times 3 \times \dfrac{1}{0.2}$

4. $\dfrac{1.3 \times 8.2}{1.3}$

5. $\dfrac{4}{5}\left(\dfrac{10}{3} + \dfrac{15}{6}\right)$

6. $-\dfrac{3}{5}\left(-\dfrac{8}{21}\right)\left(-\dfrac{5}{3}\right)$

7. $1.6 \times \dfrac{5}{8} - 2.4 \times \dfrac{5}{8}$

8. $\dfrac{-2.4 \times \frac{4}{7}}{\frac{4}{7}}$

Problem 3.3 *continued*

H Recall that some fractions have decimals that terminate. For example, $\frac{3}{4} = 0.75$. Other fractions have decimals that repeat. For example, $\frac{1}{3} = 0.333\ldots = 0.\overline{3}$. The 3 repeats.

1. State whether each fraction will *terminate* or *repeat*. Then write each fraction as a decimal.

   a. $\frac{2}{5}$

   b. $\frac{3}{8}$

   c. $\frac{-5}{6}$

   d. $\frac{35}{10}$

   e. $\frac{8}{-9}$

   f. $\frac{-3}{-11}$

2. List two other fractions that will terminate and two that will repeat. Give their decimal representations.

A C E Homework starts on page 66.

Note on Notation You know that a rational number is any number that you can write in the form $\frac{p}{q}$, where p and q are integers and $q \neq 0$. When a rational number is negative, the negative sign can be associated with the numerator, the denominator, or the entire fraction. For positive integers a and b,

$$\frac{-a}{b} = \frac{a}{-b} = -\frac{a}{b}$$

For example, suppose $a = 6$ and $b = 2$.

$$\frac{-6}{2} = \frac{6}{-2} = -\frac{6}{2} = -3$$

3.4 Playing the Integer Product Game
Applying Multiplication and Division of Integers

 You have developed algorithms for adding, subtracting, multiplying, and dividing integers. You will apply your multiplication and division algorithms in the Integer Product Game.

The game board consists of a list of factors and a grid of products. To play, you need a game board, two paper clips, and colored markers or chips.

Integer Product Game

Rules

1. Player A puts a paper clip on a number in the factor list.

2. Player B puts the other paper clip on any number in the factor list, including the number chosen by Player A. Player B then marks the product of the two factors on the product grid.

3. Player A moves *either one* of the paper clips to another number. He or she then marks the new product with a different color than Player B.

4. Each player takes turns moving a paper clip and marking a product. A product can only be marked by one player.

5. The winner is the first player to mark four squares in a row (up and down, across, or diagonally).

−36	−30	−25	−24	−20	−18
−16	−15	−12	−10	−9	−8
−6	−5	−4	−3	−2	−1
1	2	3	4	5	6
8	9	10	12	15	16
18	20	24	25	30	36

Factors:

−6 −5 −4 −3 −2 −1 1 2 3 4 5 6

- What product would give the least number? What product would give the greatest number?

Problem 3.4

Play the Integer Product Game with positive and negative factors.
Look for strategies for picking the factors and products.

A What strategies did you find useful in playing the game? Explain.

B What pair(s) of numbers from the factor list will give each product?

   1. 5

   2. −12

   3. 12

   4. −25

C Your opponent puts a paper clip on −4. List five products that you can form, assuming they are not marked. Tell where you would need to put your paper clip in each case.

D Describe the moves to make in each case.

   1. The paper clips are on −5 and −2. You want a product of −15.

   2. The paper clips are on −3 and −2. You want a product of −6.

   3. Your opponent will win with 24. What numbers should you avoid with your paper clip moves?

E Mia thinks the game could also be called the Division Game. Explain why Mia might think this.

ACE Homework starts on page 66.

Applications

1. At some international airports, trains carry passengers between the separate terminal buildings. Suppose that one such train system moves along a track like the one below.

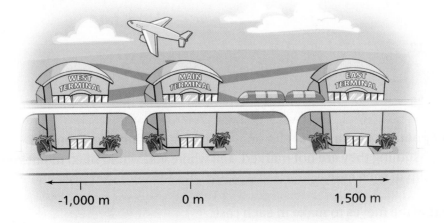

a. A train leaves the main terminal going east at 10 meters per second. Where will it be in 10 seconds? When will it reach the east terminal?

b. A train passes the main terminal going east at 10 meters per second. Where was that train 15 seconds ago? When was it at the west terminal?

c. A train leaves the main terminal going west at 10 meters per second. Where will it be in 20 seconds? When will it reach the west terminal?

d. A train passes the main terminal going west at 10 meters per second. When was it at the east terminal? Where was it 20 seconds ago?

2. Julia thinks a bit more about how to use red and black chips to model operations with integers. She draws the following chip board. She decides it represents $8 \times (-5) = -40$ and $-40 \div 8 = -5$. Explain why Julia's reasoning makes sense.

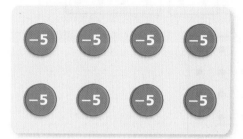

Use Julia's reasoning from Exercise 2 to find each value.

3. $10 \times (-5)$

4. $4 \times (-15)$

5. $3 \times (-5)$

6. $-14 \div 2$

7. $-14 \div 7$

8. $-35 \div 7$

9. Find each product.

   a. $7 \cdot 2$

   b. $-7 \cdot (-2)$

   c. $7 \cdot (-2)$

   d. $-7 \cdot 2$

   e. $8 \cdot 2.5$

   f. $-9 \cdot (-4)$

   g. $12 \cdot (-3)$

   h. $-1.5 \cdot 4$

   i. $3.5 \cdot 7$

   j. $-8.1 \cdot (-1)$

   k. $1 \cdot (-6)$

   l. $-2\frac{1}{2} \cdot 1$

10. Tell whether each product is greater than or less than zero.

   a. $5 \cdot (-7)$

   b. $-3.2 \cdot 1.5$

   c. $10.5 \cdot (-4)$

   d. $-2 \cdot (-3) \cdot (-1)$

   e. $-\frac{2}{3} \cdot 2\frac{3}{4}$

   f. $-\frac{3}{4} \cdot \left(-1\frac{5}{6}\right) \cdot \left(-\frac{7}{4}\right)$

   g. $-\frac{3}{4} \cdot \left(-1\frac{5}{6}\right) \cdot \frac{7}{4}$

   h. $-\frac{3}{4} \cdot \left(-1\frac{5}{6}\right) \cdot \left(-\frac{7}{4}\right) \cdot \left(-2\frac{3}{8}\right)$

   i. $\frac{3}{4} \cdot \left(-1\frac{5}{6}\right) \cdot \frac{7}{4} \cdot \left(-2\frac{3}{8}\right)$

   j. $\frac{3}{4} \cdot 1\frac{5}{6} \cdot \frac{7}{4} \cdot \left(-2\frac{3}{8}\right)$

The dot patterns illustrate commutative properties for operations on whole numbers. Write a number sentence for each case.

11.

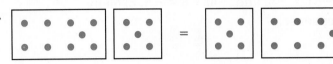

12.

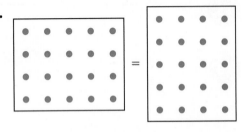

13. Find the values for each pair.

a. $4 \cdot (-3)$ and $-3 \cdot 4$

b. $2 \cdot (-4)$ and $-4 \cdot 2$

c. $-2 \cdot (-3)$ and $-3 \cdot (-2)$

d. $\frac{1}{5} \cdot \left(-\frac{4}{9}\right)$ and $-\frac{4}{9} \cdot \frac{1}{5}$

e. What can you conclude about multiplication with negative numbers?

14. You have located fractions such as $-\frac{5}{7}$ on a number line. You have also used fractions to show division: $\frac{-5}{7} = -5 \div 7$ and $\frac{5}{-7} = 5 \div (-7)$. Tell whether each statement is *true* or *false*. Explain.

a. $\frac{-1}{2} = \frac{1}{-2}$

b. $-\frac{1}{2} = \frac{-1}{-2}$

15. For each number sentence, find a value for n that makes the sentence true.

a. $24 \div 2 = n$

b. $-24 \div (-2) = n$

c. $24 \div n = -12$

d. $n \div 2 = -12$

e. $5 \div 2.5 = n$

f. $-12 \div n = 3$

g. $n \div (-3) = -4$

h. $(-16) \div \frac{1}{4} = n$

For Exercises 16–18, write four related multiplication and division facts for each set of integers.

Sample 27, 9, 3

$$9 \cdot 3 = 27$$

$$3 \cdot 9 = 27$$

$$27 \div 9 = 3$$

$$27 \div 3 = 9$$

16. 7, −3, −21

17. −4, −5, 20

18. 1.5, −3, −4.5

For Exercises 19–24, determine whether the product of or quotient of each expression is greater than, less than, or equal to 0 without doing any calculations. Explain your reasoning.

19. $-1{,}105.62 \div 24.3$

20. $0 \cdot (-67)$

21. $-27.5 \cdot (-63)$

22. $0 \div 89$

23. $-54.9 \div (-3)$

24. $-2{,}943 \cdot 1.06$

25. Use the multiplication and division algorithms you developed to find each value.

a. $12 \cdot 9$

b. $5 \cdot (-25)$

c. $-220 \div (-50)$

d. $48 \div (-6)$

e. $-63 \div 9$

f. $\frac{2}{-3} \cdot \left(\frac{-4}{5}\right)$

g. $\frac{-99}{33}$

h. $-2.7 \div (-0.3)$

i. $-36 \cdot 5$

j. $52.5 \div (-7)$

k. $-2\frac{1}{2} \cdot \left(-\frac{2}{3}\right)$

l. $9 \div 5$

m. $-9 \cdot (-50)$

n. $\frac{-96}{24}$

o. $6 \cdot 1\frac{1}{2}$

p. $-\frac{5}{8} \cdot \frac{8}{5}$

q. $4 \cdot \left(-1\frac{1}{4}\right)$

r. $-2.5 \cdot 2\frac{1}{5}$

Multiple Choice For Exercises 26 and 27, find each value.

26. $-24 \div 4$

    A. -96 **B.** -6 **C.** 6 **D.** 96

27. $-10 \cdot (-5)$

    F. -50 **G.** -2 **H.** 2 **J.** 50

Use properties of multiplication and division to find each value. State
which properties you use.

28. $\dfrac{\frac{2}{7} \cdot 9}{\frac{2}{7}}$ **29.** $\frac{3}{8} \cdot (-4) \cdot 3.5 \cdot \frac{8}{3}$

30. $-1.3 \cdot 5 \cdot (-6) \cdot 0.2$ **31.** $\dfrac{4.9 \cdot 5.8}{4.9}$

For Exercises 32–35, state whether each fraction will *terminate* or
repeat. Write each fraction as a decimal.

32. $\dfrac{-5}{9}$ **33.** $\dfrac{7}{-8}$ **34.** $\dfrac{-4}{-11}$ **35.** $\dfrac{5}{16}$

36. Chris and Elizabeth are making a version of the Integer Product
Game in which players need three products in a row to win.

**Chris and Elizabeth's
Product Game**

4	–4	6	–6
9	–9	10	–10
15	–15	25	–25

Factors:

What six factors do they need for their game? Explain your reasoning.

Connections

37. The temperature changed $-2°F$ per hour from noon on Tuesday until 10:00 A.M. the next morning. The temperature at noon on Tuesday is shown.

    a. What was the temperature at 4:00 P.M. on Tuesday?

    b. What was the temperature at 9:00 A.M. on Wednesday?

Write a number sentence to represent each situation. Then answer the question.

38. The Extraterrestrials have a score of -300. They answer four 50-point questions incorrectly. What is their new score?

39. The Super Computers answered three 100-point questions incorrectly. They now have 200 points. What was their score before answering the three questions incorrectly?

40. A football team is at its own 25-yard line. In the next three plays, it loses an average of 4 yards per play. Where is the team after the three plays?

41. A new convenience store wishes to attract customers. For a one-day special, the store sells gasoline for $.25 per gallon below its regular cost per gallon. Suppose the store sells 5,750 gallons of gas that day. What is the store's profit or loss in comparison to the amount the store would have made without the special?

42. Multiply or divide. Show your work.

    a. $52 \cdot 75$ **b.** $52 \cdot (-75)$ **c.** $-2,262 \div (-58)$

    d. $\frac{2}{3} \cdot \frac{4}{5}$ **e.** $-9,908 \div 89$ **f.** $-7.77 \div (-0.37)$

    g. $-34 \cdot 15$ **h.** $53.2 \div (-7)$ **i.** $\frac{-2}{3} \cdot \frac{6}{8}$

    j. $90 \div 50$ **k.** $-90 \cdot (-50)$ **l.** $-108 \div 24$

    m. $19.5 \div (-3)$ **n.** $-8.4 \cdot 6$ **o.** $6 \cdot 2\frac{1}{2}$

    p. $-3\frac{2}{3} \cdot (-9)$ **q.** $4 \cdot \left(-1\frac{1}{4}\right)$ **r.** $-2.5 \cdot 2\frac{1}{5}$

43. The list below gives average temperatures (in °C) for a city for each month of the year, from January through December.

$$-25, -20, -13, -2, 9, 15, 17, 14, 7, -4, -16, -23$$

a. What is the median?

b. What is the range?

c. What is the mean?

d. Number the months from 1 (for January) through 12 (for December). Plot a graph of the (month, temperature) data.

44. Find the sum, difference, product, or quotient.

a. $-5 - 18$

b. $-23 + 48$

c. $\frac{3}{4} \cdot \left(-\frac{5}{9}\right)$

d. $119 + (-19.3)$

e. $-1.5 - (-32.8)$

f. $12 \div 15$

g. $-169 \div (-1.3)$

h. $0.47 - 1.56$

i. $6 \cdot (-3.5)$

j. $\frac{2}{-3} \div \frac{5}{6}$

k. $\frac{7}{12} - \left(-\frac{2}{3}\right)$

l. $-\frac{4}{5} \div \left(-\frac{1}{4}\right)$

45. Estimate the sum, difference, product, or quotient.

a. $-52 - 5$

b. $-43 + (-108)$

c. $2\frac{3}{4} \cdot \left(-\frac{5}{9}\right)$

d. $79 + (-25.3)$

e. $-12.5 - (-37.3)$

f. $89 \div 15$

g. $-169 \div (-13)$

h. $6.3 - 1.86$

i. $61 \cdot (-3.9)$

j. $-\frac{2}{3} \div \left(1\frac{5}{6}\right)$

k. $5\frac{7}{12} - \left(-\frac{2}{3}\right)$

l. $-\frac{4}{5} \div \left(-\frac{1}{4}\right)$

Find integers to make each sentence true.

46. ▨ · ▨ = 30

47. ▨ · ▨ = −30

48. −24 ÷ ▨ = ▨

Extensions

Determine whether each statement is *always*, *sometimes*, or *never* *true*. Explain.

49. If m and n are positive rational numbers, then $m + n$ is positive.

50. If m and n are negative rational numbers, then $m + n$ is negative.

51. If m is a positive rational number and n is a negative rational number, then $m + n$ is negative.

52. If m and n are positive rational numbers, then $m \times n$ is positive.

53. If m and n are negative rational numbers, then $m \times n$ is negative.

54. To add $5 + 3 + 2$, you might think that it is easier to add the $3 + 2$ and then add the answer to the 5. The mathematical property that allows you to change the grouping of addends (or factors) is called the *Associative Property*.

Test the Associative Property for addition and multiplication of integers by simplifying the expressions below. Find the values within the parentheses first. When you need a grouping symbol like parentheses inside another set of parentheses, you can use brackets to make it easier to read. For example, $(4 - (-6))$ can be written as $[4 - (-6)]$.

a. $[3 \cdot (-3)] \cdot 4$ and $3 \cdot (-3 \cdot 4)$

b. $(-5 \cdot 4) \cdot (-3)$ and $-5 \cdot [4 \cdot (-3)]$

c. $[-2 \cdot (-3)] \cdot (-5)$ and $-2 \cdot [-3 \cdot (-5)]$

d. $(3 \cdot 4) \cdot (-5)$ and $3 \cdot [4 \cdot (-5)]$

e. $[3 + (-3)] + 4$ and $3 + (-3 + 4)$

f. $(-5 + 4) + (-3)$ and $-5 + [4 + (-3)]$

g. $[-2 + (-3)] + (-5)$ and $-2 + [-3 + (-5)]$

h. $(3 + 4) + (-5)$ and $3 + [4 + (-5)]$

i. Does the Associative Property work for addition and multiplication of integers?

Tell whether each statement is *true* or *false*. Explain.

55. $-1 = -1 + 0$

56. $-3\frac{3}{8} = -\frac{21}{8}$

57. $-6.75 = -6 + \left(-\frac{3}{4}\right)$

For Exercises 58 and 59, write a story for a problem that is answered by finding the value of *n*.

58. $-4n = -24$

59. $\frac{n}{2} = 16$

60. Find a set of addends to make a Sum Game. Each sum on the board below should be the sum of two numbers (possibly a single number added to itself). Each pair of numbers should add to a sum on the board.

Hint: You need 11 numbers, all with different absolute values.

Sum Game

-24	-22	-20	-18	-16	-14
-12	-11	-10	-9	-8	-7
-6	-5	-4	-3	-2	-1
0	1	2	3	4	5
6	7	8	9	10	11
12	14	16	18	20	22

Factors:

In this Investigation, you studied ways to use multiplication and division of rational numbers to answer questions about speed, time, distance, and direction of motion. You used the results of those calculations to develop algorithms for multiplying and dividing any two rational numbers. The following questions will help you summarize what you have learned.

Think about these questions. Discuss your ideas with other students and your teacher. Then write a summary of your findings in your notebook.

1. **Give** an example of a multiplication problem, involving two integers, in which the product is

   a. less than 0.   **b.** greater than 0.   **c.** equal to 0.

   d. In general, describe the signs of the factors for each product in parts (a)–(c).

2. **Give** an example of a division problem, involving two integers, in which the quotient is

   a. less than 0.   **b.** greater than 0.   **c.** equal to 0.

   d. In general, describe the signs of the dividend and divisor for each quotient in parts (a)–(c).

3. **a.** Suppose three numbers are related by an equation of the form $a \cdot b = c$, where a, b, and c are not equal to 0. Write two related number sentences using division.

   b. Suppose three numbers are related by an equation of the form, $a \div b = c$, where a, b, and c are not equal to 0. Write two related number sentences using multiplication.

4. **Which** operations on integers are commutative? Give numerical examples to support your answer.

Common Core Mathematical Practices

As you worked on the Problems in this Investigation, you used prior knowledge to make sense of them. You also applied Mathematical Practices to solve the Problems. Think back over your work, the ways you thought about the Problems, and how you used Mathematical Practices.

Hector described his thoughts in the following way:

Jake and I knew that a negative number times a negative number is positive. This helped us predict the sign of the product of a set of numbers in Problem 3.2. If there is an even number of numbers that are negative, we can group these numbers in pairs. The product of each pair is positive. Then we are left with positive numbers, so the final product is positive. If there are an uneven number of negative numbers, the product is negative because there will always be a negative number that is not paired with another negative number. And a negative times a positive is negative.

Common Core Standards for Mathematical Practice

MP2 Reason abstractly and quantitatively.

- What other Mathematical Practices can you identify in Hector's reasoning?

- Describe a Mathematical Practice that you and your classmates used to solve a different Problem in this Investigation.

Properties of Operations

When you study new types of numbers, you need to know what properties apply to them. You know that both addition and multiplication of rational numbers are commutative.

$$-\frac{2}{3} + \frac{1}{6} = \frac{1}{6} + \left(-\frac{2}{3}\right) \text{ and } -\frac{2}{3} \cdot \frac{1}{6} = \frac{1}{6} \cdot \left(-\frac{2}{3}\right)$$

You also used a set of conventions called the *Order of Operations* to help you decide how to carry out a computation.

1. Compute all expressions within parentheses or brackets first.
   Note: To avoid confusion, you use brackets in sentences that contain many parentheses.

2. Compute all numbers with exponents.

3. Then compute all multiplications and divisions in order from left to right.

4. Then compute all additions and subtractions in order from left to right.

....

Common Core State Standards

7.NS.A.1d Apply properties of operations as strategies to add and subtract rational numbers.

7.NS.A.2a Understand that multiplication is extended from fractions to rational numbers by requiring that operations continue to satisfy the properties of operations, particularly the distributive property, leading to products such as $(-1)(-1) = 1$ and the rules for multiplying signed numbers. Interpret products of rational numbers by describing real-world contexts.

7.NS.A.2c Apply properties of operations as strategies to multiply and divide rational numbers.

7.NS.A.3 Solve real-world and mathematical problems involving the four operations with rational numbers.

7.EE.B.3 Solve multi-step real-life and mathematical problems posed with positive and negative rational numbers in any form (whole numbers, fractions, and decimals), using tools strategically . . .

Also 7.NS.A.1, 7.NS.A.2, 7.NS.A.2d

Using the Order of Operations, you get results like this:

$$7\frac{1}{2} + \left(6 \cdot 4\frac{1}{2} - 9\right) \div 3 = 7\frac{1}{2} + (27 - 9) \div 3$$

$$= 7\frac{1}{2} + 18 \div 3$$

$$= 7\frac{1}{2} + 6$$

$$= 13\frac{1}{2}$$

The following example shows why these conventions are necessary.

The soccer team orders 20 new jerseys from Custom Jersey Designs. The total cost is represented by the equation $C = 100 + 15n$, where C is the cost in dollars and n is the number of jerseys ordered. Pedro and David calculate the total cost.

Custom Jersey Designs

your logo here

$100 setup fee

$15 per shirt

Pedro's calculation: $C = 100 + 15 \cdot 20$

$$= 100 + 300$$

$$= \$400$$

David's calculation: $C = 100 + 15 \cdot 20$

$$= 115 \cdot 20$$

$$= \$2,300$$

• Who did the calculation correctly?

4.1 Order of Operations

The Order of Operations applies to calculations involving positive and negative numbers. The following questions provide practice in using the Order of Operations.

In a game called Dealing Up, a player draws four cards. The player uses all four cards to write a number sentence that gives the greatest possible result.

 What is the greatest result you can make from two of the following numbers? Three? Four?

$$-25 \quad +2 \quad -3 \quad +3$$

Problem 4.1

A Jamar and Elena are playing Dealing Up. Jamar draws the following four cards:

1. Jamar writes $5 - (-6) \cdot 4 + (-3) = 41$. Elena says the result should be 26. Who is correct and why?

2. Elena starts by writing $-3 - (-6) + 5^4$. What is her result?

3. Insert parentheses into $-3 - (-6) + 5^4$ to give a greater result than in part (2).

continued on the next page >

Problem 4.1 *continued*

B Find each value.

1. $-7 \cdot 4 + 8 \div 2$
2. $(3 + 2)^2 \cdot 6 - 1$
3. $2\frac{2}{5} \cdot 4\frac{1}{2} - 5^3 + 3$
4. $8 \cdot (4 - 5)^3 + 3$
5. $-8 \cdot [4 - (-5 + 3)]$
6. $-16 \div 8 \cdot 2^3 + (-7)$

C Use parentheses, where needed, to make the greatest and least possible values.

1. $7 - 2 + 3^2$
2. $46 + 2.8 \cdot 7 - 2$
3. $25 \cdot (-3.12) + 21.3 \div 3$
4. $5.67 + 35.4 - 178 - 181$

D Rodrigo performs the following computation:

$$3 + 2 \cdot 7 - 6$$

His answer is 29.

1. Explain how Rodrigo obtained his answer.
2. Is Rodrigo's answer correct? If not, what is the correct answer? Explain.

E Use the Order of Operations to find the value. Show your work.

$$3 + 4 \cdot 5 \div 2 \cdot 3 - 7^2 + 6 \div 3 = \blacksquare$$

ACE Homework starts on page 86.

4.2 The Distributive Property

Recall that you can use the Distributive Property to rewrite an expression. The rewritten expression may be easier to calculate or may give new information.

An expression written as a sum of terms is in *expanded form*. If the terms have a common factor, then you can use the Distributive Property to write an equivalent expression. You can write the expression as a product of the common factor and the sum of the other two factors. This is called *factored form*.

With integers:
$$20 + 35 = 55$$
$$5 \cdot 4 + 5 \cdot 7 = 5 \cdot (4 + 7)$$

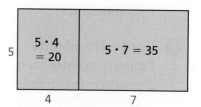

With a variable:
$$40 + 8x = 8 \cdot 5 + 8 \cdot x$$
$$8 \cdot 5 + 8 \cdot x = 8 \cdot (5 + x)$$

You can also use the Distributive Property to rewrite expressions with negative numbers. Use the Distributive Property to multiply the first factor by each number in the second factor and add the two resulting products.

With integers: $-3 \cdot (4 + 8) = -3 \cdot 4 + (-3) \cdot 8$

With a variable: $-2 \cdot (x + 6) = -2 \cdot x + (-2) \cdot 6$

When you apply the Distributive Property to rewrite $5 \cdot x + 5 \cdot (-2.5)$ as $5 \cdot [x + (-2.5)]$, you are factoring out the common factor 5 from the two parts of the sum. When you write the equivalent expression $5 \cdot [x + (-2.5)]$, you can say you have factored the expression into the product of two terms, 5 and $[x + (-2.5)]$.

- Will the values of these expressions be the same or different?

$$-2 \cdot (-3 - 7) \qquad 2 \cdot (3 + 7)$$

Problem 4.2

A The checkbook shows Juan's bank account balance at the beginning of the week. During the week he withdraws $19 and $30. How much money does he have left at the end of the week?

DATE	ITEM	DEPOSIT	WITHDRAWAL	BALANCE
				$ 100

1. Show two different ways to solve this problem.

2. Describe how the two ways are different.

B Use the Distributive Property to write each expression in expanded form.

1. $5 \cdot (3 + 2)$

2. $5 \cdot [3 + (-2)]$

3. $5 \cdot (3 - 2)$

4. $5 \cdot [3 - (-2)]$

5. For parts (1)–(4), find the value of each expression.

C Use the Distributive Property to write each expression in factored form.

1. $6 \cdot 2 + 6 \cdot 3$

2. $6 \cdot 2 - 6 \cdot 3$

3. $-6 \cdot 2 + (-6) \cdot 3$

4. $-6 \cdot 2 - (-6) \cdot 3$

5. $5x - 8x$

6. $-3x - 4x$

7. Explain how to factor an expression with subtraction.

Problem 4.2 continued

D
1. If you apply the Order of Operations to $3\frac{1}{2} \cdot 15 - 3\frac{1}{2} \cdot 5$, you get $52\frac{1}{2} - 17\frac{1}{2} = 35$. What value do you get if you use the Distributive Property first to factor $3\frac{1}{2} \cdot 15 - 3\frac{1}{2} \cdot 5$?

2. If you apply the Order of Operations to $17(8.5 - 3.5)$, you get $17 \cdot 5 = 85$. What value do you get if you apply the Distributive Property first to $17(8.5 - 3.5)$?

3. What would you say to someone who is wondering whether to apply the Distributive Property or the Order of Operations first?

E Ling claims she has another way to show that $-1(-1) = 1$. Ling wrote her reasoning:

> By the Distributive Property, I know that $-1[1 + (-1)]$ equals $-1(1) + (-1)(-1)$.
> Because $1 + (-1)$ equals 0, I also know that $-1[1 + (-1)]$ equals $-1(0)$, or 0.
> So $-1(1) + (-1)(-1)$ must equal 0. I know $-1(1)$ equals -1,
> so $-1 + (-1)(-1)$ must equal 0.
> Therefore, $-1(-1)$ must equal 1.

Do you agree with Ling's reasoning? Does $(^{-}1)(^{-}1) = {}^{+}1$?

F In parts (1) and (2), use the Order of Operations and properties of operations to compute each expression. Give your answers as decimals.

1. a. $(1 + 5 + 3) \div 4$ **b.** $\frac{1}{4} + \frac{5}{4} + \frac{3}{4}$

2. a. $(1 + 5 - 2) \div 3$ **b.** $\frac{1}{3} + \frac{5}{3} - \frac{2}{3}$

3. What can you say about the expressions in parts (1) and (2)?

4. How would you describe the relationship between the Distributive Property and division?

A C E Homework starts on page 86.

4.3 What Operations Are Needed?

In the questions below, you will use what you have learned about operations on rational numbers to solve problems. Always ask yourself the following question:

- What operation(s) do you need to solve the problem, and how do you know?

Problem 4.3

A Three friends are going hiking with Latisha. For each of the four hikers, she buys two bottles of water and three packs of trail mix. The bottles of water cost $1.50 each, and the packs of trail mix cost $3.75 each.

   1. a. Can Latisha go through the express checkout lane for customers with 15 or fewer individual items?

      b. Write a number sentence to show how you found the total number of items Latisha bought.

      c. Write a different number sentence that shows a different way to find the total number of items.

      d. Explain how you know which operation(s) to use.

   2. Latisha has $60. Does she have enough money to pay for the items?

B Mr. Chan buys a roll of paper towels for $2.19 and a bottle of window cleaner for $2.69. In his state, there is a 4% sales tax on these items. Mr. Chan also buys a gallon of milk for $3.95. There is no sales tax on milk. Mr. Chan has a $5 coupon to use at the store.

   1. Write a number sentence to find Mr. Chan's total bill. What is his total bill?

   2. Is there more than one way to compute this total?

   3. Explain how you know which operation(s) to use.

Problem 4.3 *continued*

C Eli's class held a fund raising event last month. The class's expenses were $5.75, $4.75, and $3.75. The amounts of money the class raised were $13.50, $24.70, $13.15, and $19.50.

   1. Write a number sentence to find how much money the class has after the fundraiser. Did the class make any money? If so, how much?

   2. Can you use two different orders of computation?

   3. Explain how you know which operation(s) to use.

D The following sequence of scoring occurred during a Math Fever game between the Super Brains and the Rocket Scientists.

Super Brains: −50, +150, −100, +250, −150
Rocket Scientists: −150, +250, −50, −50, +100

   1. Write a number sentence to find each team's score. Who is ahead at this stage of the game? By how many points?

   2. Can you use a different number sentence to find each team's score?

E The table shows the hourly amount of water flowing into and out of a water tower for given time periods. For example, for the first 4 hours, 5,000 gallons flowed into the tower each hour.

Water Tower Water Flow

Water Flow In (gallons per hour)	Water Flow Out (gallons per hour)	Time (hours)
5,000	0	4
4,000	0	7
0	7,500	3
5,000	3,000	6.5

   1. a. If there are 5,000 gallons of water at the start, how much is there at the end of the entire time period?

      b. What number sentence shows your reasoning?

   2. a. What was the average rate of water flow per hour in the first 11 hours?

      b. What was the average rate of flow of water per hour in the last 9.5 hours?

      c. At the end of the entire time period, what was the average rate of flow (in or out) per hour?

A C E Homework starts on page 86.

Applications

1. Find the values of each pair of expressions.

   a. $-12 + (-4 + 9)$ $[-12 + (-4)] + 9$

   b. $(14 - 20) - 8$ $14 - (20 - 8)$

   c. $[14 + (-20)] + (-8)$ $14 + [-20 + (-8)]$

   d. $-1 - [-1 + (-1)]$ $[-1 - (-1)] + (-1)$

   e. Which cases lead to expressions with different results? Explain.

For Exercises 2–7, find the value of each expression.

2. $(5 - 3) \div (-2) \cdot (-1)$ 3. $2 + (-3) \cdot 4 - (-5)$

4. $4 \cdot 2 \cdot (-3) + (-10) \div 5$ 5. $-3 \cdot [2 + (-10)] - 2^2$

6. $(4 - 20) \div 2^2 - 5 \cdot (-2)$ 7. $10 - [50 \div (-2 \cdot 25) - 7] \cdot 2^2$

For Exercises 8–11, rewrite each expression in an equivalent form to show a simpler way to do the arithmetic. Explain how you know the two results are equal without doing any calculations.

8. $(-150 + 270) + 30$ 9. $(43 \cdot 120) + [43 \cdot (-20)]$

10. $23 + (-75) + 14 + (-23) - (-75)$ 11. $[0.8 \cdot (-23)] + [0.8 \cdot (-7)]$

12. Without doing any calculations, determine whether each number sentence is true. Explain. Then check your answer.

    a. $50 \cdot 432 = (50 \cdot 400) + (50 \cdot 32)$

    b. $50 \cdot 368 = (50 \cdot 400) - (50 \cdot 32)$

    c. $-50 \cdot 998 = [-50 \cdot (-1{,}000)] + [-50 \cdot 2]$

    d. $-50 + (400 \cdot 32) = (-50 + 400) \cdot (-50 + 32)$

    e. $(-70 \cdot 20) + (-50 \cdot 20) = (-120 \cdot 20)$

    f. $6 \cdot 17 = 6 \cdot 20 - 6 \cdot 3$

For each part, use the Distributive Property to write an equivalent expression.

13. $-2 \cdot [5 + (-8)]$

14. $(-3 \cdot 2) - [-3 \cdot (-12)]$

15. $x \cdot (-3 + 5)$

16. $-7x + 4x$

17. $2x \cdot [2 - (-4)]$

18. $x - 3x$

19. A grocery store receipt shows 5% state tax due on laundry detergent and a flower bouquet. Does it matter whether the tax is calculated on each separate item or the total cost? Explain.

RECEIPT

Laundry
Detergent .... $ 7.99 T

Flower
Bouquet .... $ 3.99 T

Sales Tax ....

Connections

For Exercises 20–37, find the sum, difference, product, or quotient.

20. $3 \cdot 12$

21. $3 \cdot (-12)$

22. $-3 \div (-12)$

23. $-10 \cdot (-11)$

24. $-10 + 11$

25. $10 - 11$

26. $-24 - (-12)$

27. $\frac{-24}{-12}$

28. $-18 \div 6$

29. $50 \cdot 70$

30. $50 \cdot (-70)$

31. $2,200 \div (-22)$

32. $-50 \cdot (-120)$

33. $-139 + 899$

34. $5,600 - 7,800$

35. $-4,400 - (-1,200)$

36. $\frac{-9,900}{-99}$

37. $-580 + (-320)$

38. When using negative numbers and exponents, you sometimes need parentheses to make it clear what you are multiplying.

You can think of -5^4 as "the opposite of 5^4" or
$-(5^4) = -(5 \cdot 5 \cdot 5 \cdot 5) = -625$

You can think of $(-5)^4$ as "negative five to the fourth power" or
$(-5)^4 = -5 \cdot (-5) \cdot (-5) \cdot (-5) = 625$

Indicate whether the following expressions will be negative or positive. Explain your answers.

a. -3^2　　　　**b.** $(-6)^3$　　　　**c.** $(-4)^4$

d. -1^6　　　　**e.** $(-3)^4$　　　　**f.** -2^3

39. This list shows the yards gained and lost during the first several plays of a football game:

$$8, 4, 3, 7, -15, 20, 5, -12, 32, 1$$

Write an expression that shows how to compute the team's average gain or loss per play. Then compute the average.

40. Complete each number sentence.

a. $-34 + (-15) = \blacksquare$

b. $-12 \cdot (-23) = \blacksquare$

c. $-532 \div \blacksquare = -7$

d. $-777 - \blacksquare = -740$

e. Write a fact family for part (a).

f. Write a fact family for part (b).

For Exercises 41–44, write a related fact. Use it to find the value of n that makes the sentence true.

41. $n - (-5) = 35$　　　　**42.** $4 + n = -43$

43. $-2n = -16$　　　　**44.** $\frac{n}{4} = -32$

45. Insert parentheses (or brackets) in each expression if needed to make the equation true.

   a. $1 + (-3) \cdot (-4) = 8$ **b.** $1 + (-3) \cdot (-4) = 13$

   c. $-6 \div (-2) + (-4) = 1$ **d.** $-6 \div (-2) + (-4) = -1$

   e. $-4 \cdot 2 - 10 = -18$ **f.** $-4 \cdot 2 - 10 = 32$

46. **Multiple Choice** Which set of numbers is in order from least to greatest?

   A. $31.4, -14.2, -55, 75, -0.05, 0.5, 3.140$

   B. $\frac{2}{5}, \frac{-3}{5}, \frac{8}{7}, \frac{-9}{8}, \frac{-3}{2}, \frac{5}{3}$

   C. $-0.2, -0.5, 0.75, 0.6, -1, 1.5$

   D. None of these

47. Find the absolute values of the numbers for each set in Exercise 46. Write them in order from least to greatest.

For Exercises 48–50, decide whether each statement is correct, and explain your answer.

48. $|-2 + 3| = |-2| + |3|$

49. $5 - |-2 + 3| = 5 - |-2| + |3|$

50. $|-2 - 3| = |-2| + |-3|$

51. You can use dot patterns to illustrate the distributive properties for operations on whole numbers. Write a number sentence to represent the pair of dot patterns.

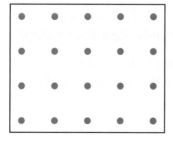 $=$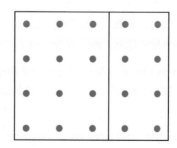

52. A trucking company carries freight along a highway from New York City to San Francisco. Its home base is in Omaha, Nebraska, which is about halfway between the two cities. Truckers average about 50 miles per hour on this route.

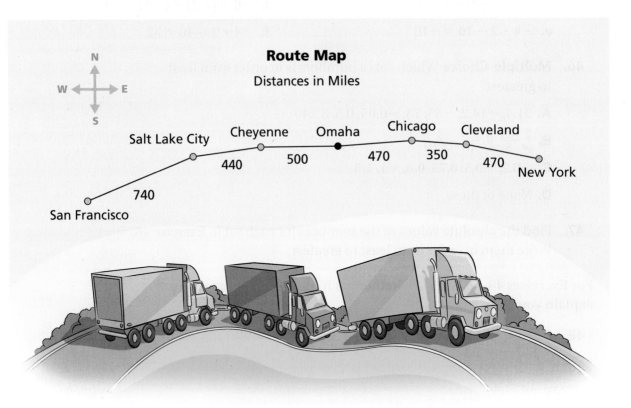

Route Map

Distances in Miles

Make a number line to represent this truck route. Put Omaha at 0. Use positive numbers for cities east of Omaha and negative numbers for cities west of Omaha. Then write number sentences to answer each question.

a. A truck leaves Omaha heading east and travels for 7 hours. About how far does the truck go? Where on the number line does it stop?

b. A truck leaves Omaha heading west and travels for 4.5 hours. About how far does the truck go? Where on the number line does it stop?

c. A truck heading east arrives in Omaha. About where on the number line was the truck 12 hours earlier?

d. A truck heading west arrives in Omaha. About where on the number line was the truck 11 hours earlier?

Extensions

Copy each pair of expressions in Exercises 53–57. Insert $<$ or $>$ to make a true statement.

53. $-23 \blacksquare -45$

54. $-23 + 10 \blacksquare -45 + 10$

55. $-23 - 10 \blacksquare -45 - 10$

56. $-23 \cdot 10 \blacksquare -45 \cdot 10$

57. $-23 \cdot (-10) \blacksquare -45 \cdot (-10)$

For Exercises 58–60, refer to your results in Exercises 53–57. Complete each statement. Test your ideas with other numerical cases, or develop another kind of explanation, perhaps using chip board or number line ideas.

58. If $a > b$, then $a + c \blacksquare b + c$.

59. If $a > b$, then $a - c \blacksquare b - c$.

60. If $a > b$, then $a \cdot c \blacksquare b \cdot c$.

For Exercises 61–63, find the value for n that makes the sentence true.

61. $n - (-24) = 12$

62. $2.5n = -10$

63. $2.5n + (-3) = -13$

64. Complete each pair of calculations.

  a. $12 \div (-8 + 4) = \blacksquare$ $[12 \div (-8)] + (12 \div 4) = \blacksquare$

  b. $-12 \div [-5 - (-3)] = \blacksquare$ $[-12 \div (-5)] - [-12 \div (-3)] = \blacksquare$

  c. $(-2 - 6) \div 4 = \blacksquare$ $(-2 \div 4) - (6 \div 4) = \blacksquare$

  d. $(5 + 6) \div 3 = \blacksquare$ $(5 \div 3) + (6 \div 3) = \blacksquare$

  e. What can you conclude from parts (a)–(d) about the Distributive Property?

65. When you find the mean (average) of two numbers, you add them together and divide by 2.

    a. Does the order in which you do the operations matter? Give examples.

    b. Does multiplication distribute over the averaging operation? That is, will a number a times the average of two numbers, x and y, give the same result as the average of ax and ay? Give examples.

For Exercises 66–69, write equivalent expressions to show two different ways to find the area of each rectangle. Use the ideas of the Distributive Property.

66.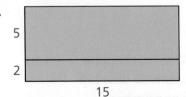

67.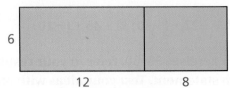

68.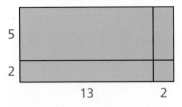

69.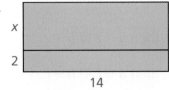

For Exercises 70–73, draw and label the edges and areas of a rectangle to illustrate each pair of equivalent expressions.

70. $(3 + 2) \cdot 12 = 3 \cdot 12 + 2 \cdot 12$

71. $9 \cdot 3 + 9 \cdot 5 = 9 \cdot (3 + 5)$

72. $x \cdot (5 + 9) = 5x + 9x$

73. $2 \cdot (x + 8) = 2x + 16$

In this Investigation, you compared important properties of arithmetic with positive numbers to properties of arithmetic with negative numbers. The following questions will help you summarize what you have learned.

Think about these questions. Discuss your ideas with other students and your teacher. Then write a summary of your findings in your notebook.

1. **a. What** is the Order of Operations? Why is the Order of Operations important?

   b. Give an example of a numerical expression in which the use of parentheses changes the result of the computation.

2. **Describe** how the Distributive Property relates addition and multiplication. Give numerical examples.

Common Core Mathematical Practices

As you worked on the Problems in this Investigation, you used prior knowledge to make sense of them. You also applied Mathematical Practices to solve the Problems. Think back over your work, the ways you thought about the Problems, and how you used Mathematical Practices.

Elena described her thoughts in the following way:

> While working on Problem 4.1, we noticed the importance of where the parentheses are in an expression. We were given an expression and had to put parentheses in to make the greatest and least possible values. To help us with this, we needed a good understanding of the Order of Operations, so we would know where to put the parentheses.
>
> ....
>
> **Common Core Standards for Mathematical Practice**
> **MP6** Attend to precision.

 • What other Mathematical Practices can you identify in Elena's reasoning?

• Describe a Mathematical Practice that you and your classmates used to solve a different Problem in this Investigation.

Unit Project

Dealing Down

Dealing Down is a mathematics card game that tests your creative skill at writing expressions. Play several rounds. Then write a report on the strategies you used.

How to Play Dealing Down

- Work in small groups.

- Shuffle the 25 cards marked with the following numbers.

  $-10, -9, -8, -7, -6, -5, -4, -3, -2, -1, -\frac{1}{2}, -\frac{1}{3}, -\frac{1}{4}, 0, 0.25, \frac{1}{3},$
  $0.5, 1, 2, 3, 4, 5, 7, 8, 10$

- Deal four cards to the center of the table.

- All players use the four numbers to write an expression with the least possible quantity. The numbers can be used in any order and with any operation.

- Players compare answers. Each player explains why his or her answer is accurate and the least possible quantity.

- Each player with an expression for the least quantity gets 1 point.

- Record the results in a table such as the one below. Play more rounds and update the table.

Round 1

Cards Dealt	Expression With the Least Quantity	Who Scored a Point
Why That Expression Has the Least Quantity:		

- The player with the most points at the end of the game wins.

In Your Notebook

Write a report about strategies for writing an expression for the least possible quantity using four numbers. Consider the following ideas as you look at the strategies in Dealing Down.

- Operations with negative and positive numbers
- Order of Operations including the use of parentheses and exponents
- Commutative properties of addition and multiplication
- Distributive Property

In this Unit, you investigated properties, operations, and applications of integers and rational numbers. You learned how to

- Add, subtract, multiply, and divide integers and rational numbers

- Represent operations with integers and rational numbers on a number line, and represent operations with integers on a chip board

- Use integers and rational numbers in real-world problems

Use Your Understanding: Rational Numbers

Test your understanding of rational numbers by solving the following problems.

1. An absent-minded scorekeeper writes the number sentences below. Find the value of n that makes each sentence true. Explain what each sentence tells about the team's performance.

   a. BrainyActs: $-250 + (-100) + 200 + n = 50$

   b. Xtremes: $450 + (-250) + n = 0$

   c. ExCells: $n + 50 + 200 + (-150) = -250$

   d. AmazingM's: $350 + (-300) + n = -150$

2. Irving goes to college 127 miles away from home. When he drives home for vacation, he plans to drop off his friend, Whitney. Her exit is 93 miles before his.

   Irving and Whitney are so busy talking that they miss the exit to her house. They are now only 36 miles from Irving's exit! They turn around and drive back to Whitney's exit. How far did Irving and Whitney travel in total from when they left college to when they finally reached Whitney's exit? Model this problem on a number line.

3. For each number sentence:
   - Write a fact family.
   - Identify the member of each fact family that is easiest to use to solve for n. Explain your reasoning.
   - Find the value for n that makes each sentence true.

   a. $-2\frac{1}{2} + n = -3\frac{3}{4}$

   b. $\frac{2}{3}n = 10$

Explain Your Reasoning

Answer the following questions to summarize what you now know.

4. Describe what a number line looks like now that you have learned about negative numbers.

5. Which number is greater? Explain.

   a. $-20, -35$

   b. $-2\frac{3}{4}, -2\frac{1}{3}$

   c. $-12.5, 10.5$

6. Use a number line or chip model to check each calculation. Show your work.

   a. $5 + (-7) = -2$ b. $-2 + (-9) = -11$

   c. $3 \cdot (-2) = -6$ d. $-3 \cdot (-2) = 6$

   e. Describe how a number line and a chip model can be used to model an addition or multiplication problem.

7. Suppose you are given two integers. How do you find their

   a. sum?   b. difference?

   c. product?   d. quotient?

8. Which operations have the following properties? Give numerical examples.

   a. commutative   b. distributive

English / Spanish Glossary

A **absolute value** The absolute value of a number is its distance from 0 on the number line. Numbers that are the same distance from 0 have the same absolute value. For example, −3 and 3 both have an absolute value of 3.

valor absoluto El valor absoluto de un número es su distancia del 0 en una recta numérica. Se puede interpretar como el valor de un número cuando no importa su signo. Por ejemplo, tanto −3 como 3 tienen un valor absoluto de 3.

additive identity Zero is the additive identity for rational numbers. Adding zero to any rational number results in a sum identical to the original rational number. For any rational number a, $0 + a = a$. For example, $0 + 4.375 = 4.375$.

identidad de suma El cero es la identidad de suma para los números racionales. Sumarle cero a cualquier número racional da como resultado un total idéntico al número racional original. Para cualquier número racional a, $0 + a = a$. Por ejemplo, $0 + 4.375 = 4.375$.

additive inverses Two numbers, a and b, that satisfy the equation $a + b = 0$. For example, 3 and −3 are additive inverses, and $\frac{1}{2}$ and $-\frac{1}{2}$ are additive inverses.

inversos de suma Dos números, a y b, que cumplen con la ecuación $a + b = 0$. Por ejemplo, 3 y −3 son inversos de suma, y $\frac{1}{2}$ y $-\frac{1}{2}$ son inversos de suma.

algorithm A set of rules for performing a procedure. Mathematicians invent algorithms that are useful in many kinds of situations. Some examples of algorithms are the rules for long division or the rules for adding two fractions.

algoritmo Un conjunto de reglas para realizar un procedimiento. Los matemáticos crean algoritmos que son útiles en muchos tipos de situaciones. Las reglas para realizar una división larga o para sumar dos fracciones son algunos ejemplos de algoritmos.

C **Commutative Property** The order of the addition or multiplication of two numbers does not change the result. For two numbers a and b, $a + b = b + a$ and $a \cdot b = b \cdot a$. For example, $\frac{3}{7} + 8 = 8 + \frac{3}{7}$ and $\frac{3}{7} \cdot 8 = 8 \cdot \frac{3}{7}$.

Propiedad conmutativa El orden de dos números cuando se los suma o se los multiplica no altera el resultado. Para dos números a y b, $a + b = b + a$ y $a \cdot b = b \cdot a$. Por ejemplo, $\frac{3}{7} + 8 = 8 + \frac{3}{7}$ y $\frac{3}{7} \cdot 8 = 8 \cdot \frac{3}{7}$.

D **describe** Academic Vocabulary

To explain or tell in detail. A written description can contain facts and other information needed to communicate your answer. A diagram or a graph may also be included.

related terms *express, explain*

sample Given the pair of points (5, 7) and (−4, 7), describe the direction and the distance between the first point and the second point on a coordinate graph.

> The direction from ($^+5$, $^+7$) to ($^-4$, $^+7$) is to the left. The distance between the two points is the distance between the x-coordinates because the y-coordinates are the same. The distance between the x-coordinates is the distance from $^+5$ to the y-axis plus the distance from the y-axis to $^-4$: $5 + 4 = 9$.

describir Vocabulario académico

Explicar o decir con detalle. Una descripción escrita puede contener datos y otro tipo de información necesaria para comunicar tu respuesta. También puede incluir un diagrama o una gráfica.

términos relacionados *expresar, explicar*

ejemplo Dados los pares de los puntos ($+5$, $+7$) y (−4, $+7$), describe la dirección y la distancia entre el primer punto y el segundo punto en una gráfica de coordenadas.

> La dirección desde ($^+5$, $^+7$) a ($^-4$, $^+7$) es hacia la izquierda. La distancia entre los dos puntos es la distancia entre las coordenadas x, porque las coordenadas y son iguales. La distancia entre las coordenadas x es la distancia desde $^+5$ al eje de y más la distancia del eje de y a $^-4$: $5 + 4 = 9$.

Distributive Property A mathematical property used to rewrite expressions involving addition and multiplication. The Distributive Property states that for any three real numbers a, b, and c, $a(b + c) = ab + ac$. If an expression is written as a factor multiplied by a sum, you can use the Distributive Property to multiply the factor by each term in the sum.

$$4(5 + x) = 4(5) + 4(x) = 20 + 4x$$

If an expression is written as a sum of terms and the terms have a common factor, you can use the Distributive Property to rewrite the expression as the common factor multiplied by a sum. This process is called factoring.

$$20 + 4x = 4(5) + 4(x) = 4(5 + x)$$

Propiedad distributiva Una propiedad matemática que se usa para volver a escribir expresiones que incluyen la suma y la multiplicación. La propiedad distributiva establece que para tres números reales cualesquiera, a, b, y c, $a(b + c) = ab + ac$. Si una expresión se escribe como la multiplicación de un factor por una suma, la propiedad distributiva se puede usar para multiplicar el factor por cada término de esa suma.

$$4(5 + x) = 4(5) + 4(x) = 20 + 4x$$

Si una expresión se escribe como una suma de términos y los términos tienen un factor común, la propiedad distributiva se puede usar para volver a escribir la expresión como la multiplicación del factor común por una suma. Este proceso se llama descomponer en factores.

$$20 + 4x = 4(5) + 4(x) = 4(5 + x)$$

E **expanded form** The form of an expression made up of sums or differences of terms rather than products of factors. The expressions $20 + 30$, $5(4) + 5(21)$, $x^2 + 7x + 12$ and $x^2 + 2x$ are in expanded form.

forma desarrollada La forma de una expresión que está compuesta de sumas o diferencias de términos en vez de productos de factores. Las expresiones $20 + 30$, $5(4) + 5(21)$, $x^2 + 7x + 12$ y $x^2 + 2x$ están representadas en forma desarrollada.

explain Academic Vocabulary
To give facts and details that make an idea easier to understand. Explaining can involve a written summary supported by a diagram, chart, table, or any combination of these.

related terms *describe, show, justify, tell, present*

sample Explain how to multiply two negative numbers.

> To multiply two negative numbers, multiply as if both numbers were positive. The product will always be a positive number.

explicar Vocabulario académico
Dar datos y detalles que hacen que una idea sea más fácil de comprender. Explicar puede incluir un resumen escrito apoyado por un diagrama, una gráfica, una tabla o una combinación de éstos.

términos relacionados *describir, demostrar, justificar, decir, presentar*

ejemplo Explica cómo se multiplican dos números negativos.

> Para multiplicar dos números negativos, multiplica como si ambos números fueran positivos. El producto siempre será un número positivo.

F **factored form** The form of an expression made up of products of factors rather than sums or differences of terms. The expressions $2 \times 2 \times 5$, $3(2 + 7)$, $(x + 3)(x + 4)$ and $x(x-2)$ are in factored form.

forma factorizada La forma de una expresión que está compuesta de productos de factores en lugar de sumas o diferencias de términos. Las expresiones $2 \times 2 \times 5$, $3(2 + 7)$, $(x + 3)(x + 4)$ y $x(x-2)$ están representadas en forma factorizada.

I **integers** The whole numbers and their opposites. 0 is an integer, but is neither positive nor negative. The integers from -4 to 4 are shown on the number line below.

enteros Los números enteros y sus opuestos. El 0 es un entero, pero no es positivo ni negativo. En la siguiente recta numérica se muestran los enteros comprendidos entre -4 y 4.

L **locate** Academic Vocabulary
To find or identify a value, usually on a
number line or coordinate graph.

related terms *find, identify*

sample Locate and label the points $(-3, 4)$,
$(-3, -4)$ and $(3, 4)$ on the coordinate graph.

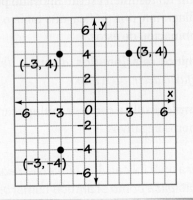

ubicar Vocabulario académico
Hallar o identificar un valor, generalmente
en una recta numérica o en una gráfica de
coordenadas.

términos relacionados *hallar, identificar*

ejemplo Ubica y rotula los puntos $(-3, 4)$,
$(-3, -4)$ y $(3, 4)$ en una gráfica de
coordenadas.

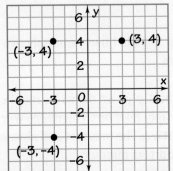

M **multiplicative identity** The multiplicative
identity for rational numbers is 1 or any
rational expression equal to 1. Multiplying
any rational number by 1 results in a product
identical to the original rational number.
For any rational number N, $N \times 1 = N$,
or for any rational numbers R and $\frac{a}{b}$, $\frac{a}{b} \times \frac{R}{R} = \frac{a}{b}$.
For example, $\frac{4}{9} \times 1 = \frac{4}{9}$, and $\frac{5}{8} \times \frac{3}{3} = \frac{5}{8}$.

identidad multiplicativa La identidad
multiplicativa para los números racionales
es 1 o cualquier otra expresión racional igual
a 1. Multiplicar cualquier número racional
por 1 da como resultado un producto
idéntico al número racional original. Para
cualquier número racional, N, $N \times 1 = N$, o
para cualquiera de los números racionales
R y $\frac{a}{b}$, $\frac{a}{b} \times \frac{R}{R} = \frac{a}{b}$. Por ejemplo, $\frac{4}{9} \times 1 = \frac{4}{9}$ y
$\frac{5}{8} \times \frac{3}{3} = \frac{5}{8}$.

---

multiplicative inverses Two numbers, a
and b, that satisfy the equation $ab = 1$. For
example, 3 and $\frac{1}{3}$ are multiplicative inverses,
and $-\frac{1}{2}$ and -2 are multiplicative inverses.

inversos multiplicativos Dos números, a y
b, que cumplen con la ecuación $ab = 1$. Por
ejemplo, 3 y $\frac{1}{3}$ son inversos multiplicativos, y
$-\frac{1}{2}$ y -2 son inversos multiplicativos.

negative number A number less than 0. On a number line, negative numbers are located to the left of 0 (on a vertical number line, negative numbers are located below 0).

número negativo Un número menor que 0. En una recta numérica, los números negativos están ubicados a la izquierda del 0 (en una recta numérica vertical, los números negativos están ubicados debajo del 0).

number sentence A mathematical statement that gives the relationship between two expressions that are composed of numbers and operation signs. For example, $3 + 2 = 5$ and $6 \times 2 > 10$ are number sentences; $3 + 2$, 5, 6×2, and 10 are expressions.

oración numérica Enunciado matemático que describe la relación entre dos expresiones compuestas por números y signos de operaciones. Por ejemplo, $3 + 2 = 5$ y $6 \times 2 > 10$ son oraciones numéricas. $3 + 2$, 5, 6×2, y 10 son expresiones.

opposites Two numbers whose sum is 0. For example, -3 and 3 are opposites. On a number line, opposites are the same distance from 0 but in different directions from 0. The number 0 is its own opposite.

opuestos Dos números cuya suma da 0. Por ejemplo, -3 y 3 son opuestos. En una recta numérica, los opuestos se encuentran a la misma distancia de 0 pero en direcciones opuestas del 0 en la recta numérica. El número 0 es su propio opuesto.

Order of Operations A set of agreements or conventions for carrying out calculations with one or more operations, parentheses, or exponents.

1. Work within parentheses.

2. Write numbers written with exponents in standard form.

3. Do all multiplication and division in order from left to right.

4. Do all addition and subtraction in order from left to right.

Orden de las operaciones Un conjunto de acuerdos o convenciones para llevar a cabo cálculos con más de una operación, paréntesis o exponentes.

1. Resolver lo que está entre paréntesis.

2. Escribir los números con exponentes en forma estándar.

3. Multiplicar y dividir en orden de izquierda a derecha.

4. Sumar y dividir en orden de izquierda a derecha.

positive number A number greater than 0. (The number 0 is neither positive nor negative.) On a number line, positive numbers are located to the right of 0 (on a vertical number line, positive numbers are located above 0).

número positivo Un número mayor que 0. (El número 0 no es positivo negativo.) En una recta numérica, los números positivos se ubican a la derecha del 0 (en una recta numérica vertical, los números positivos están arriba del 0).

rational numbers Numbers that can be expressed as a quotient of two integers where the divisor is not zero. For example, $\frac{1}{2}$, $\frac{9}{11}$, and $-\frac{7}{5}$ are rational numbers. Also, 0.799 is a rational number, since $0.799 = \frac{799}{1,000}$.

números racionales Números que se pueden expresar como el cociente de dos números enteros donde el divisor no es cero. Por ejemplo, $\frac{1}{2}$, $\frac{9}{11}$, y $-\frac{7}{5}$ son números racionales. También 0.799 es un número racional, porque $0.799 = \frac{799}{1,000}$.

....

represent Academic Vocabulary
To stand for or take the place of something else. Symbols, equations, charts, and tables are often used to represent particular situations.

related terms *symbolize, stand for*

representar Vocabulario académico
Significar o tomar el lugar de algo. Con frecuencia, se usan símbolos, ecuaciones, gráficas y tablas para representar situaciones determinadas.

términos relacionados *simbolizar, significar*

sample Players spin a 0–5 spinner to see how far and in which direction they will move. Sally started at zero, spun a 5, and picked a negative card. She then spun a 3 and picked a positive card. Which of the following expressions represents her distance from zero on the number line?

A. $|3 + 5|$

B. $|-3 - 5|$

C. $|-5 + 3|$

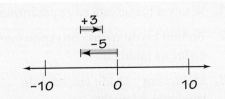

Sally moved five units in a negative direction and then three units in a positive direction. Absolute value signs are used to show distance, so the answer is C.

ejemplo Los jugadores hacen girar una rueda giratoria numerada del 0 al 5 para ver cuánto y en qué dirección se tienen que mover. Sally empezó en el cero, le salió un 5 en la rueda giratoria y sacó una tarjeta negativa. Después, le salió un 3 y sacó una tarjeta positiva. ¿Cuál de las siguientes expresiones representa la distancia que ella recorrió desde el cero en una recta numérica?

A. $|3 + 5|$

B. $|-3 - 5|$

C. $|-5 + 3|$

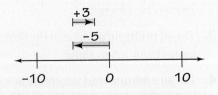

Sally se movió cinco unidades en dirección negativa y después tres unidades en dirección positiva. Para mostrar la distancia se usan signos de valor absoluto, por lo tanto la respuesta es la C.

Index

Index

Acknowledgments

Cover Design

Three Communication Design, Chicago

Text

Temperature data on page 15 are from Temperatures in Spearfish South Dakota. Source: National Weather Service.

Photographs

Photo locators denoted as follows: Top (T), Center (C), Bottom (B), Left (L), Right (R), Background (Bkgd)

2TR Stephanie Maze/Encyclopedia/Corbis; **2BR** Jorg Hackemann/Shutterstock; **3T** ArteSub/Alamy; **13BR** Patrick Foto/Shutterstock; **14C** Stephanie Maze/Encyclopedia/Corbis; **21BR** Katrina Brown/Shutterstock; **21BL** Accent Alaska.com/Alamy; **23C** Matt Tilghman/Shutterstock; **71TR** Migstock/Alamy; **85BC** Jorg Hackemann/Shutterstock.

Stretching
-and-
Shrinking

Understanding Similarity

Lappan, Phillips, Fey, Friel

Understanding Similarity

Looking Ahead

A map is a scale drawing of the place it represents. You can use a map to find actual distances to any place in the world. **How** can you estimate the distance from Cape Town, South Africa to Port Elizabeth, South Africa?

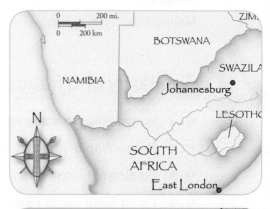

Suppose that you want to find the width of a river that is too wide to measure directly. **How** can you use similar triangles to find the distance across the river?

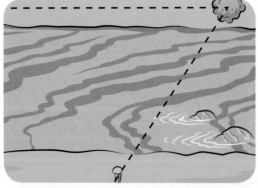

Here is a picture of Duke, a real dog. If you know the scale factor between Duke and the picture, **how** can you determine how long Duke is from his nose to the tip of his tail?

You probably use the word *similar* in everyday conversation. For example, you might say that one song sounds similar to another song. You may also say that your friend's bike is similar to yours.

In many cases, you might use the word *similar* to describe objects and images that are the same shape but not the same size.

A floor plan of a house has the same shape as the actual house, but it is much smaller. The images on a movie screen are the same shape as the real people and objects they depict, but they are much larger. You can order your school portrait in a variety of sizes, but your face will have the same shape in each photo.

In this Unit, you will learn what it means for two shapes to be mathematically similar. The ideas you learn can help you answer questions like those on the previous page.

Mathematical Highlights

Understanding Similarity

I n *Stretching and Shrinking*, you will learn the mathematical meaning of similarity, explore the properties of similar figures, and use similarity to solve problems.

You will learn how to

- Identify similar figures by comparing corresponding sides and angles

- Use scale factors and ratios to describe relationships among the side lengths, perimeters, and areas of similar figures

- Construct similar figures (scale drawings) using informal methods, scale factors, and geometric tools

- Use algebraic rules to produce similar figures and recognize when a rule shrinks or enlarges a figure

- Predict the ways that stretching or shrinking a figure will affect side lengths, angle measures, perimeters, and areas

- Use the properties of similarity to find distances and heights that cannot be measured directly

- Use scale factors or ratios to find missing side lengths in a pair of similar figures

When you encounter a new problem, it is a good idea to ask yourself questions. In this Unit, you might ask questions such as:

What determines whether two shapes are similar?

What is the same and what is different about two similar figures?

When figures are similar, **how** are the side lengths, areas, and scale factors related?

How can I use similar figures to find missing measurements?

Mathematical Practices and Habits of Mind

In the *Connected Mathematics* curriculum you will develop an understanding of important mathematical ideas by solving problems and reflecting on the mathematics involved. Every day, you will use "habits of mind" to make sense of problems and apply what you learn to new situations. Some of these habits are described by the *Common Core State Standards for Mathematical Practices* (MP).

MP1 Make sense of problems and persevere in solving them.

When using mathematics to solve a problem, it helps to think carefully about

- data and other facts you are given and what additional information you need to solve the problem;
- strategies you have used to solve similar problems and whether you could solve a related simpler problem first;
- how you could express the problem with equations, diagrams, or graphs;
- whether your answer makes sense.

MP2 Reason abstractly and quantitatively.

When you are asked to solve a problem, it often helps to

- focus first on the key mathematical ideas;
- check that your answer makes sense in the problem setting;
- use what you know about the problem setting to guide your mathematical reasoning.

MP3 Construct viable arguments and critique the reasoning of others.

When you are asked to explain why a conjecture is correct, you can

- show some examples that fit the claim and explain why they fit;
- show how a new result follows logically from known facts and principles.

When you believe a mathematical claim is incorrect, you can

- show one or more counterexamples—cases that don't fit the claim;
- find steps in the argument that do not follow logically from prior claims.

MP4 Model with mathematics.

When you are asked to solve problems, it often helps to

- think carefully about the numbers or geometric shapes that are the most important factors in the problem, then ask yourself how those factors are related to each other;
- express data and relationships in the problem with tables, graphs, diagrams, or equations, and check your result to see if it makes sense.

MP5 Use appropriate tools strategically.

When working on mathematical questions, you should always

- decide which tools are most helpful for solving the problem and why;
- try a different tool when you get stuck.

MP6 Attend to precision.

In every mathematical exploration or problem-solving task, it is important to

- think carefully about the required accuracy of results; is a number estimate or geometric sketch good enough, or is a precise value or drawing needed?
- report your discoveries with clear and correct mathematical language that can be understood by those to whom you are speaking or writing.

MP7 Look for and make use of structure.

In mathematical explorations and problem solving, it is often helpful to

- look for patterns that show how data points, numbers, or geometric shapes are related to each other;
- use patterns to make predictions.

MP8 Look for and express regularity in repeated reasoning.

When results of a repeated calculation show a pattern, it helps to

- express that pattern as a general rule that can be used in similar cases;
- look for shortcuts that will make the calculation simpler in other cases.

You will use all of the Mathematical Practices in this Unit. Sometimes, when you look at a Problem, it is obvious which practice is most helpful. At other times, you will decide on a practice to use during class explorations and discussions. After completing each Problem, ask yourself:

- What mathematics have I learned by solving this Problem?
- What Mathematical Practices were helpful in learning this mathematics?

Enlarging and Reducing Shapes

In this Investigation, you will make **scale drawings** of figures. Your scale drawings will have the same shape as the original figure, but may be larger or smaller. The drawings will help you explore how some properties of a shape change when the shape is enlarged or reduced.

Common Core State Standards

7.RP.A.2 Recognize and represent proportional relationships between quantities.

7.G.A.1 Solve problems involving scale drawings of geometric figures, including computing actual lengths and areas from a scale drawing and reproducing a scale drawing at a different scale.

7.G.A.2 Draw (freehand, with ruler and protractor, and with technology) geometric shapes with given conditions. Focus on constructing triangles from three measures of angles or sides, noticing when the conditions determine a unique triangle, more than one triangle, or no triangle.

Also 7.RP.A.2b, 7.G.B.6

1.1 Solving a Mystery
An Introduction to Similarity

The Mystery Club at P.I. Middle School meets monthly. Members watch videos, discuss novels, play "whodunit" games, and talk about real-life mysteries. One day, a member announces that the school is having a contest. A teacher in disguise will appear for a few minutes at school each day for a week. Any student can pay $1 for a guess at the identity of the mystery teacher. The student with the first correct guess wins a prize.

The Mystery Club decides to enter the contest together. Each member brings a camera to school in hopes of getting a picture of the mystery teacher.

One of Daphne's photos looks like the picture below. Daphne has a copy of the *P.I. Monthly* magazine shown in the picture. The *P.I. Monthly* magazine is 10 inches high. She thinks she can use the magazine and the picture to estimate the teacher's height.

- What do you think Daphne has in mind? Use the picture and the information about the height of the magazine to estimate the teacher's height. Explain your reasoning.

- The teacher advisor to the Mystery Club says that the picture is similar to the actual scene. What do you suppose the adviser means by *similar*? Is it different from saying that two students in your class are similar?

Michelle, Daphne, and Mukesh are the officers of the Mystery Club. Mukesh designs this flier to attract new members.

Daphne wants to make a large poster to publicize the next meeting. She wants to redraw the club's logo, "Super Sleuth," in a larger size. Michelle shows her a clever way to enlarge the figure by using rubber bands.

Instructions for Stretching a Figure

1. Make a "two-band stretcher" by tying the ends of two identical rubber bands together. (The rubber bands should be the same width and length.) Bands about 3 inches long work well.

2. Take the sheet with the figure you want to enlarge and tape it to your desk. Next to it, tape a blank sheet of paper. If you are right-handed, put the blank sheet on the right. If you are left-handed, put it on the left (see the diagram below).

3. With your finger, hold down one end of the rubber-band stretcher on point *P*. Point *P* is called the *anchor point*. It must stay in the same spot.

4. Put a pencil in the other end of the stretcher. Stretch the rubber bands with the pencil until the knot is on the outline of your picture.

5. Keep the rubber bands taut (stretched). Move your pencil to guide the knot around the picture. Your pencil will draw a copy of the picture. The new picture is called the **image** of the original. It is also a scale drawing of the original.

Left-handed setup

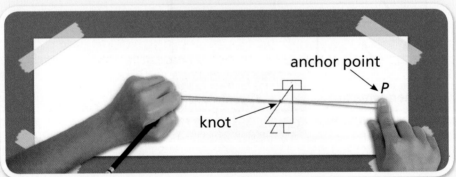

Right-handed setup

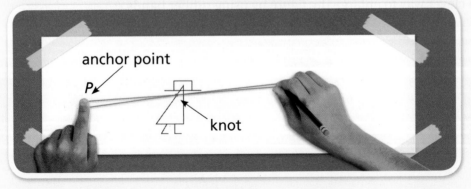

• How are the original shape and its image alike? Different?

Problem 1.1

Use the rubber-band method to enlarge the figure on the Mystery Club flier. Draw the figure as carefully as you can, so you can compare the size and shape of the image to the size and shape of the original figure.

Ⓐ Describe how the original figure and the image are alike and how they are different. Compare these features:

  • the general shapes of the two figures

  • the lengths of the line segments in the hats and bodies

  • the areas and perimeters of the hats and bodies

  • the angles in the hats and bodies

  • the distance of corresponding points on each figure from *P*

Explain each comparison you make. For example, you may find that two lengths are different. Be sure to tell which lengths you are comparing and explain how they are different.

Ⓑ Use your rubber-band stretcher to enlarge another simple figure, such as a circle or a square.

  1. Compare the general shapes, lengths, areas, perimeters, and angles of the original figure and the image.

  2. Would your comparisons in part (1) change if the location of *P* were changed? Explain why or why not.

Ⓒ The original figure and its image are *similar figures*. What do you think similar means in mathematical terms? What things are the same about these similar figures? What is different?

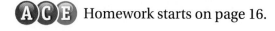 Homework starts on page 16.

1.2 Scaling Up and Down
Corresponding Sides and Angles

In the last Problem, you worked with images, or scale drawings, that were similar to the original. Those scale drawings were larger than the original figure. In this Problem, you will work with scale drawings that are smaller than the original. You will also learn more about what it means for figures to be *similar*.

When you study similar figures, you often compare their sides and angles. To compare the parts correctly, mathematicians use the terms **corresponding sides** and **corresponding angles.** In every pair of similar figures, each side of one figure has a corresponding side in the other figure. Also, each angle has a corresponding angle.

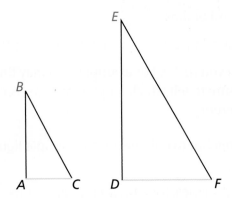

Corresponding angles
B and *E*
A and *D*
C and *F*

Corresponding sides
AC and *DF*
AB and *DE*
BC and *EF*

Recall that there are two ways to identify angles.

You can identify an angle with three letters. The angles in the small triangle on the previous page have the following names:

Angle BAC or $\angle BAC$
Angle BCA or $\angle BCA$
Angle ABC or $\angle ABC$

Notice that the letter identifying the vertex of an angle is always the middle letter in its name. For example, point A is the vertex of $\angle BAC$.

You can also name an angle by its vertex. It is important to use this method only when it is clear which angle you are referring to.

$\angle BAC$ can also be called $\angle A$
$\angle BCA$ can also be called $\angle C$
$\angle ABC$ can also be called $\angle B$

- What names would you give the angles of the large triangle?

Did You Know?

Measurement is often used in police work. For example, some stores with cameras place a spot on the wall 6 feet from the floor. When a person standing near the wall is filmed, this makes it easier to estimate the person's height. Investigators take measurements of tire marks at the scene of auto accidents to help them estimate the speed of the vehicles involved. Photographs and molds of footprints help the police determine the shoe size, type of shoe, and weight of the person who made the prints.

Daphne thinks the rubber-band method is clever, but she believes the
school copier can make more accurate copies in a greater variety of sizes.
She makes a copy of "Super Sleuth" with the size factor set at 75%. Then,
she makes a copy with a setting of 150%. The results are shown below.

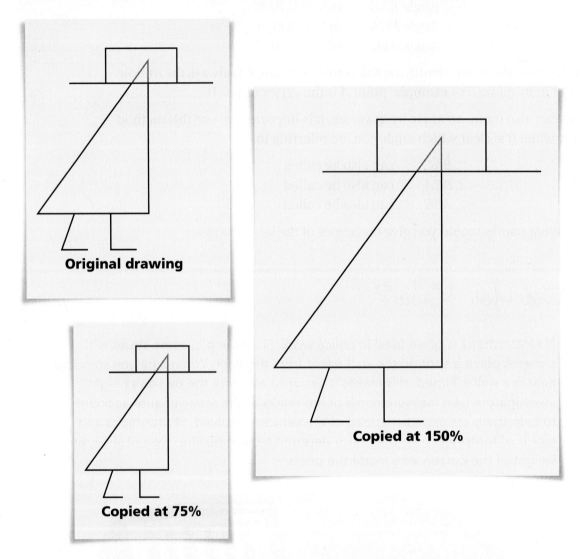

Original drawing

Copied at 75%

Copied at 150%

- How are these copies of the original logo like the copy you made with
  the rubber-band stretchers? How are these copies different from the
  rubber-band stretcher copy?

- How are these copies like the original? How are they different?

Problem 1.2

A Use the figures on the previous page. For each copy of Super Sleuth, do the following:

1. Describe how the side lengths compare to the corresponding side lengths in the original figure.

2. Describe how the angle measures compare to the corresponding angle measures in the original figure.

3. Describe how the perimeter of the triangle in each copy compares to the perimeter of the triangle in the original figure.

4. Describe how the area of the triangle in each copy compares to the area of the triangle in the original figure.

B How do the relationships in the size comparisons you made in Question A relate to the copier size factors used?

C 1. If two figures are similar, what is the same about the figures and what is different?

2. If you wanted to achieve a 150% increase with the rubber-band method, what would you do?

A C E Homework starts on page 16.

Applications

For Exercises 1 and 2, use the drawing at the right, which shows a person standing next to a ranger's outlook tower.

1. Find the approximate height of the tower if the person is

   a. 6 feet tall

   b. 5 feet 6 inches tall

2. Find the approximate height of the person if the tower is

   a. 28 feet tall

   b. 36 feet tall

3. Copy square *ABCD* and anchor point *P* onto a sheet of paper. Use the rubber-band method to enlarge the figure. Then, answer parts (a)–(e) below.

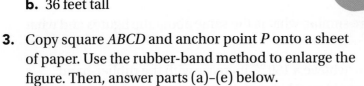

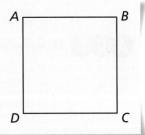

   a. How do the side lengths of the original figure compare to the side lengths of the image?

   b. How does the perimeter of the original figure compare to the perimeter of the image?

   c. How do the angle measures of the original figure compare to the angle measures of the image?

   d. How does the area of the original figure compare to the area of the image? How many copies of the original figure would it take to cover the image?

   e. How does the distance between each point in the original figure and *P* compare to the corresponding distances in the image?

4. Copy parallelogram *ABCD* and anchor point *P* onto a sheet of paper. Use the rubber-band method to enlarge the figure. Then, answer parts (a)–(e) from Exercise 3 for your diagram.

5. The diagram on the left is the floor plan for a model house. The diagram on the right is a scale drawing of the floor plan. The scale drawing was made by reducing the original on a copy machine.

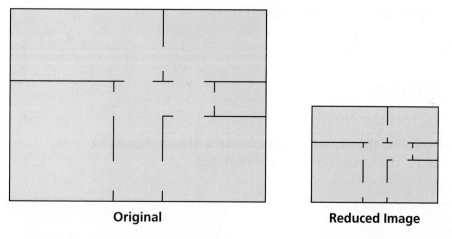

Original   Reduced Image

a. Estimate the copier size factor used. Give your answer as a percent.

b. How do the segment lengths in the original plan compare to the corresponding segment lengths in the reduced image?

c. Compare the area of the entire original floor plan to the area of the entire reduced image. Then, do the same with one room in the plan. Is the relationship between the areas of the rooms the same as the relationship between the areas of the whole plans? Explain.

d. The scale on the original plan is 1 inch = 1 foot. This means that 1 inch on the floor plan represents 1 foot on the model house. What is the scale on the reduced plan?

6. **Multiple Choice** Suppose you reduce the design below with a copy machine. Which of the following can be the image?

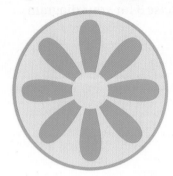

A.    B.   C.   D.

7. Suppose you copy a drawing of a polygon using the given size factor. How will the side lengths, angle measures, and perimeter of the image compare to those of the original?

   a. 200%   **b.** 150%   **c.** 50%   **d.** 75%

Connections

For Exercises 8–11, find the perimeter and the area of each figure. In Exercises 10 and 11, the measurements are rounded.

8.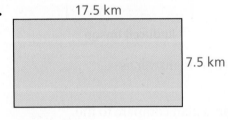

9.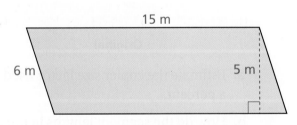

10.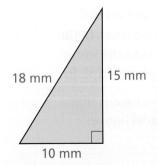

11.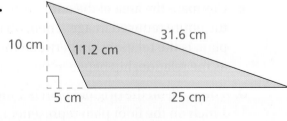

12. Copy hexagon *ABCDEF* and anchor point *P* onto a sheet of paper. Make an enlargement of the hexagon using your two-band stretcher.

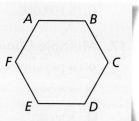

    a. How do the side lengths of the two hexagons compare?

    b. How do the angles of the hexagons compare?

    c. How do the areas of the hexagons compare?

    d. How do the perimeters of the hexagons compare?

13. Find the given percent of each number. Show your work.

    a. 25% of 120   **b.** 80% of 120

    c. 120% of 80   **d.** 70% of 150

    e. 150% of 200   **f.** 200% of 150

14. Multiple Choice What is the 5% sales tax on a $14.00 compact disc?

    A. $0.07   **B.** $ 0.70

    C. $7.00   **D.** $70.00

15. Multiple Choice What is the 15% service tip on a $25.50 dinner in a restaurant?

    F. $1.70   **G.** $ 3.83

    H. $5.10   **J.** $38.25

16. Multiple Choice What is the 28% tax on a $600,000 cash prize?

    A. $16,800   **B.** $ 21,429

    C. $168,000   **D.** $214,290

17. Multiple Choice What is the 7.65% Social Security/Medicare tax on a paycheck of $430?

    F. $3.29   **G.** $5.62

    H. $32.90   **J.** $60.13

18. One angle measure is given for each of the parallelograms below.

- Find the measure of the other three angles in the parallelogram.

- List all pairs of supplementary angles in the diagram. Then, classify each angle as *acute, right,* or *obtuse.*

- For each parallelogram, find the measures of the angles formed by extending two adjacent sides through their common vertex.

    a.    **b.**

19. While shopping for sneakers, Ling finds two pairs she likes. One pair costs $55 and the other costs $165. She makes the following statements about the prices.

"The expensive sneakers cost $110 more than the cheaper sneakers."

"The cost of the expensive sneakers is 300% of the cost of the cheaper sneakers."

"The cheaper sneakers are $\frac{1}{3}$ the cost of the expensive sneakers."

    a. Are all her statements accurate? Explain.

    b. How are the comparison methods Ling uses like the methods you use to compare the sizes and shapes of similar figures?

    c. Which statements are appropriate for comparing the size and shape of an image to the original figure? Explain.

Extensions

20. A movie projector that is 6 feet away from a large screen shows a rectangular picture that is 3 feet wide and 2 feet high.

    a. Suppose the projector is moved to a point 12 feet from the screen. What size will the picture be (width, height, and area)?

    b. Suppose the projector is moved to a point 9 feet from the screen. What size will the picture be (width, height, and area)?

21. Amy's friend gave her a picture from Field Day. The picture is 3 in. by 2 in. Amy has a picture frame that is 6 in. by 4 in. She wants the photo to fit in the frame exactly. What percent enlargement does she need to make?

22. Make a three-band stretcher by tying three rubber bands together. Use this stretcher to enlarge the "Super Sleuth" drawing from Problem 1.1.

    a. How does the shape of the image compare to the shape of the original figure?

    b. How do the lengths of the segments in the two figures compare?

    c. How do the areas of the two figures compare?

    d. How do the distances from P compare?

23. Suppose you enlarge some triangles and squares with a two-band stretcher. You use an anchor point inside the original figure, as shown in the sketches below.

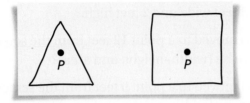

   a. In each case, how do the shape and position of the image compare to the shape and position of the original?

   b. What relationships do you expect to find among the side lengths, angle measures, perimeters, and areas of the figures, and the distances from P?

   c. Test your ideas with larger copies of the given shapes. Make sure the shortest distance from the anchor point to any side of a shape is at least one band length.

24. Suppose you make a stretcher with two different-sized rubber bands. Suppose the band attached to the anchor point is twice as long as the band attached to the pencil.

   a. If you used the stretcher to enlarge polygons, what relationships would you expect to find among the side lengths, angle measures, perimeters, and areas of the figures?

   b. Test your ideas with copies of some basic geometric shapes.

In this Investigation, you solved problems that involved enlarging (stretching) and reducing (shrinking) figures. You used rubber-band stretchers and copy machines to make scale drawings. The following questions will help you summarize what you have learned.

Think about these questions. Discuss your ideas with other students and your teacher. Then write a summary of your findings in your notebook.

1. a. **When** you enlarge or reduce a figure, what features stay the same?

   b. **When** you enlarge or reduce a figure, what features change?

2. Rubber-band stretchers, copy machines, and projectors all make images that are similar to the original shapes. **What** does it mean for two shapes to be similar? Complete the sentence below.

   "Two geometric shapes are similar when . . ."

Common Core Mathematical Practices

As you worked on the Problems in this Investigation, you used prior knowledge to make sense of them. You also applied Mathematical Practices to solve the Problems. Think back over your work, the ways you thought about the Problems, and how you used Mathematical Practices.

Tori described her thoughts in the following way:

In Problem 1.1, we had to describe how our original figure and the new image were alike and different. We had to compare the general shapes of the figures, the lengths of the line segments, the areas and perimeters, the angles, and the distance of each figure from a point.

Since our rubber band stretchers produced rough images, we used the edges of a piece of paper to make estimates of the lengths. Some other groups used rulers. To compare angle sizes, we used tracing paper to copy an angle. We compared this angle with a corresponding angle in the image.

Common Core Standards for Mathematical Practice
MP5 Use appropriate tools strategically

- What other Mathematical Practices can you identify in Tori's reasoning?

- Describe a Mathematical Practice that you and your classmates used to solve a different Problem in this Investigation.

Similar Figures

Zack and Marta want to design a computer game that involves several animated characters. They ask Marta's uncle, Carlos, a programmer for a video game company, about computer animation.

Carlos explains that the computer screen can be thought of as a grid made up of thousands of tiny points, called pixels. To animate a figure, you need to enter the coordinates of key points on the figure. The computer uses these points to draw the figure in different positions.

Each of the tiny dots on this screen is a *pixel*, which is a shortened form of "picture element."

Common Core State Standards

7.RP.A.2b Identify the constant of proportionality (unit rate) in tables, graphs, equations, diagrams, and verbal descriptions of proportional relationships.

7.G.A.1 Solve problems involving scale drawings of geometric figures, including computing actual lengths and areas from a scale drawing and reproducing a scale drawing at a different scale.

7.G.B.6 Solve real-world and mathematical problems involving area, volume and surface area of two- and three-dimensional objects composed of triangles, quadrilaterals, polygons, cubes, and right prisms.

Also 7.RP.A.2, 7.RP.A.2a and essential for 7.EE.B.4, 7.EE.B.4a

Sometimes the figures in a computer game need to change size. A computer can make a figure larger or smaller. You can give it a rule for finding key points on the new figure, using key points from the original figure.

Did You Know?

You can make figures and then rotate, slide, flip, stretch, and copy them using a computer graphics program. There are two basic kinds of graphics programs. Paint programs make images out of pixels. Draw programs make images out of lines that are drawn from mathematical equations.

The images you make in a graphics program are displayed on the computer screen. A beam of electrons activates a chemical in the screen, called phosphor, to make the images appear on your screen. If you have a laptop computer with a liquid crystal screen, an electric current makes the images appear on the screen.

2.1 Drawing Wumps
Making Similar Figures

Zack and Marta's computer game involves a family called the Wumps. The members of the Wump family are various sizes, but they all have the same shape. That is, they are *similar*. Mug Wump is the game's main character. By enlarging or reducing Mug, a player can transform him into other Wump family members.

Zack and Marta experiment with enlarging and reducing figures on a coordinate grid. First, Zack draws Mug Wump on graph paper. Then, he labels the key points from *A* to *X* and lists the coordinates for each point. Marta writes the rules that will change Mug's size.

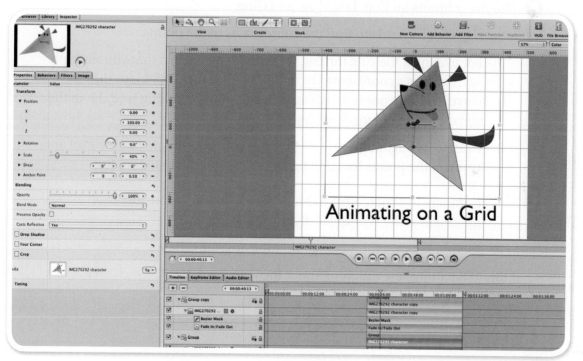

Problem 2.1

Marta tries several rules for transforming Mug into different sizes. At first glance, all the new characters look like Mug. They look like they might be mathematically similar to Mug. Some of the new characters are quite different, however. They are not mathematically similar to Mug.

Ⓐ To draw Mug on a coordinate graph, refer to the "Mug Wump" column in the table on the next page.

- For Parts 1–3 of the figure, plot the points in order. Connect them as you go along.

- For Part 4, plot the two points, but do not connect them.

- When you are finished, describe Mug's shape.

Ⓑ Use the columns for Zug, Lug, Bug, and Glug.

    1. Use the given rule to find the coordinates of the points.

        For example, the rule for Zug is $(2x, 2y)$. This means that you multiply each of Mug's coordinates by 2. Point A on Mug is $(0, 1)$, so the corresponding point A on Zug is $(0, 2)$. Point B on Mug is $(2, 1)$, so the corresponding point B on Zug is $(4, 2)$.

    2. Draw Zug, Lug, Bug, and Glug on separate coordinate planes. Plot and connect the points for each figure just as you did to draw Mug.

Ⓒ **1.** Compare the characters to Mug. Which are the impostors (*not* members of the Wump family)?

    2. What things are the same about Mug and the others?

    3. What things are different about the five characters?

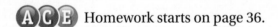 Homework starts on page 36.

Coordinates of Game Characters

	Mug Wump	Zug	Lug	Bug	Glug
Rule	(x, y)	$(2x, 2y)$	$(3x, y)$	$(3x, 3y)$	$(x, 3y)$
Point	Part 1				
A	(0, 1)	(0, 2)	▪	▪	▪
B	(2, 1)	(4, 2)	▪	▪	▪
C	(2, 0)	▪	▪	▪	▪
D	(3, 0)	▪	▪	▪	▪
E	(3, 1)	▪	▪	▪	▪
F	(5, 1)	▪	▪	▪	▪
G	(5, 0)	▪	▪	▪	▪
H	(6, 0)	▪	▪	▪	▪
I	(6, 1)	▪	▪	▪	▪
J	(8, 1)	▪	▪	▪	▪
K	(6, 7)	▪	▪	▪	▪
L	(2, 7)	▪	▪	▪	▪
M	(0, 1)	▪	▪	▪	▪
	Part 2 (Start Over)				
N	(2, 2)	▪	▪	▪	▪
O	(6, 2)	▪	▪	▪	▪
P	(6, 3)	▪	▪	▪	▪
Q	(2, 3)	▪	▪	▪	▪
R	(2, 2)	▪	▪	▪	▪
	Part 3 (Start Over)				
S	(3, 4)	▪	▪	▪	▪
T	(4, 5)	▪	▪	▪	▪
U	(5, 4)	▪	▪	▪	▪
V	(3, 4)	▪	▪	▪	▪
	Part 4 (Start Over)				
W	(2, 5) (make a dot)	▪	▪	▪	▪
X	(6, 5) (make a dot)	▪	▪	▪	▪

2.2 Hats Off to the Wumps
Changing a Figure's Size and Location

Zack experiments with multiplying Mug's coordinates by different whole numbers to make other characters. Marta asks her uncle how multiplying the coordinates by a decimal or adding numbers to or subtracting numbers from each coordinate will affect Mug's shape. He gives her a sketch for a new shape (a hat for Mug) and some rules to try.

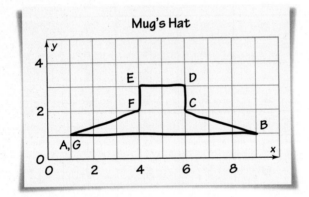

? • Which rules will produce similar hats?

• How can you use a rule to predict side lengths of the image?

Problem 2.2

Ⓐ Look at the rules for Hats 1 to 5 in the table. Before you find any coordinates, predict how each rule will change Mug's hat.

Rules for Mug's Hat

Point	Mug's Hat (x, y)	Hat 1 (x + 2, y + 3)	Hat 2 (x − 1, y + 4)	Hat 3 (x + 2, 3y)	Hat 4 (0.5x, 0.5y)	Hat 5 (2x, 3y)
A	(1, 1)	▪	▪	▪	▪	▪
B	(9, 1)	▪	▪	▪	▪	▪
C	▪	▪	▪	▪	▪	▪
D	▪	▪	▪	▪	▪	▪
E	▪	▪	▪	▪	▪	▪
F	▪	▪	▪	▪	▪	▪
G	▪	▪	▪	▪	▪	▪

Ⓑ Copy and complete the table.

  1. Give the coordinates of Mug's hat and the five other hats.

  2. Plot each new hat on a separate coordinate grid and connect each point as you go.

Ⓒ **1.** Compare the angles and side lengths of the hats.

  2. Which hats are similar to Mug's hat? Explain why.

Ⓓ Write rules that will make hats similar to Mug's in each of these ways.

  1. The side lengths are one third as long as Mug's.

  2. The side lengths are 1.5 times as long as Mug's.

  3. The hat is the same size as Mug's, but has moved right 1 unit and up 5 units.

Ⓔ Write a rule that makes a hat that is *not* similar to Mug's.

Ⓐ Ⓒ Ⓔ Homework starts on page 36.

2.3 Mouthing Off and Nosing Around
Scale Factors

 How did you decide which of the computer game characters were members of the Wump family? How did you decide which were impostors?

- In general, how can you decide whether or not two shapes are similar?

You have experimented with rubber-band stretchers, copiers, and coordinate plots. Your experiments suggest that for two figures to be **similar,** there must be the following correspondence between the figures.

- The side lengths of one figure are multiplied by the same number to get the corresponding side lengths in the second figure.

- Corresponding angles are the same size.

The **scale factor** is the number that the side lengths of one figure can be multiplied by to give the corresponding side lengths of the other figure.

The rectangles below are similar. The scale factor from the smaller rectangle to the larger rectangle is 3.

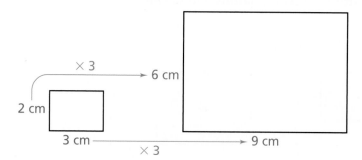

- What is the scale factor from the larger rectangle to the smaller rectangle? Explain how you found it.

Chicago Model City is a 1 : 600 scale model of the city. The buildings were made using a 3D printer. Each building is made of many thin layers of resin, hardened by a laser and then painted.

Problem 2.3

The diagram shows a collection of mouths (rectangles) and noses (triangles). Some are from the Wump family. Others are from impostors.

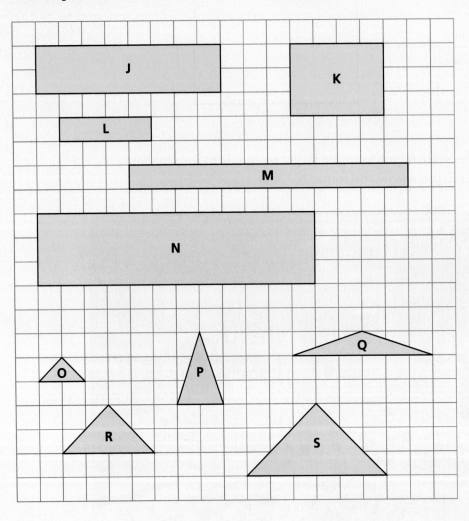

Problem 2.3 continued

Use the rectangles on the previous page.

A **1.** Which pairs of rectangles are similar? Explain how you know.

2. For each pair of similar rectangles, find the scale factor and the perimeter and area of each rectangle.

3. Describe the relationship between the perimeters of two similar rectangles and the scale factor.

4. Describe the relationship between the areas of two similar rectangles and the scale factor.

B **1.** Which pairs of triangles are similar? Explain how you know.

2. For each pair of similar triangles, find the scale factor. Then find the area of each triangle.

3. Does the same relationship between the scale factor of similar rectangles and their area apply for similar triangles? Explain.

4. Draw three right triangles such that exactly two of the right triangles are similar. Explain how each triangle is similar or not similar to the other two.

C **1.** After studying the mouths in the diagram, Marta and Zack agree that Rectangles J and L are similar. Marta says the scale factor is 2. Zack says it is 0.5. Is either of them correct? How would you describe the scale factor so there is no confusion?

2. Explain how to find the scale factor from a figure to a similar figure.

3. Does the scale factor change the angle sizes? Explain.

4. You have used rubber bands and coordinate graphs to make similar figures. How does the scale factor show up in each of these methods?

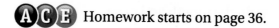 Homework starts on page 36.

Applications

1. The table below gives key coordinates for drawing Mug Wump's mouth and nose. It also gives rules for finding the corresponding points for four other characters—some members of the Wump family and some impostors.

Coordinates of Characters

Rule	Mug Wump (x, y)	Glum (1.5x, 1.5y)	Sum (3x, 2y)	Tum (4x, 4y)	Crum (2x, y)
Point	**Mouth**				
M	(2, 2)	▦	▦	▦	▦
N	(6, 2)	▦	▦	▦	▦
O	(6, 3)	▦	▦	▦	▦
P	(2, 3)	▦	▦	▦	▦
Q	(2, 2) (connect Q to M)	▦	▦	▦	▦
	Nose (Start Over)				
R	(3, 4)	▦	▦	▦	▦
S	(4, 5)	▦	▦	▦	▦
T	(5, 4)	▦	▦	▦	▦
U	(3, 4) (connect U to R)	▦	▦	▦	▦

a. Before you find the coordinates or plot points, predict which characters are the impostors.

b. Copy and complete the table. Then, plot the figures on grid paper. Label each figure.

c. Which of the new characters (Glum, Sum, Tum, and Crum) are members of the Wump family? Which are impostors?

d. Choose one of the new Wumps. How do the mouth and nose measurements (side lengths, perimeter, area, angle measures) compare with those of Mug Wump?

e. Choose one of the impostors. What are the dimensions of this impostor's mouth and nose? How do the mouth and nose measurements compare with those of Mug Wump?

f. Do your findings in parts (b)–(e) support your prediction from part (a)? Explain.

2. a. Design a Mug-like character of your own on grid paper. Give your character eyes, a nose, and a mouth.

   b. Give coordinates so that someone else could draw your character.

   c. Write a rule for finding coordinates of a member of your character's family. Check your rule by plotting the figure.

   d. Write a rule for finding the coordinates of an impostor. Check your rule by plotting the figure.

3. a. On grid paper, draw triangle *ABC* with vertex coordinates *A*(0, 2), *B*(6, 2), and *C*(4, 4).

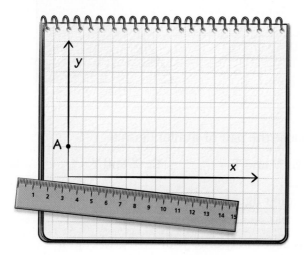

   b. Apply the rule (1.5*x*, 1.5*y*) to the vertices of triangle *ABC* to get triangle *PQR*. Compare the corresponding measurements (side lengths, perimeters, areas, area, angle measures) of the two triangles.

   c. Apply the rule (2*x*, 0.5*y*) to the vertices of triangle *ABC* to get triangle *FGH*. Compare the corresponding measurements (side lengths, perimeters, areas, angle measures) of the two triangles.

   d. Which triangle, *PQR* or *FGH*, seems similar to triangle *ABC*? Why?

4. a. On grid paper, draw parallelogram *ABCD* with vertex coordinates *A*(0, 2), *B*(6, 2), *C*(8, 6), and *D*(2, 6).

   b. Write a rule to find the vertex coordinates of a parallelogram *PQRS* that is larger than, but similar to, *ABCD*. Test your rule to see if it works.

   c. Write a rule to find the vertex coordinates of a parallelogram *TUVW* that is smaller than, but similar to, *ABCD*. Test your rule to see if it works.

For Exercises 5 and 6, study the size and shape of the polygons below.

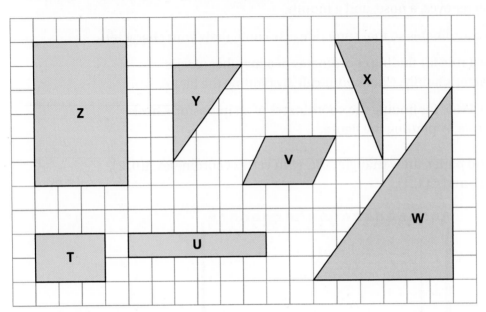

5. **Multiple Choice** Choose the pair of similar figures.

   A. Z and Y **B.** V and T **C.** X and Y **D.** Y and W

6. Find another pair of similar figures. Explain your reasoning.

7. Copy the figures below accurately onto your own grid paper.

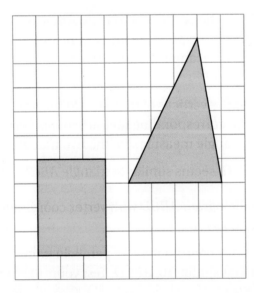

   a. Draw a figure similar, but not identical, to the rectangle.

   b. Draw a figure similar, but not identical, to the triangle.

   c. How do you know your scale drawings are similar to the given figures?

8. The diagram below shows two similar polygons.

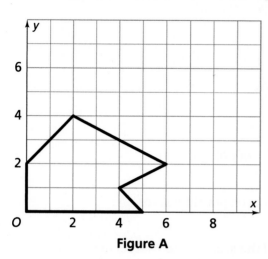

Figure A

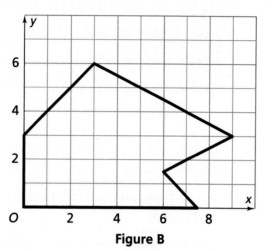

Figure B

a. Write a rule for finding the coordinates of a point on Figure B from the corresponding point on Figure A.

b. Write a rule for finding the coordinates of a point on Figure A from the corresponding point on Figure B.

c. i. What is the scale factor from Figure A to Figure B?

ii. Use the scale factor to describe how the perimeter and area of Figure B are related to the perimeter and area of Figure A.

d. i. What is the scale factor from Figure B to Figure A?

ii. Use the scale factor to describe how the perimeter and area of Figure A are related to the perimeter and area of Figure B.

9. a. Suppose you make Figure C by applying the rule $(2x, 2y)$ to the points on Figure A from Exercise 8. Find the coordinates of the vertices of Figure C.

b. i. What is the scale factor from Figure A to Figure C?

ii. Use the scale factor to describe how the perimeter and area of Figure C are related to the perimeter and area of Figure A.

c. i. What is the scale factor from Figure C to Figure A?

ii. Use the scale factor to describe how the perimeter and area of Figure A are related to the perimeter and area of Figure C.

iii. Write a coordinate rule of the form (mx, my) that can be used to find the coordinates of any point of Figure A from the corresponding points of Figure C.

10. What is the scale factor from an original figure to its image if the image is made using the given method?

   a. a two-rubber-band stretcher

   b. a copy machine with size factor 150%

   c. a copy machine with size factor 250%

   d. the coordinate rule $(0.75x, 0.75y)$

11. a. Use the polygons below. Which pairs of polygons are similar figures?

   b. For each pair of similar figures, list corresponding sides and angles.

   c. For each pair of similar figures, find the scale factor that relates side lengths of the larger figure to the corresponding side lengths of the smaller figure.

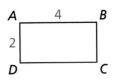

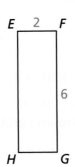

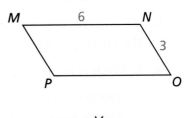

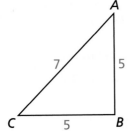

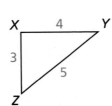

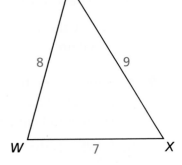

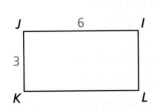

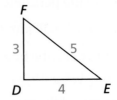

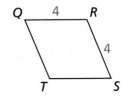

12. On grid paper, draw a rectangle with an area of 14 square centimeters. Label it *ABCD*.

   a. Write and use a coordinate rule that will make a rectangle similar to rectangle *ABCD* that is three times as long and three times as wide. Label it *EFGH*.

   b. How does the perimeter of rectangle *EFGH* compare to the perimeter of rectangle *ABCD*?

   c. How does the area of rectangle *EFGH* compare to the area of rectangle *ABCD*?

   d. How do your answers to parts (b) and (c) relate to the scale factor from rectangle *ABCD* to rectangle *EFGH*?

13. A student drew the figures below. The student says the two shapes are similar because there is a common scale factor for all of the sides. The sides of the figure on the right are twice as long as those of the figure on the left. What do you say to the student to explain why the figures are *not* similar?

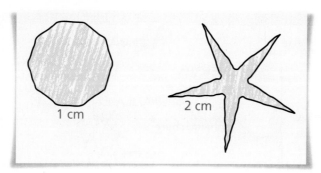

Connections

For Exercises 14 and 15, the rule $(x, \frac{3}{4}y)$ is applied to a polygon.

14. Is the image similar to the original polygon? Explain.

15. Each of the following points is on the original polygon. Find the coordinates of each corresponding point on the image.

   a. (6, 8)

   b. (9, 8)

   c. $\left(\frac{3}{2}, \frac{4}{3}\right)$

Multiple Choice For Exercises 16 and 17, what is the percent reduction or enlargement that will result if the rule is applied to a figure on a coordinate grid?

16. $(1.5x, 1.5y)$

    A. 150%   **B.** 15%   **C.** 1.5%   **D.** None of these

17. $(0.7x, 0.7y)$

    F. 700%   **G.** 7%   **H.** 0.7%   **J.** None of these

18. The rule $\left(x + \frac{2}{3}, y - \frac{3}{4}\right)$ is applied to a polygon. For each vertex below of the polygon, find the coordinates of the corresponding vertex on the image.

    a. $(5, 3)$ **b.** $\left(\frac{1}{6}, \frac{11}{12}\right)$ **c.** $\left(\frac{9}{12}, \frac{4}{5}\right)$

19. An accurate map is a scale drawing of the place it represents. Below is a map of South Africa.

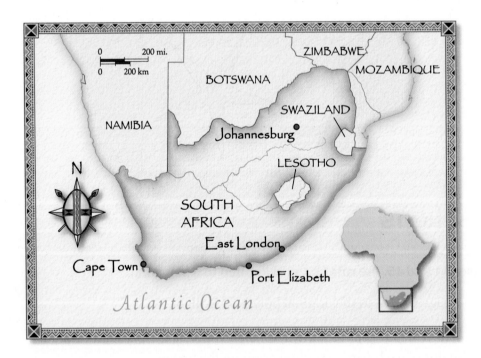

    a. Use the scale to estimate the distance from Cape Town to Port Elizabeth.

    b. Use the scale to estimate the distance from Johannesburg to East London.

    c. What is the relationship between the scale for the map and a "scale factor"?

Find each quotient.

20. $\frac{1}{2} \div \frac{1}{4}$

21. $\frac{1}{4} \div \frac{1}{2}$

22. $\frac{3}{7} \div \frac{4}{7}$

23. $\frac{4}{7} \div \frac{3}{7}$

24. $\frac{3}{2} \div \frac{3}{5}$

25. $1\frac{1}{2} \div \frac{3}{8}$

26. At a bake sale, 0.72 of a pan of corn bread has not been sold. A serving is 0.04 of a pan.

    a. How many servings are left?

    b. Use a hundredths grid to show your reasoning.

27. Each pizza takes 0.3 of a large block of cheese. Charlie has 0.8 of a block of cheese left.

    a. How many pizzas can he make?

    b. Use a diagram to show your reasoning.

28. a. What part of the grid below is shaded?

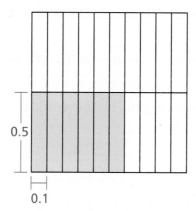

    b. The grid shows the part of a pan of spinach appetizers remaining. How many servings are left if a serving is 0.04?

    c. Draw a picture to confirm your answer to part (b).

Extensions

29. Select a drawing of a comic strip character from a newspaper or magazine. Draw a grid over the figure or tape a transparent grid on top of the figure. Identify key points on the figure and then enlarge it using each of these rules. Which figures are similar? Explain.

    a. $(2x, 2y)$ **b.** $(x, 2y)$ **c.** $(2x, y)$

30. Suppose you use the rule $(3x + 1, 3y - 4)$ to transform Mug Wump into a new figure.

   a. How will the angle measures in the new figure compare to corresponding angle measures in Mug?

   b. How will the side lengths of the new figure compare to corresponding side lengths of Mug?

   c. How will the area and perimeter of this new figure compare to the area and perimeter of Mug?

31. The vertices of three similar triangles are given.

   - triangle *ABC*: $A(1, 2)$, $B(4, 3)$, $C(2, 5)$
   - triangle *DEF*: $D(3, 6)$, $E(12, 9)$, $F(6, 15)$
   - triangle *GHI*: $G(5, 9)$, $H(14, 12)$, $I(8, 18)$

   a. Find a rule that changes the vertices of triangle *ABC* to the vertices of triangle *DEF*.

   b. Find a rule that changes the vertices of triangle *DEF* to the vertices of triangle *GHI*.

   c. Find a rule that changes the vertices of triangle *ABC* to the vertices of triangle *GHI*.

32. If you drew Mug and his hat on the same grid, his hat would be at his feet instead of on his head.

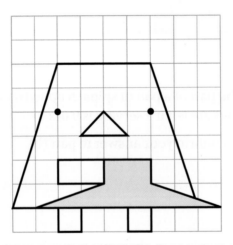

   a. Write a rule that puts Mug's hat centered on his head.

   b. Write a rule that changes Mug's hat to fit Zug and puts the hat on Zug's head.

   c. Write a rule that changes Mug's hat to fit Lug and puts the hat on Lug's head.

33. Films are sometimes modified to fit a TV screen. Find out what that means. What exactly is modified? If Mug is in a movie, is he still a Wump when you see the video on TV?

34. The diagram below shows Mug Wump drawn on a coordinate grid. Use this diagram to answer the questions on the next page.

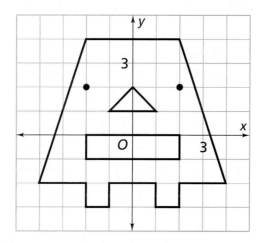

a. Use the diagram on the previous page. Complete the first column of a table like the one shown to record coordinates of key points needed to draw Mug. (You will need to determine the number of points needed for each body part.)

b. Suppose you make scale drawings with rules $(2x, 2y)$ and $(-2x, -2y)$. Complete the table to give coordinates for the images of Mug.

c. On graph paper, plot the images of Mug Wump produced by the new sets of coordinates in part (b).

d. Compare the length, width, and area of Mug's mouth to those of the figures drawn in part (c). Explain how you could have predicted those results by studying the coordinate rules for the drawings.

Coordinates for Mug and Variations

Rule	(x, y)	$(2x, 2y)$	$(-2x, -2y)$
Head Outline	$(-4, -2)$	▨	▨
	$(-2, -2)$	▨	▨
	$(-2, 3)$	▨	▨
	▨	▨	▨
	▨	▨	▨
Nose	$(-1, 1)$	▨	▨
	▨	▨	▨
	▨	▨	▨
Mouth	$(-2, -1)$	▨	▨
	▨	▨	▨
	▨	▨	▨
	▨	▨	▨
Eyes	$(-2, 2)$	▨	▨
	▨	▨	▨

35. Explain how each rule changes the original shape, size, and location of Mug Wump.

a. $(-x, y)$

b. $(x, -y)$

c. $(-0.5x, -0.5y)$

d. $(-0.5x, y)$

e. $(-3x, -3y)$

f. $(3x + 5, -3y - 4)$

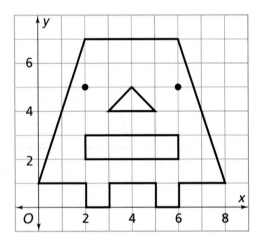

36. The diagram below shows Mug Wump drawn at the center of a coordinate grid and in four other positions.

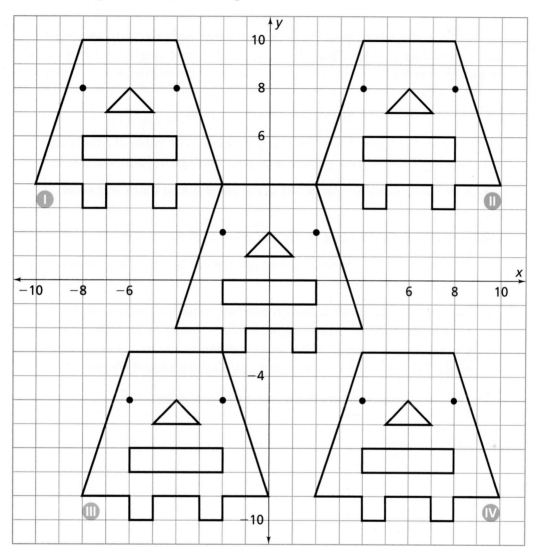
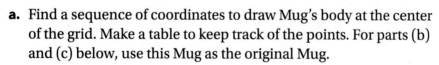

a. Find a sequence of coordinates to draw Mug's body at the center of the grid. Make a table to keep track of the points. For parts (b) and (c) below, use this Mug as the original Mug.

b. You can write a coordinate rule to describe the movement of points from one location to another. For example, the coordinate rule $(x - 2, y + 3)$ moves a point (x, y) to the left 2 units and up 3 units from its original location. Which of the other drawings is produced by the coordinate rule $(x + 6, y - 7)$?

c. Find coordinate rules for moving the original Mug to the other positions on the grid.

Mathematical Reflections 2

In this Investigation, you drew a character named Mug Wump on a coordinate grid. Then you used rules to transform Mug into other characters. Some of the characters you made were similar to Mug Wump, and some were not. The following questions will help you summarize what you have learned.

Think about these questions. Discuss your ideas with other students and your teacher. Then write a summary of your findings in your notebook.

1. If two shapes are similar, **what** is the same about them and what is different?

2. **a. What** does the scale factor tell you about two similar shapes?

   b. How does the coordinate rule for making two similar shapes relate to the scale factor?

3. Rubber-band stretchers, copy machines, movie projectors, and coordinate grids all make images that are similar to (or scale drawings of) the original shapes. **What** does it mean to say two shapes are similar? Build on your statement from Mathematical Reflection 1:

   "Two geometric shapes are similar when . . ."

Common Core Mathematical Practices

As you worked on the Problems in this Investigation, you used prior knowledge to make sense of them. You also applied Mathematical Practices to solve the Problems. Think back over your work, the ways you thought about the Problems, and how you used Mathematical Practices.

Hector described his thoughts in the following way:

> We noticed a relationship between the areas of similar figures. For example, in Problem 2.3, Question A, the scale factor from Rectangle L to Rectangle N is 3, and 9 of Rectangle L fit into Rectangle N. Therefore, the scale factor for the area is 3×3. This is the same as the "square of the scale factor" of the sides: 3^2.
>
> The same rule works for triangles. This confirms the claims we made about areas of triangles and rectangles in Problem 1.2.
>
> ....
>
> **Common Core Standards for Mathematical Practice**
>
> **MP7** Look for and make use of structure

- What other Mathematical Practices can you identify in Hector's reasoning?

- Describe a Mathematical Practice that you and your classmates used to solve a different Problem in this Investigation.

3

Scaling Perimeter and Area

In *Shapes and Designs*, you learned that some polygons fit together to cover, or tile, a flat surface. For example, the surface of a honeycomb has a pattern of regular hexagons. Many bathroom and kitchen floors are covered with a pattern of square tiles. These patterns of polygons that fit together are called *tessellations*.

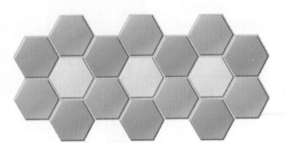 

Common Core State Standards

7.RP.A.2b Identify the constant of proportionality . . . in diagrams and verbal descriptions of proportional relationships.

7.G.A.1 Solve problems involving scale drawings of geometric figures, including computing actual lengths and areas from a scale drawing and reproducing a scale drawing at a different scale.

7.G.A.2 Draw (freehand, with ruler and protractor, and with technology) geometric shapes with given conditions. Focus on constructing triangles from three measures of angles or sides . . .

7.G.B.6 Solve real-world and mathematical problems involving area, volume, and surface area of two- and three-dimensional objects composed of triangles, quadrilaterals, polygons, cubes, and right prisms.

Also 7.RP.A.2, 7.RP.A.2a, and essential for 7.RP.A.3, 7.EE.B.4, 7.EE.B.4a

Look closely at the pattern of squares on the previous page. You can see that the large square consists of nine small squares. The large square is similar to each of the nine small squares. The large square has sides formed by the sides of three small squares, so the scale factor from the small square to the large square is 3.

You can also put four small squares together to make a four-tile square. This four-tile square is similar to both the large nine-tile square and the small single-tile square. The scale factor from the single-tile square to the four-tile square is 2. The scale factor from the four-tile square to the single-tile square is $\frac{1}{2}$.

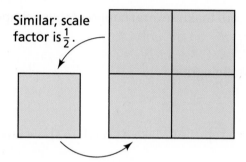

Similar; scale factor is $\frac{1}{2}$.

Similar; scale factor is 2.

No matter how closely you look at the hexagon pattern, however, you cannot find a large hexagon made up of similar smaller hexagons.

A shape is a **rep-tile** if you can put together *congruent* (same size and shape) copies of the shape to make a larger, similar shape. The congruent copies may be rotated in order to fit together. A square is a rep-tile, but a regular hexagon is not.

- Which quadrilaterals are rep-tiles?

- For those that are, how might you subdivide them into smaller, similar figures?

3.1 Rep-Tile Quadrilaterals
Forming Rep-Tiles With Similar Quadrilaterals

In this Problem, you will discover which rectangles and non-rectangular quadrilaterals are rep-tiles.

Problem 3.1

Sketch or use your Shapes Set to make several copies of these shapes:

- a non-square rectangle
- a non-rectangular parallelogram
- a trapezoid

A Which of these shapes is a rep-tile? Make a sketch to show how the copies fit together.

B Look at your sketches from Question A.

1. What is the scale factor from the original figure to the larger figure? Explain your reasoning.

2. How does the perimeter of the larger figure relate to the perimeter of the original figure?

3. How does the area of the larger figure relate to the area of the original figure?

C 1. Extend the rep-tile patterns you drew for Question A. Do this by sketching additional copies of the original figure to make even larger figures that are similar to the original. Show how the copies fit together.

2. Find the scale factor from each original figure to each new figure. Explain your reasoning.

3. What do the scale factors tell you about the corresponding side lengths, perimeters, angles, and areas?

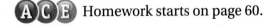 Homework starts on page 60.

3.2 Rep-Tile Triangles
Forming Rep-Tiles With Similar Triangles

Rep-tiles must tessellate, but not every shape that tessellates is a rep-tile.

- Are the birds in the tessellation below rep-tiles?

In Problem 3.1, you determined which quadrilaterals are rep-tiles. In this Problem, you will investigate which triangles are rep-tiles.

 Which types of triangles are rep-tiles?

Did You Know?

Mathematicians and scientists are very interested in rep-tiles. They share many properties with strange, newly discovered, crystal-like figures called quasicrystals. Quasicrystals do not have the translational symmetry of ordinary crystals, but they have other properties that ordinary crystals do not have. Scientists are currently researching the properties of quasicrystals and why they work. Quasicrystals are used to insulate wires and to coat mechanical parts to prevent erosion and wear. Quasicrystals even work well as a coating for non-stick frying pans!

Problem 3.2

Sketch or use your Shapes Set to make several copies of these shapes:

- a right triangle
- an isosceles triangle
- a scalene triangle

Ⓐ Which of these triangles is a rep-tile? Make a sketch to show how copies of the original figure fit together to make a larger, similar triangle.

Ⓑ Look at your sketches from Question A.

1. What is the scale factor from each original triangle to each larger triangle? Explain your reasoning.

2. How is the perimeter of the larger triangle related to the perimeter of the original?

3. How is the area of the larger triangle related to the area of the original?

Ⓒ 1. Extend the rep-tile patterns you made in Question A. Do this by sketching additional copies of the original triangle to make even larger triangles that are similar to the original. Show how the copies fit together.

2. Find the scale factor from each original triangle to each new triangle.

3. What do the scale factors tell you about the corresponding side lengths, perimeters, angles, and areas?

Problem 3.2 *continued*

D Study the rep-tile patterns you sketched for Questions A and C. Copy each of the triangles below. Then divide each triangle into four or more smaller, similar triangles.

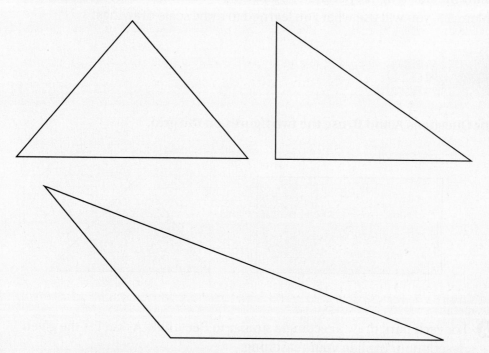

E 1. Suppose you are given a rectangle or triangle rep-tile and a scale factor of 5. How many copies of your rep-tile would be needed to make the scale copy? Explain your reasoning.

2. It takes nine copies of a certain rep-tile to make a similar figure. What is the scale factor between the original rep-tile and the image? Explain.

3. Tomoko claims that all triangles are rep-tiles. Is this true? Explain.

A C E Homework starts on page 60.

3.3 Designing Under Constraints
Scale Factors and Similar Shapes

The scale factor from one figure to a similar figure gives you information about how the side lengths, perimeters, and areas of the figures are related. In Problem 3.3, you will use what you learned to draw scale drawings.

Problem 3.3

For Questions A and B, use the two figures on the grid.

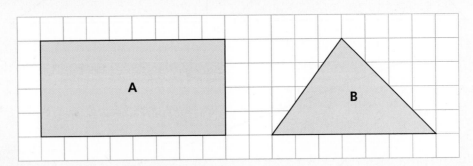

A For each part, draw a rectangle similar to Rectangle A that fits the given description. Explain your reasoning.

1. The scale factor from Rectangle A to the new rectangle is 2.5.

2. The area of the new rectangle is $\frac{1}{4}$ the area of Rectangle A.

3. The perimeter of the new rectangle is three times the perimeter of Rectangle A.

B For each part, draw a triangle similar to Triangle B that fits the given description. Explain your reasoning.

1. The area of the new triangle is 16 times the area of Triangle B.

2. The scale factor from Triangle B to the new triangle is $\frac{1}{2}$.

Problem **3.3** *continued*

C **1.** Rectangles *ABCD* and *EFGH* are similar. Find the length of side *AD*. Explain how you found the length.

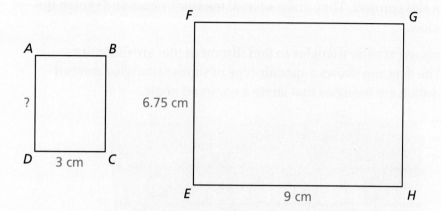

2. Triangles *ABC* and *DEF* are similar. Find the missing side lengths and angle measures. Explain.

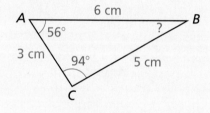

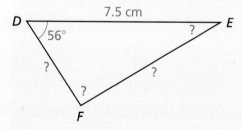

A C E Homework starts on page 60.

3.4 Out of Reach
Finding Lengths With Similar Triangles

Durell, Angie, and Tonya are designing a triangular boardwalk that crosses a river for a class project. They make several measurements and sketch the diagram below.

The students use similar triangles to find distances that are difficult to measure. The diagram shows a specific type of similar triangles, **nested triangles,** which are triangles that share a common angle.

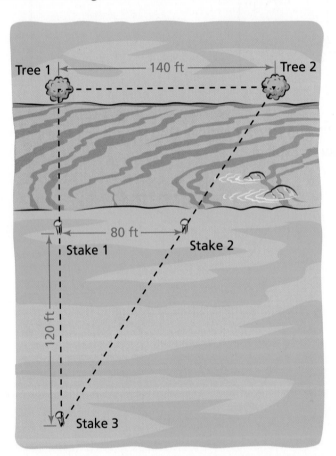

- The angles that look like right angles are right angles. How are the angles in the smaller triangle related to the angles in the larger triangle?

- Durell claims that he can use rep-tiles to show that the smaller right triangle is similar to the larger right triangle. Is he correct?

Two triangles are similar if corresponding angles are congruent. In a later Unit, you will prove this fact. For now, we will assume that it is true.

Problem 3.4

Ⓐ The triangles in the diagram on the previous page are similar. What is the distance across the river from Stake 1 to Tree 1? Explain your reasoning.

Ⓑ Describe the relationship between the perimeter of the smaller triangle and the perimeter of the larger triangle.

Ⓒ The diagram on the previous page shows three stakes and two trees. In what order do you think Durell, Angie, and Tonya located the key points and measured the segments and angles? Explain your reasoning.

Ⓓ Another group of students sketches a different diagram with similar triangles. They put their stakes in different places. Use the diagram below. Does the second group get the same measurement for the width of the river? Explain.

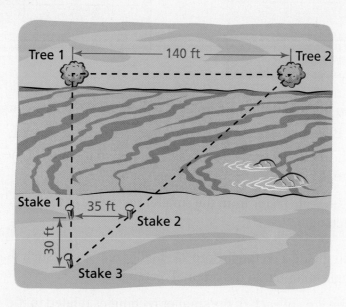

Ⓐ Ⓒ Ⓔ Homework starts on page 60.

Applications

1. Look for rep-tile patterns in the designs below. For each design,

   - Decide whether the small quadrilaterals are similar to the large quadrilateral. Explain.

   - If the quadrilaterals are similar, give the scale factor from each small quadrilateral to the large quadrilateral.

   a.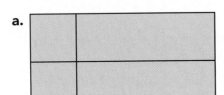

   b.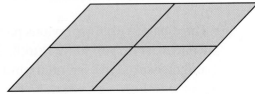

   c.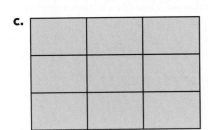

   d.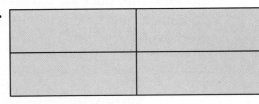

2. Suppose you put together nine copies of a rectangle to make a larger, similar rectangle.

   a. How is the area of the larger rectangle related to the area of the smaller rectangle?

   b. What is the scale factor from the smaller rectangle to the larger rectangle?

3. Suppose you divide a rectangle into 25 smaller rectangles such that each rectangle is similar to the original rectangle.

   a. How is the area of each of the smaller rectangles related to the area of the original rectangle?

   b. What is the scale factor from the original rectangle to each of the smaller rectangles?

4. Look for rep-tile patterns in the figures below.

   • Tell whether the small triangles are similar to the large triangle. Explain.

   • If the triangles are similar, give the scale factor from each small triangle to the large triangle.

   a.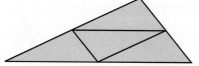

   b.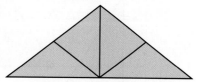

   c.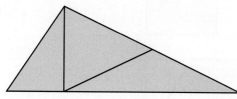

   d.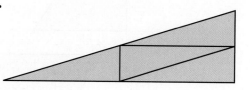

5. **a.** For rectangles E–G, give the length and width of a different, similar rectangle. Explain how you know the new rectangles are similar.

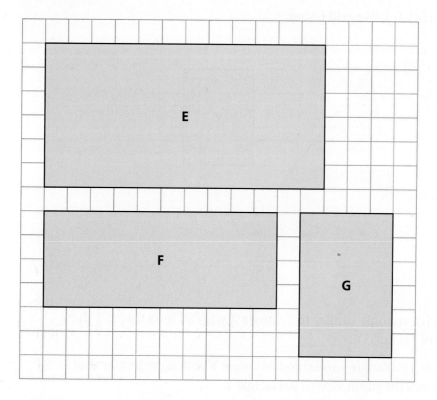

   b. Give the scale factor from each original rectangle in part (a) to the similar rectangles you described. Explain what the scale factor tells you about the corresponding lengths, perimeters, and areas.

6. Copy polygons A–D onto grid paper. Draw line segments that divide each of the polygons into four congruent polygons that are similar to the original polygon.

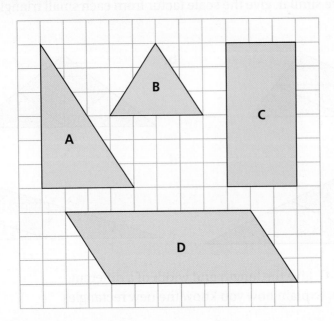

7. For parts (a)–(c), use grid paper.

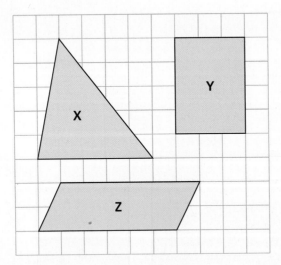

a. Sketch a triangle similar to Triangle X with an area that is $\frac{1}{4}$ the area of Triangle X.

b. Sketch a rectangle similar to Rectangle Y with a perimeter that is 0.5 times the perimeter of Rectangle Y.

c. Sketch a parallelogram similar to Parallelogram Z with side lengths that are 1.5 times the side lengths of Parallelogram Z.

8. Use the polygons below.

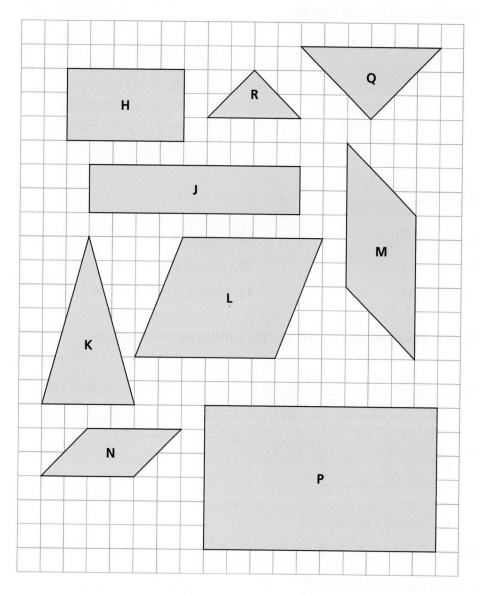

a. List pairs of similar shapes.

b. For each pair of similar shapes, find the scale factor from the smaller shape to the larger shape.

Triangle ABC is similar to triangle PQR. For Exercises 9–14, find the indicated angle measure or side length.

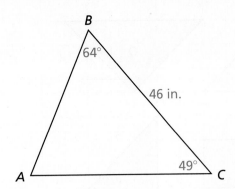
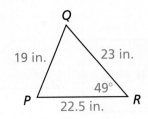

9. angle *A*

10. angle *Q*

11. angle *P*

12. length of side *AB*

13. length of side *AC*

14. perimeter of triangle *ABC*

Multiple Choice For Exercises 15–18, use the similar parallelograms below.

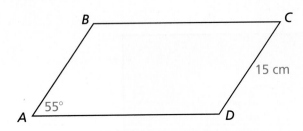
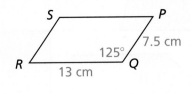

15. What is the measure of angle *D*?

    A. 55°   **B.** 97.5°   **C.** 125°   **D.** 135°

16. What is the measure of angle *R*?

    F. 55°   **G.** 97.5°   **H.** 125°   **J.** 135°

17. What is the measure of angle *S*?

    A. 55°   **B.** 97.5°   **C.** 125°   **D.** 135°

18. What is length of side *AB*?

    F. 3.75 cm   **G.** 13 cm   **H.** 15 cm   **J.** 26 cm

19. Suppose Rectangle B is similar to Rectangle A below. The scale factor from Rectangle A to Rectangle B is 4. What is the area of Rectangle B?

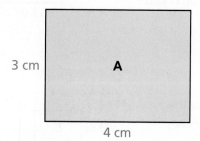

3 cm

A

4 cm

20. Suppose Rectangle E has an area of 9 square centimeters and Rectangle F has an area of 900 square centimeters. The two rectangles are similar. What is the scale factor from Rectangle E to Rectangle F?

21. Suppose Rectangles X and Y are similar. Rectangle X is 5 centimeters by 7 centimeters. The area of Rectangle Y is 140 square centimeters. What are the dimensions of Rectangle Y?

22. Anya and Jalen disagree about whether the two figures below are similar. Do you agree with Anya or with Jalen? Explain.

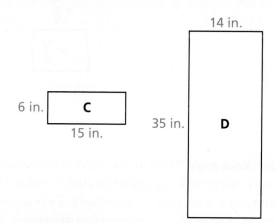

14 in.

6 in.   **C**

15 in.

35 in.   **D**

Anya's Reasoning

The two rectangles are not similar. The height of Rectangle D is almost 6 times the height of Rectangle C, but the widths are almost the same. Similar rectangles must have the same scale factor for the base and the height.

OR

Jalen's Reasoning

The two rectangles are similar. The scale factor from C to D is $\frac{7}{3}$. You can multiply the short side of C (the height) by to get 14 inches, which is the short side of D (the base). This scale factor also works for the long sides of the rectangles since $15 \times \frac{7}{3} = 35$.

23. Evan, Melanie, and Wyatt discuss whether the two figures at the right are similar. Do you agree with Evan, Melanie, or Wyatt? Explain.

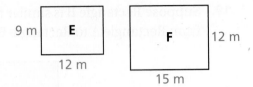

Evan's Reasoning

Rectangles E and F are similar because each shape has four right angles. Also, each rectangle has at least one side that is 12 meters long.

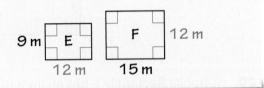

Melanie's Reasoning

The scale factor for the height from rectangle E to rectangle F is $\frac{12}{9}$, or $\frac{4}{3}$.

The scale factor for the base is $\frac{15}{12}$, or $\frac{5}{4}$. $\frac{4}{3} \neq \frac{5}{4}$, so the rectangles are not similar.

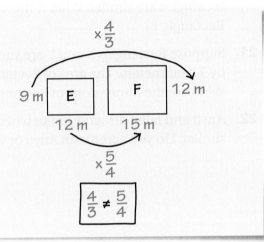

Wyatt's Reasoning

Rectangles E and F are similar. Rectangle F is 3 meters taller than Rectangle E since 9 meters + 3 meters = 12 meters. Rectangle F is also 3 meters wider than Rectangle E since 12 meters + 3 meters = 15 meters. Each dimension of Rectangle F is 3 meters greater than the corresponding dimension of Rectangle E, so the rectangles are similar.

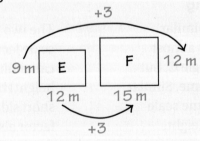

24. Janine, Trisha, and Jeff drew parallelograms that are similar to
Parallelogram *P* below.

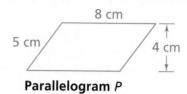

Parallelogram *P*

Each student claims that the scale factor from *P* to the sketched
parallelogram is 4. Are any of the students correct in their reasoning?
Explain.

Janine's Method

I divided the original
parallelogram into four similar
parallelograms. Parallelogram
P is four times as large as each
of the new parallelograms.

Trisha's Method

I sketched four copies of parallelogram P.
The shape has four times the area of
parallelogram P.

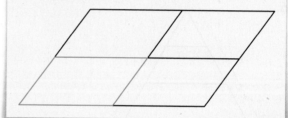

Jeff's Method

I wanted a scale factor of 4. The perimeter of the original shape
is 26 centimeters. I drew a parallelogram with a perimeter of
4 × 26 centimeters = 104 centimeters.

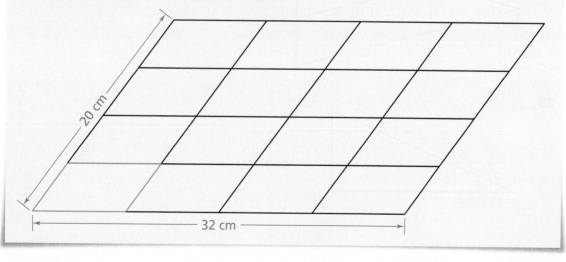

25. Judy lies on the ground 45 feet from her tent. Both the top of the tent and the top of a tall cliff are in her line of sight. Her tent is 10 feet tall. About how high is the cliff? Assume the two triangles are similar.

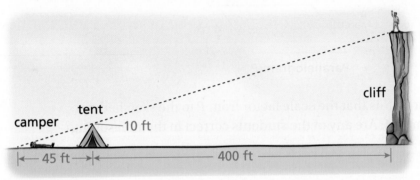

Not drawn to scale

For Exercises 26–28, each triangle has been subdivided into triangles that are similar to the original triangle. Copy each triangle and label as many side lengths as you can.

26.

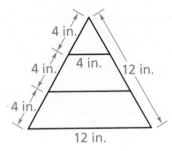

27.

28.

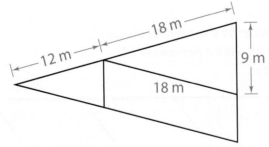

Connections

29. In the figure below, lines L_1 and L_2 are parallel.

    a. Use what you know about parallel lines to find the measures of angles *a* through *g*.

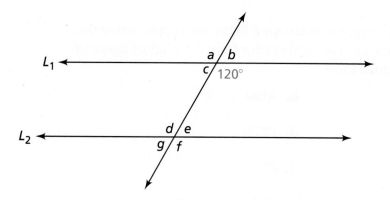

    b. List all pairs of *supplementary* angles in the diagram.

30. For each of the following angle measures, find the measure of its supplementary angle.

    a. $160°$ **b.** $90°$ **c.** $x°$

31. The right triangles below are similar.

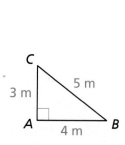 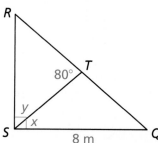

    a. Find the length of side *RS*.

    b. Find the length of side *RQ*.

    c. The measure of angle *x* is about $40°$. If the measure of angle *x* were exactly $40°$, what would be the measure of angle *y*?

    d. Use your answer from part (c) to find the measure of angle *R*. Explain how you can find the measure of angle *C*.

    e. Angle *x* and angle *y* are *complementary angles*. Find two additional pairs of complementary angles in Triangles *ABC* and *QRS*.

32. For parts (a)–(f), find the number that makes the fractions equivalent.

a. $\frac{1}{2} = \frac{3}{\blacksquare}$

b. $\frac{5}{6} = \frac{\blacksquare}{24}$

c. $\frac{3}{4} = \frac{6}{\blacksquare}$

d. $\frac{8}{12} = \frac{2}{\blacksquare}$

e. $\frac{3}{5} = \frac{\blacksquare}{100}$

f. $\frac{6}{4} = \frac{\blacksquare}{10}$

33. For parts (a)–(f), suppose you copy a figure on a copier using the given scale factor. Find the scale factor from the original figure to the copy in decimal form.

a. 200%

b. 50%

c. 150%

d. 125%

e. 75%

f. 25%

34. Write each fraction as a decimal and as a percent.

a. $\frac{2}{5}$

b. $\frac{3}{4}$

c. $\frac{3}{10}$

d. $\frac{1}{4}$

e. $\frac{7}{10}$

f. $\frac{7}{20}$

g. $\frac{4}{5}$

h. $\frac{7}{8}$

i. $\frac{15}{20}$

j. $\frac{3}{5}$

35. For parts (a)–(d), tell whether the figures are mathematically similar. Explain your reasoning. If the figures are similar, give the scale factor from the left figure to the right figure.

a.

b.

c.

d.

For Exercises 36–38, decide whether the statement is true or false. Explain your reasoning.

36. All squares are similar.

37. All rectangles are similar.

38. If the scale factor between two similar shapes is 1, then the two shapes are the same size.

39. a. Suppose the following rectangle is reduced by a scale factor of 50%. What are the dimensions of the reduced rectangle?

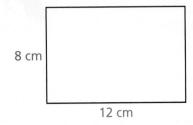

8 cm

12 cm

b. Suppose the reduced rectangle from part (a) is reduced again by a scale factor of 50%. What are the dimensions of the new rectangle? Explain your reasoning.

c. How does the reduced rectangle from part (b) compare to the original rectangle from part (a)?

40. Multiple Choice What is the value of x? The diagram is not to scale.

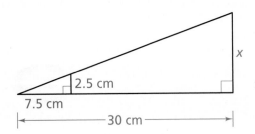

2.5 cm

7.5 cm

x

30 cm

A. 3 cm

B. 10 cm

C. 12 cm

D. 90 cm

For Exercises 41 and 42, find the missing side length. The diagrams are not to scale.

41.

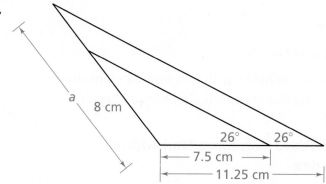

42.

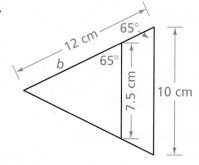

Extensions

43. Trace each shape. Divide each shape into four smaller, identical pieces that are similar to the original shape.

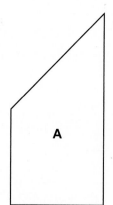

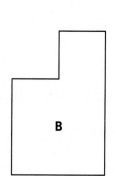

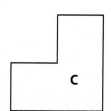

44. The **midpoint** of a line segment is a point that divides the segment into two segments of equal length. Draw a figure on grid paper by following these steps:

Step 1: Draw a large square.

Step 2: Mark the midpoint of each side.

Step 3: Connect the midpoints, in order, with four line segments to form a new figure. (The line segments should not intersect inside the square.)

Step 4: Repeat Steps 2 and 3 three more times. Work with the newest figure each time.

a. What kind of figure is formed when the midpoints of the sides of a square are connected?

b. Find the area of the original square you drew in Step 1.

c. Find the area of each of the new figures that was formed.

d. How do the areas change between successive figures?

e. Are there any similar figures in your final drawing? Explain.

45. Repeat Exercise 44 starting with an equilateral triangle, connecting three line segments to form a new triangle each time.

46. Suppose Rectangle A is similar to Rectangle B and to Rectangle C. Can you conclude that Rectangle B is similar to Rectangle C? Explain. Use drawings and examples to illustrate your answer.

47. You can subdivide figures to get smaller figures that are mathematically similar to the original. The mathematician Benoit Mandelbrot called these figures *fractals*. A famous example is the Sierpinski triangle.

Sierpinski Triangle

You can follow these steps to make the Sierpinski triangle.

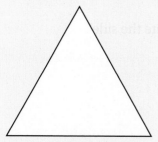

Step 1: Draw a triangle. (It does not have to be an equilateral triangle.)

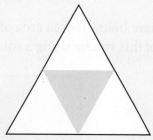

Step 2: Mark the midpoint of each side. Connect the midpoints to form four identical triangles that are similar to the original. Shade the center triangle.

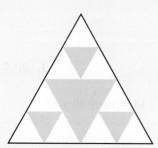

Step 3: For each unshaded triangle, mark the midpoints. Connect them in order to form four identical triangles. Shade the center triangle in each case.

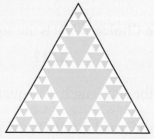

Step 4: Repeat Steps 2 and 3 over and over. To make a real Sierpinski triangle, you need to repeat the process an infinite number of times! This triangle shows five subdivisions.

a. Follow the steps for making the Sierpinski triangle until you subdivide the original triangle three times.

b. Describe any patterns you observe in your figure.

c. Mandelbrot used the term *self-similar* to describe fractals like the Sierpinski triangle. What do you think this term means?

Use the paragraph below for Exercises 48–52.

When you find the area of a square, you multiply the length of one side by itself. For a square with a side length of 3 units, you multiply 3×3 to get 9 square units. For this reason, mathematicians call 9 the *square* of 3.

The *square root* of 9 is 3. The symbol $\sqrt{\ }$ is used for the square root. This gives the fact family below.

$$3^2 = 9$$
$$\sqrt{9} = 3$$

48. The square below has an area of 10 square units. Write the side length of this square using a square root symbol.

49. Multiple Choice What is the square root of 144?

    F. 7   **G.** 12   **H.** 72   **J.** 20,736

50. What is the side length of a square with an area of 144 square units?

51. You have learned that if a figure grows by a scale factor of s, the area of the figure grows by a factor of s^2. If the area of a figure grows by a factor of f, what is the scale factor?

52. Find three examples of squares and square roots in the work you have done so far in this Unit.

53. Song makes a copy of the poster below.

12 in.

9 in.

a. She presses the 50% button on the copy machine. Now the length and width of the poster are each half of their original sizes. Song thinks that if she enlarges the copy by 150%, the new copy will be the same size as the original. Is she correct?

b. Suppose Song had done the opposite in part (a), first enlarging the poster by 150%, and then reducing the copy by 50%. Will the final copy be the same size as the original? Will it be the same size as the copy made in part (a)?

c. Song uses the same process from parts (a) and (b) with a different-sized poster. Does she get similar results?

d. Song applied a scale factor of 25% to shrink the original poster. Now she wants to get the poster back to the original size. What scale factor should she use? Explain your reasoning.

e. Suppose Song had used 75% and 125% in parts (a) and (b) instead of 50% and 150%. What would have happened?

f. What general statements can you make about applying any pair of two scale factors one after the other? Consider a pair of two enlargements, a pair of two reductions, and a pair consisting of one enlargement and one reduction.

In this Investigation, you explored similar polygons and scale factors. The following questions will help you summarize what you have learned.

Think about these questions. Discuss your ideas with other students and your teacher. Then write a summary of your findings in your notebook.

1. **a.** If two polygons are similar, **how** can you find the scale factor from one polygon to the other? Give specific examples.

   b. Suppose you are given a polygon. **How** can you draw a similar figure?

2. **What** does the scale factor between two similar figures tell you about the

   a. side lengths?

   b. perimeters?

   c. areas?

   d. angles?

3. If two figures are similar, **how** can you find a missing side length?

4. **Describe** how you can find the measure of a distance that you cannot measure directly.

5. **What** does it mean to say two shapes are similar? After completing Investigation 3, how can you build on your statements from Mathematical Reflections 1 and 2?

   "Two geometric shapes are similar when . . ."

Common Core Mathematical Practices

As you worked on the Problems in this Investigation, you used prior knowledge to make sense of them. You also applied Mathematical Practices to solve the Problems. Think back over your work, the ways you thought about the Problems, and how you used Mathematical Practices.

Elena described her thoughts in the following way:

We were trying to solve a realistic problem in Problem 3.4. We needed to find the distance across a river.

We looked at a diagram where some distances and angles were labeled. The diagram included similar triangles. We used properties of similar triangles to help us find the distance across the river. We presented our work to the class.

Matt wondered how we knew which sides were corresponding. We used the picture to explain which sides were corresponding and why.

Common Core Standards for Mathematical Practice
MP4 Model with mathematics

• What other Mathematical Practices can you identify in Elena's reasoning?

• Describe a Mathematical Practice that you and your classmates used to solve a different Problem in this Investigation.

Similarity and Ratios

You can enhance a report or story by adding photographs, drawings, or diagrams. If you place a graphic in an electronic document, you can enlarge, reduce, or move it. When you click on the graphic, it appears inside a frame with handles along the sides, such as th figure shown below.

You can change the size and shape of the image by dragging the handles.

Common Core State Standards

7.RP.A.2 Recognize and represent proportional relationships between quantities.

7.RP.A.3 Use proportional relationships to solve multistep ratio and percent problems.

7.EE.B.4 Use variables to represent quantities in a real-world or mathematical problem, and construct simple equations and inequalities to solve problems by reasoning about the quantities.

7.G.A.1 Solve problems involving scale drawings of geometric figures, including computing actual lengths and areas from a scale drawing and reproducing a scale drawing at a different scale.

Also 7.G.B.6, 7.RP.A.2a, 7.RP.A.2b, 7.EE.B.3, and 7.EE.B.4a

Here are examples of the image after it has been resized.

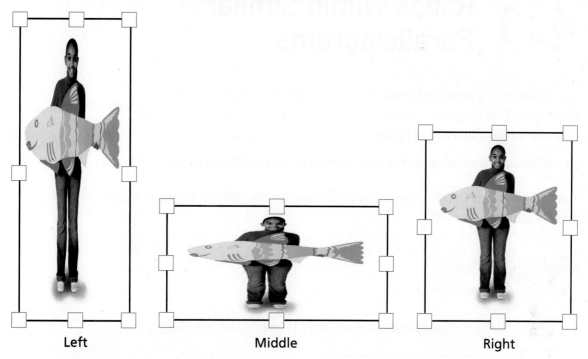

Left   Middle   Right

- How did this technique produce these variations of the original shape?
- Which of these images appears to be similar to the original? Why?

You can use ratios to describe and compare shapes. A **ratio** is a comparison of two quantities, such as two lengths. The rectangle around the original figure is about 10 centimeters tall and 8 centimeters wide. You can say, "The ratio of height to width is 10 to 8."

This table gives the ratios of height to width for the images.

Image Information

Figure	Height (cm)	Width (cm)	Height-to-Width Ratio
Original	10	8	10 to 8
Left	8	3	8 to 3
Middle	3	6	3 to 6
Right	5	4	5 to 4

- What do you notice about the height-to-width ratios?

The comparisons "10 to 8" and "5 to 4" are *equivalent ratios*. **Equivalent ratios** are like equivalent fractions. In fact, ratios are often written in fraction form. You can express equivalent ratios with equations. A **proportion** is an equation stating that two ratios are equal.

$$\frac{10}{8} = \frac{5}{4} \qquad\qquad \frac{8}{10} = \frac{4}{5}$$

4.1 Ratios Within Similar Parallelograms

You know that a scale factor relates each length in a figure to the corresponding length in its image. You can also write a ratio to compare any two lengths in a single figure.

- What information does the ratio of side lengths within a figure give?

For the diagrams in this Investigation, all measurements are drawn to scale unless otherwise noted.

Problem 4.1

A **1.** Which rectangles are similar? Explain your reasoning.

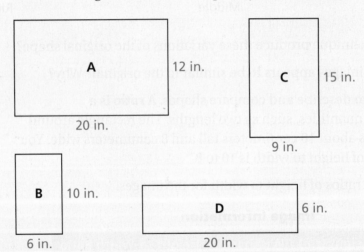

2. a. For each rectangle, find the ratio of the length of a short side to the length of a long side.

  b. What do you notice about the ratios in part (a) for similar rectangles? About the ratios for non-similar rectangles?

3. Choose two similar rectangles. Find the scale factor from the smaller rectangle to the larger rectangle. What does the scale factor tell you?

4. Compare the information given by the scale factor from part (3) to the information given by the ratios of side lengths from part (2).

Problem 4.1 *continued*

B **1.** Which of the parallelograms below are similar? Explain.

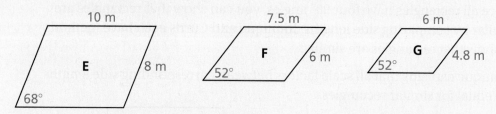

2. For each parallelogram, find the ratio of the length of a long side to the length of a short side. How do the ratios compare?

C **1.** Suppose you find the ratio of the lengths of **adjacent sides,** two sides that meet at a vertex, in a rectangle. This ratio is equivalent to the ratio of the corresponding side lengths in another rectangle. Are the figures similar? Explain your reasoning.

2. Suppose you find the ratio of the lengths of adjacent sides in a parallelogram. This ratio is equivalent to the ratio of the adjacent sides in another parallelogram. Are the figures similar? Explain.

A C E Homework starts on page 90.

Did You Know?

Hancock Place is an office building in Boston, Massachusetts. The tower of the building has a unique shape. While most office buildings are rectangular, the base of the tower of Hancock Place is a parallelogram. This makes the tower look two-dimensional from some vantage points.

4.2 Ratios Within Similar Triangles

Since all rectangles have four 90° angles, you can show that rectangles are similar by comparing side lengths. Jounique and Curtis each have methods to show that rectangles are similar.

Jounique explains that all scale factors between corresponding side lengths are equal for similar rectangles.

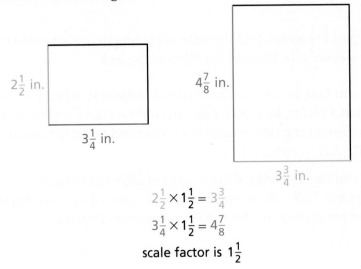

$$2\tfrac{1}{2} \times 1\tfrac{1}{2} = 3\tfrac{3}{4}$$
$$3\tfrac{1}{4} \times 1\tfrac{1}{2} = 4\tfrac{7}{8}$$

scale factor is $1\tfrac{1}{2}$

Curtis says that rectangles are similar if the ratios of corresponding adjacent sides within each shape are proportional.

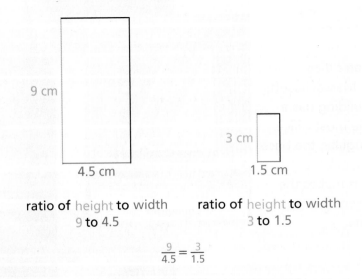

ratio of height to width   ratio of height to width
9 to 4.5   3 to 1.5

$$\frac{9}{4.5} = \frac{3}{1.5}$$

You need to compare more than just side lengths of polygons to understand their shapes. In this Problem, you will use angle measures and side-length ratios to find similar triangles.

Problem 4.2

For Questions A and B, use the triangles below. The triangles are drawn to scale.

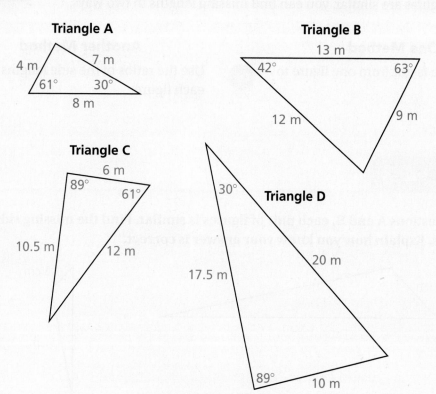

Triangle A

4 m   7 m

61°   30°

8 m

Triangle B

13 m

42°   63°

12 m   9 m

Triangle C

6 m

89°   61°

10.5 m   12 m

Triangle D

30°

20 m

17.5 m

89°   10 m

A Which triangles are similar? Explain your reasoning.

B **1.** Within each triangle, find the ratio of shortest side to longest side. Find the ratio of shortest side to "middle" side.

2. What do you notice about the ratios in part (1) for similar triangles? About the ratios for non-similar triangles?

C Choose two similar triangles. Find the scale factor from the smaller triangle to the larger triangle. What information does the scale factor give?

D Compare the information given by the ratios of side lengths in Question B to the information given by the scale factor in Question C.

A C E Homework starts on page 90.

4.3 Finding Missing Parts
Using Similarity to Find Measurements

When two figures are similar, you can find missing lengths in two ways.

One Method

Use the scale factor from one figure to the other.

OR

Another Method

Use the ratios of the side lengths within each figure.

Problem 4.3

For Questions A and B, each pair of figures is similar. Find the missing side lengths. Explain how you know your answer is correct.

A

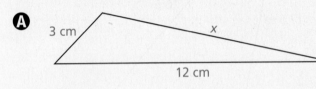

3 cm

x

12 cm

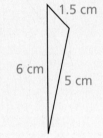

1.5 cm

6 cm

5 cm

B

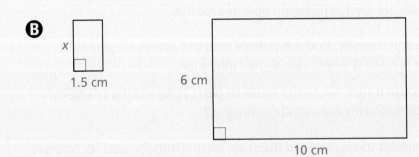

x

1.5 cm

6 cm

10 cm

Problem 4.3 *continued*

C The figures below are similar. Find the missing measurements. Explain how you found your answers.

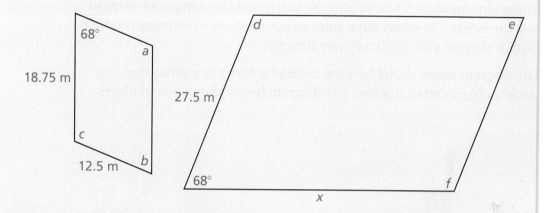

D The figures below are similar. Each side length is in centimeters.

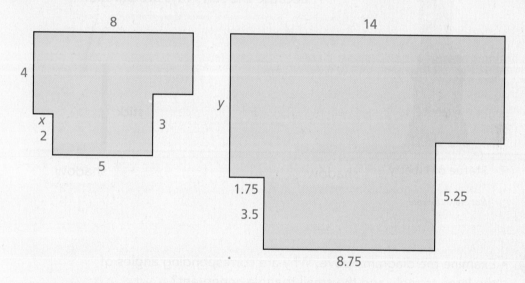

1. Find the value of *x*. Explain how you found it.

2. Find the value of *y*. Explain.

3. Find the area and perimeter of one of the figures.

4. Use your answer to part (3) and the scale factor. Find the area and perimeter of the other figure. Explain.

A C E Homework starts on page 90.

4.4 Using Shadows to Find Heights
Using Similar Triangles

You can find the height of a school building by climbing a ladder and using a long tape measure. You can also use easier and less dangerous ways to find the height. On sunny days, you can use shadows to estimate outdoor heights that are difficult to measure directly.

The diagram below shows how the method works. On a sunny day, any upright object casts a shadow. The diagram below shows two triangles.

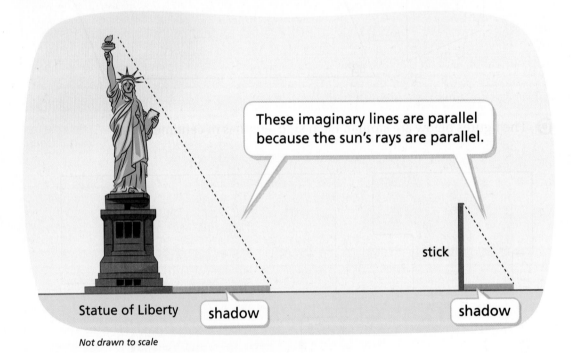

These imaginary lines are parallel because the sun's rays are parallel.

stick

Statue of Liberty | shadow | shadow

Not drawn to scale

- Examine the diagram above. Why are corresponding angles of the large triangle and the small triangle congruent?

- What does this suggest about the similarity of the triangles?

- How can you use the shadows to find the height of the Statue of Liberty?

To use the shadow method, measure the following:

- the length of the stick
- the length of the stick's shadow
- the length of the building's shadow

Problem 4.4

Your teacher will assign you an object such as a flagpole, clock tower, or school. Use the shadow method to find the height of the object.

A Make the necessary measurements. Sketch a diagram and record your measurements on the sketch.

B Use similar triangles and your sketch to find the height of the object.

C When you use the shadow method, what problems might affect the accuracy of your answer? Explain.

D A tree casts a 25-foot shadow. At the same time, a 6-foot stick casts a shadow 4.5 feet long. How tall is the tree?

ACE Homework starts on page 90.

The Statue of Liberty is about 111 feet tall from head to toe. When she casts a 600-foot-long shadow, her head casts a shadow about 93½ feet long. You can use that information to find the height of her head.

Applications

1. For parts (a)–(c), use the parallelograms below.

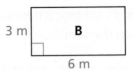

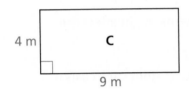

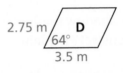

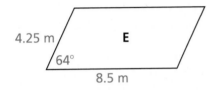

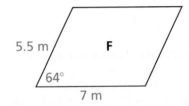

   a. List all the pairs of similar parallelograms. Explain your reasoning.

   b. For each pair of similar parallelograms, find the ratio of two adjacent side lengths in one parallelogram. Find the ratio of the corresponding side lengths in the other parallelogram. How do these ratios compare?

   c. For each pair of similar parallelograms, find the scale factor from one shape to the other. Explain how the information given by the scale factors is different from the information given by the ratios of adjacent side lengths.

2. a. On grid paper, draw two similar rectangles where the scale factor from one rectangle to the other is 2.5. Label the length and width of each rectangle.

   b. For each rectangle, find the ratio of the length to the width.

   c. Draw a third rectangle that is similar to one of the rectangles in part (a). Find the scale factor from the new rectangle to the one from part (a).

   d. Find the ratio of the length to the width for the new rectangle.

   e. What can you say about the length-to-width ratios of the three rectangles? Is this true for another rectangle that is similar to one of the three rectangles? Explain.

3. For parts (a)–(d), use the triangles below. The drawings are not to scale.

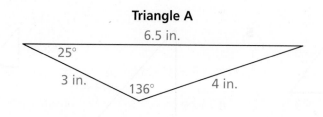

Triangle A

6.5 in.

25°

3 in.

136°

4 in.

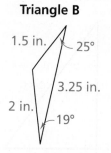

Triangle B

1.5 in.

25°

3.25 in.

2 in.

19°

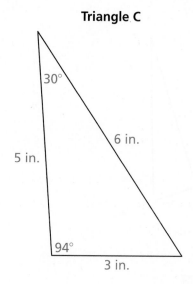

Triangle C

30°

6 in.

5 in.

94°

3 in.

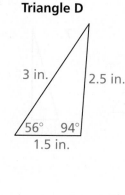

Triangle D

3 in.

2.5 in.

56° 94°

1.5 in.

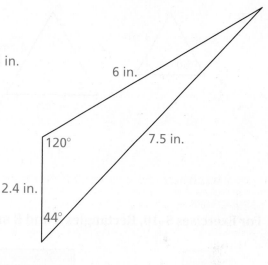

Triangle E

6 in.

120°

7.5 in.

2.4 in.

44°

a. List all the pairs of similar triangles. Explain why they are similar.

b. For each pair of similar triangles, find the ratio of two side lengths in one triangle. Find the ratio of the corresponding side lengths in the other. How do these ratios compare?

c. For each pair of similar triangles, find the scale factor from one shape to the other. Explain how the information given by the scale factors is different than the information given by the ratios of side lengths.

d. How are corresponding angles related in similar triangles? Is it the same relationship as for corresponding side lengths? Explain.

For Exercises 4–7, each pair of figures is similar. Find the missing measurement. Explain your reasoning. (Note: The figures are not drawn to scale.)

4.

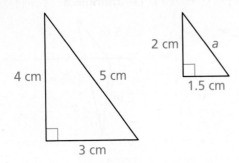

5.

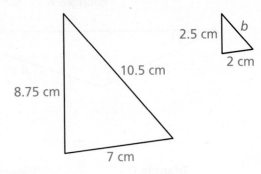

6.

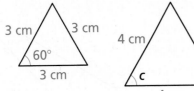

7.

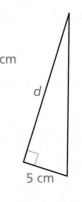

For Exercises 8–10, Rectangles A and B are similar.

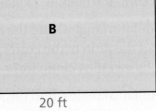

8. Multiple Choice What is the value of x?

   A. 4   **B.** 12   **C.** 15   **D.** $33\frac{1}{3}$

9. What is the scale factor from Rectangle B to Rectangle A?

10. Find the area of each rectangle. How are the areas related?

11. Rectangles C and D are similar.

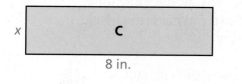

a. What is the value of *x*?

b. What is the scale factor from Rectangle C to Rectangle D?

c. Find the area of each rectangle. How are the areas related?

12. Suppose you want to buy new carpeting for your bedroom. The bedroom floor is a 9-foot-by-12-foot rectangle. Carpeting is sold by the square yard.

a. How much carpeting do you need to buy?

b. Carpeting costs $22 per square yard. How much will the carpet cost?

13. Suppose you want to buy the carpet described in Exercise 12 for a library. The library floor is similar to the floor of the 9-foot-by-12-foot bedroom. The scale factor from the bedroom to the library is 2.5.

a. What are the dimensions of the library? Explain.

b. How much carpeting do you need for the library?

c. How much will the carpet for the library cost?

14. The Washington Monument is the tallest structure in Washington, D.C. At a certain time, the monument casts a shadow that is about 500 feet long. At the same time, a 40-foot flagpole nearby casts a shadow that is about 36 feet long. About how tall is the monument? Sketch a diagram.

15. Darius uses the shadow method to estimate the height of a flagpole. He finds that a 5-foot stick casts a 4-foot shadow. At the same time, he finds that the flagpole casts a 20-foot shadow. What is the height of the flagpole? Sketch a diagram.

16. **a.** Greg and Zola are trying to find the height of their school building. Zola takes a picture of Greg standing next to the building. How might this picture help them determine the height of the building?

     b. Greg is 5 feet tall. The picture Zola took shows Greg as $\frac{1}{4}$ inch tall. If the building is 25 feet tall in real life, how tall should the building be in the picture? Explain.

     c. In part (a), you thought of ways to use a picture to find the height of an object. Think of an object in your school that is difficult to measure directly, such as a high wall, bookshelf, or trophy case. Describe how you might find the height of the object.

17. Movie screens often have an *aspect ratio* of 16 by 9. This means that for every 16 feet of width along the base of the screen there are 9 feet of height. The width of the screen at a local drive-in theater is about 115 feet wide. The screen has a 16 : 9 aspect ratio. About how tall is the screen?

18. Triangle A has sides that measure 4 inches, 5 inches, and 6 inches. Triangle B has sides that measure 8 feet, 10 feet, and 12 feet. Taylor and Landon are discussing whether the two triangles are similar. Do you agree with Taylor or with Landon? Explain.

Taylor's Explanation

The triangles are similar. If you double each of the side lengths of Triangle A, you get the side lengths for Triangle B.

OR

Landon's Explanation

The triangles are not similar. Taylor's method works when the two measures have the same units. However, the sides of Triangle A are measured in inches, and the sides of Triangle B are measured in feet. So, they cannot be similar.

Connections

For Exercises 19–24, tell whether each pair of ratios is equivalent.

19. 3 to 2 and 5 to 4

20. 8 to 4 and 12 to 8

21. 7 to 5 and 21 to 15

22. 1.5 to 0.5 and 6 to 2

23. 1 to 2 and 3.5 to 6

24. 2 to 3 and 4 to 6

25. Use a pair of equivalent ratios from Exercises 19–24. Write a similarity problem using the ratios. Explain how to solve the problem.

For each ratio in Exercises 26–29, write two other equivalent ratios.

26. 5 to 3

27. 4 to 1

28. 3 to 7

29. 1.5 to 1

30. Here is a picture of Duke. The scale factor from Duke to the picture is 12.5%. Use an inch ruler to make any measurements.

a. How long is Duke from his nose to the tip of his tail? Explain how you used the picture to find your answer.

b. To build a doghouse for Duke, you need to know his height. How tall is Duke? Explain.

c. A copy center has a machine that prints on poster-size paper. You can resize an image from 50% to 200%. How can you use the machine to make a life-size picture of Duke?

31. Paloma draws triangle *ABC* on a grid. She applies a rule to make the triangle on the right.

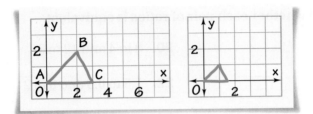

a. What rule did Paloma apply to make the new triangle?

b. Is the new triangle similar to triangle *ABC*? Explain your reasoning. If the triangles are similar, give the scale factor from triangle *ABC* to the new triangle.

For Exercises 32 and 33, use the paragraph below.

The Rosavilla School District wants to build a new middle school building. They ask architects to make scale drawings of possible layouts for the building. Two possibilities are shown below.

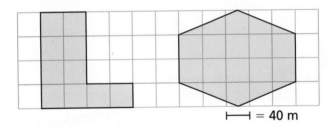

$\vdash\!\!\dashv$ = 40 m

32. **a.** What is the area of each scale drawing in square units?

b. What would the area of the ground floor of each building be?

33. **Multiple Choice** The school board likes the L-shaped layout but wants a building with more space. They increase the L-shaped layout by a scale factor of 2. For the new layout, choose the correct statement.

F. The area is two times the original.

G. The area is four times the original.

H. The area is eight times the original.

J. None of the statements above are correct.

34. The school principal visits Ashton's class one day. Ashton uses the mirror method to estimate the principal's height. This diagram shows the measurements he records.

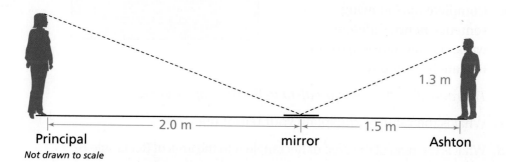

Principal   ←—— 2.0 m ——→   mirror   ←—— 1.5 m ——→   1.3 m   Ashton

Not drawn to scale

a. What estimate should Ashton give for the principal's height?

b. Is your answer to part (a) a reasonable height for an adult?

35. Use the table for parts (a)–(c).

Student Heights and Arm Spans

Height (in.)	60	65	63	50	58	66	60	63	67	65
Arm Span (in.)	55	60	60	48	60	65	60	67	62	70

a. Find the ratio of arm span to height for each student. Write the ratio as a fraction. Then write the ratio as an equivalent decimal. What patterns do you notice?

b. Find the mean of the ratios.

c. Use your answer from part (b). Predict the arm span of a person who is 62 inches tall. Explain your reasoning.

36. For each angle measure, find the measure of its complement and the measure of its supplement.

Sample: 30°   complement: 60°; supplement: 150°

a. 20°   **b.** 70°   **c.** 45°

37. The rectangles at the right are similar.

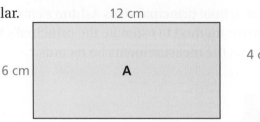

12 cm

6 cm   **A**

4 cm   **B**   x

a. What is the scale factor from Rectangle A to Rectangle B?

b. Complete the following sentence in two different ways. Use the side lengths of Rectangles A and B.

The ratio of ▨ to ▨ is equivalent to the ratio of ▨ to ▨.

c. What is the value of *x*? Explain your reasoning.

d. What is the ratio of the area of Rectangle A to the area of Rectangle B?

For Exercises 38 and 39, use the rectangles below.

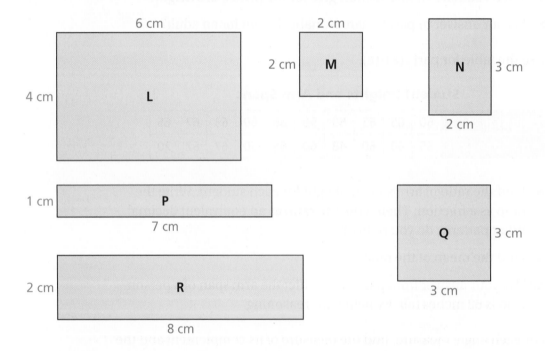

6 cm

4 cm   **L**

2 cm

2 cm   **M**

N   3 cm

2 cm

1 cm   **P**

7 cm

Q   3 cm

2 cm   **R**

8 cm

3 cm

38. Multiple Choice Which pair of rectangles listed below is similar?

A. L and M   **B.** L and Q   **C.** L and N   **D.** P and R

39. a. Find at least one more pair of similar rectangles.

b. For each pair of similar rectangles, find the scale factor from the larger rectangle to the smaller rectangle. Find the scale factor from the smaller rectangle to the larger rectangle.

c. For each similar pair of rectangles, find the ratio of the area of the larger rectangle to the area of the smaller rectangle.

Extensions

40. For parts (a)–(e), use the similar triangles below.

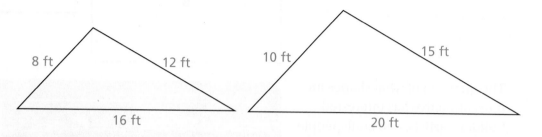

a. What is the scale factor from the smaller triangle to the larger triangle? Write your answer as a fraction and a decimal.

b. Choose any side of the larger triangle. Find the ratio of this side length to the corresponding side length in the smaller triangle. Write your answer as a fraction and as a decimal. How does the ratio compare to the scale factor from part (a)?

c. What is the scale factor from the larger triangle to the smaller triangle? Write your answer as a fraction and a decimal.

d. Choose any side of the smaller triangle. Find the ratio of this side length to the corresponding side length in the larger triangle. Write your answer as a fraction and as a decimal. How does the ratio compare to the scale factor from part (c)?

e. What patterns do you notice in parts (a)–(d)? Are these patterns the same for any pair of similar figures? Explain.

41. For parts (a) and (b), use a straightedge and an angle ruler or protractor.

a. Draw two different triangles that each have angle measures of 30°, 60°, and 90°. Do the triangles appear to be similar?

b. Draw two different triangles that each have angle measures of 40°, 80°, and 60°. Do the triangles appear to be similar?

c. Based on your findings for parts (a) and (b), make a conjecture about triangles with congruent angle measures.

42. One of these rectangles is "most pleasing to the eye."

A

B

C

The question of what shapes are most attractive has interested builders, artists, and craftspeople for thousands of years.

The ancient Greeks were particularly attracted to rectangular shapes similar to Rectangle B above. They referred to such shapes as "golden rectangles." They used golden rectangles frequently in buildings and monuments. The ratio of the length to the width in a golden rectangle is called the "golden ratio."

This photograph of the Parthenon (a temple in Athens, Greece) shows several golden rectangles.

a. Measure the length and width of Rectangles A, B, and C above in centimeters. For each rectangle, estimate the ratio of the length to the width as accurately as possible. The ratio for Rectangle B is an approximation of the golden ratio.

b. You can divide a golden rectangle into a square and a smaller rectangle similar to the original rectangle.

Golden Rectangle

The smaller rectangle is similar to the larger rectangle.

smaller rectangle

Copy Rectangle B above. Divide this golden rectangle into a square and a rectangle. Is the smaller rectangle a golden rectangle? Explain.

43. For parts (a) and (b), use the triangles below.

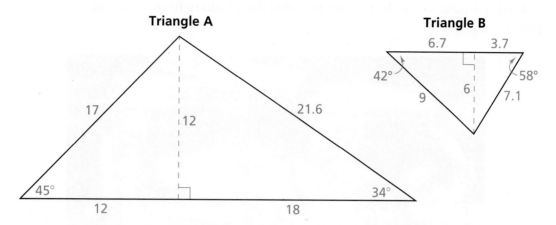

Triangle A

17   12   21.6   45°   12   18   34°

Triangle B

6.7   3.7   42°   6   58°   9   7.1

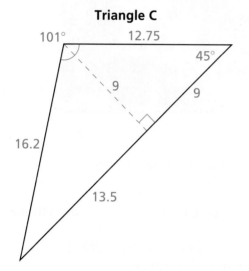

Triangle C

101°   12.75   45°   9   9   16.2   13.5

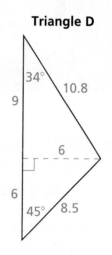

Triangle D

34°   10.8   9   6   6   45°   8.5

a. Identify the triangles that are similar to each other. Explain your reasoning.

b. For each triangle, find the ratio of the base to the height. How do these ratios compare for the similar triangles? How do these ratios compare for the non-similar triangles?

For Exercises 44–48, suppose a photographer for the school newspaper took this picture. The editors want to resize the photo to fit in a specific space on a page.

4 in.

6 in.

44. Can the original photo be changed to a similar rectangle with the given measurements (in inches)?

   a. 8 by 12   **b.** 9 by 11   **c.** 6 by 9   **d.** 3 by 4.5

45. Suppose that the school copier only has three paper sizes (in inches): $8\frac{1}{2}$ by 11, 11 by 14, and 11 by 17. You can enlarge or reduce documents by specifying a percent from 50% to 200%. Can you make copies of the photo that fit exactly on any of the three paper sizes? Explain your reasoning.

46. A copy machine accepts scale factors from 50% to 200%. How can you use the copy machine to produce a copy that is 25% of the original photo's size? How does the area of the copy relate to the area of the original photo?

47. How can you use the copy machine to reduce the photo to a copy that is 12.5% of the original photo's size? 36% of the original photo's size? How does the area of the reduced figure compare to the area of the original in each case?

48. What is the greatest enlargement of the photo that will fit on paper that is 11 inches by 17 inches?

49. The following sequence of numbers is called the *Fibonacci sequence*. It is named after an Italian mathematician from the 14th century who contributed to the early development of algebra.

1, 1, 2, 3, 5, 8, 13, 21, 34, 55, 89, 144, 233, 377 . . .

a. Look for patterns in this sequence. How are the numbers found? Use your ideas to find the next four terms.

b. Find the ratio of each term to the term before it. For example, 1 to 1, 2 to 1, 3 to 2, and so on. Write each of the ratios as a fraction and as an equivalent decimal. Compare the results to the golden ratios you found in Exercise 44. Describe similarities and differences.

50. Francisco, Katya, and Peter notice that all squares are similar. They wonder if other shapes that have four sides are *all-similar*. Who is correct?

Francisco's Work

Squares are the only type of *all-similar* polygon with four sides. This is because all the sides have equal length, and all the angles are right angles.

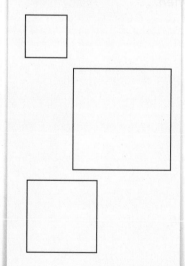

Katya's Work

All rectangles are *all-similar*. Just like squares, all the angles in rectangles are congruent.

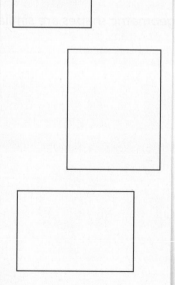

Peter's Work

I know that rhombi are four-sided shapes with sides that are all the same length. Rhombi must be *all-similar* because, for two rhombi, there is a consistent scale factor for all corresponding side lengths.

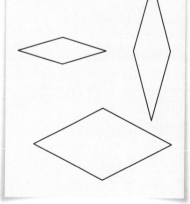

51. Ernie and Vernon are having a discussion about *all-similar* shapes. Ernie says that regular polygons and circles are the only types of *all-similar* shapes. Vernon claims isosceles right triangles are *all-similar*, but they are not regular polygons. Who is correct? Explain.

In this Investigation, you used ratios to describe and compare the size and shape of rectangles, triangles, and other figures. The following questions will help you summarize what you have learned.

Think about these questions. Discuss your ideas with other students and your teacher. Then write a summary of your findings in your notebook.

1. If two triangles, rectangles, or parallelograms are similar,

   a. **How** does the ratio of two side lengths within one figure compare to the ratio of the corresponding side lengths in the other figure?

   b. **What** does the scale factor from one figure to the other tell you about the figures?

2. a. **Describe** at least two ways to find a missing side length in a pair of similar figures.

   b. **How** can you find the height of an object that cannot be measured directly?

3. **What** does it mean to say that two shapes are similar? After exploring with ratios, build on your statements from Mathematical Reflections 1, 2, and 3:

   "Two geometric shapes are similar when. . ."

Common Core Mathematical Practices

As you worked on the Problems in this Investigation, you used prior knowledge to make sense of them. You also applied Mathematical Practices to solve the Problems. Think back over your work, the ways you thought about the Problems, and how you used Mathematical Practices.

Shawna described her thoughts in the following way:

We looked at two similar rectangles in Problem 4.1. For each rectangle, we determined the ratio of length to width. We noticed that the ratios were equal. This was not true for two non-similar rectangles.

We also looked at the ratio of a side length in one rectangle to the corresponding side length in a similar rectangle. This ratio always gave us the scale factor between the two rectangles. This makes sense since you multiply each side length of one rectangle by the scale factor to find the corresponding side length in the similar rectangle.

We noticed that these patterns are true for parallelograms and triangles, too.

Common Core Standards for Mathematical Practice

MP2 Reason abstractly and quantitatively

- What other Mathematical Practices can you identify in Shawna's reasoning?

- Describe a Mathematical Practice that you and your classmates used to solve a different Problem in this Investigation.

Unit Project

Shrinking or Enlarging Pictures

Your final project for this Unit involves two parts:

1. the drawing of a similar image of a picture
2. a written report on making similar figures

Part 1: Drawing

You will enlarge or shrink a picture or cartoon of your choice. Be sure to choose a picture that has lengths, angles, and areas that you will be able to measure and compare. You will use coordinate graphing rules to produce a similar image.

If you enlarge the picture, the image must have a scale factor of at least 4.

If you shrink the picture, the image must have a scale factor of at most $\frac{1}{4}$.

Your final project must be presented in a display for others. Both the original picture and the image need to be in the display, and you must do the following:

- identify the scale factor and show how the lengths compare between the picture and the image;

- identify two pairs of corresponding angles and show how the angles compare between the picture and the image;

- compare some area of the picture with the corresponding area of the image.

Part 2: Write a Report

Write a report describing how you made your similar figure. Your report should include the following:

- a description of the technique or method you used to make the image;

- a description of changes in the lengths, angles, and area between the original picture and the image;

- a paragraph (or more) on other details that you think are interesting or that help the reader understand what they see (for example, a description of any problems or challenges you had and decisions you made as a result).

The Problems in this Unit helped you understand the concept of similarity as it applies to geometric shapes. You learned how to

- make similar shapes or scale drawings

- determine whether or not two shapes are similar

- relate side lengths, perimeters, angle measures, and areas of similar shapes to each other

- use similarity to solve problems

Use Your Understanding: Similarity

Test your understanding of similarity by solving the following problems.

1. The square below is subdivided into triangles and parallelograms. Some of the shapes are similar.

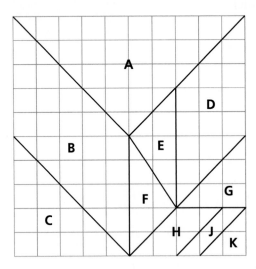

a. List all the pairs of similar triangles in the figure. For each pair, give the scale factor from one figure to the other.

b. Pick a pair of similar triangles. Explain how their perimeters are related and how their areas are related.

c. List several pairs of triangles in the figure that are *not* similar.

d. List all pairs of similar parallelograms in the figure. For each pair, give the scale factor from one figure to the other.

e. Pick a pair of similar parallelograms. Explain how their perimeters are related and how their areas are related.

f. List several pairs of parallelograms in the figure that are *not* similar.

2. a. Suppose a triangle is drawn on a coordinate grid. Which of the following rules will change the triangle into a similar triangle?

i. $(3x, 3y)$ **ii.** $(x + 3, y + 2)$

iii. $(2x, 4y)$ **iv.** $(2x, 2y + 1)$

v. $(1.5x, 1.5y)$ **vi.** $(x - 3, 2y - 3)$

b. For each of the rules in part (a) that will produce a similar triangle, give the scale factor from the original triangle to its image.

3. A photo of the after-school pottery class measures 12 centimeters by 20 centimeters. The class officers want to enlarge the photo to fit on a large poster.

a. Can the original photo be enlarged to 60 centimeters by 90 centimeters?

b. Can the original photo be enlarged to 42 centimeters by 70 centimeters?

12 cm

20 cm

Explain Your Reasoning

Answer the following questions to summarize what you know.

4. What questions do you ask yourself when deciding whether two shapes are similar?

5. Suppose Shape A is similar to Shape B. The scale factor from Shape A to Shape B is k.
   a. How are the perimeters of the two figures related?
   b. How are the areas of the two figures related?

6. If two triangles are similar, what do you know about the following measurements?
   a. the side lengths of the two figures
   b. the angle measures of the two figures

7. Tell whether each statement is true or false. Explain.
   a. Any two equilateral triangles are similar.
   b. Any two rectangles are similar.
   c. Any two squares are similar.
   d. Any two isosceles triangles are similar.

English / Spanish Glossary

A adjacent sides Two sides that meet at a vertex. In this rectangle, sides *AB* and *AD* are adjacent because they meet at vertex A.

lados adyacentes Son dos lados que coinciden en un vértice. En este rectángulo, los lados *AB* y *AD* son adyacentes porque coinciden en el vértice *A*.

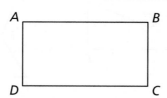

....

C compare Academic Vocabulary To tell or show how two things are alike and different.

related terms *analyze, relate, resemble*

sample: Compare the ratios of each of the corresponding side lengths for the similar triangles shown below.

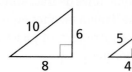

> The ratios of the corresponding side lengths of two triangles are $\frac{3}{6}$, $\frac{4}{8}$, and $\frac{5}{10}$. Each of these ratios equals $\frac{1}{2}$, so all of the ratios of the corresponding side lengths are equal.

comparar Vocabulario académico Decir o mostrar en qué se parecen y en qué se diferencian dos cosas.

términos relacionados *analizar, relacionar, parecerse*

ejemplo: Compara las razones de las longitudes de lado correspondientes para los triángulos que se muestran.

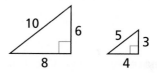

> Las razones de las langitudes de lado correspondientes de dos triángulos son $\frac{3}{6}$, $\frac{4}{8}$ y $\frac{5}{10}$. Cada una de estas razones es igual a $\frac{1}{2}$, por lo tanto todas las razones de las longitudes de lado correspondientes son iguales.

corresponding angles Corresponding angles have the same relative position in similar figures. In this pair of similar shapes, angle *BCD* corresponds to angle *JKF*.

ángulos correspondientes Los ángulos correspondientes tienen la misma posición relativa en figuras semejantes. En el siguiente par de figuras semejantes, el ángulo *BCD* corresponde al ángulo *JKF*.

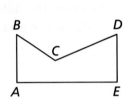
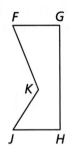

corresponding sides Corresponding sides have the same relative position in similar figures. In the pair of similar shapes above, side *AB* corresponds to side *HJ*.

lados correspondientes Los lados correspondientes tienen la misma posición relativa en figuras semejantes. En las dos figuras semejantes que se muestran abajo, el lado *AB* corresponde al lado *HJ*.

E **equivalent ratios** Ratios whose fraction representations are equivalent are called equivalent ratios. For instance, the ratios 3 to 4 and 6 to 8 are equivalent because $\frac{3}{4} = \frac{6}{8}$.

razones equivalentes Las razones cuyas representaciones de fracciones son equivalentes se llaman razones equivalentes. Por ejemplo, las razones 3 a 4 y 6 a 8 son equivalentes porque $\frac{3}{4} = \frac{6}{8}$.

estimate Academic Vocabulary To find an approximate answer that is relatively close to an exact amount.

related terms *approximate, guess*

sample: Estimate the scale factor for the similar rectangles shown below.

hacer una estimación Vocabulario académico Hallar una respuesta aproximada que esté relativamente cerca de una cantidad exacta.

términos relacionados *aproximar, suponer*

ejemplo: Estima el factor de escala para los rectángulos semejantes que se muestran.

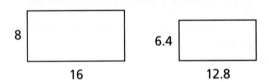

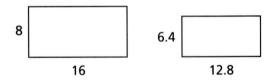

The side length 6.4 in the smaller rectangle corresponds to the side length 8 in the larger rectangle. Since 6.4 is about $\frac{3}{4}$ of 8, the scale factor is about $\frac{3}{4}$.

La longitud de lado 6.4 del rectángulo más pequeño corresponde a la longitud de lado 8 en el rectángulo más grande. Como 6.4 es aproximadamente $\frac{3}{4}$ de 8. El factor de escala es aproximadamente $\frac{3}{4}$.

explain Academic Vocabulary To give facts and details that make an idea easier to understand. Explaining can involve a written summary supported by a diagram, chart, table, or any combination of these.

related terms *describe, show, justify, tell, present*

sample: Consider the following similar rectangles. Is it possible to find the missing value *x*? Explain.

explicar Vocabulario académico Proporcionar datos y detalles que hagan que una idea sea más fácil de comprender. Explicar puede incluir un resumen escrito apoyado por un diagrama, una gráfica, una tabla o una combinación de estos.

términos relacionados *describir, mostrar, justificar, decir, presentar*

ejemplo: Observa los siguientes rectángulos semejantes. ¿Se puede hallar el valor de x? Explica tu respuesta.

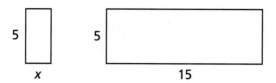

Since I know the two rectangles are similar, I can find the scale factor. Once I know the scale factor, I can divide the side length of the larger rectangle that corresponds to the missing side length *x* by the scale factor. This will give me the value of *x*.
I can also find the value of *x* by writing a proportion using the scale factor as one of the ratios, $\frac{x}{5} = \frac{5}{15}$, and then solve for *x*.

Como sé que los dos rectángulos son semejantes, puedo hallar el factor de escala. Una vez que sepa el factor de escala, puedo dividir la longitud de lado del rectángulo más grande, que corresponde a la longitud de lado x, por el factor de escala. Eso me dará el valor de x.
También puedo hallar el valor de x al escribir una proporción usando el factor escala como una de las razones, $\frac{x}{5} = \frac{5}{15}$, y después resolver para x.

image The figure that results from some transformation of a figure. It is often of interest to consider what is the same and what is different about a figure and its image.

imagen La figura que resulta al realizar la transformación de una figura. A menudo es interesante tener en cuenta en qué se parecen y en qué se diferencian una figura y su imagen.

M **midpoint** A point that divides a line segment into two segments of equal length. In the figure below *M* is the midpoint of the segment *LN*.

punto medio Punto que divide un segmento de recta en dos segmentos de igual longitud. En la figura de abajo, *M* es el punto medio del segmento de recta *LN*.

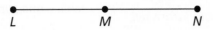

N **nested triangles** Triangles that share a common angle are sometimes called nested. In the figure below, triangle *ABC* is nested in triangle *ADE*.

triángulos semejantes Los triángulos que comparten un ángulo común a veces se llaman *semejantes*. En la siguiente figura, el triángulo *ABC* es semejante al triángulo *ADE*.

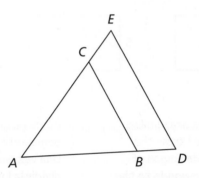

P **proportion** An equation stating that two ratios are equal.

proporción Una ecuación que enuncia que dos razones son iguales.

R **ratio** A ratio is a comparison of two quantities. It is sometimes expressed as a fraction. For example, suppose the length AB is 2 inches and the length *CD* is 3 inches. The ratio of the length of side *AB* to the length of side *CD* is 2 to 3, or $\frac{2}{3}$. The ratio of the length of side *CD* to the length of side *AB* is 3 to 2, or $\frac{3}{2}$.

razón La razón es una comparación de dos cantidades. A veces se expresa como una fracción. Por ejemplo, supón que la longitud de *AB* es 2 pulgadas y la longitud de *CD* es 3 pulgadas. La razón de la longitud del lado *AB* a la longitud del lado *CD* es de 2 a 3, es decir, $\frac{2}{3}$. La razón de la longitud del lado CD a la longitud del lado *AB* es 3 a 2, es decir, $\frac{3}{2}$.

relate Academic Vocabulary To have a connection or impact on something else.

related terms *connect, correlate*

sample: Find the area of the similar triangles below. Relate the area of triangle A to the area of triangle B.

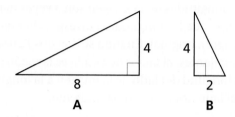

The area of triangle A is $\frac{1}{2}(4)(8) = 16$. The area of triangle B is $\frac{1}{2}(2)(4) = 4$. The area of triangle A is 4 times the area of triangle B.

relacionar Vocabulario académico Tener una conexión o un impacto en algo.

términos relacionados *conectar, correlacionar*

ejemplo: Halla el área de los triángulos semejantes de abajo. Relaciona el área del triángulo A con el área del triángulo B.

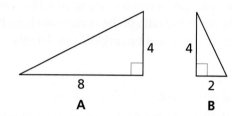

El área del triángulo A es $\frac{1}{2}(4)(8) = 16$. El área del triángulo B es $\frac{1}{2}(2)(4) = 4$. El área del triángulo A es 4 veces el área del triángulo B.

rep-tile A figure you can use to make a larger, similar version of the original is called a rep-tile. The smaller figure below is a rep-tile because you can use four copies of it to make a larger similar figure.

baldosa autosimilar Una figura que puedes usar para hacer una version más grande y semejante a la original, se llama baldosa autosimilar. La figura más pequeña de abajo es una baldosa autosimilar porque se pueden usar cuatro copias de ella para hacer una figura semejante más grande.

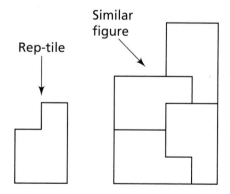

scale drawing An image of a figure that is similar to the original.

dibujo a escala La imagen de una figura que es semejante a la figura original.

scale factor The number used to multiply the lengths of a figure to stretch or shrink it to a similar image. If we use a scale factor of 3, all lengths in the image are 3 times as long as the corresponding lengths in the original. When you are given two similar figures, the scale factor is the ratio of the image side length to the corresponding original side length.

factor de escala El número utilizado para multiplicar las longitudes de una figura para ampliarla o reducirla a una imagen semejante. Si el factor de escala es 3, todas las longitudes de la imagen son 3 veces más largas que las longitudes correspondientes de la figura original. Cuando se dan dos figuras semejantes, el factor de escala es la razón de la longitud del lado de la imagen a la longitud del lado original correspondiente.

similar Similar figures have corresponding angles of equal measure and the ratios of each pair of corresponding sides are equivalent.

semejante Las figuras semejantes tienen ángulos correspondientes de igual medida y las razones de cada par de lados correspondientes son equivalentes.

Index

Acknowledgments

Cover Design

Three Communication Design, Chicago

Photographs

Photo locators denoted as follows: Top (T), Center (C), Bottom (B), Left (L), Right (R), Background (Bkgd)

003 Mirek Weichsel/Glow Images; **007** Martin Heitner/Purestock/SuperStock; **010** Pearson Education, Inc.; **021** Bob Daemmrich/Alamy; **025** Tetra Images/ Alamy; **027** Pearson Education, Inc.; **033** Nikreates/Alamy; **053** AFP/Getty Images/Newscom; **080** Pearson Education, Inc.; **081** Pearson Education, Inc.; **083** Nikreates/Alamy; **089** Christian Carollo/Shutterstock; **093** Gary Blakeley/ Fotolia; **100** Izzet Keribar/Lonely planet Images/Getty Images; **102** Kevin Radford/Superstock; **109** Ableimages/Digital Vision/Thinkstock.

Comparing and Scaling

Ratios, Rates, Percents, and Proportions

Lappan, Phillips, Fey, Friel

Ratios, Rates, Percents, and Proportions

Markups, Markdowns, and Measures: Using Ratios, Percents, and Proportions   62

Looking Ahead

More for Your Money has pasta on sale at 7 boxes for $6. FreshFoods sells the same pasta at 6 boxes for $5. **Which** is the better deal?

A dealer's buying price on a used car is marked up by 15% to the selling price for customers. Suppose that the selling price is later marked down by 15%. **How** can you determine whether the new selling price is the same as the dealer's buying price?

Ming's job is to take care of chimps at the zoo. She has a mix of 20 scoops of high-fiber food and 30 scoops of high-protein food. **How** can she adjust this to make the mix 60% high fiber and 40% high protein?

Many everyday problems and decisions call for comparisons. *Which runner is faster? Which Internet service is cheaper? Which cranberry bog yields the most berries?* In some cases, the comparisons involve only counting, measuring, or rating, and then ordering the results from least to greatest. In other cases, more complex reasoning is required. All of the questions on the previous page involve comparisons. In this Unit you will explore many ways to compare numbers and to analyze comparisons. You will learn both how to choose and how to use comparison strategies for solving problems and making decisions.

Mathematical Highlights

Comparing and Scaling

In this Unit, you will extend your knowledge of ratios, proportions, and proportional reasoning. You will learn how to:

- Analyze comparison statements for correctness and quality;

- Use ratios, rates, and percents to write comparison statements;

- Distinguish between and use part-to-part and part-to-whole ratios to make comparisons;

- Scale a ratio, rate, or percent to solve a problem;

- Set up and solve proportions;

- Find unit rates and use them to solve problems;

- Recognize proportional situations from a table, graph, or equation;

- Connect a unit rate and a constant of proportionality to a table, graph, or equation representing a situation.

As you work on the Problems in this Unit, ask yourself these questions about situations that involve comparisons.

What quantities are being compared?

Why does the situation involve a proportional relationship (or not)?

How might ratios, rates, or a proportion be used to solve the problem?

Mathematical Practices and Habits of Mind

In the *Connected Mathematics* curriculum you will develop an understanding of important mathematical ideas by solving problems and reflecting on the mathematics involved. Every day, you will use "habits of mind" to make sense of problems and apply what you learn to new situations. Some of these habits are described by the *Common Core State Standards for Mathematical Practices* (MP).

MP1 Make sense of problems and persevere in solving them.

When using mathematics to solve a problem, it helps to think carefully about

- data and other facts you are given and what additional information you need to solve the problem;
- strategies you have used to solve similar problems and whether you could solve a related simpler problem first;
- how you could express the problem with equations, diagrams, or graphs;
- whether your answer makes sense.

MP2 Reason abstractly and quantitatively.

When you are asked to solve a problem, it often helps to

- focus first on the key mathematical ideas;
- check that your answer makes sense in the problem setting;
- use what you know about the problem setting to guide your mathematical reasoning.

MP3 Construct viable arguments and critique the reasoning of others.

When you are asked to explain why a conjecture is correct, you can

- show some examples that fit the claim and explain why they fit;
- show how a new result follows logically from known facts and principles.

When you believe a mathematical claim is incorrect, you can

- show one or more counterexamples—cases that don't fit the claim;
- find steps in the argument that do not follow logically from prior claims.

MP4 Model with mathematics.

When you are asked to solve problems, it often helps to

- think carefully about the numbers or geometric shapes that are the most important factors in the problem, then ask yourself how those factors are related to each other;
- express data and relationships in the problem with tables, graphs, diagrams, or equations, and check your result to see if it makes sense.

MP5 Use appropriate tools strategically.

When working on mathematical questions, you should always

- decide which tools are most helpful for solving the problem and why;
- try a different tool when you get stuck.

MP6 Attend to precision.

In every mathematical exploration or problem-solving task, it is important to

- think carefully about the required accuracy of results; is a number estimate or geometric sketch good enough, or is a precise value or drawing needed?
- report your discoveries with clear and correct mathematical language that can be understood by those to whom you are speaking or writing.

MP7 Look for and make use of structure.

In mathematical explorations and problem solving, it is often helpful to

- look for patterns that show how data points, numbers, or geometric shapes are related to each other;
- use patterns to make predictions.

MP8 Look for and express regularity in repeated reasoning.

When results of a repeated calculation show a pattern, it helps to

- express that pattern as a general rule that can be used in similar cases;
- look for shortcuts that will make the calculation simpler in other cases.

You will use all of the Mathematical Practices in this Unit. Sometimes, when you look at a Problem, it is obvious which practice is most helpful. At other times, you will decide on a practice to use during class explorations and discussions. After completing each Problem, ask yourself:

- What mathematics have I learned by solving this Problem?
- What Mathematical Practices were helpful in learning this mathematics?

Ways of Comparing: Ratios and Proportions

Surveys are used to determine people's preferences for many things. You may have seen surveys about food, cars, consumer products, or political candidates. From survey results, it can be easy to determine popular choices. Explaining how much more popular one choice is than another may not be as easy. In this Investigation, you will explore strategies for comparing numbers in accurate and useful ways.

1.1 Surveying Opinions
Analyzing Comparison Statements

Companies that sell soft drinks often report survey results about customers' preferences.

Common Core State Standards

7.RP.A.3 Use proportional relationships to solve multistep ratio and percent problems.

7.RP.A.2 Recognize and represent proportional relationships between quantities.

7.EE.B.4 Use variables to represent quantities in a real-world or a mathematical problem and construct simple equations and inequalities to solve problems by reasoning about quantities.

Also 7.RP.A.2a and 7.RP.A.2c, essential for 7.RP.A.1 and 7.RP.A.2b

The Marketing Club at Neilson Middle School is studying surveys and other marketing strategies. One of the surveys is about people's preferences for two different kinds of cola. Club members have various opinions about ways to report the results from the cola taste test.

Problem 1.1

Here are four statements about the cola taste-test results.

> 1. In a taste test, people who preferred Bolda Cola outnumbered those who preferred Cola-Nola by a ratio of 17,139 to 11,426.
>
> 2. In a taste test, 5,713 more people preferred Bolda Cola.
>
> 3. In a taste test, 60% of the people preferred Bolda Cola.
>
> 4. In a taste test, people who preferred Bolda Cola outnumbered those who preferred Cola-Nola by a ratio of 3 to 2.

A **1.** Describe what you think each statement above means.

2. Which of the above statements do you think would be best in an advertisement for Bolda Cola? Why?

3. Is it possible that all four statements are based on the same survey data? Explain your reasoning.

4. In what other ways could you express the claims in the four statements? Explain your reasoning.

5. Suppose you surveyed 1,000 cola drinkers. What numbers of Bolda Cola and Cola-Nola drinkers would you expect? Explain your reasoning.

Problem **1.1** *continued*

B Students at Neilson Middle School are planning an end-of-year event. Of the 150 students in the school, 100 would like an athletic event and 50 would like a concert. Decide whether each statement below accurately reports the results of the Neilson Middle School survey.

  1. At Neilson Middle School, $\frac{1}{3}$ of the students prefer a concert to an athletic event.

  2. Students prefer an athletic event to a concert by a ratio of 2 to 1.

  3. The **ratio** of students who prefer a concert to students who prefer an athletic event is 1 to 2.

  4. The number of students who prefer an athletic event is 50 more than the number who prefer a concert.

  5. The number of students who prefer an athletic event is two times the number who prefer a concert.

  6. At Neilson Middle School, 50% of the students prefer a concert to an athletic event.

C **1.** Study each correct comparison statement from Question B. What information does each statement give you about the situation? What information is left out?

  2. Use the Neilson Middle School survey results above. Suppose you consider a sample of students at a larger school. How might you predict the number of students who prefer an athletic event to a concert?

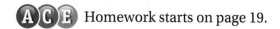 Homework starts on page 19.

1.2 Mixing Juice
Comparing Ratios

Every year, the Grade 7 students at Langston Hughes School go on an outdoor education camping trip. During the week-long trip, the students study nature and participate in recreational activities. Everyone pitches in to help with the cooking and cleanup.

This year, Arvin and Mariah were in charge of making orange juice for the campers. They planned to make the juice by mixing water and frozen orange juice concentrate. To find the mix that would taste best, they decided to test some mixes.

Mix A

| 2 cups concentrate | 3 cups cold water |

Mix B

| 5 cups concentrate | 9 cups cold water |

Mix C

| 1 cup concentrate | 2 cups cold water |

Mix D

| 3 cups concentrate | 5 cups cold water |

 Which mix will make juice that is the most "orangey?" Explain.

Problem 1.2

A 1. Which mix will make juice that is the most "orangey"? Explain your reasoning.

2. Which mix will make juice that is the least "orangey"? Explain your reasoning.

B 1. Isabelle and Doug used fractions to express their reasoning.

> Isabelle:
>
> $\frac{5}{9}$ of Mix B is concentrate.

> Doug:
>
> $\frac{5}{14}$ of Mix B is concentrate.

Do you agree with either of them? Explain.

2. Max thinks that Mix A and Mix C are the same. Max says "They are both the most 'orangey' since the difference between the number of cups of water and the number of cups of concentrate is 1." Is Max's thinking correct? Explain.

C Assume that each camper will get $\frac{1}{2}$ cup of juice. Answer Questions (1) and (2) below for *each* of the four recipes.

1. How many batches are needed to make juice for 240 campers?

2. How much concentrate and how much water are needed to make juice for 240 campers?

D For each recipe, how much concentrate is needed to make 1 cup of juice? How much water is needed?

A C E Homework starts on page 19.

1.3 Time to Concentrate
Scaling Ratios

In Problem 1.2, you may have used the ratios below to determine which recipe was the most "orangey." Below are two ratios describing Mix A.

two cups of concentrate
to
three cups of water

$2:3$ or $\frac{2}{3}$

OR

two cups of concentrate
to
five cups of juice

$2:5$ or $\frac{2}{5}$

The first ratio is a **part-to-part ratio.** It compares one part (the water) of the whole (the juice) to the other part (the concentrate). The second ratio is a **part-to-whole ratio.** It compares one part (the concentrate) to the whole (the juice).

For Mix B, you can write the part-to-part ratio as 5 cups concentrate to 9 cups water, or $5:9$, or $\frac{5}{9}$. You can write the part-to-whole ratio as 5 cups concentrate to 14 cups juice, or $5:14$, or $\frac{5}{14}$.

Scaling ratios was one of the comparison strategies Sam used in Problem 1.2. He wrote

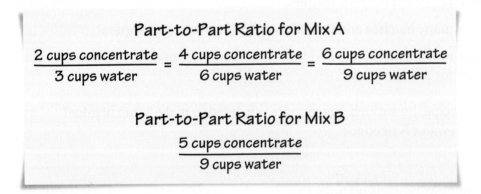

Part-to-Part Ratio for Mix A

$$\frac{2 \text{ cups concentrate}}{3 \text{ cups water}} = \frac{4 \text{ cups concentrate}}{6 \text{ cups water}} = \frac{6 \text{ cups concentrate}}{9 \text{ cups water}}$$

Part-to-Part Ratio for Mix B

$$\frac{5 \text{ cups concentrate}}{9 \text{ cups water}}$$

- How could Sam use these ratios to compare the Mix A and Mix B recipes?

In the next Problem you will look at several more mixes for orange juice and lemonade.

Problem 1.3

A A typical can of orange juice concentrate holds 12 fluid ounces. The standard recipe is shown below.

Mix one can of concentrate
with three cans of cold water.

How large a pitcher will you need to hold the juice made from a typical can? Show or explain how you arrived at your answer.

B A typical can of lemonade concentrate holds 12 fluid ounces. The standard recipe is shown below.

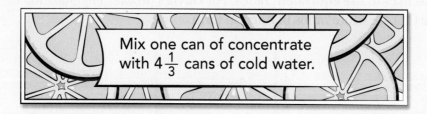

Mix one can of concentrate
with $4\frac{1}{3}$ cans of cold water.

1. How large a pitcher will you need to hold the lemonade from a typical can? Show or explain how you arrived at your answer.

2. The pitchers below hold $\frac{1}{2}$ gallon, 60 ounces, and 1 gallon. Which container should you use for the lemonade from one can? Explain your reasoning.
   Note: 1 gallon = 128 ounces

continued on the next page >

Problem 1.3 *continued*

C Solve these mixing problems.

1. a. Cece is making orange juice using one 16-ounce can of concentrate. She is using the standard ratio of one can of concentrate to three cans of cold water. How large a pitcher will she need?

b. Olivia has a one-gallon pitcher to fill with orange juice. She uses the standard ratio of one can of concentrate to three cans of cold water. How much concentrate does she need?

2. August has some leftover cans of lemonade concentrate in his freezer. He uses $1\frac{1}{2}$ ten-ounce cans of concentrate and the standard ratio of one can of concentrate to $4\frac{1}{3}$ cans of cold water. How large a pitcher does he need?

D Otis likes to use equivalent ratios. For Olivia's problem in Question C, part (1), he wrote ratios in fraction form:

$$\frac{1}{4} = \frac{x}{128}$$

1. What do the numbers 1, 4, and 128 mean in each ratio? What does *x* mean in this *equation*?

2. How can Otis find the correct value of *x*?

A C E Homework starts on page 19.

1.4 Keeping Things in Proportion
Scaling to Solve Proportions

In Problem 1.3 you used ratios and scaling to solve problems. When you write two equivalent ratios in fraction form and set them equal to each other, you form a **proportion.**

Otis's strategy for solving a problem involving a ratio of orange concentrate to juice was to write this proportion:

$$\frac{1}{4} = \frac{x}{128}$$

- Would it have made sense for Otis to write $\frac{1}{x} = \frac{4}{128}$?

- What are some other ways Otis might have written a proportion?

- Otis solved the proportion $\frac{1}{4} = \frac{x}{128}$ by scaling up. He wrote $\frac{1 \cdot 32}{4 \cdot 32} = \frac{x}{128}$.

- How did he know to scale up by $\frac{32}{32}$?

In *Stretching and Shrinking,* you worked with ratios to find missing lengths in similar figures. There are many other situations in which setting up a proportion can help you solve a problem. For example, suppose that among American doctors men outnumber women by a ratio of 12 to 5.

- If about 600,000 American doctors are men, how can you figure out how many are women?

There are four ways to write this as a proportion.

Write the known ratio of men to women doctors. Complete the proportion with the ratio of actual numbers of doctors.

$$\frac{12 \text{ men}}{5 \text{ women}} = \frac{600{,}000 \text{ men}}{x \text{ women}}$$

Write a ratio of men to men data. Complete the proportion with women to women data.

$$\frac{12 \text{ men}}{600{,}000 \text{ men}} = \frac{5 \text{ women}}{x \text{ women}}$$

Write the known ratio of women to men doctors. Complete the proportion with the ratio of actual numbers of doctors.

$$\frac{5 \text{ women}}{12 \text{ men}} = \frac{x \text{ women}}{600{,}000 \text{ men}}$$

Write a different ratio of men to men data. Complete the proportion with women to women data.

$$\frac{600{,}000 \text{ men}}{12 \text{ men}} = \frac{x \text{ women}}{5 \text{ women}}$$

Using what you know about equivalent ratios, you can find the number of women doctors from any one of these proportions. Finding the missing value in a proportion is called *solving the proportion*.

- Does one of the proportions seem easier to solve than the others?

- How many women doctors are there?

Problem 1.4

For each question, set up a proportion that shows the relationship between known and unknown quantities. Then use equivalent fractions, ratios, and scaling to solve each proportion.

A Imani gives vitamins to her dogs. The recommended dosage is 1 teaspoon per day for adult dogs weighing 10 pounds. She needs to give vitamins to Bruiser, who weighs 80 pounds and to Dust Ball, who weighs 7 pounds. What is the correct dosage for each dog?

B **1.** Jogging 5 miles burns about 500 Calories. How many miles does Tanisha need to jog to burn off the 1,200-Calorie lunch she ate?

 2. Tanisha jogs about 8 miles in 2 hours. How long will it take her to jog 12 miles?

C The triangles in this picture are similar. Find the height of the tree.

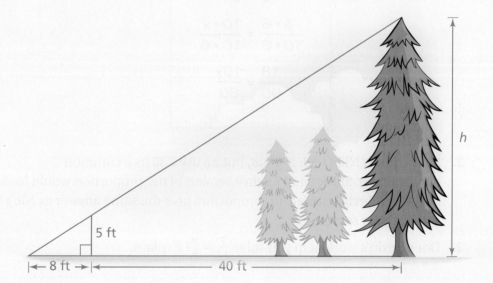

continued on the next page >

Problem 1.4 continued

D Solve these proportions for the variable x. Use the reasoning you applied in Questions A through C.

1. $\frac{8}{5} = \frac{32}{x}$ 2. $\frac{7}{12} = \frac{x}{9}$ 3. $25 : x = 5 : 7$

4. $\frac{x}{3} = \frac{8}{9}$ 5. $\frac{x}{5} = \frac{120}{3}$ 6. $x : 6 = 10 : 150$

E 1. Nic was working on the proportion below.

$$\frac{3}{10} = \frac{x}{6}$$

He could not see a way to scale 10 to make 6. Instead, he scaled both sides of the proportion. His work is shown below. How could Nic complete his solution?

$$\frac{3}{10} = \frac{x}{6}$$

$$\frac{3 \cdot 6}{10 \cdot 6} = \frac{10 \cdot x}{10 \cdot 6}$$

$$\frac{18}{60} = \frac{10x}{60}$$

2. Kevin thinks Nic's idea is great, but he used 30 as a common denominator. Show what Kevin's version of the proportion would look like. Does Kevin's scaled-up proportion give the same answer as Nic's? Explain your reasoning.

3. Does Kevin's work help you solve $\frac{7}{12} = \frac{x}{9}$? Explain.

A C E Homework starts on page 19.

Applications

1. In a comparison taste test of two juice drinks, 780 people preferred Cranberry Blast. Only 220 people preferred Melon Splash. Complete each statement.

   a. There were ■ more people who preferred Cranberry Blast.

   b. In the taste test, ■% of the people preferred Cranberry Blast.

   c. People who preferred Cranberry Blast outnumbered those who preferred Melon Splash by a ratio of ■ to ■.

2. In a taste test of new ice creams invented at Moo University, 750 freshmen preferred Cranberry Bog ice cream, while 1,250 freshmen preferred Coconut Orange ice cream. Complete each statement.

   a. The fraction of freshmen who preferred Cranberry Bog is ■.

   b. The percent of freshmen who preferred Coconut Orange is ■%.

   c. The ratio of freshmen preferring Coconut Orange to those who preferred Cranberry Bog was ■ to ■.

3. A town is debating whether to put in curbs along the streets. The ratio of town residents who support putting in curbs to those who oppose it is 2 to 5.

   a. What fraction of the residents oppose putting in curbs?

   b. If 210 people in the town are surveyed, how many do you expect to favor putting in curbs?

   c. What percent of the residents oppose putting in curbs?

Students at a middle school are asked to record how they spend their time from midnight on Friday to midnight on Sunday. Carlos records his data on his phone. Use his phone screen for Exercises 4–7.

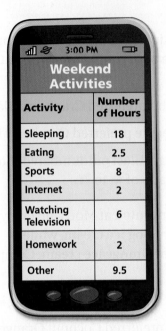

3:00 PM

Weekend Activities

Activity	Number of Hours
Sleeping	18
Eating	2.5
Sports	8
Internet	2
Watching Television	6
Homework	2
Other	9.5

4. How would you compare the way Carlos spent his time on various activities over the weekend?

5. Decide whether each statement is an accurate description of how Carlos spent his time that weekend. Explain your reasoning.

  a. Carlos spent one-sixth of his time watching television.

  b. The ratio of hours spent watching television to hours spent doing chores or homework was 3 to 1.

  c. Sports, Internet, and watching television took about 33% of his time.

  d. Time spent doing homework was only 20% of the time spent watching television.

  e. Sleeping, eating, and "other" activities took up 12 hours more than all other activities combined.

6. Estimate the numbers of hours that would be in your weekend activity table. Then write a ratio statement such as the one in Exercise 5, part (b), to fit your data.

7. Use each concept below at least once. Write statements to compare the weekend time Carlos spent on his various activities.

   a. ratio   **b.** difference

   c. fraction   **d.** percent

8. A class at Middlebury Middle School collected data on the types of movies students prefer. Complete each statement using the table.

   Types of Movies Preferred by Middlebury Students

Type of Movie	7th Grade	8th Grade
Action	75	90
Comedy	105	150
Total	180	240

   a. The ratio of seventh-graders who prefer comedies to eighth-graders who prefer comedies is ▣ to ▣.

   b. The fraction of total students (both seventh- and eighth-graders) who prefer action movies is ▣.

   c. The fraction of seventh-graders who prefer action movies is ▣.

   d. The percent of total students who prefer comedies is ▣.

   e. The percent of eighth-graders who prefer action movies is ▣.

   f. Grade ▣ has the greater percent of students who prefer action movies.

9. In a survey, 100 students were asked whether they prefer watching television or listening to the radio. The results show that 60 students prefer watching television while 40 prefer listening to the radio. Use each concept at least once to express the student preferences.

   a. ratio   **b.** percent

   c. fraction   **d.** difference

10. Compare these four mixes for apple juice.

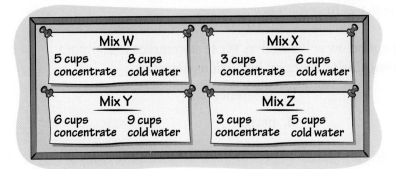

Mix W	
5 cups concentrate	8 cups cold water

Mix X	
3 cups concentrate	6 cups cold water

Mix Y	
6 cups concentrate	9 cups cold water

Mix Z	
3 cups concentrate	5 cups cold water

   a. Which mix would make the most "appley" juice? Explain your reasoning.

   b. Suppose you make a single batch of each mix. What fraction of each batch is concentrate?

   c. Rewrite your answers to part (b) as percents.

   d. Suppose you make only 1 cup of Mix W. How much water and how much concentrate do you need?

11. Examine these statements about the apple juice mixes in Exercise 10. Decide whether each is accurate. Give reasons for your answers.

   a. Mix Y has the most water per batch, so it will taste the least "appley."

   b. Mix Z is the most "appley" because the difference between the concentrate and water is 2 cups. It is 3 cups for each of the others.

   c. Mix Y is the most "appley" because it has only $1\frac{1}{2}$ cups of water for each cup of concentrate. The others have more water per cup.

   d. Mix X and Mix Y taste the same because you just add 3 cups of concentrate and 3 cups of water to turn Mix X into Mix Y.

12. If possible, write each comparison of concentrate to water as a ratio. If not possible, explain why.

   a. The mix is 60% concentrate.

   b. The fraction of the mix that is water is $\frac{3}{5}$.

   c. The difference between the amount of concentrate and water is 4 cups.

A can of concentrated grapefruit juice includes the instructions "Mix one can of concentrate with 4 cans of cold water." For Exercises 13–16, use these mixing instructions.

13. Write a ratio for each situation. Then decide whether the situation is part-to-part or part-to-whole.

　a. water to concentrate

　b. concentrate to juice

　c. water to juice

14. Determine which of the situations described in Exercise 13 can be represented by the following ratios. Explain your reasoning.

　a. $\frac{12}{60}$　　　**b.** $\frac{3}{12}$　　　**c.** $\frac{2}{2\frac{1}{2}}$　　　**d.** $\frac{5}{10}$

15. Orlando and Tanya are experimenting with different mix ratios. Determine whether each mix below will result in a more concentrated (more "grapefruity") or a less concentrated (less "grapefruity") mix than the original mix instructions.

Mix A	Mix B
3 cans concentrate : 15 cans water	3 cans concentrate : 15 cans juice

Mix C	Mix D
10 cans cold water : 7 cans concentrate	$\frac{1}{4}$ can concentrate : $1\frac{1}{2}$ cans water

16. Jonathan and Samantha are making grapefruit juice from concentrate for a carnival. Jonathan mixes 10 cans of concentrate with 40 cans of water. Samantha mixes 8 cans of concentrate with 32 cans of water. Their teacher asks them to combine the two mixes into one large container.

Determine whether their new mixture will be less grapefruity, more grapefruity, or the same as the recipe on the can of concentrate. Explain your reasoning.

A can of concentrated grapefruit juice includes the instructions "Mix one can of concentrate with 4 cans of cold water." For Exercises 17 and 18, use these mixing instructions.

17. Find the missing value in each situation. State the scale factor you used.

   a. 24 cans concentrate : ▓ cans water   **b.** 24 cans concentrate : ▓ cans juice

   c. 24 cans juice : ▓ cans water   **d.** 24 cans juice : ▓ cans concentrate

18. Raina, Amelia, and Krista wanted to find the number of cans of concentrate they would need if they used 128 cans of water. They knew the problem they were trying to solve was $\frac{1}{4} = \frac{x}{128}$. Which of the following strategies would work? Explain.

Raina's Strategy

I was looking for $\frac{1}{4}$ of 128. I took 128

and divided it by 4 to find the value of x.
x = 32

Amelia's Strategy

I wrote a series of equivalent fractions
by doubling the numerator and denominator.

$\frac{1}{4} = \frac{2}{8} = \frac{4}{16} = \frac{8}{32} = \frac{16}{64} = \frac{32}{128}$ so x = 32

Krista's Strategy

I factored the denominator of the right
side of the equation to determine x.

$\frac{1}{4} = \frac{x}{128} = \frac{1 \cdot 1 \cdot 2}{4 \cdot 4 \cdot 8}$ so x = 2

19. Jared and Pedro walk 1 mile in about 15 minutes. They can keep up this pace for several hours.

  a. About how far can they walk in 90 minutes?

  b. About how far can they walk in 65 minutes?

20. Swimming $\frac{1}{4}$ of a mile uses about the same number of Calories as running 1 mile.

  a. Gilda ran a 26-mile marathon. About how far would her sister have to swim to use the same number of Calories Gilda used during the marathon?

  b. Juan swims 5 miles a day. About how many miles would he have to run to use the same number of Calories used during his swim?

21. After testing many samples, an electric company determined that approximately 2 of every 1,000 light bulbs on the market are defective. Americans buy more than 1 billion light bulbs every year. Estimate how many of these bulbs are defective.

22. The organizers of an environmental conference order buttons for the participants. They pay $18 for 12 dozen buttons. Write and solve proportions to answer each question. Assume that price is proportional to the size of the order.

  a. How much do 4 dozen buttons cost?

  b. How much do 50 dozen buttons cost?

  c. How many dozens of buttons can the organizers buy for $27?

  d. How many dozens of buttons can the organizers buy for $63?

23. Denzel makes 10 of his first 15 shots in a basketball free-throw contest. His success rate stays about the same for his next 100 free throws. Write and solve a proportion for each part. Round your answer to the nearest whole number.

Free-Throw Contest Contest		
Player	Attempts	Baskets
Denzel	15	10
Mitchell	10	5
Rachael	15	7
Zoe	15	6

2:30 PM

a. About how many baskets do you expect Denzel to make in his next 60 attempts?

b. About how many free throws do you expect him to make in his next 80 attempts?

c. About how many attempts do you expect Denzel to take to make 30 free throws?

d. About how many attempts do you expect him to take to make 45 free throws?

For Exercises 24–31, solve each equation.

24. $12.5 = 0.8x$

25. $\frac{x}{15} = \frac{20}{30}$

26. $\frac{x}{18} = 4.5$

27. $\frac{15.8}{x} = 0.7$

28. $245 = 0.25x$

29. $\frac{18}{x} = \frac{4.5}{1}$

30. $\frac{0.1}{48} = \frac{x}{960}$

31. $\frac{x}{900} = \frac{3.5}{15}$

32. **Multiple Choice** Middletown sponsors a two-day conference for selected middle-school students to study government. There are three middle schools in Middletown.

Suppose 20 student delegates will attend the conference. Each school should be represented fairly in relation to its population. How many should be selected from each school?

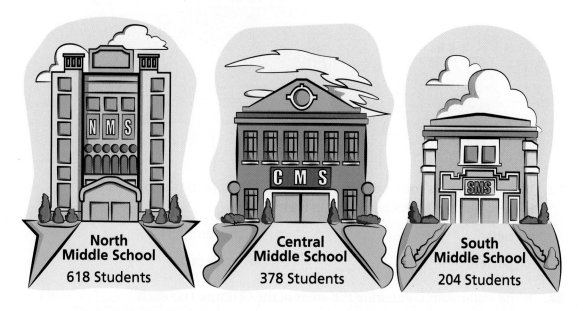

North
Middle School
618 Students

Central
Middle School
378 Students

South
Middle School
204 Students

A. North: 10 delegates, Central: 8 delegates, South: 2 delegates

B. North: 11 delegates, Central: 7 delegates, South: 2 delegates

C. North: 6 delegates, Central: 3 delegates, South: 2 delegates

D. North: 10 delegates, Central: 6 delegates, South: 4 delegates

Connections

The sketches below show two members of the Grump family. The Grumps are geometrically similar. Use the figures for Exercises 33–36.

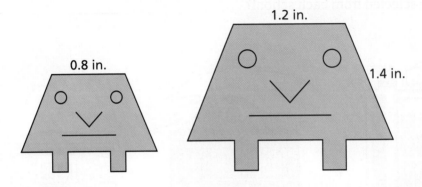

0.8 in.   1.2 in.   1.4 in.

33. Write statements comparing the lengths of corresponding segments in the Grumps. Use each concept at least once.

   a. ratio   **b.** fraction

   c. percent   **d.** scale factor

34. Write statements comparing the areas of the Grumps. Use each concept at least once.

   a. ratio   **b.** fraction

   c. percent   **d.** scale factor

35. How long is the segment in the smaller Grump that corresponds to the 1.4-inch segment in the larger Grump?

36. Multiple Choice The mouth of the smaller Grump is 0.6 inches wide. How wide is the mouth of the larger Grump?

   A. 0.4 in.   **B.** 0.9 in.

   C. 1 in.   **D.** 1.2 in.

37. Suppose a news story reports "A survey found that $\frac{4}{7}$ of all Americans watched the Super Bowl on television." Bishnu thinks this means the survey reached seven people and four of them watched the Super Bowl on television. Do you agree with him? If not, what does the statement mean?

38. A fruit bar is 5 inches long. The bar will be split into two pieces. For each situation, find the lengths of the two pieces.

   a. One piece is $\frac{3}{10}$ of the whole bar.

   b. One piece is 60% of the bar.

   c. One piece is 1 inch longer than the other.

39. Exercise 38 includes several numbers or quantities: 5 inches, 3, 10, 60%, and 1 inch. Determine whether each number or quantity refers to the whole, a part, or the difference between two parts.

40. If possible, change each comparison of red paint to white paint to a percent comparison. If it is not possible, explain why.

   a. The fraction of a mix that is red paint is $\frac{1}{4}$.

   b. The ratio of red to white paint in a different mix is 2 to 5.

41. If possible, change each comparison to a fraction comparison. If it is not possible, explain why.

   a. A nut mix is 30% peanuts.

   b. The ratio of almonds to other nuts in a mix is 1 to 7.

42. Find a value that makes each sentence correct.

   a. $\frac{3}{10} = \frac{\blacksquare}{30}$ **b.** $\frac{1}{2} < \frac{\blacksquare}{20}$

   c. $\frac{\blacksquare}{20} > \frac{3}{5}$ **d.** $\frac{9}{30} \leq \frac{\blacksquare}{15}$

   e. $\frac{\blacksquare}{12} \geq \frac{3}{4}$ **f.** $\frac{9}{21} = \frac{12}{\blacksquare}$

43. Use the table for parts (a)–(e).

Participation in Walking for Exercise

	Age 12–17	Age 55–64
People Who Walk	5,520,000	12,595,000
Total in Group	25,056,000	31,556,000

Source: *U.S. Census Bureau*

a. What percent of the 55–64 age group walk for exercise?

b. What percent of the 12–17 age group walk for exercise?

c. Write a ratio statement to compare the number of 12- to 17-year-olds who walk to the number of 55- to 64-year-olds who walk. Use approximate numbers to simplify the ratio.

d. Write a ratio statement to compare the percent of 12- to 17-year-olds who walk for exercise to the percent of 55- to 64-year-olds who walk for exercise.

e. Which form of data—numbers of walkers or percents—would you use to compare the popularity of walking for exercise among various groups? Explain.

44. Copy the number line below. Add labels for 0.25, $\frac{6}{8}$, $1\frac{3}{4}$, and 1.3.

45. Write two unequal fractions with different denominators. Which fraction is greater? Explain.

46. Write a fraction and a decimal such that the fraction is greater than the decimal. Explain.

Copy each pair of numbers in Exercises 47–55. Insert <, >, or = to
make a true statement.

47. $\frac{4}{5} \blacksquare \frac{11}{12}$

48. $\frac{14}{21} \blacksquare \frac{10}{15}$

49. $\frac{7}{9} \blacksquare \frac{3}{4}$

50. 2.5 $\blacksquare$ 0.259

51. 30.17 $\blacksquare$ 30.018

52. 0.006 $\blacksquare$ 0.0060

53. 0.45 $\blacksquare \frac{9}{20}$

54. $1\frac{3}{4} \blacksquare 1.5$

55. $\frac{1}{4} \blacksquare 1.3$

56. Suppose a news story reports "90% of the people in the Super Bowl
stadium were between the ages of 25 and 55." Alicia thinks this
means only 100 people were in the stadium, and 90 of them were
between 25 and 55 years of age. Do you agree with her? If not, what
does the statement mean?

57. Multiple Choice Choose the value that makes $\frac{18}{32} = \frac{\blacksquare}{16}$ correct.

F. 7

G. 8

H. 9

J. 10

58. Multiple Choice Choose the value that makes $\frac{\blacksquare}{30} \leq \frac{6}{20}$ correct.

A. 9

B. 10

C. 11

D. 12

59. Find a value that makes each sentence correct. Explain your
reasoning in each case.

a. $\frac{3}{4} = \frac{\blacksquare}{12}$

b. $\frac{3}{4} < \frac{\blacksquare}{12}$

c. $\frac{3}{4} > \frac{\blacksquare}{12}$

d. $\frac{9}{12} = \frac{12}{\blacksquare}$

60. Find values that make each sentence correct.

a. $\frac{6}{8} = \frac{\blacksquare}{12} = \frac{\blacksquare}{16}$

b. $\frac{\blacksquare}{9} = \frac{8}{12} = \frac{\blacksquare}{21}$

c. $\frac{\blacksquare}{60} = \frac{\blacksquare}{75} = \frac{6}{90}$

d. $\frac{\blacksquare}{4} = \frac{15}{\blacksquare} = \frac{24}{16}$

61. Multiple Choice Ayanna is making a circular spinner to be used at the school carnival. She wants the spinner to be divided so that 30% of the area is blue, 20% is red, 15% is green, and 35% is yellow. Choose the spinner that fits the description.

A.

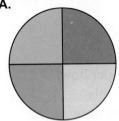

B.

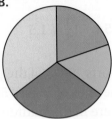

C.

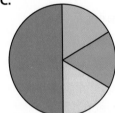

D.

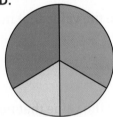

62. Hannah is making her own circular spinner. She makes the ratio of green to yellow 2 : 1, the ratio of red to yellow 3 : 1, and the ratio of blue to green 2 : 1. Make a sketch of her spinner.

63. a. Plot the points (8, 6), (8, 22), and (24, 14) on a coordinate plane. Connect them to form a triangle.

b. Draw the triangle you get when you apply the rule (0.5x, 0.5y) to the three points from part (a).

c. How are lengths of corresponding sides in the triangles from parts (a) and (b) related?

d. The area of the smaller triangle is what percent of the area of the larger triangle?

e. The area of the larger triangle is what percent of the area of the smaller triangle?

64. The polygons below are similar.

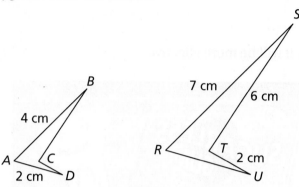

a. What is the length of side *BC*? Explain your reasoning.

b. What is the length of side *RU*? Explain your reasoning.

c. What is the length of side *CD*? Explain your reasoning.

65. Yoshi and Kai are trying to earn a certificate in their Outdoor Education Class. They have the task of measuring the width of a river. Their report includes a diagram that shows their work.

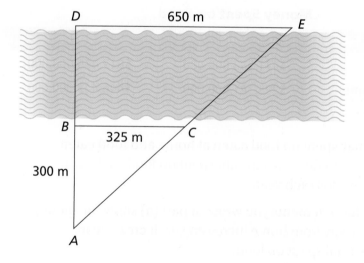

a. How do you think they came up with the lengths of the segments *AB*, *BC*, and *DE*?

b. How can they use segments *AB*, *BC*, and *DE* to find the width of the river?

Extensions

66. Rewrite this ad so that it will be more effective.

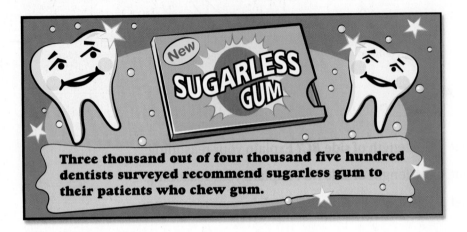

Three thousand out of four thousand five hundred dentists surveyed recommend sugarless gum to their patients who chew gum.

67. Use the table below.

Money Spent on Food

Where Food Is Eaten	2002	2010
Home	$471,533,000,000	$617,475,000,000
Away from Home	$295,341,000,000	$446,442,000,000

SOURCE: *U.S. Census Bureau*

a. Compare money spent on food eaten at home and food eaten away from home to the total amount spent on food each year. Write statements for each year.

b. Explain how the statements you wrote in part (a) show the money spent on food away from home increasing or decreasing in relation to the total spent on food.

68. The two histograms below display information about gallons of water used per person in 24 households in a week.

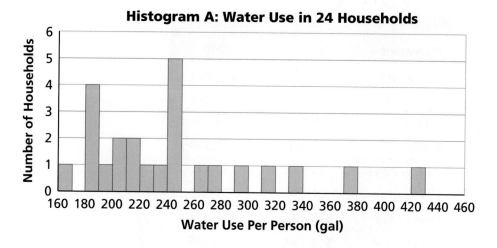

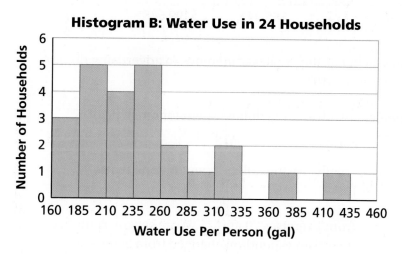

a. Compare the two histograms and explain how they differ.

b. Where do the data seem to clump in Histograms A and B?

The table below shows advertising spending for a small media company. Use the table for Exercises 69–74.

Advertising Spending		
Placement	**2000**	**2010**
Newspapers	$32,415	$18,203
Magazines	$4,973	$7,728
Television	$19,318	$35,718
Radio	$5,126	$11,318
Yellow Pages	$4,984	$1,327
Internet	$1,934	$7,548
Direct Mail	$13,497	$8,458
Other	$13,194	$19,345
Total	$95,441	$109,645

69. Which placement has the greatest difference in advertising dollars between 2000 and 2010?

70. Find the percent of advertising dollars spent for one type of placement in 2000.

71. Find the percent of advertising dollars spent for one type of placement in 2010.

72. Use your results from Exercises 70 and 71. Write several sentences describing how advertising spending changed from 2000 to 2010.

73. Suppose you were thinking about investing in Internet advertising or radio station advertising. Which method of comparing advertising costs (differences or percents) makes the Internet seem the better investment? Which makes the radio station seem the better investment?

74. Suppose you are a reporter writing an article about trends in advertising over time. Which method of comparison would you choose? Explain.

75. Angela, a biologist, spends summers on an island in Alaska. For several summers she studied puffins. Two summers ago, Angela captured, tagged, and released 20 puffins. This past summer, she captured 50 puffins and found that 2 of them were tagged. Using Angela's findings, estimate the number of puffins on the island. Explain your reasoning.

Puffins
- Live about 20 years
- About 10 inches tall
- Weigh about 500 grams
- Can fly about 50 mi/h
- Beaks are most colorful in spring and summer

76. Rita wants to estimate the number of beans in a large jar. She takes out 100 beans and marks them. Then she returns them to the jar and mixes them with the unmarked beans. She then gathers some data by taking a sample of beans from the jar. Use her data to predict the number of beans in the jar.

Sample

Number of marked beans: 2

Beans in sample: 30

77. The picture below is drawn on a centimeter grid.

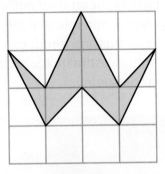

a. On a grid made of larger squares than those shown here, draw a figure similar to this figure. What is the scale factor from the original figure to your drawing?

b. Draw another similar figure, but use a grid of smaller squares than those shown here. What is the scale factor from the original figure to your drawing?

c. Compare the perimeters and areas of the original figure and its copy in each case (enlargement and reduction). Explain how these values are related to the scale factor in each case.

78. The people of the United States are represented in Congress, which is made up of the House of Representatives and the Senate.

a. In the House of Representatives, the number of representatives from each state varies. From what you know about Congress, how is the number of representatives from each state determined?

b. How is the number of senators from each state determined?

c. Compare the two methods of determining representation in Congress. What are the advantages and disadvantages of these two forms of representation for states with large populations? How about for states with small populations?

In this Investigation, you used ratios to make comparisons. You also used ratios and developed proportions to solve mixture problems. You used scaling techniques to solve proportions and determine relationships between known and unknown quantities. The questions below will help you summarize what you learned.

Think about your answers to these questions, and discuss your ideas with other students and your teacher. Then write a summary of your findings in your notebook.

1. **a.** In this Investigation you have used ratios, percents, fractions, and differences to make comparison statements. **How** have you found these ideas helpful?

   b. Give examples to explain how part-to-part ratios are different from, but related to, part-to-whole ratios.

2. **How** can you use scaling or equivalent ratios

   a. to solve a proportion? Give an example.

   b. to make a decision? Give an example.

Common Core Mathematical Practices

As you worked on the Problems in this Investigation, you used prior knowledge to make sense of them. You also applied Mathematical Practices to solve the Problems. Think back over your work, the ways you thought about the Problems and how you used Mathematical Practices.

Jayden described his thoughts in the following way:

In our class there were many different strategies for solving Problem 1.2. Our group scaled down each recipe to find how much water is needed for 1 cup of concentrate.

For A, we need 1 cup concentrate for $\frac{3}{2}$ cups of water.

For B, we need 1 cup concentrate for $\frac{9}{5}$ cups of water.

For C, we need 1 cup concentrate for 2 cups of water.

For D, we need 1 cup concentrate for $\frac{5}{3}$ cups of water.

The recipe with the least amount of water for 1 cup of concentrate is the most orangey. It is recipe A.

....

Common Core Standards for Mathematical Practice

MP2 Reason abstractly and quantitatively

- What other Mathematical Practices can you identify in Jayden's reasoning?

- Describe a Mathematical Practice that you and your classmates used to solve a different Problem in this Investigation.

Investigation 2

Comparing and Scaling Rates

In Investigation 1, you explored strategies for comparing quantities. You used ratios, fractions, percents, and differences. Knowing several methods of comparison is not enough. You also need to be able to choose an appropriate and effective method of comparison for any given situation.

2.1 Sharing Pizza
Comparison Strategies

The dining room at a camp has two sizes of table. A large table seats ten people, and a small table seats eight people. When the campers come for dinner one night, there are four pizzas on each large table and three pizzas on each small table.

Large Table

Small Table

Common Core State Standards

7.RP.A.2a Decide whether two quantities are in a proportional relationship, e.g., by testing for equivalent ratios in a table or graphing on a coordinate plane . . .

7.RP.A.2b Identify the constant of proportionality (unit rate) in tables, graphs, equations, diagrams, and verbal descriptions of proportional relationships.

7.RP.A.2c Represent proportional relationships by equations.

Also 7.RP.A.1, 7.RP.A.2, 7.RP.A.2a, 7.RP.A.2d, 7.RP.A.3, 7.EE.B.4, and 7.EE.B.4a

Problem 2.1

A The campers at each table share the pizzas equally. Does a person sitting at a small table get the same amount of pizza as a person sitting at a large table? Explain your reasoning.

B Selena wonders whether a person at a small table or a person at a large table gets more pizza. She uses two ratios, 8 : 3 and 10 : 4, and says

> The difference of 10 and 4 is 6. The difference of 8 and 3 is 5. The large table has more people, so the people at the small table will get more pizza.

1. Do you agree with Selena's reasoning? Explain.

2. Tony disagrees with Selena. He says

> If you place five pizzas on the large table and three pizzas on the small table, Selena's method would show that the campers at the large table and the campers at the small table get the same amount of pizza.
>
> If ten people share five pizzas, however, each person gets $\frac{1}{2}$ pizza. That's more pizza than each of the eight people who share three pizzas will get.

Do you agree with Tony's reasoning? Explain.

C There are 160 campers.

1. If everyone sits at small tables, how many pizzas should the camp director order?

2. If everyone sits at large tables, how many pizzas should the camp director order?

3. The camp director also has extra-large tables that seat 25. How many pizzas should be placed on each of these tables? Explain.

4. How many pizzas should he order if everyone sits at extra-large tables?

 Homework starts on page 51.

2.2 Comparing Pizza Prices
Scaling Rates

You have used fractions, percents, and ratios to make comparisons. Many real-world situations require another, related strategy to compare numbers.

• What is being compared in each statement below?

> We need two sandwiches for each person at the picnic.

> I earn $5.50 per hour when I babysit for my neighbor.

> The mystery meat in the cafeteria has 355 Calories per 6-ounce serving.

> Akira's top running rate is 8.5 kilometers per hour.

These statements can be written as ratios, such as 5.5 dollars to 1 hour or 355 Calories to 6 ounces of meat. Each of these ratios is a **rate,** a comparison of two quantities measured in different units.

• How are the ratios below similar? How are they different?

2 sandwiches to 1 person

2 votes for Bolda Cola to 1 vote for Cola Nola

• The ratio of the width of Mug's mouth to the width of Pug's mouth is 2 : 1. Is this a rate? Explain.

Julia is in charge of ordering pizzas for a camp dinner. She wonders whether to order the pizzas from Royal Pizza or Howdy's Pizza.

Each pizzeria allows customers to use the same pricing rate for fewer or more pizzas than the listed number.

You can use the ads to find the cost for any number of pizzas you want to purchase. One way to find the costs is to build a **rate table.** This is a table that shows the prices for different numbers of pizzas.

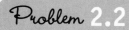 2.2

As the campers plan their pizza dinner, they need to calculate the costs for many different numbers of pizzas.

A **1.** Copy the pizza price table below. Complete the table with the prices for each of the numbers of pizzas shown.

Pizza Prices

Number of Pizzas	1	2	3	4	5	10	15	20	100	150	200
Price of Royal Pizza	▦	▦	▦	▦	▦	$120	▦	▦	▦	▦	▦
Price of Howdy's Pizza	▦	▦	▦	▦	▦	▦	$195	▦	▦	▦	▦

2. How much will 53 pizzas from Royal cost? Explain your reasoning.

3. How much will 27 pizzas from Howdy's cost? Explain.

4. The campers consider their budget. How many pizzas can they buy from Royal with $400? What if they only have $96? Explain.

B **1.** If you know the price of one pizza, how can you find the price of additional numbers of pizzas?

2. For each pizza place, use your strategy from part (1) to write an equation for the total price P for any number of pizzas n.

3. How does your equation help you solve problems such as those in Question A, part (4)?

continued on the next page >

Problem 2.2 *continued*

C Howdy's listed price is valid only if you pick up the pizza. If you request delivery, they charge a flat $5 fee for any number of pizzas.

1. **a.** Copy and complete the table below. Find the prices for Howdy's pizzas if you pick up and if they deliver.

Howdy's Pizza Prices

Number of Pizzas	1	2	3	4	5	10	15
Price if Howdy's Delivers	▪	▪	▪	▪	▪	▪	▪
Price for Pick Up	▪	▪	▪	▪	▪	▪	$195

   b. Describe the patterns you see in the table.

   c. In Question B, part (2), you wrote an equation for the cost of pizza at Howdy's. How does the information represented by the equation show up in the table? Explain.

2. **a.** On the same coordinate plane, plot the data for Howdy's prices with no delivery fee and with the delivery fee.

   b. How are the graphs similar? How are they different?

   c. For each graph, which coordinate pair represents how much one pizza costs? how much zero pizzas cost?

ACE Homework starts on page 51.

2.3 Finding Costs
Unit Rate and Constant of Proportionality

In *Comparing Bits and Pieces,* you found unit rates. Recall that a **unit rate** is a rate in which the second quantity is 1 unit. The rates *45 miles per gallon* and *$3.50 per hour* are unit rates because "per gallon" means "for one gallon" and "per hour" means "for one hour."

You may have used the following unit rates in previous Problems:

- amount of pizza per person

- number of people per pizza

- price per pizza

The unit rate for the price of one pizza at Howdy's is $13. The equation $C = 13n$ relates cost of pizza and number of pizzas.

This equation represents a *proportional relationship* because you multiply one variable by a constant number to get the value of the other variable. The constant multiplier is called the **constant of proportionality.**

$$C = 13n$$

$\uparrow$

constant of
proportionality

When a delivery charge of $5 is added to the cost, the relationship is no longer proportional: $C = 13n + 5$ is not a proportional relationship.

 How can you recognize a proportional relationship from a table or graph?

In this Problem you will find and work with unit rates.

Problem 2.3

Ⓐ FreshFoods has oranges on sale at 10 for $2. For each part, find the unit rate. Be sure to label your answers with the proper units.

1. What is the cost per orange?

2. How many oranges can you buy for $1?

3. Copy and complete the table below.

Cost of Oranges at FreshFoods

Number of Oranges, *n*	10	■	1	20	11	■
Cost, *C*	$2	$1	■	■	■	$2.60

4. How does finding a unit rate help you answer questions such as the ones below?

   • How many oranges can you buy for $5?

   • How much do 25 oranges cost?

5. The equation $n = 5C$ relates cost C to number of oranges n.

   a. What does this equation tell you about the relationship between the number of oranges and the cost of the oranges?

   b. What is another equation relating these same two variables? What information does this other equation give you?

   c. Identify two unit rates from these equations. Explain how you found the unit rates. What information do the unit rates give you?

   d. How does the constant of proportionality relate to the unit rate?

6. a. Graph the equations from Question 5 on two coordinate planes. Show values of *n* from 1 to 20.

   b. How can you use the graphs to find the unit rates?

   c. How can you use the graphs to find the constants of proportionality?

Problem 2.3 *continued*

B Noralie's car uses 20 gallons of gasoline to go 600 miles.

1. Write two unit rates relating the number of miles Noralie drives and the number of gallons her car uses. Explain your reasoning. What does each unit rate mean?

2. The graph below shows the relationship between distance d and gallons g of gasoline. Which unit rate appears on the graph? Explain.

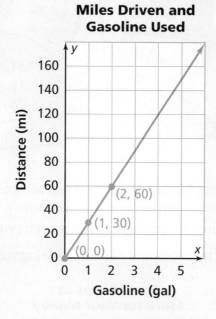

Miles Driven and Gasoline Used

3. What equation relating d and g does the graph represent?

4. Which coordinate pair represents how far Noralie can drive on 1 gallon of gas? On zero gallons of gas?

5. Josh used the proportion $\frac{600}{20} = \frac{x}{4}$ to find the number of miles Noralie's car can travel on 4 gallons of gasoline. Lisa says she can use a unit rate.

a. Do you agree with Josh or with Lisa? Explain.

b. What other strategies can you use to find the number of miles Noralie's car can travel on 4 gallons of gasoline?

continued on the next page >

Problem **2.3** *continued*

C Gus wants to determine which store has better prices for groceries.

1. At More for Your Money, pasta is on sale at 7 boxes for $6. Gus makes a rate table and writes the proportions $\frac{7}{6} = \frac{n}{1}$ and $\frac{6}{7} = \frac{C}{1}$. What information does Gus get from solving each proportion?

2. Copy the rate table below. Fill in the missing values.

**Pasta Prices at
More for Your Money**

Cost, C	$6	$1	■
Boxes, n	7	■	1

3. At FreshFoods, pasta is on sale at 6 boxes for $5. Gus decides he needs to divide. What value does the quotient $6 \div 5$ describe? What value does the quotient $5 \div 6$ describe?

4. At which store should Gus buy pasta? Explain.

 Homework starts on page 51.

Applications

1. Guests at a pizza party are seated at three tables. The small table has 5 seats and 2 pizzas. The medium table has 7 seats and 3 pizzas. The large table has 12 seats and 5 pizzas. The pizzas at each table are shared equally. At which table does a guest get the most pizza?

2. Suppose a news story about the Super Bowl claims "Men outnumbered women in the stadium by a ratio of 9 to 5." Haru thinks that this means there were 14 people in the stadium—9 men and 5 women. Do you agree with Haru? Why or why not?

3. **Multiple Choice** Which of the following is a correct interpretation of the statement "Men outnumbered women by a ratio of 9 to 5?"

   A. There were four more men than women.

   B. The number of men was 1.8 times the number of women.

   C. The number of men divided by the number of women was equal to the quotient of $5 \div 9$.

   D. In the stadium, five out of nine fans were women.

4. Each business day, news reports tell the number of stocks that gained (went up in price) and the number that declined (went down in price). For each of the following pairs of reports, determine which report is better news for investors.

   a. Gains outnumber declines by a ratio of 5 to 3. Gains outnumber declines by a ratio of 7 to 5.

   b. Gains outnumber declines by a ratio of 9 to 5. Gains outnumber declines by a ratio of 6 to 3.

   c. Gains outnumber declines by a ratio of 10 to 7. Gains outnumber declines by a ratio of 6 to 4.

Note on Notation Mathematicians use ellipses to indicate the continuation of a pattern. For example, you can refer to the list of numbers between 1 and 10 by writing 1, 2, 3, . . ., and 10, rather than listing each number. You can do this for other intervals as well. For example, 6, 9, 12, . . ., and 30 refers to the list of every multiple of 3 from 6 to 30.

For Exercises 5–11, use correct measurement units in the rates you compute.

5. Maralah can drive her car 580 miles at a steady speed using 20 gallons of gasoline. Make a rate table to show the number of miles she can drive her car for 1, 2, 3, . . ., and 10 gallons of gas.

6. Joel can drive his car 450 miles at a steady speed using 15 gallons of gasoline. Make a rate table showing the number of miles he can drive his car for 1, 2, 3, . . ., and 10 gallons of gas.

7. Franky's Trail Mix Factory gives customers the information in the table below. Use the pattern in the table to answer the questions.

   a. Fiona eats 75 grams of trail mix. How many Calories does she eat?

   b. Rico eats trail mix containing 1,000 Calories. How many grams of trail mix does he eat?

   c. Write an equation to represent the number of Calories in any number of grams of trail mix.

   d. Write an equation to represent the number of grams of trail mix that will provide any given number of Calories.

Caloric Content of Franky's Trail Mix

Grams of Trail Mix	Calories
50	150
150	450
300	900
500	1,500

8. At camp, Miriam uses a pottery wheel to make 3 bowls in 2 hours. Duane makes 5 bowls in 3 hours.

   a. Who makes bowls faster, Miriam or Duane?

   b. How long will it take Miriam to make a set of 12 bowls?

   c. How long will it take Duane to make a set of 12 bowls?

9. The dairy uses 50 pounds of milk to make 5 pounds of cheddar cheese.

   a. Make a rate table showing the amount of milk needed to make 5, 10, 15, 20, . . ., and 50 pounds of cheddar cheese.

   b. Graph the relationship between pounds of milk and pounds of cheddar cheese. First, decide which variable should go on each axis.

   c. Write an equation relating pounds of milk m to pounds of cheddar cheese c.

   d. What is the constant of proportionality in your equation from part (c)?

   e. Explain one advantage of each method (the graph, the table, and the equation) to express the relationship between milk and cheddar cheese production.

10. a. Keeley buys songs from a music website. She buys 35 songs for $26.25. What is the price per song?

   b. Regina gets a $50 gift card for the music site. She tries to estimate how many songs she can buy with the gift card. Which estimate is the most reasonable? Explain.

      i. between 30 and 50 songs

      ii. around 70 songs, but less than 70

      iii. around 70 songs, but more than 70

      iv. at least 90 songs

   c. Copy and complete the table below.

Prices of Songs

Number of Songs, n	35	▦	50	1	70	▦
Cost, C	$26.25	$3	▦	▦	▦	$15

   d. Lucius and Javier discuss how to write an equation relating price and number of songs. Lucius writes the equation $n = 0.75C$. Javier writes the equation $C = 0.75n$. Do you agree with Lucius or with Javier? Use the information from parts (a)–(c) to explain.

11. a. Several students wonder which is a better buy, a 40-pack of pencil-top erasers for $2.82 or a 2-pack of pencil-top erasers for $.12. They use different methods to arrive at an answer. Which of these methods are correct? Which method do you prefer? Explain.

Courtney

Compare the two unit rates to determine which unit rate is cheaper.

$$\frac{2.82}{40} = \frac{x}{1} \qquad x = 0.0705 \approx \$.07 \text{ per eraser}$$

$$\frac{0.12}{2} = \frac{x}{1} \qquad x = 0.06 = \$.06 \text{ per eraser}$$

The 2-packs have a cheaper per-eraser price.

Elliot

If I buy 40 of the 2-packs of erasers, the total cost will be

$40 \times 0.12 = 4.8 = \$4.80$

That is more expensive than spending $2.82 for a 40-pack of erasers. The 40-pack is the better deal.

Julio

If a 2-pack costs $.12, then twenty 2-packs would have the same number of erasers as the 40-pack. Twenty 2-packs cost

$20 \times 0.12 = 2.4 = \$2.40$

Since a 40-pack costs $2.82, the price per eraser of the 2-packs is cheaper.

Kimi

If a 40-pack costs $2.82, then half of the pack (20 erasers) should cost $1.41.
Ten 2-packs (also 20 erasers) should cost $1.20. This is cheaper.
The price per eraser is cheaper using the 2-packs.

b. Describe another method you can use to determine which is the better buy.

12. For each situation, find a unit rate and write an equation relating the two quantities.

   a. 3 dozen apples for $4.50

   b. 30 bottles of water for $4.80

   c. 24 ounces of mozzarella cheese for $2.88

13. Which of these items is the better buy?

   a. an 8-pack of glue sticks for $3.99 or 1 glue stick for $.54

   b. a 12-pack of tape for $2.50 or 1 roll of tape for $.19

   c. a 100-pack of pencils for $4.88 or 1 pencil for $.05

   d. a 50-pack of paper clips for $.89 or a 25-pack of paper clips for $.45

Connections

14. Find values that make each sentence correct.

   a. $\dfrac{6}{14} = \dfrac{\blacksquare}{21} = \dfrac{\blacksquare}{28}$

   b. $\dfrac{\blacksquare}{27} = \dfrac{8}{36} = \dfrac{\blacksquare}{63}$

   c. $\dfrac{\blacksquare}{20} = \dfrac{\blacksquare}{25} = \dfrac{6}{30}$

   d. $\dfrac{\blacksquare}{8} = \dfrac{15}{\blacksquare} = \dfrac{24}{32}$

15. For each diagram, write three statements comparing the areas of the shaded and unshaded regions. In one statement, use fractions to express the comparison. In the second, use percentages. In the third, use ratios.

   a.

   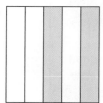

   b.

   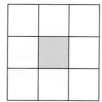

16. **Multiple Choice** Choose the value that makes $\frac{18}{30} = \frac{\blacksquare}{15}$ correct.

    F. 7   **G.** 8   **H.** 9   **J.** 10

17. **Multiple Choice** Choose the value that makes $\frac{\blacksquare}{15} \leq \frac{3}{5}$ correct.

    A. 9   **B.** 10   **C.** 11   **D.** 12

For Exercises 18–21, rewrite each equation. Replace the variable with a number that makes a true statement.

18. $\frac{4}{9} \times n = 1\frac{1}{3}$ 19. $n \times 2.25 = 90$

20. $n \div 15 = 120$ 21. $180 \div n = 15$

22. Find two fractions with a product between 10 and 11.

23. Find two decimals with a product between 1 and 2.

24. These diagrams show floor plans for two different dorm rooms. One room is for two students. The other is for one student.

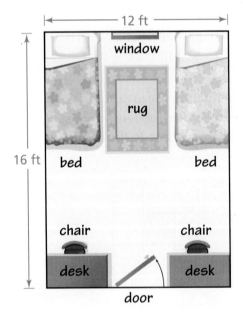
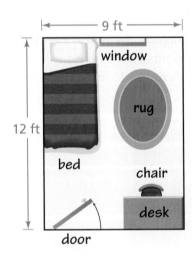

  a. Are the walls of the floor plans similar rectangles? If so, what is the scale factor? If not, why not?

  b. What is the ratio of the floor areas of the two rooms (including the space under the beds and desks)?

  c. Which room gives more space per student?

For Exercises 25 and 26, use both the table and the graph below. The table shows the mean times that students in one seventh-grade class spend on several activities during a weekend. The data are also displayed in the stacked bar graph.

Weekend Activities (hours)

Category	Boys	Girls	All Students
Sleeping	18.8	18.2	18.4
Eating	4.0	2.7	3.1
Sports	7.8	6.9	7.2
Texting	0.5	0.7	0.6
Watching TV	4.2	3.0	3.4
Chores and Homework	3.6	5.8	5.1
Other	9.1	10.7	10.2

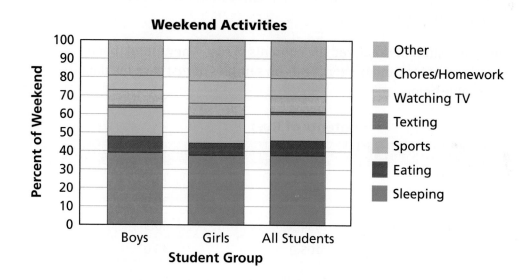

25. The stacked bar graph was made using the data from the table. Explain how it was constructed.

26. Suppose you are writing a report summarizing the class's data. You have space for either the table or the graph, but not both. What is one advantage of including the table? What is one advantage of including the bar graph?

Extensions

27. A cranberry bog owner has pressed 240 liters of cranberry juice. He has many sizes of containers in which to package the juice.

a. The owner wants to package all the cranberry juice in identical containers. Copy and complete the table to show the number of containers of each size the owner would need to package the juice.

Containers Needed by Volume

Volume of Container (liters)	10	4	2	1	$\frac{1}{2}$	$\frac{1}{4}$	$\frac{1}{10}$
Number of Containers Needed	▨	▨	▨	▨	▨	▨	▨

b. Write an equation that relates the volume V of a container and the number of containers n needed to hold 240 liters of cranberry juice.

28. Chemistry students analyzed the contents of rust. They found that it is made up of iron and oxygen. Tests on samples of rust gave the data in the table below.

Contents of Rust

Amount of Rust (g)	Amount of Iron (g)	Amount of Oxygen (g)
50	35.0	15.0
100	70.0	30.0
135	94.5	40.5
150	105.0	45.0

a. Is the ratio of iron to oxygen the same in each sample? Explain.

b. Is the ratio of iron to total rust the same in each sample? Explain.

c. The students analyze 400 grams of rust. How much iron and how much oxygen should they find?

29. Mammals vary in the length of their pregnancies, or gestations. Gestation is the time from conception to birth. Use the table to answer the questions below.

Gestation Times and Life Spans of Selected Mammals

Animal	Gestation (days)	Life Span (years)
Chipmunk	31	6
Cat	63	12
Fox	52	7
Lion	100	15
Black Bear	219	18
Gorilla	258	20
Moose	240	12
Giraffe	425	10
Elephant (African)	660	35

SOURCE: *The World Almanac and Book of Facts*

a. For each mammal listed in the table, compare life span to gestation.

b. Which animal has the greatest ratio of life span to gestation time? Which has the least ratio?

c. Plot the data on a coordinate graph using (gestation, life span) as data points. Describe any patterns that you see. Is there a relationship between the two variables? Explain.

d. What pattern would you expect to see in a graph if each statement were true?

i. Longer gestation time implies longer life span.

ii. Longer gestation time implies shorter life span.

In this Investigation, you found rates to compare two quantities. Then you used the rates to solve real-world problems. The following questions will help you summarize what you have learned.

Think about these questions. Discuss your ideas with other students and your teacher. Then write a summary of your findings in your notebook.

1. **a. How** are tables, graphs, and equations helpful when you work with proportions?

   b. How can you identify a unit rate or constant of proportionality in a table? In a graph? In an equation?

2. **How** are unit rates useful?

3. **How** is finding a unit rate similar to solving a proportion?

Common Core Mathematical Practices

As you worked on the Problems in this Investigation, you used prior knowledge to make sense of them. You also applied Mathematical Practices to solve the Problems. Think back over your work, the ways you thought about the Problems, and how you used Mathematical Practices.

Sophie described her thoughts in the following way:

In Problem 2.2, Lola doubled the cost of 10 pizzas to find the cost of 20 pizzas at Royal Pizza. I found the cost of 1 pizza at Royal. Then I multiplied that unit rate by 20 to find the cost of 20 pizzas. We both got the same answer. We decided that both methods work since we both used ratios and showed our work.

Lola's work: $\dfrac{10}{\$120} = \dfrac{10 \times 2}{\$120 \times 2}$

$= \dfrac{20}{\$240}$

My work: $\dfrac{10}{\$120} = \dfrac{1}{\$12}$

$= \dfrac{1 \times 20}{\$12 \times 20}$

$= \dfrac{20}{\$240}$

Common Core Standards for Mathematical Practice

MP3 Construct viable arguments and critique the reasoning of others

- What other Mathematical Practices can you identify in Sophie's reasoning?

- Describe a Mathematical Practice that you and your classmates used to solve a different Problem in this Investigation.

Markups, Markdowns, and Measures: Using Ratios, Percents, and Proportions

Latasha bought a concert ticket. She does not remember the price of the ticket, but she remembers that she had to pay $1 in tax. Sales tax where Latasha lives is 8%. She drew a percent bar to find the original price.

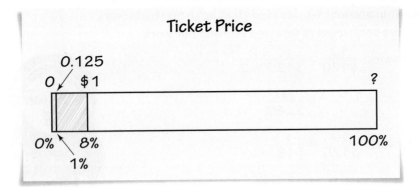

- How does Latasha know that 1% of the ticket price is $.125?

- How does knowing that 1% of the ticket price is $.125 help Latasha find the original price?

- How does knowing that 1% of the ticket price is $.125 help Latasha find the total price of the ticket?

....

Common Core State Standards

7.RP.A.1 Compute unit rates associated with ratios of fractions, including ratios of lengths, areas and other quantities measured in like or different units.

7.RP.A.2 Recognize and represent proportional relationships between quantities.

7.RP.A.2d Explain what a point (x, y) on the graph of a proportional relationship means in terms of the situation, with special attention to the points (0, 0) and (1, r), where r is the unit rate.

7.RP.A.3 Use proportional relationships to solve multistep ratio and percent problems.

Also 7.RP.A.2a, 7.RP.A.2b, 7.RP.A.2c, 7.NS.A.3, 7.EE.B.3, 7.EE.B.4, and 7.EE.B.4a

Percent bars can help you keep track of values in a problem involving percents. You can also use a percent table to organize the information in a percent problem. Latasha used a percent table to solve the same problem.

Ticket Price

Percent	8% (tax)	1%	100% (original ticket price)	108% (total price)
Dollars	1	0.125	▪	▪

- How are percent tables and rate tables similar? How are they different?

- How can Latasha find the missing values in the table?

3.1 Commissions, Markups, and Discounts
Proportions With Percents

Salespeople who sell cars, houses, and fancy jewelry often work on commission. Typically, a **commission** is a percentage of the sale price of an item.

Alternatively, a commission may be a percentage of the item's markup. The **markup** is the difference between the *buying price*, the cost for a store or dealer to buy an item, and the *selling price*, the price the store or dealer sets for their customers.

> ## Did You Know?
>
> **Car dealerships** buy cars at a certain cost. Then, they mark up the price of the car. They do this so that they can pay their salespeople and make any repairs to the used cars, but still make a profit. To make a profit, the *selling price* must be higher than the *buying price*.

Problem 3.1

Huan sells cars at Carla's Used Cars. Recently he received a job offer from Otto's Used Autos. In this Problem, you will decide whether Huan should work for Carla or for Otto.

A At Carla's Used Cars, Huan earns a commission that is 25% of the markup on the car. Huan recently sold the cars below.

1. For each car, what was Huan's commission in dollars? Explain how you found the commissions.

2. At Carla's, the markup on a car is 10% of the buying price, the price at which Carla bought the car.

   a. For each car, what was Carla's buying price? Explain.

   b. For each car, what was the selling price? Explain.

3. a. Carla buys a minivan for $20,500. She writes a proportion to find the selling price S.

   $$\frac{S}{110} = \frac{20{,}500}{100}$$

   Is Carla's method correct? Explain.

   b. Use the same four numbers as the proportion above. Write the proportion in a different way. Explain how you chose the positions of the numbers in this proportion.

Problem 3.1 continued

c. Huan checks the selling price Carla found. He uses M to represent the markup.

$$\frac{M}{10} = \frac{20{,}500}{100}$$

Is Huan's method correct? Explain.

d. A customer wants to buy the minivan. Her budget is $23,000. The selling price plus 5% sales tax goes over the customer's budget. What maximum selling price can the customer afford? Explain.

B At Otto's, the markup is 15% of the buying price. The commission at Otto's is 20% of the markup. Huan wonders whether he will get higher commissions at Carla's or at Otto's.

1. Otto also bought a minivan for $20,500. At which dealership would Huan make a higher commission on the minivan? Explain.

2. In this Unit, you have compared quantities in many ways. Write two statements comparing Huan's commission on the minivan if he works for Carla to his commission if he works for Otto.

C Huan takes the job at Otto's Used Autos. Otto has a luxury sedan for sale at a selling price of $20,700.

1. What was Otto's buying price for the luxury sedan? Explain.

2. Otto offers a discount on his cars.

Huan says that if Otto takes 15% off the $20,700 luxury sedan, the discounted selling price will be the same as the buying price. There will be no markup, so Huan will not get a commission. Do you agree with Huan's reasoning? Explain.

ACE Homework starts on page 71.

3.2 Measuring to the Unit
Measurement Conversions

 You can use unit rates, such as 3 feet per yard, to convert measurements. The following relationships may be helpful in this Problem.

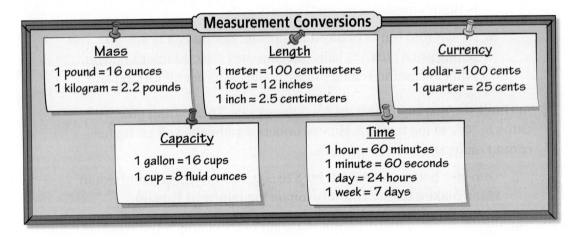

Measurement Conversions

Mass
1 pound = 16 ounces
1 kilogram ≈ 2.2 pounds

Length
1 meter = 100 centimeters
1 foot = 12 inches
1 inch ≈ 2.5 centimeters

Currency
1 dollar = 100 cents
1 quarter = 25 cents

Capacity
1 gallon = 16 cups
1 cup = 8 fluid ounces

Time
1 hour = 60 minutes
1 minute = 60 seconds
1 day = 24 hours
1 week = 7 days

You can also use proportions to convert measurements. For example,

$$\frac{1 \text{ cup}}{8 \text{ fluid ounces}} = \frac{x \text{ cups}}{50 \text{ fluid ounces}}$$

- What would solving this proportion tell you?

 Problem 3.2

A In this Unit, you have used ratios, proportions, unit rates, rate tables, and equations to solve problems. Try to use each of these strategies at least once as you solve the following problems.

1. Kate walks 5 miles in 2 hours at a steady pace. How far can she walk in 1 hour and 15 minutes? Explain your reasoning.

2. Sean walks $\frac{3}{4}$ of a mile in 15 minutes. At the same pace, how far can Sean walk in 1 hour and 20 minutes? Explain.

3. One cup of whole milk has 8 grams of fat. How many grams of fat are in a gallon of whole milk? Explain.

4. Nathan's lawnmower uses $\frac{2}{3}$ of a tank of gas to cut three one-acre lawns. How many one-acre lawns can he cut with a full tank of gas? Explain.

Problem 3.2 | *continued*

5. There are 276 Calories in 6 ounces of chicken. How many Calories are in 1 pound of chicken?

6. Chetan makes a necklace for his sister. Twelve beads take up 5 inches of string. How many beads fit on 1 foot of string? Explain.

7. Chetan wants to make a necklace with 50 beads. He knows that 12 beads take up 5 inches of string, but the store only sells string by the centimeter. How many centimeters should he buy? Explain.

B Sean walks $\frac{3}{4}$ of a mile in 15 minutes. He wants to know how far he can walk in 1 hour and 20 minutes.

1. Sean writes the expression $\frac{3}{4} \div \frac{1}{4}$ and completes the division. What information does this expression give Sean?

2. Consider Question A, part (6). Explain how Chetan can use Sean's method to find how many beads fit on a foot of string.

3. Davina tells Sean to use a proportion to find how far he can walk in 1 hour and 20 minutes. She writes

$$\frac{3}{1} = \frac{\frac{3}{4}}{\frac{1}{4}} = \frac{x}{1\frac{1}{3}}$$

How is Davina's strategy similar to Sean's strategy? How is it different?

4. How is Sean's strategy similar to using a rate table? How is it different?

Sean's Walking Rate

Distance (miles)	$\frac{3}{4}$	▪	▪
Time (hours)	$\frac{1}{4}$	1	$1\frac{1}{3}$

A C E Homework starts on page 71.

3.3 Mixing It Up
Connecting Ratios, Rates, Percents, and Proportions

You have learned to scale ratios and rates, make percent and rate tables, solve proportions, write equations, and use unit rates. These strategies are related. You can often solve ratio and rate problems in more than one way.

Problem **3.3**

Ming works at the zoo. She mixes food for the baby chimpanzees. Ming mixes up large batches of baby chimp food from sacks of high-fiber food and sacks of high-protein food. She uses the mix information above.

Problem 3.3 *continued*

A 1. Copy and complete the table to find unit rates for the baby chimp mix.

Baby Chimp Food Mix

Scoops of High-Fiber Food	▨	▨	1
Scoops of High-Protein Food	▨	1	▨
Total Scoops in Mix	100	▨	▨

2. Write two equations relating the number of scoops of high-fiber food *F* and the number of scoops of high-protein food *P*.

3. a. Ming uses 48 scoops of high-protein food in one batch. How many scoops of high-fiber food does she use? Explain your reasoning.

   b. Ming mixes a batch of baby chimp food with a total of 125 scoops. How many scoops of high-fiber food does she use? Explain.

   c. For parts (a) and (b), describe another way to solve each problem.

B Some new chimps arrive at the zoo. Ming had already mixed 20 scoops of high-fiber food and 30 scoops of high-protein food. She finds out that the new chimps are adults. Adult chimps need food that has more fiber.

1. Ming needs to add more high-fiber food to the mix she already has. She uses the information on the previous page to adjust the mix. How many more scoops of high-fiber food should she add? Explain.

2. Ming's original mix contained 20 scoops of high-fiber food. By what percentage did the amount of high-fiber food increase when Ming added more high-fiber food to the mix?

continued on the next page >

Problem 3.3 *continued*

C Ming graphs the equation $P = \frac{2}{3}F$ to show the relationship between the amounts of high-protein food and high-fiber food for adult chimps.

1. How do you know the graph matches this equation?

2. Explain how Ming can use the graph to answer Question B, part (1).

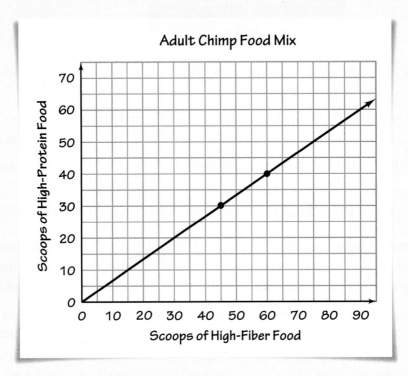

Adult Chimp Food Mix

D 1. Ming wants to use a unit rate to find how many more scoops of high-fiber food to add to the adult mix. She writes a proportion.

$$\frac{x \text{ scoops of high fiber}}{30 \text{ scoops of high protein}} = \frac{60\%}{40\%}$$

Ming says that $\frac{60\%}{40\%}$ is equal to the unit rate 1.5. Is she correct? Explain.

2. Ming replaces $\frac{60\%}{40\%}$ with the unit rate 1.5. Solve $\frac{x}{30} = 1.5$.

3. What would be Ming's first step in solving $\frac{x}{4.24} = \frac{6.82}{2.2}$?

4. Solve the proportion $\frac{x}{4.24} = \frac{6.82}{2.2}$. Describe the method you used.

 Homework starts on page 71.

Applications

For Exercises 1–5, find the sales tax.

1. a sweater for $36.00 at 7% sales tax

2. a skateboard for $62.80 at 6% sales tax

3. a baseball hat for $22.90 at 5% sales tax

4. a digital camera for $249.99 at 4% sales tax

5. a board game for $29.95 at 8% sales tax

6. Bennett bought a $21 meal. The sales tax was 5%. Bennett tried to find the sales tax in a few different ways. Which of his methods are correct? Of the correct methods, which makes the most sense to you? Explain.

A. 5% sales tax means that for every dollar you spend, you need to pay a nickel in tax. If you buy something for $21, you need to pay 21 nickels in tax.

B. You can set up a proportion and solve for the missing value.

$$\frac{\$.05}{\$1.00} = \frac{x}{\$21.00}$$

C. I know that 10% of $21.00 is $2.10, so 5% would be half of $2.10.

D. 5% is equal to $\frac{1}{20}$. To find the amount of tax on $21, find $21 ÷ 20.

E. 1% of $21.00 is $.21, so 5% of $21.00 is 5 × $.21.

7. A group of friends orders pizza at a restaurant. Each person gives some money to Chris before they order.

   a. Chris has $63 to spend on the order, including tax. The tax at the restaurant is 5%. What is the maximum cost of food the group can order and not go over $63? Explain your reasoning.

   b. Chris wants to leave a 15% tip on the price of the food, calculated before sales tax. What is the maximum cost of food the group can order and not go over $63? Explain.

For Exercises 8–10, identify which estimate seems the most reasonable. Explain.

8. 5% tax on a $42.00 purchase

   under $2.00   exactly $2.00   over $2.00

9. 9% tax on a $59.99 purchase

   under $6.00   exactly $6.00   over $6.00

10. 5.5% tax on a $309.95 purchase

    under $15.00   exactly $15.00   over $15.00

For Exercises 11–14, use the following information.

Bill's Bikes sells new and used bikes. Bill buys used bikes, fixes them, and marks up the prices by 80%. The salesperson selling the bike gets a 25% commission on the markup.

11. Find the missing values in the table.

Costs and Revenue for Roberto's Sales

Buying Price	Markup (80% of buying price)	Selling Price	Commission (25% of markup)	Profit (money the shop makes on the sale)
$100	$80	$180	$20	$60
$10	▦	▦	▦	▦
$55	▦	▦	▦	▦
$125	▦	▦	▦	▦

12. Find the missing values in the table.

Costs and Revenue for Linda's Sales

Buying Price	Markup (80% of buying price)	Selling Price	Commission (25% of markup)	Profit (money the shop makes on the sale)
▦	$48	▦	▦	▦
▦	▦	$252	▦	▦
▦	▦	▦	$14.40	▦
▦	▦	▦	▦	$54
$N	▦	▦	▦	▦

13. For each arrow in the figure below, write a mathematical rule describing how to get from one value to the next value. The first one is done for you.

14. For each part, write two equations for the listed relationship.

a. the markup amount and the buying price

b. the buying price and the selling price

c. the commission and the markup amount

d. the profit and the commission

For Exercises 15–18, solve the conversion problem.

15. Allen runs 8 miles in 3 hours at a steady pace. How long does it take him to run 3 miles?

16. Maren walks $\frac{3}{5}$ mile in 24 minutes at a steady pace. How long does it take her to walk 2 miles?

17. Half an avocado has about 160 Calories. How many Calories do a dozen avocados have?

18. There are about 1.5 grams of fat in 1 tablespoon of hummus. How many grams of fat are in $2\frac{1}{2}$ cups of hummus? (**Note:** 16 tablespoons = 1 cup)

19. The United States uses the English system of measurement. The English system has many old conversions that are rarely used.

English System Measurement Conversions

1 foot = 12 inches	1 furlong = 220 yards	1 rod = 5.5 yards
1 yard = 3 feet	1 furlong = 10 chains	1 yard = 16 nails
1 mile = 5,280 feet	1 furlong = 1,000 links	1 foot = 4 palms
1 mile = 1,760 yards	1 furlong = 40 rods	1 foot = 3 hands

Use the measurement conversions to complete the table below.

Time Predictions

	Distance and Time	Prediction
a.	1,584 feet in 3 minutes	1 mile in ▨
b.	2 furlongs in 10 minutes	1 mile in ▨
c.	1,500 links in 12 minutes	1 mile in ▨
d.	4 rods in 11 seconds	1 mile in ▨
e.	5 chains in 1 minute	1 mile in ▨

For Exercises 20–22, describe what value x represents. Then solve for x.

20. $\dfrac{16 \text{ ounces}}{1 \text{ pound}} = \dfrac{x}{3\frac{1}{2} \text{ pounds}}$

21. $\dfrac{1 \text{ gallon}}{16 \text{ cups}} = \dfrac{x}{36 \text{ cups}}$

22. $\dfrac{x}{12.5 \text{ cups}} = \dfrac{8 \text{ fluid ounces}}{1 \text{ cup}}$

For Exercises 23–25, use the conversions chart in Problem 3.2. Write a proportion and solve the conversion problem.

23. How many ounces are in $10\frac{1}{2}$ pounds?

24. How many cups are in 55 gallons?

25. About how many pounds are in 60 kilograms?

26. **a.** Alicia, Brandon, and Charlene wanted to solve the proportion $\frac{x}{4.24} = \frac{6.82}{2.2}$. Which of the students used a correct method?

Alicia

First, I simplified the fraction on the right.

$$\frac{x}{4.24} = 3.1$$

Then, I multiplied 3.1 by 4.24 to find x.

Charlene

I figured out that 6.82 − 2.2 = 4.62. So, the numerator in the right fraction was 4.62 greater than the denominator. This means that x = 4.24 + 4.62, or 8.86.

Brandon

I multiplied all the values by 100 to eliminate the decimals.

$$\frac{100x}{424} = \frac{682}{220}$$

Then I multiplied both sides by 424.

$$100x = \frac{682 \cdot 424}{220}$$

I simplified the fraction on the right.

$$100x = 1,314.4$$

Then I divided both sides by 100.

$$x = \frac{1,314.4}{100}$$

---

b. Of the correct methods, which makes the most sense to you? Explain.

For Exercises 27–30, find the unit rate for the chimp food mix. Consider the unit rate to be the number of scoops of high-fiber food per 1 scoop of high-protein food.

27. 75% high-fiber chimp food to 25% high-protein chimp food

28. 80% high-fiber chimp food to 20% high-protein chimp food

29. 85% high-fiber chimp food to 15% high-protein chimp food

30. 95% high-fiber chimp food to 5% high-protein chimp food

For Exercises 31–33, find the percentage of the chimp food mix that is high fiber and the percentage of the mix that is high protein. Note: The unit rate is the number of scoops of high-fiber food per one scoop of high-protein food.

31. unit rate: 1

32. unit rate: $\frac{1}{3}$

33. unit rate: 9

34. Lealani has 24 scoops of high-fiber chimp food.

   a. How many scoops of high-protein food should Lealani add to the mix if she wants to give it to baby chimps? Recall that baby chimps need 40% high-fiber food and 60% high-protein food.

   b. How many scoops of high-protein food should Lealani add to the mix if she wants to give it to adult chimps? Recall that adult chimps need 60% high-fiber food and 40% high-protein food.

Grown chimpanzees are about 4 feet tall. You can use that information to estimate the height of this baby chimp.

Connections

35. Claire and Pam consider the two situations below.

- marking up the price 25% and getting a 10% commission on the markup

- marking up the price 10% and getting a 25% commission on the markup

Will these situations result in the same commission, or will one commission be greater? If one commission is greater, which one?

36. Erin finds 5% sales tax for a shirt that costs $21. She calculates the tax as $0.05 \times 21 = 1.05$, or $1.05.

Erin notices that she can add $21 + 1.05 = 22.05$ to find the total cost, $22.05. She uses the Distributive Property to write $(1 \times 21) + (0.05 \times 21) = 1.05 \times 21$.

For each item below, write the total cost of the item as the product of two numbers.

Item Name	Price	Tax Rate	Tax
shirt	$21.00	5%	1.05 × 21
a. bicycle	$45.90	7%	
b. shoes	$67.50	6%	
c. laptop	$299.99	8%	
d. video game	$39.95	4%	

Credit	Debit	Subtotal	$474.34
Check	Cash	Tax	
Print Receipt		Order total	
		Cash	

37. In Exercise 36, you used the Distributive Property to find the total cost of a product and sales tax. You can also use the Distributive Property to find the total cost after a discount.

Suppose there is a 5% discount on a shirt that was originally priced at $21. Write an expression that shows the discounted price of the shirt as the product of two numbers. Explain your reasoning.

38. Bill's bike shop has a sale where the bike shop pays the customer's tax. By law, Bill has to charge a 6% sales tax, so he finds a different way to take the tax off the bill. Bill decides to give each customer a 6% discount.

   a. The customer pays the discounted price plus tax. Will this amount be the same as the original price? Explain your reasoning.

   b. Does it matter which is applied first, the discount or the tax? Explain.

Multiple Choice For Exercises 39–44, choose the best estimate for the division problem. Explain your reasoning.

39. $1\frac{2}{5} \div \frac{3}{4}$

   A. less than 1   **B.** between 1 and 2   **C.** between 2 and 3   **D.** greater than 3

40. $10 \div 1\frac{7}{8}$

   F. less than 1   **G.** between 1 and 5   **H.** between 5 and 10   **J.** greater than 10

41. $5\frac{9}{10} \div 1\frac{1}{2}$

   A. less than 1   **B.** between 1 and 4   **C.** between 4 and 12   **D.** greater than 12

42. $14\frac{2}{7} \div \frac{8}{10}$

   F. less than 1   **G.** between 1 and 7   **H.** between 7 and 14   **J.** greater than 14

43. $\frac{3}{4} \div \frac{7}{8}$

   A. less than 1   **B.** between 1 and 2   **C.** between 2 and 8   **D.** greater than 8

44. $\frac{19}{20} \div \frac{6}{10}$

   F. less than 1   **G.** between 1 and 2   **H.** between 2 and 10   **J.** greater than 10

45. Felipe walks $2\frac{1}{4}$ miles in 45 minutes at a constant rate. Use the model below to answer the questions about how far Felipe walks.

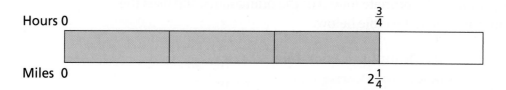

Hours 0 $\frac{3}{4}$

Miles 0 $2\frac{1}{4}$

   a. How far does Felipe walk in 15 minutes?

   b. How far does Felipe walk in 1 hour?

   c. How long does it take Felipe to walk $4\frac{1}{2}$ miles?

   d. How long does it take for Felipe to walk $3\frac{1}{4}$ miles?

For Exercises 46–49, solve each proportion.

46. $\dfrac{\frac{4}{5}}{\frac{1}{5}} = \dfrac{x}{1\frac{1}{2}}$

47. $\dfrac{\frac{5}{6}}{\frac{2}{3}} = \dfrac{x}{\frac{4}{9}}$

48. $\dfrac{\frac{6}{5}}{\frac{6}{10}} = \dfrac{x}{1\frac{2}{10}}$

49. $\dfrac{2}{\frac{1}{3}} = \dfrac{x}{\frac{5}{6}}$

50. The table below shows the conversion between liters and quarts.

Conversion Table

Liters	Quarts
1	1.06
4	4.24
5	5.30
9	9.54

   a. About how many liters are in 5.5 quarts?

   b. About how many quarts are in 5.5 liters?

   c. Write an equation that relates liters L to quarts Q.

Exercises 51–53 are about ways to mix food for different primates at the zoo.

51. Pilar mixes the primate food. For the orangutans, she uses the information in the table below.

Orangutan Food Mix

| Scoops of High-Protein Food | 21 | 24 | 27 | 18 | 33 |
| Scoops of High-Fiber Food | 7 | 8 | 9 | 6 | 11 |

a. What is the ratio of high-protein food to high-fiber food?

b. Write an equation that relates the number of scoops of high-protein food to the number of scoops of high-fiber food.

c. If Pilar mixes 12 scoops of high-protein food, how many scoops of high-fiber food should she add?

d. For every 1 scoop of high-protein food, how many scoops of high-fiber food does Pilar need?

e. Draw a graph with the amounts of high-protein food on the y-axis and the amounts of high-fiber food on the x-axis.

52. The ratio of high-fiber food to high-protein food for baby gorillas is 30% to 70%.

a. What is the unit rate for this mixture?

b. Copy and complete the table below.

Baby Gorilla Food Mix

| Scoops of High-Protein Food | ▪ | 14 | 1 | ▪ | x |
| Scoops of High-Fiber Food | 3 | ▪ | ▪ | 1 | ▪ |

c. Graph the relationship of high-protein food to high-fiber food for baby gorillas.

d. Write an equation relating the number of scoops of high-protein food to the number of scoops of high-fiber food.

53. Pilar was given the following graph of the mix ratio for adult baboon food at the zoo.

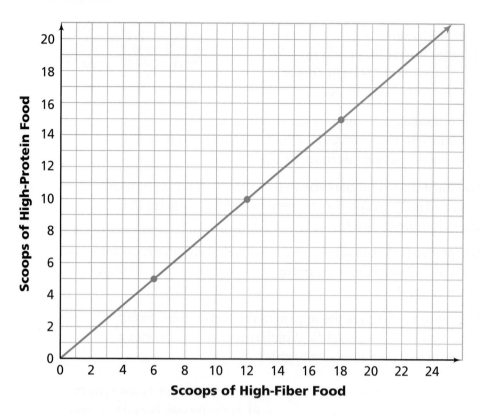

a. What is a good estimate for the number of scoops of high-protein food Pilar should use with 5 scoops of high-fiber food?

b. Pilar wants to remember a ratio of high-protein food to high-fiber food that uses small whole numbers. What ratio should she remember?

c. Write an equation that represents the graph above.

d. Pilar uses 45 scoops of high-protein food in a mix. How many scoops of high-fiber food should she use?

Extensions

54. The city of Spartanville runs two summer camps, the Green Center and the Blue Center. The table at the right shows recent attendance at the two camps.

	Green	Blue
Boys	125	70
Girls	75	30

   a. Use differences to compare the two centers' camp programs for boys and girls. Which center seems to offer a program that appeals more to girls?

   b. Use fractions to compare the two centers' camp programs for boys and girls. Which center seems to offer a program that appeals more to girls?

   c. Use percents to compare the two centers' camp programs for boys and girls. Which center seems to offer a program that appeals more to girls?

   d. Use ratios to compare the appeal of the two centers' camp programs for boys and girls. Which center seems to offer a program that appeals more to girls?

55. Use the table at the right.

   a. In which sport do boys most outnumber girls?

   b. In which sport do girls most outnumber boys?

   c. The participation in these team sports is about the same for students at Key Middle School.

Participation in Team Sports at Springbrook Middle School

Sport	Girls	Boys
Basketball	30	80
Football	10	60
Soccer	120	85
Total surveyed	160	225

     i. Suppose 250 boys at Key play sports. How many boys would you expect to play each of the three sports?

    ii. Suppose 240 girls at Key play sports. How many girls would you expect to play each of the three sports?

In this Investigation, you used your knowledge of proportions to solve consumer math problems and convert measurements. You also related graphs, equations, ratios, and unit rates. The following questions will help you summarize what you have learned.

Think about these questions. Discuss your ideas with other students and your teacher. Then write a summary of your findings in your notebook.

1. **What** strategies have you learned for solving proportions?

2. **Describe** a strategy for converting a rate measured in one pair of units to a rate measured in a different pair of units. For example, how would you convert ounces per cup to pounds per gallon?

3. You learned about scaling in *Stretching and Shrinking*. You learned about proportions and rates in *Comparing and Scaling*. **How** are the ideas in these two Units the same? How are they different?

4. **Describe** the connections you have found among unit rates, proportions, and rate tables.

Common Core Mathematical Practices

As you worked on the Problems in this Investigation, you used prior knowledge to make sense of them. You also applied Mathematical Practices to solve the Problems. Think back over your work, the ways you thought about the Problems, and how you used Mathematical Practices.

Ken described his thoughts in the following way:

In our group, Bill made a rate table for the adult chimp mix. He said that the information in the table matched the information in the graph for Problem 3.3, Question B.

For the same Question, Mary claimed that $\frac{2}{3}$ was the unit rate for the mix according to the graph. She said that the mix contained $\frac{2}{3}$ cup of high-protein food for every 1 cup of high-fiber food. This also matched the ratio of 40 cups of high-protein food : 60 cups of high-fiber food.

We knew that the graph shows pairs that fit this proportional relationship.

· ·

Common Core Standards for Mathematical Practice

MP4 Model with mathematics

- What other Mathematical Practices can you identify in Ken's reasoning?

- Describe a Mathematical Practice that you and your classmates used to solve a different Problem in this Investigation.

Unit Project

Paper Pool

This project is a mathematical investigation of a game called Paper Pool. For a pool table, use grid-paper rectangles such as the one shown at the right. Each outside corner is a pocket where a "ball" could "fall."

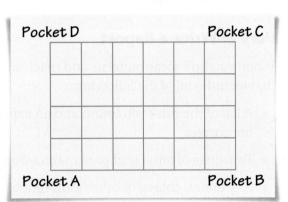

How to Play Paper Pool

- The ball always starts at Pocket A.
- To move the ball, "hit" it as if you were playing pool.
- The ball always moves on a 45° diagonal across the grid.
- When the ball hits a side of the table, it bounces off at a 45° angle and continues to move.
- If the ball moves to a corner, it falls into the pocket at that corner.

The dotted lines on the pool table below show the ball's path.

- The ball falls in Pocket D.

- There are five "hits," including the starting hit and the final hit.

- The dimensions of this pool table are 6 by 4 (always mention the horizontal length first).

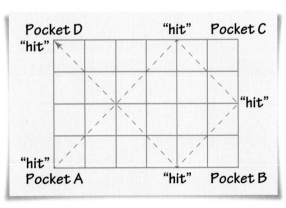

Part 1: Investigate Two Questions

Use the three Paper Pool labsheets to play the game. Try to find rules that tell you (1) the pocket into which the ball will fall and (2) the number of hits along the way. Keep track of the dimensions because they may give you clues to a pattern.

Part 2: Write a Report

When you find some patterns and reach some conclusions, write a report that includes all of the following:

- A list of the rules you found and an explanation of why you think they are correct

- Drawings of other grid paper tables that follow your rule

- Any tables, charts, or other tools that helped you find patterns

- Other patterns or ideas about Paper Pool

Extension Question

Can you predict the length of the ball's path on any size Paper Pool table? Each time the ball crosses a square, the length is 1 diagonal unit. Find the length of the ball's path in diagonal units for any set of dimensions.

Looking Back

In this Unit, you compared measured quantities in the Problems using ratios and proportions. You learned when it is best to use subtraction, division, percents, rates, ratios, and proportions to make those comparisons. You developed a variety of strategies for writing and solving proportions. These strategies include writing equivalent ratios to scale a ratio up or down. You also learned to compute and reason with unit rates.

Use Your Understanding: Ratios, Rates, Percents, and Proportions

Test your understanding of ratio, rates, percents, and proportions by solving the following problems.

1. There are 300 students in East Middle School. To plan transportation services for the new West Middle School, the school system surveyed East students. The survey asked whether students ride a bus to school or walk.

   - In Mr. Archer's homeroom, 20 students ride the bus and 15 students walk.

   - In Ms. Brown's homeroom, 14 students ride the bus and 9 students walk.

   - In Mr. Chavez's homeroom, 20 students ride the bus and the ratio of bus riders to walkers is 5 to 3.

   a. In what ways can you compare the number of students in Mr. Archer's homeroom who are bus riders to the number who are walkers? Which seems to be the best comparison statement?

   b. In what ways can you compare the numbers of bus riders and walkers in Ms. Brown's homeroom to those in Mr. Archer's homeroom? Again, which seems the best way to make the comparison?

   c. How many students in Mr. Chavez's homeroom walk to school?

d. Use the information from the three homerooms. About how many East Middle School students would you expect to walk to school? How many would you expect to ride a bus?

e. Suppose the new West Middle School will have 450 students and a ratio of bus riders to walkers that is about the same as that in East Middle School. About how many West students can be expected in each category?

2. The Purr & Woof Kennel buys food for animals that are boarded. The amounts of food eaten and the cost of the food are shown below.

a. Is cat food or dog food cheaper per pound?

b. Is it cheapest to feed a cat, a small dog, or a large dog?

c. On an average day, the kennel has 20 cats, 30 small dogs, and 20 large dogs. Which will last longer: a bag of cat food or a bag of dog food?

d. How many bags of dog food will be used in one month? How many bags of cat food will be used?

e. The owner finds a new store that sells Bow Chow in 15-pound bags for $6.75 per bag. How much does that store charge for 50 pounds of Bow Chow?

f. Which is the better buy on Bow Chow, the original source or the new store?

Explain Your Reasoning

Answering comparison questions often requires knowledge of rates, ratios, percents, and proportional reasoning. Answer the following questions about your reasoning strategies. Use the preceding problems and other examples from this Unit to illustrate your ideas.

3. How do you decide when it makes sense to compare numbers using ratios, rates, or percents rather than by finding the difference of the two numbers?

4. Suppose you are given information that the ratio of two quantities is 3 to 5. How can you express that relationship in other written forms?

5. Suppose that the ratio of two quantities is 24 to 18.
   a. State five other equivalent ratios in the form "p to q."
   b. Use whole numbers to write an equivalent ratio that cannot be scaled down without using fractions or decimals.

6. What strategies can you use to solve proportions such as $\frac{5}{8} = \frac{12}{x}$ and $\frac{5}{8} = \frac{x}{24}$?

7. How does proportional reasoning enter into the solution of each problem below?
   a. You want to prepare enough of your favorite recipe to serve a large crowd.
   b. You want to use the scale of a map to find the actual distance between two points in a park from their locations on the map.
   c. You want to find which package of raisins in a store is the best value.
   d. You want to use a design drawn on a coordinate grid to make several larger copies and several smaller copies of that design.

C **commission** The amount earned, based on the percent of total sales. For example, a car salesperson who earns 10% on car sales and sells $60,000 worth of cars would earn a commission of $6,000 (10% of $60,000).

comisión La cantidad ganada, basada en el porcentaje de las ventas totales. Por ejemplo, un vendedor de carros que gana el 10% de las ventas de carros y vende $60,000 en carros ganaría una comisión de $6,000 (10% de $60,000).

....

compare Academic Vocabulary
To tell or show how two things are alike or different.

comparar Vocabulario académico
Decir o mostrar en qué se parecen y en qué se diferencian dos cosas.

related terms *analyze, relate*

términos relacionados *analizar, relacionar*

sample Compare the fraction of boys and the fraction of girls who voted for blue.

ejemplo Compara la fracción de ninos y la fracción de ninas que votaron por el color azul.

Class Color Vote

	Blue	White	Red
Boys	19	22	16
Girls	21	16	26

Voto para el color de la clase

	Azul	Blanco	Rojo
Niños	19	22	16
Niñas	21	16	26

A total of 57 boys and 63 girls voted. So, $\frac{19}{57}$ boys and $\frac{21}{63}$ girls voted for Blue. Both $\frac{19}{57}$ and $\frac{21}{63}$ simplify to $\frac{1}{3}$. The same fraction of boys and girls voted for Blue.

En total, de 57 niños y 63 niñas votaron. Así que $\frac{19}{57}$ de los niños y $\frac{21}{63}$ de las niñas votaron por el azul. Tanto $\frac{19}{57}$ como $\frac{21}{63}$ se simplifican a $\frac{1}{3}$. La misma fracción de niños y de niñas votó por el azul.

constant of proportionality The constant ratio of two proportional quantities, x and y; usually written as $y = kx$, where k is the constant of proportionality. For example, in the equation $y = \frac{3}{4}x$, the constant of proportionality is $\frac{3}{4}$. The graph is shown below.

constante de proporcionalidad La relación constante de dos cantidades proporcionales, x y y; se escribe generalmente como $y = kx$, donde k es la constante de proporcionalidad. Por ejemplo, en la ecuacion $y = \frac{3}{4}x$, la constante de proporcionalidad es $\frac{3}{4}$. Se muestra la gráfica a continuación.

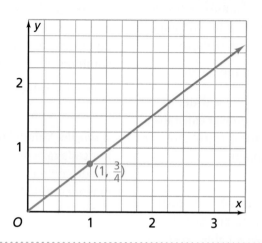

D **describe** Academic Vocabulary
To explain or tell in detail. A written description can contain facts and other information needed to communicate your answer. A diagram or a graph may also be included.

related terms *express, explain*

sample A craft store sells 15 beads for $4.50. Describe how to find the unit rate for the beads.

describir Vocabulario académico
Explicar o decir con detalles. Una descripción escrita puede tener datos y otra información necesaria para comunicar tu respuesta. También se puede incluir un diagrama o una gráfica.

términos relacionados *expresar, explicar*

ejemplo En una tienda de artesanías venden 15 cuentas por $4.50. Describe cómo se halla la tasa por unidad de las cuentas.

The unit rate is the price for one bead. To find the unit rate divide the total cost by the number of items. Divide 4.50 by 15. $4.50 \div 15 = 0.30$. The unit rate for the beads is $0.30. You can also scale down the rate by dividing the rate, 15 beads for $4.50, by 5 to get 3 beads for $0.90 and then dividing by 3 to get 1 bead for $0.30.

La tasa unitaria es el precio de una cuenta. Para hallar la tasa unitaria, divide el costo total por el número de artículos. Divide 4.50 por 15. $4.50 \div 15 = 0.30$. La tasa unitaria de las cuentas es $0.30. También puedes reducir la tasa al dividir la tasa, 15 cuentas por $4.50, por 5 para obtener 3 cuentas por $0.90 y después dividir por 3 para obtener 1 cuenta por $0.30.

E **equation** A rule containing variables that represent a mathematical relationship. An example is the equation $\frac{2}{7} = \frac{x}{42}$.

explain Academic Vocabulary

To give facts and details that make an idea easier to understand. Explaining can involve a written summary supported by a diagram, chart, table, or a combination of these.

related terms *describe, show, justify*

sample Valerie uses 1.5 cups of water for every cup of rice. Her rice cooker can cook a total of 10 cups. What is the greatest amount of rice she can cook? Explain.

1.5 cups of water and 1 cup of rice total 2.5 cups. The ratio of rice to the total amount is 1 : 2.5. I can use a table to show she can cook 4 cups of rice.

Cups of Rice	1	2	3	4
Total Cups	2.5	5	7.5	10

I can also use a proportion.

$$\frac{1}{2.5} = \frac{x}{10}$$
$$2.5x = 10$$
$$x = 4$$

Valerie can cook 4 cups of rice.

ecuación Una regla que contiene variables que representan una relación matemática. Un ejemplo de una ecuación es $\frac{2}{7} = \frac{x}{42}$.

explicar Vocabulario académico

Dar datos y detalles que hacen que una idea sea más fácil de comprender. Explicar puede implicar un resumen escrito apoyado por un diagrama, una gráfica, una tabla, o una combinación de estos.

términos relacionados *describir, mostrar, justificar*

ejemplo Valerie usa 1.5 tazas de agua por cada taza de arroz. En su olla de arroz puede cocina un total de 10 tazas. ¿Cuál es la mayor cantidad de arroz que puede cocinar? Explícalo.

1.5 tazas de agua y una taza de arroz es igual a 2.5 tazas. La razón de arroz al total es 1 : 2.5. Puedo usar una tabla para demostrar que debe usar 4 tazas de arroz.

Tazas de arroz	1	2	3	4
Tazas en total	2.5	5	7.5	10

También puedo usar una razón.

$$\frac{1}{2.5} = \frac{x}{10}$$
$$2.5x = 10$$
$$x = 4$$

Valerie puede cocinar 4 tazas de arroz.

M **markup** The amount added to the buying price of an item. It is usually a percent of the buying price.

marcado La cantidad que se agrega al precio de compra de un artículo. Por lo general es un porcentaje del precio de compra.

part-to-part ratio A part-to-part ratio represents a relationship between one part of a whole and another part of the whole. For example, in a recipe that calls for 2 cans of juice concentrate and 3 cans of water, the ratios 2 : 3 and 3 : 2 are part-to-part ratios.

razón de parte a parte Una razón de parte a parte representa una relación entre una parte de un entero y otra parte del entero. Por ejemplo, en una receta que requiera 2 latas de concentrado de jugo y 3 latas de agua, las razónes de 2 : 3 y 3 : 2 son razónes de parte a parte.

part-to-whole ratio A part-to-whole ratio represents a relationship between one part of a whole and the whole. For example, in a recipe that calls for 2 cans of juice concentrate and 3 cans of water, the ratios 2 : 5 and 3 : 5 are part-to-whole ratios, because there are 5 cans in all.

razón de parte a todo Una razón de parte a todo representa la relación entre una parte de un entero y el entero. Por ejemplo, en una receta que requiera 2 latas de concentrado de jugo y 3 latas de agua, las razónes 2 : 5 y 3 : 5 son razónes de parte a todo.

proportion An equation stating that two ratios are equal. For example,

$$\frac{\text{hours spent on homework}}{\text{hours spent in school}} = \frac{2}{7}$$

Note that this does not necessarily imply that "hours spent on homework" = 2 or that "hours spent in school" = 7. During a week, 10 hours may have been spent on homework while 35 hours were spent in school. The proportion is still true because $\frac{10}{35} = \frac{2}{7}$.

proporción Una ecuación que enuncia que dos razones son iguales. Por ejemplo,

$$\frac{\text{horas dedicadas a la tarea}}{\text{horas en la escuela}} = \frac{2}{7}$$

Observa que esto no implica necesariamente que las "horas dedicadas a la tarea" = 2, o que las "horas en la escuela" = 7. Durante una semana, puedes haber pasado 10 horas haciendo tarea y 35 horas en la escuela. La proporción sigue siendo verdadera porque $\frac{10}{35} = \frac{2}{7}$.

rate A comparison of quantities measured in two different units is called a rate. A rate can be thought of as a direct comparison of two sets (20 cookies for 5 children) or as an average amount (4 cookies per child). A rate such as 5.5 miles per hour can be written as $\frac{5.5 \text{ miles}}{1 \text{ hour}}$, or 5.5 miles : 1 hour.

tasa La comparación de cantidades que se miden en dos unidades diferentes se llama tasa. Una tasa se puede interpretar como una comparación directa entre dos grupos (20 galletas para 5 niños) o como una cantidad promedio (4 galletas por niño). Una tasa como 5.5 millas por hora se puede escribir como $\frac{5.5 \text{ millas}}{1 \text{ hora}}$, ó 5.5 millas : 1 hora.

rate table You can use a rate to find and organize equivalent rates in a rate table. For example, you can use the rate "five limes for $1.00" to make this rate table.

tabla de tasas Puedes usar una tasa para hallar y organizar tasas equivalentes en una tabla de tasas. Por ejemplo, puedes usar la tasa "cinco limones por $1.00" para hacer esta tabla de tasas.

Cost of Limes

Number of Limes	1	2	3	4	5	10	15	20
Cost of Limes	$0.20	$0.40	$0.60	$0.80	$1.00	$2.00	$3.00	$4.00

ratio A ratio is a number, often expressed as a fraction, used to make comparisons between two quantities. Ratios may also be expressed as equivalent decimals or percents, or given in the form $a : b$. Here are some examples of uses of ratios:

- The ratio of females to males on the swim team is 2 to 3, or $\frac{2\ \text{females}}{3\ \text{males}}$.

- The train travels at a speed of 80 miles per hour, or $\frac{80\ \text{miles}}{1\ \text{hour}}$.

- If a small figure is enlarged by a scale factor of 2, the new figure will have an area 4 times its original size. The ratio of the small figure's area to the large figure's area will be $\frac{1}{4}$. The ratio of the large figure's area to the small figure's area will be $\frac{4}{1}$, or 4.

- In the example above, the ratio of the length of a side of the small figure to the length of the corresponding side of the large figure is $\frac{1}{2}$. The ratio of the length of a side of the large figure to the length of the corresponding side of the small figure is $\frac{2}{1}$, or 2.

razón La razón es el número, a menudo expresado como fracción, que se usa para hacer comparaciones entre dos cantidades. Las rezones también se pueden expresar como números decimales equivalentes o como porcentajes, o en la forma $a : b$. Estos son algunos ejemplos de razones:

- La razón entre mujeres y hombres en el equipo de natación es 2 a 3, es decir, $\frac{2\ \text{mujeres}}{3\ \text{hombres}}$.

- El tren viaja a una velocidad de 80 millas por hora, o sea $\frac{80\ \text{millas}}{1\ \text{hora}}$.

- Si se amplía una figura pequeña en un factor de escala 2, la nueva figura tendrá un área cuatro veces mayor que su tamaño original. La razón entre el área de la figura pequeña y el área de la figura grande será $\frac{1}{4}$. La razón entre el área de la figura grande y el área de la figura pequeña será $\frac{4}{1}$, ó 4.

- En el ejemplo anterior, la razón entre la longitud de un lado de la figura pequeña y la longitud del lado correspondiente de la figura grande es $\frac{1}{2}$. La razón entre la longitud de un lado de la figura grande y la longitud del lado correspondiente de la figura pequeña es $\frac{2}{1}$, ó 2.

relate Academic Vocabulary
To have a connection or impact on something else.

related terms *connect, correlate*

sample Aman bikes 14 miles in 2 hours. Relate the time Aman bikes to the distance he travels.

> The unit rate for Aman's speed is $\frac{14}{2} = 7$ miles per hour. The equation relating the distance he bikes d to time in hours h is $d = 7h$.
>
>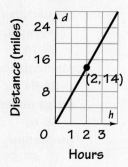

The graph and the equation both show a linear relationship between distance and time.

relacionar Vocabulario académico
Tener una conexion con algo o un impacto en algo.

términos relacionados *conectar, correlacionar*

ejemplo Adrián recorre 14 millas en 2 horas en su bicicleta. Relaciona el tiempo que Adrián monta en bicicleta con la distancia que recorre.

> La tasa unitaria de la velocidad de Aman es $\frac{14}{2} = 7$ millas por hora. La ecuación que relacions la distancia que anda en bicicleta d con el tiempo en horas h es $d = 7h$.
>
>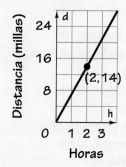

La gráfica y la ecuación demuestran una relación lineal entre distanceia y tempo.

U **unit rate** A unit rate is a rate in which the second number (usually written as the denominator) is 1, or 1 of a quantity. For example, 1.9 children per family, 32 miles per gallon, and $\frac{3 \text{ flavors of ice cream}}{1 \text{ banana split}}$ are unit rates. Unit rates are often found by scaling other rates.

tasa por unidad Una tasa por unidad es una tasa en la que el segundo número (normalmente escrito como el denominador) es 1 ó 1 de una cantidad. Por ejemplo, 1.9 niños por familia, 32 millas por galón, y $\frac{3 \text{ sabores de helado}}{1 \text{ banana split}}$ son tasas por unidad. Las tasas por unidad se calculan a menudo poniendo a escala otras tasas.

Index

Acknowledgments

Cover Design

Three Communication Design, Chicago

Photographs

Every effort has been made to secure permission and provide appropriate credit for photographic material. The publisher deeply regrets any omission and pledges to correct errors called to its attention in subsequent editions.

Unless otherwise acknowledged, all photographs are the property of Pearson Education, Inc.

Photo locators denoted as follows: Top (T), Center (C), Bottom (B), Left (L), Right (R), Background (Bkgd)

002 neelsky/Shutterstock; **003** D. Hurst/Alamy; **019** (BL) rSnapshotPhotos/Shutterstock, (BR) Ruth Peterkin/Alamy; **037** Kevin Schafer/Corbis; **053** (TL) Hemera/Thinkstock, (TR) Exactostock/SuperStock; **058** Claudisea/Fotolia; **076** neelsky/Shutterstock.

CONNECTED MATHEMATICS® 3

Moving Straight Ahead

Linear Relationships

Lappan, Phillips, Fey, Friel

Linear Relationships

3 Solving Equations
54

4 Exploring Slope: Connecting Rates and Ratios
87

Looking Ahead

Grace's walking rate is 1.5 meters per second. Her house is 90 meters from the fountain. **How** many seconds will it take her to reach the fountain? It takes Allie 45 seconds to walk from Grace's house to the fountain. **What** is Allie's walking rate?

Grace's House

Forensic scientists can estimate a person's height by measuring the lengths of certain bones. **What** is the approximate height of a male whose tibia is 50.1 centimeters long?

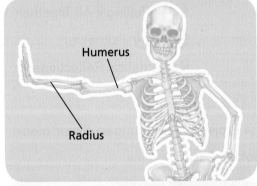

Humerus

Radius

Robert is installing a patio in his backyard. At 2:00 P.M., he has 120 stones laid in the ground. At 3:30 P.M., he has 180 stones in the ground. **When** will he be done?

All around you, things occur in patterns. Once you observe a pattern, you can use it to predict information beyond and between the data observed. The ability to use patterns to make predictions makes it possible for a baseball player to run to the right position to catch a fly ball or for a pilot to estimate the flying time for a trip.

In *Variables and Patterns*, you investigated relationships between variables. The relationships were displayed as verbal descriptions, tables, graphs, and equations. Some of the graphs, such as the graph of distance and time for a van traveling at a steady rate, were straight lines. Relationships with graphs that are straight lines are called *linear relationships*.

In this Unit, you will study linear relationships. You will learn about the characteristics of a linear relationship. You will determine whether a relationship is linear by looking at its equation or at a table of values. You will also learn how to solve linear equations. You will use what you learn about linear relationships to answer questions like those on the facing page.

Mathematical Highlights

Linear Relationships

In *Moving Straight Ahead*, you will explore properties of linear relationships and linear equations.

You will learn how to:

- Recognize problem situations that involve linear relationships

- Construct tables, graphs, and symbolic equations that represent linear relationships

- Translate information about linear relations given in a verbal description, a table, a graph, or an equation to one of the other forms

- Connect equations that represent linear relationships to the patterns in tables and graphs of those equations

- Identify the rate of change, slope, and *y*-intercept from the graph of a linear relationship

- Solve linear equations

- Write and interpret equivalent expressions as well as determine whether two or more expressions are equivalent

- Solve problems and make decisions about linear relationships using information given in tables, graphs, and equations

- Solve problems that can be modeled with inequalities and graph the solution set

When you encounter a new problem, it is a good idea to ask yourself questions. In this Unit, you might ask questions such as:

What are the variables in the problem?

Do the variables in the problem have a linear relationship to each other?

What patterns in the problem suggest that the relationship is linear?

How can the linear relationship in a situation be represented with a verbal description, a table, a graph, or an equation?

How do changes in one variable affect changes in a related variable?

How are these changes captured in a table, a graph, or an equation?

How can tables, graphs, and equations of linear relationships be used to answer questions?

Common Core State Standards
Mathematical Practices and Habits of Mind

In the *Connected Mathematics* curriculum you will develop an understanding of important mathematical ideas by solving problems and reflecting on the mathematics involved. Every day, you will use "habits of mind" to make sense of problems and apply what you learn to new situations. Some of these habits are described by the *Common Core State Standards for Mathematical Practices* (MP).

MP1 Make sense of problems and persevere in solving them.

When using mathematics to solve a problem, it helps to think carefully about

- data and other facts you are given and what additional information you need to solve the problem;
- strategies you have used to solve similar problems and whether you could solve a related simpler problem first;
- how you could express the problem with equations, diagrams, or graphs;
- whether your answer makes sense.

MP2 Reason abstractly and quantitatively.

When you are asked to solve a problem, it often helps to

- focus first on the key mathematical ideas;
- check that your answer makes sense in the problem setting;
- use what you know about the problem setting to guide your mathematical reasoning.

MP3 Construct viable arguments and critique the reasoning of others.

When you are asked to explain why a conjecture is correct, you can

- show some examples that fit the claim and explain why they fit;
- show how a new result follows logically from known facts and principles.

When you believe a mathematical claim is incorrect, you can

- show one or more counterexamples—cases that don't fit the claim;
- find steps in the argument that do not follow logically from prior claims.

MP4 Model with mathematics.

When you are asked to solve problems, it often helps to

- think carefully about the numbers or geometric shapes that are the most important factors in the problem, then ask yourself how those factors are related to each other;
- express data and relationships in the problem with tables, graphs, diagrams, or equations, and check your result to see if it makes sense.

MP5 Use appropriate tools strategically.

When working on mathematical questions, you should always

- decide which tools are most helpful for solving the problem and why;
- try a different tool when you get stuck.

MP6 Attend to precision.

In every mathematical exploration or problem-solving task, it is important to

- think carefully about the required accuracy of results; is a number estimate or geometric sketch good enough, or is a precise value or drawing needed?
- report your discoveries with clear and correct mathematical language that can be understood by those to whom you are speaking or writing.

MP7 Look for and make use of structure.

In mathematical explorations and problem solving, it is often helpful to

- look for patterns that show how data points, numbers, or geometric shapes are related to each other;
- use patterns to make predictions.

MP8 Look for and express regularity in repeated reasoning.

When results of a repeated calculation show a pattern, it helps to

- express that pattern as a general rule that can be used in similar cases;
- look for shortcuts that will make the calculation simpler in other cases.

You will use all of the Mathematical Practices in this Unit. Sometimes, when you look at a Problem, it is obvious which practice is most helpful. At other times, you will decide on a practice to use during class explorations and discussions. After completing each Problem, ask yourself:

- What mathematics have I learned by solving this Problem?

- What Mathematical Practices were helpful in learning this mathematics?

Walking Rates

In *Variables and Patterns*, you read about a bicycle touring business. You used contextual situations, tables, graphs, and equations to represent patterns relating variables such as cost, income, and profit. You looked at some linear relationships, like the relationship between cost and number of rental bikes represented in this graph:

A relationship between two variables for which all points lie on a straight line is called a **linear relationship.** From the graph, you see that the relationship between the number of bikes rented and the total rental cost is a linear relationship. In this Investigation, consider these questions:

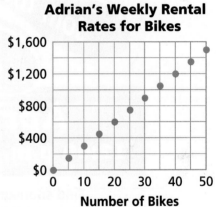

Adrian's Weekly Rental Rates for Bikes

- How can you determine whether a relationship is linear by examining a table of data or an equation?

- How do changes in one variable affect changes in a related variable? How are these changes captured in a table, a graph, or an equation?

Common Core State Standards

7.RP.A.2b Identify the constant of proportionality (unit rate) in tables, graphs, equations, diagrams, and verbal descriptions of proportional relationships.

7.RP.A.2c Represent proportional relationships by equations.

7.EE.B.4 Use variables to represent quantities in a real-world or mathematical problem, and construct simple equations and inequalities to solve problems by reasoning about the quantities.

Also 7.RP.A.2, 7.RP.A.2a, 7.EE.B.4a

1.1 Walking Marathons
Finding and Using Rates

Ms. Chang's class decides to participate in a walkathon. Each participant must find sponsors to pledge a certain amount of money for each kilometer the participant walks. Leanne suggests that they determine their walking rates in meters per second so they can make predictions.

- Do you know what your walking rate is?

- How can you determine your walking rate?

Problem 1.1

One way to define your walking rate is the distance you walk for every second of walking time.

To determine your walking rate:

- Line up ten meter sticks, end to end (or mark off 10 meters), in the hall of your school.

- Have a partner time your walk.

- Start at one end and walk the length of the ten meter sticks using your normal walking pace.

A What is your walking rate in meters per second?

B Assume you continue to walk at this constant rate.

1. How long would it take you to walk 500 meters?

2. How far could you walk in 30 seconds? In 10 minutes? In 1 hour?

3. Describe in words the distance in meters you could walk in a given number of seconds.

4. Write an equation that represents the distance d in meters that you could walk in t seconds if you maintain this pace.

5. Use the equation to predict the distance you would walk in 45 seconds.

A C E Homework starts on page 16.

1.2 Walking Rates and Linear Relationships

Tables, Graphs, and Equations

Think about the effect a walking rate has on the relationship between time walked and distance walked. This will provide some important clues about how to identify linear relationships from tables, graphs, and equations.

Problem 1.2

Here are the walking rates that Gilberto, Alana, and Leanne found in their experiment.

Ⓐ

1. Make a table showing the distance walked by each student for the first ten seconds. How does the walking rate appear as a pattern in the table?

Name	Walking Rate
Alana	1 meter per second
Gilberto	2 meters per second
Leanne	2.5 meters per second

2. Graph the times and distances for the three students on the same coordinate axes. Use a different color for each student's data. How does the walking rate affect the graph?

3. Write an equation that gives the relationship between the time t and the distance d walked for each student. How is the walking rate represented in the equations?

4. How can you predict that the graph will be a straight line from the patterns in the table? In the equation? Explain.

5. Are any of these proportional relationships? If so, what is the constant of proportionality?

Ⓑ For each student:

1. If time t increases by 1 second, by how much does the distance d change? How is this change represented in a table? In a graph?

2. If t increases by 5 seconds, by how much does d change? How is this change represented in a table? In a graph?

3. What is the walking rate per minute? The walking rate per hour?

Problem **1.2** *continued*

C Four other friends who are part of the walkathon made the following representations of their data. Could any of these relationships be linear relationships? Explain.

George's Walking Rate

Time (seconds)	Distance (meters)
0	0
1	2
2	9
3	11
4	20
5	25

Elizabeth's Walking Rate

Time (seconds)	Distance (meters)
0	0
2	3
4	6
6	9
8	12
10	15

Billie's Walking Rate
$$D = 2.25t$$

D represents distance
t represents time

Bob's Walking Rate
$$t = \frac{100}{r}$$

t represents time
r represents walking rate

 A C E Homework starts on page 16.

1.3 Raising Money
Using Linear Relationships

In *Variables and Patterns*, you looked at situations that involved *dependent* and *independent* variables. In Problem 1.2, the distance walked depended on the time. This tells you that distance is the **dependent variable** and time is the **independent variable**. In this Problem, you will look at relationships between two other variables in a walkathon.

Each participant in the walkathon must find sponsors to pledge a certain amount of money for each kilometer the participant walks.

The students in Ms. Chang's class are trying to estimate how much money they might be able to raise. Several questions come up in their discussions:

- What variables can affect the amount of money that is collected?

- How can you use these variables to estimate the amount of money each student will collect?

- Will the amount of money collected be the same for each walker?

Each student found sponsors who are willing to pledge money according to the following descriptions.

- Leanne's sponsors will donate $10 regardless of how far she walks.

- Gilberto's sponsors will donate $2 per kilometer (km).

- Alana's sponsors will make a $5 donation plus 50¢ per kilometer.

The class refers to these as *pledge plans*.

Tables, graphs, and equations will help you predict how much money might be raised with each plan.

- What are the dependent and independent variables?

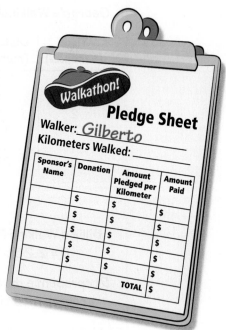

? Who will raise the most money after *d* kilometers?

Problem 1.3

A 1. Make a table for each student's pledge plan. Show the amount of money each of his or her sponsors would donate if he or she walked distances from 0 to 6 kilometers. What are the dependent and independent variables?

2. Graph the three pledge plans on the same coordinate axes. Use a different color for each plan.

Problem **1.3** *continued*

3. For each pledge plan, write an equation that represents the relationship between the distance walked and the amount of money donated. Explain what information each number and variable in the equations represents.

4. For each plan:

   a. What pattern of change between the two variables do you observe in the table?

   b. How does this pattern appear in the graph? In the equation?

   c. How can you determine if a relationship is linear from a table, a graph, or an equation?

   d. Does this relationship represent a proportional relationship?

B 1. Suppose each student walks 8 kilometers in the walkathon. How much money does each sponsor donate? Explain how you found your answer.

2. Suppose each student raises $10 from a sponsor. How many kilometers does each student walk? Explain.

3. On which graph does the point (12, 11) lie? What information does this point represent?

4. In Alana's plan, how is the fixed $5 donation represented in

   a. the table?

   b. the graph?

   c. the equation?

C Gilberto decides to give a T-shirt to each of his sponsors. Each shirt costs him $4.75. He plans to pay for each shirt with some of the money he raises from each sponsor.

1. Write an equation that represents the amount of money Gilberto raises from each sponsor after he has paid for the T-shirt. Explain what information each number and variable represents.

2. Graph the equation for distances from 0 to 5 kilometers. Compare this graph to the graph of Gilberto's pledge plan in Question A, part (2).

3. Is this relationship linear? Explain.

ACE Homework starts on page 16.

1.4 Using the Walkathon Money
Recognizing Linear Relationships

In previous Problems, you noticed that, as the independent variable changes by a constant amount, there is a pattern of change in the dependent variable. You can use this pattern of change to identify other linear relationships.

Ms. Chang's class decides to use their money from the walkathon to provide books for the children's ward at the hospital. The class puts the money in the school safe and withdraws a fixed amount each week to buy new books. To keep track of the money, Isabella makes a table of the amount of money in the account at the end of each week.

Week	Amount of Money at the End of Each Week
0	$144
1	$132
2	$120
3	$108
4	$96
5	$84

- What do you think the graph of this data would look like?

- Does this table represent a linear relationship? How did you decide?

 Problem 1.4

Ⓐ 1. How much money is in the account at the start of the project? Explain.

2. How much money is withdrawn from the account each week?

3. Suppose the students continue withdrawing the same amount of money each week. Sketch a graph of this relationship.

4. Write an equation that represents the relationship. Explain what information each number and variable represents.

5. Is the relationship between the number of weeks and the amount of money left in the account linear? Explain.

Problem 1.4 continued

B Mr. Mamer's class also raised money from the walkathon. They use the money to buy games and puzzles for the children's ward. Keenan uses a graph to keep track of the amount of money in the account at the end of each week.

Money in Mr. Mamer's Class Account

Amount of Money vs *Week*

$100, $90, $80, $70, $60, $50, $40, $30, $20, $10, $0

0 1 2 3 4 5 6 7 8 9 10

1. What information does the graph represent about the money in Mr. Mamer's class account?

2. Make a table of data for the first 10 weeks. Explain why this table represents a linear relationship.

3. Write the equation that models the linear relationship. Explain what information each number and variable represents.

C **1.** How can you determine whether a relationship is linear from a graph, a table, or an equation?

2. Compare the patterns of change for the linear relationships in this Problem to those in previous Problems in this Investigation.

A C E Homework starts on page 16.

Applications

1. Hoshi walks 10 meters in 3 seconds.

   a. What is her walking rate?

   b. At this rate, how long does it take her to walk 100 meters?

   c. She walks at this same rate for 50 seconds. How far does she walk?

   d. Write an equation that represents the distance d that Hoshi walks in t seconds.

2. Milo walks 40 meters in 15 seconds. Mira walks 30 meters in 10 seconds. Whose walking rate is greater?

For Exercises 3–5, Jose, Mario, Melanie, Mike, and Alicia are on a weeklong cycling trip. The table below gives the distance Jose, Mario, and Melanie each travel for the first 3 hours. Cycling times include only biking time, not time to eat, rest, and so on.

Cycling Distance

Cycling Time (hours)	Distance (miles)		
	Jose	Mario	Melanie
0	0	0	0
1	5	7	9
2	10	14	18
3	15	21	27

3. a. Assume that each person cycles at a constant rate. Find the rate at which each person travels during the first 3 hours. Explain.

   b. Find the distance each person travels in 7 hours.

   c. Graph the time and distance data for all three riders on the same coordinate axes.

   d. Use the graphs to find the distance each person travels in $6\frac{1}{2}$ hours.

   e. Use the graphs to find the time it takes each person to travel 70 miles.

f. How does the rate at which each person rides affect each graph?

g. For each rider, write an equation that can be used to calculate the distance traveled after a given number of hours.

h. Use your equations from part (g) to calculate the distance each person travels in $6\frac{1}{2}$ hours.

i. How does a person's cycling rate show up in his or her equation?

j. Are any of these proportional relationships? If so, what is the constant of proportionality?

4. Mike makes the following table of the distances he travels during the first day of the trip.

a. Suppose Mike continues riding at this rate. Write an equation for the distance Mike travels after t hours.

b. Sketch a graph of the equation. How did you choose the range of values for the time axis? For the distance axis?

c. How can you find the distances Mike travels in 7 hours and in $9\frac{1}{2}$ hours, using the table? Using the graph? Using the equation?

d. How can you find the numbers of hours it takes Mike to travel 100 miles and 237 miles, using the table? Using the graph? Using the equation?

e. For parts (c) and (d), what are the advantages and disadvantages of using each model—a table, a graph, and an equation—to find the answers?

f. Compare the rate at which Mike rides with the rates at which Jose, Mario, and Melanie ride. Who rides the fastest? How can you determine this from the tables? From the graphs? From the equations?

Cycling Distance

Time (hours)	Distance (miles)
0	0
1	6.5
2	13
3	19.5
4	26
5	32.5
6	39

5. The distance in miles Alicia travels in t hours is represented by the equation $d = 7.5t$.

a. At what rate does Alicia travel? Explain.

b. Suppose the graph of Alicia's distance and time is put on the same set of axes as Mike's, Jose's, Mario's, and Melanie's graphs. Where would it be located in relationship to each of the graphs? Describe the location without actually making the graph.

6. The graph below represents the walkathon pledge plans for three sponsors.

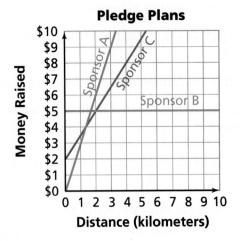

Pledge Plans

a. Describe each sponsor's pledge plan.

b. What is the number of dollars per kilometer each sponsor pledges?

c. What does the point where the line crosses the *y*-axis mean for each sponsor?

d. Write the coordinates of two points on each line. What information does each point represent for the sponsor's pledge plan?

e. Does each relationship represent a proportional relationship?

7. The students in Ms. Chang's class decide to order water bottles that advertise the walkathon. Hyun obtains two different quotes for the costs of the bottles.

a. For each company, write an equation Hyun could use to calculate the cost for any number of bottles.

b. On the same set of axes, graph both equations from part (a). Which variable is the independent variable? Which is the dependent variable?

c. From which company do you think the class should buy water bottles? What factors influenced your decision?

d. For what number of water bottles is the cost the same for both companies? Explain.

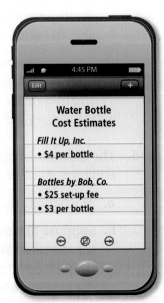

8. **Multiple Choice** The equation $C = 5n$ represents the cost C in dollars for n caps that advertise the walkathon. Which of the following ordered pairs could represent a number of caps and the cost for that number of caps, (n, C)?

   A. $(0, 5)$ **B.** $(3, 15)$ **C.** $(15, 60)$ **D.** $(5, 1)$

9. The equation $d = 3.5t + 50$ gives the distance d in meters that a cyclist is from his home after t seconds.

   a. Which of the following ordered pairs represents a point on the graph of this equation? Explain your answer.

   i. $(10, 85)$ **ii.** $(0, 0)$ **iii.** $(3, 60.5)$

   b. What information do the coordinates tell you about the cyclist?

10. Examine the pattern in each table.

Table 1

x	y
−2	3
−1	3
0	3
1	3
2	3

Table 2

x	y
−3	9
−2	4
−1	1
0	0
1	1

Table 3

x	y
0	10
3	19
5	25
10	40
12	46

Table 4

x	y
0	−3
2	−6
4	−9
6	−12
8	−15

   a. Describe the similarities and differences in Tables 1–4.

   b. Explain how you can use each table to decide whether the data indicate a linear relationship between the two quantities.

   c. Sketch a graph of the data in each table.

   d. Write an equation that represents the relationship between the independent and dependent variables for each linear relationship. Explain what information the numbers and variables tell you about the relationship.

11. **a.** The temperature at the North Pole is 30°F and is expected to drop 5°F per hour for the next several hours. Write an equation that represents the relationship between temperature and time. Explain what information your numbers and variables represent.

   b. Is this a linear relationship? Explain your reasoning.

12. Jamal's parents give him money to spend at camp. Jamal spends the same amount of money on snacks each day. The table below shows the amount of money, in dollars, he has left at the end of each day.

Snack Money

Days	0	1	2	3	4	5	6
Money Left	$20	$18	$16	$14	$12	$10	$8

a. How much money does Jamal have at the start of camp? Explain.

b. How much money does he spend each day? Explain.

c. Is the relationship between the number of days and the amount of money left in Jamal's wallet a linear relationship? Explain.

d. Assume that Jamal's spending pattern continues. Check your answer to part (c) by sketching a graph of this relationship.

e. Write an equation that represents the relationship. Explain what information the numbers and variables represent.

13. Write an equation for each graph.

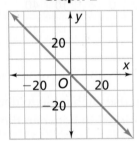

14. a. Describe a situation that involves a linear relationship between an independent variable and a dependent variable for which the rate of change is:

   i. positive.   **ii.** zero (no change).   **iii.** negative.

b. Write an equation that models each situation in part (a).

Connections

15. Jelani is in a walking race at his school. In the first 20 seconds, he walks 60 meters. In the next 30 seconds, he walks 60 meters. In the next 10 seconds, he walks 35 meters. In the last 40 seconds, he walks 80 meters.

   a. Describe how Jelani's walking rate changes during the race.

   b. What would a graph of Jelani's walking race look like?

16. Insert parentheses in the expression on the left side of each equation to make each number sentence true.

   a. $2 + -3 \times 4 = -10$

   b. $4 + -3 \times -4 = -4$

   c. $-12 \div 2 + -4 = 6$

   d. $8 \div -2 + -2 = -6$

17. Which of the following number sentences are true? In each case, explain how you could answer without any calculation. Check your answers by doing the indicated calculations.

   a. $20 \times 410 = (20 \times 400) + (20 \times 10)$

   b. $20 \times 308 = (20 \times 340) - (20 \times 32)$

   c. $-20 \times -800 = (-20 \times -1{,}000) + (-20 \times 200)$

   d. $-20 + (300 \times 32) = (-20 + 300) \times (-20 + 32)$

18. Fill in the missing parts to make each number sentence true.

   a. $15 \times (6 + 4) = (15 \times \blacksquare) + (15 \times 4)$

   b. $2 \times (x + 6) = (2 \times \blacksquare) + (\blacksquare \times 6)$

   c. $(x \times 2) + (x \times 6) = \blacksquare \times (2 + 6)$

19. a. Draw a rectangle whose area can be represented by the expression $5 \times (12 + 6)$.

   b. Write another expression to represent the area of the rectangle in part (a).

20. Find the unit rate and use it to write an equation relating the two quantities.

    a. 150 dollars for 50 T-shirts

    b. 62 dollars to rent 14 video games

    c. 18 tablespoons of sugar in 3 glasses of Bolda Cola

21. The longest human-powered sporting event is the Tour de France cycling race. In a particular year, the average speed for the winner of this race was 23.66 miles per hour.

    a. In that same year, the race was 2,292 miles long. How long did it take the winner to complete the race?

    b. Suppose the winner had reduced his average cycling rate by 0.1 mile per hour. By how much would his time have changed?

22. **a.** In 1990, Nadezhda Ryashkina set the record for the 10,000 m race-walking event. She finished this race in 41 minutes 56.23 seconds. What was Ryashkina's average walking rate, in meters per second?

    b. In 2001, Olimpiada Ivanova set the record for the 20,000 m race-walking event. She finished the race in 86 minutes 52.3 seconds. What was Ivanova's average walking speed, in meters per second?

23. A recipe for orange juice calls for 2 cups of orange juice concentrate and 3 cups of water. The table below shows the amount of concentrate and water needed to make a given number of batches of juice.

Orange Juice Mixture Amounts

Batches of Juice (b)	Concentrate (c)	Water (w)	Juice (j)
1	2 cups	3 cups	5 cups
2	4 cups	6 cups	10 cups
3	6 cups	9 cups	15 cups
4	8 cups	12 cups	20 cups

The relationship between the number of batches of juice b and the number of cups of concentrate c is linear. The equation that represents this linear relationship is $c = 2b$. Are there other relationships in this table that are linear? Sketch graphs or write equations for any you find.

24. The table below shows the number of cups of orange juice, pineapple juice, and soda water needed for different quantities of punch.

Pineapple Punch Recipe

J (orange juice, cups)	*P* (pineapple juice, cups)	*S* (soda water, cups)
1	▨	▨
2	▨	▨
3	▨	▨
4	12	6
5	▨	▨
6	▨	▨
7	▨	▨
8	24	12

The relationship between cups of orange juice and cups of pineapple juice is linear. The relationship between cups of orange juice and cups of soda water is also linear.

a. Zahara makes the recipe using 6 cups of orange juice. How many cups of soda water does she use? Explain your reasoning.

b. Patrick makes the recipe using 6 cups of pineapple juice. How many cups of orange juice and cups of soda water does he use? Explain.

25. The graph at the right represents the distance John runs in a race. Use the graph to describe John's progress during the course of the race. Does he run at a constant rate during the race? Explain.

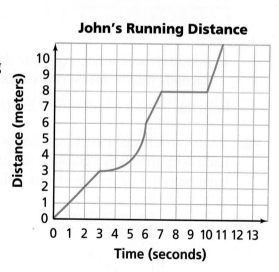

John's Running Distance

26. **a.** Does this graph represent a linear relationship? Explain.

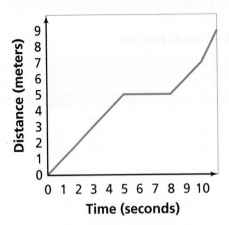

b. Could this graph represent a walking pattern? Explain.

For Exercises 27–29, students conduct an experiment to investigate the rate at which a leaking faucet loses water. They fill a paper cup with water, make a small hole in the bottom, and collect the dripping water in a measuring container, measuring the amount of water in the container at the end of each 10-second interval.

27. Students conducting the leaking-faucet experiment produce the table below. The measuring container they use has a capacity of 100 milliliters.

Leaking Faucet Experiment

Time (seconds)	10	20	30	40	50	60	70
Water Loss (milliliters)	2	5	8.5	11.5	14	16.5	19.5

a. Suppose the students continue their experiment. After how many seconds will the measuring container overflow?

b. Is this a linear relationship? Explain.

28. Denise and Takashi work together on the leaking-faucet experiment. Each of them makes a graph of the data they collect. What might have caused their graphs to look different?

Denise's Graph

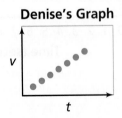

Takashi's Graph

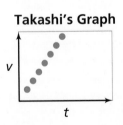

29. What might the graph below represent in the leaking-faucet experiment?

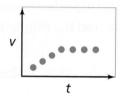

Extensions

30. a. The table below shows the populations of four cities for the past eight years. Describe how the population of each city changed over the eight years.

City Populations

Year	Population			
	Deep Valley	Nowhere	Swampville	Mount Silicon
0 (start)	1,000	1,000	1,000	1,000
1	1,500	900	1,500	2,000
2	2,000	800	2,500	4,000
3	2,500	750	3,000	8,000
4	3,000	700	5,000	16,000
5	3,500	725	3,000	32,000
6	4,000	900	2,500	64,000
7	4,500	1,500	1,500	128,000
8	5,000	1,700	1,000	256,000

b. Use the table to determine which relationships are linear.

c. Graph the data for each city. Describe how you selected ranges of values for the variables on the horizontal and vertical axes.

d. What are the advantages of using a table or a graph to represent the data?

31. In the walkathon, José asks his sponsors to donate $10 for the first 5 kilometers he walks and $1 per kilometer after 5 kilometers.

a. Sketch a graph that represents the relationship between the money collected from each sponsor and the number of kilometers walked.

b. Compare this graph to the graphs of the other pledge plans in Problem 1.3.

32. The cost C to make T-shirts for the walkathon is given by the equation $C = 20 + 5n$, where n is the number of T-shirts.

a. Find the coordinates of a point that lies on the graph of this equation. Explain what information the coordinates represent in this context.

b. Find the coordinates of a point above the line. Explain what information the coordinates represent in this context.

c. Find the coordinates of a point below the line. Explain what information the coordinates represent in this context.

33. Reggie is looking forward to walking in a walkathon. He writes some equations to use to answer some questions he has about the walkathon. For each of parts (a)–(c), do the following two things:

• Tell what information you think he was trying to find with the equation.

• Write one question he could use the equation to answer.

a. $y = 3x + 20$

b. $y = 0.25x$

c. $y = 4x$

Mathematical Reflections 1

In this Investigation, you began to explore linear relationships. You examined the patterns of change between two variables. The following questions will help you summarize what you have learned.

Think about these questions. Discuss your ideas with other students and your teacher. Then write a summary of your findings in your notebook.

1. **Describe** how the dependent variable changes as the independent variable changes in a linear relationship. Give examples.

2. **How** does the pattern of change between two variables in a linear relationship show up in

   a. a contextual situation?

   b. a table?

   c. a graph?

   d. an equation?

Common Core Mathematical Practices

As you worked on the Problems in this Investigation, you used prior knowledge to make sense of them. You also applied Mathematical Practices to solve the Problems. Think back over your work, the ways you thought about the Problems, and how you used Mathematical Practices.

Elena described her thoughts in the following way:

At the end of Problem 1.3, we noticed that the linear relationship with the greatest positive pattern of change had the steepest line. For example, $A_{Gilberto} = 2n$ and $A_{Alana} = 5 + 0.5n$. The line of Gilberto's equation is steeper since it has a greater rate of change.

This makes sense since as the number of kilometers increases by one unit, the money each sponsor donates to Gilberto increases by $2. The money each sponsor donates to Alana increases by $.50.

For Leanne, the equation is $A_{Leanne} = 10$, so the change is 0. As the number of kilometers increases by one unit, the money each sponsor donates to Leanne does not change. The graph is a horizontal line.

· ·

Common Core Standards for Mathematical Practice

MP8 Look for and express regularity in repeated reasoning.

- What other Mathematical Practices can you identify in Elena's reasoning?

- Describe a Mathematical Practice that you and your classmates used to solve a different Problem in this Investigation.

Exploring Linear Relationships With Graphs and Tables

In the last Investigation, you examined linear relationships. For example, the distance, d, a person walks at a constant rate depends on the amount of time, t, the person walks. Also, the amount of money, A, a person raises from each sponsor depends on the distance, d, walked in the walkathon. Both of these relationships are linear. You might have written the following equations to represent these two relationships for Alana.

$$d = 1t$$
$$\text{and}$$
$$A = 5 + 0.5d$$

In this Investigation, you will continue to solve problems involving walking rates and other linear relationships.

· ·

Common Core State Standards

7.RP.A.2b Identify the constant of proportionality (unit rate) in tables, graphs, equations, diagrams, and verbal descriptions of proportional relationships.

7.RP.A.2c Represent proportional relationships by equations.

7.EE.B.3 Solve multi-step real-life and mathematical problems posed with positive and negative rational numbers in any form (whole numbers, fractions, and decimals), using tools strategically. Apply properties of operations to calculate with numbers in any form; convert between forms as appropriate; and assess the reasonableness of answers using mental computation and estimation strategies.

7.EE.B.4 Use variables to represent quantities in a real-world or mathematical problem, and construct simple equations and inequalities to solve problems by reasoning about the quantities.

Also 7.RP.A.2d, 7.EE.B.4a

2.1 Henri and Emile's Race
Finding the Point of Intersection

In Ms. Chang's class, Emile found out that his walking rate is 2.5 meters per second. That is, Emile walks 2.5 meters every 1 second. When he gets home from school, he times his little brother Henri as Henri walks 100 meters. He figures out that Henri's walking rate is 1 meter per second. Henri walks 1 meter every second.

Problem 2.1

Henri challenges Emile to a walking race. Because Emile's walking rate is faster, Emile gives Henri a 45-meter head start. Emile knows his brother would enjoy winning the race, but he does not want to make the race so short that it is obvious his brother will win.

A How long should the race be so that Henri will win in a close race?

B Describe your strategy for finding your answer to Question A. Give evidence to support your answer.

A C E Homework starts on page 38.

2.2 Crossing the Line
Using Tables, Graphs, and Equations

Your class may have found some very interesting strategies for solving Problem 2.1, such as:

- Making a table showing time and distance data for both brothers

- Graphing time and distance data for both brothers on the same set of axes

- Writing an equation for each brother representing the relationship between time and distance

? How can each of these strategies be used to solve the Problem?

Problem 2.2

A For each brother in Problem 2.1:

1. Make a table showing the distance from the starting line at several different times during the first 40 seconds. How can the table be used to find the length of the race?

2. Graph the time and the distance from the starting line on the same set of axes. How can the graph be used to find the length of the race?

3. Write an equation representing the relationship between time and distance. Explain what information each variable and number represents.

4. How does the walking rate of each brother show up in the graph, the table, and the equation?

B 1. How far does Emile walk in 20 seconds?

2. After 20 seconds, how far apart are the brothers? How is this distance represented in the table and on the graph?

3. Is the point (26, 70) on either graph?

4. When will Emile overtake Henri? Explain.

C How can you determine which of two lines will be steeper from

1. a table of the data?

2. an equation?

D 1. At what points do Emile's and Henri's graphs cross the y-axis?

2. What information do these points represent in terms of the race?

3. How can these points be found in a table? In an equation?

A C E Homework starts on page 38.

Did You Know?

Have you ever seen a walking race? You may have thought the walking style of the racers seemed rather strange. Race walkers must follow two rules:

- The walker must always have one foot in contact with the ground.

- The walker's leg must be straight from the time it strikes the ground until it passes under the body.

A champion race walker can cover a mile in about 6.5 minutes. It takes most people 15 to 20 minutes to walk a mile.

2.3 Comparing Costs
Comparing Relationships

All of the linear relationships you have studied so far can be written in the form $y = mx + b$, or $y = b + mx$. In this equation, y depends on x.

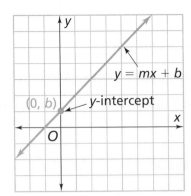

In Problem 2.2, you found the points at which Emile's and Henri's graphs cross the y-axis. These points are called the *y-intercepts*. The **y-intercept** is the point where the line crosses the y-axis, or when $x = 0$. The coordinates of the y-intercept for the graph shown above are $(0, b)$. To save time, we sometimes refer to the number b, rather than the coordinates of the point $(0, b)$, as the y-intercept.

A **coefficient** is the number that multiplies a variable in an equation. The m in $y = mx + b$ is the coefficient of x, so mx means m times x.

- You can represent the distance d_{Emile} that Emile walks after t seconds with the equation, $d_{\text{Emile}} = 2.5t$. The y-intercept is $(0, 0)$, and the coefficient of t is 2.5. You multiply Emile's walking rate by the time t he walks. He starts at a distance of 0 meters.

Emile

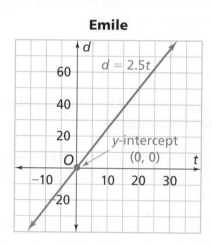

- You can represent the distance d_{Henri} that Henri is from where Emile started with the equation, $d_{\text{Henri}} = 45 + t$, where t is the time in seconds. The y-intercept is $(0, 45)$, and the coefficient of t is 1.

Henri

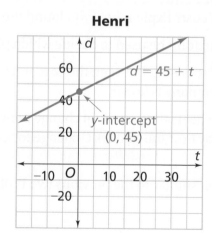

A **solution of an equation** is an ordered pair that makes the equation true and lies on the graph of the line.

- Is $(0, 45)$ a solution of the equation $d_{\text{Henri}} = 45 + t$? Explain.

- What would t be if $(t, 48)$ is a solution? Explain.

- What would d be if $(10, d)$ is a solution? Explain.

In this Problem, you will look at situations represented by an equation or a table.

Problem 2.3

Ms. Chang's class decides to give T-shirts to each person who participates in the walkathon. They receive bids for the cost of the T-shirts from two different companies. Mighty Tee charges $49 plus $1 per T-shirt. No-Shrink Tee charges $4.50 per T-shirt. Ms. Chang writes the following equations to represent the relationships relating cost to the number of T-shirts:

$$C_{\text{Mighty}} = 49 + n$$

$$C_{\text{No-Shrink}} = 4.5n$$

The number of T-shirts is n. C_{Mighty} is the cost in dollars for Mighty Tee. $C_{\text{No-Shrink}}$ is the cost in dollars for No-Shrink Tee.

Ⓐ 1. For each equation, explain what information the y-intercept and the coefficient of n represent. What is the independent variable? What is the dependent variable?

2. For each company, what is the cost for 12 T-shirts? For 20 T-shirts?

3. Lani calculates that the school has about $120 to spend on T-shirts. From which company will $120 buy the most T-shirts? Explain your answer.

4. **a.** For what number of T-shirts is the cost of the two companies equal? What is that cost? Explain how you found the answers.

   b. How can this information be used to decide which plan to choose?

5. **a.** Explain why the relationship between the cost and the number of T-shirts for each company is linear.

   b. In each equation, what is the pattern of change between the two variables? That is, by how much does C change for every 1 unit that n increases?

   c. How is this situation similar to the previous two Problems?

Problem 2.3 *continued*

B The following table represents the costs from another company, The Big T.

T-Shirt Costs

n	C
0	34
3	41.5
5	46.5
8	54
10	59

1. Compare the costs for this company to the costs for the two companies in Question A.

2. Is the relationship between the two variables in this plan linear? If so, what is the pattern of change between the two variables?

3. **a.** Would the point (20, 84) lie on the graph of this cost plan? Explain.

   b. What information about the number of T-shirts and cost do the coordinates of the point (20, 84) represent?

   c. What equation relates C and n?

   d. Would (20, 80) be a solution of the equation? Would (14, 69) be a solution? Explain.

ACE Homework starts on page 38.

2.4 Connecting Tables, Graphs, and Equations

Look again at Alana's pledge plan from Problem 1.3. Suppose A represents the amount raised in dollars and d represents the distance walked in kilometers. You can express this plan with the equation $A = 5 + 0.5d$.

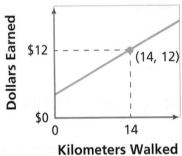

Alana's Pledge Plan

- Explain why the point (14, 12) is on the graph of Alana's pledge plan.

- Write a question you could answer by locating this point.

- How can you use the equation for Alana's pledge plan to check the answer to the question you made up?

- How can you use a graph to find the number of kilometers that Alana walks if a sponsor donates $17? How could you use an equation to answer this question?

In this Problem, you will investigate similar questions relating to pledge plans for a walkathon.

Problem 2.4

Consider the following pledge plans. In each equation, y is the amount pledged in dollars by each sponsor, and x is the distance walked in kilometers.

Plan 1	**Plan 2**	**Plan 3**
$y = 5x - 3$	$y = -x + 6$	$y = 2$

Problem 2.4 continued

A For each pledge plan:

1. What information does the equation give about the pledge plan? Does the plan make sense?

2. Make a table of values of x from -5 to 5.

3. Sketch a graph of the relationship. What part of each graph is relevant to the situation?

4. Do the y-values increase, decrease, or stay the same as the x-values increase? Explain how you can find the answer using a table, a graph, or an equation.

B **1.** Which graph from Question A, part (3) contains the point $(2, 4)$?

2. How do the coordinates $(2, 4)$ relate to the equation of the line? To the corresponding table of data?

3. Write a question you could answer by locating this point.

C **1.** Which relationship has a graph you can use to find the value of x that makes $8 = 5x - 3$ a true statement?

2. How does finding the value of x in $8 = 5x - 3$ help you find the coordinates for a point on the graph of the relationship?

D The following three points all lie on the graph of the same plan:

$$(-7, 13) \qquad (1.2, \blacksquare) \qquad (\blacksquare, -4)$$

1. Two of the points have a missing coordinate. Find the missing coordinate. Explain how you found it.

2. Write a question you could answer by finding the missing coordinate.

E **1.** Describe how a point on a graph is related to a table and an equation that represent the same relationship.

2. How can you use a table, a graph, or an equation that represents the relationship $y = 5x - 3$ to

a. find the value of y when $x = 7$?

b. find the value of x when $y = 23$?

 Homework starts on page 38.

Applications

1. Grace and Allie are going to meet at the fountain near their houses. They both leave their houses at the same time. Allie passes Grace's house on her way to the fountain.

   - Allie's walking rate is 2 meters per second.
   - Grace's walking rate is 1.5 meters per second.

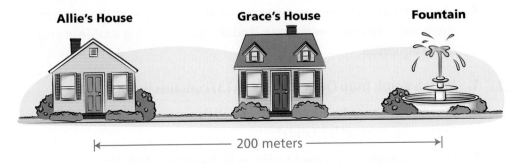

Allie's House   **Grace's House**   **Fountain**

|← ———————————— 200 meters ———————————— →|

   a. How many seconds will it take Allie to reach the fountain?

   b. Suppose Grace's house is 90 meters from the fountain. Who will reach the fountain first, Allie or Grace? Explain your reasoning.

2. In Problem 2.2, Emile's friend, Gilberto, joins the race. Gilberto has a head start of 20 meters and walks at 2 meters per second.

   a. Write an equation that gives the relationship between Gilberto's distance d from where Emile starts and the time t.

   b. How would Gilberto's graph compare to Emile's and Henri's graphs?

3. Ingrid stops at Tara's house on her way to school. Tara's mother says that Tara left 5 minutes ago. Ingrid leaves Tara's house, walking quickly to catch up with Tara. The graph below shows the distance each girl is from Tara's house, starting from the time Ingrid leaves Tara's house.

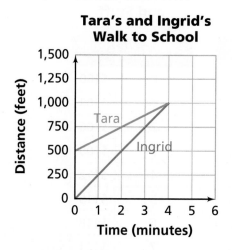

Tara's and Ingrid's Walk to School

a. In what way is this situation like the race between Henri and Emile? In what way is it different?

b. After how many minutes does Ingrid catch up with Tara?

c. How far from Tara's house does Ingrid catch up with Tara?

d. Each graph intersects the distance axis (the *y*-axis). What information do these points of intersection give about the situation?

e. Which line is steeper? How can you tell from the graph? How is the steepness of each line related to the rate at which the person travels?

f. What do you think the graphs would look like if we extended them to show distance and time after the girls meet?

In Exercises 4 and 5, the student council asks for cost estimates for a skating party to celebrate the end of the school year.

4. The following tables represent the costs from two skating companies.

Rollaway Skates

Number of People	Cost
0	$0
1	$5
2	$10
3	$15
4	$20
5	$25
6	$30
7	$35
8	$40

Wheelie's Skates and Stuff

Number of People	Cost
0	$100
1	$103
2	$106
3	$109
4	$112
5	$115
6	$118
7	$121
8	$124

a. For each company, is the relationship between the number of people and cost a linear relationship? Explain.

b. For each company, write an equation that represents the relationship between the cost and the number of people. What is the dependent variable? What is the independent variable?

c. Describe how you can use the table or a graph to find when the costs of the two plans are equal. How can this information help the student council decide which company to choose?

5. A third company, Wheels to Go, gives their quote in the form of the equation $C_W = 35 + 4n$, where C_W is the cost in dollars for n students.

a. What information do the numbers 35 and 4 represent in this situation?

b. For 60 students, which of the three companies is the cheapest? Explain how you could determine the answer using tables, graphs, or equations.

c. Suppose the student council wants to keep the cost of the skating party to $500. How many people can they invite under each of the three plans?

d. The points below lie on one or more of the graphs of the three cost plans. Decide to which plan(s) each point belongs.

   i. (20, 115)   **ii.** (65, 295)   **iii.** (50, 250)

e. Pick one of the points in part (d). Write a question that could be answered by locating this point.

6. A band decides to sell protein bars to raise money for an upcoming trip. The cost (the amount the band pays for the protein bars) and the income the band receives for the protein bars are represented on the graph.

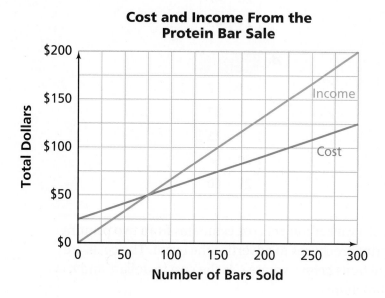

a. How many protein bars must be sold for the cost to equal the income?

b. What is the income from selling 50 protein bars? 125 bars?

c. Suppose the income is $200. How many protein bars were sold? How much of this income is profit?

7. Suppose each of the following patterns continues.

- Which represent linear relationships? Explain your answer.

- For those that are linear relationships, write an equation that expresses the relationship.

a.

x	y
-10	-29
0	1
10	31
20	61
30	91

b.

x	y
1	9
5	17
7	21
20	47
21	49

c.

x	y
1	1
2	4
3	9
4	16
5	25

d.

x	y
1	9
5	22
7	25
20	56
21	60

8. The organizers of a walkathon get cost estimates from two printing companies to print brochures to advertise the event. The costs are given by the equations below, where C is the cost in dollars and n is the number of brochures.

Company A

$$C = 15 + 0.10n$$

Company B

$$C = 0.25n$$

a. For what number of brochures are the costs the same for both companies? What method did you use to get your answer?

b. The organizers have $65 to spend on brochures. How many brochures can they have printed if they use Company A? If they use Company B?

c. What information does the y-intercept of the graph represent for each equation?

d. What information does the coefficient of n represent for each equation?

e. For each company, describe the change in the cost as the number of brochures increases by 1.

9. A school committee is assigned the task of selecting a DJ for the end-of-school-year party. Darius obtains several quotes for the cost of three DJs.

Compare DJs

$60 per hour

$100 set-up fee
plus
$40 per hour

$175 set-up fee
plus
$30 per hour

a. For each DJ, write an equation that shows how the total cost C relates to the number of hours x.

b. What information does the coefficient of x represent for each DJ?

c. For each DJ, what information does the y-intercept of the graph represent?

d. Suppose the DJ will need to work eight and one half hours. What is the cost of each DJ?

e. Suppose the committee has only $450 dollars to spend on a DJ. For how many hours could each DJ play?

10. A local department store offers two installment plans for buying a $270 skateboard.

> **Plan 1** A fixed weekly payment of $10.80
>
> **Plan 2** A $120 initial payment plus $6.00 per week

a. For each plan, how much money is owed after 12 weeks?

b. Which plan requires the least number of weeks to pay for the skateboard? Explain.

c. Write an equation for each plan. Explain what information the variables and numbers represent.

d. Suppose the skateboard costs $355. How would the answers to parts (a)–(c) change?

For each equation in Exercises 11–14, answer parts (a)–(d).

    a. What is the rate of change?

    b. State whether the *y*-values are increasing, decreasing, or neither as *x* increases.

    c. Give the *y*-intercept.

    d. List the coordinates of two points that lie on the graph of the equation.

11. $y = 1.5x$ **12.** $y = -3x + 10$

13. $y = -2x + 6$ **14.** $y = 2x + 5$

15. Dani earns $7.50 per hour when she babysits.

    a. Draw a graph that relates the number of hours she babysits and the total amount of money she earns.

    b. Choose a point on the graph. Ask two questions that can be answered by finding the coordinates of this point.

16. Martel wants to use his calculator to find the value of *x* when $y = 22$ in the equation $y = 100 - 3x$. Explain how he can use each table or graph to find the value of *x* when $100 - 3x = 22$.

    a.

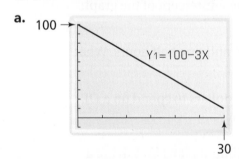

    b.

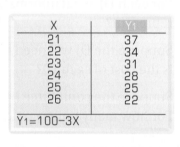

    c.

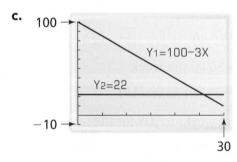

17. Match each equation to a graph.

   a. $y = 3x + 5$ **b.** $y = x - 7$ **c.** $y = -x - 10$

Graph 1

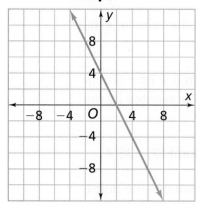

Graph 2

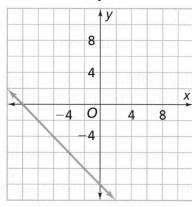

Graph 3

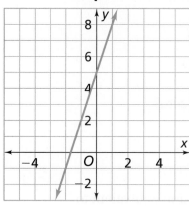

Graph 4

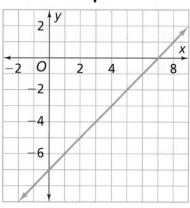

   d. Write an equation for the graph that has no match.

For each equation in Exercises 18–21, give two values for x for which the value of y is negative.

18. $y = -2x - 5$

19. $y = -5$

20. $y = 2x - 5$

21. $y = \frac{3}{2}x - \frac{1}{4}$

For Exercises 22–28, consider the following equations:

    i. $y = 2x$ **ii.** $y = -5x$ **iii.** $y = 2x - 6$

    iv. $y = -2x + 1$ **v.** $y = 7$

22. Which equation has a graph you can use to find the value of x that makes $8 = 2x - 6$ a true statement?

23. How does finding a solution for x in the equation $8 = 2x - 6$ help you find the coordinates of a point on the line represented by the equation $y = 2x - 6$?

24. Which equation has a graph that contains the point $(7, -35)$?

25. The following two points lie on the graph that contains the point $(7, -35)$. Find the missing coordinate for each point.

    $(-1.2, \blacksquare)$ $(\blacksquare, -15)$

26. Which equations have a positive rate of change?

27. Which equations have a negative rate of change?

28. Which equations have a rate of change equal to zero?

Connections

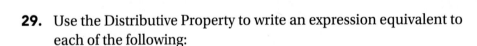

29. Use the Distributive Property to write an expression equivalent to each of the following:

    a. $x(-2 + 3)$ **b.** $(-4x) + (2x)$ **c.** $(x) - (4x)$

30. Decide whether each statement is true or false. Explain your reasoning.

    a. $15 - 3x = 15 + -3x$

    b. $3.5x + 5 = 5(0.7x + 5)$

    c. $3(2x + 1) = (2x + 1) + (2x + 1) + (2x + 1)$

31. The Ferry family decides to buy a new television that costs $215. The store has an installment plan that allows them to make a $35 down payment and then pay $15 a month. Use the graph to answer the questions below.

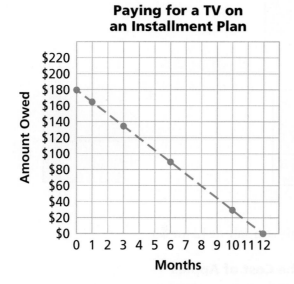

Paying for a TV on an Installment Plan

a. Write an equation that represents the relationship between the amount the Ferry family still owes and the number of months after the purchase. Explain what information the numbers and variables represent.

b. The point where the graph of an equation intersects the x-axis is called the **x-intercept**. What are the x- and y-intercepts of the graph for this payment plan? Explain what information each intercept represents.

32. Shallah Middle School is planning a school trip. The cost is $5 per person. The organizers know that three adults are going on the trip, but they do not yet know the number of students who will go. Write an expression that represents the total costs for x students and three adults.

33. Use the Distributive Property to write two expressions that show two different ways to compute the area of each rectangle.

a.

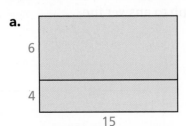

b.

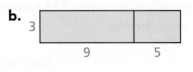

c.

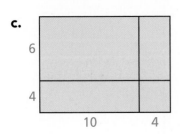

d.

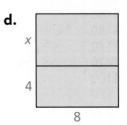

34. Harvest Foods has apples on sale at 12 for $3.

The Cost of Apples

Number of Apples	12	■	1	48	10	■
Cost	$3	$1.50	■	■	■	$4.50

a. What is the cost per apple?

b. Complete the rate table to show the costs of different numbers of apples.

c. How many apples can you buy for $1?

d. Is the relationship between number of apples and cost linear? Explain.

35. Lamar bought some bagels for his friends. He paid $15 for 20 bagels.

a. How much did Lamar pay per bagel?

b. Write an equation relating the number of bagels, n, to the total cost, C.

c. Use your equation to find the cost of 150 bagels.

36. DeAndre says that $x = -1$ makes the equation $-8 = -3 + 5x$ true. Tamara checks this value for x in the equation. She says DeAndre is wrong because $-3 + 5 \times (-1)$ is -2, not -8. Why do you think these students disagree?

37. Determine whether the following mathematical sentences are true or false.

    a. $5 + 3 \times 2 = 16$ **b.** $3 \times 2 + 5 = 16$

    c. $5 + 3 \times 2 = 11$ **d.** $3 \times 2 + 5 = 11$

    e. $\frac{3}{2} \div \frac{4}{3} - \frac{1}{8} = 1$ **f.** $\frac{1}{2} + \frac{3}{2} \div \frac{1}{2} = 2$

38. Jamal feeds his dog the same amount of dog food each day from a very large bag. The number of cups left on the 3rd day and the number of cups left on the 11th day are shown below.

Day 3

Day 11

44 cups

28 cups

    a. How many cups of food does he feed his dog a day?

    b. How many cups of food were in the bag when he started?

    c. Write an equation for the total amount of dog food Jamal has left after feeding his dog for d days.

39. a. Match the following connecting paths for the last 5 minutes of Jalissa's race.

1. 2. 3. 4. 5.

    i. Jalissa finishes running at a constant rate.

    ii. Jalissa runs slowly at first and gradually increases her speed.

   iii. Jalissa runs quickly and then gradually decreases her speed.

    iv. Jalissa runs quickly and reaches the finish line early.

    v. After falling, Jalissa runs at a constant rate.

b. Which of the situations in part (a) was most likely to represent Jalissa's running for the entire race? Explain your answer.

40. In *Stretching and Shrinking,* you plotted the points $(8, 6)$, $(8, 22)$, and $(24, 14)$ on grid paper to form a triangle.

a. Draw the triangle you get when you apply the rule $(0.5x, 0.5y)$ to the three points.

b. Draw the triangle you get when you apply the rule $(0.25x, 0.25y)$ to the three points.

c. How are the three triangles you have drawn related?

d. What are the areas of the three triangles?

e. Do you notice any linear relationships among the data of the three triangles, such as the area, scale factor, lengths of sides, and so on?

41. In *Covering and Surrounding,* you looked at perimeters of rectangles.

a. Make a table of possible whole number values for the length and width of a rectangle with a perimeter of 20 meters.

b. Write an equation that represents the data in this table. Make sure to define your variables.

c. Is the relationship between length and width linear in this case? Explain.

d. Find the area of each rectangle.

Extensions

42. For each equation below, decide whether it models a linear relationship. Explain how you decided.

a. $y = 2x$ **b.** $y = \frac{2}{x}$ **c.** $y = x^2$

43. a. Write equations for three lines that intersect to form a triangle.

    b. Sketch the graphs and label the coordinates of the vertices of the triangle.

    c. Will any three lines intersect to form a triangle? Explain.

44. a. Which one of the following points is on the line $y = 3x - 7$: $(3, 3)$, $(3, 2)$, $(3, 1)$, or $(3, 0)$? Describe where each of the other three points is in relation to the line.

    b. Find another point on the line $y = 3x - 7$ and three more points above the line.

    c. The equation $y = 3x - 7$ is true for $(4, 5)$ and $(7, 14)$. Use this information to find two points that make the inequality $y < 3x - 7$ true and two points that make the inequality $y > 3x - 7$ true.

45. Ms. Chang's class decides to order posters that advertise the walkathon. Ichiro obtains quotes from two different companies.

           Clear Prints charges $2 per poster.

           Posters by Sue charges $15 plus $.50 per poster.

    a. For each company, write an equation Ichiro could use to calculate the cost for any number of posters.

    b. For what number of posters is the cost the same for both companies? Explain.

    c. Which company do you think the class should buy posters from? Explain your reasoning.

    d. If Ms. Chang's class has an $18 budget for posters, which company do you think the class should buy posters from? If Ms. Chang donates an additional $10 for ordering posters, does it impact the decision made? What factors influenced your decision?

    e. Use the information from parts (a)–(c) to find an ordered pair that makes the inequality $C < 20$ true for Clear Prints. Find an ordered pair that makes the inequality $C > 20$ true for Posters by Sue.

In this Investigation, you continued to explore patterns of change between the independent and dependent variables in a linear relationship. You learned how to use tables, graphs, and equations to solve problems that involve linear relationships. The following questions will help you summarize what you have learned.

Think about these questions. Discuss your ideas with other students and your teacher. Then write a summary of your findings in your notebook.

1. a. **Explain** how the information about a linear relationship is represented in a table, a graph, or an equation.

   b. **Describe** several real-world situations that can be modeled by equations of the form $y = mx + b$ or $y = mx$. Explain how the latter equation represents a proportional relationship.

2. a. **Explain** how a table or a graph that represents a linear relationship can be used to solve a problem.

   b. **Explain** how you have used an equation that represents a linear relationship to solve a problem.

Common Core Mathematical Practices

As you worked on the Problems in this Investigation, you used prior knowledge to make sense of them. You also applied Mathematical Practices to solve the Problems. Think back over your work, the ways you thought about the Problems, and how you used Mathematical Practices.

Tori described her thoughts in the following way:

In Problem 2.1, we looked at how far apart the brothers were after t seconds. For example, at the start of the race, they are 45 meters apart. After 1 second, they are $45 - 1.5 = 43.5$ meters apart. After 2 seconds, they are 42 meters apart. After 10 seconds, they are 30 meters apart.

We made a table and found the time it took for Emile to catch up to Henri, or when the distance between them is 0, which is 30 seconds. We used this to choose the length of the race so that Henri wins the race.

Another group member made a graph of the data (time, distance apart), and we saw that it is a line that is decreasing. It started at the y-intercept of 45 meters and crossed the x-axis at 30 seconds.

··

Common Core Standards for Mathematical Practice

MP2 Reason abstractly and quantitatively.

- What other Mathematical Practices can you identify in Tori's reasoning?

- Describe a Mathematical Practice that you and your classmates used to solve a different Problem in this Investigation.

Solving Equations

In the last Investigation, you examined the patterns in the table and graph for the relationship relating Alana's distance d and money earned A in the walkathon.

The equation $A = 5 + 0.5d$ is another way to represent that relationship. The graph of the relationship is a line that contains infinitely many points. The coordinates of each point can be substituted into the equation to make a true statement. The coordinates of these points are solutions to the equation.

Common Core State Standards

7.EE.A.1 Apply properties of operations as strategies to add, subtract, factor, and expand linear expressions with rational coefficients.

7.EE.A.2 Understand that rewriting an expression in different forms in a problem context can shed light on the problem and how the quantities in it are related.

7.EE.B.4a Solve word problems leading to equations of the form $px + q = r$ and $p(x + q) = r$, where p, q, and r are specific rational numbers. Solve equations of these forms fluently. Compare an algebraic solution to an arithmetic solution, identifying the sequence of the operations used in each approach.

7.EE.B.4b Solve word problems leading to inequalities of the form $px + q > r$ or $px + q < r$, where p, q, and r are specific rational numbers. Graph the solution set of the inequality and interpret it in the context of the problem.

Also 7.EE.B.4

For example, the point (3, 6.5) lies on the line of $A = 5 + 0.5d$. This means that $d = 3$, $A = 6.5$, and $6.5 = 5 + 0.5(3)$ is a true statement. So, the coordinate pair (3, 6.5) is a solution to the equation.

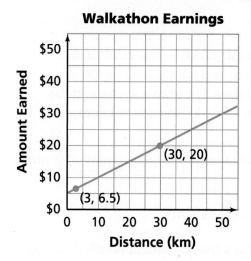

Walkathon Earnings

- Does the point (30, 20) lie on the line? Is it a solution to the equation? Explain.

- Does the point (20, 20) lie on the line? Is it a solution to the equation? Explain.

- What happens if you choose a point that is not visible on this section of the graph, such as (70, 40)? Is it on the line? Explain.

The corresponding entries in a table are the coordinates of points on the line representing the equation $A = 5 + 0.5d$. So, we can also find a solution to an equation by using a table.

- How could you find the value of d that corresponds to $A = 30$ in the table?

d	A
0	5
1	5.5
2	6
3	6.5
4	7
20	15
25	17.5
30	20

3.1 Solving Equations Using Tables and Graphs

In a relationship between two variables, if you know the value of one variable, you can use a table or a graph to find the value of the other variable. For example, suppose Alana raises $10 from a sponsor in the walkathon from Problem 1.3. Then you can ask: How many kilometers does Alana walk?

In the equation $A = 5 + 0.5d$, this means that $A = 10$. The equation is now $10 = 5 + 0.5d$.

- What value of d will make this a true statement?

Finding the value of d that will make this a true statement is called *solving the equation* for d. You can use tables or graphs to find the missing value. In this Investigation, you will develop strategies for solving equations symbolically, using properties of operations and equality.

Problem 3.1

A Use the equation $A = 5 + 0.5d$.

1. a. Suppose Alana walks 23 kilometers. Show how you can use a table and a graph to find the amount of money each sponsor donates.

b. Write an equation that represents the amount of money Alana collects if she walks 23 kilometers. Can you use the equation to find the amount? Explain.

2. Suppose Alana writes the equation $30 = 5 + 0.5d$.

a. What question is she trying to ask?

b. Show how you can answer Alana's question by reasoning with a table of values, a graph of the relationship $A = 5 + 0.5d$, or with the equation $30 = 5 + 0.5d$ itself.

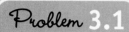 *continued*

B The equation $D = 25 + 2.5t$ is related to situations that you have explored. In parts (1) and (2) below, the value of one variable in the equation is known. Find the solution (the value of the unknown variable) in each part. Then, describe another way you can find the solution.

    1. $D = 25 + 2.5(7)$ **2.** $70 = 25 + 2.5t$

A C E Homework starts on page 69.

3.2 Mystery Pouches in the Kingdom of Montarek
Exploring Equality

In the Kingdom of Montarek, money takes the form of $1 gold coins called rubas. Messengers carry money between the king's castles in sealed pouches that always hold equal numbers of coins.

$1 gold coin   sealed pouch

One day a messenger arrived at one of the castles with a box containing two sealed pouches and five loose $1 coins. The ruler thanked the messenger for the money, which equaled $11.

- Can you figure out the number of coins in each pouch?

- Does the following visual equation help in finding the number of coins in each pouch?

In this Problem, you will solve more problems involving mystery pouches.

Problem **3.2**

A In parts (1)–(6) below, each pouch contains the same number of $1 gold coins. Also, the total number of coins on each side of the equation is the same.

- Find the number of gold coins in each pouch. Write down your steps so that someone else could follow your steps to find the number of coins in a pouch.

- Describe how you can check your answer. That is, how do you know you have found the correct number of gold coins in each pouch?

1.

2.

3.

4.

5.

6.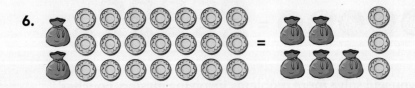

Problem 3.2 *continued*

B In Question A, part (2), Nichole thought of the left-hand side of the situation as having two groups. Each group contained one pouch and two coins. She visualized the following steps to help her find the number of coins in a pouch.

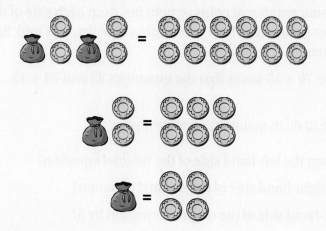

1. Is Nichole correct? Explain.

2. Noah looked at Nichole's strategy and claimed that she was applying the Distributive Property. Is Noah's claim correct? Explain.

3. Are there other situations in which Nichole's method might work? Explain.

ACE Homework starts on page 69.

3.3 From Pouches to Variables
Writing Equations

In the last Problem, you used pictures of pouches and gold coins to solve equations. Your solutions maintained the equality of the coins on both sides of the equal sign. For example, you might have removed (or subtracted) the same number of coins or pouches from each side of the equation. To better understand how to maintain equality, let's look first at numerical statements.

The equation $85 = 70 + 15$ states that the quantities 85 and $70 + 15$ are equal.

What do you have to do to maintain equality if you:

- subtract 15 from the left-hand side of the original equation?

- add 10 to the right-hand side of the original equation?

- divide the left-hand side of the original equation by 5?

- multiply the right-hand side of the original equation by 4?

Try your methods on another example of equality. Summarize what you know about maintaining equality between two quantities.

Throughout this Unit, you have been solving equations with two variables. Sometimes the value of one variable is known, and you want to find the value of the other variable. In this Problem, you will continue to find the value of a variable without using a table or a graph. You will learn to use *symbolic* methods to solve a linear equation.

The picture below shows a situation from Problem 3.2.

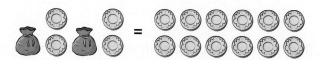

Because the number of gold coins in each pouch is unknown, you can let *x* represent the number of coins in one pouch. You can let 1 represent the value of one gold coin.

You can write the following equation to represent the situation:

$$2x + 4 = 12$$

Or, you can use Nichole's method from Problem 3.2 to write this equation:

$$2(x + 2) = 12$$

The expressions $2x + 4$ and $2(x + 2)$ are **equivalent expressions.** Two or more expressions are equivalent if they have the same value, regardless of what number is substituted for the variable. These two expressions are an example of the Distributive Property for numbers.

$$2(x + 2) = 2x + 4$$

In this Problem, you will revisit situations with pouches and coins, but you will use symbolic equations to represent your solution process.

Problem 3.3

Ⓐ For each situation, find the number of coins in each pouch. Record your answers in a table like the one shown.

Picture	Steps for Finding the Coins in Each Pouch	Solution Using Equations
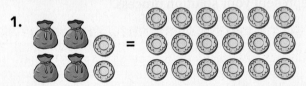		

- In the second column, use your method from Problem 3.2 to find the number of gold coins in each pouch. Record your steps.

- In the third column, write an equation that represents the situation. Use *x* to represent the number of gold coins in each pouch. Use the number 1 to represent each coin. Then, use your equation to find the number of gold coins in each pouch.

- Check your answers.

1.

2.

3.

Problem 3.3 *continued*

4.

5. Describe two situations in Question A for which you could write more than one equation to represent the situation.

B For each equation:

- Use your strategies from Question A to solve the equation.

- Check your answer.

  1. $30 = 6 + 4x$

  2. $7x = 5 + 5x$

  3. $7x + 2 = 12 + 5x$

  4. $2(x + 4) = 16$

C Describe a general method for solving equations using what you know about equality.

A C E Homework starts on page 69.

3.4 Solving Linear Equations

To maintain the equality of two expressions, you can add, subtract, multiply, or divide each side of the equality by the same number. These are called the **properties of equality**. In the last Problem, you applied properties of equality and numbers to find a solution to an equation.

So far in this Investigation, all of the situations have involved positive whole numbers.

- Does it make sense to think about negative numbers in a coin situation?

- Does it make sense to think about fractions in a coin situation?

 What strategies do you have for solving an equation like $-2x + 10 = 15$?

You have used the properties of equality to solve equations involving pouches and coins. These properties are also useful in solving all linear equations.

Problem 3.4

A For parts 1–3:

- Record each step you take to find your solution.

- Then, check your answer.

1. **a.** $5x + 10 = 20$ **b.** $5x - 10 = 20$ **c.** $5x + 10 = -20$

   d. $5x - 10 = -20$ **e.** $10 - 5x = 20$ **f.** $10 - 5x = -20$

2. **a.** $\frac{1}{4}x + 6 = 12$ **b.** $1\frac{1}{2} + 2x = 6\frac{1}{2}$ **c.** $\frac{3}{5} = -x + 1$

   d. $3.5x = 130 + 10x$ **e.** $15 - 4x = 10x + 45$

3. **a.** $3(x + 1) = 21$ **b.** $2 + 3(x + 1) = 6x$ **c.** $-2(2x - 3) = -2$

Problem 3.4 *continued*

B Below are examples of students' solutions the equations from Question A, part (3) above. Is each solution correct? If not, explain what the error is.

$$3(x + 1) = 21$$

Corry's Solution

3 times something in the parentheses must be 21.
So 3( ) = 21.
The something is 7.
So x + 1 = 7, and
x = 6.

$$2 + 3(x + 1) = 6x$$

Hadden's Solution

2 + 3(x + 1) is equivalent to 5(x + 1).
So I can rewrite the original equation as 5(x + 1) = 6x.
Using the Distributive Property, this is the same as
    5x + 5 = 6x.
Subtracting 5x from each side, I get 5 = 1x.
So x = 5.

$$-2(2x - 3) = -2$$

Jackie's Solution

By using the Distributive Property on the left-hand
    side of the equality, I get −4x − 6 = −2.
By adding 6 to each side, I get −4x = 4.
By dividing both sides by −4, I get x = −1.

C Describe the strategies you have used for solving linear equations. When might you use one over another?

ACE Homework starts on page 69.

3.5 Finding the Point of Intersection
Equations and Inequalities

In Problem 2.3, you used graphs and tables to find when the costs of two different plans for buying T-shirts were equal. The graphs of the two cost plans are shown below. C_n represents the costs of the No-Shrink Tee. C_m represents the costs of the Mighty Tee. The **point of intersection** of the two lines tells us when the costs for the two T-shirt plans are equal.

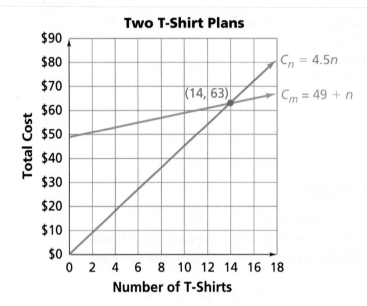

Two T-Shirt Plans

$C_n = 4.5n$

$C_m = 49 + n$

(14, 63)

Total Cost — Number of T-Shirts

- What information do the coordinates of the point of intersection of the two lines give you about this situation?

- Show how you could use the two equations to find the coordinates of the point of intersection of the two lines. That is, for what number of T-shirts n is $C_m = C_n$?

- For what number(s) of T-shirts is plan C_m less than plan C_n? That is, when is $C_m < C_n$?

Statements like $C_m = C_n$ are called equality statements or equations. You learned how to solve these equations symbolically in this Investigation.

Statements like $C_m < C_n$, $x < 5$, and $x > -5$ are called **inequality statements** or inequalities.

In this Problem, you will answer questions about points of intersection and about when the cost of one plan is less than or greater than that of another plan.

Problem 3.5

At Fabulous Fabian's Bakery, the expenses E to make n cakes per month is given by the equation $E = 825 + 3.25n$. The income I for selling n cakes is given by the equation $I = 8.20n$.

A 1. In the equations for I and E, what information do the y-intercepts give you?

   2. What do the coefficients of n represent?

B Fabian sells 100 cakes in January.

   1. What are his expenses and his income?

   2. What is his profit? Describe how you found your answer.

   3. Kevin drew the graph below. Explain how he could use his graph to determine Fabian's profit.

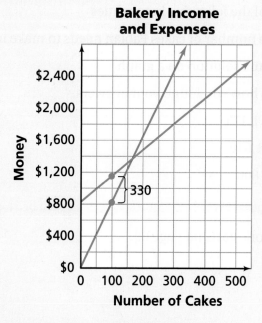

Bakery Income and Expenses

C 1. Write an equation that represents the profit, P, for selling n cakes. Describe how you can use this equation to find the profit.

   2. Fabian uses the equation $P = 4.95n - 825$ to predict the profit. Does this equation make sense? Explain.

continued on the next page >

Problem 3.5 continued

D The *break-even* point is when expenses equal income ($E = I$). Fabian thinks that this information is useful.

  1. Write an equation to find the number of cakes n needed to break even. How many cakes does Fabian need to make in order to break even?

  2. Describe how you could use a table or graph to find the break-even point.

E **1.** How many cakes can Fabian make if he wants his expenses to be less than $2,400 a month?

  2. How many cakes can he make if he wants to his income to be greater than $2,400 a month?

  3. Fabian's sister Mariah wrote the following inequality statements to answer parts (1) and (2) above.

$$825 + 3.25n < 2,400 \quad \text{and} \quad 8.20n > 2,400$$

  Do these statements make sense? Why?

  4. For each of the following inequalities

  • find the number of cakes Fabian needs to make in a month.

  • record the solution on a graph.

  • explain how you found your answers.

    a. $E < 1,475$

    b. $I > 1,640$

    c. $P > 800$

A C E Homework starts on page 69.

Applications

1. Ms. Chang's class decides to use the *Cool Tee's* company to make their T-shirts. The following equation represents the relationship between the cost *C* and the number of T-shirts *n*.

$$C = 2n + 20$$

   a. The class wants to buy 25 T-shirts from *Cool Tee's*. Describe how you can use a table and a graph to find the cost for 25 T-shirts.

   b. Suppose the class has $80 to spend on T-shirts. Describe how you can use a table and a graph to find the number of T-shirts the class can buy.

   c. Taleah writes the following equation in her notebook:

   $$C = 2(15) + 20$$

   What information is Sophia looking for?

   d. Keisha uses the coordinates (30, 80) to find information about the cost of the T-shirts. What information is she looking for?

2. Mary uses the following equations to find some information about three walkathon pledge plans.

Plan 1	**Plan 2**	**Plan 3**
$14 = 2x$	$y = 3.5(10) + 10$	$100 = 1.5x + 55$

   In each equation, *y* is the amount donated in dollars, and *x* is the number of kilometers walked. For each equation:

   a. What information is Mary trying to find?

   b. Describe how you could find the information.

3. Find the solution (the value of the variable) for each equation.

   a. $y = 3(10) + 15$ b. $24 = x + 2$ c. $10 = 2x + 4$

4. Consider the equation $y = 5x - 15$.

   a. Find *y* if $x = 1$.   b. Find *x* if $y = 50$.

   c. Describe how you can use a table or a graph to answer parts (a) and (b).

For each situation in Exercises 5–8, find the number of coins in each pouch. Each pouch contains the same number of $1 gold coins, and the total number of coins on each side of the equation is the same.

5.

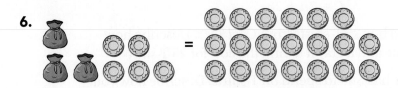

6.

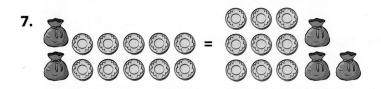

7.

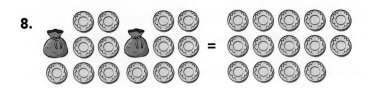

8.

9. For each equation, sketch a picture using pouches and coins. Then, determine how many coins are in a pouch.

   a. $3x = 12$

   b. $2x + 5 = 19$

   c. $4x + 5 = 2x + 19$

   d. $x + 12 = 2x + 6$

   e. $3(x + 4) = 18$

10. Gilberto's grandfather gives him $5 for his birthday and then 50¢ for each math question he answers correctly on his math exams for the year.

    a. Write an equation that represents the amount of money that Gilberto receives during a school year. Explain what the variables and numbers mean.

    b. Use the equation to find the number of correct answers Gilberto needs to buy a new shirt that costs $25. Show your work.

    c. Gilberto answered all 12 problems correctly on his first math exam. How much money is he assured of receiving for the year? Show your work.

11. For parts (a) and (b), find the mystery number and explain your reasoning.

    a. If you add 15 to 3 times the mystery number, you get 78. What is the mystery number?

    b. If you subtract 27 from 5 times the mystery number, you get 83. What is the mystery number?

    c. Make up clues for a riddle whose mystery number is 9.

12. Use properties of equality and numbers to solve each equation for x. Check your answers.

    a. $7 + 3x = 5x + 13$ **b.** $3x - 7 = 5x + 13$

    c. $7 - 3x = 5x + 13$ **d.** $3x + 7 = 5x - 13$

13. Multiple Choice Which of the following is a solution to the equation $11 = -3x - 10$?

    A. 1.3   **B.** $-\frac{1}{3}$ **C.** -7 **D.** 24

14. Solve each equation for x. Check your answers.

    a. $3x + 5 = 20$ **b.** $3x - 5 = 20$ **c.** $3x + 5 = -20$

    d. $-3x + 5 = 20$ **e.** $-3x - 5 = -20$

15. Determine whether each expression is *always, sometimes,* or *never* equal to $-2(x - 3)$.

    a. $-2x + 6$ **b.** $-2x - 6$ **c.** $2x + 6$

    d. $-2x - 3$ **e.** $-2(x + 3)$ **f.** $2(3 - x)$

16. For each equation in Group 1, find a matching equation in Group 2 that has the same solution. Write down any strategies you used.

Group 1

A: $3x + 6 = 12$

B: $3x - 6 = 12$

C: $-3x + 6 = 12$

D: $3x + 6 = -12$

E: $6x - 3 = 12$

Group 2

F: $x = 6$

G: $3(2 - x) = 12$

H: $3x = 6$

J: $x - \frac{1}{2} = 2$

K: $x + 2 = -4$

17. Solve each equation. Check your answers.

a. $3(x + 2) = 12$

b. $3(x + 2) = x - 18$

c. $3(x + 2) = 2x$

d. $3(x + 2) = -15$

18. Solve each equation for x.

a. $5 - 2(x - 1) = 12$

b. $5 + 2(x - 1) = 12$

c. $5 - 2(x + 2) = 12$

d. $5 - 2x + 2 = 12$

19. Solve each equation for x.

a. $2x + 6 = 6x + 2$

b. $2x + 6 = 6x - 2$

c. $2x - 6 = -6x + 2$

d. $-2x - 6 = -6x - 2$

For Exercises 20 and 21, use the equation $y = 4 - 3x$.

20. Find y when:

a. $x = 4$

b. $x = -3$

c. $x = 2$

d. $x = -\frac{4}{3}$

e. $x = 0$

21. Find x when:

a. $y = 0$

b. $y = 21$

c. $y = -15$

d. $y = 3.5$

22. Explain how the information you found for Exercises 20 and 21 relates to locating points on a line representing $y = 4 - 3x$.

23. In each part below, identify the equations that have the same solution.

a. A: $x = 8$

    B: $-x = 8$

    C: $x + 3x = 8$

    D: $1x = 8$

    E: $8 = 4x$

    F: $8 = -1x$

b. G: $x - 1 = 6$

    H: $x - 1 = -6$

    J: $-x + 1 = -6$

    K: $-x + 1 = 6$

    L: $6 = 1 - x$

    M: $-1 + x = 6$

c. N: $x - \frac{1}{2} = 4$

    O: $\frac{1}{2}x = -4$

    P: $x = 4 + \frac{1}{2}$

    Q: $-\frac{1}{2}x = 4$

    R: $\frac{1}{2} - x = 4$

    S: $-x + \frac{1}{2} = 4$

24. Two students' solutions to the equation $6(x + 4) = 3x - 2$ are shown below. Both students made an error. Find the errors and give a correct solution.

Student 1

$6(x + 4) = 3x - 2$

$x + 4 = 3x - 2 - 6$

$x + 4 = 3x - 8$

$x + 4 + 8 = 3x - 8 + 8$

$x + 12 = 3x$

$12 = 2x$

$x = 6$ ✗

Student 2

$6(x + 4) = 3x - 2$

$6x + 4 = 3x - 2$

$3x + 4 = -2$

$3x + 4 - 4 = -2 - 4$

$3x = -6$

$x = -2$ ✗

25. Two students' solutions to the equation $58.5 = 3.5x - 6$ are shown below. Both students made an error. Find the errors and give a correct solution.

Student 1

$58.5 = 3.5x - 6$

$58.5 - 6 = 3.5x$

$52.5 = 3.5x$

$\dfrac{52.5}{3.5} = x$

so, $x = 15$ ✗

Student 2

$58.5 = 3.5x - 6$

$58.5 + 6 = 3.5x - 6 + 6$

$64.5 = 3.5x$

$\dfrac{64.5}{3.5} = \dfrac{3.5}{3.5}x$

so, $x \approx 1.84$ ✗

26. Describe how you could use a graph or a table to solve each equation.

a. $5x + 10 = -20$

b. $4x - 9 = -7x + 13$

27. Use the equation $P = 10 - 2.5c$.

a. Find P when $c = 3.2$.

b. Find c when $P = 85$.

c. Describe how you can use a table or a graph to answer parts (a) and (b).

28. Use the equation $m = 15.75 + 3.2d$.

a. Find m when:

i. $d = 20$ **ii.** $d = 0$ **iii.** $d = 3.2$

b. Find d when:

i. $m = 54.15$ **ii.** $m = 0$ **iii.** $m = 100$

29. Khong thinks he has a different way to solve equations, by first factoring out both sides of the equation by the greatest common factor. This is how he solved the first equation in Problem 3.4.

> $5x + 10 = 20$ is the same as $5(x + 2) = 5(4)$.
> So, If I divide both sides by 5, I get $x + 2 = 4$.
> This means that $x = 2$.

a. Is Khong correct, that this method works for this problem? Explain.

b. Use Khong's method to solve the equation $40x + 20 = 120$.

c. Khong says his method won't work to solve $7x + 3 = 31$. Why is that?

d. Write an equation that can be solved using Khong's method. Then solve your equation.

30. The expenses E and income I for making and selling T-shirts with a school logo are given by the equations $E = 535 + 4.50n$ and $I = 12n$, where n is the number of T-shirts.

   a. How many T-shirts must be made and sold to break even? Explain.

   b. Suppose only 50 shirts are sold. Is there a profit or a loss? Explain.

   c. Suppose the income is $1,200. Is there a profit or a loss? Explain.

   d. i. For each equation, find the coordinates of a point that lies on the graph of the equation.

      ii. What information does this point give you?

      iii. Describe how to use the equation to show that the point lies on the graph.

31. The International Links long-distance phone company charges no monthly fee but charges 18 cents per minute for long-distance calls. The World Connections' long-distance company charges $50 per month plus 10 cents per minute for long-distance calls. Compare the World Connections long-distance plan to that of International Links.

   a. Under what circumstances is it cheaper to use International Links? Explain your reasoning.

   b. Write an inequality that describes when each company is cheaper. Represent the solution to the inequality on a graph.

32. Two cell-phone providers have different charges per month for text-messaging plans. Driftless Region Telephone has a plan charging $1\frac{1}{2}$ cents per text, with a monthly rate of $10. Walby Communications charges $16 per month for unlimited texting.

   a. If you were paying for a plan, which one would you purchase? Explain.

   b. Would you make the same recommendation for anyone else?

   c. Write an inequality that would help someone decide which plan to purchase. Then, represent the solution on a graph.

33. Students at Hammond Middle School are raising money for the end-of-year school party. They decide to sell roses for Valentine's Day. The students can buy the roses for 50 cents each from a wholesaler. They also need $60 to buy ribbon and paper to protect the roses as well as materials for advertising the sale. They sell each rose for $1.30.

a. How many roses must they sell to break even? Explain.

b. What is the students' profit if they sell 50 roses? 100 roses? 200 roses?

34. Ruth considers buying a cell phone from two different companies. Company A has a cost plan given by the equation $C_A = 32n$, where n is the number of months she has the phone and C_A is the total cost. Company B has a cost plan represented by the equation $C_B = 36 + 26n$, where n is the number of months she is on the plan and C_B is the total cost.

a. Graph both equations on the same set of axes.

b. What is the point of intersection of the two graphs? What information does this give you?

Connections

35. Describe what operations are indicated in each expression. Then, write each expression as a single number.

a. $-8(4)$

b. $-2 \cdot 4$

c. $6(-5) - 10$

d. $2(-2) + 3(5)$

36. Find each quotient.

a. $\frac{12}{-3}$

b. $\frac{-12}{3}$

c. $\frac{-12}{-3}$

d. $\frac{0}{-10}$

e. $\frac{-5}{5}$

f. $\frac{5}{-5}$

g. $\frac{-5}{-5}$

37. Decide whether each pair of quantities is equal. Explain your reasoning.

a. $6(5) + 2$ and $6(5 + 2)$

b. $8 - 3x$ and $3x - 8$

c. $4 + 5$ and $5 + 4$

d. $-2(3)$ and $3(-2)$

e. $3 - 5$ and $5 - 3$

f. 2 quarters and 5 dimes

g. 1.5 liters and 15 milliliters

h. 2 out of 5 students prefer wearing sneakers to school and 50% of the students prefer wearing sneakers to school

38. **a.** Use fact families to write a related sentence for $n - (-3) = 30$. Does this related sentence make it easier to find the value for n? Why or why not?

  b. Use fact families to write a related sentence for $5 + n = -36$. Does this related sentence make it easier to find the value for n? Why or why not?

  c. Solve the equations in parts (a) and (b) using properties of equality. How does this method compare to using the fact families?

39. Write two different expressions to represent the area of each rectangle.

a.

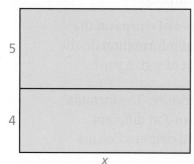

b.

40. Find the value of x that makes each equation true.

  a. $3\frac{1}{2}x = \frac{3}{4}$

  b. $3\frac{1}{2} = \frac{3}{4}x$

  c. $\frac{7}{8}x = \frac{1}{8}$

  d. $\frac{5}{6} = \frac{3}{4}x$

41. Fill in the missing representation for each inequality.

	In Symbols	On a Number Line	In Words
a.	$x > -4$	![number line with open circle at -4, marks -8 -6 -4 -2 0 2]	▦
b.	$x \leq 2$	▦	all numbers less than or equal to 2
c.	$3 < x$	▦	▦
d.	▦	![number line with closed circle at 3, marks -3 0 3 6]	▦
e.	▦	▦	all numbers greater than negative 3

42. The number of times a cricket chirps in a minute is related to the temperature. You can use the formula

$$n = 4t - 160$$

to determine the number of chirps n a cricket makes in a minute when the temperature is t degrees Fahrenheit. If you want to estimate the temperature by counting cricket chirps, you can use the following form of the equation:

$$t = \tfrac{1}{4}n + 40$$

a. At 60°F, how many times does a cricket chirp in a minute?

b. What is the temperature if a cricket chirps 150 times in a minute?

c. At what temperature does a cricket stop chirping?

d. Sketch a graph of the equation with number of chirps on the x-axis and temperature on the y-axis. What information do the y-intercept of the graph and the coefficient of n give you?

43. The higher the altitude, the colder the temperature. The formula $T = t - \frac{d}{150}$ is used to estimate the temperature T at different altitudes, where t is the ground temperature in degrees Celsius and d is the altitude in meters.

a. Suppose the ground temperature is 0 degrees Celsius. What is the temperature at an altitude of 1,500 meters?

b. Suppose the temperature at 300 meters is 26 degrees Celsius. What is the ground temperature?

44. The sum S of the angles of a polygon with n sides is $S = 180(n - 2)$. Find the angle sum of each polygon.

a. triangle   **b.** quadrilateral   **c.** hexagon

d. decagon (10-sided polygon)

e. icosagon (20-sided polygon)

45. Suppose the polygons in Exercise 44 are regular polygons. Find the measure of an interior angle of each polygon.

46. How many sides does a polygon have if its angle sum is

a. 540 degrees?   **b.** 1,080 degrees?

47. The perimeter of each shape is 24 cm. Find the value of x.

a.

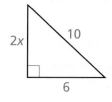

b.

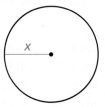

c.

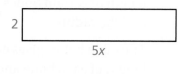

d. Find the area of the triangle in part (a) and the rectangle in part (c).

48. World Connections long-distance phone company charges $50 per month plus 10 cents per minute for each call.

a. Write an equation for the total monthly cost C for t minutes of long-distance calls.

b. Dwayne makes $10\frac{1}{2}$ hours of long-distance calls in a month. How much is his bill for that month?

c. If Andrea receives a $75 long-distance bill for last month's calls, how many minutes of long-distance calls did she make?

d. Should the solution to part (c) be written as an equality or inequality? Is it possible that the total number of minutes Andrea was charged was not equal to the amount of time she actually talked on the phone? Explain.

49. As a person ages beyond 30, his or her height can start to decrease by approximately 0.06 centimeter per year.

a. Write an equation that represents a person's height h after the age of 30. Let t be the number of years beyond 30 and H be the height at age 30.

b. A 60-year-old female is 160 centimeters tall. About how tall was she at age 30? Explain how you found your answer.

c. Suppose a basketball player is 6 feet, 6 inches tall on his thirtieth birthday. About how tall will he be at age 80? Explain. (Remember, 1 inch $\approx$ 2.54 centimeters.)

d. Jena says that in part (a), the equation should actually be written as an inequality. Why might Jena use an inequality to represent this relationship? What inequality do you think Jena has in mind?

50. Forensic scientists can estimate a person's height by measuring the length of certain bones, including the femur, the tibia, the humerus, and the radius.

The table below gives equations for the relationships between the length of each bone and the estimated height of males and females. These relationships were found by scientists after much study and data collection. In the table, F represents the length of the femur, T the length of the tibia, H the length of the humerus, R the length of the radius, and h the person's height. All measurements are in centimeters.

Bone	Male	Female
Femur	$h = 69.089 + 2.238F$	$h = 61.412 + 2.317F$
Tibia	$h = 81.688 + 2.392T$	$h = 72.572 + 2.533T$
Humerus	$h = 73.570 + 2.970H$	$h = 64.977 + 3.144H$
Radius	$h = 80.405 + 3.650R$	$h = 73.502 + 3.876R$

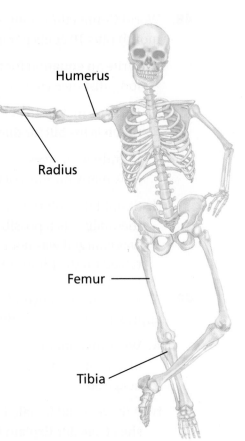

Humerus

Radius

Femur

Tibia

a. About how tall is a female if her femur is 46.2 centimeters long?

b. About how tall is a male if his tibia is 50.1 centimeters long?

c. Suppose a woman is 152 centimeters tall. About how long is her femur? Her tibia? Her humerus? Her radius?

d. Suppose a man is 183 centimeters tall. About how long is his femur? His tibia? His humerus? His radius?

e. Describe generally what the graph would look like for each equation without drawing the specific graph. What do the x- and y-intercepts represent in this problem? Does this make sense? Why?

Extensions

51. The maximum weight allowed in an elevator is 1,500 pounds.

   a. The average weight per adult is 150 pounds, and the average weight per child is 40 pounds. Write an equation for the number of adults A and the number of children C the elevator can hold.

   b. Suppose ten children are in the elevator. How many adults can get in?

   c. Suppose six adults are in the elevator. How many children can get in?

52. Solve each equation. Explain what your answers might mean.

   a. $2(x + 3) = 3x + 3$ **b.** $2(x + 3) = 2x + 6$ **c.** $2(x + 3) = 2x + 3$

53. Frank thinks he can solve inequalities the same way he can solve equations. He uses the method shown below.

> $2x + 6 < 16$
> First, I subtract 6 from both sides. Then I divide by 2.
> This simplifies the inequality to $x < 5$.
>
> My last step is to check my answer.
> $x = 4$ $2(4) + 6 = 14$ $14 < 16$
> $x = 6$ $2(6) + 6 = 18$ $18 \not< 16$

   a. Does Frank's method work in general for other inequalities?

   b. Frank runs into some difficulties trying to solve the following problem:

$$-2x + 1 > 5$$
$$-2x > 4$$

He thinks the answer is $x > -2$. He knows that if this is true, then $x = 0$ should be a solution, because $0 > -2$. But when he checks his work, he notices that $-2(0) + 1 \not> 5$. What numbers should be solutions for the original inequality?

54. Wind can affect the speed of an airplane. Suppose a plane is flying round-trip from New York City to San Francisco. The plane has a cruising speed of 300 miles per hour. The wind is blowing from west to east at 30 miles per hour. When the plane flies into (in the opposite direction of) the wind, its speed decreases by 30 miles per hour. When the plane flies with (in the same direction as) the wind, its speed increases by 30 miles per hour.

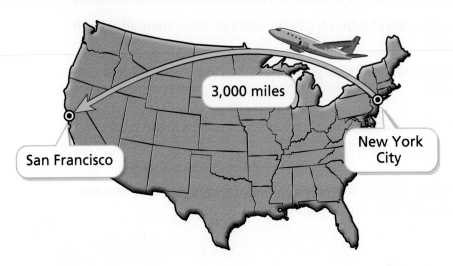

3,000 miles

San Francisco

New York City

a. Make a table that shows the total time the plane has traveled after each 200-mile interval on its trip from New York City to San Francisco and back.

Airplane Flight Times

Distance (mi)	NYC to SF Time (h)	SF to NYC Time (h)
0	▩	▩
200	▩	▩
400	▩	▩
600	▩	▩
▩	▩	▩

b. For each direction, write an equation for the distance d traveled in t hours.

c. On the same set of axes, sketch graphs of the time and distance data for travel in each direction.

d. How long does it take a plane to fly 5,000 miles against a 30-mile-per-hour wind? With a 30-mile-per-hour wind? Explain how you found your answers.

55. Students in Mr. Rickman's class are asked to solve the equation $\frac{2}{3}(6x - 9) + \frac{1}{3}(6x - 9) = 3$. Look at the three solutions below. Are they correct? Explain which method makes the most sense to you.

Jess's Solution

I began by distributing the numbers outside the parentheses on the left side.

$$\frac{2}{3}(6x - 9) + \frac{1}{3}(6x - 9) = 3$$
$$4x - 6 + 2x - 3 = 3$$
$$6x - 9 = 3$$
$$6x = 12$$
$$x = 2$$

Terri's Solution

I began by multiplying each side of the equation by 3.

$$3\left[\frac{2}{3}(6x - 9) + \frac{1}{3}(6x - 9)\right] = 3(3)$$
$$2(6x - 9) + 1(6x - 9) = 9$$
$$12x - 18 + 6x - 9 = 9$$
$$18x - 27 = 9$$
$$18x = 36$$
$$x = 2$$

Brian's Solution

I knew that $\frac{2}{3} + \frac{1}{3} = 1$, so I simplified the right side to $6x - 9$.

$$\frac{2}{3}(6x - 9) + \frac{1}{3}(6x - 9) = 3$$
$$1(6x - 9) = 3$$
$$6x - 9 = 3$$
$$6x = 12$$
$$x = 2$$

56. Multiple Choice Dorine solves the equation $3x + 3 = 3x + 9$ and is trying to make sense of her answer.

$$3x + 3 = 3x + 9$$
$$\underline{-3x - 3 \quad -3x - 3}$$
$$0 = 6$$

Which of the following should Dorine say is the correct solution?

A. $x = 6$, because 6 is the final number in the equation.

B. $x = 6$ or $x = 0$, because both of these numbers are in the last equation.

C. There is no solution, because each value of x will lead to $0 = 6$, which is not true.

D. The solution is all numbers, because x will satisfy the equation.

57. Multiple Choice Flora solves an equation similar to Dorine's:

$$3(x + 1) = 3x + 3$$

Flora uses the following method.

$$3(x + 1) = 3x + 3$$
$$3x + 3 = 3x + 3$$
$$\underline{-3x - 3 \quad -3x - 3}$$
$$0 = 0$$

Which of the following should Flora say is the correct solution?

A. $x = 0$, since $0 = 0$ is the last line of the equation.

B. No solution, because x does not show up in the equation $0 = 0$.

C. Any number x will work.

58. Fill in the missing representation for each inequality.

	In Symbols	On a Number Line	In Words
a.	▣	–4 –2 0 2 4	all positive numbers
b.	$x^2 < 9$	▣	all numbers whose squares are less than 9
c.	▣	▣	all numbers whose absolute values are greater than or equal to 2
d.	$x^3 > x$	▣	all numbers for which the cube of the number is greater than the number itself
e.	$x + \frac{1}{x} > 1$	▣	all numbers for which the sum of the number and its reciprocal is greater than 1

59. The Small World long-distance phone company charges 55¢ for the first minute of a long-distance call and 23¢ for each additional minute.

a. Write an equation for the total cost C of an m-minute long-distance call. Explain what your variables and numbers mean.

b. How much does a 10-minute long-distance call cost?

c. Suppose a call costs $4.92. How long does the call last?

Mathematical Reflections 3

In this Investigation, you learned how to solve equations by operating on the symbols. The following questions will help you summarize what you have learned.

Think about these questions. Discuss your ideas with other students and your teacher. Then write a summary of your findings in your notebook.

1. **a.** Suppose that, in an equation with two variables, you know the value of one of the variables. Describe a method for finding the value of the other variable using the properties of equality. Give an example to illustrate your method.

   b. Compare the method you described in part (a) to the methods of using a table or a graph to solve linear equations.

2. **a.** Explain how an inequality can be solved by methods similar to those used to solve linear equations.

   b. Describe a method for finding the solution to an inequality using graphs.

3. Give an example of two equivalent expressions that were used in this Investigation. Explain why they are equivalent.

Common Core Mathematical Practices

As you worked on the Problems in this Investigation, you used prior knowledge to make sense of them. You also applied Mathematical Practices to solve the Problems. Think back over your work, the ways you thought about the Problems, and how you used Mathematical Practices.

Nick described his thoughts in the following way:

In Problem 3.2, Question A, part (1), we first noted that there are 10 coins on the left and there are 4 coins and 3 bags on the right. So, the three bags must contain a total of 6 coins so that the total number of coins on the right is 10. We figured out that each bag must have 2 coins in it.

But then another group showed us their method. They took four coins off of each side. Now they had 6 coins on the left and 3 bags on the right. They also found that each bag must have 2 coins. Both methods are correct.

Common Core Standards for Mathematical Practice

MP3 Construct viable arguments and critique the reasoning of others.

- What other Mathematical Practices can you identify in Nick's reasoning?

- Describe a Mathematical Practice that you and your classmates used to solve a different Problem in this Investigation.

Exploring Slope: Connecting Rates and Ratios

All of the patterns of change you have explored in this Unit involved constant rates. For example, you worked with walking rates expressed in meters per second and pledge rates expressed in dollars per kilometer. In these situations, you found that the rate affects the following things:

- the steepness of the graph

- the coefficient, m, of x in the equation $y = mx + b$

- how the y-values in the table change for each unit change in the x-values

In this Investigation, you will explore another way to express the constant rate.

. . . .

Common Core State Standards

7.RP.A.2d Explain what a point (x, y) on the graph of a proportional relationship means in terms of the situation, with special attention to the points $(0, 0)$ and $(1, r)$, where r is the unit rate.

7.EE.A.2 Understand that rewriting an expression in different forms in a problem context can shed light on the problem and how the quantities in it are related.

Also 7.EE.A.1, 7.EE.B.4, 7.EE.B.4a

4.1 Climbing Stairs
Using Rise and Run

Climbing stairs is good exercise, so some athletes run up and down stairs as part of their training. The steepness of stairs determines how difficult they are to climb. By investigating the steepness of stairs, you can find another important way to describe the steepness of a line.

Consider these questions about the stairs you use at home, in your school, and in other buildings.

- How can you describe the steepness of the stairs?

- Is the steepness the same between any two consecutive steps?

Carpenters have developed the guidelines below to ensure that the stairs they build are relatively easy for a person to climb. Steps are measured in inches.

- The ratio of rise to run for each step should be between 0.45 and 0.60.

- The rise plus the run for each step should be between 17 and $17\frac{1}{2}$ inches.

The steepness of stairs is determined by the ratio of the rise to the run for each step. The rise and run are labeled in the diagram below.

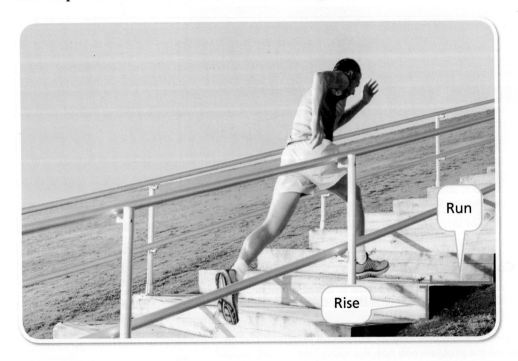

Problem 4.1

(A) **1.** Determine the steepness of a set of stairs in your school or home. To calculate the steepness you will need to

- measure the rise and run of at least two steps in the set of stairs.

- make a sketch of the stairs, and label the sketch with the measurements you found.

- find the ratio of rise to run.

2. How do the stairs you measured compare to the carpenters' guidelines on the previous page?

(B) A set of stairs is being built for the front of the new Arch Middle School. The ratio of rise to run is 3 to 5.

1. Is this ratio within the carpenters' guidelines?

2. Make a sketch of a set of stairs that meet this ratio. Label the lengths of the rise and run of a step.

3. Sketch the graph of a line that passes through the origin and whose y-values change by 3 units for each 5-unit change in the x-values.

4. **a.** Write an equation for the line in part (3).

b. What is the coefficient of x in the equation?

c. How is the coefficient related to the steepness of the line represented by the equation?

d. How is the coefficient related to the steepness of a set of stairs with this ratio?

ACE Homework starts on page 98.

4.2 Finding the Slope of a Line

The method for finding the steepness of stairs suggests a way to find the steepness of a line. A line drawn from the bottom step of a set of stairs to the top step touches each step at one point. The rise and the run of a step are the vertical and the horizontal changes, respectively, between two points on the line.

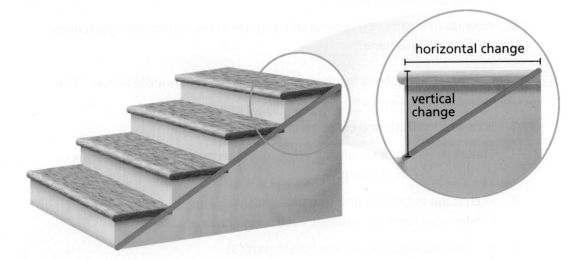

horizontal change

vertical change

The steepness of the line is the ratio of rise to run, or vertical change to horizontal change, for this step. We call this ratio the **slope** of the line.

$$\text{slope} = \frac{\text{vertical change}}{\text{horizontal change}} = \frac{\text{rise}}{\text{run}}$$

- Does the slope change if we take two stairs at a time?

- Is the slope the same between any two stairs?

Unlike the steepness of stairs, the slope of a line can be negative. To determine the slope of a line, you need to consider the direction, or sign, of the vertical and horizontal changes from one point to another. If vertical change is negative for positive horizontal change, the slope will be negative. Lines that slant *upward* from left to right have *positive slope*. Lines that slant *downward* from left to right have *negative slope*.

The following situations all represent linear relationships.

- For each graph, describe how you can find the slope of the line.

Line With Positive Slope

x	2	5
y	2	4

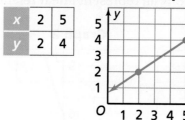

Line With Negative Slope

x	1	4
y	4	2

- Describe how you can find the slope of the line that represents the data in the table below.

x	−1	0	1	2	3	4
y	0	3	6	9	12	15

Information about a linear relationship can be given in several different representations, such as a table, a graph, an equation, or a contextual situation. These representations are useful in answering questions about linear situations.

Problem 4.2

A The graphs, tables, and equations all represent linear relationships.

Graph 1   **Graph 2**

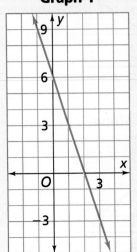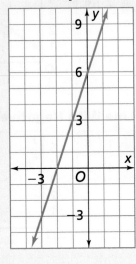

Table 1

x	−6	−4	−2	0	2	4
y	−10	−7	−4	−1	2	5

Table 2

x	1	2	3	4	5	6
y	4.5	4.0	3.5	3.0	2.5	2.0

Equation 1

$y = 2.5x + 5$

Equation 2

$y = 20 - 3x$

1. Find the slope and y-intercept of the line associated with each of these representations.

2. Write an equation for each graph and table.

Problem 4.2 *continued*

B The points (3, 5) and (–2, 10) lie on a line.

1. What is the slope of the line?

2. Find two more points that lie on this line. Explain your method.

3. Eun Mi observed that any two points on a line can be used to find the slope. How is Eun Mi's observation related to the idea of "linearity?"

C 1. John noticed that for lines represented by equations of the form $y = mx$, the points (0, 0) and (1, m) are always on the line. Is he correct? Explain.

2. What is the slope of a horizontal line? A vertical line? Explain your reasoning.

D 1. Compare your methods for finding the slope of a line from a graph, a table, and an equation.

2. In previous Investigations, you learned that linear relationships have a constant rate of change. As the independent variable changes by a constant amount, the dependent variable also changes by a constant amount. How is the constant rate of change of a linear relationship related to the slope of the line that represents that relationship?

ACE Homework starts on page 98.

4.3 Exploring Patterns With Lines

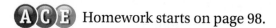

Your understanding of linear relationships can be used to explore some ideas about groups of lines.

For example, suppose the slope of a line is 3.

- Sketch a line with this slope.

- Can you sketch a different line with this slope? Explain.

In this Problem, you will use slope to explore some patterns among linear relationships.

Problem 4.3

A Consider the two groups of lines shown below.

Group 1 $y = 3x$ $y = 5 + 3x$ $y = 10 + 3x$ $y = -5 + 3x$

Group 2 $y = -2x$ $y = 4 - 2x$ $y = 8 - 2x$ $y = -4 - 2x$

1. What features do the equations in each group have in common?

2. For each group, graph the equations on the same coordinate axes. What patterns do you observe in the graphs?

3. Describe another group of lines that have the same pattern.

B Consider the three pairs of lines shown below.

Pair 1

$y = 2x$

$y = -\frac{1}{2}x$

Pair 2

$y = 4x$

$y = -0.25x$

Pair 3

$y = -3x + 5$

$y = \frac{1}{3}x - 1$

1. What features do the equations in each pair have in common?

2. For each pair, graph both equations on the same coordinate axes. What patterns do you observe in the graphs?

3. Describe another pair of lines that have the same pattern.

C Consider the three pairs of lines shown below.

Pair 1

$y = 2x + 1$

$y = 2(x + 1) - 1$

Pair 2

$y = 5 - 2x$

$y = 3 - 2(x - 1)$

Pair 3

$y = 2(x - 1)$

$y = 4x - 2x - 2$

1. For each pair, graph both equations on the same coordinate axes.

2. What do you notice about the graphs of each pair of equations? How might you have predicted this from the equations?

Ⓐ Ⓒ Ⓔ Homework starts on page 98.

4.4

Pulling It All Together
Writing Equations for Linear Relationships

Throughout this Unit, you have learned several ways to model linear relationships. You have also learned ways to move back and forth between tables, graphs, and equations to solve problems. The next Problem pulls some of these ideas together.

Problem 4.4

Ⓐ Today is Chantal's birthday. Her grandfather gave her some money as a birthday gift. Chantal plans to put her birthday money in a safe place and add part of her allowance to it each week. Her sister, Chanice, wants to know how much their grandfather gave her and how much of her allowance she is planning to save each week. As usual, Chantal does not answer her sister directly. Instead, she wants her to figure out the answer for herself. She gives her these clues:

> After five weeks, I will have saved a total of $175
>
> After eight weeks, I will have saved $190.

1. How much of her allowance is Chantal planning to save each week?

2. How much birthday money did Chantal's grandfather give her?

3. Write an equation for the total amount of money A Chantal will have saved after n weeks. What information do the y-intercept and coefficient of n represent in this context?

continued on the next page >

Problem 4.4 continued

B In the United States, temperature is measured using the Fahrenheit scale. Some countries, such as Canada, use the Celsius temperature scale. In cities near the border of these two countries, weather forecasts present the temperature using both scales.

The relationship between degrees Fahrenheit and degrees Celsius is linear. Two important reference points for this relationship are:

- Water freezes at 0°C, which is 32°F.
- Water boils at 100°C, which is 212°F.

1. Use this information to write an equation relating degrees Fahrenheit and degrees Celsius.

2. How did you find the *y*-intercept? What does the *y*-intercept tell you about this situation?

3. A news Web site uses the image below to display the weather forecast. However, some of the temperatures are missing. Use your equation from part (1) to find the missing temperatures.

? °F	**?** °F	63° F	70° F	58° F
13° C	14° C	**?** °C	**?** °C	**?** °C
Mon	**Tues**	**Wed**	**Thurs**	**Fri**

Problem 4.4 *continued*

C Square tiles were used to make the pattern below:

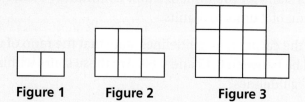

Figure 1   **Figure 2**   **Figure 3**

1. Write an equation that gives the perimeter P of the nth figure.

2. Compare your equation with that of your classmates. Are the expressions for perimeter equivalent? Explain.

3. Is the relationship linear? Explain.

4. Hachi observed that there was an interesting pattern for the number of square tiles needed to build each figure.

   a. What pattern might she have observed?

   b. Write an equation that gives the number of square tiles T in the nth figure.

   c. Is this relationship linear?

D 1. Look back to the equations you wrote in Question A, part (3); Question B, part (1); and Question C, part (1). Without graphing any of the equations, describe what the graph of each would look like. Which variable would be on the x-axis? Which variable would be on the y-axis? Would the line have a positive slope or a negative slope?

2. When it is helpful to represent a relationship as an equation? A table? A graph?

ACE Homework starts on page 98.

Applications

1. Plans for a set of stairs for the front of a new community center use the ratio of rise to run of 2 units to 5 units.

   a. Recall that the carpenters' guidelines state that the ratio of rise to run should be between 0.45 and 0.60. Are these stairs within the carpenters' guidelines?

   b. Sketch a set of stairs that meets the rise-to-run ratio of 2 units to 5 units.

   c. Sketch the graph of a line where the y-values change by 2 units for each 5-unit change in the x-values.

   d. Write an equation for your line in part (c).

2. a. Find the horizontal distance and the vertical distance between the two labeled points on the graph below.

   b. What is the slope of the line?

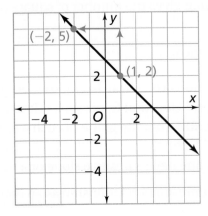

For Exercises 3–6, find the slope and the y-intercept of the line associated with the equation.

3. $y = 10 + 3x$

4. $y = 0.5x$

5. $y = -3x$

6. $y = -5x + 2$

7. Seven possible descriptions of lines are listed below.

  i. positive slope   **ii.** negative slope

  iii. y-intercept equals 0   **iv.** passes through the point $(1, 2)$

  v. slope of zero   **vi.** positive y-intercept

  vii. negative y-intercept

For each equation, list *all* of the descriptions i–vii that describe the graph of that equation.

  a. $y = 2x$ **b.** $y = 3 - 3x$

  c. $y = 2x + 3$ **d.** $y = 5x - 3$

  e. $y = 2$

In Exercises 8–12, the tables represent linear relationships. Give the slope and the y-intercept of the graph of each relationship. Then match each of the following equations with the appropriate table.

  $y = 5 - 2x$ $y = 2x$ $y = -3x - 5$

  $y = 2x - 1$ $y = x + 3.5$

8.

x	0	1	2	3	4
y	0	2	4	6	8

9.

x	0	1	2	3	4
y	3.5	4.5	5.5	6.5	7.5

10.

x	1	2	3	4	5
y	1	3	5	7	9

11.

x	0	1	2	3	4
y	5	3	1	-1	-3

12.

x	2	3	4	5	6
y	-11	-14	-17	-20	-23

13. a. Find the slope of the line represented by the equation $y = x - 1$.

    b. Make a table of x- and y-values for the equation $y = x - 1$. How is the slope related to the table entries?

14. a. Find the slope of the line represented by the equation $y = -2x + 3$.

    b. Make a table of x- and y-values for the equation $y = -2x + 3$. How is the slope related to the table entries?

15. In parts (a) and (b), the equations represent linear relationships. Use the given information to find the value of b.

    a. The point $(1, 5)$ lies on the line representing $y = b - 3.5x$.

    b. The point $(0, -2)$ lies on the line representing $y = 5x - b$.

    c. What are the y-intercepts in parts (a) and (b)? What are the patterns of change in parts (a) and (b)?

    d. Find the x-intercepts for the linear relationships in parts (a) and (b). (The x-intercept is the point where the graph intersects the x-axis.)

For each pair of points in Exercises 16–19, answer parts (a)–(e).

    a. Plot the points on a coordinate grid and draw a line through them.

    b. Find the slope of the line.

    c. Find the y-intercept of the line. Explain how you found the y-intercept.

    d. Use your answers from parts (b) and (c) to write an equation for the line.

    e. Find one more point that lies on the line.

16. $(0, 0)$ and $(3, 3)$

17. $(-1, 1)$ and $(3, -3)$

18. $(0, -5)$ and $(-2, -3)$

19. $(3, 6)$ and $(5, 6)$

For Exercises 20–22, determine which of the linear relationships A–K
fit the description given.

A.

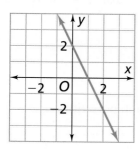

B.

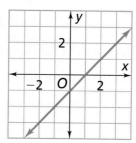

C.

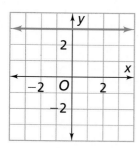

D.

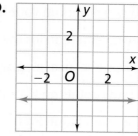

E.

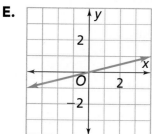

F.

x	−3	−2	−1	0
y	7	5	3	1

G.

x	−4	−2	−1	0
y	2	2	2	2

H. $y = 1.5$ **J.** $y = -5 + 3x$ **K.** $y = 4 + -2x$

20. The line corresponding to this relationship has positive slope.

21. The line corresponding to this relationship has a slope of −2.

22. The line corresponding to this relationship has a slope of 0.

23. Decide which graph from Exercises 20–22 matches each equation.

  a. $y = x - 1$ **b.** $y = -2$ **c.** $y = \frac{1}{4}x$

For each equation in Exercises 24–26, answer parts (a)–(d).

24. $y = x$ **25.** $y = 2x - 2$ **26.** $y = -0.5x + 2$

   a. Make a table of x- and y-values for the equation.

   b. Sketch a graph of the equation.

   c. Find the slope of the line.

   d. Make up a problem that can be represented by each equation.

27. **a.** Graph a line with slope 3.

     i. Find two points on your line.

     ii. Write an equation for the line.

   b. On the same set of axes, graph a line with slope $-\frac{1}{3}$.

     i. Find two points on your line.

     ii. Write an equation for the line.

   c. Compare the two graphs you made in parts (a) and (b).

28. Use the line in the graph below to answer each question.

   a. Find the equation of a line that is parallel to this line.

   b. Find the equation of a line that is perpendicular to this line.

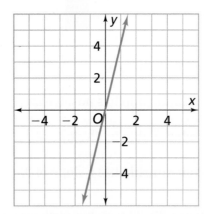

29. a. Find the slope of each line below. Then write an equation for the line.

i.

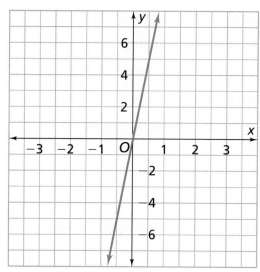

ii.

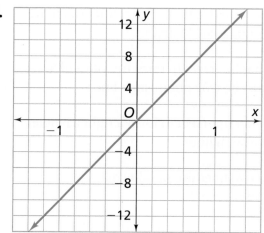

iii.

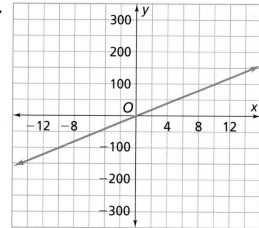

b. Compare the slopes of the three lines.

c. How are the three graphs similar? How are they different?

30. Descriptions of three possible lines are listed below.

    i. a line that *does not* pass through the first quadrant

    ii. a line that passes through exactly two quadrants

    iii. a line that passes through only one quadrant

  a. For each, decide whether such a line exists. Explain.

  b. If such a line exists, what must be true about the equation of the line that satisfies the conditions?

  c. If such a line exists, sketch its graph. Then write the equation of the line next to the graph.

31. Suppose the slopes of two lines are the negative reciprocal of each other. For example:

$$y = 2x \text{ and } y = -\frac{1}{2}x$$

What must be true about the two lines? Is your conjecture true if the *y*-intercept of either equation is not zero? Explain.

32. Write equations for four lines that intersect to form the sides of a parallelogram. Explain what must be true about such lines.

33. Write equations for three lines that intersect to form a right triangle. Explain what must be true about such lines.

34. Describe how you can decide if two lines are parallel or perpendicular from the equations of the lines.

35. Meifeng is taking a bike repair class. She pays the bike shop $15 per week for the class. At the end of the third week, Meifeng still owes the bike shop $75.

  a. How many payments does Meifeng have left?

  b. How much did the class cost?

  c. Write an equation that models the relationship between the time in weeks and the amount of money Meifeng owes.

  d. Without graphing, describe what the graph of this relationship would look like.

36. Robert is installing a patio in his backyard. At 2:00 P.M., he has 120 stones laid in the ground. At 3:30 P.M., he has 180 stones in the ground. His design for the patio says he needs 400 stones total.

   a. When would you predict he will be done?

   b. What is a reasonable estimate for when he started?

   c. If you wanted to know how many stones he would have in the ground at any time, what would be most helpful to you: an equation, a graph, or a table? Explain.

37. At noon, the temperature is 30°F. For the next several hours, the temperature falls by an average of 3°F an hour.

   a. Write an equation for the temperature T, n hours after noon.

   b. What is the y-intercept of the line the equation represents? What does the y-intercept tell you about this situation?

   c. What is the slope of the line the equation represents? What does the slope tell you about this situation?

38. Damon never manages to make his allowance last for a whole week, so he borrows money from his sister. Suppose Damon borrows 50 cents every week.

   a. Write an equation for the amount of money m Damon owes his sister after n weeks.

   b. What is the slope of the graph of the equation from part (a)?

39. In 2000, the small town of Cactusville was destined for obscurity. However, due to hard work by its city officials, it began adding manufacturing jobs at a fast rate. As a result, the city's population grew 239% from 2000 to 2010.

WELCOME TO
CACTUSVILLE
2010 Population
37,000

   a. What was the population of Cactusville in 2000?

   b. Suppose the same rate of population increase continues. What might the population be in the year 2020?

40. Terrance and Katrina share a veterinary practice. They each make farm visits two days a week. They take cellular phones on these trips to keep in touch with the office. Terrance makes his farm visits on weekdays. His cellular phone rate is $14.95 a month plus $.50 a minute. Katrina makes her visits on Saturday and Sunday and is charged a weekend rate of $34 a month.

   a. Write an equation for each billing plan.

   b. Is it possible for Terrance's cellular phone bill to be more than Katrina's? Explain how you know this.

   c. Suppose Terrance and Katrina made the same number of calls in the month of May. Is it possible for Terrance's and Katrina's phone bills to be for the same amount? If so, how many minutes of phone calls would each person have to make for their bills to be equal?

   d. Katrina finds another phone company that offers one rate for both weekday and weekend calls. The billing plan for this company is given by the equation $A = 25 + 0.25m$, where A is the total monthly bill and m is the number of minutes of calls. Compare this billing plan with the other two plans.

41. Three students build the following pattern using the least number of toothpicks possible. For example, Figure 2 uses 5 toothpicks. Suppose that this pattern continues beyond Figure 3.

Figure 1   Figure 2   Figure 3

a. The students are trying to figure out the perimeter of Figure 6 without building it. For each student's method, tell whether you agree or disagree. If you agree, explain why. If you disagree, describe what is incorrect about the student's reasoning.

Juan's Method

From one figure to the next, you are adding one unit of perimeter. Figure 3 has a perimeter of 5 units, so Figure 6 will have a perimeter of 5 + 1 + 1 + 1 = 8 units.

Natalie's Method

Figure 3 has a perimeter of 5 units. 6 is twice as great as 3. So Figure 6 has twice the perimeter, or 10 units.

Steven's Method

Figure 6 will have 6 triangles, and each triangle has a perimeter of 3 units. So Figure 6 will have a perimeter of 6 • 3 = 18 units.

b. The students want to figure out a way to calculate how many toothpicks T they would need to build any figure number F. Which students wrote correct equations? Explain.

Juan's Equation

$T = (F + 1) + F$

There are $(F + 1)$ slanted toothpicks. There are F toothpicks on the top and bottom.

Natalie's Equation

$T = 2F + 1$

There are F of this shape

in each figure plus one extra toothpick at the end.

Steven's Equation

$T = 3F - (F - 1)$

There are F triangles, each with 3 toothpicks. But, there are $F - 1$ toothpicks double-counted.

42.

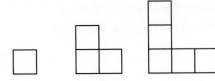

Figure 1   Figure 2   Figure 3

a. Assume that this pattern continues beyond Figure 3.Write an equation that represents the number of squares S in figure n.

b. Explain how you know your equation will work for any figure number.

c. Write two different equations that represent the perimeter P for any given figure number n.

Connections

43. Some hills have signs indicating their steepness, or slope. Here are some examples:

On a coordinate grid, sketch hills with each of these slopes.

44. Solve each equation and check your answers.

a. $2x + 3 = 9$

b. $\frac{1}{2}x + 3 = 9$

c. $x + 3 = \frac{9}{2}$

d. $x + \frac{1}{2} = 9$

e. $\frac{x + 3}{2} = 9$

45. Use properties of equality and numbers to solve each equation for x. Check your answers.

a. $3 + 6x = 4x + 9$

b. $6x + 3 = 4x + 9$

c. $6x - 3 = 4x + 9$

d. $3 - 6x = 4x + 9$

46. Use the graph below to answer each question.

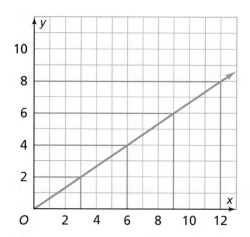

a. Are any of the rectangles in the picture above similar? If so, tell which rectangles, and explain why they are similar.

b. Find the slope of the diagonal line. How is it related to the similar rectangles?

c. Which of these rectangles belong to the set of rectangles in the graph? Explain.

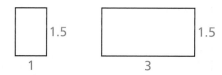

47. The graph below shows the height of a rocket from 10 seconds before liftoff through 7 seconds after liftoff.

a. Describe the relationship between the height of the rocket and time.

b. What is the slope for the part of the graph that is a straight line? What does this slope represent in this situation?

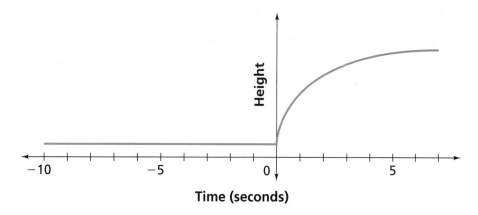

48. Solve each equation. Check your answers.

    a. $2(x + 5) = 18$ **b.** $2(x + 5) = x - 8$

    c. $2(x + 5) = x$ **d.** $2(x + 5) = -15$

49. Multiple Choice Which equation has a graph that contains the point $(-2, 7)$?

    A. $y = 4x + 1$ **B.** $y = -x + 5$

    C. $y = 3x - 11$ **D.** $y = -3x + 11$

50. Each pair of figures is similar. Find the lengths of the sides marked x.

    a.

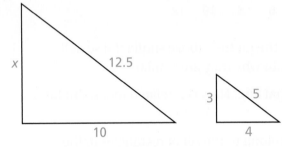

    b.

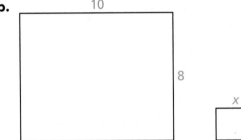

51. Find a value of n that will make each statement true.

    a. $\dfrac{n}{10} = \dfrac{3}{2}$ **b.** $\dfrac{5}{6} = \dfrac{n}{18}$ **c.** $-\dfrac{4}{6} = \dfrac{n}{3}$ **d.** $\dfrac{5}{18} = \dfrac{20}{n}$

    e. Write an equation for a line whose slope is $-\dfrac{4}{6}$.

52. Find a value of n that will make each statement true.

    a. 15% of 90 is n.   **b.** 20% of n is 80.   **c.** n% of 50 is 5.

Extensions

53. On a March flight from Boston to Detroit, a monitor displayed the altitude and the outside air temperature. Two passengers that were on that flight tried to find a formula for temperature t in degrees Fahrenheit at an altitude of a feet above sea level. One passenger said the formula was $t = 46 - 0.003a$, and the other said it was $t = 46 + 0.003a$.

a. Which formula makes more sense to you? Why?

b. The Detroit Metropolitan Airport is 620 feet above sea level. Use the formula you chose in part (a) to find the temperature at the airport on that day.

c. Does the temperature you found in part (b) seem reasonable? Why or why not?

54. Jada's track team decides to convert their running rates from miles per hour to kilometers per hour (1 mile $\approx$ 1.6 kilometers).

a. Which method would you use to help the team do their converting: graph, table, or equation? Explain why you chose your method.

b. One of Jada's teammates said that she could write an equation for her spreadsheet program that could convert any team member's running rate from miles per hour to kilometers per hour. Write an equation that each member could use for this conversion.

In this Investigation, you learned that graphs of linear relationships are straight lines. You also learned about the slope, or steepness, of a line. You learned how slope is related to an equation of the line and to a table or a graph of the equation. These questions will help you summarize what you have learned.

Think about these questions. Discuss your ideas with other students and your teacher. Then, write a summary of your findings in your notebook.

1. Explain what the slope of a line is. **How** does finding the slope compare to finding the rate of change between two variables in a linear relationship?

2. **How** can you find the slope of a line from

   a. an equation?

   b. a graph?

   c. a table of values of the line?

   d. the coordinates of two points on the line?

3. For parts (a) and (b), **explain** how you can write an equation of a line from the information. Use examples to illustrate your thinking.

   a. the slope and the *y*-intercept of the line

   b. two points on the line

Common Core Mathematical Practices

As you worked on the Problems in this Investigation, you used prior knowledge to make sense of them. You also applied Mathematical Practices to solve the Problems. Think back over your work, the ways you thought about the Problems, and how you used Mathematical Practices.

Hector described his thoughts in the following way.

It took our group many steps to solve Problem 4.4, Question A. First, since the amount of money Chantal saved from her weekly allowance is the same each week, we reasoned that the amount of money for each of the weeks between weeks 5 and 8 is a constant.

During this time she saved $190 – $175 or $15. So $15 ÷ 3 weeks is $5 per week. To find the amount of money her grandfather gave her, we found the amount of money she saved from her allowance for the first five weeks, which is 5 × $5 or $25.

Then, we subtracted this amount from $175, and this gave us $150. This is the amount her grandfather gave her for her birthday. We think her grandfather is very generous.

....

Common Core Standards for Mathematical Practice

MP1 Make sense of problems and persevere in solving them.

 • What other Mathematical Practices can you identify in Hector's reasoning?

• Describe a Mathematical Practice that you and your classmates used to solve a different Problem in this Investigation.

Conducting an Experiment

In many situations, patterns become apparent only after sufficient data are collected, organized, and displayed. Your group will be carrying out one of these experiments.

- In Project 1, you will investigate the rate at which a leaking faucet loses water.

- In Project 2, you will investigate how the drop height of a ball is related to its bounce height.

You will examine and use the patterns in the data collected from these experiments to make predictions.

Project 1: Wasted Water Experiment

In this experiment, you will simulate a leaking faucet and collect data about the volume of water lost at 5-second intervals. You will then use the patterns in your results to predict how much water is wasted when a faucet leaks for one month.

Read the directions carefully before you start. Be prepared to explain your findings to the rest of the class.

Materials:

- a watch or clock with a second hand
- a styrofoam or paper cup
- water
- a paper clip
- a clear measuring container (such as a graduated cylinder)

Directions:

Divide the work among the members of your group.

1. Make a table with columns for recording time and the amount of water lost. Fill in the time column with values from 0 seconds to 60 seconds in 5-second intervals (that is, 5, 10, 15, and so on).

2. Use the paper clip to punch a hole in the bottom of the paper cup. Cover the hole with your finger.

3. Fill the cup with water.

4. Hold the paper cup over the measuring container.

5. When you are ready to begin timing, uncover the hole so that the water drips into the measuring container, simulating the leaky faucet.

6. Record the amount of water in the measuring container at 5-second intervals for a minute.

Use this experiment to write an article for your local paper, trying to convince the people in your town to conserve water and fix leaky faucets.

In your article, include the following information:

- a coordinate graph of the data you collected;

- a description of the variables you investigated in this experiment and a description of the relationship between the variables;

- a list showing your predictions for:

  - the amount of water that would be wasted in 15 seconds, 2 minutes, in 2.5 minutes, and in 3 minutes if a faucet dripped at the same rate as your cup does;

  - how long it would take for the container to overflow if a faucet dripped into the measuring container at the same rate as your cup;

  Explain how you made your predictions. Did you use the table, the graph, or some other method? What clues in the data helped you?

- a description of other variables, besides time, that affect the amount of water in the measuring container;

- a description of how much water would be wasted in one month if a faucet leaked at the same rate as your paper cup (explain how you made your predictions);

- the cost of the water wasted by a leaking faucet in one month. (To do this, you will need to find out how much water costs in your area. Then, use this information to figure out the cost of the wasted water.)

Project 2: Ball Bounce Experiment

In this experiment, you will investigate how the height from which a ball is dropped is related to the height it bounces. Read the directions carefully before you start. Be prepared to explain your findings to the rest of the class.

Materials:

- a meter stick
- a ball that bounces

Directions:

Divide the work among the members of your group.

1. Make a table with columns for recording drop height and bounce height.
2. Hold the meter stick perpendicular to a flat surface, such as an uncarpeted floor, a table, or a desk.
3. Choose and record a height on the meter stick as the height from which you will drop the ball. Hold the ball so that either the top of the ball or the bottom of the ball is at this height.
4. Drop the ball and record the height of the first bounce. If the *top* of the ball was at your starting height, look for the height of the *top* of the ball. If the *bottom* of the ball was at your starting height, look for the height of the *bottom* of the ball. (You may have to do this several times before you feel confident you have a good estimate of the bounce height.)
5. Repeat this for several different starting heights.

After you have completed the experiment, write a report that includes the following:

- a coordinate graph of the data you collected;

- a description of the variables you investigated in this experiment and a description of the relationship between the variables;

- a list showing your predictions for:

  - the bounce height for a drop height of 2 meters;

  - the drop height needed for a bounce height of 2 meters;

- a description of how you made your prediction, whether you used a table, a graph, or some other method, and the clues in the data that helped you make your predictions;

- an explanation of the bounce height you would expect for a drop height of 0 centimeters and where you could find this on the graph;

- a description of any other variables besides the drop height, which may affect the bounce height of the ball.

In this Unit, you explored many examples of linear relationships between variables. You learned how to recognize linear patterns in graphs and in tables of numerical data. You also learned how to express those patterns in words and in symbolic equations or formulas. Most importantly, you learned how to interpret tables, graphs, and equations to answer questions about linear relationships.

Use Your Understanding: Algebraic Reasoning

Test your understanding of linear relationships by solving the following problems about the operation of a movie theater.

1. Suppose that a theater charges a school group $4.50 per student to show a special film. Suppose that the theater's operating expenses include $130 for the staff and a film rental fee of $1.25 per student.

   a. What equation relates the number of students x to the theater's income I?

   b. What equation relates the theater's operating expenses E to the number of students x?

   c. Copy and complete the table below.

   Theater Income and Expenses

Number of Students, x	0	10	20	30	40	50	60	70
Income, I ($)	▦	▦	▦	▦	▦	▦	▦	▦
Expenses, E ($)	▦	▦	▦	▦	▦	▦	▦	▦

   d. On the same set of axes, graph the theater's income and operating expenses for any number of students from 0 to 100.

   e. Describe the patterns by which income and operating expenses increase as the number of students in a group increases.

   f. Write and solve an equation that you can use to answer the question "How many students need to attend the movie so that the theater's income will equal its operating expenses?"

   g. Write an equation that represents the theater's profit. Compare your equation to those your classmates wrote.

h. Find the number of students that make each of the following inequality statements true.

   i. $E < 255$

   ii. $I > 675$

2. At another theater, the income and expenses combine to give the equation $y = 3x - 115$. This equation relates operating profit and the number of students in a group.

  a. What do the numbers 3 and -115 tell you about:

    i. the relationship between the number of students and the theater's profit?

    ii. the pattern of entries that would appear in a table of sample (*students, profit*) data?

    iii. a graph of the relationship between the number of students and the profit?

  b. Write and solve equations to find the number of students needed for the theater to:

    i. break even (make a profit of $0).

    ii. make a profit of $100.

  c. Write and solve an equation you can use to find the number of students for which the theaters in Exercise 1 and Exercise 2 make the same profit. Then find the amount of that profit.

Explain Your Reasoning

When you use mathematical calculations to solve a problem or make a decision, it is important to be able to justify each step in your reasoning. For Exercises 1 and 2:

3. Consider the variables and relationships.

    a. What are the variables?

    b. Which pairs of variables are related to each other?

    c. In each pair of related variables, how does a change in the value of one variable cause a change in the value of the other variable?

4. Which relationships are linear and which are not linear? What patterns in the tables, graphs, and equations support your conclusions?

5. For a linear relationship, what information do the slope and *y*-intercept of the graph indicate about the relationship?

6. For a linear relationship, how do the slope and *y*-intercept relate to data patterns in the table?

7. Consider the strategies for solving linear equations such as those in Problem 1, part (f) and Problem 2, part (c).

    a. How can you solve the equations using tables of values?

    b. How can you solve the equations using graphs?

    c. How can you solve the equations using symbolic reasoning alone?

8. Suppose you were asked to write a report describing the relationships among the number of students in the group, the theater's income, and the theater's operating expenses. What value might be gained by including the table? Including the graph? Including the equation? What are the limitations of each representation?

C **coefficient** A number that is multiplied by a variable in an equation or expression. In a linear equation of the form $y = mx + b$, the number m is the coefficient of x as well as the slope of the line. For example, in the equation $y = 3x + 5$, the coefficient of x is 3. This is also the slope of the line.

coeficiente Un número que se multiplica por una variable en una ecuación o expresión. En una ecuación lineal de la forma $y = mx + b$, el número m es el coeficiente de x así como la pendiente de la recta. Por ejemplo, en la ecuación $y = 3x + 5$, el coeficiente de x es 3. También representa la pendiente de la recta.

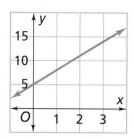

constant term A number in an equation that is not multiplied by a variable, or an amount added to or subtracted from the terms involving variables. In an equation of the form $y = mx + b$, the y-intercept, b, is a constant term. The effect of the constant term on a graph is to raise or lower the graph. The constant term in the equation $y = 3x + 5$ is 5. The graph of $y = 3x$ is raised vertically 5 units to give the graph of $y = 3x + 5$.

término constante Un número en una ecuación que no está multiplicado por una variable o una cantidad sumada o restada a los términos que contienen variables. En una ecuación de la forma $y = mx + b$, el intercepto en y, b, es un término constante. El efecto del término constante hace que una gráfica suba o baje. El término constante en la ecuación $y = 3x + 5$ es 5. Para obtener la gráfica de $y = 3x + 5$, la gráfica $y = 3x$ se sube 5 unidades sobre el eje vertical.

coordinates An ordered pair of numbers used to locate a point on a coordinate grid. The first number in a coordinate pair is the value for the *x*-coordinate, and the second number is the value for the *y*-coordinate. A coordinate pair for the graph shown below is (0, 60).

coordenadas Un par ordenado de números que se usa para ubicar un punto en una gráfica de coordenadas. El primer número del par de coordenadas es el valor de la coordenada *x* y el segundo número es el valor de la coordenada *y*. Un par de coordenadas para la gráfica que se muestra es (0, 60).

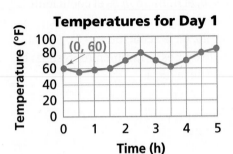

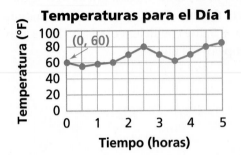

• •

D

dependent variable One of the two variables in a relationship. Its value depends upon or is determined by the other variable called the *independent variable*. For example, the distance you travel on a car trip (dependent variable) depends on how long you drive (independent variable).

variable dependiente Una de las dos variables de una relación. Su valor depende o está determinado por el valor de la otra variable, llamada *variable independiente*. Por ejemplo, la distancia que recorres durante un viaje en carro (variable dependiente) depende de cuánto conduces (variable independiente).

describe Academic Vocabulary

To explain or tell in detail. A written description can contain facts and other information needed to communicate your answer. A diagram or a graph may also be included.

related terms *express, explain, illustrate*

sample Describe how to solve the equation $3x + 14 = 23$.

I can sketch a graph of the line $y = 3x + 14$. When y is 23, the value of x is 3.

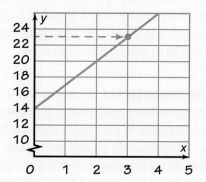

I can also solve for x in the equation $3x + 14 = 23$ by subtracting 14 from both sides to get $3x = 9$. Then I can divide both sides by 3 to get $x = 3$.

describir Vocabulario académico

Explicar o decir con detalle. Una descripción escrita puede contener datos y otra información necesaria para comunicar tu respuesta. También se puede incluir un diagrama o una gráfica.

términos relacionados *expresar, explicar, illustrar*

ejemplo Describe cómo se resuelve la ecuación $3x + 14 = 23$.

Puedo bosquejar una gráfica de la recta $y = 3x + 14$. Cuando y es 23, el valor de x es 3.

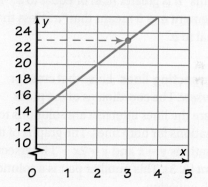

También puedo resolver x en la ecuación $3x + 14 = 23$ restando 14 de cada lado para obtener $3x = 9$. Luego puedo dividir ambos lados por 3 para obtener $x = 3$.

E

equivalent expressions Expressions that represent the same quantity. For example, $2 + 5$, $3 + 4$, and 7 are equivalent expressions. You can apply the Distributive Property to $2(x + 3)$ to write the equivalent expression $2x + 6$. You can apply the Commutative Property to $2x + 6$ to write the equivalent expression $6 + 2x$.

expresiones equivalentes Expresiones que representan la misma cantidad. Por ejemplo, $2 + 5$, $3 + 4$ y 7 son expresiones equivalentes. Puedes aplicar la propiedad distributiva a $2(x + 3)$ para escribir la expresión equivalente $2x + 6$. Puedes aplicar la propiedad conmutativa a $2x + 6$ para escribir la expresión equivalente $6 + 2x$.

independent variable One of the two variables in a relationship. Its value determines the value of the other variable called the *dependent variable*. If you organize a bike tour, for example, the number of people who register to go (independent variable) determines the cost for renting bikes (dependent variable).

variable independiente Una de las dos variables en una relación. Su valor determina el de la otra variable, llamada *variable dependiente*. Por ejemplo, si organizas un recorrido en bicicleta, el número de personas inscritas (variable independiente) determina el costo del alquiler de las bicicletas (variable dependiente).

inequality A statement that two quantities are not equal. The symbols $>$, $<$, $\geq$, and $\leq$ are used to express inequalities. For example, if a and b are two quantities, then "a is greater than b" is written as $a > b$, and "a is less than b" is written as $a < b$. The statement $a \geq b$ means "a is greater than or equal to b." The statement $a \leq b$ means that "a is less than or equal to b."

desigualdad Enunciado que indica que dos cantidades no son iguales. Los símbolos $>$, $<$, $\geq$ y $\leq$ se usan para expresar desigualdades. Por ejemplo, si a y b son dos cantidades, entonces "a es mayor que b" se escribe como $a > b$ y "a es menor que b" se escribe como $a < b$. El enunciado $a \geq b$ significa "a es mayor que o igual a b". El enunciado $a \leq b$ significa "a es menor que o igual a b".

intersecting lines Lines that cross or *intersect*. The coordinates of the point where the lines intersect are solutions to the equations for both lines. The graphs of the equations $y = x$ and $y = 2x - 3$ intersect at the point (3, 3). This number pair is a solution to each equation.

rectas intersecantes Rectas que se cruzan o *intersecan*. Las coordenadas del punto en el que las rectas se intersecan son la solución de las ecuaciones de las dos rectas. Las gráficas de las ecuaciones $y = x$ e $y = 2x - 3$ se intersecan en el punto (3, 3). Este par de números es la solución de las dos ecuaciones.

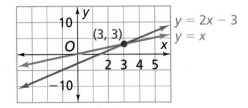

linear relationship A relationship in which there is a constant rate of change between two variables. A linear relationship can be represented by a straight-line graph and by an equation of the form $y = mx + b$. In the equation, m is the slope of the line, and b is the y-intercept.

relación lineal Una relación en la que hay una tasa de variación constante entre dos variables. Una relación lineal se puede representar con una gráfica de línea recta y con una ecuación de la forma $y = mx + b$. En la ecuación, m es la pendiente de la recta y b es el intercepto en y.

origin The point where the x- and y-axes intersect on a coordinate graph. With coordinates $(0, 0)$, the origin is the center of the coordinate plane.

origen El punto en que los ejes de las x y las y se intersecan en una gráfica de coordenadas. Si las coordenadas son $(0, 0)$, el origen es el centro del plano de coordenadas.

point of intersection The point where two lines intersect. If the lines are represented on a coordinate grid, the coordinates for the point of intersection can be read from the graph.

punto de intersección El punto en el que dos rectas se intersecan. Si las rectas están representadas en una gráfica de coordenadas, las coordenadas del punto de intersección se pueden leer en la gráfica.

properties of equality For all real numbers a, b, and c:

Addition: If $a = b$, then $a + c = b + c$.

Subtraction: If $a = b$, then $a - c = b - c$.

Multiplication: If $a = b$, then $a \cdot c = b \cdot c$.

Division: If $a = b$ and $c \neq 0$, then $\frac{a}{c} = \frac{b}{c}$.

propiedades de la igualdad Para todos los números reales a, b y c:

Suma: Si $a = b$, entonces $a + c = b + c$.

Resta: Si $a = b$, entonces $a - c = b - c$.

Multiplicación: Si $a = b$, entonces $a \cdot c = b \cdot c$.

División: Si $a = b$ y $c \neq 0$, entonces $\frac{a}{c} = \frac{b}{c}$.

relate Academic Vocabulary
To have a connection to or impact on something else.

related terms *connect, correlate*

sample Hannah raises $12 for every 3 pies she sells. Write an equation that shows how the total number of pies p she sells relates to the amount of money she raises r.

relacionar Vocabulario académico
Tener una conexión o un impacto en algo.

términos relacionados *unir, correlacionar*

ejemplo Hannah recauda $12 por cada 3 pasteles que vende. Escribe una ecuación que muestre cómo se relaciona el número total de pasteles p que vende con la cantidad que recauda r.

If she raises $12 for selling 3 pies, she raises $4 for every pie, because $\frac{\$12}{4} = 3$. The equation $r = 4p$ shows the relationship.

Si recauda $12 por vender 3 pasteles, recauda $4 por cada pastel, porque $\frac{\$12}{4} = 3$. La ecuación $r = 4p$ muestra la relación.

represent Academic Vocabulary
To stand for or take the place of something else. For example, an equation can represent a given situation, and a graph can represent an equation.

related terms *symbolize, correspond to*

sample A company charges $15 per sweatshirt plus a total shipping fee of $10. Does this represent a linear relationship?

representar Vocabulario académico
Significar o tomar el lugar de algo más. Por ejemplo, una ecuación puede representar una situación dada y una gráfica puede representar una ecuación.

términos relacionados *simbolizar, corresponder*

ejemplo Una compañía cobra $15 por sudadera más una tarifa de envío de $10. ¿Representa esto una relación lineal?

This represents a linear relationship because there is a constant rate of change between the number of sweatshirts and the amount the company will charge.

Esto representa una relación lineal porque hay una tasa de cambio constante entre el número de sudaderas y la cantidad que la compañía cobra.

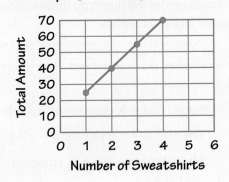

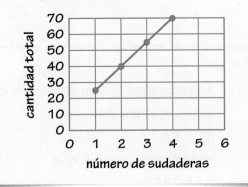

---

rise The vertical change between two points on a graph. The slope of a line is the rise divided by the run.

distancia vertical La variación vertical entre dos puntos de una gráfica. La pendiente de una recta es la distancia vertical dividida por la distancia horizontal.

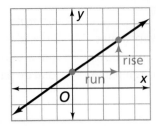

---

run The horizontal change between two points on a graph. The slope of a line is the rise divided by the run.

distancia horizontal La variación horizontal entre dos puntos de una gráfica. La pendiente de una recta es la distancia vertical dividida por la distancia horizontal.

S

scale The distance between two consecutive tick marks on the *x*- and *y*-axes of a coordinate grid. When graphing, an appropriate scale must be selected so that the resulting graph will be clearly shown. For example, when graphing the equation $y = 60x$, a scale of 1 for the *x*-axis and a scale of 15 or 30 for the *y*-axis would be reasonable.

escala La distancia entre dos marcas consecutivas en los ejes *x* y *y* de una gráfica de coordenadas. Cuando se hace una gráfica, se debe seleccionar una escala apropiada de manera que represente con claridad la gráfica resultante. Por ejemplo, cuando se grafica la ecuación $y = 60x$, una escala razonable sería 1 para el eje de las *x* y una escala de 15 ó 30 para el eje de las *y*.

slope The number that expresses the steepness of a line. The slope is the ratio of the vertical change to the horizontal change between any two points on the line. Sometimes this ratio is referred to as *the rise over the run*. The slope of a horizontal line is 0. Slopes are positive if the *y*-values increase from left to right on a coordinate grid and negative if the *y*-values decrease from left to right. The slope of a vertical line is undefined. The slope of a line is the same as the constant rate of change between the two variables. For example, the points (0, 0) and (3, 6) lie on the graph of $y = 2x$. Between these points, the vertical change is 6 and the horizontal change is 3, so the slope is $\frac{6}{3} = 2$, which is the coefficient of *x* in the equation.

pendiente El número que expresa la inclinación de una recta. La pendiente es la razón entre la variación vertical y la horizontal entre dos puntos cualesquiera de la recta. A veces, a esta razón se la llama *distancia vertical sobre distancia horizontal.* La pendiente de una recta horizontal es 0. Las pendientes son positivas si los valores de *y* aumentan de izquierda a derecha en una gráfica de coordenadas y negativas si los valores de *y* disminuyen de izquierda a derecha. La pendiente de una recta vertical es indefinida. La pendiente de una recta es igual a la tasa de variación constante entre las dos variables. Por ejemplo, los puntos (0, 0) y (3, 6) están representados en la gráfica de $y = 2x$. Entre estos puntos, la variación vertical es 6 y la variación horizontal es 3, de manera que la pendiente es $\frac{6}{3} = 2$, que es el coeficiente de *x* en la ecuación.

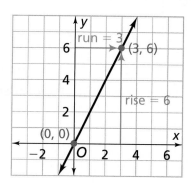

solution of an equation The value or values that make an equation true.

solución de una ecuación El valor o valores que hacen que una ecuación sea verdadera.

solve Academic Vocabulary

To determine the value or values that make a given statement true. Several methods and strategies can be used to solve a problem including estimating, isolating the variable, drawing a graph, or using a table of values.

related terms *calculate, solution*

sample Solve the equation
$4(x - 3) = 2x$.

resolver Vocabulario académico

Determinar el valor o valores que hacen verdadero un enunciado. Se pueden usar varios métodos o estrategias para resolver un problema, entre ellos la estimación, aislar la variable, hacer una gráfica o usar una tabla de valores.

términos relacionados *calcular, solución*

ejemplo Resuelve la ecuación
$4(x - 3) = 2x$.

I can solve the equation by isolating x on the left side of the equation.

$$4(x - 3) = 2x$$
$$4x - 12 = 2x$$
$$2x - 12 = 0$$
$$2x = 12$$
$$x = 6$$

I can also solve for x by using a table.

x	$4(x-3)$	$2x$
0	-12	0
3	0	6
5	8	10
6	12	12

The answer is $x = 6$.

Puedo resolver la ecuación despejando x en el lado izquierdo de la ecuación.

$$4(x - 3) = 2x$$
$$4x - 12 = 2x$$
$$2x - 12 = 0$$
$$2x = 12$$
$$x = 6$$

También puedo resolver x usando una tabla.

x	$4(x-3)$	$2x$
0	-12	0
3	0	6
5	8	10
6	12	12

La respuesta es $x = 6$.

x-intercept The point where a graph crosses the *x*-axis. In the graph, the *x*-intercept is $(-4, 0)$ or -4.

intercepto en x El punto en el que la gráfica atraviesa el eje de las *x*. En la gráfica, el intercepto en *x* es $(-4, 0)$ ó -4.

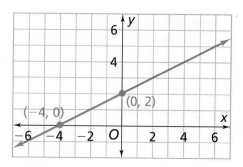

y-intercept The point where the graph crosses the *y*-axis. In a linear equation of the form $y = mx + b$, the *y*-intercept is the constant, *b*. In the graph, the *y*-intercept is $(0, 2)$ or 2.

intercepto en y El punto en el que la gráfica atraviesa el eje de las *y*. En una ecuación lineal de la forma $y = mx + b$, el intercepto en *y* es la constante, *b*. En la gráfica, el intercepto en *y* es $(0, 2)$ ó 2.

Index

Acknowledgments

Cover Design

Three Communication Design, Chicago

Text

Grateful acknowledgment is made to the following for copyrighted material:

080 National Council of Teachers of Mathematics

From *"Mathematics in Forensic Science: Male and Female Bone Measurements"* by George Knill from MATHEMATICS TEACHER, FEBRUARY 1981.

Photographs

Photo locators denoted as follows: Top (T), Center (C), Bottom (B), Left (L), Right (R), Background (Bkgd)

002 Christina Richards/Shutterstock; **003** Westend61/Westend61/Corbis; **032** Michael Steele/Staff/Getty Images; **087** Dudarev Mikhail/Shutterstock; **088** Les and Dave Jacobs/cultura/Corbis; **105** Christina Richards/Shutterstock; **108** (L) Powered by Light/Alan Spencer/Alamy, (R) Taweesak Jarearnsin/ Shutterstock.

CONNECTED ✺ MATHEMATICS® 3

What Do You Expect?

Probability and Expected Value

Lappan, Phillips, Fey, Friel

Probability and Expected Value

Looking Ahead

For a game, each player guesses a color and chooses a block from a bucket. A player who correctly predicts the color wins. After each selection, the block is returned to the bucket. **What** are the chances of winning the game?

A scratch-off prize card has five spots. Two of the spots have a matching prize. You scratch off only two spots. If the prize under both spots match, you win. **How** likely is it that you will win?

Nishi is going to take a free throw. If she is successful, she is allowed to attempt a second free throw. **How** can you determine whether Nishi is most likely to score 0, 1, or 2 points?

Probabilities can help you make decisions. If there is a 75% chance of rain, you might decide to carry an umbrella. If a baseball player has a 0.245 batting average, you expect that he is more likely not to get a hit than to get a hit on a given at-bat.

Probabilities can also help you to predict what will happen over the long run. Suppose you and a friend toss a coin before each bus ride to decide who will sit by the window. You can predict that you will sit by the window about half of the time.

Many probability situations involve a payoff—points scored in a game, lives saved by promoting good health, or profit earned from a business venture. You can sometimes find the long-term average payoff. For example, when deciding whether to make an investment, a company might figure out how much it can expect to earn over the long run.

In this Unit, you will look at questions involving probability and expected value, including the three questions on the opposite page.

Mathematical Highlights

In this Unit, you will deepen your understanding of basic probability concepts. You will learn about the expected value of situations involving chance.

You will learn how to

- Use probabilities to predict what will happen over the long run

- Distinguish between equally likely events and those that are not equally likely

- Use strategies for identifying possible outcomes and analyzing probabilities, such as using lists or tree diagrams

- Develop two kinds of probability models:

    (1) Gather data from experiments (experimental probability)

    (2) Analyze possible outcomes (theoretical probability)

- Understand that experimental probabilities are better estimates of theoretical probabilities when they are based on larger numbers of trials

- Determine if a game is fair or unfair

- Use models to analyze situations that involve two stages (or actions)

- Determine the expected value of a chance situation

- Analyze situations that involve binomial outcomes

- Interpret statements of probability to make decisions and answer questions

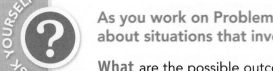

As you work on Problems in this Unit, ask yourself questions about situations that involve analyzing probabilities:

What are the possible outcomes for the event(s) in this situation?

Are these outcomes equally likely?

Is this a fair or unfair situation?

Can I compute the theoretical probabilities or do I conduct an experiment?

How can I determine the probability of one event followed by a second event: two-stage probabilities?

How can I use expected value to help me make decisions?

Mathematical Practices and Habits of Mind

In the *Connected Mathematics* curriculum you will develop an understanding of important mathematical ideas by solving problems and reflecting on the mathematics involved. Every day, you will use "habits of mind" to make sense of problems and apply what you learn to new situations. Some of these habits are described by the *Common Core State Standards for Mathematical Practices* (MP).

MP1 Make sense of problems and persevere in solving them.

When using mathematics to solve a problem, it helps to think carefully about

- data and other facts you are given and what additional information you need to solve the problem;
- strategies you have used to solve similar problems and whether you could solve a related simpler problem first;
- how you could express the problem with equations, diagrams, or graphs;
- whether your answer makes sense.

MP2 Reason abstractly and quantitatively.

When you are asked to solve a problem, it often helps to

- focus first on the key mathematical ideas;
- check that your answer makes sense in the problem setting;
- use what you know about the problem setting to guide your mathematical reasoning.

MP3 Construct viable arguments and critique the reasoning of others.

When you are asked to explain why a conjecture is correct, you can

- show some examples that fit the claim and explain why they fit;
- show how a new result follows logically from known facts and principles.

When you believe a mathematical claim is incorrect, you can

- show one or more counterexamples—cases that don't fit the claim;
- find steps in the argument that do not follow logically from prior claims.

MP4 Model with mathematics.

When you are asked to solve problems, it often helps to

- think carefully about the numbers or geometric shapes that are the most important factors in the problem, then ask yourself how those factors are related to each other;
- express data and relationships in the problem with tables, graphs, diagrams, or equations, and check your result to see if it makes sense.

MP5 Use appropriate tools strategically.

When working on mathematical questions, you should always

- decide which tools are most helpful for solving the problem and why;
- try a different tool when you get stuck.

MP6 Attend to precision.

In every mathematical exploration or problem-solving task, it is important to

- think carefully about the required accuracy of results; is a number estimate or geometric sketch good enough, or is a precise value or drawing needed?
- report your discoveries with clear and correct mathematical language that can be understood by those to whom you are speaking or writing.

MP7 Look for and make use of structure.

In mathematical explorations and problem solving, it is often helpful to

- look for patterns that show how data points, numbers, or geometric shapes are related to each other;
- use patterns to make predictions.

MP8 Look for and express regularity in repeated reasoning.

When results of a repeated calculation show a pattern, it helps to

- express that pattern as a general rule that can be used in similar cases;
- look for shortcuts that will make the calculation simpler in other cases.

You will use all of the Mathematical Practices in this Unit. Sometimes, when you look at a Problem, it is obvious which practice is most helpful. At other times, you will decide on a practice to use during class explorations and discussions. After completing each Problem, ask yourself:

- What mathematics have I learned by solving this Problem?
- What Mathematical Practices were helpful in learning this mathematics?

A First Look At Chance

Decisions, decisions, decisions—you make decisions every day. You choose what to wear, with whom to have lunch, what to do after school, and maybe what time to go to bed.

To make some decisions, you consider the chance, or likelihood, that something will happen. You may listen to the weather forecast to decide whether you will wear a raincoat to school. In some cases, you may even let chance make a decision for you, such as when you roll a number cube to see who goes first in a game.

A number cube shows the numbers 1, 2, 3, 4, 5, and 6 on its faces.

Common Core State Standards

7.SP.C.6 Approximate the probability of a chance event by collecting data on the chance process that produces it and observing its long-run relative frequency, and predict the approximate relative frequency given the probability.

7.SP.C.7a Develop a uniform probability model by assigning equal probability to all outcomes, and use the model to determine probabilities of events.

7.SP.C.7b Develop a probability model (which may not be uniform) by observing frequencies in data generated from a chance process.

Also 7.RP.A.2, 7.SP.C.8, 7.SP.C.8a, 7.SP.C.8b

Think about these questions. They are examples of probability situations to help you consider the likelihood of particular events.

- What are the chances of getting a 2 when you roll a number cube? Are you more likely to roll a 2 or a 6? How can you decide?

- The weather forecaster says the chance of rain tomorrow is 40%. What does this mean? Should you wear a raincoat?

- When you toss a coin, what are the chances of getting tails?

- Suppose you toss seven tails in a row. Are you more likely to get heads or tails on the next toss?

1.1 Choosing Cereal
Tossing Coins to Find Probabilities

Kalvin always has cereal for breakfast. He likes Cocoa Blast cereal, but his mother wants him to eat Health Nut Flakes at least some mornings.

Kalvin and his mother agree to leave the cereal problem to chance. Each morning in June, Kalvin tosses a coin. If the coin lands on heads, he will have Cocoa Blast. If the coin lands on tails, he will have Health Nut Flakes.

 Predict how many days Kalvin can expect to eat Cocoa Blast in June.

Problem 1.1

A **1.** Test your prediction. Toss a coin 30 times (one for each day in June). Record your results in a table with the headings below. Your table will have 30 rows.

Coin-Toss Results

Day	Result of Toss (H or T)	Number of Heads So Far	Fraction of Heads So Far	Percent of Heads So Far
1				
2				

2. As you add more data, what happens to the percent of tosses that are heads?

B Work with your classmates to combine the results from all the groups.

1. What percent of the total number of tosses for your class is heads?

2. As your class adds more data, what happens to the percent of tosses that are heads?

3. Based on what you found for June, how many times do you expect Kalvin to eat Cocoa Blast in July? Explain your reasoning.

C Kalvin's mother tells him that the chance of a coin showing heads when he tosses it is $\frac{1}{2}$. Does this mean that every time he tosses a coin twice, he will get one head and one tail? Explain.

A C E Homework starts on page 17.

1.2 Tossing Paper Cups
Finding More Probabilities

Kalvin wants to find something else to toss that will give him a better chance of eating his favorite cereal each morning. He wonders if a paper cup would be a good thing to toss.

Because Kalvin wants to eat Cocoa Blast cereal more of the time, he needs to determine if the cup lands in one position more often than another. If so, he will ask to toss a paper cup instead of a coin.

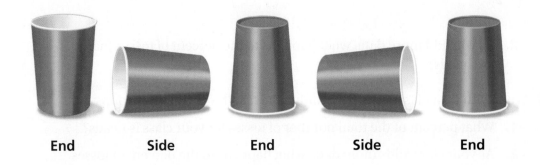

End	**Side**	**End**	**Side**	**End**

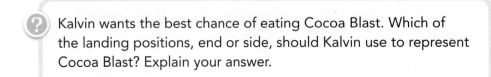

? Kalvin wants the best chance of eating Cocoa Blast. Which of the landing positions, end or side, should Kalvin use to represent Cocoa Blast? Explain your answer.

Problem 1.2

A Conduct an experiment to test your prediction about how a paper cup lands. Toss a paper cup 50 times. Make a table to record your data.

B Use your results to answer the following questions:

  1. For what fraction of your 50 tosses did the cup land on one of its ends? What percent is this?

  2. For what fraction of your 50 tosses did the cup land on its side? What percent is this?

  3. Do the landing positions *end* and *side* have the same chance of occurring? If not, which is more likely? Explain.

  4. Which of the cup's landing positions should Kalvin use to represent Cocoa Blast? Explain your reasoning.

C Combine the data from all the groups in your class. Based on these data, would you change your answers to parts (3) and (4) of Question B? Explain.

D Kalvin's mother agrees to let him use a cup to decide his cereal each morning. On the first morning, the cup lands on its end. On the second morning, it lands on its side. Kalvin says, "This cup isn't any better than the coin. It lands on an end 50% of the time!" Do you agree or disagree with Kalvin? Explain.

A C E Homework starts on page 17.

1.3 One More Try
Finding Experimental Probabilities

In the last two Problems, you conducted experiments to find the chances of particular results. You represented those chances as fractions or percents. The mathematical word for chance is **probability.** A probability that you find by conducting an experiment and collecting data is called an **experimental probability.**

Suppose you toss a paper cup 50 times, and it lands on its side 31 times. Each toss of the cup is a **trial.** In this experiment, there are 50 trials. **Favorable outcomes** are the trials in which a desired result occurs.

In this case, a favorable result, *landed on side,* occurred 31 times. To find the experimental probability, use the ratio below.

$$\frac{\text{number of favorable outcomes}}{\text{total number of trials}}$$

You can write "the probability of the cup landing on its side" as $P(\text{side})$. The equation below gives the results of the experiment just described.

$$P(\text{side}) = \frac{\text{number of times cup landed on its side}}{\text{number of times cup was tossed}} = \frac{31}{50}$$

The ratio of number of desired results to the total number of trials is also called **relative frequency.**

Kalvin has come up with one more way to use probability to decide his breakfast cereal. This time, he tosses two coins.

- If the coins match, he gets to eat Cocoa Blast.

Match

Match

- If the coins do not match, he eats Health Nut Flakes.

No Match

(?) Suppose Kalvin's mother agrees to let him use this method. How many days in June do you think Kalvin will eat Cocoa Blast?

Problem 1.3

A 1. Conduct an experiment by tossing a pair of coins 30 times. Keep track of the number of times the coins *match* and the number of times *no match* occurs.

2. Based on your data, what is the experimental probability of getting a match? Of getting a no-match?

B Combine your data with your classmates' data.

1. Find the experimental probabilities for the combined data. Compare these probabilities with the probabilities in Question A.

2. Based on the class data, do you think a match and a no-match have the same chance of occurring? Explain.

C Think about the possible results when you toss two coins.

1. In how many ways can a match occur?

2. In how many ways can a no-match occur?

3. Based on the number of ways each result can occur, do a match and a no-match have the same chance of occurring? Explain.

D Kalvin's friend Asta suggests that he toss a thumbtack. If it lands on its side, he eats Cocoa Blast. If it lands on its head, he eats Health Nut Flakes. She says they must first experiment to find the probabilities involved. Asta does 11 tosses. Kalvin does 50 tosses. Here are the probabilities they find based on their experiments.

$$\text{Asta: } P(\text{heads}) = \frac{6}{11} \qquad \text{Kalvin: } P(\text{heads}) = \frac{13}{50}$$

Which result do you think better predicts the experimental probability of the thumbtack landing on its head when tossed? Explain.

 Homework starts on page 17.

1.4 Analyzing Events
Understanding *Equally Likely*

Kalvin finds a coin near a railroad track. It looks flat and a little bent, so he guesses it has been run over by a train. He decides to use this unusual coin to choose his breakfast cereal during November. By the end of the month, he has had Health Nut Flakes only seven times. His mother is suspicious of the coin.

- Why is Kalvin's mother suspicious of the coin?

- What does it mean for a coin to be "fair"?

She says, "You call a coin a fair coin if heads and tails are **equally likely** results of a coin toss." This means that you have the same chance of getting heads as getting tails. Kalvin and his mother wonder if Kalvin's coin is a fair coin.

Kalvin's mother says, "Suppose each person in our family writes his or her name on a card and puts the card in a hat. If you mix up the three cards and pull one out, all three names are equally likely to be picked. But suppose I put my name in the hat ten times. Then the names are not equally likely to be picked. My name has a greater chance of being chosen."

- Why is each card equally likely to be chosen, but each name is not?

- Kalvin and his father want all three names equally likely to be chosen. How many cards should they add to the hat so that each name is equally likely to be chosen? What should be on each card?

Problem 1.4

A The list below gives several actions and possible results. In each case, decide whether the possible results are equally likely and explain. For actions 5 and 6, start by listing all the possible results.

Action	Possible Results
1. You toss an empty juice can.	The can lands on its side, the can lands upside-down, or the can lands right-side-up.
2. A baby is born.	The baby is a boy or the baby is a girl.
3. A baby is born.	The baby is right-handed or the baby is left-handed.
4. A high school team plays a football game.	The team wins or the team loses.
5. You roll a six-sided number cube.	_____
6. You guess an answer on a true-or-false test.	_____

B For which of the actions in Question A did you find the results to be equally likely? Does this mean that the probability of each result is $\frac{1}{2}$ (or 50%)? Explain your reasoning.

C Describe an action for which the results are equally likely. Then, describe an action for which the results are *not* equally likely.

A C E Homework starts on page 17.

Applications

1. **a.** Miki tosses a coin 50 times, and the coin shows heads 28 times. What fraction of the 50 tosses is heads? What percent is this?

   b. Suppose the coin is fair, and Miki tosses it 500 times. About how many times can she expect it to show heads? Explain your reasoning.

2. Suppose Kalvin tosses a coin to determine his breakfast cereal every day. He starts on his twelfth birthday and continues until his eighteenth birthday. About how many times would you expect him to eat Cocoa Blast cereal?

3. Kalvin tosses a coin five days in a row and gets tails every time. Do you think there is something wrong with the coin? How can you find out?

4. Len tosses a coin three times. The coin shows heads every time. What are the chances the coin shows tails on the next toss? Explain.

5. Is it possible to toss a coin 20 times and have it land heads-up 20 times? Is this likely to happen? Explain.

6. Kalvin tosses a paper cup once each day for a year to determine his breakfast cereal. Use your results from Problem 1.2 to answer the following.

   a. How many times do you expect the cup to land on its side? On one of its ends?

   b. How many times do you expect Kalvin to eat Cocoa Blast in a month? In a year? Explain.

7. Dawn tosses a pawn from her chess set five times. It lands on its base four times and on its side only once.

   Andre tosses the same pawn 100 times. It lands on its base 28 times and on its side 72 times. Based on their data, if you toss the pawn one more time, is it more likely to land on its base or its side? Explain.

8. Kalvin flips a small paper cup 50 times and a large paper cup 30 times. The table below displays the results of his experiments. Based on these data, should he use the small cup or the large cup to determine his breakfast each morning? Explain.

Cup-Toss Results

Where Cup Lands	Small Paper Cup	Large Paper Cup
Side	39 times	22 times
One of Its Ends	11 times	8 times

9. Kalvin's sister Kate finds yet another way for him to pick his breakfast. She places one blue marble and one red marble in each of two bags. She says that each morning he can choose one marble from each bag. If the marbles are the same color, he eats Cocoa Blast. If not, he eats Health Nut Flakes. Explain how selecting one marble from each of the two bags and tossing two coins are similar.

10. Adsila and Adahy have to decide who will take out the garbage. Adahy suggests they toss two coins. He says that if at least one head comes up, Adsila takes out the garbage. If no heads come up, Adahy takes out the garbage. Should Adsila agree to Adahy's proposal? Explain why or why not.

For Exercises 11–15, decide whether the possible results are equally likely. Explain.

Action	**Possible Results**
11. Your phone rings at 9:00 P.M.	The caller is your best friend, the caller is a relative, or the caller is someone else.
12. You check the temperature at your home tomorrow morning.	The temperature is 30°F or above, or the temperature is below 30°F.
13. You spin the pointer once.	The pointer lands on yellow, the pointer lands on red, or the pointer lands on blue.

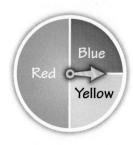

Action	**Possible Results**
14. You find out how many car accidents occurred in your city or town yesterday.	There were fewer than five accidents, there were exactly five accidents, or there were more than five accidents.
15. You choose a card from a standard deck of playing cards (with no jokers).	The card is a spade, the card is a heart, the card is a diamond, or the card is a club.

For Exercises 16–17, first list all the possible results for each action. Then decide whether the results are equally likely.

16. You choose a block from a bag containing one red block, three blue blocks, and one green block.

17. You try to steal second base during a baseball game.

18. For parts (a)–(f), give an example of a result that would have a probability near the percent given.

   a. 0%   **b.** 25%   **c.** 50%

   d. 75%   **e.** 80%   **f.** 100%

Connections

19. Colby rolls a number cube 50 times. She records the result of each roll and organizes her data in the table below.

Number Cube Results

Number	Frequency
1	☰☰ |
2	☰☰ ||||
3	☰☰ |
4	☰☰ |||
5	☰☰ ☰☰ |
6	☰☰ ☰☰

a. What fraction of the rolls are 2's? What percent is this?

b. What fraction of the rolls are odd numbers? What percent is this?

c. What percent of the rolls is greater than 3?

d. Suppose Colby rolls the number cube 100 times. About how many times can she expect to roll a 2? Explain.

e. If Colby rolls the number cube 1,000 times, about how many times can she expect to roll an odd number? Explain.

20. Find a fraction between each pair of fractions.

  a. $\frac{1}{10}$ and $\frac{8}{25}$ 　　　　　　　　　**b.** $\frac{3}{8}$ and $\frac{11}{40}$

For Exercises 21–23, use the bar graph below.

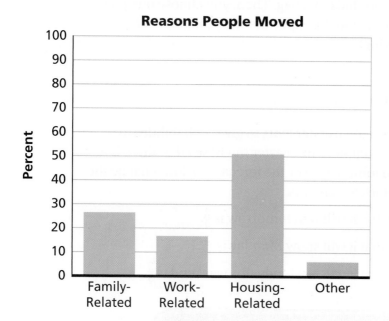

Reasons People Moved

21. **Multiple Choice** Suppose 41,642 people moved. About how many of those people moved for family-related reasons?

   A. 28   **B.** 11,000   **C.** 21,000   **D.** 31,000

22. **Multiple Choice** What fraction of the people represented in the graph moved for reasons other than work-related, housing-related, or family-related?

   F. $\frac{6}{10}$ **G.** $\frac{6}{100}$ **H.** $\frac{52}{100}$ **J.** $\frac{94}{100}$

23. **Multiple Choice** Suppose 41,642 people moved. About how many moved for housing-related reasons?

   A. 52   **B.** 11,000   **C.** 21,000   **D.** 31,000

24. Suppose you write all the factors of 42 on pieces of paper and put them in a bag. You shake the bag. Then, you choose one piece of paper from the bag. Find the experimental probability of choosing the following.

  a. an even number

  b. a prime number

25. Weather forecasters often use percents to give probabilities in their forecasts. For example, a forecaster might say that there is a 50% chance of rain tomorrow. For the forecasts below, change the fractional probabilities to percents.

  a. The probability that it will rain tomorrow is $\frac{2}{5}$.

  b. The probability that it will snow Monday is $\frac{3}{10}$.

  c. The probability that it will be cloudy this weekend is $\frac{3}{5}$.

For Exercises 26–29, use the graph below.

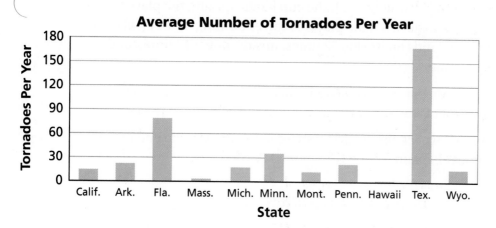

Average Number of Tornadoes Per Year

26. Is a tornado equally likely to occur in California and in Florida? Explain your reasoning.

27. Is a tornado equally likely to occur in Arkansas and in Pennsylvania?

28. Is a tornado equally likely to occur in Massachusetts and in Texas?

29. Based on these data, is a person living in Montana more likely to experience a tornado than a person living in Massachusetts? Explain.

Extensions

30. Monday is the first day Kalvin tosses a coin to determine his cereal. During the first five days, he has Cocoa Blast only twice. One possible pattern of Kalvin's coin tosses is shown.

Coin-Toss Results

Monday	Tuesday	Wednesday	Thursday	Friday
H	H	T	T	T

Find every way Kalvin can toss the coin during the week and have Cocoa Blast cereal twice. Explain how you know that you found every possible way.

31. Yolanda watches a carnival game in which a paper cup is tossed. It costs $1 to play the game. If the cup lands upright, the player receives $5. Otherwise, the player receives nothing. The cup is tossed 50 times. It lands on its side 32 times, upside-down 13 times, and upright 5 times.

    a. If Yolanda plays the game ten times, about how many times can she expect to win? How many times can she expect to lose?

    b. Do you expect her to have more or less money at the end of ten games? Explain.

Mathematical Reflections

1

In this Investigation, you conducted experiments with coins and paper cups. You used fractions and percents to express the chances, or probabilities, that certain results would occur. You also considered several actions and determined whether the possible results were equally likely. The questions below will help you summarize what you have learned.

Think about these questions. Discuss your ideas with other students and your teacher. Then write a summary of your findings in your notebook.

1. **How** do you find the experimental probability that a particular result will occur? **Why** is it called the experimental probability?

2. In an experiment, are 30 trials as good as 500 trials to predict the chances of a result? **Explain**.

3. **What** does it mean for results to be equally likely?

Common Core Mathematical Practices

As you worked on the Problems in this Investigation, you used prior knowledge to make sense of them. You also applied Mathematical Practices to solve the Problems. Think back over your work, the ways you thought about the Problems, and how you used Mathematical Practices.

Hector described his thoughts in the following way:

> Our group noticed that in Problem 1.2, Kalvin tries another method for choosing his cereal. He flips a cup and records how the cup lands, on either an end or a side.
>
> At first we thought that the results would be the same as those for tossing a coin. After we tossed the cup 50 times, we were not so sure. It landed on its side 27 times and on its end 23 times.
>
> After we combined the class data, we were fairly certain that the two events were not equally likely. The cup would land on its side more often than on its end.

Common Core Standards for Mathematical Practice

MP7 Look for and make use of structure.

- What other Mathematical Practices can you identify in Hector's reasoning?

- Describe a Mathematical Practice that you and your classmates used to solve a different Problem in this Investigation.

Experimental and Theoretical Probability

Investigation

In the last Investigation, you collected the results of many coin tosses. You found that the experimental probability of a coin landing on heads is $\frac{1}{2}$ $\left(\text{or very close to } \frac{1}{2}\right)$.

You assume that the coins are fair coins for which there are two equally likely results of a toss, heads or tails. The word **outcome** means an individual result of an action or event.

The coin-tossing experiment had two possible outcomes, heads and tails. Heads was a favorable outcome for Kalvin. A probability calculated by examining possible outcomes, rather than by experimenting, is a **theoretical probability.**

$$P(\text{heads}) = \frac{\text{number of ways heads can occur}}{\text{number of outcomes}} = \frac{1}{2}$$

The probability of tossing heads is 1 of 2, or $\frac{1}{2}$. The probability of tossing tails is also $\frac{1}{2}$.

Common Core State Standards

7.SP.C.5 Understand that the probability of a chance event is a number between 0 and 1 that expresses the likelihood of the event occurring.

7.SP.C. 8 Find probabilities of compound events using organized lists, tables, tree diagrams, and simulation.

7.SP.C.8c Design and use a simulation to generate frequencies for compound events.

Also 7.RP.A.2, 7.RP.A.2a, 7.RP.A.3, 7.SP.C.6, 7.SP.C.7b, 7.SP.C.8b, 7.SP.C.8a

But all experiments do not result in equally likely outcomes. When you tossed a cup, the two outcomes were not equally likely. The chances of landing on the side and landing in an upright position were not the same.

In this Investigation, you will explore some other situations in which probabilities are found both by experimenting and by analyzing the possible outcomes.

2.1 Predicting to Win
Finding Theoretical Probabilities

In the last 5 minutes of the *Gee Whiz Everyone Wins!* game show, all the members of the audience are called to the stage. Each one chooses a block *at random* from a bucket containing an unknown number of red, yellow, and blue blocks. Each block has the same size and shape.

Before choosing, each contestant predicts the color of his or her block. If the prediction is correct, the contestant wins. After each selection, the block is put back into the bucket and the bucket is shaken. That way, the probabilities do not change as blocks are removed.

- What do you think *random* means?

- Suppose you are a member of the audience. Would you rather be called to the stage first or last? Explain.

- Does it matter that the block is returned to the bucket and the bucket is shaken after each contestant? Explain.

Problem 2.1

(A) 1. Play the block-guessing game with your class. Keep a record of the number of times a color is chosen. Play the game until you think you can predict the chances of each color being chosen.

2. Based on the data you collect during the game, find the experimental probabilities of choosing red, choosing yellow, and choosing blue.

(B) 1. Suppose you counted the red blocks, the blue blocks, and the yellow blocks in the bucket. How would you use this information to calculate the theoretical probability of drawing a red, a blue, or a yellow block?

2. How do the theoretical probabilities compare to the experimental probabilities in Question A?

3. What is the sum of the theoretical probabilities in Question B part (1)?

(C) 1. Does each individual block, without regard to color, have the same chance of being chosen? Explain.

2. Does each color have the same chance of being chosen? Explain.

3. If you choose a block, is it equally likely that it will be red or blue?

4. Which person has the advantage—the first person to choose from the bucket or the last person? Explain.

(D) Suppose you have a different bucket. You can't see inside, but you know there are 30 blocks in all. How can you use your observations of others picking blocks to predict how many of each color there are?

(A)(C)(E) Homework starts on page 36.

2.2 Choosing Marbles
Developing Probability Models

Sammy collects marbles. He asks his teacher if the class could experiment with marbles instead of blocks. The teacher says, "What really matters is whether we can predict the probabilities in a situation using marbles. Let's try a bag with marbles of different colors."

Problem 2.2

A A bag contains two yellow marbles, four blue marbles, and six red marbles. You choose a marble from the bag at random. Answer the following questions and explain your reasoning.

1. What is the probability the marble is yellow? The probability it is blue? The probability it is red?

2. What is the sum of the probabilities from part (1)?

3. What color is the selected marble most likely to be?

4. What is the probability the marble is not blue?

5. What is the probability the marble is either red or yellow?

6. What is the probability the marble is white?

7. Jakayla says the probability the marble is blue is $\frac{12}{4}$. Adsila says $\frac{12}{4}$ is impossible. Which girl is correct?

Problem 2.2 *continued*

B Suppose a new bag has twice as many marbles of each color.

   1. Do the probabilities change? Explain.

   2. How many blue marbles should you add to this bag to have the probability of choosing a blue marble equal to $\frac{1}{2}$?

C A different bag contains several marbles. Each marble is red or white or blue. The probability of choosing a red marble is $\frac{1}{3}$, and the probability of choosing a white marble is $\frac{1}{6}$.

   1. What is the probability of choosing a blue marble? Explain.

   2. What is the least number of marbles that can be in the bag? Suppose the bag contains the least number of marbles. How many of each color does the bag contain?

   3. Can the bag contain 48 marbles? If so, how many of each color does it contain?

   4. Suppose the bag contains 8 red marbles and 4 white marbles. How many blue marbles does it contain?

D **1.** Do you think the experimental probabilities would be different with blocks instead of marbles? How about theoretical probabilities?

   2. Design a fair way for Kalvin to choose his breakfast cereal using blocks or marbles.

A C E Homework starts on page 36.

2.3 Designing a Fair Game
Pondering Possible and Probable

Santo and Tevy are playing a game with coins. They take turns tossing three coins. If all three coins match, Santo wins. Otherwise, Tevy wins. Each player has won several turns in the game. Tevy, however, seems to be winning more often. Santo thinks the game is unfair. A **fair game** is a game in which all players have equal chances of winning.

Santo drew the tree diagram below to represent tossing three coins. A **tree diagram** is an illustration using branches to show the sample space of an event. The **sample space** is another name for the set of possible outcomes of an event.

Coin 1	Coin 2	Coin 3	Outcome
		H	HHH
	H	T	HHT
H		H	HTH
	T	T	HTT
		H	THH
	H	T	THT
T		H	TTH
	T	T	TTT

 How can you decide if a game is fair or not?

Problem 2.3

A Use the tree diagram from above to answer the following questions:

   1. What is the sample space for tossing three coins?

   2. How many possible outcomes are there when you toss three coins? Are the outcomes equally likely?

   3. What is the theoretical probability that the three coins will match?

   4. What is the theoretical probability that exactly two coins will match?

   5. Is the game played by Santo and Tevy a fair game? If so, explain why. If not, explain how to make it fair.

B Suppose you tossed three coins for 24 trials. How many times would you expect two coins to match?

C Santo said, "It is *possible* to toss three coins and have them match." Tevy replied, "Yes, but is it *probable*?" What do you think each boy meant?

ACE Homework starts on page 36.

2.4 Winning the Bonus Prize
Using Strategies to Find Theoretical Probabilities

All the winners from the *Gee Whiz Everyone Wins!* game show have the opportunity to compete for a bonus prize. Each winner chooses one block from each of two bags. Each bag contains one red, one yellow, and one blue block. This bonus game consists of two events, which can also be called a **compound event.**

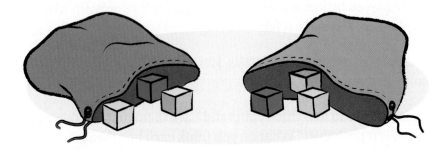

The contestant must predict which color she or he will choose from each of the two bags. If the prediction is correct, the contestant wins a $10,000 bonus prize!

- What color choice gives you the best chance of winning?

Problem 2.4

(A) 1. Conduct an experiment with 36 trials for the situation above. Record the pairs of colors that you choose.

2. Find the experimental probability of choosing each possible pair of colors.

(B) 1. Find all of the possible color pairs that can be chosen. Are these outcomes equally likely? Explain your reasoning.

2. Find the theoretical probability of choosing each pair of colors.

3. How do the theoretical probabilities compare with your experimental probabilities? Explain any differences.

(C) 1. Brelynn and Akimi change the rules of the game. Each contestant must predict which color combination will result from choosing a block from each bag. Brelynn and Akimi make the following predictions for this game.

> Akimi: I predict 2 reds.
>
> Brelynn: I predict 1 blue and 1 red, in either order.

Who has the better chance of winning? Explain.

2. Does a contestant have a chance to win the bonus prize? Is it likely a contestant will win the bonus prize? Explain.

3. If you play this game 18 times, how many times do you expect to win?

(A)(C)(E) Homework starts on page 36.

Applications

1. A bucket contains one green block, one red block, and two yellow blocks. You choose one block from the bucket.

   a. Find the theoretical probability that you will choose each color.

   P(green) = 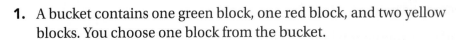 P(yellow) = ▨ P(red) = ▨

   b. Find the sum of the probabilities in part (a).

   c. What is the probability that you will *not* choose a red block? Explain how you found your answer.

   d. What is the sum of the probability of choosing a red block and the probability of not choosing a red block?

2. A bubble-gum machine contains 25 gumballs. There are 12 green, 6 purple, 2 orange, and 5 yellow gumballs.

   a. Find each theoretical probability.

   P(green) = ▨ P(purple) = ▨

   P(orange) = ▨ P(yellow) = ▨

   b. Find the sum.

   P(green) + P(purple) + P(orange) + P(yellow) = ▨

   c. Write each of the probabilities in part (a) as a percent.

   P(green) = ▨ P(purple) = ▨

   P(orange) = ▨ P(yellow) = ▨

   d. What is the sum of all the probabilities as a percent?

   e. What do you think the sum of the probabilities for all the possible outcomes must be for any situation? Explain.

3. Bailey uses the results from an experiment to calculate the probability of each color of block being chosen from a bucket. He says $P(\text{red}) = 35\%$, $P(\text{blue}) = 45\%$, and $P(\text{yellow}) = 20\%$. Jarod uses theoretical probability because he knows how many of each color block is in the bucket. He says $P(\text{red}) = 45\%$, $P(\text{blue}) = 35\%$, and $P(\text{yellow}) = 20\%$. On Bailey's turn, he predicts blue. On Jarod's turn, he predicts red. Neither boy makes the right prediction.

   a. Did the boys make reasonable predictions based on their own probabilities? Explain.

   b. Did they do something wrong with their calculations? Explain.

4. A bag contains two white blocks, one red block, and three purple blocks. You choose one block from the bag.

   a. Find each probability.

   $P(\text{white}) = \blacksquare$ $P(\text{red}) = \blacksquare$ $P(\text{purple}) = \blacksquare$

   b. What is the probability of *not* choosing a white block? Explain how you found your answer.

   c. Suppose the number of blocks of each color is doubled. What happens to the probability of choosing each color?

   d. Suppose you add two more blocks of each color to the original bag. What happens to the probability of choosing each color?

   e. How many blocks of which colors should you add to the original bag to make the probability of choosing a red block equal to $\frac{1}{2}$?

5. A bag contains exactly three blue blocks. You choose a block at random. Find each probability.

   a. $P(\text{blue})$

   b. $P(\textit{not}\ \text{blue})$

   c. $P(\text{yellow})$

6. A bag contains several marbles. Some are red, some are white, and some are blue. You count the marbles and find the theoretical probability of choosing a red marble is $\frac{1}{5}$. You also find the theoretical probability of choosing a white marble is $\frac{3}{10}$.

   a. What is the least number of marbles that can be in the bag?

   b. Can the bag contain 60 marbles? If so, how many of each color does it contain?

   c. If the bag contains 4 red marbles and 6 white marbles, how many blue marbles does it contain?

   d. How can you find the probability of choosing a blue marble?

7. Decide whether each statement is *true* or *false*. Justify your answers.

   a. The probability of an outcome can be 0.

   b. The probability of an outcome can be 1.

   c. The probability of an outcome can be greater than 1.

8. Patricia and Jean design a coin-tossing game. Patricia suggests tossing three coins. Jean says they can toss one coin three times. Are the outcomes different for the two situations? Explain.

9. Pietro and Eva are playing a game in which they toss a coin three times. Eva gets a point if no two consecutive toss results match (as in H-T-H). Pietro gets a point if exactly two consecutive toss results match (as in H-H-T). If all three toss results match, no one scores a point. The first player to get 10 points wins. Is this a fair game? Explain. If it is not a fair game, change the rules to make it fair.

10. Silvia and Juanita are designing a game. A player in the game tosses two number cubes. Winning depends on whether the sum of the two numbers is odd or even. Silvia and Juanita make a tree diagram of possible outcomes.

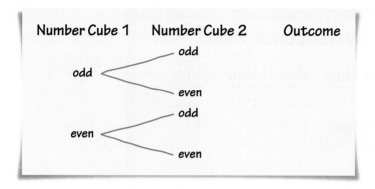

   a. List all the outcomes for the sums.

   b. Design rules for a two-player game that is fair.

   c. Design rules for a two-player game that is not fair.

   d. How is this situation similar to tossing two coins and seeing if the coins match or don't match?

11. Melissa is designing a birthday card for her sister. She has a blue, a yellow, a pink, and a green sheet of paper. She also has a black, a red, and a purple marker. Suppose Melissa chooses one sheet of paper and one marker at random.

   a. Make a tree diagram to find all the possible color combinations.

   b. What is the probability that Melissa chooses pink paper and a red marker?

   c. What is the probability that Melissa chooses blue paper? What is the probability she does not choose blue paper?

   d. What is the probability that she chooses a purple marker?

12. Lunch at school consists of a sandwich, a vegetable, and a fruit. Each lunch combination is equally likely to be given to a student. The students do not know what lunch they will get. Sol's favorite lunch is a chicken sandwich, carrots, and a banana.

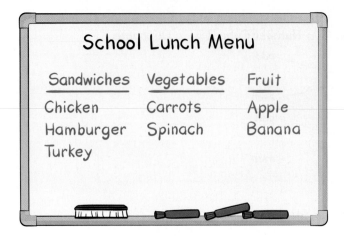

School Lunch Menu

Sandwiches	Vegetables	Fruit
Chicken	Carrots	Apple
Hamburger	Spinach	Banana
Turkey		

a. Make a tree diagram to determine how many different lunches are possible. List all the possible outcomes.

b. What is the probability that Sol gets his favorite lunch? Explain your reasoning.

c. What is the probability that Sol gets at least one of his favorite lunch items? Explain.

13. Suppose you spin the pointer of the spinner at the right once and roll the number cube. (The numbers on the cube are 1, 2, 3, 4, 5, and 6.)

a. Make a tree diagram of the possible outcomes of a spin of the pointer and a roll of the number cube.

b. What is the probability that you get a 2 on both the spinner and the number cube? Explain your reasoning.

c. What is the probability that you get a *factor* of 2 on both the spinner and the number cube?

d. What is the probability that you get a *multiple* of 2 on both the number cube and the spinner?

Connections

14. Find numbers that make each sentence true.

   a. $\frac{1}{8} = \frac{\blacksquare}{32} = \frac{5}{\blacksquare}$

   b. $\frac{3}{7} = \frac{\blacksquare}{21} = \frac{6}{\blacksquare}$

   c. $\frac{8}{20} = \frac{\blacksquare}{5} = \frac{16}{\blacksquare}$

15. Which of the following sums is equal to 1?

   a. $\frac{1}{6} + \frac{3}{6} + \frac{2}{6}$

   b. $\frac{4}{18} + \frac{1}{9} + \frac{2}{3}$

   c. $\frac{1}{5} + \frac{1}{3} + \frac{1}{5}$

16. Describe a situation in which events have a theoretical probability that can be represented by the equation $\frac{1}{12} + \frac{1}{3} + \frac{7}{12} = 1$.

17. Kara and Bly both perform an experiment. Kara gets a probability of $\frac{125}{300}$ for a particular outcome. Bly gets a probability of $\frac{108}{320}$.

   a. Whose experimental probability is closer to the theoretical probability of $\frac{1}{3}$? Explain your reasoning.

   b. Give two possible experiments that Kara and Bly can do and that have a theoretical probability of $\frac{1}{3}$.

For Exercises 18–25, estimate the probability that the given event occurs. Any probability must be between 0 and 1 (or 0% and 100%). If an event is impossible, the probability it will occur is 0, or 0%. If an event is certain to happen, the probability it will occur is 1, or 100%.

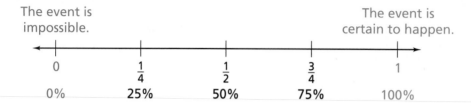

Sample

> Samantha: I watch some television every night, unless I have too much homework. So far, I do not have much homework today. I am about 95% sure that I will watch television tonight.

18. You are absent from school at least one day during this school year.

19. You have pizza for lunch one day this week.

20. It snows on July 4 this year in Mexico.

21. You get all the problems on your next math test correct.

22. The next baby born in your local hospital is a girl.

23. The sun sets tonight.

24. You take a turn in a game by tossing four coins. The result is all heads.

25. You toss a coin and get 100 tails in a row.

26. Karen and Mia play games with coins and number cubes. No matter which game they play, Karen loses more often than Mia. Karen is not sure if she just has bad luck or if the games are unfair. The games are described in this table. Review the game rules and complete the table.

Game	Can Karen Win?	Karen Likely to Win?	Game Fair or Unfair?
Game 1 Roll a number cube. • Karen scores a point if the roll is even. • Mia scores a point if the roll is odd.			
Game 2 Roll a number cube. • Karen scores a point if the roll is a multiple of 4. • Mia scores a point if the roll is a multiple of 3.			
Game 3 Toss two coins. • Karen scores a point if the coins match. • Mia scores a point if the coins do not match.			
Game 4 Roll two number cubes. • Karen scores a point if the number cubes match. • Mia scores a point if the number cubes do not match.			
Game 5 Roll two number cubes. • Karen scores a point if the product of the two numbers is 7. • Mia scores a point if the sum of the two numbers is 7.			

27. Karen and Mia invent another game. They roll a number cube twice and read the two digits shown as a two-digit number. So, if Karen gets a 6 and then a 2, she has 62.

Roll 1: 6

Roll 2: 2

Result: 62

   a. What is the least number possible?

   b. What is the greatest number possible?

   c. Are all numbers equally likely?

   d. Suppose Karen wins on any prime number and Mia wins on any multiple of 4. Explain how to decide who is more likely to win.

Multiple Choice For Exercises 28–31, choose the fraction closest to the given decimal.

   28. 0.39

      A. $\frac{1}{2}$ **B.** $\frac{1}{4}$ **C.** $\frac{1}{8}$ **D.** $\frac{1}{10}$

   29. 0.125

      F. $\frac{1}{2}$ **G.** $\frac{1}{4}$ **H.** $\frac{1}{8}$ **J.** $\frac{1}{10}$

   30. 0.195

      A. $\frac{1}{2}$ **B.** $\frac{1}{4}$ **C.** $\frac{1}{8}$ **D.** $\frac{1}{10}$

   31. 0.24

      F. $\frac{1}{2}$ **G.** $\frac{1}{4}$ **H.** $\frac{1}{8}$ **J.** $\frac{1}{10}$

32. Koto's class makes the line plot shown below. Each mark represents the first letter of the name of a student in her class.

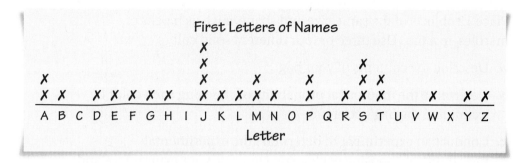

First Letters of Names

Suppose you choose a student at random from Koto's Class.

a. What is the probability that the student's name begins with J?

b. What is the probability that the student's name begins with a letter after F and before T in the alphabet?

c. What is the probability that you choose Koto?

d. Suppose two new students, Melvin and Theo, join the class. You now choose a student at random from the class. What is the probability that the student's name begins with J?

33. A bag contains red, white, blue, and green marbles. The probability of choosing a red marble is $\frac{1}{7}$. The probability of choosing a green marble is $\frac{1}{2}$. The probability of choosing a white marble is half the probability of choosing a red one. You want to find the number of marbles in the bag.

a. Why do you need to know how to multiply and add fractions to proceed?

b. Why do you need to know about multiples of whole numbers to proceed?

c. Can there be seven marbles in the bag? Explain.

34. Write the following as one fraction.

a. $\frac{1}{2}$ of $\frac{1}{7}$

b. $\frac{1}{7} + \frac{1}{14} + \frac{1}{2}$

Extensions

35. Place 12 objects of the same size and shape, such as blocks or marbles, in a bag. Use three or four different solid colors.

   a. Describe the contents of your bag.

   b. Determine the theoretical probability of choosing each color by examining the bag's contents.

   c. Conduct an experiment to determine the experimental probability of choosing each color. Describe your experiment and record your results.

   d. How do the two types of probability compare?

36. Suppose you toss four coins.

   a. List all the possible outcomes.

   b. What is the probability of each outcome?

   c. Design a game for two players that involves tossing four coins. What is the probability that each player wins? Is one player more likely to win than the other player?

37. Suppose you are a contestant on the *Gee Whiz Everyone Wins!* game show in Problem 2.4. You win a mountain bike, a vacation to Hawaii, and a one-year membership to an amusement park. You play the bonus round and lose. Then the host makes this offer:

Would you accept this offer? Explain.

38. Suppose you compete for the bonus prize on the *Gee Whiz Everyone Wins!* game in Problem 2.4. You choose one block from each of two bags. Each bag contains one red, one yellow, and one blue block.

a. Make a tree diagram to show all the possible outcomes.

b. What is the probability that you choose two blocks that are *not* blue?

c. Jason made the tree diagram shown below to find the probability of choosing two blocks that are not blue. Using his tree, what probability do you think Jason got?

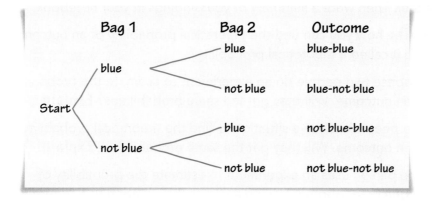

d. Does your answer in part (b) match Jason's? If not, why do you think Jason gets a different answer?

In this Investigation, you explored two ways to get information about probability. One method is to design an experiment and collect data. (The result is an experimental probability.) The other method is to analyze a situation carefully to see exactly what might happen. (The result is a theoretical probability.) The questions below will help you summarize what you have learned.

Think about these questions. Discuss your ideas with other students and your teacher. Then write a summary of your findings in your notebook.

1. **Describe** how you can find the theoretical probability of an outcome. **Why** is it called a theoretical probability?

2. **a.** Suppose two people do an experiment to estimate the probability of an outcome. Will they get the same probabilities? **Explain**.

   b. Two people analyze a situation to find the theoretical probability of an outcome. Will they get the same probabilities? **Explain**.

   c. One person uses an experiment to estimate the probability of an outcome. Another person analyzes the situation to find the theoretical probability of the outcome. Will they get the same probabilities? **Explain**.

3. **What** does it mean for a game to be fair?

4. **What** is a sample space, and how can it be represented?

Common Core Mathematical Practices

As you worked on the Problems in this Investigation, you used prior knowledge to make sense of them. You also applied Mathematical Practices to solve the Problems. Think back over your work, the ways you thought about the Problems, and how you used Mathematical Practices.

Shawna described her thoughts in the following way:

In Problem 2.2, we had to decide if Jakayla or Adsila was correct about the probability of choosing a blue marble.

Once we decided which girl was correct, we had to justify why we chose that student. We agreed with Adsila, since the probability is always less than or equal to 1. It cannot be greater than 1.

Common Core Standards for Mathematical Practice

MP3 Construct viable arguments and critique the reasoning of others.

- What other Mathematical Practices can you identify in Shawna's reasoning?

- Describe a Mathematical Practice that you and your classmates used to solve a different Problem in this Investigation.

Making Decisions with Probability

Spring vacation has arrived! Kalvin thinks he can stay up until 11:00 P.M. every night. His father thinks Kalvin will have more energy for his activities during the vacation if he goes to bed at 9:00 P.M.

3.1 Designing a Spinner to Find Probabilities

Kalvin makes the three spinners shown below. Kalvin is negotiating with his father to use one of the spinners to determine his bedtime.

Spinner 1 **Spinner 2** **Spinner 3**

- Which spinner gives Kalvin the best chance of going to bed at 11:00? Explain your reasoning.

Common Core State Standards

7.SP.C.7 Develop a probability model and use it to find probabilities of events. Compare probabilities from a model to observed frequencies . . .

7.SP.C.7b Develop a probability model (which may not be uniform) by observing frequencies in data generated from a chance process.

7.SP.C.8c Design and use a simulation to generate frequencies for compound events.

Also 7.RP.A.2, 7.RP.A.2a, 7.RP.A.3, 7.SP.C.5, 7.SP.C.6, 7.SP.C.7a, 7.SP.C.8, 7.SP.C.8a, 7.SP.C.8b

Problem 3.1

A Kalvin decides to design a spinner that lands on 11:00 most often. To convince his father to use this spinner, Kalvin puts three 9:00 spaces, two 10:00 spaces, and one 11:00 space on the spinner. However, he uses the biggest space for 11:00. Kalvin hopes the pointer lands on that space most often.

1. Which time do you think is most likely to occur?

2. Is Kalvin's father likely to agree to use this spinner? Explain why or why not.

B 1. Find the experimental probability that the pointer lands on 9:00, on 10:00, and on 11:00.

2. After how many spins did you decide to stop spinning? Explain why.

3. Suppose Kalvin spins the pointer 64 times. Based on your experiment, how many times can he expect the pointer to land on 9:00, on 10:00, and on 11:00?

C 1. What is the theoretical probability that the pointer lands on 9:00, on 10:00, and on 11:00? Explain.

2. Compare your answers to Question B, part (3) and Question C, part (1).

3. Suppose Kalvin spins the pointer 64 times. Based on your theoretical probabilities, how many times can he expect the pointer to land on 9:00, on 10:00, and on 11:00?

D Describe one way Kalvin's father can design a spinner so that Kalvin is most likely to go to bed at 9:00.

A C E Homework starts on page 58.

3.2 Making Decisions
Analyzing Fairness

One day at school, Kalvin's teacher has to decide which student to send to the office for an important message. Billie, Evo, and Carla volunteer. Kalvin suggests they design a quick experiment to choose the student fairly.

- What does it mean to choose the student fairly?

Problem 3.2

A 1. How could the class use each of these ways to choose a messenger?

    a. a coin   **b.** a number cube   **c.** colored cubes

    d. playing cards   **e.** a spinner   **f.** drawing straws

2. Is each a fair way to make a choice? Explain why or why not.

In Questions B and C, three suggestions for making a decision are given. Decide whether each suggestion is a fair way to make the decision. If not, explain why.

B At lunch, Kalvin and his friends discuss whether to play kickball, soccer, baseball, or dodgeball. Ethan, Ava, and Beno all have suggestions.

Ethan: We can make a spinner like this.

Ava: We can roll a number cube. If it lands on 1, we play kickball. If it lands on 2, we play soccer. Landing on 3 means baseball, 4 means dodgeball, and we can roll again if it's a 5 or a 6.

Beno: We can put 1 red straw, 2 yellow straws, 3 green straws, and 4 purple straws in a container. If the straw drawn is red, we play soccer, and if it's yellow, we play baseball. If it's green, we play dodgeball, and if it's purple, we play kickball.

1. Which method would you choose and why?

2. Which method would you *not* choose and why?

3. Are all three methods fair?

Problem 3.2 *continued*

C The group decides to play baseball. Tony and Meda are the team captains. Now they must decide who bats first. Examine each method, and then decide which method you would choose. Explain why.

Tony: We can roll a number cube. If the number is a multiple of 3, my team bats first. Otherwise, Meda's team bats first.

Meda: Yes, let's roll a number cube, but my team bats first if the number is even and Tony's team bats first if it's odd.

Jack: Each team rolls two number cubes, and the team that rolls two numbers that add to make an even number bats first.

D There are 60 sixth-grade students at Kalvin's school. The students need to choose someone to wear the mascot costume on field day. Huey and Sal are texting about it.

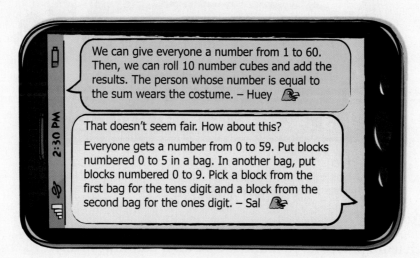

We can give everyone a number from 1 to 60. Then, we can roll 10 number cubes and add the results. The person whose number is equal to the sum wears the costume. – Huey

That doesn't seem fair. How about this?

Everyone gets a number from 0 to 59. Put blocks numbered 0 to 5 in a bag. In another bag, put blocks numbered 0 to 9. Pick a block from the first bag for the tens digit and a block from the second bag for the ones digit. – Sal

1. Is Huey's plan unfair, as Sal claims? If so, why is it unfair?

2. Is Sal's plan fair or unfair? Explain your answer.

3. a. Design a new and fair plan for choosing someone to wear the mascot costume.

b. Explain why your new plan will work.

 Homework starts on page 58.

3.3 Roller Derby
Analyzing a Game

Have you ever figured out a strategy for winning a game?

Now that you know about making tables and diagrams to find probabilities, you can use these tools to find winning strategies for games. In this Problem, you play a two-team game called Roller Derby.

Each team needs a game board with columns numbered 1–12, a pair of number cubes, and 12 markers (such as coins, buttons, or small blocks).

- As you play, think about strategies for winning and how probability relates to your strategies.

Roller Derby

Rules

1. Each team places its 12 markers into their columns in any way it chooses.

2. Each team rolls a number cube. The team with the highest roll goes first.

3. Teams take turns rolling the two number cubes. They remove a marker from the column on their board with the same number as the sum of the numbers on the number cubes. If the column is empty, the team does not get to remove a marker.

4. The first team to remove all the markers from its board wins.

Problem 3.3

Ⓐ **1.** Play the game at least twice. For each game, record the strategies you use to place your markers on the board.

2. Record how many times each sum is rolled.

3. Which sums seem to occur most often?

4. Which sums do not come up very often?

5. What is a good strategy for placing your markers on the game board?

Ⓑ **1.** Find all the possible pairs of numbers you can get from rolling two number cubes.

2. Find the sum for each of these outcomes.

3. Are all of the sums equally likely? Explain.

4. How many ways can you get a sum of 2?

5. What is the probability of getting a sum of 4?

6. What is the probability of getting a sum of 6?

7. Which sums occur most often?

Ⓒ Now that you have looked at the possible outcomes of the Roller Derby game, do you have any new strategies for winning? Explain.

Ⓐ Ⓒ Ⓔ Homework starts on page 58.

Did You Know?

Galileo was an Italian physicist, astronomer, and mathematician. Among other things, he is famous for discovering the moons of Jupiter. He also studied problems in probability similar to the ones you have seen.

A famous problem he worked on involved rolling three number cubes. He looked at the possibilities for getting a sum of 9 or a sum of 10. A sum of 9 is made using six groups of numbers:

(1, 2, 6), (1, 3, 5), (1, 4, 4), (2, 2, 5), (2, 3, 4), and (3, 3, 3).

A sum of 10 is made using six other groups of numbers:

(1, 3, 6), (1, 4, 5), (2, 2, 6), (2, 3, 5), (2, 4, 4), and (3, 3, 4).

What puzzled people is that, when they did experiments, the sum of 10 occurred more often. By making a diagram similar to a counting tree, Galileo showed the theoretical probability matched the experimental results. There are actually 25 combinations that have a sum of 9, and 27 combinations that have a sum of 10.

3.4 Scratching Spots
Designing and Using a Simulation

People in different kinds of jobs find simulations useful to their business. A **simulation** is a model used to find experimental probabilities when it is not possible to work with a real situation. For example, when the first astronauts flew in space, they practiced in simulators to give them a sense of what it would be like in space.

In this Problem, you will play a simple game to help you think about simulation. After you play the game, you will be challenged to create a simulation for a situation that interests you.

• In what other situations would a simulation be helpful?

Problem 3.4

Tawanda's Toys is having a contest. Any customer who spends at least $10 receives a scratch-off prize card.

- Each card has five silver spots that reveal the names of video games when you scratch them.

- Exactly two spots match on each card.

- A customer may scratch off only two spots on a card.

- If the spots match, the customer wins that video game.

Prize cards are only given to paying customers. So, acquiring many of them for a valid experiment is not sensible. Instead, we can design an experiment using a model with the same characteristics as the prize cards. There are five equally likely choices, of which exactly two match. So, you can design an experiment using simulation to find the probability of each outcome.

One way you can simulate the scratch-off card is by using five playing cards, or by making your own cards. First, make sure that exactly two out of the five cards match. Place the cards facedown on a table. With your eyes closed, have a friend mix up the cards. Then open your eyes and choose two cards. If the cards match, you win. Otherwise, you lose.

A Use a simulation to find the experimental probability of winning.

B Examine the different ways you can scratch off two spots. Then use what you found to determine the theoretical probability of winning.

C 1. How much do you need to spend to get 100 prize cards?

   2. How many video games can you expect to win with 100 prize cards?

D Describe a situation in which it would be very difficult to directly determine the probability of an event happening. Show how you could use simulation to help you figure out the approximate probabilities for the outcomes of the event.

 Homework starts on page 58.

Applications

1. For parts (a)–(g), use a spinner similar to the one at the right.

   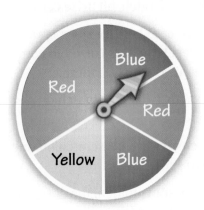

   a. Use a paper clip or bobby pin as a pointer. Spin the pointer 30 times. What fraction of your spins land on red? On blue? On yellow?

   b. Use an angle ruler or another method to examine the spinner. What fraction of the spinner is red? What fraction is blue? What fraction is yellow? Explain.

   c. Compare your answers to parts (a) and (b). Do you expect these answers to be the same? Explain why or why not.

   d. Suppose you spin 300 times instead of 30 times. Do you expect your answers to become closer to or further from the fractions you found in part (b)? Explain your reasoning.

   e. When you spin, is it equally likely that the pointer will land on red, on blue, or on yellow? Explain.

   f. Suppose you use the spinner to play a game with a friend. Your friend scores a point every time the pointer lands on red. To make the game fair, for what outcomes should you score a point? Explain.

   g. Suppose you use this spinner to play a three-person game. Player A scores if the pointer lands on yellow. Player B scores if the pointer lands on red. Player C scores if the pointer lands on blue. How can you assign points so the game is fair?

2. The cooks at Kyla's school make the spinners below to help them choose the lunch menu. They let the students take turns spinning. For parts (a)–(c), decide which spinner you would choose. Explain your reasoning.

Spinner A

Spinner B

a. Your favorite lunch is pizza.

b. Your favorite lunch is lasagna.

c. Your favorite lunch is hot dogs.

3. When you use each of the spinners below, the two possible outcomes are landing on 1 and landing on 2. Are the outcomes equally likely? If not, which outcome has a greater theoretical probability? Explain.

a.

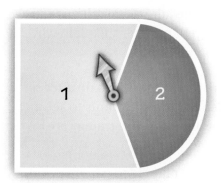

b.

4. Molly designs a game for a class project. She makes the three spinners shown. She tests to see which one she likes best for her game. She spins each pointer 20 times and writes down her results, but she forgets to record which spinner gives which set of data. Match each spinner with one of the data sets. Explain your answer.

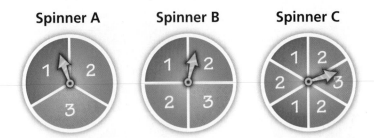

Spinner A   **Spinner B**   **Spinner C**

First data set: 1, 2, 3, 2, 1, 1, 2, 1, 2, 2, 2, 3, 2, 1, 2, 2, 2, 3, 2, 2

Second data set: 2, 3, 1, 1, 3, 3, 3, 1, 1, 2, 3, 2, 2, 2, 1, 1, 1, 3, 3, 3

Third data set: 1, 2, 3, 3, 1, 2, 2, 2, 3, 2, 1, 2, 2, 2, 3, 2, 2, 3, 2, 1

5. Three people play a game on each spinner in Exercise 4.
   Player 1 scores a point if the pointer lands on 1.
   Player 2 scores a point if the pointer lands on 2.
   Player 3 scores a point if the pointer lands on 3.

   a. On which spinner(s) is the game a fair game? Explain.

   b. Choose a spinner that you think doesn't make a fair game. Then, change the scoring rules to make the game fair by assigning different points for landing on the different numbers. Explain why your point system works.

6. **Multiple Choice** Jake, Carl, and John are deciding what to do after school. Jake thinks they should play video games. Carl wants to see a movie. John thinks they should ride their bikes. Which strategy is a fair way to decide?

   A. Let's toss three coins. If they all match, we play video games. If there are exactly two heads, we see a movie. If there are exactly two tails, we ride our bikes.

   B. Let's roll a number cube.
      If we roll a 1 or 2, we play video games.
      If we roll a 3 or 4, we go to the movies.
      Otherwise, we ride bikes.

   C. Let's use this spinner.

   D. None of these is fair.

7. **Multiple Choice** The Millers can't decide whether to eat pizza or burritos for dinner. Which strategy is a fair way to decide?

   F. Let's roll a number cube and toss a coin. If the number cube is even and the coin is heads, then we eat pizza. If the number cube is odd and the coin is tails, then we eat burritos. If neither happens, we try again.

   G. Let's toss a coin. If it is heads, we eat pizza. If it is tails, we do *not* eat burritos.

   H. Each of these is fair.

   J. Neither of these is fair.

8. **a.** Make a spinner and a set of rules for a fair two-person game. Explain why your game is fair.

   b. Make a spinner and a set of rules for a two-person game that is *not* fair. Explain why your game is not fair.

For Exercises 9 and 10, use your list of possible outcomes for rolling two number cubes from Problem 3.3.

9. **Multiple Choice** What is the probability of getting a sum of 5 when you roll two number cubes?

   A. $\frac{1}{9}$ **B.** $\frac{1}{6}$ **C.** $\frac{1}{4}$ **D.** $\frac{1}{3}$

10. **Multiple Choice** What is the probability of getting a sum greater than 9 when you roll two number cubes?

   F. $\frac{1}{9}$ **G.** $\frac{1}{6}$ **H.** $\frac{1}{4}$ **J.** $\frac{1}{3}$

Ella is playing Roller Derby with Carlos. Ella places all her markers in column 1 and Carlos places all of his markers in column 12.

11. **Multiple Choice** What is the probability that Ella will win?

   A. 0   **B.** $\frac{1}{3}$ **C.** $\frac{1}{2}$ **D.** 1

12. **Multiple Choice** What is the probability that Carlos will win?

   F. 0   **G.** $\frac{1}{3}$ **H.** $\frac{1}{2}$ **J.** 1

13. In some board games, you can end up in "jail." One way to get out of jail is to roll doubles (two number cubes that match). What is the probability of getting out of jail on your turn by rolling doubles? Use your list of possible outcomes of rolling two number cubes that you created for Problem 3.3. Explain your reasoning.

14. Tawanda wants fewer winners for her scratch-off cards. She decides to order new cards with six spots. Two of the spots on each card match. What is the probability that a person who plays once will win on the card?

Connections

Copy and complete the following table. Write each probability as a fraction, decimal, or percent.

Probabilities

	Fraction	Decimal	Percent
15.	$\frac{1}{4}$	■	25%
16.	$\frac{1}{8}$	■	■
17.	■	■	$33\frac{1}{3}\%$
18.	■	■	10%
19.	■	0.1666...	■
20.	■	0.05	■

21. The cooks at Kyla's school let students make spinners to determine the lunch menu.

    a. Make a spinner for which the chance of selecting lasagna is 25%, the chance of selecting a hamburger is $16\frac{2}{3}$%, and the chance of selecting a tuna sandwich is $33\frac{1}{3}$%. The last choice is hot dogs.

    b. What is the chance of selecting hot dogs?

22. Three of the following situations have the same probability of getting "spinach." What is the probability for these three situations?

    a. Spin the pointer on this spinner once.

    b. Roll a number cube once. You get spinach when you roll a multiple of 3.

    c. Toss two coins. You get spinach with one head and one tail.

    d. Roll a number cube once. You get spinach when you roll a 5 or 6.

Rewrite each pair of numbers. Insert $<$, $>$, or $=$ to make a true statement.

    23. $\dfrac{1}{3\frac{1}{2}}$ ▦ $\dfrac{1}{4}$

    24. $\dfrac{3.5}{7}$ ▦ $\dfrac{1}{2}$

    25. 0.30 ▦ $\dfrac{1}{3}$

26. Use the table of historic baseball statistics to answer parts (a)–(d).

Batting Averages

Player	At-bats	Hits
Player A	4,089	1,317
Player B	5,457	1,715
Player C	4,877	1,518

a. What percent of Player A's at-bats resulted in a hit?

b. What percent of Player B's at-bats resulted in a hit?

c. What percent of Player C's at-bats resulted in a hit?

d. Suppose each player comes to bat today with the same skill his record shows. Who has the greatest chance of getting a hit? Explain your reasoning.

27. A–1 Trucks used this graph to show that their trucks last longer than other trucks.

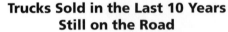
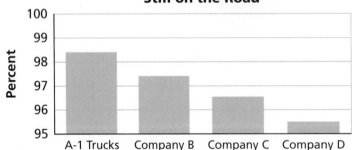

Trucks Sold in the Last 10 Years Still on the Road

a. The bar for A–1 Trucks is about six times the height of the bar for Company D. Does this mean that the chance of one of A–1's trucks lasting ten years is about six times as great as the chance of one of Company D's trucks lasting ten years? Explain.

b. If you wanted to buy a truck, would this graph convince you to buy a truck from A–1 Trucks? Why or why not?

For Exercises 28–30, find an equivalent fraction with a denominator of 10 or 100. Then, write a decimal number for each fraction.

28. $\frac{3}{20}$ **29.** $\frac{2}{5}$ **30.** $\frac{11}{25}$

31. Aran knows that if you roll a number cube once, there is a 50% chance of getting an even number. He says that if you roll a number cube twice, the chance of getting at least one even number is doubled. Is he correct?

32. a. Suppose you fold this shape along the dashed lines to make a three-dimensional shape. How many faces will it have?

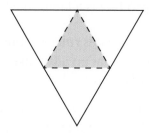

     b. Suppose you roll the shape in part (a). What is the probability that the shaded face lands on the bottom?

     c. Suppose you fold the below. Can you use it in a fair game in which you roll it? Explain.

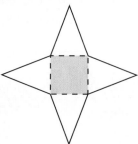

Use your list of possible outcomes when you roll two number cubes from Problem 3.3.

33. What is the probability that the sum is a multiple of 4?

34. What is the probability that the sum is a common multiple of 2 and 3?

35. What is the probability that the sum is a prime number? Explain.

36. Which has a greater probability of being rolled on a pair of number cubes, a sum that is a factor of 6 or a sum that is a multiple of 6? Explain your reasoining.

37. Suppose Humberto and Nina play the game Evens and Odds. They roll two number cubes and find the product of the numbers. If the product is odd, Nina scores a point. If the product is even, Humberto scores a point.

    a. Make a table of the possible products of two number cubes.

    b. What is the probability that Nina wins? What is the probability that Humberto wins? Explain your reasoning.

    c. Is this a fair game? If not, how could you change the points scored by each player so that it would be fair?

    d. What is the probability that the product is a prime number?

    e. What is the probability that the product is a factor of 4?

38. The Federal Trade Commission (FTC) makes rules for businesses that buy and sell things. One rule states that an advertisement may be found unlawful if it can deceive a person.

To decide whether an ad is deceptive, the FTC considers the "general impression" it makes on a "reasonable person." Even if every statement is true, the ad is deceptive if it gives an overall false impression. For example, cows can't appear in margarine ads because they give the false impression that margarine is a dairy product.

    a. Tawanda places this ad in a newspaper. According to the FTC, is it legal for Tawanda to say, "Every card is a winner"? Explain.

    b. Design a better ad that excites people but does not lead some to think they will win every time.

    c. Find an ad that might be deceptive. Why do you think it is deceptive? What proof could the company provide to change your mind?

39. A sugarless gum company used to have an advertisement that included the following statement:

> Four out of five dentists surveyed recommend sugarless gum for their patients who chew gum.

Do you think this statement means that 80% of dentists believe their patients should chew sugarless gum? Explain your reasoning.

40. Portland Middle School students make a flag as shown. After it hangs outside for a month, it looks dirty, and they examine it. They find more insects stuck on the yellow part than on the green part. Cheng says insects are more attracted to yellow than to green.

a. Students in a science class test Cheng's idea. They simulate the flag by using a piece of plywood painted with the same design. What is the chance that an insect landing at random on the plywood will hit the yellow part?

b. Suppose the result of the students' simulation is that 13 insects land on the yellow part and 12 insects land on the green part. Does this evidence support Cheng's conjecture?

Extensions

41. Design a spinner with five regions. You want the pointer to be equally likely to land in all of the regions. Give the number of degrees in the central angle of each region.

42. Design a spinner with five regions such that the chance of landing in one region is twice the chance of landing in each of the other four regions. Give the number of degrees in the central angle of each region.

For Exercises 43–45, design a contest for each company. Each contest should help the company attract customers, but not make the company lose money. Explain the rules, including any requirements for entering the contest.

43. The manager of a small clothing store wants to design a contest in which 1 of every 30 players wins a prize.

44. The director of operations for a chain of supermarkets wants to design a contest with a $100,000 grand prize!

45. An auto dealer sells new and used cars. The owner wants to have a contest with many winners and big prizes. She wants about one of every ten players to win a $500 prize.

In this Investigation, you used spinners and number cubes in probability situations. You used both experimental and theoretical probabilities to help you make decisions. You also examined a game to determine winning strategies for playing the game. The questions below will help you summarize what you learned.

Think about these questions. Discuss your ideas with other students and your teacher. Then write a summary of your findings in your notebook.

1. **Describe** a situation in which you and a friend can use probability to make a decision. Can the probabilities of the outcomes be determined both experimentally and theoretically? **Why** or why not?

2. **Describe** a situation in which it is difficult or impossible to find the theoretical probabilities of the outcomes.

3. **Explain** what it means for a probability situation to be fair.

4. **Describe** some of the strategies for determining the theoretical probabilities for situations in this Unit. Give an example of a situation for each of the strategies.

Common Core Mathematical Practices

As you worked on the Problems in this Investigation, you used prior knowledge to make sense of them. You also applied Mathematical Practices to solve the Problems. Think back over your work, the ways you thought about the Problems, and how you used Mathematical Practices.

Ken described his thoughts in the following way:

We were making decisions about fairness in Problem 3.2. We had several tools:

- coin
- number cube
- colored cubes
- playing cards
- spinner
- drawing straws

We had to determine which one was the most reasonable for choosing a messenger.

We also explained how we decided each tool was fair or not. To determine the fairness of each tool, we had to understand how each tool was used. We wanted to make sure each of the three students had the same chance of being chosen.

Our group used a number cube. Billie goes if 1 or 2 comes up. Evo goes if 3 or 4 comes up. Carla goes if 5 or 6 comes up. As a class, we found a way to make each tool work.

Common Core Standards for Mathematical Practice

MP5 Use appropriate tools strategically.

- What other Mathematical Practices can you identify in Ken's reasoning?

- Describe a Mathematical Practice that you and your classmates used to solve a different Problem in this Investigation.

Analyzing Compound Events Using an Area Model

Each turn in the games of chance in Investigation 3 involved two actions. Recall the Roller Derby game in Problem 3.3. In this game, you rolled two number cubes and then determined the outcomes. You determined the theoretical probabilities of these games using a variety of strategies.

Situations involving chance occur in many of the games we love to play. We always want to know what our chances are of winning in each situation. It helps if we have some ideas that help us analyze a situation.

An area model is a useful tool for analyzing situations with two stages. The goal is to divide the area into parts that correctly reflect the chances we have to win.

In this Investigation, you encounter probability situations that involve more than one action on a turn.

··

Common Core State Standards

7.SP.C.6. Approximate the probability of a chance event by collecting data on the chance process that produces it and observing its long-run relative frequency, and predict the approximate relative frequency given the probability.

7.SP.C.7b. Develop a probability model (which may not be uniform) by observing frequencies in data generated from a chance process.

7.SP.C.8. Find probabilities of compound events using organized lists, tables, tree diagrams, and simulation.

7.SP.C.8c Design and use a simulation to generate frequencies for compound events.

Also 7.RP.A.2, 7.RP.A.2a, 7.RP.A.3, 7.SP.C.5, 7.SP.C.7, 7.SP.C.7a, 7.SP.C.8a, 7.SP.C.8b

4.1 Drawing Area Models to Find the Sample Space

Bucket 1 contains three marbles—one red and two green. Bucket 2 contains four marbles—one red, one blue, one green, and one yellow. The player draws a marble from each bucket.

Bucket 1

Bucket 2

 How can we analyze this two-stage situation so that we can predict what outcomes can occur and with what frequency?

 Problem 4.1

Miguel draws a square to represent an area of 1 square unit. He will use the square's area to represent a probability of 1. The square represents the sum of all of the probabilities for all of the possible outcomes.

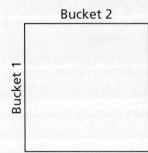

Bucket 2

Bucket 1

Problem 4.1 continued

A Miguel adds to his diagram to help him find the theoretical probabilities of drawing marbles from Bucket 1.

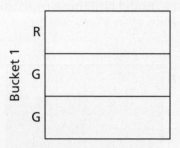

1. Explain what Miguel has done so far. Does this look reasonable?

2. Use the top edge to represent Bucket 2. How many sections do you need to represent the marbles in Bucket 2? Draw the lines and label the sections you need to represent Bucket 2.

3. Now label each of the sections inside the square with two letters to represent the results of choosing two marbles. RR in a section would mean that two red marbles were drawn from the buckets.

B Use your probability area model from Question A to answer each part.

1. What are the probabilities for selecting each pair of marbles?

   a. RR   **b.** RB   **c.** RG

   d. RY   **e.** GR   **f.** GB

   g. GG   **h.** GY   **i.** YY

2. Use your drawing to answer these questions:

   What is the probability of choosing a marble from each bucket and

   a. getting at least one red?

   b. getting at least one blue?

   c. getting at least one green?

   d. getting at least one yellow?

Problem 4.1 continued

C The area model below represents a different situation from Questions A and B. In this area model, $P(RY) = \frac{1}{10}$, $P(RB) = \frac{1}{10}$, $P(GY) = \frac{4}{10}$, and $P(GB) = \frac{4}{10}$. Use the area model and these probabilities to answer the following questions:

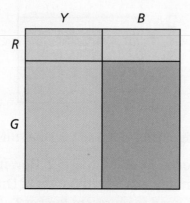

1. What is the area of each section?

2. For each section, what fraction of the whole square is this?

3. How do the fractions in part (2) compare to the probabilities of each section?

4. Which of the following could be the contents of the two buckets? Explain your reasoning.

    a. 2 red and 8 green in Bucket 1
    5 yellow and 5 blue in Bucket 2

    b. 2 red and 8 green in Bucket 1
    10 yellow and 10 blue in Bucket 2

    c. 1 red and 4 green in Bucket 1
    3 yellow and 3 blue in Bucket 2

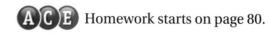 Homework starts on page 80.

4.2 Making Purple
Area Models and Probability

Making Purple is a popular game at the school carnival. A player spins the pointer of each spinner below once. Getting red on one spinner and blue on the other spinner wins, because red and blue together make purple.

- Suppose you take ten turns with the two spinners. How often would you expect to get red and blue?

Problem 4.2

A Play the Making Purple game several times. Based on your results, what is the experimental probability that a player will "make purple" on a turn?

B Construct an area model. Determine the theoretical probability that a player will make purple on a turn.

C How do your answers to Questions A and B compare?

D The cost to play the game is $2. The winner gets $6 for making purple. Suppose 36 people play the game.

1. How much money will the school take in from this game?

2. How many people do you expect will win a prize?

3. How much money do you expect the school to pay out in prizes?

4. How much profit do you expect the school to make from this game?

5. Should the school include this game in the carnival? Justify your answer using your answers to parts (1)–(4).

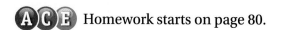 Homework starts on page 80.

4.3 One-and-One Free Throws
Simulating a Probability Situation

In the district finals, Nishi's basketball team is 1 point behind with 2 seconds left. A player on the other team fouls Nishi. Now she is in a one-and-one free-throw situation. This means that Nishi will try one free throw. If she makes it, she tries a second free throw. If she misses the first free throw, she does not get to try a second free throw.

- What are the possible scores Nishi can make in a one-and-one free-throw situation?

- How can each score be made?

- How would you design an experiment to analyze this situation?

Problem 4.3

A **1.** Is it most likely that Nishi will score 0 points, 1 point, or 2 points? Record what you think before you analyze the situation.

2. Is the spinner below a good model for Nishi's free-throw record? Explain your reasoning.

3. Simulate Nishi's one-and-one situation 20 times using a spinner like the one above. Record the result of each trial.

4. Based on your results, what is the experimental probability that Nishi will score 0 points? 1 point? 2 points?

B **1.** Make an area model for this situation using a 10 × 10 grid. What is the theoretical probability that Nishi will score 0 points? 1 point? 2 points? Compare the three theoretical probabilities with the three experimental probabilities.

2. How does the spinner in Question A, part (2) reflect Nishi's free-throw record? How does the area model in Question B, part (1) reflect Nishi's free-throw record? Which of these models is the better model for Nishi's free-throw record? Explain.

3. Refer to the area model in Question B, part (1). How does this help you predict the number of times Nishi will score 2 points in 100 one-and-one situations? In 200 one-and-one situations?

C Suppose Nishi's free-throw percentage is 70%. Explain how the new percentage affects the outcome.

A C E Homework starts on page 80.

4.4 Finding Expected Value

In the last Problem, you looked at different probabilities. These probabilities represented different outcomes of Nishi's one and-one free-throw situation. You might have been surprised about which outcome is most likely. In this Problem, you will look at the number of points Nishi can expect to make each time she is in a one-and-one free-throw situation.

- What is Nishi most likely to score? What is Nishi least likely to score?

The mean, or average, number of points for each one-and-one free-throw situation is called the **expected value.**

- What do you think her average score, or expected value, will be for a one-and-one free-throw situation?

Problem 4.4

Suppose Nishi has a 60% free-throw percentage and is in a one-and-one free-throw situation 100 times during the season.

Ⓐ 1. How many times can she expect to score 0 points? What is the total number of points for these situations?

2. How many times can she expect to score 1 point? What is the total number of points for these situations?

3. How many times can she expect to score 2 points? What is the total number of points for these situations?

4. What total number of points do you expect Nishi to score in these 100 situations at the free-throw line?

5. Find Nishi's average number of points for a one-and-one situation.

6. Use the data you collected from the spinner simulation in Problem 4.3. Calculate the average score for the experimental results for Nishi. How does the theoretical average compare with the experimental average?

Problem 4.4 *continued*

B **1.** Copy and complete the table below for the players whose free-throw percentages are 20%, 40%, 60%, and 80% in 100 one-and-one situations. You will fill in the Expected Value column in part (2).

Points Expected in 100 One-and-One Situations

Player's Free-Throw Percentage	Points			
	0	**1**	**2**	**Expected Value, or Average**
20%	▪	▪	▪	▪
40%	▪	▪	▪	▪
60%	▪	▪	▪	▪
80%	▪	▪	▪	▪

2. Calculate the mean, or average, number of points for each situation. Record these values in the table in part (1). Describe any patterns.

C **1.** Use the data from the table in Question B, part (1). Complete a graph like the one below.

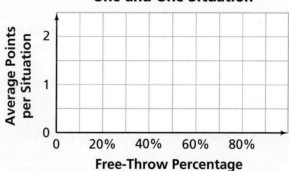

Points Expected in a One-and-One Situation

2. How does the mean, or average, number of points compare for players with a 20% free-throw percentage? 40%? 60%? 80%?

3. Nishi's dad makes an average of about 1 point in each one-and-one free-throw situation. Find his free-throw percentage.

4. Nishi's older sister has a 70% free-throw percentage. What is her average number of points in a one-and-one situation? Check by making an area model.

 Homework starts on page 80.

Applications

A school carnival committee features a different version of the Making Purple game, as shown below.

Making Purple
$1 to play
Draw a red marble
and a blue marble.
Win $3!

marbles
- 1 red
- 1 blue
- 1 green
- 1 yellow

marbles
- 1 red
- 1 yellow
- 1 green

1. Before playing the game, do you predict that the school will make money on this game? Explain.

2. Use an area model to show the possible outcomes for this game. Explain how your area model shows all the possible outcomes.

3. What is the theoretical probability of choosing a red and a blue marble on one turn?

4. Suppose one marble is chosen from each bucket. Find the probability of each situation.

   a. You choose a green marble from Bucket 1 and a yellow marble from Bucket 2.

   b. You do not choose a blue marble from either bucket.

   c. You choose two blue marbles.

   d. You choose at least one blue marble.

5. Parker Middle School is having a Flag Day Festival. In a contest, students choose one block from each of two different bags. A student wins if he or she picks a red and a blue block. James makes the tree diagram below to find the probability of winning.

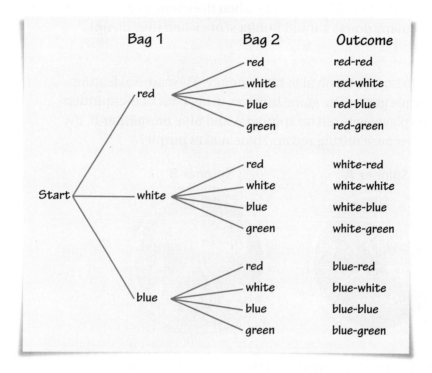

a. Draw an area model that represents this contest.

b. What is the probability of winning this contest?

6. There are two No-Cavity prize bins at a dentist's office. One bin has two hot-pink toothbrushes and three neon-yellow toothbrushes. The other bin has four packages of sugar-free gum, three grape and one strawberry. Kira has no cavities. The dentist tells her to close her eyes and choose a prize from each bin.

a. What is the probability that Kira will choose a neon-yellow toothbrush and a pack of grape gum? Draw an area model to support your solution.

b. The dental assistant refills the bins after every patient. Suppose the next 100 patients have no cavities. How many times do you expect the patients to get a neon-yellow toothbrush and a pack of grape gum?

7. Bonita and Deion are using the spinners from the Making Purple game in Problem 4.2. They take turns spinning. If the colors on the two spinners make purple, Deion scores. If the colors do not make purple, Bonita scores. They want to make their game a fair game. How many points should Deion score when the spinners make purple? How many points should Bonita score when they do not make purple?

8. A science club hosts a carnival to raise money. The carnival features a Making Purple game. The game involves using both of the spinners shown. If the player gets red on spinner A and blue on spinner B, the player wins, because mixing red and blue makes purple.

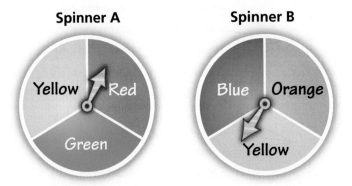

a. List the possible outcomes when you spin both pointers. Are these outcomes equally likely? Explain your reasoning.

b. What is the theoretical probability that a player "makes purple"? Show or explain how you arrived at your answer.

c. Suppose 100 people play the Making Purple game. How many people do you expect to win?

d. The club charges $1 per turn. A player who makes purple receives $5. The club expects 100 people to play. How much money do you expect the club to make?

For Exercises 9–11, a bag contains three green marbles and two
blue marbles. You choose a marble, return it to the bag, and then
choose again.

9. a. Which method (*make a tree diagram, make a list, use an area
model,* or *make a table or chart*) would you use to find the
possible outcomes? Explain your choice.

   b. Use your chosen method to find all of the possible outcomes.

10. Suppose you do this experiment 50 times. Predict the number of
times you will choose two marbles of the same color. Use the method
you chose in Exercise 9.

11. Suppose this experiment is a two-person game. One player scores
if the marbles match. The other player scores if the marbles do not
match. Describe a scoring system that makes this a fair game.

12. Al is at the top of Morey Mountain. He wants to make choices that
will lead him to the lodge. He does not remember which trails to take.

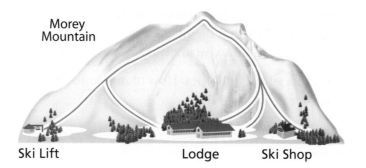

Morey
Mountain

Ski Lift   Lodge   Ski Shop

   a. Design an experiment using a number cube or drawing the
numbers 1–6 from a hat. Find the experimental probability of
Al ending at the lodge. Conduct the experiment 20 times.

   b. What is the experimental probability of Al ending at the lodge?
At the lift? At the ski shop?

   c. Find the theoretical probability of ending at the lodge, the lift,
and the ski shop. Compare the experimental and theoretical
probabilities. Do you have more confidence in the experimental
or the theoretical probability? Why?

13. Kenisha is designing a game involving paths through the woods that lead to caves. A player first chooses Cave A or Cave B. Next, the player starts at the beginning and chooses a path at random at each fork. If the player lands in the cave that was chosen in the beginning, he or she wins a prize.

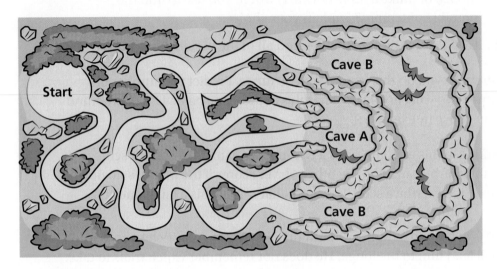

a. Suppose a player chooses a path at random at each fork. What is the theoretical probability that the player ends up in Cave A? In Cave B? Show or explain how you arrived at your answer.

b. Suppose you play this game 100 times. How many times do you expect to end in Cave A? In Cave B?

14. Kenisha designed another version of the cave paths game. The new version has a different arrangement of paths leading into Caves A and B. She makes an area model to analyze the probabilities of landing in each room. For Kenisha's new version, what is the probability that a player will end up in Cave A? In Cave B?

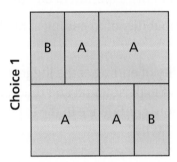

15. Multiple Choice Choose the map that the area model in Exercise 14 could represent.

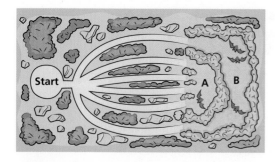

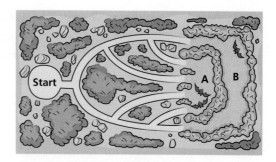

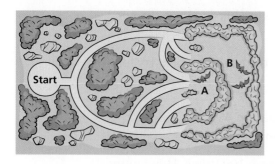

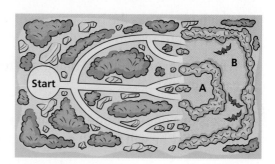

For Exercises 16 and 17, a basketball player participates in a one-and-one free-throw situation. Determine if each player with the given free-throw percentage will most likely score 0 points, 1 point, or 2 points. Make an area model to support each answer.

16. 80%

17. 40%

18. Nishi, who has a 60% free-throw percentage, is in a two-attempt free-throw situation. This means that she will attempt the second free throw no matter what happens on the first.

   a. Is Nishi most likely to score 0 points, 1 point, or 2 points? Explain.

   b. Nishi plans to keep track of her score on two-attempt free-throw situations. What average number of points can she expect to score per two-attempt situation?

19. Repeat Exercise 18 for a player with each free-throw percentage.

   a. 50%

   b. 80%

Use the information in the table. It shows free-throw statistics for some of the players on a basketball team.

Free-Throw Statistics

Name	Free Throws Attempted	Free Throws Made
Gerrit	54	27
David	49	39
Ken	73	45
Alex	60	42

20. a. Which player has the best chance of making his next free throw? Explain your reasoning.

   b. What is the probability of making a free throw on the next try for each person?

21. a. Alex is in a one-and-one free-throw situation. What is the probability he will score 0 points? 1 point? 2 points?

   b. Suppose Alex is in a one-and-one situation 100 times. How many times do you expect each outcome in part (a) to occur?

   c. What is the average number of points you expect Alex to make in a one-and-one situation?

   d. Repeat part (a) using Gerrit.

22. a. In a two-attempt free-throw situation, a player gets a second attempt even if the first attempt is missed. Suppose Gerrit is in a two-attempt free-throw situation. What is the probability that he will score 0 points? 1 point? 2 points?

   b. Compare your answers to Exercise 21. Explain why the answers are not exactly the same.

Connections

For Exercises 23–28, Megan is designing a computer game called *Treasure Hunt*. The computer chooses a square at random on the grid. Then, it hides a treasure in the room containing the square. Find the probability that the computer will hide the treasure in each room.

	Library	Den
Great hall	Front hall	Dining hall

23. Library

24. Den

25. Dining hall

26. Great hall

27. Front hall

28. Multiple Choice Megan enlarges the floor plan in the game grid above by a scale factor of 2. How does this affect the probabilities that the treasure is in each room?

   F. They are unchanged.

   G. They are $\frac{1}{2}$ the original probability.

   H. They are twice the original.

   J. They are four times the original.

29. Carlos is also designing a *Treasure Hunt* game. He keeps track of the number of times the computer hides the treasure in each room. Here is a line plot of his results.

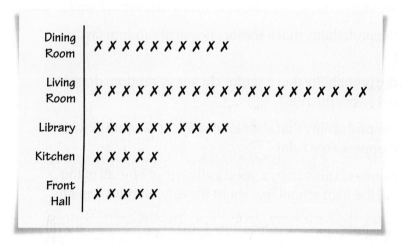

Design a floor plan that could give this data. State the area of each room on your floor plan.

30. Seniors at a high school took a survey. The results are shown below.

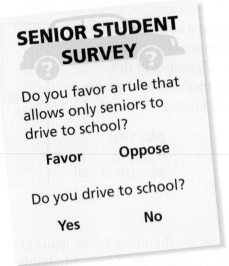

Driving Survey

	Drives to School	Does Not Drive to School	Row Totals
Favors Rule	40	30	70
Opposes Rule	20	10	30
Total	60	40	100

a. How many seniors drive to school?

b. How many seniors favor the rule?

c. How many seniors favor the rule and do not drive to school?

d. What is the probability that a senior chosen at random favors the rule?

e. What is the probability that a senior chosen at random drives to school and favors the rule?

f. What is the probability that a senior chosen at random drives to school or opposes the rule?

g. Are the results of this survey a good indicator of how all of the students at the high school feel about the driving rule? Explain.

31. Marni and Ira are playing a game with this square spinner. A game is ten turns. Each turn is two spins. The numbers for the two spins are added. Marni scores 1 point for a sum that is negative. Ira scores 1 point for a sum that is positive. After ten turns, each player totals their points. The player with more points wins.

a. List all of the possible outcomes.

b. Is this game fair? Explain.

32. Fergus designs a dartboard for a school carnival. His design is shown below. He must decide how much to charge a player and how much to pay out for a win. To do this, he needs to know the probabilities of landing in sections marked A and B. Assume the darts land at random on the dartboard.

A	A	A	A	A	A
A					A
A					A
A		B			A
A					A
A	A	A	A	A	A

a. What is the probability of landing in a section marked A?

b. What is the probability of landing in a section marked B?

33. Fergus designs two more dartboards for the school carnival. A player pays $1 to play and wins $2 if the dart lands in sections marked B. If the dart lands in sections marked A, the player wins no money.

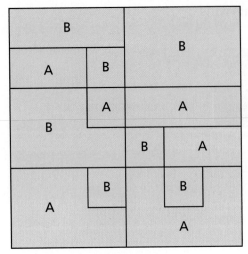

Dartboard 1   **Dartboard 2**

a. What is the probability of landing in sections marked A on Dartboard 1? On Dartboard 2? Explain.

b. How much money will the player expect to make (or lose) after 36 turns using Dartboard 1? Using Dartboard 2? Explain.

c. How much money will the carnival expect to make (or lose) after 36 turns using Dartboard 1? Using Dartboard 2?

d. Can the carnival expect to make a profit on this game with either board? Explain.

34. a. If you roll one number cube two times, what is the probability of getting a factor of 5 both times?

b. Suppose you roll two different number cubes. What is the probability of getting a factor of 5 on both cubes?

c. How do your answers to parts (a) and (b) compare? Explain why the answers have this relationship.

For Exercises 35–37, a game show uses a large spinner with many equal-sized sections. One section is labeled *Bankrupt*. If a player spins and lands on *Bankrupt*, she loses all of her money. Carlota makes a version of the spinner below. Answer each question and explain your reasoning.

35. What is the probability that a player who spins the spinner one time will land on *Bankrupt*?

36. What is the probability that a player who spins the spinner one time will get $500 or more?

37. Sam just spun the spinner and landed on $350. What is the probability he will land on $350 on his next spin?

Multiple Choice For Exercises 38–40, choose the answer that is the correct percent of the given number.

38. 30% of 90

    A. 60   **B.** 27   **C.** 30   **D.** 18

39. 25% of 80

    F. 20   **G.** 3.2   **H.** 15   **J.** 25

40. 45% of 180

    A. 70   **B.** 40   **C.** 81   **D.** 53

41. Wanda, the Channel 1 weather person, uses previous data and a computer model to predict the weather. By looking at many previous days with the same weather conditions, she saw that it rained 30 out of 100 days. So, she predicted that there is a 30% chance of rain on Saturday and a 30% chance of rain on Sunday. Then, it rained both days.

    a. Suppose Wanda's calculations were correct, and there was a 30% chance of rain each day. What was the probability that there would be rain on both days?

    b. How should Wanda explain this to her manager?

    c. Wanda is working on her predictions for the next few days. She calculates that there is a 20% chance of rain on Monday and a 20% chance of rain on Tuesday. If she is correct, what is the probability that it will rain on at least one of these days?

42. A lake has 10,000 fish. When a fisherman scoops up his net, he catches 500 fish. Suppose 150 of the 500 fish in his net are salmon. How many salmon do you predict are in the lake?

43. a. Copy the table below. Use your answers from Problem 4.5 to fill in your table.

Average Points per Attempt for Different Free-Throw Percentages

Probability of One Basket	20%	40%	60%	80%	100%
Average Points per One-and-One Attempt	0.24	▦	0.96	▦	▦

b. Is the average for an 80% percentage twice that of 40%? Explain.

c. Use this table or your graph from Problem 4.4, Question C. Is the average for 100% twice the average of 50%? Explain.

d. A player with a 20% free-throw percentage makes 0.24 points, on average, in a one-and-one situation. Copy and complete this table. How are the relationships in this table different from the table in part (a)?

Average Points for a Player With a 20% Free-Throw Percentage

Number of One-and-One Situations	1	10	20	100
Average Points Made	0.24	▦	▦	▦

Suppose you spin the pointer on each spinner once.

44. Suppose you add the results.

    a. What is the probability of getting a positive number?

    b. What is the average value?

45. Suppose you multiply the results.

    a. What is the probability of getting a positive number?

    b. What is the average value?

Extensions

Use the information below to answer Exercises 46–48.

Gee Whiz Everybody Wins!

Rules

One player waits backstage.

The other player places two green marbles and two blue marbles in two containers in any arrangement.

The player backstage comes out and chooses one of the containers at random.

The player chooses a marble at random without looking.

If the marble is green both players win a prize.

46. Suppose Brianna is given two green marbles and two blue marbles to distribute between the two containers. Emmanuel waits backstage.

   a. List all of the different ways Brianna can place the four marbles in the two containers.

   b. For each arrangement, what is the probability that Emmanuel chooses a green marble?

   c. Which arrangement will give Brianna and Emmanuel the greatest chance of winning? The least chance of winning? Explain.

47. Brianna is given two blue marbles and three green marbles to distribute between the two containers. Which arrangement gives Emmanuel the best chance of choosing a green marble?

48. Suppose Brianna is given two green marbles, two blue marbles, and three buckets. How can she put the marbles in the three buckets to have the best chance of choosing a green marble?

49. Della is chosen as a contestant on a game show. The host gives her two red marbles, two green marbles, and two yellow marbles.

Della will put the marbles into two identical cans in any way she chooses. The host will then rearrange the cans. He will leave the marbles as Della placed them. Della will then select a can and choose a marble. If she chooses a red marble, she wins a prize.

How should Della arrange the marbles so she has the best chance of choosing a red marble?

50. Make up your own marbles-and-buckets problem. Find the solution.

51. For the game below, you use the two spinners shown. You get two spins. You may spin each spinner once, or you may spin one of the spinners twice. If you get a red on one spin and a blue on the other spin (the order makes no difference), you win. To have the greatest chance of winning, should you spin Spinner A twice, spin Spinner B twice, or spin each spinner once? Explain.

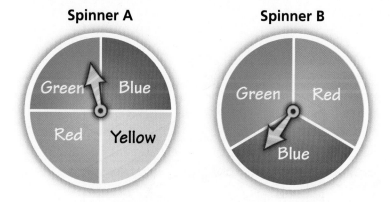

Spinner A

Spinner B

Use the data about the basketball team from Exercises 20–22.

52. What is the probability that Alex will make all of his next three free throws? Explain your reasoning.

53. David is in a one-and-one free-throw situation. What is the probability that he will make both free throws?

54. Emilio increases his free-throw average to 50%. His coach makes a deal with him. At tomorrow's practice, Emilio can attempt either to make three free throws in a row or to make at least four out of five free throws. If he is successful, he will start every game for the rest of the season. Which option should he choose? Explain.

55. a. Curt has made 60% of his free throws during recent practice sessions. The coach says that if Curt makes three free throws in a row, he can start Saturday's game. What is the probability that Curt will start Saturday's game?

   b. Curt has a difficult time making three free throws in a row. The coach tells him to instead try making three out of four free throws. What is the probability that Curt will make at least three out of four free throws?

56. When a player is fouled while attempting a three-point basket, three free throws are awarded. Luis has an 80% free-throw percentage. He draws the diagrams below to analyze the probability of getting 1, 2, or 3 baskets.

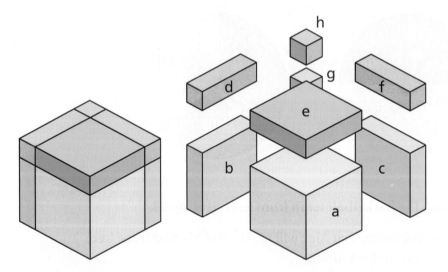

   a. Which parts of the lettered diagram represent Luis making all three baskets? Exactly two baskets? Exactly one basket? Missing all three baskets?

   b. What is the probability of Luis getting 1 point in a three free-throw situation? 2 points? 3 points? No points?

In this Investigation, you analyzed probabilities of two-stage events by dividing the area of a square. You also learned how to find the average outcome for events, such as a basketball player attempting free throws in a one-and-one situation. The following questions will help you summarize what you have learned.

Think about these questions. Discuss your ideas with other students and your teacher. Then write a summary of your findings in your notebook.

1. **Describe** four probability situations that involve two actions. **Describe** the outcomes for these situations.

2. You can use an area model or a simulation to determine the probability of a situation that involves two actions. **Explain** how each of these is used.

3. **Describe** how you would calculate the expected value for a probability situation.

4. Expected value is sometimes called the long-term average. **Explain** why this makes sense.

Common Core Mathematical Practices

As you worked on the Problems in this Investigation, you used prior knowledge to make sense of them. You also applied Mathematical Practices to solve the Problems. Think back over your work, the ways you thought about the Problems, and how you used Mathematical Practices.

Hector described his thoughts in the following way:

We found the expected value for players with different free-throw percentages in Problem 4.4. We had to focus on the important information necessary to complete our table. Then we described the pattern we noticed in the data.

For the players with 20%, 40%, 60%, and 80% free-throw percentages, we noticed that the numbers of missed baskets out of 100 were in reverse order (80, 60, 40, and 20).

We thought about how the expected value increased by 0.48 when the free-throw percentage increased from 60% to 80%. We guessed that half of that increase would be from 60% to 70%. This gave us an estimated value of 1.2 for the expected value of a player with a 70% free-throw percentage.

....

Common Core Standards for Mathematical Practice

MP2 Reason abstractly and quantitatively.

 • What other Mathematical Practices can you identify in Hector's reasoning?

• Describe a Mathematical Practice that you and your classmates used to solve a different Problem in this Investigation.

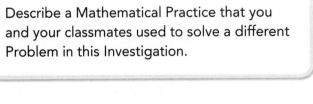

Binomial Outcomes

In some situations, there are only two outcomes. In Investigation 1, you flipped a paper cup to determine which cereal Kalvin would eat for breakfast. The two outcomes, *end* or *side,* were not equally likely.

You also flipped a coin to determine which cereal Kalvin would eat for breakfast. The two outcomes, *heads* or *tails,* were equally likely.

- What are other examples of situations with two outcomes?
- Which of these are equally likely?

Situations like tossing a coin or a cup that have exactly two outcomes are binomial situations. If a situation has *n* identical trials and each trial results in one of two outcomes, then the probability of a given outcome is called a **binomial probability.**

- What are some other examples of binomial probability situations?
- What probability questions might you ask about these situations?

In this Investigation you will explore situations that are binomial situations.

Common Core State Standards

7.SP.C.5 Understand that probability of a chance event is a number between 0 and 1 that expresses the likelihood of the event occurring. Large numbers indicate greater likelihood. A probability near 0 indicates an unlikely event, a probability around 1 indicates an event that is neither unlikely nor likely, and a probability near 1 indicates a likely event.

7.SP.C.8.a Understand that, just as with simple events, the probability of a compound event is the fraction of outcomes in the sample space for which the compound event occurs.

7.SP.C.8.b Represent sample spaces for compound events using methods such as organized lists, tables, and tree diagrams. For an event described in everyday language (e.g. "rolling double sixes"), identify the outcomes in the sample space which compose the event.

Also 7.RP.A.2, 7.RP.A.2a, 7.RP.A.3, 7.SP.C.7, 7.SP.C.7a, 7.SP.C.7b, 7.SP.C.8, 7.SP.C.8c

5.1 Guessing Answers
Finding More Expected Values

Have you ever forgotten to study for a true/false quiz? Have you then tried to guess at the answers? If this happens, you might decide to flip a coin and choose Heads = True and Tails = False.

- What is your chance of getting Question 1 correct?

- What are your chances of getting every question correct?

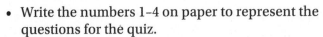
Problem 5.1

A quiz has four true/false questions. Each question is worth 25 points.

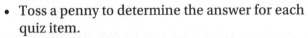
Directions

- Write the numbers 1–4 on paper to represent the questions for the quiz.
- Toss a penny to determine the answer for each quiz item.
- Write T *(true)* if a head shows and F *(false)* if a tail shows.
- After you have written your answers, your teacher will give you the correct answer.
- Mark your answers *correct* or *incorrect*. Record your score.

A Compare answers with your classmates. How many papers had

1. exactly 4 correct (all correct)?

2. exactly 3 correct (3 correct and 1 incorrect)?

3. exactly 2 correct (2 correct and 2 incorrect)?

4. exactly 1 correct (1 correct and 3 incorrect)?

5. none correct (0 correct and 4 incorrect)?

6. What is the experimental probability of getting all 4 correct? Exactly 3 correct? Exactly 2 correct? Exactly 1 correct? None correct?

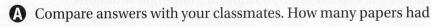

Problem 5.1 *continued*

B **1.** How many different ways can you get all 4 correct? Exactly 3 correct? Exactly 2 correct? Exactly 1 correct? None correct?

2. Find the theoretical probability of each score below.

    a. 100 (all correct)

    b. 75 (exactly three correct)

    c. 50 (exactly two correct)

    d. 25 (exactly one correct)

    e. 0 (all incorrect)

C **1.** Suppose you take the quiz 32 times. How many times do you expect to get 4 correct answers? 3 correct answers? 2 correct answers? 1 correct answer? 0 correct answers?

2. What would your total score be in each case?

3. If you take the quiz 32 times, what is the expected average score? Will the expected value change if you take the quiz 100 times? Explain.

D Suppose the true/false quiz has five questions and you guess each one. What is the probability that you will get them all correct? Explain.

A C E Homework starts on page 105.

5.2 Ortonville
Binomial Probability

In this Problem, you will explore another binomial situation that has equally likely outcomes.

- Suppose you know that a family with five children is moving in next door. What is the probability that the five children are all boys?

Problem 5.2

Ortonville is a very special town. Each family is named Orton and has exactly five children. Below are the names given to the Ortonville children.

The Orton Children

	Girl	Boy
First-Born Child	Gloria	Benson
Second-Born Child	Gilda	Berndt
Third-Born Child	Gail	Blair
Fourth-Born Child	Gerri	Blake
Fifth-Born Child	Gina	Brett

A List all of the possible outcomes for a family with five children.

B What is the probability that a family has children named Gloria, Gilda, Blair, Blake, and Gina?

C Find the probability that a family has

1. exactly five girls or five boys.

2. two girls and three boys.

3. the first or last child a boy.

4. at least one boy.

5. at most one boy.

 Homework starts on page 105.

5.3 A Baseball Series
Expanding Binomial Probability

Every fall the best baseball team in the American League plays the best team in the National League. The series has up to seven games. The first team to win four games wins the series.

Suppose the Bobcats are playing the Gazelles in a youth baseball championship 7-game series. The teams enter the series evenly matched. That is, they each have an equally likely chance of winning each game.

The Gazelles have won the first two games of the series.

- What is a likely ending for this series?

Let us consider *all* of the possible outcomes for the last 5 games.

Label the outcomes with a G for a Gazelles win or a B for a Bobcats win. For example, BBGG means that, after the Gazelles won the first two games, the Bobcats win the third and fourth games, and the Gazelles win the fifth and sixth games. In this example, the series ends in six games (6), when the Gazelles have won four games (G). In baseball notation, this is written G-6.

- What does BBBGG mean? Who won the series?

- What does BBBB mean? Do they need to play a seventh game?

- What does BBGB mean? Who is more likely to win this series?

- What is the probability that the series will end in 4 games? 5 games? 6 games? 7 games?

- What is the probability that the Bobcats win the series?

Problem 5.3

A Before you analyze the rest of the series, predict whether it is more probable that the series will end in 4, 5, 6, or 7 games.

B Suppose all five remaining games are played. What are all of the possible outcomes for these five games? Include all possibilities even if there is a winner before all seven games are played.

C 1. For each outcome, determine the length of the series.

   2. What is the probability that the series ends in four games? In five games? In six games? In seven games?

D Analyze the outcomes in Question C for wins. What is the probability that the Gazelles win the series? That the Bobcats with the series?

A C E Homework starts on page 105.

Did You Know?

The World Series started in 1903 as a best-of-nine-game series. From 1905 until 1919, the series changed to the best-of-seven games.

After World War I ended, the series temporarily changed back to the best-of-nine games in 1919 to 1921. From 1922 until now, the series has remained a best-of-seven series.

Between 1922 and 2012 the World Series ended in four games nineteen times. It ended in five games eighteen times. It ended in six games eighteen times and in seven games thirty-five times. There was no World Series in 1994.

Applications

1. It costs six tickets to play the Toss-a-Penny game at the school carnival. For each turn, a player tosses a penny three times. If the penny lands heads up two or more times in a turn, the player wins ten tickets to spend on food and games.

   a. Suppose Benito plays the game 80 times. How many tickets can he expect to win?

   b. What is the average number of tickets Benito can expect to win or to lose per turn?

2. a. Suppose you toss three coins at the same time. Your friend tosses one coin three times in a row.

   Is the probability of your getting three heads the *same as* or *different from* your friend's? Explain your reasoning.

   b. Suppose you toss three coins and get three tails. What is the probability you will get three tails the next time you toss the three coins? Explain.

   c. Is the probability of getting three heads in three tosses the same, greater, or less than the probability of getting three tails in three tosses?

   d. Is the probability of getting two heads in three tosses the same, greater, or less than the probability of getting one head in three tosses?

For Exercises 3–9, use this information: Scout, Ms. Rodriguez's dog, is about to have puppies. The vet thinks Scout will have four puppies. Assume that for each puppy, a male and female are equally likely.

3. a. List all of the possible combinations of female and male puppies that Scout might have.

    b. Is Scout more likely to have four male puppies or two male and two female puppies? Explain.

4. Multiple Choice What is the probability that Scout will have four female puppies?

    A. $\frac{1}{2}$ **B.** $\frac{1}{4}$ **C.** $\frac{1}{8}$ **D.** $\frac{1}{16}$

5. Multiple Choice What is the probability that Scout will have two male and two female puppies?

    F. $\frac{1}{4}$ **G.** $\frac{3}{4}$ **H.** $\frac{1}{8}$ **J.** $\frac{3}{8}$

6. Multiple Choice What is the probability that Scout will have at least one male puppy?

    A. $\frac{15}{16}$ **B.** $\frac{7}{8}$ **C.** $\frac{3}{4}$ **D.** $\frac{1}{2}$

7. Multiple Choice What is the probability that Scout will have at least one female puppy?

    F. $\frac{15}{16}$ **G.** $\frac{7}{8}$ **H.** $\frac{3}{4}$ **J.** $\frac{1}{2}$

8. Ms. Rodriguez plans to sell her dog's female puppies for $250 each and her male puppies for $200 each. How much money can she expect to make from a litter of four puppies?

9. Suppose the vet thinks Scout will have a litter of five puppies. How much money can Ms. Rodriguez expect to make from selling the puppies?

10. Rajan's physical education class divides into two teams. The two teams are evenly matched. One team is the Champs, and the other team is the Stars. The series is five games. The first team to win three games wins the series. The Champs win the first game.

    a. What is the probability that the series will end in 3, 4, or 5 games?

    b. What is the probability that the Stars will win the series?

Connections

11. You might find that a tree diagram is a helpful model in this Exercise.

   a. List the possible outcomes when you toss a coin three times.

   b. How many outcomes are there when you toss a coin four times? (You do not have to list them all.) Five times?

   c. How many ways can you get five heads in five tosses? How many ways can you get zero heads in five tosses? How many ways can you get four heads? Three heads? Two heads? One head?

   d. Explain why some symmetry in your answers in part (c) makes sense.

12. The largest hamster litter on record consisted of 26 babies. Suppose a hamster has 26 babies. Assume that for each baby, females and males are equally likely. What is the theoretical probability that all 26 babies will be male? Explain your reasoning.

13. Drew walks her neighbors' dogs. She collects $10 per week from each neighbor. One neighbor offers her these deals.

   a. Toss five coins. If there are four or more heads, the customer pays $18. Otherwise, he pays $4. Find the expected value for this deal. Decide if it is a fair deal.

   b. Toss five coins. If they are all the same, the customer pays $80. Otherwise, he pays $4. Find the expected value for this deal. Decide if it is a fair deal.

14. King George's home, Castle Warwick, is under siege. King George must escape to Castle Howard. The only escape route is through a series of canals, shown below.

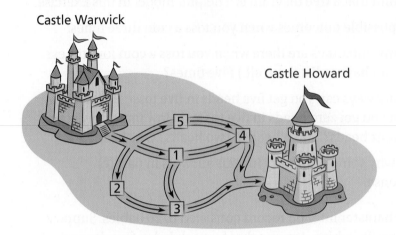

Castle Warwick

Castle Howard

There are five gates in the series of canals. Each gate opens and closes at random and is open half the time and closed the other half. The arrows show the way the water is flowing.

a. What is the probability that a water route from Castle Warwick to Castle Howard is open?

b. How is this problem similar to Problem 5.3?

15. Ethan makes a game played on the number line.

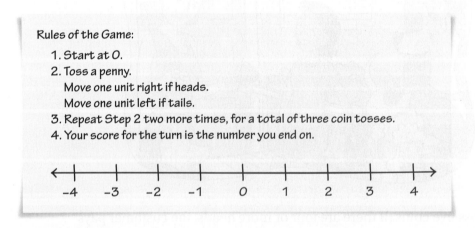

Rules of the Game:
1. Start at 0.
2. Toss a penny.
   Move one unit right if heads.
   Move one unit left if tails.
3. Repeat Step 2 two more times, for a total of three coin tosses.
4. Your score for the turn is the number you end on.

a. What scores are possible after one turn (three tosses)?

b. Suppose Ethan changes his game so that a turn consists of four tosses. What scores are possible after one turn?

16. a. For the spinner below, what are the possible outcomes of a single spin? What is the probability of each outcome?

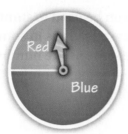

b. Spinning the spinner from part (a) three times is also a binomial situation. What is the probability of RBB (in this order)?

c. Using this spinner below once is not a binomial situation. What are the possible outcomes? What is the probability of each?

d. Does spinning the spinner below make a binomial situation? Explain your reasoning.

e. Suppose you spin the spinner in part (d) three times. What is the probability of RBB (in this order)?

Extensions

Pascal's Triangle (on the left, below) can be used to summarize binomial probabilities and answer new questions in some binomial situations. The sum of each row is the same as the number of outcomes in a binomial probability. For example, some binomial situations are written across from their corresponding row.

Pascal's Triangle	Coin	True/False Test
1	Tossing 1 coin	1 question
1 1	Tossing 2 coins	2 questions
1 2 1	Tossing 3 coins	3 questions
1 3 3 1	Tossing 4 coins	4 questions
1 4 6 4 1	Tossing 5 coins	5 questions
1 5 10 10 5 1		

For Exercises 17 and 18, use Pascal's Triangle above.

17. Describe some patterns in Pascal's Triangle.

18. What is the sixth row (the next row in the diagram above) of Pascal's Triangle? Describe what probabilities each number represents in a situation that involves tossing 6 coins.

For Exercises 19–21, tell which row from Pascal's Triangle you used.

19. On a five-question true/false test, what is the probability that you will guess exactly two correct answers?

20. A coin is tossed six times. What is the probability that at least two heads occur?

21. On a nine-question true/false test, what is the probability that you will guess exactly three correct answers?

In this Investigation, you looked at probabilities for situations involving a series of actions, each with two equally likely outcomes. The following questions will help you summarize what you have learned.

Think about these questions. Discuss your ideas with other students and your teacher. Then write a summary of your findings in your notebook.

1. **Describe** five different binomial situations. **Explain** why they are binomial situations.

2. Tossing a coin three times is an example of a situation involving a series of three actions, each with two equally likely outcomes.

   a. **Pick** one of the situations in Question 1. **Describe** a series of three actions, each with two equally likely outcomes. Make a list of all the possible outcomes.

   b. **Write** a question about your situation that can be answered by your list.

3. As you increase the number of actions for a binomial situation, what happens to the total number of possible outcomes? For example, suppose you increase the number of times a coin is tossed. **What** happens to the total number of outcomes?

Common Core Mathematical Practices

As you worked on the Problems in this Investigation, you used prior knowledge to make sense of them. You also applied Mathematical Practices to solve the Problems. Think back over your work, the ways you thought about the Problems, and how you used Mathematical Practices.

Tori described her thoughts in the following way:

We analyzed a baseball series in Problem 5.3. We had to predict which number of games was likely to end the series. We guessed 5 games.

We determined the different options for how the series could play out. Then, we looked at different ways each team could win the series.

Then, we listed all of the options and found the actual probabilities for ending in 4, 5, 6, or 7 games. We had to use strategies similar to the ones we used in the Problems 5.1 and 5.2.

Common Core Standards for Mathematical Practice

MP1 Make sense of problems and persevere in solving them

- What other Mathematical Practices can you identify in Tori's reasoning?

- Describe a Mathematical Practice that you and your classmates used to solve a different Problem in this Investigation.

The Carnival Game

This Project requires you to use the mathematics you have studied in several Units, including this one. You will make a game for a school carnival and test your game. Then, you will write a report to the carnival committee about your game.

Part 1: Design a Carnival Game

You can design a new game or redesign one of the games you analyzed in this Unit. Keep these guidelines in mind.

- The game should make a profit for the school.
- The game should be easy to set up and use at a school carnival. It should not require expensive equipment.
- The game should take a relatively short time to play.
- Your friends and peers should easily understand the rules of the game.

Part 2: Test Your Game

After you have drafted a game design, you will need to try out your game. You should play the game several times until you feel confident that you can predict what will happen in the long run. Keep track of your trials and include that information in your report.

Part 3: Submit Your Game Design to the Carnival Committee

Once you are satisfied that your game is reasonable, prepare to submit your design. Your submission to the committee should include two things: a model or a scale model of the game and a written report.

Model or Scale Model

If you build a scale model instead of an actual model, give the scale factor from the scale model to the actual game.

You can either construct the model out of materials similar to those you would use for the actual game, or you can prepare scale drawings of the game. If you make drawings, be sure to include enough views of your game so that anyone could look at the drawings and construct the game.

Rules

Include a set of rules with your model that explains how the game is played, how much it costs to play, how a player wins, and the value of what a player wins.

Part 4: Write a Report

Write a report about your game to the carnival committee. Assume that the committee consists of teachers in the building (not just mathematics teachers), parents, and other students. Your report should include:

- The experimental probability of winning the game you found from playing the game several times

- The theoretical probability of winning the game, if possible

- An explanation of why you were unable to calculate the theoretical probability, if unable to find it

- The amount of money the school will collect and how much they should expect to pay out if the game is played many times

- Explanations for how you determined the amounts of money collected and paid out

- An explanation of why your game should be chosen, why the game is worth having in the carnival, and why you think people would want to play it

In this Unit, you studied some basic ideas of probability and some ways to use those ideas to solve problems about probability and expected value. In particular, you studied how to

- Find and interpret experimental and theoretical probabilities

- Use simulations to gather experimental data

- Use tree diagrams and other listing techniques to find all of the possible outcomes

- Use area models in which probabilities are shown as parts of a whole square

Use Your Understanding: Probability Reasoning

To test your understanding and skill with probability ideas and strategies, consider the following problem situations.

1. Maria's homework problem is to design two dartboards that match these conditions:

   - The probability of landing in region A is 30%.

   - The probability of landing in region B is 25%.

   - The probability of landing in region C is 20%.

   - The remaining space on the dartboard is region D.

   a. Draw a square dartboard that meets the given conditions.
   b. Find the probability that a dart will land in region D.
   c. Find the probability that a dart will land in a region other than D.
   d. Find the probability that a dart will *not* land in region A.

2. Gabrielle and Nick are playing the Match/No Match game. On each turn, the players spin the two spinners shown below. Gabrielle scores 1 point if the spins match, and Nick scores 1 point if they do not match.

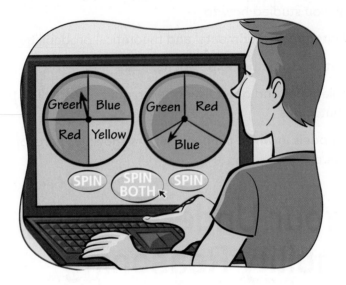

   a. Use a tree diagram to show all of the possible outcomes for this game.

   b. What is the theoretical probability of getting a match?

   c. What is the theoretical probability of getting a nonmatch?

   d. Does each player have an equally likely chance of winning? Explain your reasoning.

   e. Is this a fair game? If so, explain why. If not, explain how you could change the rules to make it fair.

3. Kali designed a new computer game. She programmed the game so the probability that a player will win is $\frac{1}{4}$ on each turn. If the player wins, the score increases by four points. If the player loses, two points are deducted from the score.

   a. Matthew plans to play 12 rounds of the game. How many points can he expect to score?

   b. How many points per round can Matthew expect to win or lose?

   c. Is this a fair game? If not, how would you change the points won or lost so that it is a fair game?

Explain Your Reasoning

When you use mathematical calculations or diagrams to solve a problem or make a decision, it is important to justify your reasoning. Answer these questions about your work.

4. What does it mean to say that the probability of an event is $\frac{1}{2}$, $\frac{2}{3}$, or $\frac{5}{8}$?

5. How are experimental and theoretical probabilities of an event related to each other?

6. What does it mean when a set of outcomes is *not* equally likely?

7. Explain and illustrate with a specific example how you could use each strategy to analyze probabilities.
   a. tree diagrams
   b. area models

8. What does it mean to find the expected value of a chance activity with numerical outcomes? Give three examples of Problems in this Unit for which you had to find the expected value.

A **area model** A diagram in which fractions of the area of the diagram correspond to probabilities in a situation. For example, suppose there are three blue blocks and two red blocks in a container. If one block is drawn out at a time, and the block drawn each time is replaced, the area model below shows that the probability of getting two red blocks is $\frac{4}{25}$.

Area models are particularly helpful when the outcomes being analyzed are not equally likely, because more likely outcomes take up larger areas. Area models are also helpful for outcomes involving more than one stage, such as rolling a number cube and then tossing a coin.

modelo de área Un diagrama en el que las fracciones del área del diagrama corresponden a las probabilidades de una situación. Por ejemplo, supón que hay tres bloques azules y dos bloques rojos en un recipiente. Si se saca un bloque a la vez, reemplazando el bloque que se saca cada vez, el modelo de área de abajo muestra que la probabilidad de sacar dos bloques rojos es $\frac{4}{25}$.

Los modelos de área son especialmente útiles cuando los resultados que se analizan no son igualmente probables, porque los resultados más probables ocupan áreas más grandes. Los modelos de área son también útiles para resultados que incluyen más de un paso, como lanzar un cubo numérico y luego lanzar una moneda al aire.

Second Choice

		B	B	B	R	R
	B	BB	BB	BB	BR	BR
First Choice	B	BB	BB	BB	BR	BR
	B	BB	BB	BB	BR	BR
	R	RB	RB	RB	RR	RR
	R	RB	RB	RB	RR	RR

B **binomial probability** The probability of getting one of two possible outcomes over many trials. For example, the probability of getting a heads or tails when tossing a coin or the probability of getting a 5 or not 5 when rolling a number cube.

probabilidad del binomio La probabilidad de obtener uno de dos resultados posibles en varias pruebas. Por ejemplo, la probabilidad de obtener cara o cruz cuando se lanza una moneda al aire o la probabilidad de obtener o no un 5 cuando se lanza un cubo numérico.

C **compound event** An event that consists of two or more simple events. For example, tossing a coin is a simple event. Tossing two coins, and examining combinations of outcomes, is a compound event.

evento compuesto Evento que consiste de dos o más eventos simples. Por ejemplo, lanzar una moneda al aire es un evento simple. Lanzar dos monedas al aire y examinar combinaciones de resultados, es un evento compuesto.

D **describe** Academic Vocabulary To explain or tell in detail. A written description can contain facts and other information needed to communicate an answer. A diagram or a graph may also be included.

related terms *explain, present*

sample Three of ten rolls of a number cube result in a 5. Describe the theoretical and experimental probability of rolling a 5.

Since a number cube has six identical sides and the number 5 appears once, the theoretical probability of rolling a 5 is $\frac{1}{6}$. The experimental probability of rolling a 5 is $\frac{3}{10}$.

describir Vocabulario académico Explicar o decir con detalle. Una descripción escrita puede contener datos y otra información necesaria para comunicar una respuesta. También se puede incluir un diagrama o una gráfica.

términos relacionados *explicar, presentar*

ejemplo En tres de diez lanzamientos de un cubo numérico obtienes un 5. Describe la probabilidad teórica y experimental de obtener un 5.

Como un cubo numérico tiene seis caras iguales y el número 5 aparece una sola vez, la probabilidad teórica de que salga un 5 es $\frac{1}{6}$. La probabilidad experimental de que salga un 5 es $\frac{3}{10}$.

---

design Academic Vocabulary To make using specific criteria.

related terms *draw, plan, outline, model*

sample A computer game randomly hides a treasure chest. The probability that the treasure chest will be hidden in the sand is 50%, in the water 30%, in the rocks 10%, or in the grass 10%. Design a computer screen for this game.

I'll draw 50 of the 100 square units as sand, 30 as water, and 10 each as rocks and grass to match each probability.

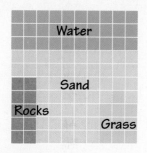

diseñar Vocabulario académico Crear algo usando criterios específicos.

términos relacionados *dibujar, planear, bosquejar, representar*

ejemplo Un juego de computadora oculta al azar un cofre del tesoro. La probabilidad de que el cofre del tesoro esté escondido en la arena es de 50%, en el agua de 30%, en las rocas de 10% o en el pasto de 10%. Diseña una pantalla de computadora para este juego.

Dibujaré 50 de los 100 cuadrados unitarios para la arena, 30 para el agua, 10 para las rocas y 10 para el pasto, para representar cada probabilidad.

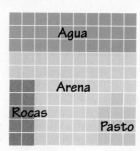

determine Academic Vocabulary To use the given information and any related facts to find a value or make a decision.

related terms *solve, evaluate, examine*

sample Eugene's favorite shirts are red, black, orange, and white. His favorite hats are red, gold, and black. Eugene randomly selects one shirt and one hat. Make a chart to determine the probability that they are the same color.

determinar Vocabulario académico Usar la información dada y cualquier dato relacionado para hallar un valor o tomar una decisión.

términos relacionados *resolver, evaluar, examinar*

ejemplo Las camisetas favoritas de Eugene son rojas, negras, anaranjadas y blancas. Sus gorras favoritas son rojas, doradas y negras. Eugene selecciona al azar una camiseta y una gorra. Haz una gráfica para determinar la probabilidad de que sean del mismo color.

The chart shows 12 possible combinations.

The probability of the same color is $\frac{2}{12}$, or $\frac{1}{6}$.

	Hats		
	R	G	B
R	RR	RG	RB
B	BR	BG	BB
O	OR	OG	OB
W	WR	WG	WB

Shirts

La tabla muestra 12 combinaciones posibles. La probabilidad de que sean del mismo color es de $\frac{2}{12}$ ó $\frac{1}{6}$.

	Gorras		
	R	D	N
R	RR	RD	RN
N	NR	ND	NN
A	AR	AD	AN
B	BR	BD	BN

Camisetas

E **equally likely** Two or more events that have the same probability of occurring. For example, when you toss a fair coin, heads and tails are equally likely; each has a 50% chance of happening. Rolling a six-sided number cube gives a $\frac{1}{6}$ probability for each number to come up. Each outcome is equally likely.

igualmente probables Dos o más eventos que tienen la misma probabilidad de ocurrir. Por ejemplo, cuando lanzas una moneda al aire, la probabilidad de obtener cara es igual a la de obtener cruz; es decir, cada caso tiene una probabilidad del 50% de ocurrir. Lanzar un cubo numérico de 6 lados supone $\frac{1}{6}$ de probabilidad de que salga cada número. Cada resultado es igualmente probable.

expected value (or long-term average) Intuitively, the average payoff over the long run. For example, suppose you are playing a game with two number cubes. You score 2 points when a sum of 6 is rolled, 1 point for a sum of 3, and 0 points for anything else. If you roll the cubes 36 times, you could expect to roll a sum of 6 five times, a sum of 3 twice, and the other sums 29 times. This means that you could expect to score $(5 \times 2) + (2 \times 1) + (29 \times 0) = 12$ points for 36 rolls, an average of $\frac{12}{36} = \frac{1}{3}$ point per roll. Here, $\frac{1}{3}$ is the expected value, or long-term average, of one roll.

valor esperado (o promedio a largo plazo) El promedio de puntos o recompensas que se espera obtener a largo plazo. Por ejemplo, imagínate un juego con dos cubos numéricos en el que obtienes 2 puntos por una suma de 6, 1 punto por una suma de 3 y 0 puntos por cualquier otra suma. Si lanzas los cubos numéricos 36 veces, puedes esperar obtener una suma de 6 cinco veces, una suma de 3 dos veces, y las otras sumas 29 veces. Esto significa que puedes esperar conseguir $(5 \times 2) + (2 \times 1) + (29 \times 0) = 12$ puntos por 36 lanzamientos, o sea un promedio de $\frac{12}{36} = \frac{1}{3}$ de punto por lanzamiento. Aquí $\frac{1}{3}$ es el valor esperado, o promedio a largo plazo, de un lanzamiento.

experimental probability A probability that is determined through experimentation. For example, you could find the experimental probability of getting a head when you toss a coin by tossing a coin many times and keeping track of the outcomes. The experimental probability would be the ratio of the number of heads to the total number of tosses, or trials. Experimental probability may not be the same as the theoretical probability. However, for a large number of trials, they are likely to be close. Experimental probabilities are used to predict behavior over the long run.

probabilidad experimental La probabilidad que se determina mediante la experimentación. Por ejemplo, puedes hallar la probabilidad experimental de obtener cara cuando lanzas una moneda al aire al efectuar numerosos tiros y llevar la cuenta de los resultados. La probabilidad experimental sería la razón del número de caras al número total de tiros o pruebas. La probabilidad experimental puede no ser igual a la probabilidad teórica. Sin embargo, en un gran número de pruebas, es probable que estén cerca. Las probabilidades experimentales se usan para predecir lo que ocurrirá largo plazo.

explain Academic Vocabulary To give facts and details that make an idea easier to understand. Explaining can involve a written summary supported by a diagram, chart, table, or a combination of these.

related terms *clarify, describe, justify*

sample Find the probability of tossing a coin 3 times and getting heads exactly two times. Explain your reasoning.

I can use a tree diagram to look at all eight possible outcomes when tossing a coin three times.

Toss 1	Toss 2	Toss 3	Results
H	H	H	HHH
		T	**HHT**
	T	H	**HTH**
		T	HTT
T	H	H	**THH**
		T	THT
	T	H	TTH
		T	TTT

There are 3 outcomes in which there are exactly two heads. The probability is $\frac{3}{8}$.

explicar Vocabulario académico Dar datos y detalles que hacen que una idea sea más fácil de comprender. Explicar puede incluir un resumen escrito apoyado por un diagrama, una gráfica, una tabla o una combinación de estos.

términos relacionados *aclarar, describir, justificar*

ejemplo Halla la probabilidad de lanzar una moneda al aire tres veces y obtener cara exactamente dos veces. Explica tu razonamiento.

Puedo usar un diagrama arborescente para observar los ocho resultados posibles al lanzar una moneda al aire tres veces.

Tirada 1	Tirada 2	Tirada 3	Resultados
C	C	C	CCC
		Cr	**CCCr**
	Cr	C	**CCrC**
		Cr	CCrCr
Cr	C	C	**CrCC**
		Cr	CrCCr
	Cr	C	CrCrC
		Cr	CrCrCr

Hay 3 resultados en que hay exactamente dos caras. La probabilidad es de $\frac{3}{8}$.

fair game A game in which each player is equally likely to win. The probability of winning a two-person fair game is $\frac{1}{2}$. An unfair game can be made fair by adjusting the scoring system, or the payoffs. For example, suppose you play a game in which two fair coins are tossed. You score when both coins land heads up. Otherwise, your opponent scores. The probability that you will score is $\frac{1}{4}$, and the probability that your opponent will score is $\frac{3}{4}$. To make the game fair, you might adjust the scoring system so that you receive 3 points each time you score and your opponent receives 1 point when he or she scores. This would make the expected values for each player equal, which results in a fair game.

juego justo Un juego en el que cada jugador tiene igual probabilidad de ganar. La probabilidad de ganar en un juego justo entre dos personas es $\frac{1}{2}$. Para hacer justo un juego injusto se puede ajustar el sistema de reparto de puntos o de recompensas. Por ejemplo, imagina un juego que consiste en lanzar dos monedas al aire. Si salen dos caras, tú obtienes puntos. Si no, los obtiene el otro jugador. La probabilidad de que tú obtengas los puntos es $\frac{1}{4}$ y la probabilidad de que los obtenga el otro jugador es $\frac{3}{4}$. Para hacer que el juego sea justo, podrías ajustar el sistema de reparto de puntos de manera que, cada vez que salgan dos caras, tú recibas 3 puntos y en las demás ocasiones el otro jugador reciba 1 punto. Esto haría que los valores esperados para cada jugador fueran iguales, lo que daría como resultado en un juego justo.

favorable outcome An outcome that gives a desired result. A favorable outcome is sometimes called a *success*. For example, when you toss two coins to find the probability of the coins matching, HH and TT are favorable outcomes.

resultado favorable Un resultado que proporciona una consecuencia deseada. A veces, a un resultado favorable se le llama un éxito. Por ejemplo, cuando lanzas dos monedas al aire para hallar la probabilidad de que las dos coincidan, los resultados CC y CrCr son resultados favorables.

Law of Large Numbers This law states, in effect, that as more trials of an experiment are conducted, the experimental probability more closely approximates the theoretical probability. It is not at all unusual to have 100% heads after three tosses of a fair coin, but it would be extremely unusual to have even 60% heads after 1,000 tosses. This is expressed by the Law of Large Numbers.

Ley de números grandes Esta ley establece, en efecto, que a medida que se realicen más pruebas de un experimento, más se acercar· la probabilidad experimental a la probabilidad teórica. No es inusual obtener el 100% de caras después de tres lanzamientos de una moneda justa al aire, pero sería extremadamente inusual obtener incluso el 60% de caras después de 1,000 lanzamientos. Esto se expresa en la ley de los números grandes.

outcome A possible result. For example, when a number cube is rolled, the possible outcomes are 1, 2, 3, 4, 5, and 6. Other possible outcomes are even or odd. Others are three and not three. When determining probabilities, it is important to be clear about what the possible outcomes are.

resultado Una consecuencia posible. Por ejemplo, cuando se lanza un cubo numérico, los resultados posibles son 1, 2, 3, 4, 5 y 6. Otros resultados posibles son pares o impares. Incluso otro es tres y no tres. Cuando se determinan las probabilidades, es importante definir cuáles son los resultados posibles.

payoff The number of points (or dollars or other objects of value) a player in a game receives for a particular outcome.

recompensa El número de puntos (o dólares u otros objetos de valor) que recibe un jugador por un resultado particular.

probability A number between 0 and 1 that describes the likelihood that an outcome will occur. For example, when a fair number cube is rolled, a 2 can be expected $\frac{1}{6}$ of the time, so the probability of rolling a 2 is $\frac{1}{6}$. The probability of a certain outcome is 1, while the probability of an impossible outcome is 0.

probabilidad Un número comprendido entre 0 y 1 que describe la probabilidad de que ocurra un resultado. Por ejemplo, cuando se lanza un cubo numérico justo, se puede esperar un 2 cada $\frac{1}{6}$ de las veces, por tanto, probabilidad de obtener un 2 es $\frac{1}{6}$. La probabilidad de un cierto resultado es 1, mientras que la probabilidad de un resultado imposible es 0.

random Outcomes that are uncertain when viewed individually, but which exhibit a predictable pattern over many trials. For example, when you roll a fair number cube, you have no way of knowing what the next roll will be, but you do know that, over the long run, you will roll each number on the cube about the same number of times.

aleatorio(s) Resultados que son inciertos cuando se consideran individualmente, pero que presentan un patrón predecible a lo largo de muchas pruebas. Por ejemplo, cuando lanzas un cubo numérico, es imposible saber cuál será el resultado del siguiente lanzamiento, pero sabes que, a la larga, obtendrás cada uno de los números del cubo numérico aproximadamente el mismo número de veces.

relative frequency The ratio of the number of desired results to the total number of trials.

frecuencia relativa La razón del número de resultados deseados al número total de pruebas.

sample space The set of all possible outcomes in a probability situation. When you toss two coins, the sample space consists of four outcomes: HH, HT, TH, and TT.

espacio muestral El conjunto de todos los resultados posibles en una situación de probabilidad. Cuando lanzas dos monedas al aire, el espacio muestral consiste en cuatro resultados: CC, CCr, CrC y CrCr.

simulation An experiment using objects that represent the relevant characteristics of a real-world situation.

simulación Experimento en el que se usan objetos para representar las características relevantes de una situación de la vida diaria.

theoretical probability A probability obtained by analyzing a situation. If all the outcomes are equally likely, you can find a theoretical probability of an event by listing all the possible outcomes and then finding the ratio of the number of outcomes producing the desired event to the total number of outcomes. For example, there are 36 possible equally likely outcomes (number pairs) when two fair number cubes are rolled. Of these, six have a sum of 7, so the probability of rolling a sum of 7 is $\frac{6}{36}$, or $\frac{1}{6}$. Since the sum of the probabilities of all possible events must be 1, theoretical probability can be applied to events that are not equally likely. The probability of rolling a sum of 7 is $\frac{1}{6}$, and the probability of not rolling a 7 is $\frac{5}{6}$.

probabilidad teórica La probabilidad que se obtiene mediante el an·lisis de una situación. Si todos los resultados son igualmente probables, puedes hallar una probabilidad teórica de un evento haciendo una lista de todos los resultados posibles y luego hallando la razón del número de resultados que produce el evento deseado al número total de resultados. Por ejemplo, al lanzar dos cubos numéricos, hay 36 resultados igualmente probables (pares de números). De estos, seis tienen una suma de 7, por tanto, la probabilidad de obtener una suma de 7 es $\frac{6}{36}$ ó $\frac{1}{6}$. Dado que la suma de las probabilidades de todos los eventos posibles debe ser 1, la probabilidad teórica también se puede aplicar a eventos que no son igualmente probables. La probabilidad de obtener una suma de 7 es $\frac{1}{6}$ y la probabilidad de *no* obtener un 7 es $\frac{5}{6}$.

tree diagram A diagram used to determine the number of possible outcomes in a probability situation. The number of final branches is equal to the number of possible outcomes. The tree diagram below shows all the possible outcomes for randomly choosing a yellow or a red rose and then a white or a pink ribbon. The four possible outcomes are listed in the last column. Tree diagrams are handy to use when outcomes are equally likely.

diagrama de árbol Un diagrama que se usa para determinar el número de resultados posibles en una situación de probabilidad. El número de ramas finales es igual al número de resultados posibles. El siguiente diagrama de árbol muestra todos los resultados posibles de escoger al azar una rosa amarilla o roja, y luego una cinta blanca o rosada. Los cuatro resultados posibles aparecen en la última columna. Los diagramas de árbol son útiles cuando los resultados son igualmente probables.

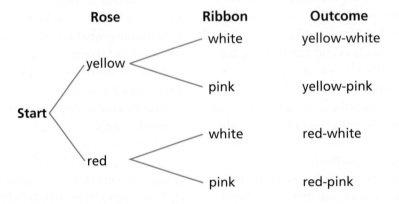

trial One round of an experiment. For example, if you are interested in the behavior of a coin, you might experiment by tossing a coin 50 times and recording the results. Each toss is a trial, so this experiment consists of 50 trials.

prueba Una ronda de un experimento. Por ejemplo, si te interesan los resultados de lanzar una moneda al aire, puedes hacer un experimento lanzando una moneda al aire 50 veces y anotando los resultados. Cada lanzamiento es una prueba, por tanto, este experimento consiste en 50 pruebas.

Index

Index

Acknowledgments

Cover Design

Three Communication Design, Chicago

Photographs

Photo locators denoted as follows: Top (T), Center (C), Bottom (B), Left (L), Right (R), Background (Bkgd)

002 Pearson Education; **003** Shaun Wilkinson/Shutterstock; **013** Rsooll/Fotolia; **028** Pearson Education; **036** Brian Hagiwara/BrandX Pictures/Getty Images; **104** Chicago History Museum/Contributor/Getty Images.

CONNECTED MATHEMATICS 3

Filling and Wrapping

Three-Dimensional Measurement

Lappan, Phillips, Fey, Friel

Three-Dimensional Measurement

Looking Ahead

A rectangular compost box with dimensions 1 foot by 2 feet by 3 feet can decompose 0.5 pound of garbage a day. **What** are the dimensions of boxes that will decompose 1, 2, and 5 pounds of garbage a day?

A pizzeria owner surveyed her lunch customers and found that $6 was a fair price for a 9-inch pizza with one topping. Based on this price, **what** prices would you suggest for 12- and 15-inch pizzas with one topping?

What do you think is a fair price for a 9-inch, cheese-filled crust pizza with one topping?

(Please check one price.)

○ $4.00 ○ $8.00
○ $6.00 ○ $10.00

Thanks!
Pizzeria Management

Esther buys a scoop of ice cream in a cone, and Jasmine gets a scoop in a cylindrical cup. Suppose they both allow their ice cream to melt. **Will** the melted ice cream fill each container exactly?

The way a product is packaged is important. Stores are filled with containers such as boxes, cans, bags, and bottles that come in interesting three-dimensional shapes. A unique shape can attract shoppers to take a closer look at the product.

When a company plans the packaging for a product, it must consider several questions. The company must determine how much of the product should be sold in each package, what and how much material is needed to make the package, and what package design is best for the product.

Thinking about how products are packaged can make you a smarter consumer. You can usually save money by comparing the cost of products in different-sized packages.

In this Unit, you will explore measurement of surface area and volume for a variety of three-dimensional shapes. You will learn how to calculate the amount of material it takes to *fill* a shape and the amount of material needed to *wrap* the shape. As you work through the Investigations, you will consider questions like those on the opposite page.

Mathematical Highlights

Three-Dimensional Measurement

In *Filling and Wrapping*, you will explore surface area and volume of three-dimensional objects.

You will learn how to:

- Develop the ability to visualize and draw three-dimensional shapes

- Develop strategies for finding volumes of three-dimensional objects, including prisms, cylinders, pyramids, cones, and spheres

- Design and use nets to develop formulas for finding surface areas of prisms and cylinders

- Develop formulas and strategies for finding the area and circumference of a circle

- Explore patterns relating the volumes of prisms, cylinders, cones, spheres, and pyramids

- Understand that three-dimensional figures may have the same volume but different surface areas

- Investigate the effects of scaling dimensions of figures on the volume and surface area

- Recognize and solve problems involving volume and surface area

When you encounter a new problem, it is a good idea to ask yourself questions. In this Unit, you might ask questions such as:

What are the shapes and properties of the figures in the problem?

Which measures of a figure are involved—length, surface area, or volume?

What measurement strategies or formulas might help in using given information to find unknown measurements?

Mathematical Practices and Habits of Mind

In the *Connected Mathematics* curriculum you will develop an understanding of important mathematical ideas by solving problems and reflecting on the mathematics involved. Every day, you will use "habits of mind" to make sense of problems and apply what you learn to new situations. Some of these habits are described by the *Common Core State Standards for Mathematical Practices* (MP).

MP1 Make sense of problems and persevere in solving them.

When using mathematics to solve a problem, it helps to think carefully about

- data and other facts you are given and what additional information you need to solve the problem;
- strategies you have used to solve similar problems and whether you could solve a related simpler problem first;
- how you could express the problem with equations, diagrams, or graphs;
- whether your answer makes sense.

MP2 Reason abstractly and quantitatively.

When you are asked to solve a problem, it often helps to

- focus first on the key mathematical ideas;
- check that your answer makes sense in the problem setting;
- use what you know about the problem setting to guide your mathematical reasoning.

MP3 Construct viable arguments and critique the reasoning of others.

When you are asked to explain why a conjecture is correct, you can

- show some examples that fit the claim and explain why they fit;
- show how a new result follows logically from known facts and principles.

When you believe a mathematical claim is incorrect, you can

- show one or more counterexamples—cases that don't fit the claim;
- find steps in the argument that do not follow logically from prior claims.

MP4 Model with mathematics.

When you are asked to solve problems, it often helps to

- think carefully about the numbers or geometric shapes that are the most important factors in the problem, then ask yourself how those factors are related to each other;
- express data and relationships in the problem with tables, graphs, diagrams, or equations, and check your result to see if it makes sense.

MP5 Use appropriate tools strategically.

When working on mathematical questions, you should always

- decide which tools are most helpful for solving the problem and why;
- try a different tool when you get stuck.

MP6 Attend to precision.

In every mathematical exploration or problem-solving task, it is important to

- think carefully about the required accuracy of results; is a number estimate or geometric sketch good enough, or is a precise value or drawing needed?
- report your discoveries with clear and correct mathematical language that can be understood by those to whom you are speaking or writing.

MP7 Look for and make use of structure.

In mathematical explorations and problem solving, it is often helpful to

- look for patterns that show how data points, numbers, or geometric shapes are related to each other;
- use patterns to make predictions.

MP8 Look for and express regularity in repeated reasoning.

When results of a repeated calculation show a pattern, it helps to

- express that pattern as a general rule that can be used in similar cases;
- look for shortcuts that will make the calculation simpler in other cases.

You will use all of the Mathematical Practices in this Unit. Sometimes, when you look at a Problem, it is obvious which practice is most helpful. At other times, you will decide on a practice to use during class explorations and discussions. After completing each Problem, ask yourself:

- What mathematics have I learned by solving this Problem?
- What Mathematical Practices were helpful in learning this mathematics?

Building Smart Boxes: Rectangular Prisms

Nearly everything for sale in stores is wrapped in some sort of package. Packages come in a wide variety of shapes and sizes. The most common and simplest are boxes in the shape of *rectangular prisms.* You learned about rectangular prisms in *Covering and Surrounding.* A **rectangular prism** is a three-dimensional shape with a top and bottom (base) that are congruent rectangles and *lateral* (side) faces that are parallelograms.

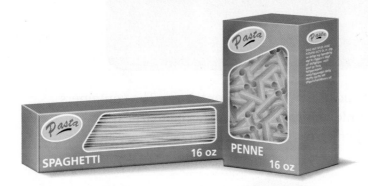

Because so much packaging involves rectangular prisms, it is helpful to know the properties of rectangular prisms. Your work in this Investigation will reveal the most important properties. It will also help you develop strategies for working with nonrectangular prisms.

Common Core State Standards

7.G.A.1 Solve problems involving scale drawings of geometric figures, including computing actual lengths and area from a scale drawing and reproducing a scale drawing at a different scale.

7.G.B.6 Solve real-world and mathematical problems involving area, volume and surface area of two- and three-dimensional objects composed of triangles, quadrilaterals, polygons, cubes, and right prisms.

7.RP.A.2 Recognize and represent proportional relationships between quantities.

Also 7.EE.A.2

1.1 How Big Are Those Boxes?
Finding Volume

 In this globalized world, people enjoy products from many different countries. The most economical way to transport goods is by water on large container ships.

The ships are loaded with individual shipping containers. The containers can be easily loaded and unloaded and then transferred to trucks for delivery. The containers themselves are also used for temporary storage in many places.

Standard shipping containers are rectangular prisms. To decide on the right container for any particular use, it is important to know the size of the things you want to store and the size of the containers available.

 • What measurements would help you decide how you might use the container for shipping or storage?

• How can you determine the capacity of the container?

Problem 1.1

Some students came up with this list of ways to measure a shipping container: (1) Length; (2) Width; (3) Height; (4) Diagonals; (5) Surface Area; and (6) Volume.

A How does each measurement 1–6 relate to the parts of the container?

B Match each of the possible measurements 1–6 to the questions they would help to answer. Explain your reasoning.

1. How much paint would you use to paint the container in a new color?

2. Could you store a small car in the container?

3. How many sacks of rice, corn, or beans could you store in the container?

4. Could you store pipes for a farm sprinkler system in the container?

5. Could you store a long flagpole in the container?

C The filled shipping containers are stacked on a ship. The load is built up in layers.

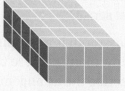

1 Layer   2 Layers   5 Layers

1. How could you calculate the number of containers in each layer of such a load?

2. How could you then calculate the total number of containers in the load?

3. Suppose a ship's load has 10 containers in each row from one side to the other, 15 containers in each row from front to back, and 8 layers of containers. How many containers are in the whole load?

continued on the next page >

Problem 1.1 continued

D Basketballs are spheres, but they are often packaged in boxes in the shape of cubes.

1. How many of these boxes would fit into a shipping container that is 6 feet long by 5 feet wide by 4 feet high? Describe the arrangement of the boxes.

2. What are the dimensions of some other rectangular containers that would hold the same number of basketball boxes? Describe the arrangement of the boxes in each case. Which containers make the most sense? The least sense?

3. Suppose that your classroom is a shipping container that is a rectangular prism. How many of these basketball boxes would fit in your classroom? Describe the arrangement of the boxes.

E 1. Find the surface area and volume of each prism in Question C.

2. Describe a strategy for finding volume and surface area of a rectangular prism.

A C E Homework starts on page 15.

1.2 Optimal Containers I
Finding Surface Area

A toy company is planning to market a Wump Family and Imposter Characters collector set. Each character will be sold separately. The Mug Wump character comes in a cube-shaped package with 1-inch edges.

The toy company has to ship packages of the Mug Wump characters to many different toy stores. It plans to ship in large boxes, each holding 24 of the cube-shaped packages.

> **?** What are the dimensions of a box that will hold 24 of the cube-shaped packages and be least expensive to make?

Problem 1.2

A Find all the ways that 24 unit cubes can be packed in a rectangular prism. Sketch each possibility. Record the dimensions, volume, surface area, and sketches in a table like this:

Possible Arrangements of 24 Cubes

Length (in.)	Width (in.)	Height (in.)	Volume (in.³)	Surface Area (in.²)	Sketch
▪	▪	▪	▪	▪	▪
▪	▪	▪	▪	▪	▪
▪	▪	▪	▪	▪	▪

B Which arrangement of cubes requires the box that can be made with the least material? Which requires the box that needs the most material?

C Which box shape would you recommend for shipping the Mug Wump characters? Explain your reasoning.

D Why do you think the shipping directions called for 24, rather than 26, Mug Wump characters in a box?

 Homework starts on page 15.

1.3 Optimal Containers II
Finding the Least Surface Area

The challenge of designing inexpensive packaging also applies to many other products. To find a packaging strategy that will work for any product, it is helpful to explore different cases and look for a pattern in the results.

> ? How would you design a rectangular box that holds a given volume but uses the least packaging material?

Problem 1.3

A For each part, do the following:

- Find the dimensions of the large boxes that require the least packaging material to enclose the given number of cube-shaped boxes for the Mug Wump characters.

- Explain your strategy and how you know you have designed the box with the least packaging material.

1. 8 cube-shaped boxes

2. 27 cube-shaped boxes

3. 12 cube-shaped boxes

4. 30 cube-shaped boxes

B Suppose you need to design a box to hold a liquid, such as juice or milk, or a material, such as rice, cake mix, or pasta. Because the contents of the box are not identical unit cubes, it is possible to consider dimensions other than whole numbers.

For each given volume, find the dimensions of the box that uses the least packaging material.

1. 1,000 cubic centimeters

2. 30 cubic centimeters

3. 500 cubic centimeters

 Homework starts on page 15.

1.4 Compost Containers
Scaling Up Prisms

Finding enough landfill space for garbage is becoming a problem for many communities. Some communities are considering composting as a way to recycle garbage into productive soil. Composting is a method for turning organic waste into rich soil. Today, many people have compost boxes that break down kitchen waste quickly and with little odor. The secret is in the worms!

The Science Club wants to promote environmental awareness in the community. It organizes a campaign to have families build and use compost containers called 1-2-3 boxes.

Recipe for a 1-2-3 Compost Box

- Start with an open rectangular wood box that is 1 foot high, 2 feet wide, and 3 feet long. This is a 1-2-3 box.

- Mix 10 pounds of shredded newspaper with 15 quarts of water. Put the mixture in the 1-2-3 box.

- Add a few handfuls of soil.

- Add about 1,000 redworms (about 1 pound).

Every day, mix collected kitchen waste with the soil in the box. The worms will do the rest of the work, turning the waste into new soil. A 1-2-3 box will decompose about 0.5 pound of garbage a day.

- If you want to double the amount of garbage you can compost, what would be the dimensions of the new box?

- How many worms would you need?

Problem 1.4

A Use grid paper to make a scale model of the 1-2-3 box that will decompose 0.5 pound of garbage each day.

B Assume that the number of worms used increases to match the increase in box volume. What changes in the dimensions of the basic design would produce a box that could compost 1 pound of garbage each day? 2 pounds of garbage? 5 pounds of garbage?

C **1.** The Science Club wants to scale up the basic 1-2-3 design to a larger box that is similar in shape. Copy and complete the following table that shows the cost and capacity of several larger boxes.

Compost Box Project

Open Box (h-w-ℓ)	Scale Factor	Surface Area (ft²)	Volume (ft³)	Amount of Garbage Decomposed in a Day (lb)	Worms Needed
1-2-3	▪	▪	▪	▪	▪
2-4-6	▪	▪	▪	▪	▪
3-6-9	▪	▪	▪	▪	▪
4-8-12	▪	▪	▪	▪	▪
▪	▪	▪	▪	▪	▪
▪	▪	1,024	▪	▪	▪
▪	▪	▪	▪	▪	▪
▪	▪	▪	6,000	▪	▪

2. What growth patterns do you see in the volume and surface area?

D Suppose a large compost box is similar to a 1-2-3 box with scale factor f.

1. How is the surface area of the large box related to that of the 1-2-3 box?

2. If both boxes had tops, would the relationship of surface areas change? Explain.

3. How is the volume of the 4-8-12 box related to that of the 1-2-3 box?

4. How is the amount of decomposed garbage related to the volume of the 1-2-3 box?

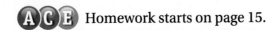

ACE Homework starts on page 15.

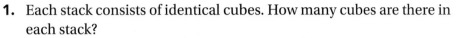

Applications

1. Each stack consists of identical cubes. How many cubes are there in each stack?

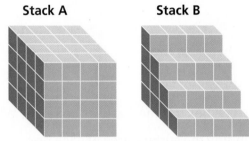

Stack A   Stack B

2. Bags of sand, cement, or fertilizer are often packed on wooden pallets for shipping.

   a. Estimate the number of bags on the wooden pallet pictured above.

   b. How many loaded pallets in the shape of 1-meter cubes could you load in a semitrailer that has inner dimensions 2 meters wide by 10 meters long by 3 meters high?

   c. How many loaded pallets in the shape of 1-meter cubes could you ship in a railroad boxcar that has inner dimensions 3 meters wide by 15 meters long by 4 meters high?

3. Suppose you plan to make a box that will hold exactly 40 one-inch cubes.

   a. Give the dimensions of all the possible boxes you can make.

   b. Which of the boxes you described in part (a) has the least surface area? Explain.

4. Each of these boxes holds 36 table-tennis balls.

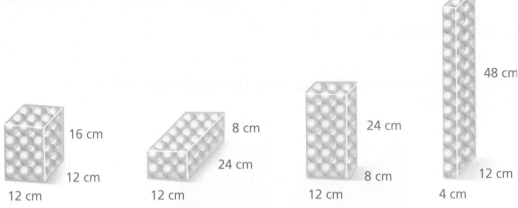

16 cm
12 cm
12 cm

8 cm
24 cm
12 cm

24 cm
8 cm
12 cm

48 cm
12 cm
4 cm

   a. Without calculating, which box has the least surface area? Why?

   b. Check your guess by finding the surface area of each box.

5. Liquids, such as juice or milk, and solids, such as rice or cake mix, are often packaged in rectangular boxes. Because the material settles easily into a box of any dimensions, there are many packaging possibilities.

   a. What are the volume and surface area of a box that has width 3.5 centimeters, length 10 centimeters, and height 15 centimeters?

   b. What are the dimensions of the box that would hold 250 cubic centimeters of juice and have minimum surface area?

6. The box below is a $6 \times 1 \times 2$ arrangement of drink cans. Suppose the dimensions of the box are, in centimeters, $39 \times 13 \times 12.25$.

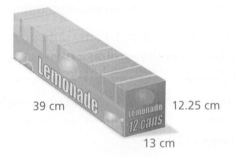

39 cm   12.25 cm

13 cm

   a. What is the surface area of the box?

   b. What is the surface area of a box with the more traditional $4 \times 3 \times 1$ arrangement, which measures, in centimeters, $26 \times 19.5 \times 12.25$?

7. The box below is a 4 × 3 × 2 arrangement of drink cans. Suppose the dimensions of the box are, in centimeters, 26 × 19.5 × 24.5.

24.5 cm

26 cm

19.5 cm

24 cans

a. What is the surface area of the box?

b. What is the surface area of a box with the more traditional 6 × 4 × 1 arrangement, which measures, in centimeters, 39 × 26 × 12.25?

8. Suppose that a company sells laundry soap in boxes that measure 4 inches by 8 inches by 12 inches. The company wants to offer larger economy size boxes.

a. What changes in dimensions would give a box with double the volume?

b. What changes in dimensions would give a box with triple the volume?

c. What changes in dimensions would give a box with half the volume?

d. Given each scale factor below, find the volume of the box similar to the basic box.

   i. scale factor of 2

   ii. scale factor of 1.5

   iii. scale factor of 0.5

Explain how you can find these answers without calculating the separate dimensions of each new box design.

9. You want to make a compost box bigger than the basic 1-2-3 foot size. Your friend says, 'If you double each dimension, you'll be able to double the capacity at only double the cost of the materials to build it.'

  a. Is your friend correct about doubling the capacity? Why or why not?

  b. Is your friend correct about doubling the cost? Why or why not?

10. The city of Centerville plans to dig a landfill in the shape of a rectangular prism. The landfill is 85 feet deep, 200 feet wide, and 700 feet long.

  a. How many cubic feet of garbage will the landfill hold?

  b. What information do you need to determine how long the landfill can be used until it is full?

  c. The city manager says that an increase of only 10% in each dimension would increase the capacity of the landfill by 33%. Is she correct? Explain.

11. Shaun's hobby is building model airplanes and ships from kits. One of his projects is an historic sailing ship. The actual ship is related to the model by a scale factor of 200.

  a. If the length of the model is 25 centimeters, what is the length of the actual ship?

  b. If the length of one mast on the actual ship is 30 meters, what is the length of the mast on the model?

  c. If the area of the deck on the model is 20 square centimeters, what is the area of the deck on the actual ship?

  d. If the model ship's interior has volume 100 cubic centimeters, what is the volume of the interior of the actual ship?

Connections

12. Find all the factor pairs and the prime factorizations of each number.

    a. 11   **b.** 18   **c.** 42

13. Suppose you enlarge the triangle below by a scale factor of 2.4.

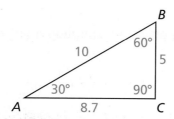

  a. What is the perimeter of the image? How can you find this without finding the lengths of each side of the image?

  b. What is the area of the image? How can you find this without finding the lengths of each side of the image?

  c. What are the measures of the angles in the image? How can you find these measures without measuring the angles in the image?

For Exercises 14–16, find the area and perimeter of each figure. Figures are not drawn to scale.

14.

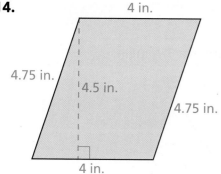

15.

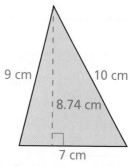

16.

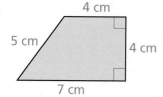

17. Angles *m* and *n* below are supplementary angles. Angle *m* has a measure of 78°. What is the measure of angle *n*?

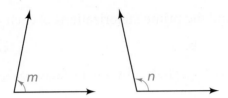

18. Multiple Choice Which pair of angles are complementary angles?

A.

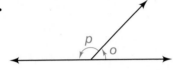

B.

C.

19. Multiple Choice Which angle is supplementary to a 57° angle?

A.   **B.**

C.   **D.**

20. Ms. Zhou is making wooden slats for doll beds from a strip of thin board. She cuts $\frac{1}{12}$ of the strip for another project. Bed slats for one doll bed take $\frac{1}{8}$ of a strip.

$\frac{1}{12}$

How many beds can Ms. Zhou make from the remaining board?

21. Calculations of surface areas and volumes often require combining measurements in different units. You can almost always make the conversions by use of rules in the form $y = kx$. Write formulas for these unit conversions.

   a. Feet F to inches I (This means to convert any given number of feet to the equivalent number of inches.)

   b. Inches I to feet F

   c. Centimeters C to meters M

   d. Meters M to centimeters C

   e. Inches I to centimeters C
   Hint: Use 1 inch = 2.54 centimeters.

22. A company that makes compost boxes of various sizes charges $500 to set up its equipment for production. It then adds a charge per box of $.15 per square foot based on the surface area of the box.

   a. The Science Club plans to order compost boxes to sell at Back-to-School Night. The boxes have length 3 feet, width 2 feet, and height 1 foot. What is the surface area of each box (without tops)?

   b. How much will it cost the club to buy 100 boxes? 200 boxes? 1,000 boxes?

   c. What equation relates cost of a box order C to number of boxes ordered n? Is this a linear relationship? Explain.

   d. If the club wants to spend at most $750 on its box order, how many boxes can it purchase?

23. The square prism below has a volume of 100 cubic centimeters. What is its height?

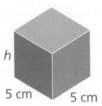

5 cm   5 cm

24. The rectangular prism below has a surface area of 158 square centimeters. What is its height?

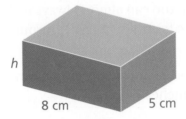

8 cm   5 cm

25. Four friends share $\frac{3}{5}$ of a rectangular pizza.

    a. What fraction of the pizza did each receive?

    b. Draw a diagram to illustrate your answer.

26. Mr. Bouck is making snack bars for a camping trip. The recipe calls for $\frac{3}{8}$ stick of butter. Mr. Bouck has $3\frac{1}{2}$ sticks on hand.

    a. How many batches of the recipe can Mr. Bouck make?

    b. Draw a diagram to illustrate your answer.

27. Taye plans to plant an herb garden in a glass tank. A scoop of dirt fills 0.15 of the volume of the tank. Taye needs to put in dirt equal to 65% of the volume. How many scoops of dirt does he need?

0.15 of volume

28. a. The dimensions of a recreation center floor are 150 feet by 90 feet. The walls of the recreation center are 20 feet high. A gallon of paint will cover about 400 square feet. About how much paint is needed to paint the walls of the recreation center?

b. If a gallon of paint costs $25.50, about how much will it cost to buy the paint for the recreation center walls?

Extensions

29. The number cubes used in many games of chance have the special property that the numbers on opposite faces always add to 7.

a. Draw a net that you can assemble into a cube.

b. Enter the numbers 1, 2, 3, 4, 5, and 6 on the net in a way that guarantees the number cube made from that net meets the condition of opposite faces adding to 7.

c. Is there more than one way to enter the numbers on your particular net? Why or why not?

30. The net for any 1-inch cube will have six 1-inch squares arranged in some pattern.

a. Considering only area, how many nets for 1-inch cubes should you be able to cut from a rectangle that is 9 inches long and 4 inches wide?

b. Can you find a way to actually cut that number of cube nets in the pattern shown below from a 9×4 rectangle? Why or why not?

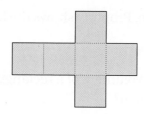

31. Each expression below will help you to find either the volume or surface area of one of the boxes pictured. Simplify each expression. Decide whether you have found a volume or a surface area, and for which box.

   a. $2 \times (3.5 \times 5.7) + 2 \times (5.7 \times 12) + 2 \times (3.5 \times 12)$

   b. $6\frac{1}{4} \times 6$

   c. $6 \times 6\frac{1}{2}$

   d. $2\frac{1}{3} \times 2\frac{2}{5} \times 5$

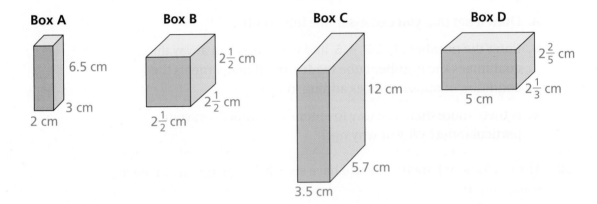

Box A   **Box B**   **Box C**   **Box D**

Box A: 6.5 cm, 3 cm, 2 cm

Box B: $2\frac{1}{2}$ cm, $2\frac{1}{2}$ cm, $2\frac{1}{2}$ cm

Box C: 12 cm, 5.7 cm, 3.5 cm

Box D: $2\frac{2}{5}$ cm, $2\frac{1}{3}$ cm, 5 cm

32. **a.** What is the formula for the surface area of a rectangular prism with length ℓ, width w, and height h?

   b. If you stretch or shrink a rectangular prism with dimensions ℓ, w, and h by a scale factor of f, what will be the surface area of the new rectangular prism?

   c. Explain how the Distributive Property shows the following:

$$\text{Area}_{\text{new}} = f^2 \cdot \text{Area}_{\text{original}}$$

33. **a.** What is the formula for the volume V of a rectangular prism with length ℓ, width w, and height h?

   b. If you stretch or shrink a rectangular prism with dimensions ℓ, w, and h by a scale factor of f, what will be the volume V of the new rectangular prism?

   c. Explain how the expression in part (b) shows the following:

$$\text{Volume}_{\text{new}} = f^3 \cdot \text{Volume}_{\text{original}}$$

In this Investigation you reviewed basic properties of rectangular prisms. You also explored the connections between surface area and volume of those three-dimensional figures. The following questions will help you summarize what you have learned.

Think about these questions. Discuss your ideas with other students and your teacher. Then write a summary of your findings in your notebook.

1. **How** can you calculate the volume and surface area of a rectangular prism from measures of its length, width, and height? Explain why this works.

2. **How** are the surface area and volume of a rectangular prism related to each other?

3. **How** will the surface area and volume of a prism change in each of the following cases?

   a. You increase or reduce one dimension by a scale factor of f.

   b. You increase or reduce two dimensions by a scale factor of f.

   c. You increase or reduce all three dimensions by a scale factor of f.

Common Core Mathematical Practices

As you worked on the Problems in this Investigation, you used prior knowledge to make sense of them. You also applied Mathematical Practices to solve the Problems. Think back over your work, the ways you thought about the Problems, and how you used Mathematical Practices.

Hector described his thoughts in the following way:

> In all the Problems of this Investigation, we had to reason about what type of measure we needed to answer the questions. Did we need to count square units or cubic units?
>
> Sometimes we counted the units. Other times, we realized it was more efficient to use the formulas for volume and surface area of rectangular prisms. Then we had to make sure that our answers made sense for the Problems.
>
> **Common Core Standards for Mathematical Practice**
> **MP2** Reason abstractly and quantitatively.

 • What other Mathematical Practices can you identify in Hector's reasoning?

• Describe a Mathematical Practice that you and your classmates used to solve a different Problem in this Investigation.

Polygonal Prisms

A **right prism** is a three-dimensional shape with a top and a base that are congruent polygons and lateral faces that are rectangles. The boxes you studied in Investigation 1 were all right prisms. In each case the congruent base and top were rectangles, so they could also be called right rectangular prisms. There are many other interesting and useful types of right prisms. If the bases are regular polygons, then the prism is called a **regular prism**. The prisms below all have the same height.

- How does a prism change as the number of sides of its base increases?

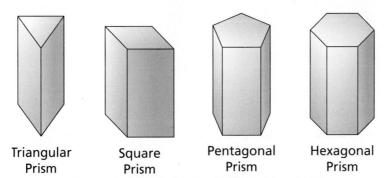

| Triangular Prism | Square Prism | Pentagonal Prism | Hexagonal Prism |

Suppose you filled the triangular prism with rice and poured the rice into each of the other prisms.

- How do you think the volumes compare?

- What about the surface area?

Common Core State Standards

7.NS.A.3 Solve real-world and mathematical problems involving the four operations with rational numbers.

7.G.A.3 Describe the two-dimensional figures that result from slicing three-dimensional figures, as in plane sections of right rectangular prisms and right rectangular pyramids.

7.G.B.6 Solve real-world and mathematical problems involving area, volume and surface area of two- and three-dimensional objects composed of triangles, quadrilaterals, polygons, cubes, and right prisms.

In this Investigation, you will discover ways to make different kinds of prisms. You will also develop strategies for measuring their surface areas and volumes.

2.1 Folding Paper
Surface Area and Volume of Prisms

You can make models of prisms (with open tops and bottoms) by folding paper. For example, the next sketch shows how to make a triangular prism.

Directions for Making Paper Prisms
(These paper models are open at the top and bottom.)

- Start with four identical sheets of paper.

- Use the shorter dimension as the height for each prism.

- Make a *triangular* prism by marking and folding one of the sheets of paper into three congruent rectangles. Tape the paper into the shape of a triangular prism.

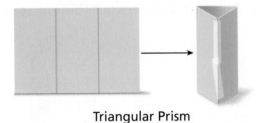

Triangular Prism

- Make a *square* prism by marking, folding, and taping a sheet of paper into four congruent rectangles.

- Make a *pentagonal* prism by marking, folding, and taping a sheet of paper into five congruent rectangles.

- Make a *hexagonal* prism by marking, folding, and taping a sheet of paper into six congruent rectangles.

- Make an *octagonal* prism by marking, folding, and taping a sheet of paper into eight congruent rectangles.

Models like this are very helpful in studying patterns in the surface area and volume of different prisms.

 How is finding the surface area of any prism like finding the surface area of a rectangular prism?

Problem 2.1

A Assume the prisms have a top and bottom. Make any measurements needed to find the surface area of each prism you construct.

1. Complete this table:

Surface Areas of Prisms

Prism Type	Area of Sides	Area of Top and Bottom	Total Surface Area
Triangular	▪	▪	▪
Square	▪	▪	▪
Pentagonal	▪	▪	▪
Hexagonal	▪	▪	▪
Octagonal	▪	▪	▪

2. How do the surface areas of the five prisms compare as the number of faces in the prisms increases?

3. Describe a strategy for finding the surface area of a prism.

B How do the volumes of the five prisms compare as the number of faces in a prism increases? Explain.

C 1. How could you use another identical sheet of paper to make a figure whose volume is greater than the volume of any of the polygonal prisms in Question A? What might it look like?

2. How would the surface area of that figure compare to the surface areas of the polygonal prisms in Question A?

Note: Keep your prism models for use later in this Unit.

 Homework starts on page 35.

2.2 Packing a Prism
Calculating Volume of Prisms

To calculate the exact volume of a rectangular prism, you could visualize packing it with layers of identical cubes. This works well for square prisms.

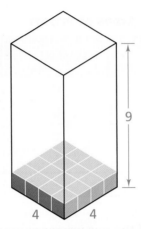

It is impossible to pack a triangular prism with cubes in the same way. But, consider the special case of a prism whose base is a right triangle. The figure below shows how you could visualize packing this prism with cubes and parts of cubes.

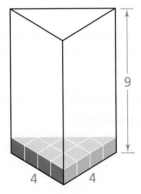

• How many cubes would you need to fill the prism?

• How can you find the volume of any prism?

• Compare it to finding the volume of a rectangular prism.

Problem 2.2

A Use these prisms to answer the questions below.

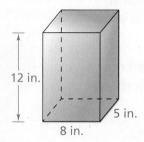
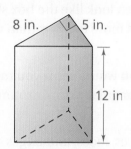

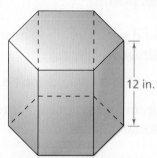

Area of the Base: about 166 in.²

1. How are the volumes of the prisms related?

2. Describe a general strategy for finding the volume of each prism. How does your strategy help you compare the volumes of the prisms?

B 1. A triangular prism has a right triangle base with one leg 4 inches and the other leg 7 inches. The height of the prism is 11 inches. What is its volume?

2. What is the volume of an octagonal prism whose base area is 15 square centimeters and whose height is 4.5 centimeters?

C Describe a strategy for finding the volume of any prism. Give examples.

A C E Homework starts on page 35.

2.3 Slicing Prisms and Pyramids

Pictures of boxes often look like the box shown at the right. But there is more to a box than what you see in a picture.

Think about what you would see if you turned the box, or another rectangular prism, around to show all of its sides.

- How many vertices, faces, and edges does the pastry box have? Would these answers be different for larger or smaller prisms?

Now, think about what you would see if you stood near a very large rectangular prism such as a railroad freight car.

- How many vertices, edges, and faces would you be able to see?

- What shapes would result from making one cut through the pastry box, the freight car, or another rectangular prism?

 Many cities in cold climates celebrate winter with a carnival. Ice sculptures are often among the highlights of winter celebrations. Sculptors start with blocks of ice in the shape of rectangular prisms. Then, they use tools to create spectacular frozen works of art.

• What shapes would result from making one cut through a rectangular prism?

• Can you make triangular, pentagonal, hexagonal, and other prisms by carving parts off a rectangular prism?

To figure out strategies for carving polygonal prisms out of rectangular prisms, you can experiment with a block of clay and a wire clay cutter. However, once a cut is made it is hard to put the pieces back together. So it helps to think before carving.

Problem 2.3

Think about each question and then test your ideas with actual cuts applied to blocks of clay.

A Start with a square prism. For each part, explain how you could make each prism with a minimum number of cuts into the square prism.

1. A triangular prism

2. A pentagonal prism

3. A hexagonal prism

B Some interesting shapes result when you cut prisms from different angles. Suppose that you start with a square prism like those shown below and make one cut in the directions indicated by the dashed lines. Answer the following questions for each prism.

• What are the shapes of the two resulting figures?

• What are the shapes of the faces of the figures?

• How many vertices, edges, and faces does each figure have?

 1. 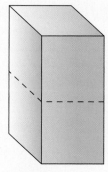   **2.**    **3.**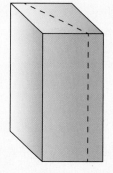

continued on the next page >

Problem 2.3 *continued*

C A **pyramid** is a solid figure with a polygonal base and triangular faces that rise to a common vertex. There are many famous pyramids, such as the ancient great pyramids of Egypt. Some modern buildings are also shaped like pyramids.

1. How could you make cuts into a cube to produce a square pyramid with one side of the cube as its base? Sketch your ideas.

2. How could you make cuts into a cube to produce a triangular pyramid—a pyramid that has triangles for all four sides? Sketch your ideas.

3. Suppose you start with a square pyramid and make one slice. Predict the shape of the two solids that result from the cut. Confirm your conjecture by cutting such a pyramid.

 Homework starts on page 35.

Applications

1. Suppose that the polygons below were drawn on centimeter grid paper. How many 1-centimeter cubes (some cut in pieces) would it take to cover each polygon?

   a.

   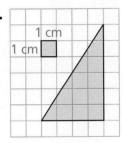

   b.

   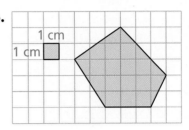

   c.

   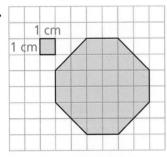

2. Using the method from Problem 2.1, Darius and Mariana made paper prisms from 4 inch-by-6 inch pieces of paper. One has an equilateral triangle for its base, another has a square base, and the third has a regular hexagon for its base. The height of each prism is 4 inches.

   To find the areas of the base and top polygons, they traced and measured those figures, as accurately as they could, to get the data shown below. The figures are not drawn to scale.

   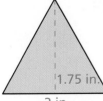
   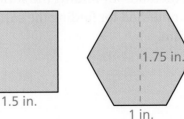

   a. What are the areas of the sides of each prism?

   b. What are the perimeters of the bases (and tops) of the each prism?

   c. What are the areas of the bases (and tops) of each prism?

For Exercises 3–5, use a copy of each of the figures on centimeter grid paper. Cut out each figure and tape it together to make a prism. Use the resulting prisms to answer parts (a) and (b) for each figure.

3.

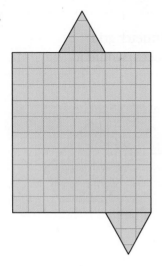

4.

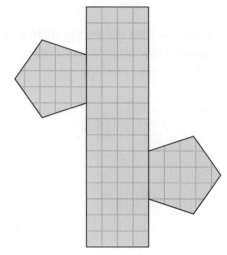

5.

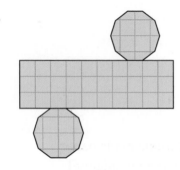

   a. What is the surface area of each prism? Explain your reasoning.

   b. What is the volume of each prism? Explain your reasoning.

6. **a.** Describe how to find the surface area of any prism.

    b. Compare your methods for finding the surface area of any prism with your method for finding the surface area of a rectangular prism.

7. **a.** Describe how to find the volume of any prism.

    b. Compare your methods for finding the volume of any prism with your method for finding the volume of a rectangular prism.

8. Suppose that the figures shown in Exercise 1 are the bases of prisms that are 10 centimeters tall (a triangular prism, a pentagonal prism, and an octagonal prism). What is the volume of each prism?

9. Use your answers to Exercise 2 to find the volumes of the prisms that Darius and Mariana created.

    a. The triangular prism

    b. The square prism

    c. The hexagonal prism

    d. Do the results in parts (a)–(c) fit the same pattern relating areas and volumes of the three prisms as your work in Problem 2.1? Why or why not?

10. Side and top views of a prism whose base and top are equilateral triangles are shown below.

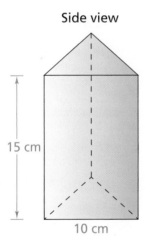

Side view

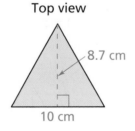

Top view

15 cm

10 cm

8.7 cm

10 cm

    a. What is the surface area of the prism?

    b. What is the volume of the prism?

11. The sketch below shows side and top views of a prism with base and top that are regular pentagons.

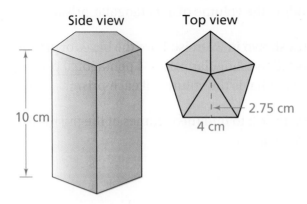

Side view   Top view

10 cm   2.75 cm   4 cm

a. What is the surface area of the prism?

b. What is the volume of the prism?

12. For Problem 2.1, Sheryl made paper prisms that were all 8.5 inches high. She traced the polygon bases on 1-inch grid paper to give a picture like the one shown below. Estimate the volume of each prism.

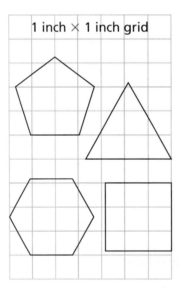

1 inch × 1 inch grid

13. Suppose that you slice three triangular prisms as shown below.

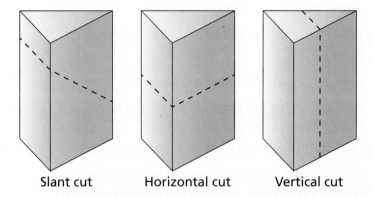

Slant cut   Horizontal cut   Vertical cut

For each cut, answer the following questions.

- How many faces will there be on each figure created by the slice?
- What different polygons appear as faces on each figure?

14. a. What kinds of figures will result if you cut a square pyramid along one edge as shown below? Describe the number and shapes of the faces of the new figures formed.

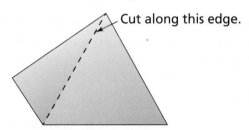

Cut along this edge.

b. What kinds of figures will result if you cut into a square pyramid as shown below? Describe the number and shapes of the faces of the new figures formed.

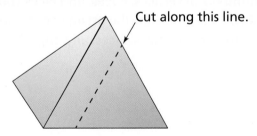

Cut along this line.

Connections

15. Suppose that you are looking at a building in the shape of a triangular prism.

a. How many vertices, edges, and faces would the prism have?

b. What are the greatest numbers of vertices, edges, and faces you would be able to see? How could you view the prism in order to see the maximum number of vertices, edges, and faces?

c. What are the smallest numbers of vertices, edges, and faces you would be able to see? How could you view the prism in order to see only the minimum number of vertices, faces, and edges?

16. Suppose that you are looking at a building in the shape of a prism with regular pentagons for base and top.

a. How many vertices, edges, and faces would the prism have?

b. What are the greatest numbers of vertices, edges, and faces you would be able to see? How could you view the prism in order to see the maximum number of vertices, edges, and faces?

c. What are the smallest numbers of vertices, edges, and faces you would be able to see? How could you view the prism in order to see only the minimum number of vertices, faces, and edges?

17. Suppose that you are looking at a large square pyramid.

a. How many vertices, edges, and faces would the pyramid have?

b. What are the greatest numbers of vertices, edges, and faces you would be able to see? How could you view the prism in order to see the maximum number of vertices, edges, and faces?

c. What are the smallest numbers of vertices, edges, and faces you would be able to see? How could you view the prism in order to see only the minimum number of vertices, faces, and edges?

18. The figure below shows a rectangle drawn on a grid of identical squares.

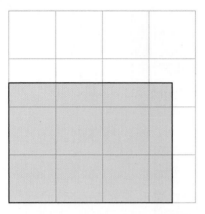

   a. What is $3\frac{1}{2} \times 2\frac{1}{2}$? How does the diagram confirm your result?

   b. What is 3.5×2.5? How does the diagram confirm your result?

19. The regular octagon in the figure below is enclosed in a square.

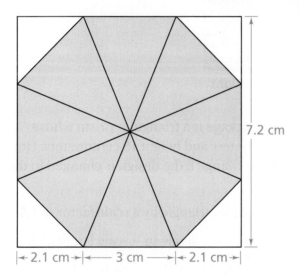

7.2 cm

|← 2.1 cm →|←——— 3 cm ———→|← 2.1 cm →|

   a. Does the calculation $8(0.5 \times 3 \times 3.6)$ give the area of the octagon? Why or why not?

   b. Does the calculation $(7.2 \times 7.2) - 4(0.5 \times 2.1 \times 2.1)$ give the area of the octagon? Why or why not?

For Exercises 20–22, use the three given views of a three-dimensional figure to sketch the figure itself. Then, find its volume.

20.

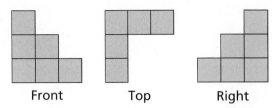

Front   Top   Right

21.

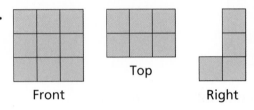

Front   Top   Right

22.

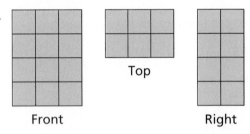

Front   Top   Right

23. Suppose that the design of a package is a triangular prism whose base has area 12 square centimeters and height 15 centimeters. How will the volume of the package change if the design is changed in the following ways?

 a. The base is stretched to a similar triangle by a scale factor of 1.5.

 b. The base is stretched to a similar triangle by a scale factor of 3.

 c. The base is shrunk to a similar triangle by a scale factor of 0.6.

 d. The height of the prism is increased by a factor of 3.

 e. The height of the prism is increased to 18 centimeters.

24. The figure below shows four rectangles on a grid of squares.

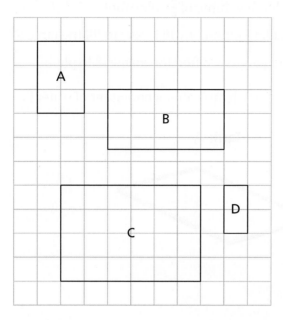

a. Which pairs of rectangles are similar? Explain.

b. Suppose that a fifth rectangle has length 12 and is similar to rectangle D in the figure above. What must be the width of the fifth rectangle?

25. Suppose you are standing inside a large rectangular prism, such as your school's gymnasium.

a. What are the greatest numbers of vertices, edges, and faces you could see by moving your eyes, but not moving your head? Where would you stand?

b. What are the smallest numbers of vertices, edges, and faces you could see by moving your eyes, but not moving your head? Where would you stand?

26. Kwan has two prism-shaped containers. One has a volume of $3\frac{3}{4}$ cubic feet. The other has a volume of $\frac{1}{3}$ cubic foot.

a. How many of the smaller container will it take to fill the larger?

b. What operation(s) did you use to find the answer? Explain.

27. Antonia has two prism-shaped containers. One has a volume of $2\frac{2}{5}$ cubic feet. The other has a volume of $\frac{2}{3}$ cubic foot.

   a. How many of the smaller container will it take to fill the larger?

   b. What operation(s) did you use to find the answer? Explain.

28. The diagram below shows a fish tank after a container of water is poured into it.

Tank A

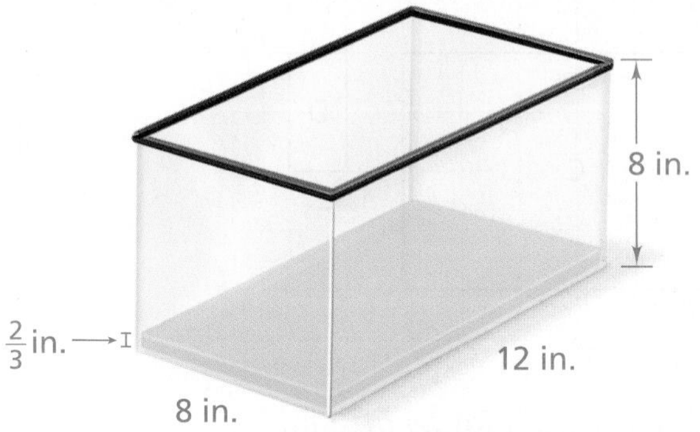

$\frac{2}{3}$ in. ⟶

8 in.

8 in.

12 in.

   a. Using the same container, how many containers of water are needed to fill the tank?

   b. What fraction of the tank does the container fill?

   c. A different container holds $12\frac{3}{4}$ cubic inches of water. How many of these containers are needed to fill the tank?

29. The diagram below shows a fish tank after a container of water is poured into it.

Tank B

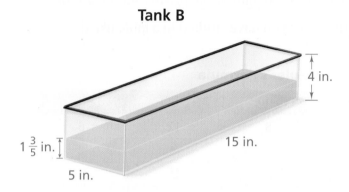

4 in.

$1\frac{3}{5}$ in.

15 in.

5 in.

a. Using the same container, how many containers of water are needed to fill the tank?

b. What fraction of the tank does the container fill?

c. A different container holds $4\frac{4}{9}$ cubic inches of water. How many of these containers are needed to fill the tank?

Extensions

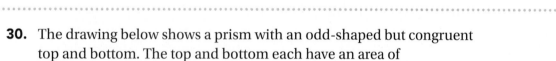

30. The drawing below shows a prism with an odd-shaped but congruent top and bottom. The top and bottom each have an area of 10 square centimeters. The height of the prism is 4 centimeters.

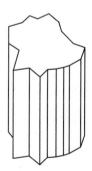

a. What is the volume of the prism? Explain your reasoning.

b. Is your estimate for the volume more than, less than, or equal to the exact volume? Explain.

31. Leonhard Euler made contributions in many areas of mathematics. One of his most widely known discoveries is a formula relating the vertices, edges, and faces of solid figures like prisms and pyramids.

a. Record data about figures you have studied in a table like the one below.

Euler's Formula

Figure	Vertices	Edges	Faces
Rectangular Prism	8	12	6
Triangular Prism	▨	▨	▨
Pentagonal Prism	▨	▨	▨
Hexagonal Prism	▨	▨	▨
Triangular Pyramid	▨	▨	▨
Square Pyramid	▨	▨	▨

b. Study the data to see if you can discover Euler's Formula relating the number of vertices V, edges E, and faces F in figures such as the prisms and pyramids you have studied.

c. Test your ideas by counting vertices, faces, and edges on other solid figures that have polygonal faces.

In this Investigation, you studied the effects of cutting right rectangular prisms. You also developed methods for finding the volumes and surface areas of prisms. The following questions will help you summarize what you learned.

Think about these questions. Discuss your ideas with other students and your teacher. Then write a summary of your findings in your notebook.

1. **How** can you find the surface area of any right prism? Explain why your method works.

2. **How** can you find the volume of any right prism? Explain why your method works.

3. **What** two- and three-dimensional shapes result when a right rectangular prism is cut by

   a. a horizontal slice?

   b. a vertical slice?

   c. a slanted slice?

Common Core Mathematical Practices

As you worked on the Problems in this Investigation, you used prior knowledge to make sense of them. You also applied Mathematical Practices to solve the Problems. Think back over your work, the ways you thought about the Problems, and how you used Mathematical Practices.

Jayden described his thoughts in the following way:

In Problem 2.1, we compared the volume of various prisms made from identical sheets of paper. We used the paper models and filled them with rice.

We conjectured that the more we increased the number of sides, the larger the volume would get. We were not able to show that this was true until we used grid paper in Problem 2.2. This helped us to be more accurate with our measurements.

....

Common Core Standards for Mathematical Practice

MP5 Use appropriate tools strategically.

- What other Mathematical Practices can you identify in Jayden's reasoning?

- Describe a Mathematical Practice that you and your classmates used to solve a different Problem in this Investigation.

Investigation 3

Area and Circumference of Circles

Many common and important three-dimensional objects are not defined by the straight edges and flat surfaces of prisms and pyramids. For example, you see *cylinders* in the shape of soup cans, pipelines, and telescopes.

The key to describing and measuring curved figures such as cylinders is understanding circles. The goal of this Investigation is to develop and apply formulas related to circles.

···

Common Core State Standards

7.G.B.4 Know the formulas for the area and circumference of a circle and use them to solve problems; give an informal derivation of the relationship between the circumference and area of a circle.

7.G.B.6 Solve real-world and mathematical problems involving area, volume and surface area of two- and three-dimensional objects composed of triangles, quadrilaterals, polygons, cubes, and right prisms.

Also 7.NS.A.3, 7.EE.A.1, 7.EE.A.2

3.1 Going Around in Circles
Circumference

The most popular shape for pizzas is a circle. Many pizza restaurants sell small, medium, and large pizzas. Of course, the prices are different for the three sizes.

- How do you think pizza makers set the prices for pizzas of different sizes?

- Is a large pizza usually the best buy?

The size of a circular pizza is usually described by its diameter. The **diameter** of a circle is any line segment from a point on a circle through the center point to another point on the circle.

Radius, area, and circumference are also useful terms for describing the size of a circle. A **radius** is any line segment from the center of a circle to a point on the circle.

Circumference means perimeter in the language of circles. It is the distance around the circle.

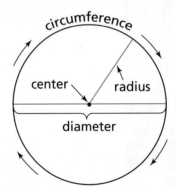

Area is a measure of how many square units it takes to exactly cover the region inside the circle.

To set the prices of pizzas, restaurants might need to find the circumference of each pizza.

 What is the relationship between the diameter or radius of a circle and its circumference?

Problem 3.1

A Use a tape measure or string to measure the circumference and diameter of several different circular objects. Make a table like the one below. Record the object name, diameter, circumference, and ratio of circumference to diameter.

Measurements of Circular Objects

Object Name	Diameter	Circumference	Ratio of $\dfrac{\text{Circumference}}{\text{Diameter}}$
▦	▦	▦	▦
▦	▦	▦	▦
▦	▦	▦	▦

B Study your results from Question A. Look for a pattern relating the circumference and the diameter. Test your ideas on some other circular objects.

1. Can you find the circumference of a circle if you know its diameter? If so, how?

2. Can you find the diameter of a circle if you know its circumference? If so, how?

ACE Homework starts on page 58.

3.2 Pricing Pizza
Connecting Area, Diameter, and Radius

A pizzeria plans to sell three sizes of its new pizza with cheese in the crust. A small pizza will be 9 inches in diameter, a medium will be 12 inches in diameter, and a large will be 15 inches in diameter.

The owner surveyed her lunch customers to find out what they would be willing to pay for a small pizza.

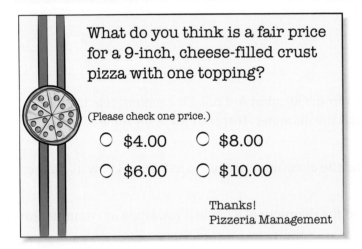

What do you think is a fair price for a 9-inch, cheese-filled crust pizza with one topping?

(Please check one price.)

○ $4.00   ○ $8.00

○ $6.00   ○ $10.00

Thanks!
Pizzeria Management

She found that $6 was a fair price for a 9-inch pizza with one topping. Based on this price, the owner wants to find fair prices for 12- and 15-inch pizzas with one topping.

• What prices would you suggest for the larger pizzas?

One of the cooks suggests making the difference in prices match the difference in pizza diameters, but the owner disagrees. She says that area is the best measurement to use to set the prices. She also says that comparing areas would suggest different prices from comparing diameters. Together, the cook and the owner wonder about the following question:

• What is the relationship, if any, between the diameter or radius of a circle and its area?

Problem 3.2

To answer this question, the owner uses the scale models of the different size pizzas shown below.

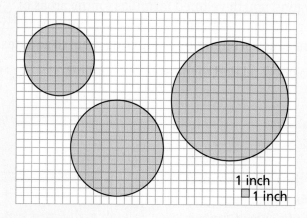

1 inch
☐ 1 inch

A Find as many different ways as you can to estimate the area of each pizza. For each method, give your estimate for the area and describe how you found it.

B Copy the table. Record each pizza's diameter, radius, and your estimate of its area.

Pizza Measurements

Size	Diameter (in.)	Radius (in.)	Area (in.²)
Small	▪	▪	▪
Medium	▪	▪	▪
Large	▪	▪	▪

C Examine the data in the table and your strategies for finding area.

1. Describe the pattern relating area to diameter or radius.

2. What would be your best estimate for the area of a circle with diameter 18 inches?

D Based on your area estimations, what would be fair prices for medium and large pizzas? Explain your reasoning.

A C E Homework starts on page 58.

3.3 Squaring a Circle to Find Its Area

In earlier study of polygons, you developed formulas for the areas of triangles and parallelograms by comparing them to rectangles. You can discover more about the areas of circles by comparing them to squares.

- How is the area of a circle related to the area of a square?

Problem 3.3

In the drawing at the right, a shaded square covers a portion of each circle. The length of a side of the shaded square is the same length as the radius of the circle. You call such a square a "radius square."

A 1. Make a table like the one below. Record the circle number, radius, area of the radius square, area of the circle, and number of radius squares needed to cover each circle.

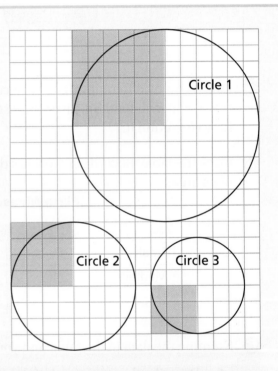

Circle 1

Circle 2   Circle 3

Circle	Radius of Circle (units)	Area of Radius Square (square units)	Area of Circle (square units)	Number of Radius Squares Needed
1	▪	▪	▪	▪
2	▪	▪	▪	▪
3	▪	▪	▪	▪

Problem 3.3 *continued*

2. Describe any patterns and relationships you see in the table that will allow you to predict the area of the circle from its radius square. Test your ideas on some other circular objects.

B 1. How can you find the area of a circle if you know the radius?

2. How can you find the radius of a circle if you know the area?

A C E Homework starts on page 58.

Did You Know?

You have discovered that the circumference of a circle is a little more than three times the diameter. The area of a circle is a little more than three times the square of the radius. The number "a little more than 3" is the same in both circumference and area calculations. It is given exactly by a decimal with infinitely many decimal digits beginning 3.14159265 …

In 1706, William Jones used the Greek letter π (also written as pi and pronounced "pie") to stand for the distance around a circle with a diameter of 1 unit.

William Jones

As early as 2000 B.C., the Babylonians knew that π was more than 3. Their estimate for π was $3\frac{1}{8}$. By the fifth century A.D., Chinese mathematician Tsu Chung-Chi wrote that π was somewhere between 3.1415926 and 3.1415927. From 1436 to 1874, the known value of π went from 14 places past the decimal point to 707 places.

In the past 50 years, mathematicians have used computers to calculate millions more digits in the decimal for π. They have shown that π cannot be expressed as a fraction with whole numbers in the numerator and denominator. Such numbers expressed as unending decimals that have no repeating pattern are called *irrational numbers*.

Tsu Chung-Chi

3.4 Connecting Circumference and Area

The special number $\pi \approx 3.14159\ldots$ plays a central role in calculating both circumferences and areas of circles. The rules for finding circumference and area of any circle are expressed in algebraic symbols by the formulas $C = \pi d$, or $C = 2\pi r$, and $A = \pi r^2$. Circumference and area tell quite different things about a circle. However, there is a clever way to show how circumference and area fit together.

 Suppose that you cut a large circular pizza into 8 identical slices. You can reposition those slices to make a shape that is very close to a parallelogram:

 How are the circle and the parallelogram related?

Problem 3.4

Ⓐ The radius of the circular pizza is 6 inches. What are its circumference and area?

Ⓑ The shape made by re-arranging the pizza slices looks like a parallelogram.

1. Estimate the height and base of the parallelogram. Explain your reasoning.

2. What is the approximate area of the parallelogram?

3. How does the approximate area of the parallelogram compare to the exact area of the circular pizza?

Ⓒ The connection between the area of the circular pizza and the area of the near-parallelogram formed when the pizza slices are rearranged is only an approximation.

Sara thinks about the parallelogram and says that the area of a circle is $A = \frac{1}{2}(\pi d)(r)$.

Evan thinks about covering the circle with radius squares and says the area is $A = \pi r^2$.

1. Do these formulas give the same area for radius 6 centimeters?

2. Would both formulas work for all values of r? Why or why not?

3. How would the accuracy of the approximation change if you cut the pizza into more slices?

Ⓓ Suppose that you have 12 meters of fencing and want to make a pen for your pet dog.

Which shape, a square or a circle, would give more area? Explain.

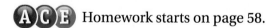

Homework starts on page 58.

Applications

For Exercises 1–4, identify the part of the circle drawn in red as
its circumference, diameter, or radius. Then, measure that part
in centimeters.

1.

2.

3.

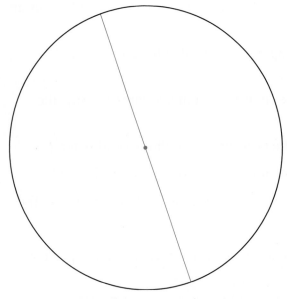

4.

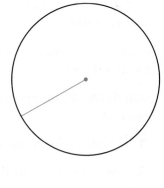

5. Use your measurements from Exercises 1–4 to find the measure of
the part of each circle in black.

6. Trace the circle at the right and draw three different diameters.

    a. What is the measure, in centimeters, of each diameter?

    b. What can you say about the measures of diameters in a circle?

    c. Estimate the circumference of this circle using the diameter measurements you found.

7. Trace this circle and draw three different radii. (RAY dee eye, the plural for radius).

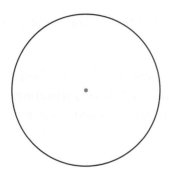

    a. What is the measure, in centimeters, of each radius?

    b. What can you say about the measures of the radii in the same circle?

    c. Estimate the circumference of this circle using the radius measurements you found.

8. Terrell says that when you know the radius of a circle, you can find the diameter by doubling the radius. Do you agree? Why or why not?

9. Enrique says that when you know the diameter of a circle you can find the radius. How can he find the length of a radius if he knows the length of the diameter?

10. **Multiple Choice** A juice can is about 2.25 inches in diameter. What is its circumference?

    A. 3.53 in.   **B.** 3.97 in.^{2}

    C. 7.065 in.   **D.** 14.13 in.

11. A pizzeria sells three different sizes of pizza. The small size has a radius of 4 inches, the medium size has a radius of 5 inches, and the large size has a radius of 6 inches.

    a. Copy and complete the table. Explain how you found the areas of the pizzas.

Pizza Measurements

Pizza Size	Diameter (in.)	Radius (in.)	Circumference (in.)	Area (in.²)
Small	▦	▦	▦	▦
Medium	▦	▦	▦	▦
Large	▦	▦	▦	▦

    b. Jamar claims the area of a pizza is about $0.75 \times (\text{diameter})^2$. Is he correct? Explain.

For Exercises 12–16, some common circular objects are described by giving their radius or diameter. Explain what useful information (if any) you would get from calculating the area or circumference of the object.

12. $4\frac{5}{8}$ -inch-diameter compact disc

13. 21-inch-diameter bicycle wheel

14. 12-inch-diameter water pipe

15. lawn sprinkler that sprays a 15-meter-radius section of lawn

16. a 9-inch-diameter round cake pan

17. Pick one of the objects from Exercises 12–16 and write a problem about it. Be sure to give the answer to your problem.

For Exercises 18–22, you may want to make scale drawings on grid paper to help find the missing measurements.

18. Derek's dinner plate has a diameter of about 9 inches. Find its circumference and area.

19. A bicycle wheel is about 26 inches in diameter. Find its radius, circumference, and area.

20. The spray from a lawn sprinkler makes a circle 40 feet in radius. What are the approximate diameter, circumference, and area of the circle of lawn watered?

21. An old-fashioned Long Play (LP) record (that people used for listening to music in the past) has a 12-inch diameter; a compact disc has a $4\frac{5}{8}$-inch diameter.

a. Find the radius, circumference, and area of each object. For the area, disregard the hole in the center of each object.

b. How many trips around the compact disc would equal one trip around the LP record?

c. How many compact discs (cut into pieces) would it take to cover the LP record? Disregard the hole in the center of each object.

22. A rectangular lawn has a perimeter of 36 meters and a circular exercise run has a circumference of 36 meters. Which shape will give Rico's dog more area to run? Explain.

23. The swimming pool at the right is a rectangle with a semicircle at one end. What are the area and perimeter of the pool?

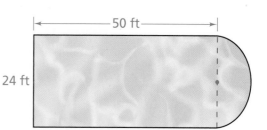

50 ft

24 ft

For Exercises 24–29, estimate the area in square centimeters and the perimeter or circumference in centimeters.

24.

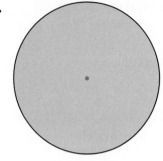

25.

26.

27.

28.

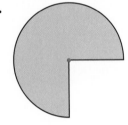

29.

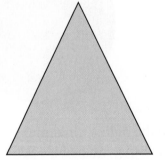

For Exercises 30 and 31, use these figures. The figures are drawn to scale.

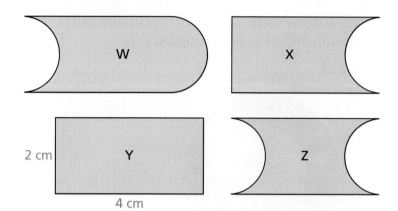

2 cm

4 cm

30. **Multiple Choice** Which answer has the figures in order from least to greatest area?

  F. W, X, Y, Z   **G.** Z, X, W or Y

  H. Y, X, Z or W   **J.** Z, Y, X, W

31. **Multiple Choice** Which answer has the figures in order from least to greatest perimeter?

  A. W, X, Y, Z   **B.** Z, X, W or Y

  C. Y, X, Z or W   **D.** Z, Y, X, W

32. A group of students submitted these designs for a school flag. The side length of each flag is 6 feet. Each flag has two colors. How much of each color of material will be needed?

  a.

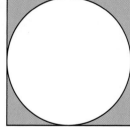

  b.

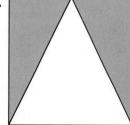

33. This circular dartboard has three circles with the same center. (These are called *concentric circles*.) The diameter of the largest circle is 20 inches. The diameters of the inner circles decrease by 4 inches as you move from the largest to the smallest. Each of the circular bands will be a different color with different points assigned to it.

Find the area of each band.

34. A circle is inscribed in a square with side length *d* units. Kaylee and Cassie were trying to find a formula for the area of a circle. They came up with two formulas for the area:

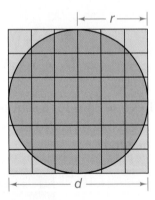

Kaylee: Area $\approx \frac{3}{4}d^2$ **Cassie:** Area $\approx 3r^2$

a. Who is correct? Explain why.

b. The class developed this formula for the area of a circle:

Area $= \pi r^2$

How do Kaylee and Cassie's formulas compare with the class formula?

c. If the diameter of a circle is 15 centimeters, what is its area?

d. If the area of a circle is 98 square inches, what is its radius?

Connections

35. Explain which measurements associated with circles would be useful in describing the size of each article of clothing.

   a. belts

   b. jeans

   c. hats

   d. shirts

36. The table shows some diameters and circumferences of circular pizzas.

Pizza Measurements

Diameter (in.)	Circumference (in.)
9	28.27
12	37.70
15	47.12
18	▓
21	▓

   a. Find the missing circumferences.

   b. Make a coordinate graph with diameter on the horizontal axis and circumference on the vertical axis.

   c. Describe the graph.

   d. Estimate the circumference of a pizza with a diameter of 20 inches.

   e. Estimate the diameter of a pizza with a circumference of 80 inches.

For Exercises 37–42, do each calculation. Then, explain how the expression could represent an area or perimeter calculation.

37. 2×10.5

38. $(4.25)^2 \times 3.14$

39. $\frac{1}{2} \times 15.25 \times 7.3$

40. $1\frac{3}{5} \times 2\frac{1}{4}$

41. $(2 \times 8) + (2 \times 10)$

42. $7\frac{1}{2} \times 3.14$

43. Kateri and Jorge are talking about the number π. Kateri says that any problem involving π has to be about circles. Jorge disagrees and shows him the example below. What do you think? Explain your reasoning.

1 in. ⬜ rectangle
π in.

For Exercises 44–46, describe the figure formed by each type of slice of the square prism.

Square Prism

44. vertical slice

45. horizontal slice

46. slanting slice

Did You Know?

You can estimate pi using probability. Take a square that is 2 units on each side. Inscribe a circle inside that has a radius of 1 unit.

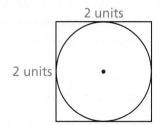

2 units

2 units

The area of the square is 4 square units. The area of the circle is πr^2 or $\pi(1)^2 = \pi$ square units.

The ratio of the area of the circle to the area of the square is $\frac{\pi}{4}$.

You can do computer simulations in which the computer randomly places a dot inside the square. A computer can place 10,000 dots inside the square in less than 30 seconds.

This ratio $\dfrac{\text{number of dots inside the circle}}{\text{total number of dots inside the square}}$ should approximate $\frac{\pi}{4}$.

So, π should equal four times the ratio $\dfrac{\text{number of dots inside the circle}}{\text{total number of dots inside the square}}$.

47. Charlie runs three computer simulations such as the one described in the *Did You Know?* box above. He records data for the three trials.

a. Copy and complete the table below of Charlie's data.

Pi Estimations

Trial	Dots Inside the Circle	Dots Inside the Square	Ratio: $\dfrac{\text{Dots in Circle}}{\text{Dots in Square}}$
1	388	500	▨
2	352	450	▨
3	373	475	▨

b. Decide which trial is closest to an approximation for $\frac{\pi}{4}$. Explain your reasoning.

Extensions

48. The diameter of Earth is approximately 42,000,000 feet. If a 6-foot-tall man walked around Earth along the equator, how much farther would his head move than his feet?

49. Suppose a piece of rope wraps around Earth. Then rope is added to make the entire rope 3 feet longer.

    a. Suppose the new rope circles Earth exactly the same distance away from the surface at all points. How far is the new rope from Earth's surface?

    b. A piece of rope is wrapped around a person's waist. Then rope is added to make it 3 inches longer. How far from the waist is the rope if the distance is the same all around?

    c. Compare the results in parts (a) and (b).

50. The Nevins want to install a circular pool with a 15-foot diameter in their rectangular patio. The patio will be surrounded by new fencing, and the patio area surrounding the pool will be covered with new tiles.

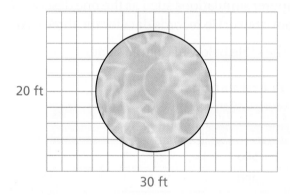

20 ft

30 ft

    a. How many feet of fencing are needed to enclose the patio?

    b. How much plastic is needed to cover the pool if there is a 1-foot overhang?

    c. How many feet of plastic tubing are needed to fit around the edge of the pool?

    d. How many square feet of ground will be covered with tiles?

In this Investigation, you explored relationships among the radius, diameter, circumference, and area of a circle. You also discovered strategies for finding the areas of circles. The following questions will help you summarize what you have learned.

Think about these questions. Discuss your ideas with other students and your teacher. Then write a summary of your findings in your notebook.

1. **How** can you find the circumference and area of a circle from measures of its radius or diameter?

2. **How** is the challenge of finding circumferences and areas of circles similar to that of finding perimeters and areas of polygons such as triangles, rectangles, and other parallelograms? **In what ways** are those tasks different?

Common Core Mathematical Practices

As you worked on the Problems in this Investigation, you used prior knowledge to make sense of them. You also applied Mathematical Practices to solve the Problems. Think back over your work, the ways you thought about the Problems, and how you used Mathematical Practices.

Tori described her thoughts in the following way:

We analyzed the best way to price a pizza in Problem 3.2. We used circles to represent the pizzas. We looked at diameter, radius, and area as ways to think about how to price a pizza in a fair way.

The prices were different depending on whether we used diameter or area. This makes sense. Since all circles are similar, the circumference (perimeter) grows by the scale factor and the area grows by the scale factor squared.

Common Core Standards for Mathematical Practice

MP4 Model with mathematics.

• What other Mathematical Practices can you identify in Tori's reasoning?

• Describe a Mathematical Practice that you and your classmates used to solve a different Problem in this Investigation.

4

Cylinders, Cones, and Spheres

A **cylinder,** such as a soup can or a barrel, is like a prism with circles for top and bottom bases. Strategies for making and measuring prisms are helpful guides to reasoning about cylinders.

The size and shape of every cylinder is set by two measurements—the height of the cylinder and either the radius or diameter of its circular base. These measurements are called the dimensions of the figure.

radius

height

base

In this Investigation, you will develop and use formulas to find the surface areas and volumes of cylinders. You will then explore relationships among the volumes of cylinders, cones, and spheres.

....

Common Core State Standards

7.NS.A.3 Solve real-world and mathematical problems involving the four operations with rational numbers.

7.G.B.4 Know the formulas for area and circumference of a circle and use them to solve problems; give an informal derivation of the relationship between the circumference and area of a circle.

7.G.B.6 Solve real-world and mathematical problems involving area, volume and surface area of two- and three-dimensional objects composed of triangles, quadrilaterals, polygons, cubes, and right prisms.

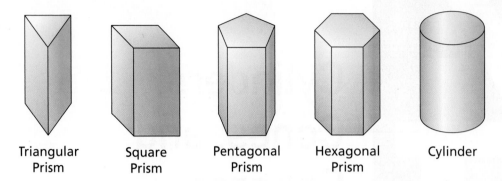

Triangular Prism Square Prism Pentagonal Prism Hexagonal Prism Cylinder

- How does the shape of a cylinder compare to the shape of a prism?

- How is finding the surface area and volume of a cylinder like, or not like, finding the surface area and volume of a prism?

4.1 Networking
Surface Area of Cylinders

When you first studied rectangular prisms in *Covering and Surrounding,* you discovered ways to make nets, or two-dimensional patterns, for prisms. From these nets, you could build boxes by folding along the edges and taping the seams together. For example, here is one possible net for a box with width 4, length 5, and height 3.

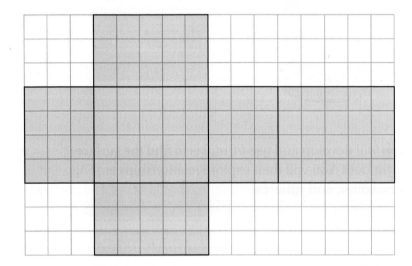

- How does the net help you find the surface area of the box?

> **?** How would a net for a cylinder help you find the surface area of the cylinder?

Problem 4.1

Nets can also help you find a formula for the surface area of any cylinder.

A Use a copy of the net shown at the right on centimeter grid paper.

1. What is the surface area of the cylinder? Explain your reasoning.

2. Cut out your net. Tape the pieces together to form a cylinder. What are the dimensions of the cylinder?

3. Describe how the dimensions of a cylinder can help you find its surface area.

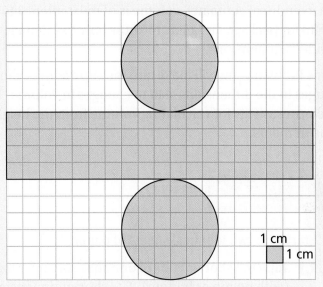

1 cm
1 cm

4. How could you change the net without changing the cylinder the plan produces?

B On centimeter grid paper, draw a net for a cylinder with a height of 5 centimeters and a base with a radius of 2 centimeters.

1. Calculate and record the dimensions of the circles and rectangle in the net.

2. Calculate the surface area of the cylinder.

C The nets you studied and designed in Questions A and B show how you can calculate the surface area of any cylinder from its dimensions.

1. Describe a strategy for calculating the surface area of any cylinder.

2. Use your strategy to find the surface area of a cylinder with a height of 7 centimeters and a base with a radius of 4 centimeters.

D Suppose you forget the formula for the surface area of a cylinder. How could you use what you just learned about nets to imagine cutting a given cylinder apart and flattening the pieces to find the surface area?

 Homework starts on page 82.

4.2 Wrapping Paper
Volume of Cylinders

Although the surface area is the best way to measure the cost of packaging for a cylindrical container, volume is of most interest to the customer. It is helpful for package designers to know how to calculate volume from a cylinder's dimensions.

In this Problem, you will make and measure some cylinders to see how changes in the dimensions lead to changes in volume. Then you will develop a strategy for calculating volume from the height and radius measurements.

Problem 4.2

Start with two identical sheets of paper.

A Tape the shorter ends of one sheet of paper together to form a cylinder (with no top or bottom). The shorter dimension of the sheet of paper is the height of the first cylinder.

1. How does the volume of this cylinder compare to the volumes of the triangular, square, pentagonal, and hexagonal prisms you made in Problem 2.1?

2. Tape the longer ends of the other sheet of paper together to form the second cylinder. The height of this cylinder is the longer dimension of the sheet of paper. Compare its volume to that of the first cylinder. Explain any differences you notice.

Problem 4.2 *continued*

B You can think about "filling" cylinders the same way that you filled prisms in Problem 2.2.

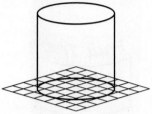 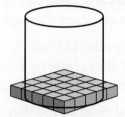 

Trace the base.   Find the number of cubes that fit in one layer.   Find the number of layers it takes to fill the cylinder.

Suppose that a cylinder has a radius of 5 centimeters and a height of 12 centimeters.

1. How many one-centimeter cubes would it take to cover that circular base? Explain.

2. How many centimeter cubes would it take to fill the entire figure? Explain.

3. If a cylinder has radius r and height h, describe a strategy for finding the volume V of the figure. Write a formula for V in terms of r and h.

C In Question A, one cylinder had a circumference equal to the length of the longer side of the sheet of paper and a height equal to the length of the shorter side. The other cylinder had the opposite dimensions. How does the formula you developed in Question B help to explain the difference in the volumes of the two cylinders?

D A cylinder with a radius of 5 cm and a height of 12 cm has a volume of 300π cm^3.

1. Which change in the dimensions of the cylinder would cause the greater change in volume: doubling the height or doubling the radius?

2. By what factor is the volume increased if both the radius and the height are increased by a factor of 2? By a factor of 3? Explain.

A C E Homework starts on page 82.

4.3 Comparing Juice Containers
Comparing Surface Areas

Fruit Tree Juice Company packages its most popular drink, cran-apple juice, in cylindrical cans. Each can is 11 centimeters high and has a radius of 2.7 centimeters.

Sales reports indicate a decline in the sales of Fruit Tree juice. At the same time, sales of juice made by a competitor, the Fruit Blast Juice Company, are on the rise.

Market researchers at Fruit Tree have determined that Fruit Blast's success is due to its new rectangular juice boxes. So, Fruit Tree has decided to package its juice in rectangular boxes.

 Problem 4.3

Fruit Tree Juice wants the new rectangular box to have the same volume as the current cylindrical can.

A On centimeter grid paper, make a net for a box that will hold the same amount of juice as the cylindrical can. Cut out your net. When you are finished, fold and tape your pattern to form a rectangular box.

  1. Give the dimensions of your juice box. Are there other possibilities for the dimensions? Explain.

  2. Compare your juice box with the boxes made by your classmates. Which rectangular box shape do you think would make the best juice container? Why?

B Compare the surface area of the cylindrical can with the surface area of your juice box.

  1. Which container has a greater surface area?

  2. If a cylinder and a rectangular box have the same volume, will the box always have a greater surface area? Explain.

 Homework starts on page 82.

4.4 Filling Cones and Spheres

Cylinders are not the only important solid figures with curved edges and faces. Balls in the shape of *spheres* play an important role in many of our most popular sports. *Cones* are used to serve ice cream and direct traffic around construction zones.

The size and shape of any **sphere** depends on the size of the radius, which is the distance from any point on the surface to its center. We can describe any sphere using this single dimension.

The size and shape of a **cone** depends on the size of two dimensions, the height and the radius of its circular base.

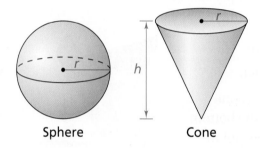

Sphere   Cone

In this Problem, you will develop strategies for calculating volumes of spheres and cones and see how changes in their dimensions cause changes in their volumes.

It is hard to measure the volume of a sphere or a cone by filling it with an exact number of unit cubes. Fortunately, there is a helpful relationship among the volumes of cylinders, spheres, and cones. A simple experiment will reveal that relationship and the formulas for the volumes of spheres and cones. In this Problem, you will make a sphere, a cone, and a cylinder, each with the same diameter and the same height.

Making the Sphere and the Cylinder

- Make a sphere from modeling clay. Measure its diameter.

- Make a cylinder with an open top and bottom from a sheet of stiff transparent plastic. Fit the cylinder snugly around the sphere. The diameter of the cylinder is equal to the diameter of the sphere.

- Trim the cylinder so that its height is equal to the vertical diameter of the sphere. Tape the sides of the cylinder together so it remains rigid.

Experimenting With the Sphere

- Flatten the clay sphere so that the clay fits snugly in the bottom of the cylinder. Mark the height of the flattened sphere on the cylinder.

- Measure and record the height and radius of the cylinder, the height of the empty space, and the height of the flattened sphere.

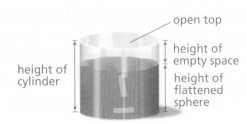

Experimenting With the Cone

- Take the clay out of the cylinder.

- Roll a piece of stiff paper into a cone shape so that the tip touches the bottom and does not have a hole at the point.

- Tape the cone shape along the seam. Trim the cone so that it is the same height (and radius) as the cylinder.

- Fill the cone to the top with sand or rice, and empty the contents into the cylinder. Repeat this as many times as needed to fill the cylinder completely. Keep track of the number of cones needed.

> **?** Do the results of the experiment suggest a relationship among the volumes of a cylinder, a sphere, and a cone? If so, describe the relationship.

Problem 4.4

A 1. Use the results of Experimenting With the Sphere to find the volume of the cylinder and the volume of the original sphere.

2. What is the relationship between the volume of the sphere and the volume of the cylinder?

Problem 4.4 *continued*

3. What formula could you use to calculate the volume of a cylinder with diameter and height both equal to *d*? What formula could you use for the volume of a sphere with diameter *d*?

4. How can the formulas in part (3) be expressed in terms of radius *r*?

B 1. What is the relationship between the volume of the cone and the volume of the cylinder?

2. How do this relationship and the formula for the volume of a cylinder suggest a formula for the volume of a cone?

C Use your formula for the volume of a sphere to complete the table.

Volumes of Spheres

Radius	Volume
1	▪
2	▪
3	▪
4	▪
5	▪
⋮	▪
10	▪

1. What pattern do you see in how the volume grows as the radius increases?

2. When the radius is doubled, how does the volume increase?

3. When the radius is tripled, how does the volume increase?

4. How is the effect of scaling up the radius similar to the patterns you noticed when you scaled up the 1-2-3 compost boxes?

D Suppose a cylinder, cone, and sphere all have the same height and that the volume of the cylinder is 64 cubic inches. Use only the relationships from Questions A and B. Describe how to find the volumes of the other shapes.

1. the sphere   2. the cone

 Homework starts on page 82.

Did You Know?

Many three-dimensional objects do not have regular shapes. According to legend, Archimedes (ahr kuh MEE deez) made an important discovery while taking a bath in the third century B.C. He noticed that the water level rose when he sat down in a tub. He determined that he could find the weight of any floating object by finding the weight of the water that the object displaced.

It is said that Archimedes was so excited about his discovery that he jumped from his bath and, without dressing, ran into the streets shouting "Eureka!," which means "I have found it!"

Archimedes

4.5 Comparing Volumes of Spheres, Cylinders, and Cones

Esther and Jasmine buy ice cream from Chilly's Ice Cream Parlor. Esther gets a scoop of ice cream in a cone, and Jasmine gets a scoop in a cylindrical cup. Each container has a height of 8 centimeters and a radius of 4 centimeters. Each scoop of ice cream is a sphere with a radius of 4 centimeters.

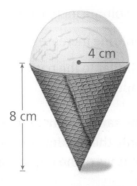

Problem 4.5

Suppose Esther and Jasmine both allow their ice cream to melt.

A Will the melted ice cream fill Esther's cone exactly?

B Will the melted ice cream fill Jasmine's cup exactly?

C How many scoops of ice cream can be packed into each container?

A C E Homework starts on page 82.

Did You Know?

Earth is nearly a sphere. You may have heard that, until 1492, most people believed Earth was flat.

Actually, as early as the fourth century B.C., scientists and mathematicians had figured out that Earth was round. When they observed the shadow of Earth as it passed across the moon during a lunar eclipse, the shadow was curved. Combining this observation with evidence gathered from observing constellations, these scientists concluded that Earth is spherical.

In the third century B.C., Eratosthenes (ayr uh TAHS thu neez), a Greek mathematician, was able to estimate the circumference of Earth.

Eratosthenes

Applications

1. Cut a sheet of paper in half so you have two identical half-sheets of paper. Tape the long sides of one sheet together to form a cylinder. Tape the short sides of the second sheet together to form another cylinder. Suppose that each cylinder has a top and a bottom.

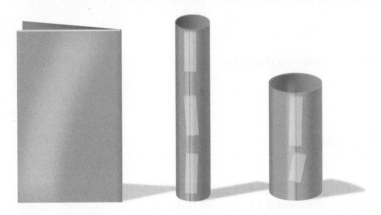

   a. Which cylinder has a greater volume? Explain.

   b. Which cylinder has a greater surface area? Explain.

2. Tennis balls are usually packaged in cylindrical containers of 3 balls like the one shown.

   a. Which measure do you think is greater—the height or the circumference of the container?

   b. How can you answer part (a) without knowing the actual diameter of a tennis ball?

3. A cylinder has a radius of 3 centimeters. Sand is poured into the cylinder to form a layer 1 centimeter deep.

    a. What is the volume of sand in the cylinder?

    b. Suppose the height of the cylinder is 20 centimeters. How many 1-centimeter deep layers of sand are needed to fill the cylinder?

    c. What is the volume of the cylinder?

For Exercises 4 and 5, find the surface area and volume of each cylinder.

    4. height = 10 cm, radius = 6.5 cm

    5. height = 6.5 cm, radius = 10 cm

6. A pipeline carrying oil is 5,000 kilometers long and has an inside diameter of 2 meters. (Remember: 1 km = 1,000 m.)

    a. How many cubic meters of oil will it take to fill 1 kilometer of the pipeline?

    b. How many cubic meters of oil will it take to fill the entire pipeline?

7. Below is a scale model of a net for a cylinder.

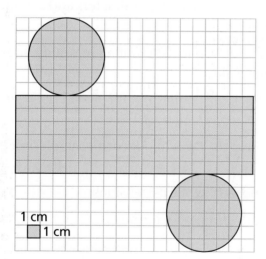

    a. Suppose the net is assembled. Find the volume of the cylinder.

    b. Find the surface area of the cylinder.

8. Suppose that a square prism is inserted into a cylinder of the same height so that side and top views of the two figures look like the diagrams below.

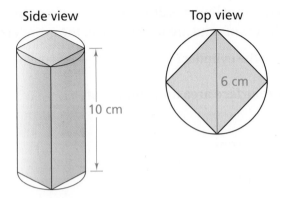

Side view   **Top view**

10 cm

6 cm

a. If the figures are both 10 centimeters in height, what are their volumes?

b. What is the ratio of cylinder volume to prism volume?

9. A popcorn vender needs to order popcorn boxes. The vendor must decide between a cylindrical box and a rectangular box (both without tops).

- The cylindrical box has a height of 20 centimeters and a radius of 7 centimeters.

- The rectangular box has a height of 20 centimeters and a square base with 12-centimeter sides.

- The cost of each box is based on the amount of material needed to make the box.

- The vendor plans to charge $2.75 for popcorn, regardless of the shape of the box.

a. Make a sketch of each box. Label the dimensions.

b. Find the volume and surface area of each box.

c. Which box would you choose? Give the reasons for your choice. What additional information might help you make a better decision?

10. A square pyramid is related to a square prism in the same way that a cone is related to a cylinder. Suppose that a square pyramid is enclosed in a square prism with base sides *s* and height *h*. What formula would you expect to give the volume of the pyramid?

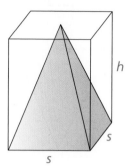

For Exercises 11 and 12, find the volume of each shape.

11.

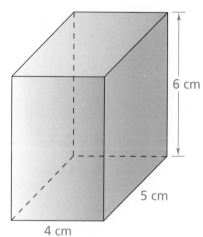

6 cm

5 cm

4 cm

12.

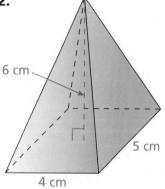

6 cm

5 cm

4 cm

13. The track and field club is planning a frozen yogurt sale to raise money. They need to buy containers to hold the yogurt. The two options are the cup and cone shown below. The two containers have the same cost. The club plans to charge $1.25 for a serving of yogurt. Which container should the club buy? Explain.

5 cm

4.5 cm

6 cm

12 cm

14. The Mathletes are planning their own frozen yogurt sale. They must choose between the prism and the square pyramid shown below, both of which have the same cost. Which container should they use? Explain.

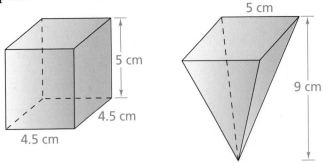

15. The prices and dimensions of several movie theater popcorn containers are shown below. Which container has the most popcorn per dollar?

| $4.00 | $2.50 | $3.75 | $3.50 |

16. Find the height of a cylinder with a radius of 3 inches and volume of 250 in.^{3}.

17. Find the height of a cone with radius of 3 inches and volume of 250 in.^{3}.

18. Suppose that a square prism and a square pyramid each have a base with sides of 3 inches and a volume of 225 in.^{3}.

a. What is the height of the prism?

b. What is the height of the pyramid?

19. A playground ball has a diameter of 18 cm.

a. Sketch a cylinder that just fits around the playground ball and label its dimensions.

b. What is the volume of the cylinder?

c. What is the volume of the ball?

For Exercises 20–21, find the volume of each sphere. In one sphere, the diameter is given. In the other, the radius is given.

20.
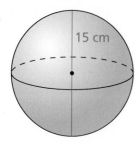
15 cm

21.
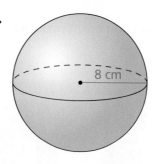
8 cm

For Exercises 22–24, each of the number sentences models the formula for the volume of a figure you have worked with in this Unit. Name, sketch, and label the dimensions of each figure. Then, find the volume.

22. $2\frac{2}{3} \times 4\frac{4}{5} \times 3\frac{7}{8}$

23. $\pi \times (2.2)^2 \times 6.5$

24. $\frac{1}{3}\pi \times (4.25)^2 \times 10$

25. Watertown has three water storage tanks in different shapes: a cylinder, a cone, and a sphere. Each tank has radius of 20 feet and height of 40 feet.

   a. Sketch each tank, and label its dimensions.

   b. Without any calculation, estimate which tank will hold the most water and which will hold the least. Explain.

   c. Find the volumes of the three tanks to confirm your answer to part (b).

26. Find the radius of a sphere with volume 250 in.³.

27. Suppose a scoop of ice cream is a sphere with a radius of 1 inch. How many scoops can be packed into the cone shown at the right?

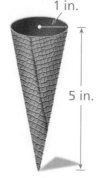
1 in.
5 in.

28. Chilly's Ice Cream Parlor is known for its root beer floats.

   • The float is made by pouring root beer over 3 scoops of ice cream until the glass is filled $\frac{1}{2}$ inch from the top.

   • A glass is in the shape of a cylinder with a radius of $1\frac{1}{4}$ inches and height of $8\frac{1}{2}$ inches.

   • Each scoop of ice cream is a sphere with a radius of $1\frac{1}{4}$ inches.

   Will there be more ice cream or more root beer in the float? Explain.

Connections

29. Suppose that you are shown two packages for sugar.

    a. Which package has the greater surface area? How do you know?

    b. Which package has the greater volume? How do you know?

For Exercises 30 and 31, Carlos plans to build a hot tub with a depth of 4 feet.

30. Carlos wants to build a circular hot tub with a volume of 1,000 ft^3. What is a good approximation for the radius of the tub?

31. Carlos decides he would rather build a rectangular hot tub that holds 400 ft^3 of water. What could be the dimensions of the base of Carlos's hot tub?

32. What two-dimensional shapes appear if you slice a cylinder in the direction shown on each figure?

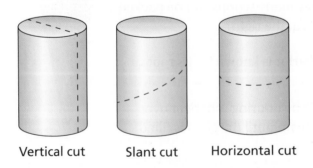

Vertical cut   Slant cut   Horizontal cut

33. If two rectangular prisms have the same height and base area, will they have the same shape? Explain.

34. If two cylinders have the same height and base area, will they have the same shape? Explain.

35. A drink can is a cylinder with radius 3 centimeters and height 12 centimeters. Ms. Doyle's classroom is 6 meters wide, 8 meters long, and 3 meters high. Estimate the number of drink cans that would fit inside Ms. Doyle's classroom. Explain your estimation strategy.

36. a. Make a table showing the relationship between the diameter and the circumference of a circle. Include data for diameters 1, 2, 3, . . . , 10 cm.

   b. Make a graph of the data (*diameter, circumference*) in your table.

   c. Suppose that each of the circles represented in your table is the base of a cylinder with height 2 cm. Some of these cylinders are shown below. Add a column to your table to show the relationship between the diameter of the base and the volume of the cylinder.

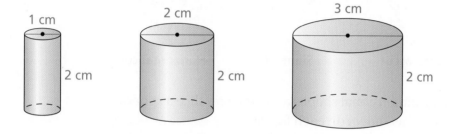

   d. Make a graph of the data (*diameter, volume*).

   e. Compare the graphs for part (b) and part (d). How are they alike? How are they different?

For Exercises 37 and 38, suppose that a scale model of a cylinder has a radius of 5 and a height of 12.

37. For each scale factor, describe how the surface area of the real cylinder is related to the surface area of the scale model.

   a. scale factor = 2   **b.** scale factor = 3.5   **c.** scale factor = *f*

38. For each scale factor, describe how the volume of the real cylinder is related to the volume of the scale model.

   a. scale factor = 2   **b.** scale factor = 3.5   **c.** scale factor = *f*

39. Five students measured the height of the same cylinder. Their measurements are listed below. What is the average of the measurements?

   5.1 centimeters   4.9 centimeters   5.15 centimeters

   5.15 centimeters   4.85 centimeters

Each number sentence in Exercises 40–42 shows calculations required to find the surface area of a three-dimensional figure. Name the figure the number sentence describes. Find the surface area.

40. $2 \times 4 \times 8.5 + 2 \times 8.5 \times 7.25 + 2 \times 7.25 \times 4$

41. $2 \times (4 \times 8.5 + 8.5 \times 7.25 + 7.25 \times 4)$

42. $2(\pi \times 4^2) + 8\pi \times 8.5$

43. What two-dimensional shapes appear if you slice a cone as shown on each figure?

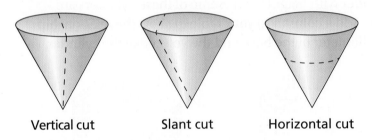

Vertical cut   Slant cut   Horizontal cut

44. What two-dimensional shapes appear if you slice a sphere horizontally as shown on each figure?

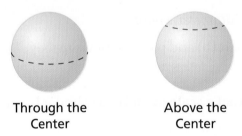

Through the   Above the
Center   Center

45. Kaiya measures the circumference of a sphere and finds that it is about 54 centimeters. What is the volume of the sphere?

Extensions

46. Suppose you know the height and volume of a cylinder. Can you make a net for the cylinder? If so, what are the dimensions of the parts of that net?

47. Some take-out drink containers have circular tops and bottoms that are not congruent. How can you estimate the volume of the container below?

4.5 cm

14 cm

3 cm

48. A cylindrical can is packed securely in a box as shown at the right.

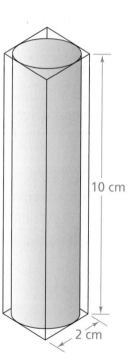

10 cm

2 cm

   a. Find the radius and height of the can.

   b. What is the volume of the empty space between the can and the box?

   c. Find the ratio of the volume of the can to the volume of the box.

   d. Make up a similar example with a can and a box of different sizes. What is the ratio of the volume of your can to the volume of your box?

   e. How does the ratio you found in part (d) compare with the ratio you found in part (c)?

49. Pyramids are named for the shapes of their bases. The left shape below is a triangular pyramid, the center shape is a square pyramid, and the right shape is a pentagonal pyramid.

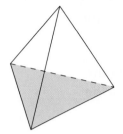 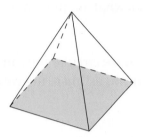 

Suppose you have a set of five pyramids whose bases are all regular polygons. The bases have 3, 4, 5, 6, and 7 sides. All pyramids have the same base perimeter, and all have the same height (with the top vertex directly above the center of the base).

a. Describe a method for finding the surface area of a regular pyramid.

b. How will the surface areas of the five pyramids be related to each other?

c. How will the volumes of the five pyramids be related to each other?

d. How would the surface area and volume of a cone with the same base perimeter and height compare to the surface areas and volumes of the five pyramids?

50. Ted made a scale model of a submarine for his science class.

a. What is the volume of Ted's model submarine in cubic inches?

b. If 1 inch on the model represents 20 feet in the actual submarine, what is the volume of the actual submarine in cubic feet?

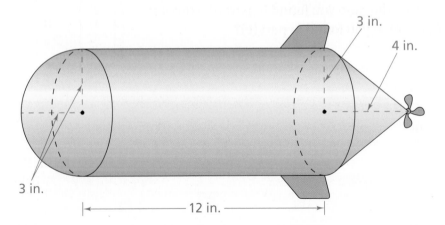

3 in.

4 in.

3 in.

12 in.

51. Some Inuit people build igloos shaped like hemispheres (halves of a sphere). Some Hopi people in Arizona build adobes shaped like rectangular prisms.

a. If the inner diameter of an Inuit igloo is 20 feet, what is the area of its floor? What is the volume of the inner space?

b. What dimensions for a Hopi dwelling would give the same floor area and the same volume of living space as the Inuit igloo?

52. For each shape, find the dimensions that will most closely fit inside a cubic box with 10-centimeter edges. Then find the volume of that shape. Assume that the base of each shape lies on a face of the cube.

a. sphere

b. cylinder

c. cone

d. pyramid

53. It may not be possible to wrap a ball smoothly with a piece of paper, but the surface area of a sphere is related to the area of a circle. You can discover this relationship with a hands-on experiment.

- Measure the diameter and radius of a spherical object.

- Make at least five paper circles that have the same diameter and radius as the sphere. Refer to these as *radius circles*.

- Tape radius circles, or pieces of the circles, on the sphere to cover it as fully as possible without overlap. Keep track of the number of radius circles needed.

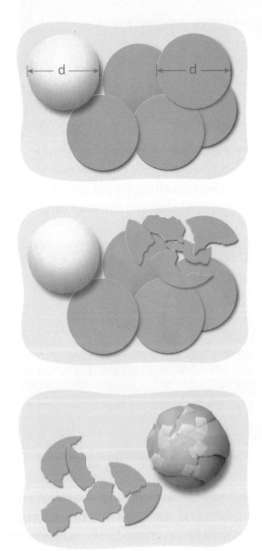

a. Repeat the experiment for multiple values of radius and surface area. About how many radius circles are needed to cover each sphere?

b. What is the approximate area of the radius circles you used to cover a sphere of radius r?

c. What does that observation suggest about a formula relating surface area S.A. and radius r for a sphere?

d. Use your formula from part (c) to complete the table.

Surface Areas of Spheres

Radius	Surface Area
1	■
2	■
3	■
4	■
5	■
⋮	■
10	■

e. What pattern do you see in the surface area as the radius increases?

f. When the radius is doubled, how does the surface area increase?

g. When the radius is tripled, how does the surface area increase?

h. How is the change in surface area from scaling up the radius of a sphere similar to the patterns you noticed when you scaled up the 1-2-3 boxes in Problem 1.4?

In this Investigation, you discovered strategies for finding the surface area and volume of a cylinder. You explored the relationships between the volumes of a cone, a sphere, and a cylinder with the same radius and height. The following questions will help you summarize what you have learned.

Think about these questions. Discuss your ideas with other students and your teacher. Then write a summary of your findings in your notebook.

1. a. **Compare** the task of finding the circumference of the base and the surface area of a cylinder to that of finding the perimeter of the base and the surface area of a prism.

    b. **Compare** the task of finding the volumes of cylinders to that of finding the volumes of prisms.

    c. **How** can you find the circumference of the base, the surface area, and the volume of a cylinder from measures of its radius or diameter and its height? **Explain** why your formulas make sense.

    d. **How** do the surface area and the volume of a cylinder change if both the radius and height are changed by a factor of f?

2. a. **How** is the task of finding the volumes of spheres and cones similar to that of finding the volumes of prisms and cylinders? **In what ways** are those tasks different?

    b. **How** can you find the volume of a sphere or a cone from measures of its dimensions?

Common Core Mathematical Practices

As you worked on the Problems in this Investigation, you used prior knowledge to make sense of them. You also applied Mathematical Practices to solve the Problems. Think back over your work, the ways you thought about the Problems, and how you used Mathematical Practices.

Elena described her thoughts in the following way:

In Problem 4.4, we increased the radius to see what it would *do* to the volume. This showed us a relationship that we saw earlier in this Unit. It was an idea that we studied in *Stretching and Shrinking*.

Using repeated multiplication, we realized that if you have a scale factor of f, the volume of a scale model grows by f^3, the surface area grows by f^2, and the lengths grow by f.

Common Core Standards for Mathematical Practice

MP8 Look for and express regularity in repeated reasoning.

- What other Mathematical Practices can you identify in Elena's reasoning?

- Describe a Mathematical Practice that you and your classmates used to solve a different Problem in this Investigation.

The Package Design Contest

The Worldwide Sporting Company (WSC) wants a new set of package designs for their table-tennis balls. The table-tennis balls are about 3.8 centimeters in diameter. WSC has decided to offer a scholarship to the students or groups of students who convince the company to use their design.

- The board of directors of WSC wants a small package, a medium package, and a large package of table-tennis balls.

- The president of the company wants the cost of the packaging to be considered.

- The marketing department wants the packages to be appealing to customers, to stack easily, and to look good on store shelves.

Part 1: Design a Contest Entry

You are to prepare an entry for the package design contest. Your task is to design three different packages for table-tennis balls. Include the following things in your contest entry:

1. A description of the shape or shapes of the packages you have designed and an explanation of why you selected these shapes.

2. Nets for each of your packages that, when they are cut out, folded, and taped together, will form models of your packages. Use centimeter grid paper to make your patterns.

3. Calculations of how much each of your package designs will cost to construct. The packaging material costs $.005 per square centimeter.

Part 2: Write a Report

You will submit your designs and a written proposal to WSC. Your written proposal should try to convince WSC that your designs are the ones they should use. Explain how you have addressed WSC's three requirements (listed above).

Remember, you are trying to persuade WSC that your designs are the best and that they should select your work. You are writing a report to the company officials, so you need to think about the presentation of your written proposal. It should be neat (preferably typed), well organized, and easy to read. The company officials should be able to follow your work and ideas easily.

In this Unit, you connected strategies for finding surface area and volume of a rectangular prism to strategies for finding measurements of other right prisms. You discovered formulas for the circumference and area of any circle and applied that knowledge to calculate surface area and volume of cylinders. You used the relationship between prisms and pyramids to find the volume of a pyramid, and you used the relationship among cylinders, spheres, and cones to find the volumes of spheres and cones. In each case, you examined the effects of enlargement and reduction on dimensions, surface area, and volume of three-dimensional figures.

Use Your Understanding: Volume and Surface Area

To test your understanding of volume and surface area, consider the following problems.

1. Below is a net for a rectangular prism.

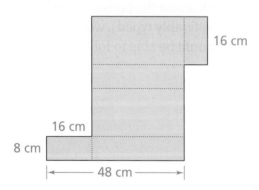

16 cm

16 cm

8 cm

48 cm

    a. What are the dimensions of the box that can be made from the net?

    b. What is the surface area of the box?

    c. What is the volume of the box?

2. A candy company is marketing a special assortment of caramels. The company wants to put 40 individual caramels into a rectangular box. Each caramel is a 1-inch cube. The caramels should completely fill the box.

   a. Which arrangement of caramels requires the most cardboard for a box? What is the surface area of that box?

   b. Which arrangement of caramels requires the least cardboard? What is the surface area of that box?

   c. Make sketches of the boxes you described in parts (a) and (b). Label the dimensions.

   d. Suppose each dimension of the box in part (b) were doubled. How many more caramels would fit in the new box?

3. A beverage company has decided to change the packaging for a juice drink. The drink used to come in a cylindrical container with a base diameter of 6 inches and a height of 10 inches. The new container is a square prism that fits inside the old cylinder, as shown in the figure.

   a. What is the volume of the original cylindrical container?

   b. How much less juice can the prism-shaped container hold than the cylindrical container?

   c. Suppose that the company wants the cost per cubic inch of juice to be the same for both containers. The original container of juice costs $2.19. How much should a new box of juice cost?

   d. The company is also considering selling the juice in a cone-shaped container with the same volume as the cylinder. Describe the possible dimensions for such a cone.

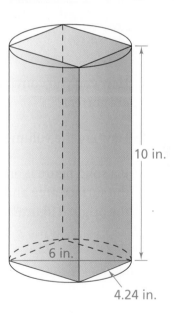

10 in.

6 in.

4.24 in.

Explain Your Reasoning

To solve problems about surface area and volume of solid figures, you have to know the meaning of those terms and some strategies for calculating the measurements from the dimensions of a figure.

4. What do *volume* and *surface area* measurements tell you about a solid figure?

5. Which formulas can you use to find the surface area and the volume of each figure?

   a. rectangular prism

   b. cylinder

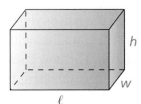

6. How can you convince someone that the formulas from Exercise 5 are correct?

7. How are the volumes of cylinders, cones, and spheres related?

8. If a solid figure is enlarged or reduced by a scale factor of f, how will the surface area and volume of the new figure be related to those of the original figure?

English / Spanish Glossary

A **area** The measure of the amount of surface enclosed by the boundary of a figure. To find the area A of a figure, you can count how many unit squares it takes to cover the figure. You can find the area of a rectangle by multiplying the length by the width. This is a shortcut method for finding the number of unit squares it takes to cover the rectangle. If a figure has curved or irregular sides, you can estimate the area. Cover the surface with a grid and count whole grid squares and parts of grid squares. When you find the area of a shape, write the units, such as square centimeters (cm^2), to indicate the unit square that was used to find the area.

área La medida de la cantidad de superficie encerrada por los límites de una figura. Para hallar el área A de una figura, puedes contar cuántas unidades cuadradas se necesitan para cubrir la figura. Puedes hallar el área de un rectángulo multiplicando el largo por el ancho. Este es un método más corto para hallar el número de unidades cuadradas que se necesitan para cubrir el rectángulo. Si una figura tiene lados curvos o irregulares, puedes estimar el área. Para ello, cubre la superficie con una cuadrícula y cuenta los cuadrados enteros y las partes de cuadrados en la cuadrícula. Cuando halles el área de una figura, escribe las unidades, por ejemplo, centímetros cuadrados (cm^2), para indicar la unidad cuadrada que se usó para hallar el área.

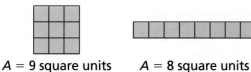

A = 9 square units A = 8 square units

 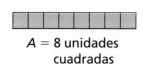

A = 9 unidades cuadradas A = 8 unidades cuadradas

B **base(s) of a three-dimensional figure** Two opposite faces of a three-dimensional shape that are parallel and congruent. For a pyramid or a cone, the base is the face opposite the vertex.

base(s) de una figura tridimensional Dos caras opuestas de una figura tridimensional que son paralelas y congruentes. En una pirámide o un cono, la base es la cara opuesta al vértice.

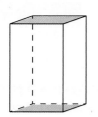 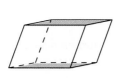

base of a two-dimensional figure See *measurements of two-dimensional figures.*

base(s) de una figura bidimensional Ver *medidas de las figuras bidimensionales.*

circle A two-dimensional figure in which every point is the same distance from a point called the *center*. Point C is the center of this circle.

círculo Una figura bidimensional en el que cada punto está a la misma distancia de un punto llamado el *centro*. El punto C es el centro del siguiente círculo.

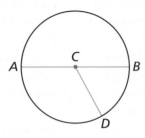

circumference The distance around (or perimeter of) a circle. It takes slightly more than three diameters to match the circumference of a circle. More formally, the circumference of a circle is pi (π) times the diameter of the circle.

circunferencia La distancia alrededor de (o el perímetro de) un círculo. Se requieren apenas más de tres diámetros para representar la circunferencia de un círculo. Más formalmente, la circunferencia de un círculo es pi (π) multiplicada por el diámetro del círculo.

compare Academic Vocabulary
To tell or show how two things are alike and different.

comparar Vocabulario académico
Decir o mostrar en qué se parecen o en qué se diferencian dos cosas.

related terms *analyze, relate, resemble*

términos relacionados *analizar, relacionar, parecerse*

sample Compare the volumes of the cube and the rectangular prism.

ejemplo Compara los volúmenes del cubo y del prisma rectangular.

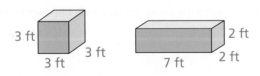

The volume of the cube is 3 ft × 3 ft × 3 ft = 27 ft³. The volume of the rectangular prism is 2 ft × 2 ft × 7ft = 28 ft³. The rectangular prism has 1 cubic foot more volume than the cube.

El volumen del cubo es 3 pies × 3 pies × 3 pies = 27 pies³. El volumen del prisma rectangular es 2 pies × 2 pies × 7 pies = 28 pies³. El prisma rectangular tiene 1 pie cúbico más de volumen que el cubo.

cone A three-dimensional shape with a circular base and a vertex opposite the base.

cono Una figura tridimensional con una base circular y un vértice opuesto a la base.

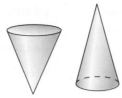

cube A three-dimensional shape with six identical square faces. A cube is also a right rectangular prism.

cubo Una figura tridimensional con seis caras cuadradas idénticas. Un cubo también es un prisma rectangular recto.

cylinder A three-dimensional shape with two opposite faces that are parallel and congruent circles. The side (lateral surface) is a rectangle that is "wrapped around" the circular faces at the ends.

cilindro Una figura tridimensional con dos caras opuestas que son círculos paralelos y congruentes. El lado (la superficie lateral) es un rectángulo que está "enrollado" alrededor de las caras circulares de los extremos.

D **describe** Academic Vocabulary
To explain or tell in detail. A written description can contain facts and other information needed to communicate your answer. A diagram or a graph may also be included.

related terms *express, explain, illustrate*

sample Describe how to find the volume of a right triangular prism.

> First, find the area of the base of the prism, a triangle, by using the formula $A = \frac{1}{2}bh$, where b is the base and h is the height of the triangle. Next, multiply the area of the base by the height of the prism. The height of the prism is the distance between the two triangular bases. The result is a quantity measured in cubic units.

describir Vocabulario académico
Explicar o decir con detalle. Una descripción escrita puede contener datos y otra información necesaria para comunicar tu respuesta. También puede incluir un diagrama o una gráfica.

términos relacionados *expresar, explicar, ilustrar*

ejemplo Describe cómo hallar el volumen de un prisma rectangular recto.

> Primero, halla el área de la base del prisma, un triángulo, usando la fórmula $A = \frac{1}{2}bh$, donde b es la base y h es la altura del triángulo. Luego, multiplica el área de la base por la altura del prisma. La altura del prisma es la distancia entre las dos bases triangulares. El resultado es una cantidad medida en unidades cúbicas.

....

diameter A segment that goes from one point on a circle through the center of the circle to another point on the circle. Also, diameter is used to indicate the length of this segment. In this circle, segment *AB* is a diameter.

diámetro Un segmento que va desde un punto en un círculo, pasando por el centro, hasta otro punto en el círculo. Además, el diámetro se usa para indicar la longitud de este segmento. En este círculo, el segmento *AB* es un diámetro.

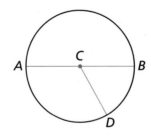

E **edge** A line segment formed where two faces of a three-dimensional shape meet.

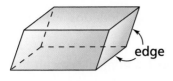
edge

edge

arista El segmento de recta que se forma en el lugar en donde se encuentran dos caras de una figura tridimensional.

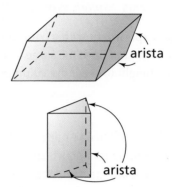
arista

arista

---

estimate Academic Vocabulary
To find an approximate answer that is relatively close to an exact amount.

related terms *approximate, guess*

sample Estimate the volume of the smoothie cup.

4 in.
6 in.
3 in.

The smoothie cup is approximately the shape of a cylinder with a height of 6 inches. I can find the average of the top and bottom base diameters, which is $(4 + 3) \div 2$ or 3.5 inches. So, I will use the radius of 1.75 inches to estimate the volume. The volume of the smoothie cup is about $6 \times 1.75^2 \times \pi$, or about 57.7 cm³.

estimar Vocabulario académico
Hallar una respuesta aproximada que esté relativamente cerca de una cantidad exacta.

términos relacionados *aproximar, suponer*

ejemplo Estima el volumen del vaso de licuado.

4 pulgs.
6 pulgs.
3 pulgs.

El vaso de licuado tiene la forma aproximada de un cilindro con una altura de 6 pulgadas. Puedo hallar el promedio de los diámetros de la parte superior y de la base, el cual es $(4 + 3) \div 2$ ó 3.5 pulgadas. Por tanto, usaré el radio de 1.75 pulgadas para estimar el volumen. El volumen del vaso de licuado es aproximadamente $6 \times 1.75^2 \times \pi$, o aproximadamente 57.7 cm³.

experiment Academic Vocabulary
To try in several different or new ways to gather information.

related terms *explore, examine, discover*

sample Experiment with a cone, a cylinder, and a sphere that have the same radius and the same height to see if the volumes are related.

> I can form all three shapes with the same radius and height and pour a material, such as sand, to determine how the volumes are related.

experimentar Vocabulario académico
Intentar varias o nuevas maneras de recopilar información.

términos relacionados *explorar, examinar, descubrir*

ejemplo Experimenta con un cono, un cilindro y una esfera que tengan el mismo radio y la misma altura para ver si los volúmenes están relacionados.

> Puedo formar las tres figuras con el mismo radio y altura y verter un material, como arena, para determinar cómo se relacionan los volúmenes.

....

explain Academic Vocabulary
To give facts and details that make an idea easier to understand. Explaining something can involve a written summary supported by a diagram, chart, table, or a combination of these.

related terms *describe, analyze, clarify, describe, justify, tell*

sample Explain what shape can be formed if the net is assembled.

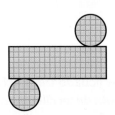

> The net has two congruent circles and a rectangle, so this is a cylinder when it is assembled. The two circles form bases, and the rectangle can be rolled to form the cylinder.

explicar Vocabulario académico
Dar datos y detalles que hacen que una idea sea más fácil de comprender. Explicar puede incluir un resumen escrito apoyado por un diagrama, una gráfica, una tabla o una combinación de estos.

términos relacionados *describir, analizar, aclarar, justificar, decir*

ejemplo Explica qué figura puedes formar si armas el modelo plano.

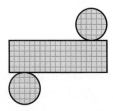

> El modelo plano tiene dos círculos congruentes y un rectángulo, por tanto, cuando se arma es un cilindro. Los dos círculos forman bases y el rectángulo se puede enrollar para formar el cilindro.

F **face** A flat two-dimensional surface of a three-dimensional shape.

cara Una superficie plana y bidimensional de una figura tridimensional.

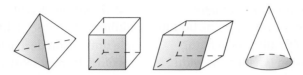

formula A rule containing variables that represents a mathematical relationship. An example is the formula for finding the area of a rectangle: $A = \ell w$, where ℓ represents the length and w represents the width.

fórmula Una regla que contiene variables y que representa una relación matemática. Un ejemplo es la fórmula para hallar el área de un rectángulo: $A = \ell a$, donde ℓ representa la longitud y a el ancho.

H **height of a three-dimensional figure** See *measurements of three-dimensional figures.*

altura de una figura tridimensional Ver *medidas de las figuras tridimensionales.*

height of a two-dimensional figure See *measurements of two-dimensional figures.*

altura de una figura bidimensional Ver *medidas de las figuras bidimensionales.*

L **lateral face** A face of a three-dimensional shape that is not a base. For a prism, the lateral faces are parallelograms. The lateral faces of a right prism are rectangles. For a pyramid, the lateral faces are triangles that meet at the vertex.

cara lateral Una cara de una figura tridimensional que no es una base. En un prisma, las caras laterales son paralelogramos. Las caras laterales de un prisma recto son rectángulos. En una pirámide, las caras laterales son triángulos que coinciden en el vértice.

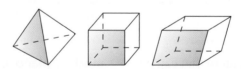

M **measurements of three-dimensional figures** Dimensions, such as length, width, and height, which describe the size of three-dimensional figures. If the base of the figure is a rectangle, *length* and *width* refer to the length and width of the figure's rectangular base. The *height* of a three-dimensional figure is the vertical distance from the bottom of the figure to its top.

medidas de las figuras tridimensionales Dimensiones como la longitud, el ancho y la altura, que describen el tamaño de las figuras tridimensionales. Si la base de la figura es un rectángulo, la *longitud* y el *ancho* se refieren a la longitud y al ancho de la base rectangular de la figura. La *altura* de una figura tridimensional es la distancia vertical desde la parte de abajo de la figura hasta la parte de arriba.

 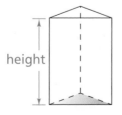 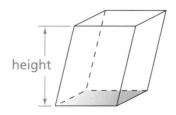 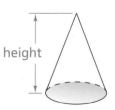

measurements of two-dimensional figures Dimensions, such as length, width, base, and height, which describe the size of two-dimensional figures. The longest dimension or the dimension along the bottom of a rectangle is usually called the length, and the other dimension is called the width, but it is not incorrect to reverse these labels. The word base is used when talking about triangles and parallelograms. The base is usually measured along a horizontal side, but it is sometimes convenient to think of one of the other sides as the base. For a triangle, the height is the perpendicular distance from a vertex opposite the base to the line containing the base. For a parallelogram, the height is the perpendicular distance from a point on the side opposite the base to the base. You need to be flexible when you encounter these terms, so you are able to determine their meanings from the context of the situation.

medidas de las figuras bidimensionales Dimensiones como la longitud, el ancho, la base y la altura, que describen el tamaño de las figuras bidimensionales. La dimensión más larga, o la dimensión de la parte inferior de un rectángulo, generalmente se llama *longitud* y la otra dimensión se llama *ancho*, sin embargo no es incorrecto intercambiar estos nombres. La palabra *base* se usa cuando se habla de triángulos y de paralelogramos. La base se mide a lo largo de un lado horizontal pero a veces es conveniente pensar en uno de los otros lados como la base. En un triángulo, la altura es la distancia perpendicular que hay desde el vértice opuesto a la base, hasta la base. En un paralelogramo, la altura es la distancia perpendicular que hay desde un punto en el lado opuesto a la base, hasta la base. Tienes que ser flexible cuando encuentres estos términos para que puedas determinar su significado dentro del contexto de la situación.

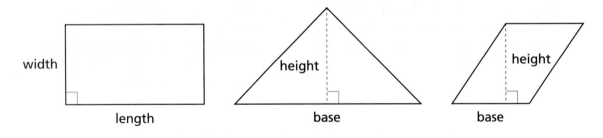

N **net** A two-dimensional pattern that can be folded into a three-dimensional figure.

modelo plano Un patrón bidimensional que se puede doblar para formar una figura tridimensional.

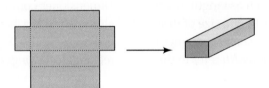

oblique prism A prism for which some or all of the lateral faces are nonrectangular parallelograms.

prisma oblicuo Un prisma en el que algunas o todas las caras laterales son paralelogramos no rectangulares.

P

perimeter The measure of the distance around a two-dimensional figure. Perimeter is a measure of length. To find the perimeter *P* of a figure, you count the number of unit lengths it takes to surround the figure. When you find the perimeter of a shape, write the units (such as centimeters, feet, or yards) to indicate the unit that was used to find the perimeter. The perimeter of the square below is 12 units, because 12 units of length surround the figure. The perimeter of the rectangle is 18 units. Notice that the rectangle has a greater perimeter, but a lesser area, than the square.

perímetro La medida de la distancia alrededor de una figura bidimensional. El perímetro es una medida de longitud. Para hallar el perímetro *P* de una figura, cuentas el número de unidades de longitud que se requieren para rodear la figura. Cuando halles el perímetro de una figura, escribe las unidades (por ejemplo, centímetros, pies o yardas) para indicar la unidad que se usó para hallar el perímetro. El perímetro del cuadrado que se muestra es de 12 unidades, porque 12 unidades de longitud rodean la figura. El perímetro del rectángulo es de 18 unidades. Observa que el rectángulo tiene un perímetro mayor, pero un área más pequeña, que el cuadrado.

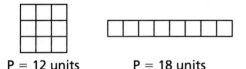

P = 12 units   P = 18 units

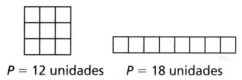

P = 12 unidades   P = 18 unidades

pi (π) The mathematical name for the ratio of a circle's circumference to its diameter. This ratio is the same for every circle, and is approximately equal to 3.1416.

pi (π) El nombre matemático para la razón de la circunferencia de un círculo a su diámetro. Esta razón es la misma para cada círculo y es aproximadamente igual a 3.1416.

prism A three-dimensional shape with a top and bottom (base) that are congruent polygons and lateral faces that are parallelograms.

prisma Una figura tridimensional que tiene una parte superior y una parte inferior (base) que son polígonos congruentes, y cuyas caras laterales son paralelogramos.

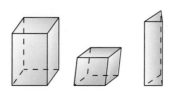

pyramid A three-dimensional shape with one polygonal base and lateral faces that are all triangles that meet at a vertex opposite the base.

pirámide Una figura tridimensional con una base que es un polígono y cuyas caras laterales son triángulos que coinciden en un vértice opuesto a la base.

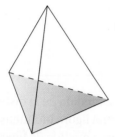  

radius A segment from the center of a circle to a point on the circle. The length of this segment is also called the radius. The radius is half of the diameter. *CD* is one radius of the circle below. The plural of radius is radii. All the radii of a circle have the same length.

radio Un segmento desde el centro de un círculo hasta un punto en el círculo. La longitud de este segmento también se llama "radio". El radio es la mitad del diámetro. *CD* es un radio del siguiente círculo. Todos los radios de un círculo tienen la misma longitud.

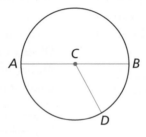

rectangular prism A prism with top and bottom bases that are congruent rectangles.

prisma rectangular Un prisma cuyas partes superior e inferior (base) son rectángulos congruentes.

right rectangular prism

oblique rectangular prism

prisma rectangular recto

prisma rectangular oblicuo

regular prism A prism whose bases are regular polygons

prisma regular Un prisma cuyas bases son polígonos regulares

right prism A prism whose vertical faces are rectangles. The bases are congruent polygons.

prisma recto Un prisma cuyas caras verticales son rectángulos. Las bases son polígonos congruentes.

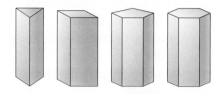

S **sphere** A three-dimensional shape whose surface consists of all the points that are a given distance from the center of the shape.

esfera Una figura tridimensional en la que todos los puntos de su superficie se encuentran a la misma distancia del centro de la figura.

surface area The area required to cover a three-dimensional shape.

área total El área que se necesita para cubrir una figura tridimensional.

U **unit cube** A cube whose edges are 1 unit long. It is the basic unit of measurement for volume.

cubo de unidades Un cubo cuyas aristas miden 1 unidad de longitud. Es la unidad básica de medición para el volumen.

V **volume** The amount of space occupied by, or the capacity of, a three-dimensional shape. The volume is the number of unit cubes that will fit into a three-dimensional shape.

volumen La cantidad de espacio que ocupa una figura tridimensional o la capacidad de dicha figura. El volumen es el número de cubos de unidades que caben en una figura tridimensional.

Index

Index

Acknowledgments

Cover Design

Three Communication Design, Chicago

Text

Grateful acknowledgment is made to the following for copyrighted material:

055 Encyclopedia Brittanica

From ENCYCLOPEDIA BRITTANNICA ONLINE, *"pi,"* Babylonians noted pi as $3\frac{1}{8}$.

055 John Wiley & Sons, Inc.

From A HISTORY OF MATHEMATICS by Carl B. Boyer: Tsu Chung-Chi discovered the value of pi (p. 202) and William Jones used the pi symbol in 1706 (p. 442).

Photographs

Photo locators denoted as follows: Top (T), Center (C), Bottom (B), Left (L), Right (R), Background (Bkgd)

003 Geri Engberg Photography; **008** (T) iStockphoto/Thinkstock, (B) tpfd/ Shutterstock; **032** (TR) sowanna/Fotolia, (BL) gtzx/Alamy, (BR) gtzx/Alamy; **034** B.S.P.I./Corbis; **049** fottoo/Fotolia; **061** (C) Photodisc/Getty Images, (CR) mbongo/Fotolia; **082** Iofoto/Fotolia; **093** (T) Digital Focus/Alamy; (B) Radius/Superstock.

Samples and Populations

Making Comparisons and Predictions

Lappan, Phillips, Fey, Friel

Making Comparisons and Predictions

3 Using Samples to Draw Conclusions 56

Looking Ahead

How can you determine whether steel-frame roller coasters or wood-frame roller coasters are faster?

A national magazine posts a survey on its Web site for its readers. **What** population do the survey results describe? Is sampling with this kind of plan a good way to draw conclusions about an entire population?

We need student volunteers for our survey.

How can you estimate the albatross population of an island?

The United States Census attempts to gather information from every household in the United States. Gathering, organizing, and analyzing data from such a large population is expensive and time-consuming. In most studies of large populations, data are gathered from a *sample* of the population.

Sampling is an important tool in statistics and data analysis. You can draw conclusions about a single population or compare samples from different populations. For example, scientists may study a sample of penguins to learn more about the entire population of penguins.

Recall that you can analyze a set of data by finding summary statistics. You can use measures of center and measures of variability to describe a distribution.

In this Unit, you will learn how to choose a sample of data from a large population and use data distributions and statistics to draw conclusions about that population. You will use these ideas to answer questions such as those on the previous page.

In *Samples and Populations*, you will learn about different ways to collect and analyze data in order to make comparisons and draw conclusions.

You will learn how to:

- Use the process of statistical investigation to answer questions

- Apply concepts from probability to select random samples from populations

- Gather information about a population by examining a sample of the population

- Use information from samples to draw conclusions about populations

- Identify how sample sizes and sampling plans influence the measures of center and variability that describe a sample distribution

- Compare samples using measures of center (mean, median), measures of variability (range, IQR, MAD), and displays that group data (histograms, box-and-whisker plots)

When you encounter a new problem, it is a good idea to ask yourself questions. In this Unit, you might ask questions such as:

What is the population?

What is the sample?

Is the sample a representative sample?

How can I describe the data I collected?

How can I use my results to draw conclusions about the population?

How can I use samples to compare two or more populations?

Mathematical Practices and Habits of Mind

In the *Connected Mathematics* curriculum you will develop an understanding of important mathematical ideas by solving problems and reflecting on the mathematics involved. Every day, you will use "habits of mind" to make sense of problems and apply what you learn to new situations. Some of these habits are described by the *Common Core State Standards for Mathematical Practices* (MP).

MP1 Make sense of problems and persevere in solving them.

When using mathematics to solve a problem, it helps to think carefully about

- data and other facts you are given and what additional information you need to solve the problem;
- strategies you have used to solve similar problems and whether you could solve a related simpler problem first;
- how you could express the problem with equations, diagrams, or graphs;
- whether your answer makes sense.

MP2 Reason abstractly and quantitatively.

When you are asked to solve a problem, it often helps to

- focus first on the key mathematical ideas;
- check that your answer makes sense in the problem setting;
- use what you know about the problem setting to guide your mathematical reasoning.

MP3 Construct viable arguments and critique the reasoning of others.

When you are asked to explain why a conjecture is correct, you can

- show some examples that fit the claim and explain why they fit;
- show how a new result follows logically from known facts and principles.

When you believe a mathematical claim is incorrect, you can

- show one or more counterexamples—cases that don't fit the claim;
- find steps in the argument that do not follow logically from prior claims.

MP4 Model with mathematics.

When you are asked to solve problems, it often helps to

- think carefully about the numbers or geometric shapes that are the most important factors in the problem, then ask yourself how those factors are related to each other;
- express data and relationships in the problem with tables, graphs, diagrams, or equations, and check your result to see if it makes sense.

MP5 Use appropriate tools strategically.

When working on mathematical questions, you should always

- decide which tools are most helpful for solving the problem and why;
- try a different tool when you get stuck.

MP6 Attend to precision.

In every mathematical exploration or problem-solving task, it is important to

- think carefully about the required accuracy of results; is a number estimate or geometric sketch good enough, or is a precise value or drawing needed?
- report your discoveries with clear and correct mathematical language that can be understood by those to whom you are speaking or writing.

MP7 Look for and make use of structure.

In mathematical explorations and problem solving, it is often helpful to

- look for patterns that show how data points, numbers, or geometric shapes are related to each other;
- use patterns to make predictions.

MP8 Look for and express regularity in repeated reasoning.

When results of a repeated calculation show a pattern, it helps to

- express that pattern as a general rule that can be used in similar cases;
- look for shortcuts that will make the calculation simpler in other cases.

You will use all of the Mathematical Practices in this Unit. Sometimes, when you look at a Problem, it is obvious which practice is most helpful. At other times, you will decide on a practice to use during class explorations and discussions. After completing each Problem, ask yourself:

- What mathematics have I learned by solving this Problem?
- What Mathematical Practices were helpful in learning this mathematics?

Making Sense of Samples

People often want to know what is typical in a given situation. For example, you might want to find out your typical math test score. You may investigate the typical number of text messages sent by students in a middle-school class. You can gather information to determine the typical batting average of a baseball player. You can collect and examine data to analyze situations such as these.

All data sets include some *variability*. Not all math scores are the same. Not all students send the same number of texts. Not all baseball players perform the same at bat. Statistical investigations pose questions with variable outcomes.

. . . .

Common Core State Standards

7.SP.B.4 Use measures of center and measures of variability for numerical data from random samples to draw informal comparative inferences about two populations.

Essential for 7.SP.B.3 Informally assess the degree of visual overlap of two numerical data distributions with similar variabilities, measuring the difference between the centers by expressing it as a multiple of a measure of variability.

Also 7.NS.A.1 and 7.NS.A.1b, essential for 7.SP.A.1 and 7.SP.A.2

1.1 Comparing Performances
Using Center and Spread

The spreadsheet below shows the math test scores earned by two students, Jun and Mia, in the first quarter of 7th grade.

| File | Edit | Tool | View | Chart | Class | Help |

Math Test Scores | Math Homework

Class	Name	Student Number	Test 1	Test 2	Test 3	Test 4	Test 5	Test 6	Test Average
001	Jun	09	80	60	100				
001	Mia	22	75	80	85				

The math test scores are *samples* of the math test scores for each student throughout the school year. You can use data from samples to make general statements about overall performance.

- Who performs better on math tests, Jun or Mia? Explain.

In Problem 1.1, you will use measures of center and measures of variability, or spread, to determine who performs more consistently on tests.

Problem 1.1

A 1. Find the *mean* and *median* of Jun's scores. What do you notice?

2. Find the mean and median of Mia's scores. What do you notice?

3. Use the measures of center you found in parts (1) and (2). Compare Jun's and Mia's test performances.

Problem 1.1 *continued*

B 1. Determine the *range* and *mean absolute deviation (MAD)* of Jun's test scores.

2. Determine the range and MAD of Mia's test scores.

3. Use the measures of spread you found in parts (1) and (2). Compare Jun's and Mia's test performances.

C Do you have enough data to make any general statements about Jun's or Mia's overall math test performance? Explain.

D The spreadsheet below shows Jun's and Mia's test scores at mid-year.

File   Edit   Tool   View   Chart   Class   Help

Math Test Scores   Math Homework

Class	Name	Student Number	Test 1	Test 2	Test 3	Test 4	Test 5	Test 6	Test Average
001	Jun	09	80	60	100	80	80	80	
001	Mia	22	75	80	85	80	80	100	

1. Find the median and mean of Jun's test data and of Mia's test data. Use each measure of center to compare Jun's scores and Mia's scores.

2. Find the range and MAD of Jun's test data and of Mia's test data. Use each measure of variability to compare Jun's scores and Mia's scores.

3. Decide whether you agree or disagree with each statement below. Use the statistics you found in parts (1) and (2). Explain your reasoning.

   • One student is a stronger math student than the other.

   • One student is more consistent than the other.

   • The two students perform equally well on math tests.

   • You can make better comparisons using the larger data set.

ACE Homework starts on page 20.

1.2 Which Team Is Most Successful?
Using the MAD to Compare Samples

A middle school's Hiking Club holds a fundraiser each spring. The club sells granola bars and packages of trail mix. The 35 club members form six fundraising teams. Each team is a *sample* of students from the club. The most successful team receives a prize.

The faculty advisor posts the money the teams raised on a bulletin board.

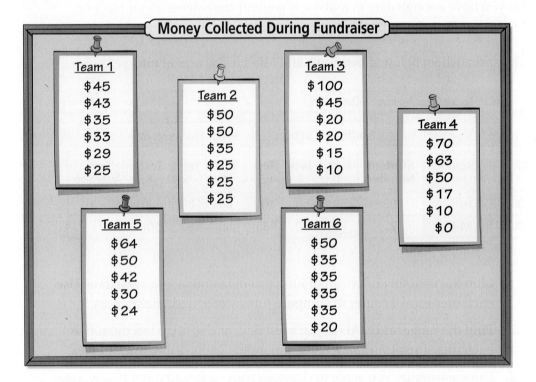

Money Collected During Fundraiser

Team 1
$45
$43
$35
$33
$29
$25

Team 2
$50
$50
$35
$25
$25
$25

Team 3
$100
$45
$20
$20
$15
$10

Team 4
$70
$63
$50
$17
$10
$0

Team 5
$64
$50
$42
$30
$24

Team 6
$50
$35
$35
$35
$35
$20

- Which team is the most successful and deserves to win the prize? Explain.

Problem 1.2

Ⓐ Make a *line plot* of each team's data. Use a scale that makes it easy to compare results among teams. Write three sentences that compare the *distributions*.

Ⓑ The Hiking Club's organizers must decide which team is awarded the prize. Each organizer has a different strategy for determining the most successful fundraising team.

For each strategy below, explain whether or not the strategy helps determine the most successful team. If the strategy helps determine the most successful team, determine who will win the prize.

1. **Bianca**

For each team, just add up all the money raised by its members. Then compare the team totals.

2. **Gianna**

Find the mean number of dollars raised by each team. Then compare the team averages.

3. **Jonah**

Compare the money raised by each member to the team's average. On average, how far does each member's amount differ from the team's mean amount? For each team, find the MAD. Then compare the MADs of the six teams.

Ⓒ What other strategies might you use? How does your strategy help you determine which team was most successful?

continued on the next page >

Problem **1.2** *continued*

D In Question A, you made line plots of the six sets of data. In Question B, part (3), you found the mean absolute deviation (MAD) of each of the six distributions.

The dot plot below shows Team 1's fundraising amounts. The red lines indicate the distances of one MAD and two MADs from the mean on either side. Count the data points located closer than, but not including, the distance of one MAD from the mean. (The △ indicates the mean, 35.)

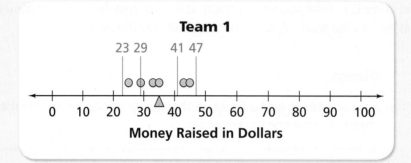

1. How many of Team 1's data values are located *within one MAD* (both less than and greater than the mean)? Write this number as a percent.

2. How many of Team 1's data values are located *within two MADs* of the mean? Write this number as a percent.

3. How many of Team 1's data values are located *more than two MADs* away from the mean? Write this number as a percent.

4. Repeat parts (1)–(3) for each of the other teams' data. For each team, use the team's MAD to analyze the distribution.

5. Use the MAD locations from parts (1)–(4). For each team, what percentage of the data values are located within two MADs of the mean of the data?

A C E Homework starts on page 20.

1.3 Pick Your Preference
Distinguishing Categorical Data From Numerical Data

In this Unit, you have worked with *numerical data,* which are counts or measures. Sometimes, however, the answers to survey questions can be sorted into categories or groups, such as your birth month, favorite movie, or eye color. These answers are *categorical data.* You can count categorical data, but you cannot place them in numerical order.

A survey about roller coasters asks these questions:

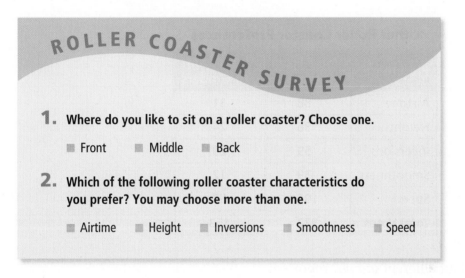

ROLLER COASTER SURVEY

1. Where do you like to sit on a roller coaster? Choose one.

■ Front   ■ Middle   ■ Back

2. Which of the following roller coaster characteristics do you prefer? You may choose more than one.

■ Airtime   ■ Height   ■ Inversions   ■ Smoothness   ■ Speed

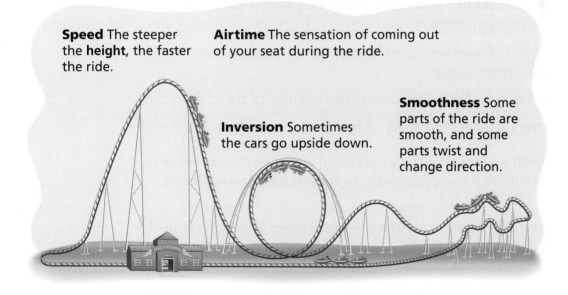

Speed The steeper the **height**, the faster the ride.

Airtime The sensation of coming out of your seat during the ride.

Inversion Sometimes the cars go upside down.

Smoothness Some parts of the ride are smooth, and some parts twist and change direction.

The tables below show the Roller Coaster Survey responses collected from Internet respondents and from a group of 7th-grade students.

Roller Coaster Seating Preferences

Preference	Votes From Internet	Votes From 7th Graders
Front	97	27
Middle	50	22
Back	18	14
Total Votes	**165**	**63**

Other Roller Coaster Preferences

Preference	Votes From Internet	Votes From 7th Graders
Airtime	88	31
Height	36	24
Inversions	59	29
Smoothness	39	12
Speed	105	57
Total Votes	**327**	**153**

Notice the four different *samples* reported:

- Answers to the first Roller Coaster Survey question from Internet respondents

- Answers to the second Roller Coaster Survey question from Internet respondents

- Answers to the first Roller Coaster Survey question from 7th graders

- Answers to the second Roller Coaster Survey question from 7th graders

The table shows that 165 people responded to the Internet survey about seating. Of those, 97 people prefer to sit at the front. The *frequency* of the response "front" is 97.

- What is the frequency of 7th graders who prefer to sit at the front of a roller coaster?

Suppose you want to find out which group includes more people who prefer to sit at the front.

The sample sizes of Internet respondents and 7th graders are different. You can use **relative frequencies**—frequencies based on percentages—to compare samples of different sizes. For example, $\frac{97}{165} \approx 0.59$, so about 59% of the people who voted online prefer to sit at the front of a roller coaster.

Relative Frequency

$\frac{97}{165} \approx 59\%$

Survey Responses

	Internet	7th Graders
Prefers Front	97	27
Total	165	63

- How can you compare the results of a survey to see whether each group responded to the questions in a similar way?

Problem 1.3

A As a class, answer the two Roller Coaster Survey questions. On a copy of the tables on the previous page, record your class data.

B For each survey question, make *bar graphs* of the three data sets: the Internet data, the 7th-grade data, and your class data. Use percents to report relative frequencies on your bar graphs.

C Which measure(s) of center—*mean, median,* or *mode*—can you use to describe these results? Explain.

D 1. For each survey question, write two statements comparing results from the three data sets.

  2. Write two statements to summarize the data collected from the Roller Coaster Survey. How are the summaries useful?

E Suppose 400 people ride a roller coaster in one day. How many of them would you predict want to sit at the front? Explain.

A C E Homework starts on page 20.

1.4

Are Steel-Frame Coasters Faster Than Wood-Frame Coasters?
Using the IQR to Compare Samples

Have you ever wondered how many roller coasters there are in the world? The table below displays data from a **census.** It shows information about the **population**, or entire collection, of roller coasters worldwide. About 95% of the coasters are steel-frame coasters; about 5% are wood-frame coasters.

Roller Coaster Census

Roller Coaster Count			Some Types of Steel-Frame Coasters			
Continent	Total	Wood	Steel	Inverted	Stand Up	Suspended	Sit Down
Africa	59	0	59	3	0	0	56
Asia	1,455	13	1,442	47	4	16	1,362
Australia	24	3	21	2	0	0	19
Europe	822	35	787	28	1	12	733
North America	764	122	642	50	10	5	561
South America	142	1	141	3	0	4	134
Total	3,266	174	3,092	133	15	37	2,865

SOURCE: *Roller Coaster DataBase*

- How do you think the roller-coaster census data were collected?

In this Problem, you will use data from a sample of 30 steel-frame roller coasters and data from a sample of 30 wood-frame roller coasters. The table below shows some data from the samples.

Roller-Coaster Sample Data

Steel-Frame Roller Coasters	Top Speed (mi/h)	Duration (min)
Steel-Frame Coaster A	22	1.50
Steel-Frame Coaster B	40	1.53
Steel-Frame Coaster C	50	2.00
Steel-Frame Coaster D	70	0.55
Wood-Frame Roller Coasters	Top Speed (mi/h)	Duration (min)
Wood-Frame Coaster A	50	1.75
Wood-Frame Coaster B	50	1.83
Wood-Frame Coaster C	55	2.00
Wood-Frame Coaster D	62	2.50

 How might you decide which are faster, steel-frame roller coasters or wood-frame roller coasters? Explain.

Problem 1.4

Use the samples of roller-coaster data provided by your teacher for Questions A–D.

 1. What do you consider to be a fast speed for a roller coaster? Explain.

2. Suppose you want to ride the faster of two roller coasters. Does knowing each roller coaster's top speed help you make the decision? Explain.

3. Do you think steel-frame roller coasters are faster than wood-frame roller coasters? Use the top-speed data to justify your answer.

continued on the next page >

Problem 1.4 *continued*

B The dot plots below show the top-speed data from the sample of 30 steel-frame coasters and 30 wood-frame coasters. The mean is marked with a blue triangle (△). Use the dot plots to answer parts (1)–(3).

Steel-Frame Roller Coaster Speeds

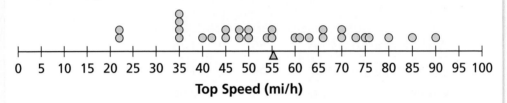

Mean = 55.03 mi/h
MAD = 14.64 mi/h

Top Speed (mi/h)

Wood-Frame Roller Coaster Speeds

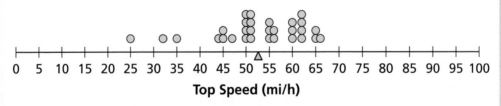

Mean = 52.6 mi/h
MAD = 7.47 mi/h

Top Speed (mi/h)

1. Identify the minimum and maximum values, ranges, and means of each distribution. Use these statistics to compare the speeds of steel-frame and wood-frame roller coasters.

2. Identify the median and the *interquartile range (IQR)* of each distribution. Use the medians and IQRs to compare the speeds of steel-frame and wood-frame roller coasters.

3. Make a *box-and-whisker plot,* or box plot, of each distribution. Use the same scale for each graph. Use the box plots to compare the speeds of steel-frame and wood-frame roller coasters.

Problem **1.4**   *continued*

C Compare your answer to Question A, part (3) with your answers to Question B. Are steel-frame roller coasters faster than wood-frame roller coasters? Explain your reasoning.

D Charlie and Rosa wrote the reports below. They used the two distributions of data to compare steel-frame roller coasters and wood-frame roller coasters. Do you agree with Charlie or with Rosa? Explain your reasoning.

Charlie

I found that the means and medians are about the same for each distribution. If I looked at the box plots and the statistics, I would say that steel-frame roller coasters are slightly faster than wood-frame roller coasters.

When I made the box plots, I noticed that the data distribution for wood-frame roller coasters has two outliers. I know that low or high data values shift the mean. In this case, the outliers made the mean speed of the wood-frame roller coasters shift down below the median.

So keeping the outliers in mind, I concluded that steel-frame roller coasters and wood-frame roller coasters have similar speeds.

Rosa

The measures of center were all pretty close, so i looked at the measures of spread. The IQR helped me see that there is greater variability in the steel-frame roller coasters than in the wood-frame roller coasters.

I looked at the top 25% of all roller-coaster speeds. The top speeds for wood-frame roller coasters are around 60–66 mi/h and steel-frame roller coasters have top speeds around 70–90 mi/h.

Steel-frame roller coasters have faster speeds than wood-frame roller coasters, but not all steel-frame roller coasters are faster than all wood-frame roller coasters.

 Homework starts on page 20.

Applications

For all Exercises, use your calculator when needed.

For Exercises 1 and 2, use the table below.

Diving Scores

Diver	Dive 1	Dive 2	Dive 3	Dive 4	Dive 5
Jarrod	8.5	8.1	6.4	9.5	10.0
Pascal	9.3	7.5	8.0	8.5	9.2

1. a. Find the mean and the median of Jarrod's diving scores. Compare the mean and the median.

 b. Find the mean and the median of Pascal's diving scores. Compare the mean and the median.

 c. Use measures of center to compare Jarrod's and Pascal's diving results. What can you say about their performances?

2. a. Find the range and the MAD of Jarrod's scores.

 b. Find the range and the MAD of Pascal's scores.

 c. Use measures of spread to compare Jarrod's and Pascal's diving results. What can you say about their performances?

The Soccer Club holds a flavored-popcorn fundraiser each fall. The 23 club members form four teams. The most successful team receives a prize. For Exercises 3–7, use the data in the table below.

Money Collected During Fundraiser
(dollars)

Team 1	Team 2	Team 3	Team 4
55	56	100	80
53	53	50	73
44	50	40	44
44	38	40	38
39	37	25	35
35	36	15	

3. Find the total amount of money collected by each team. Do the totals help you determine the most successful team? Explain.

4. a. What is the mean amount of money collected by each team? The median?

    b. Do either of these measures of center help you determine the most successful team? Explain.

5. a. For each team, find the range and MAD.

    b. Do either of these measures of spread help you determine the most successful team? Explain.

For Exercises 6 and 7, use the table above. Answer each question for Teams 1–4.

6. a. How many of the team's data values are located *within one MAD* of the mean (both less than and greater than the mean)? Write this number as a percent.

    b. How many of the team's data values are located *within two MADs* of the mean? Write this number as a percent.

    c. How many of the team's data values are located *more than two MADs* away from the mean? Write this number as a percent.

7. Use your calculations from Exercise 6. Does any team have a member who raised much more (or much less) money than the other team members? Explain your reasoning.

8. The following question was asked in a survey:

   What is your favorite amusement-park ride?

   ■ Roller Coaster   ■ Log Ride   ■ Ferris Wheel   ■ Bumper Cars

   The tablet below shows the results from an Internet survey and from surveys of 7th-grade students at East Jr. High and West Jr. High.

   ## Favorite Amusement Park Rides

Favorite Ride	Votes From the Internet	Votes From East Jr. High	Votes From West Jr. High
Roller Coaster	92	42	36
Log Ride	26	31	14
Ferris Wheel	22	3	6
Bumper Cars	20	4	4
Total Votes	**160**	**80**	**60**

   a. Make bar graphs for each of the three data sets: the Internet survey data, the data from East Jr. High, and the data from West Jr. High. Use percents to show relative frequencies.

   b. Write three or more statements comparing the data sets.

For Exercises 9–13, use the Roller Coaster Census from Problem 1.4 to complete the statements below.

9. For every one wood-frame roller coaster there are about ■ steel-frame roller coasters.

10. North America has about ■ times as many roller coasters as South America.

11. Asia has about ■ times as many roller coasters as North America.

12. North America has ▨ % of all the wood-frame roller coasters in the world.

13. Write two of your own comparison statements.

14. Use the dot plots below. For each part (a)–(c), answer the questions for each distribution.

Steel-Frame Roller Coaster Speeds

Mean = 55.03 mi/h
MAD = 14.64 mi/h

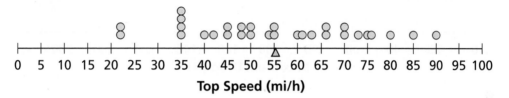

Top Speed (mi/h)

Wood-Frame Roller Coaster Speeds

Mean = 52.6 mi/h
MAD = 7.47 mi/h

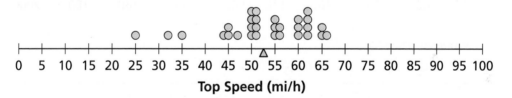

Top Speed (mi/h)

a. How many roller coasters have speeds within one MAD of the mean (both less than and greater than the mean)? Write this number as a percent.

b. How many roller coasters have speeds within two MADs of the mean? Write this number as a percent.

c. How many roller coasters have speeds more than two MADs away from the mean? Write this number as a percent.

15. The three pairs of dot plots below show data for 50 wood-frame roller coasters. Each mean is marked with a △. Each median is marked with a ⊥. Use the dot plots to answer the questions on the next page.

Maximum Drop for Each Wood-Frame Roller Coaster

Years: 1960–2004

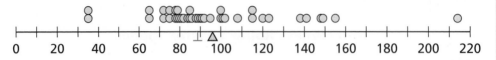

Years: 1902–1959

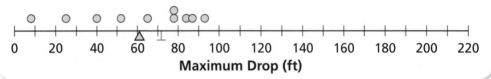

Maximum Drop (ft)

Maximum Height for Each Wood-Frame Roller Coaster

Years: 1960–2004

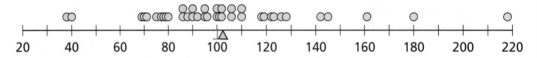

Years: 1902–1959

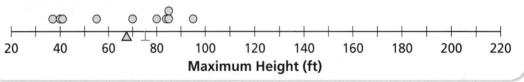

Maximum Height (ft)

Top Speed for Each Wood-Frame Roller Coaster

Years: 1960–2004

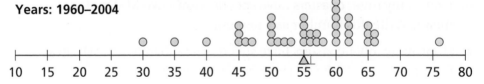

Years: 1902–1959

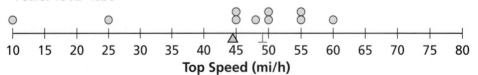

Top Speed (mi/h)

a. Write three statements comparing wood-frame roller coasters built before 1960 with wood-frame roller coasters built in 1960 or later.

b. Hector said there are too few roller coasters to make comparisons. Do you agree with Hector? Explain.

16. **Multiple Choice** Most of the data values in a distribution will be located—

   A. more than two MADs away from the mean.

   B. within two MADs of the mean.

   C. within one MAD of the mean.

Connections

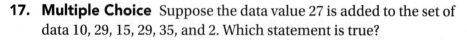

17. **Multiple Choice** Suppose the data value 27 is added to the set of data 10, 29, 15, 29, 35, and 2. Which statement is true?

   F. The mean would increase by 4.

   G. The mode would decrease by 10.

   H. The median would decrease by 1.

   J. None of the above.

18. **Multiple Choice** The mean of six numbers is 25. If one of the numbers is 15, what is the mean of the other five numbers?

   A. 15   **B.** 25   **C.** 27   **D.** 40

19. **Multiple Choice** Jasper's test scores for eight exams are below.

   84, 72, 88, 84, 92, 94, 78, and x

   If the median of his scores is 86, what is a possible value for x?

   F. 68   **G.** 84   **H.** 86   **J.** 95

20. **Multiple Choice** In Mr. Ramirez's math class, there are three times as many girls as boys. The girls' mean grade on a recent quiz was 90. The boys' mean grade was 86. What was the mean grade for the class altogether?

   A. 88   **B.** 44   **C.** 89   **D.** 95

21. The tables below show the results of a survey of children ages 5 to 15. Use the data to answer the questions on the next page.

Table 1:
Years Lived in
Current Home

Years	Children	Percent
<1	639	7.9%
1	776	9.6%
2	733	9.0%
3	735	▩
4	587	7.2%
5	612	7.5%
6	487	6.0%
7	431	5.3%
8	442	5.4%
9	412	5.1%
10	492	6.0%
11	520	6.5%
12	508	6.3%
13	339	4.1%
14	225	2.8%
15	176	2.2%
Total	8,114	100%

SOURCE: *National Geographic*

Table 2:
Apartments or Houses
Lived in Since Birth

Number of Apartments or Houses	Children	Percent
1	1,645	20.7%
2	1,957	24.7%
3	1,331	16.8%
4	968	▩
5	661	8.3%
6	487	6.1%
7	291	3.7%
8	184	2.3%
9	80	1.0%
10	330	4.2%
Total	7,934	100%

Table 3:
Cities or Towns Lived in Since Birth

Number of Cities or Towns	Boys	Girls	Ages 5–12	Ages 13–15
1	▩	42.2%	42.1%	40.9%
>1	58.9%	57.8%	▩	59.1%
Total	100%	100%	100%	100%

a. Find the missing percents in each table. Explain how you found them.

b. Make a bar graph to display the information in the third column of Table 2.

c. Write a summary paragraph about Table 2.

d. What percent of children have lived in the same home for 10 or more years? Justify your answer.

e. What percent of children have lived in only one home since they were born? Justify your answer.

f. About what fraction of the boys have lived in the same city or town all their lives? Explain.

22. The titles of the two circle graphs below are not shown. Use the data from the Roller Coaster Census in Problem 1.4. Which title goes with which graph? Explain.

Title 1: Wood-Frame Roller Coasters by Continent

Title 2: Steel-Frame Roller Coasters by Continent

a.   **b.**

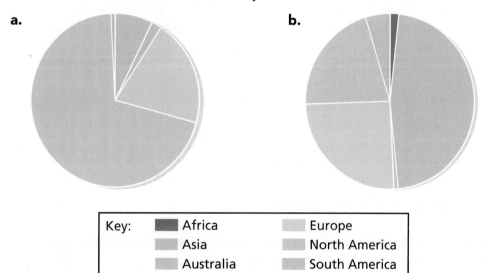

Key:	Africa	Europe
	Asia	North America
	Australia	South America

For Exercises 23 and 24, use the dot plot below. The dot plot shows the amount of sugar per serving in 47 cereals.

Sugar in Cereals

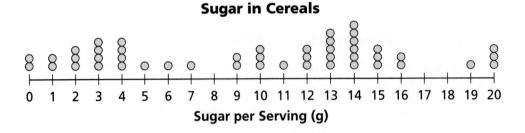

Sugar per Serving (g)

23. Describe the shape of the distribution above.

24. Estimate the locations of the mean and the median. How does the shape of the distribution influence your estimates?

For Exercises 25 and 26, use the dot plot below. The dot plot shows the serving sizes of 47 cereals.

Serving Sizes of Cereals

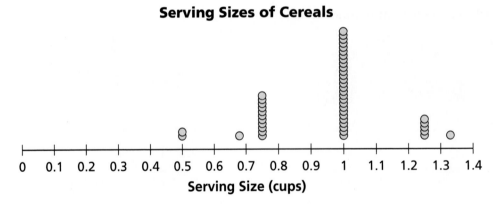

Serving Size (cups)

25. Describe the distribution of serving sizes.

26. Estimate the locations of the mean and the median. How does the shape of the distribution influence your estimates?

Extensions

For Exercises 27–32, use the dot plots and box plots below. The dot plots show the resting and exercise heart rates for a 7th-grade class.

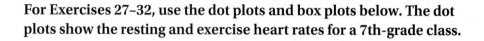

Resting Heart Rate

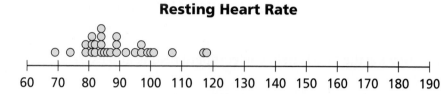

Exercise Heart Rate

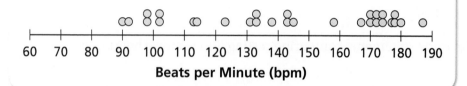

Resting Heart Rate

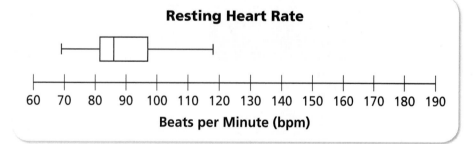

Exercise Heart Rate

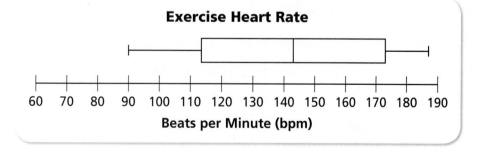

For Exercises 27–32, use the dot plots and box plots on the previous page.

27. Suppose you were given two means: 143.3 bpm and 89.4 bpm. Which mean is for the distribution of resting heart rates? Exercise heart rates? Explain.

28. Suppose you were given two MADs: 27.3 bpm and 8.9 bpm. Which MAD is for the distribution of resting heart rates? Exercise heart rates? Explain.

29. How does knowing the MADs help you compare resting and exercise heart rates?

30. Suppose you were given two IQRs: 15.5 bpm and 59.5 bpm. Which IQR is for the distribution of resting heart rates? Exercise heart rates? Explain.

31. How does knowing the IQRs help you compare resting and exercise heart rates?

32. Write three statements comparing resting and exercise heart rates.

33. The frequency table below shows the numbers of students who earned each grade in a teacher's math classes.

Letter Grade	Number of Students
A	8
B	15
C	20
D	5
F	2

a. Make a bar graph that shows the frequency of each letter grade.

b. Compute the *relative frequency* of each letter grade.

c. Make a bar graph that shows the relative frequencies.

d. Compare the two bar graphs. What do you notice about the shapes of the two distributions?

e. The teacher wants to predict about how many students might earn a letter grade of C in another math class. Should the teacher use frequency or relative frequency to help her make a prediction? Explain.

Mathematical Reflections

1

In this Investigation, you developed strategies to compare two or more distributions with equal or unequal amounts of data. The following questions will help you summarize what you have learned.

Think about these questions. Discuss your ideas with other students and your teacher. Then write a summary of your findings in your notebook.

1. **a.** A new term is used in this Investigation: *sample*. **What** do you think *sample* means?

   b. Suppose you have data from a 7th-grade class. The data are answers to the questions:

   • What is your favorite movie?

   • How many movies do you watch per week?

   i. Which statistics can you use to summarize the results of the data?

   ii. How could you use the data to predict the number of students in the entire 7th grade who would say they watch two movies per week?

2. **a. How** do graphs of distributions help you compare data sets?

   b. How do measures of center help you compare data sets?

   c. How do measures of spread help you compare data sets?

3. **When** does it make sense to compare groups using counts, or frequencies? When does it make sense to compare groups using percents, or relative frequencies? Explain.

Common Core Mathematical Practices

As you worked on the Problems in this Investigation, you used prior knowledge to make sense of them. You also applied Mathematical Practices to solve the Problems. Think back over your work, the ways you thought about the Problems, and how you used Mathematical Practices.

Sophie described her thoughts in the following way:

> Sometimes, knowing the mean is not enough when you want to compare data sets. You have to get MAD!
>
> The MAD (mean absolute deviation) is how much, on average, data values in a data set differ from the mean. When there are only a few data values, you can do the work by hand.
>
> In Problem 1.2, the mean amount collected by Team 1 was $35. We found the difference between each member's amount and the mean. We added the differences ($10 + 6 + 2 + 0 + 8 + 10 = 36$). Then we divided the sum by the total number of team members ($36 \div 6 = 6$). The MAD for Team 1 was $6. So, on average, the data values were $6 less than or greater than the mean of $35.
>
> For larger data sets, you can use special calculators. We noticed that more consistent data sets had smaller MADs.
>
> ....
>
> **Common Core Standards for Mathematical Practice**
> **MP6** Attend to precision.

? • What other Mathematical Practices can you identify in Sophie's reasoning?

• Describe a Mathematical Practice that you and your classmates used to solve a different Problem in this Investigation.

Investigation 2

Choosing a Sample From a Population

Collecting information about the students in your math class, such as their favorite foods or activities, would be fairly easy. On the other hand, collecting information about all the middle-school students in your state would be very difficult.

To make collecting information on a large group, or *population*, easier, you can collect data from a small part, or **sample**, of that population. Depending on how the sample is selected, it may be possible to use the data to make predictions or draw conclusions about an entire population. The challenge is to choose a sample that accurately represents the population as a whole.

another sample of the population

a sample of the population

Common Core State Standards

7.SP.A.1 Understand that statistics can be used to gain information about a population by examining a sample of the population; generalizations about a population from a sample are valid only if the sample is representative of that population. Understand that random sampling tends to produce representative samples and support valid inferences.

7.SP.A.2 Use data from a random sample to draw inferences about a population with an unknown characteristic of interest. Generate multiple samples (or simulated samples) of the same size to gauge the variation in estimates or predictions.

Also 7.RP.A.3, 7.SP.C.7, 7.SP.C.7a

Consider this information:

In the United States, over 75% of teens have cell phones. Almost half of the teens who own cell phones own smartphones. So, more than 35% of all teens own smartphones, compared to 23% in 2011.

From 2009 to 2011, the median number of daily texts teens sent rose from 50 to 60. Texting among older teens, ages 14–17, increased from 60 texts to 100 texts per day during that two-year span.

- How could the groups reporting this information know about the activities of all the teenagers in the United States?

- Do you think these facts were gathered from every teenager in the population? Why or why not?

Did You Know?

Thirty years ago, the first "mobile" phones were car phones that weighed over 20 pounds. Early cell phones weighed just under two pounds and cost almost $4,000 (that's roughly $9,200 in today's dollars). Today, smartphones generally weigh about 4 ounces and cost less than $1,000.

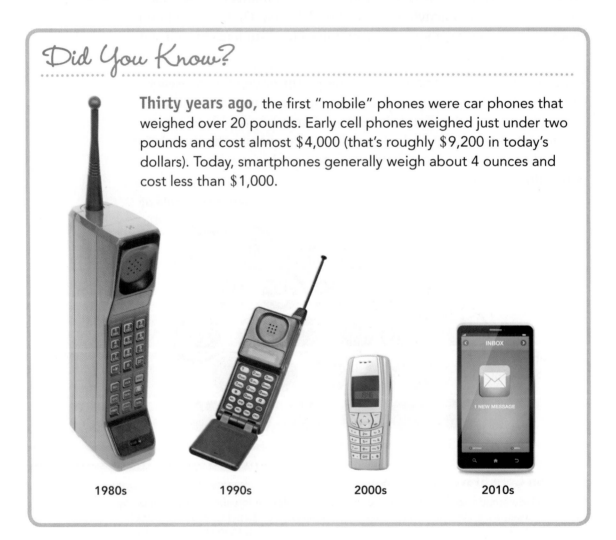

1980s   1990s   2000s   2010s

2.1 Asking About Honesty
Using a Sample to Draw Conclusions

Suppose a national magazine asks its readers to respond to the questions below about honesty. Readers take the survey on the magazine's Web site.

HONESTY SURVEY

If This Happened to You

1. **What would you do if you found someone's wallet on the street?**
   a. Try to return it to the owner
   b. Return it, but keep the money
   c. Keep the wallet and the money

2. **What would you do if a cashier mistakenly gave you $10 extra in change?**
   a. Tell the cashier about the error
   b. Say nothing and keep the cash

3. **Would you cheat on an exam if you were sure you wouldn't get caught?**
   a. Yes   b. No

4. **Would you download music from the Internet illegally instead of buying the music?**
   a. Yes   b. No

5. **Do you feel that you are an honest person in most situations?**
   a. Yes   b. No

- What is the population for the Honesty Survey?

- Is asking readers to volunteer their answers a good way for the magazine to draw conclusions about the honesty of the population? Why or why not?

Problem 2.1

A A **sampling plan** is a strategy for choosing a sample from a population. What is the population for the Honesty Survey? What is the sample? How was the sample chosen from the population?

B Suppose 5,280 people completed the survey.

   1. For the first question: 3,960 people said they would try to return the wallet to the owner; 792 said they would return the wallet but keep the money; and 528 said they would keep the wallet and the money. What is the relative frequency of each response?

   2. For the second question: 4,752 said they would tell the cashier about the error. What is the relative frequency of respondents who said they would tell the cashier about the error?

   3. For the third question: 4,224 people answered "No." What is the relative frequency of respondents said they would *not* cheat on an exam?

   4. For the fourth question: 1,584 people answered "Yes." What is the relative frequency of respondents who said they would *not* download music illegally from the Internet?

C   **1.** Make a table or graph that shows the relative frequencies of "honest" and "dishonest" answers for each of the first four questions of the Honesty Survey.

   2. Use your table or graph to analyze the responses to the four survey questions. What conclusions can you draw about people's behavior? Explain.

D Use the survey results in Question B and your answers to Question C. Suppose the United States population is about 314 million.

   1. Estimate how many people in the United States would say that they would not cheat on an exam.

   2. Estimate how many people in the United States would say that they would not download music illegally from the Internet.

Problem 2.1 continued

 1. Do you think this sample of 5,280 people accurately represents the population of the United States? Why or why not?

2. Suppose you were asked to revise the sampling plan for this survey. How could you make sure that the sample more accurately represents the U.S. population?

A C E Homework starts on page 45.

2.2 Selecting a Sample
Different Kinds of Samples

Drawing accurate conclusions about a population based on a sample can be complicated. When you choose a sample, it should be *representative* of the population. This means the sample must have characteristics similar to those of the population. Not all samples are **representative samples.**

Suppose you are doing research on students at your school. You plan to ask these questions:

> • How many hours of sleep do you get each school night?
>
> • How many movies do you watch each week?

If your school has many students, it might be difficult to gather and analyze data from every student.

- Are these questions clear enough to allow you to collect good data? Why or why not?

- How might you select a sample of your school population to survey?

Problem 2.2

Ms. Ruiz's class is conducting a survey about the number of hours students spend sleeping and the number of hours they spend watching movies. The class divides into four groups. Each group devises a plan for sampling the school population.

Group 1

Group 2

Group 3

Group 4

Problem 2.2 *continued*

Ⓐ What are the advantages and disadvantages of each sampling plan?

Ⓑ Which plan do you think will collect the most accurate data to represent students in the whole school? Explain.

Ⓒ The four sampling plans are examples of common sampling methods.

  1. Group 1's plan is an example of **convenience sampling**. What do you think convenience sampling is? Describe another sampling plan using convenience sampling.

  2. Group 2's plan is an example of **systematic sampling**. What do you think systematic sampling is? Describe another sampling plan using systematic sampling.

  3. Group 3's plan is an example of **voluntary-response sampling**. What do you think voluntary-response sampling is? Describe another sampling plan using voluntary-response sampling.

  4. Group 4's plan is an example of **random sampling**. What do you think random sampling is? Describe another sampling plan using random sampling.

Ⓓ **1.** Jahmal thinks that Group 1, Group 2, and Group 3 devised sampling plans that might not give representative samples. Do you agree or disagree? Explain.

  2. Jahmal comes up with a new plan. He thinks each teacher should select one boy and one girl and ask them the survey questions. There are four teachers for each grade (Grades 6–8), so they would end up with a sample of 24 students.

   i. What type of sampling plan is this?

   ii. Will it give a representative sample?

   iii. Do you like Jahmal's plan? Explain. If you do not like Jahmal's plan, how would you change it?

Ⓐ Ⓒ Ⓔ Homework starts on page 45.

2.3 Choosing Random Samples
Comparing Samples Using Center and Spread

In most cases, a good sampling plan is one that gives each member of the population the same chance of being selected. To do this, you may use concepts from probability, such as *equally likely* outcomes.

A random sampling plan gives each member of a population an equally likely chance of being included in the sample. The resulting sample is called a random sample.

To select a random sample from a population of 100 students, you can use spinners to generate pairs of random digits.

- How does using the two spinners help you select a random sample from a population of 100 students?

- What two-digit numbers can you generate with the spinners?

- How can you make sure Student 100 has an equally likely chance of being included in your sample?

- What ideas from probability are you using?

There are many other ways to select a random sample of students. For example, you could roll two 10-sided numbered solids or generate random numbers with your calculator.

- What other strategies could you use?

The table on the next page shows data collected from a 7th-grade class. The data include the number of hours of sleep each student got the previous night and the number of movies each student watched the previous week.

- How can you use statistics from a random sample to draw conclusions about the entire population of 7th-grade students in the school?

Responses to Grade 7 Movie and Sleep Survey

Student	Sleep Last Night (h)	Movies Last Week (no. of)	Student	Sleep Last Night (h)	Movies Last Week (no. of)	Student	Sleep Last Night (h)	Movies Last Week (no. of)
01	11.5	14	35	6.5	5	68	5.5	0
02	2.0	8	36	9.3	1	69	10.5	7
03	7.7	3	37	8.2	3	70	7.5	1
04	9.3	1	38	7.3	3	71	7.8	0
05	7.1	16	39	7.4	6	72	7.3	1
06	7.5	1	40	8.5	7	73	9.3	2
07	8.0	4	41	5.5	17	74	9.0	1
08	7.8	1	42	6.5	3	75	8.7	1
09	8.0	13	43	7.0	5	76	8.5	3
10	8.0	15	44	8.5	2	77	9.0	1
11	9.0	1	45	9.3	4	78	8.0	1
12	9.2	10	46	8.0	15	79	8.0	4
13	8.5	5	47	8.5	10	80	6.5	0
14	6.0	15	48	6.2	11	81	8.0	0
15	6.5	10	49	11.8	10	82	9.0	8
16	8.3	2	50	9.0	4	83	8.0	0
17	7.4	2	51	5.0	4	84	7.0	0
18	11.2	3	52	6.5	5	85	9.0	6
19	7.3	1	53	8.5	2	86	7.3	0
20	8.0	0	54	9.1	15	87	9.0	3
21	7.8	1	55	7.5	2	88	7.5	5
22	7.8	1	56	8.5	1	89	8.0	0
23	9.2	2	57	8.0	2	90	7.5	6
24	7.5	0	58	7.0	7	91	8.0	4
25	8.8	1	59	8.4	10	92	9.0	4
26	8.5	0	60	9.5	1	93	7.0	0
27	9.0	0	61	7.3	5	94	8.0	3
28	8.5	0	62	7.3	4	95	8.3	3
29	8.2	2	63	8.5	3	96	8.3	14
30	7.8	2	64	9.0	3	97	7.8	5
31	8.0	2	65	9.0	4	98	8.5	1
32	7.3	8	66	7.3	5	99	8.3	3
33	6.0	5	67	5.7	0	100	7.5	2
34	7.5	5						

Problem 2.3

In this Problem, you will choose a sample and then represent the data with a line plot and with a box plot. You will compare your sample's distribution with your classmates' distributions. Your class should decide on a scale for the line plot and box plot before starting.

Ⓐ 1. Select a random sample of 30 students from the table on the previous page. Your sample should include 30 different students. If you select a student who is already in your sample, select another.

2. For each student in your sample, record the number of hours slept and the number of movies watched.

Ⓑ 1. Make a line plot showing the number of movies watched by your sample.

2. a. Locate the mean.

b. Describe the shape of the distribution.

3. Find the range and MAD. Describe the variability of the number of movies watched by students in your sample.

4. Compare your sample distribution with those of your classmates. Describe any similarities or differences.

5. What can you conclude about the number of movies the population of 7th-grade students watched last week based on all the samples selected by your class? Explain.

Ⓒ 1. Find the *five-number summary* of the number of hours slept for your sample. Make a box-and-whisker plot of the data in your sample.

2. Describe the shape of the distribution.

3. Find the range and IQR. Describe the variability of the number of hours slept for the students in your sample.

4. Compare your sample distribution with those of your classmates. Describe any similarities or differences.

5. What can you conclude about the number of hours the population of 7th-grade students slept last night based on all the samples selected by your class? Explain.

 Homework starts on page 45.

2.4 Growing Samples
What Size Sample to Use?

In Problem 2.3, you used statistics from random samples to estimate the number of hours slept and the number of movies watched by 100 students.

- Are you able to make good estimates with less work by selecting smaller samples?

- How does sample size relate to the accuracy of statistical estimates?

Problem 2.4

A Use the population of 100 students from Problem 2.3. Select a random sample of 5 students and a random sample of 10 students. Record the number of hours slept and the number of movies watched for each student. **Note:** You should select a new set of students for each sample, but one or more students may happen to appear in both samples.

B Use all three samples (the 5-student sample and the 10-student sample from Question A, and the 30-student sample from Problem 2.3) to answer the questions below.

1. For each sample size (5, 10, and 30), find the mean and median number of hours slept. Find the mean and median number of movies watched. Find the IQR and the MAD of each data set.

2. Record the means, the medians, the IQRs, and the MADs in a class chart. Record the summary statistics of your classmates' samples as well.

continued on the next page >

Problem **2.4** *continued*

C **1.** Use the class data about the mean number of movies watched. For each sample size (5, 10, and 30 students), make a line plot displaying the *means* of the samples. You will have three line plots, each showing how the means vary across the samples. These are called **sampling distributions**. Compare the three sampling distributions by describing the variability in each distribution.

2. The mean number of movies watched for the population of 100 students is 4.22 movies. Write a paragraph describing how close the means of samples of different sizes are to the mean of the population.

D **1.** Use the class data about the median number of movies watched. For each sample size, make a line plot displaying the *medians* of the samples. You will have three line plots, each showing how the medians vary across the samples. Compare the three sampling distributions by describing the variability in each distribution.

2. The median number of movies watched for the population of 100 students is 3 movies. Write a paragraph describing how close the medians of samples of different sizes are to the median of the population.

E For the population of 100 students, the mean number of hours slept is 7.96 hours, and the median is 8 hours.

Follow the steps you used in Questions C and D to analyze the distribution of means and medians of samples of different sizes. Discuss how close the means and medians of samples of different sizes are to the mean and median of the whole population for the number of hours slept.

F Suppose each student in your class chose a sample of 50 students and found the means and medians of the data for the number of hours slept and the number of movies watched. What would you expect the line plots of these means and medians to look like? Explain.

G Use the class chart of summary statistics. What patterns do you see in the measures of spread for the three different sample sizes? Explain why these patterns make sense.

A C E Homework starts on page 45.

Applications

For Exercises 1–4, describe the *population*, the *sampling plan*, and the *sample*.

1. A magazine for teenagers asks its readers to write in with information about how they solve personal problems.

2. An 8th-grade class wants to find out how much time middle-school students spend on the telephone each day. Students in the class keep a record of the amount of time they spend on the phone each day for a week.

3. Ms. Darnell's class wants to estimate the number of soft drinks middle-school students drink each day. They obtain a list of students in the school and write each name on a card. They put the cards in a box and select the names of 40 students to survey.

4. The newspaper below gives information about how adults feel about global warming. The editors of the school paper want to find out how students feel about this issue. They select 26 students for their survey—one whose name begins with A, one whose name begins with B, one whose name begins with C, and so on.

A middle school has 350 students. One math class decides to investigate how many hours a typical student in the school spent doing homework last week. Several students suggest sampling plans. For Exercises 5–8, name the type of sampling plan. Then tell whether you think the sampling plan would give a representative sample.

5. Zak suggests surveying every third student on each homeroom class list.

6. Kwang-Hee suggests putting 320 white beans and 30 red beans in a bag. Each student would draw a bean as he or she enters the auditorium for an assembly. The 30 students who draw red beans will be surveyed.

7. Ushio suggests that each student in the class survey everyone in his or her English class.

8. Kirby suggests putting surveys on a table at lunch and asking students to return completed questionnaires at the end of the day.

9. A radio host asked her listeners to call in to express their opinions about a local election. What kind of sampling plan is she using? Do you think the results of this survey could be used to describe the opinions of all the show's listeners? Explain.

Manufacturers often conduct quality-control tests on samples of their products. For Exercises 10–13, describe a random sampling plan you would recommend to the company. Justify your recommendation.

10. A toy company produces 5,000 video-game systems each day.

11. A music company manufactures a total of 200,000 compact discs for about 100 recording artists each day.

12. A fireworks company produces over 1,500 rockets each day.

13. A bottling company produces 25,000 bottles of spring water each day.

14. Use the table from Problem 2.3.

   a. Suppose you select the first 30 students for a sample. A second student selects the next 30 students for a different sample, and so on. Will these samples be representative? Explain.

   b. You select students 1, 5, 9, 13, 17, 21, 25, . . . for your sample. A second student chooses students 2, 6, 10, 14, 18, 22, 26, . . . for his sample. A third student chooses students 3, 7, 11, 15, 19, 23, 27, . . . for her sample, and so on. Will this result in representative samples? Explain.

15. **a.** The homecoming committee wants to estimate how many students will attend the homecoming dance. It does not, however, want to ask every student in the school. Describe a method the committee could use to select a sample of students to survey.

   b. Describe how the committee could use the results of its survey to predict the number of students who will attend the dance.

16. Use the graph below. About how many more hours per day does a typical newborn sleep than a typical 10- to 13-year-old?

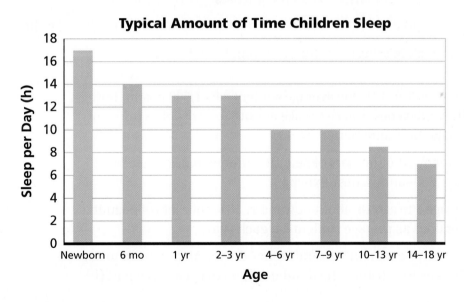

Typical Amount of Time Children Sleep

17. Suppose you want to survey students in your school to find out how many hours they sleep each night. Which would be the best sample size: 5 students, 10 students, or 30 students? Explain.

Connections

18. The scoreboard below displays Ella's diving scores from a recent competition. One score cannot be read.

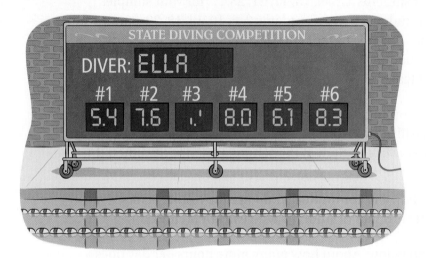

These statistics summarize Ella's diving scores:

mean = 6.75 points   median = 6.85 points   range = 3.2 points

What was Ella's missing score for the competition? Explain.

19. Between ages 5 and 18, the average student eats 1,500 peanut butter and jelly sandwiches. You can make about 15 sandwiches from an 18-ounce jar of peanut butter.

  a. How many 18-ounce jars of peanut butter would you need to make 1,500 sandwiches? Explain.

  b. From age 5 to age 18, about how many 18-ounce jars of peanut butter does an average student eat each year?

  c. How many peanut butter sandwiches does a student need to eat each week to consume the number of jars per year from part (b)?

For Exercises 20–22, use the two dot plots below. The dot plots show
the number of hours students spent doing homework on Monday.

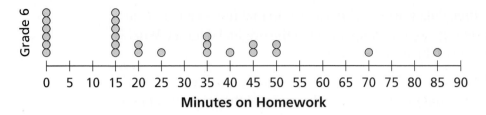

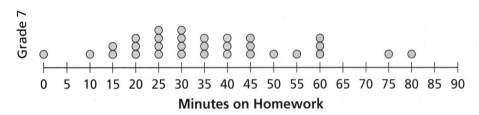

20. Find the median homework times. Copy and complete the
table below.

**Time Spent on Homework
(minutes)**

Grade	Mean	Median	MAD
6	25.8	▧	18.56
7	36.13	▧	14.53

21. a. For each grade, describe the variability in the distribution of
homework times. Use what you know about the distribution's
shape and the MAD.

    b. Use statistics to compare the times 6th graders spent doing
homework to the times 7th graders spent doing homework.

22. Could these data be used to describe the time spent on homework
on a typical school night by a typical student in each grade? Explain.

23. Consider the following data set: 20, 22, 23, 23, 24, 24, and 25.

   a. Find the mean and the range of the values.

   b. Add three data values to the data set so that the mean of the new data set is greater than the mean of the original data set. What is the range of the new data set?

   c. Add three data values to the original data set so that the mean of the new data set is less than the mean of the original data set. What is the range of the new data set?

   d. How do the ranges of the three data sets compare? Why do you think this is so?

24. Multiple Choice Suppose you survey 30 students from a population of 150 students in the 7th grade. Which statement is *false*?

   A. The ratio of those sampled to those not sampled is 30 to 120.

   B. One out of every five people in the population was sampled.

   C. Twenty-five percent of the students in the population were sampled.

   D. One-fifth of the students in the population were sampled.

25. There are 350 students in a school. Ms. Cabral's class surveys two random samples of students to find out how many went to camp last summer. The results are below.

   Sample 1: 8 of 25 attended camp.

   Sample 2: 7 of 28 attended camp.

   a. Use the results from Sample 1. What fraction of the students in the school do you think attended camp? How many students attended camp?

   b. Use the results from Sample 2. What fraction of the students in the school do you think attended camp? How many students attended camp?

   c. Which sample concludes that the greater fraction of students attended camp?

   d. One of Ms. Cabral's students says, "We were careful to choose our samples at random. Why did the two samples give us different conclusions?" How would you answer the student's question?

Use the following information for Exercises 26–31.

Annie's teacher starts each class with the names of all the students in a container. There are 12 girls and 6 boys in the class.

The teacher pulls out names at random to choose students to present answers. After choosing a name, the teacher sets the name aside. At the end of class, the teacher replaces all the names in the container. So, each student's name has a chance of being chosen the next day.

26. What is the probability Annie will be the first student chosen on Monday?

27. What is the probability Annie will be the first student chosen on Tuesday?

28. What is the probability Annie will be the first student chosen on both Monday and Tuesday?

29. What is the probability the first student chosen on a given day will be a girl?

30. Suppose Annie is chosen first. What is the probability that the next student selected will be another girl?

31. Suppose the teacher plans to choose six students during one class. Would you be surprised if only two girls were chosen? Explain.

Use the following information for Exercises 32 and 33. Alyssa wants to know what students think about replacing the candy in two vending machines in the cafeteria with more healthful snacks. Alyssa obtains a list of student names, grouped by grade, with the girls listed first in each grade.

There are 300 6th graders, 300 7th graders, and 200 8th graders. Half of the students in each grade are girls.

32. Alyssa chooses 3 different students at random from the list of 800 students.

   a. What is the probability that the first choice is a girl? The second choice is a girl? The third choice is a girl?

   b. What is the probability that Alyssa chooses three girls?

33. Alyssa decides to choose one person *from each grade* at random.

   a. What is the probability that the 6th-grade choice is a girl?

   b. What is the probability that she chooses three girls?

For Exercises 34–38, use the table below. Alyssa chooses one girl and one boy from each grade. She asks each, "Which would you prefer, a machine with healthful snacks or a machine with candy?"

Vending Machine Preferences

	Grade 6	Grade 7	Grade 8
Girl	healthful snack	healthful snack	healthful snack
Boy	candy	candy	healthful snack

34. How many 6th-grade students do you think prefer a machine with healthful snacks?

35. How many students in the whole school do you think prefer a machine with healthful snacks?

36. What is the probability that a student chosen at random from the whole school is an 8th grader who prefers a machine with healthful snacks?

37. What advice would you give Alyssa's principal about Alyssa's data and the two vending machines? Explain.

38. Alyssa's principal polls all 800 students and finds that 600 prefer a machine with healthful snacks.

  a. What is the probability that a student selected at random prefers a machine with healthful snacks?

  b. What is the probability that a student selected at random is a girl who prefers a machine with healthful snacks?

  c. What is the probability that a student selected at random is a boy who prefers a machine with healthful snacks?

  d. What advice would you give the principal about the data collected and the vending machines?

Extensions

39. Television stations, radio stations, and newspapers often use polls to predict the winners of elections long before the votes are cast. What factors might cause a pre-election poll to be inaccurate?

40. Political parties often write and then conduct their own pre-election polls to find out what voters think about their campaign and their candidates. How might such a poll be biased?

41. a. Polls conducted prior to presidential elections commonly use samples of about 1,000 eligible voters. Suppose there are 207 million eligible voters in the United States. About what percent of eligible voters are in a sample of 1,000?

  b. How do you think this small sample is chosen so that the results will predict the winner with reasonable accuracy? Consider which groups within the total population need to be represented, such as adults 65 years or older.

Did You Know?

How do pollsters decide whom to contact? When pollsters take phone polls, they use random sampling techniques to choose voters from the total voting population. Internet polls, in most cases, exclude households without Internet access. Most online polls are also completed by people who choose to participate.

In this Investigation, you learned about sampling techniques. You also drew conclusions about a population by examining data from random samples. The following questions will help you summarize what you have learned.

Think about these questions. Discuss your ideas with other students and your teacher. Then, write a summary of your findings in your notebook.

1. **Why** are data often collected from a sample rather than from an entire population?

2. **Describe** four plans for selecting a sample from a population. Discuss the advantages and disadvantages of each plan.

3. **a. How** are random samples different from convenience, voluntary-response, and systematic samples?

   b. Why is random sampling preferable to the other sampling plans?

   c. Describe three plans for selecting a random sample from a given population. **What** are the advantages and disadvantages of each plan?

4. Suppose you select several random samples of size 30 from the same population.

   a. When you compare the samples to each other, **what** similarities and differences would you expect to find among the measures of center and spread?

   b. When you compare the samples to the larger population, **what** similarities and differences would you expect to find among the measures of center and spread?

5. **How** has your idea of the term *sample* changed from what you wrote in Mathematical Reflections, Investigation 1?

Common Core Mathematical Practices

As you worked on the Problems in this Investigation, you used prior knowledge to make sense of them. You also applied Mathematical Practices to solve the Problems. Think back over your work, the ways you thought about the Problems, and how you used Mathematical Practices.

Nick described his thoughts in the following way:

In Problem 2.4, I was able to use data from all of the samples that my classmates had gathered. Instead of collecting multiple samples myself, we compiled all of our class data in one big chart.

I could use the information from all of the samples to draw conclusions about the means and medians of the larger population's data. The more data I could use, the more confident I was that my conclusions about the whole population were accurate.

Common Core Standards for Mathematical Practice
MP7 Look for and make use of structure.

• What other Mathematical Practices can you identify in Nick's reasoning?

• Describe a Mathematical Practice that you and your classmates used to solve a different Problem in this Investigation.

Using Samples to Draw Conclusions

There are many different possible samples in any population. You can use a random sampling plan to help you choose your sample fairly. In general, large random samples are more representative than small random samples or samples chosen with other sampling methods.

3.1 Solving an Archeological Mystery
Comparing Samples Using Box Plots

 Archeologists study past civilizations by excavating ancient settlements. They examine the artifacts of the people who lived there.

Common Core State Standards

7.SP.A.1 Understand that statistics can be used to gain information about a population by examining a sample of the population; generalizations about a population from a sample are valid only if the sample is representative of that population. Understand that random sampling tends to produce representative samples and support valid inferences.

7.SP.B.3 Informally assess the degree of visual overlap of two numerical data distributions with similar variabilities, measuring the difference between the centers by expressing it as a multiple of a measure of variability.

Also 7.RP.A.2, 7.NS.A.1, 7.NS.A.1b, 7.SP.A.2, 7.SP.B.4, 7.SP.C.5, and 7.SP.C.7b

On digs in southeastern Montana and north-central Wyoming, archeologists discovered the remains of two Native American settlements. They found a number of arrowheads at each site. The archeologists hoped to use the arrowheads to estimate the time period in which each site was inhabited.

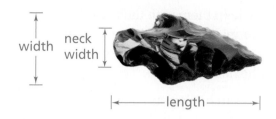

The tables below give the lengths, widths, and neck widths of the arrowheads the archeologists found. The sets of data are samples from different populations of arrowheads from two different time periods.

Site I: 15 Arrowheads

Length (mm)	Width (mm)	Neck Width (mm)
24	19	8
27	19	10
29	19	11
29	22	12
31	16	12
31	32	16
37	23	11
38	22	12
38	26	14
40	25	16
45	22	11
45	28	15
55	22	13
62	26	14
63	29	18

SOURCE: *Plains Anthropologist*

Site II: 37 Arrowheads

Length (mm)	Width (mm)	Neck Width (mm)	Length (mm)	Width (mm)	Neck Width (mm)
13	10	6	24	13	8
15	11	7	24	13	8
16	12	8	24	14	10
16	13	7	24	15	9
17	15	9	24	15	8
18	12	10	25	13	7
19	12	8	25	13	7
19	13	9	25	15	10
20	12	7	25	24	7
20	12	9	26	14	10
21	11	7	26	14	11
22	13	9	26	15	11
22	13	9	27	14	8
22	13	8	28	11	6
22	14	10	28	13	9
23	14	9	32	12	8
23	15	9	42	16	11
24	11	8	43	14	9
24	12	7			

To help them with their work, the archeologists also used samples of arrowhead data from four other settlement sites. The data from those sites are on this page and on the next page.

The archeologists knew that the Big Goose Creek and Wortham Shelter sites were settled between A.D. 500 and A.D. 1600.

Big Goose Creek: 52 Arrowheads

Length (mm)	Width (mm)	Neck Width (mm)	Length (mm)	Width (mm)	Neck Width (mm)
16	13	9	26	12	12
16	14	10	26	14	9
17	13	8	26	16	10
17	13	10	27	13	9
18	12	7	27	13	9
18	12	8	27	14	9
18	13	7	27	14	9
18	15	11	27	17	13
19	11	8	28	10	5
20	11	6	28	13	7
20	12	8	28	13	8
21	11	7	28	15	9
21	12	7	29	15	8
21	12	9	30	11	7
22	12	9	30	13	8
22	13	8	30	14	8
22	13	10	30	14	8
23	13	8	30	14	9
23	13	9	30	15	11
23	14	9	31	12	8
24	14	9	33	13	7
24	14	11	33	15	9
25	13	7	34	15	9
25	13	8	35	14	10
25	14	8	39	18	12
26	11	8	40	14	8

SOURCE: *Plains Anthropologist*

Wortham Shelter: 45 Arrowheads

Length (mm)	Width (mm)	Neck Width (mm)
18	11	8
19	12	9
19	14	10
19	14	10
19	16	14
20	13	8
20	14	10
20	15	11
22	12	9
22	14	8
23	13	11
23	14	11
23	15	11
24	12	9
24	13	10
25	14	8
25	14	10
25	15	10
25	15	10
25	15	12
26	13	9
26	13	10
26	15	12
27	14	8
27	14	10
27	15	11
28	13	11
28	14	10
28	16	12
29	13	10
29	14	9
29	14	9
29	17	12
30	14	11
30	16	9
30	17	11
31	13	10
31	14	10
31	14	11
31	16	12
31	17	12
32	14	7
32	15	10
35	18	14
42	18	7

The archeologists knew that the Laddie Creek/Dead Indian Creek and Kobold/Buffalo Creek sites were settled between 4000 B.C. and A.D. 500.

- How could you use the data to estimate the length and width of a typical arrowhead from each time period?

- How could you use the data to determine the settlement periods for the unknown sites?

Laddie Creek/Dead Indian Creek: 18 Arrowheads

Length (mm)	Width (mm)	Neck Width (mm)
25	18	13
27	20	13
27	20	14
29	14	11
29	20	13
30	23	13
31	18	11
32	16	10
32	19	10
35	20	15
37	17	13
38	17	14
39	18	15
40	18	11
41	15	11
42	22	12
44	18	13
52	21	16

Kobold/Buffalo Creek: 52 Arrowheads

Length (mm)	Width (mm)	Neck Width (mm)	Length (mm)	Width (mm)	Neck Width (mm)
25	18	15	45	22	13
30	17	12	46	17	13
30	19	15	46	20	14
31	16	13	46	23	14
31	17	12	47	19	13
32	20	13	47	20	12
32	22	17	47	22	13
32	23	18	49	20	14
35	19	11	50	21	13
35	22	14	50	23	15
37	18	12	50	23	16
37	21	11	51	18	10
38	18	9	52	17	12
38	24	15	52	22	15
39	21	14	52	24	16
40	19	15	54	24	13
40	20	12	56	19	12
40	20	13	56	21	15
40	21	12	56	25	13
41	21	13	57	21	15
42	22	14	61	19	12
42	22	15	64	21	13
44	20	11	66	20	15
44	20	12	67	21	13
44	25	14	71	24	13
45	20	13	78	26	12

Problem 3.1

The archeologists thought that Native Americans inhabiting the same area of the country during the same time period would have similar tools.

A **1.** For each known site and each unknown site, find the five-number summary of the arrowhead-length data. Then draw a box-and-whisker plot of each distribution.

   2. Use your answers to part (1). Compare the lengths of the arrowheads found at the unknown sites with the lengths of the arrowheads found at the known sites.

   a. During which time period (4000 B.C.–A.D. 500 or A.D. 500–A.D. 1600) do you think Site I was settled? Explain how your statistics and box plots support your answers.

   b. During which time period do you think Site II was settled? Explain how your statistics and box plots support your answers.

B **1.** For each known site and each unknown site, find the five-number summary of the arrowhead-width data. Then draw a box plot of each distribution.

   2. Do the box plots displaying data about arrowhead widths support your answers to Question A, part (2)? Explain.

C Suppose the archeologists had collected only a few arrowheads from each unknown site. Might they have reached a different conclusion? Explain.

 Homework starts on page 69.

3.2 Comparing Heights of Basketball Players

Using Means and MADs

Variability occurs naturally in all samples of a population. Distributions of two different samples will not be identical. When you compare two samples, you need to decide whether the samples differ more than what you would expect from natural variability.

The dot plots below show the heights of a random sample of 32 male professional basketball players and the heights of a random sample of 32 female professional basketball players.

Heights of Male Professional Basketball Players

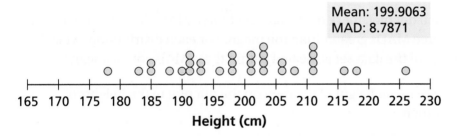

Mean: 199.9063
MAD: 8.7871

Heights of Female Professional Basketball Players

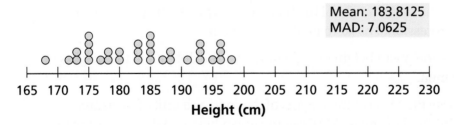

Mean: 183.8125
MAD: 7.0625

- Do these samples give enough evidence to conclude that the population of male professional basketball players is taller than the population of female professional basketball players? Or is the difference you see in these samples just due to natural variation?

In Investigation 1, you looked at how the mean and MAD are related. You found that, in many distributions, most of the data are located within two MADs of the mean.

Problem 3.2

Use the dot plots of professional basketball players' heights on the previous page.

A Compare the means of the two sets of data. Compare the variabilities of the two sets of data.

B 1. On a copy of each dot plot, mark the locations of two MADs less than the mean and two MADs greater than the mean.

2. For each distribution, what percent of the data set is located within two MADs of the mean?

3. For each dot plot, mark the locations of three MADs less than the mean and three MADs greater than the mean. For each distribution, what percent of the data set is located within three MADs of the mean?

C 1. Mark the mean height of the men on the dot plot of the heights of the women.

   a. Use the MAD of the heights of the women as a unit of measure. Within how many MADs of the mean height of the women is the mean height of the men?

   b. Is the mean height of the men an unexpected height for a female professional basketball player? Explain.

2. Mark the mean height of the women on the dot plot of the heights of the men.

   a. Use the MAD of the heights of the men as a unit of measure. Within how many MADs of the mean height of the men is the mean height of the women?

   b. Is the mean height of the women an unexpected height for a male professional basketball player? Explain your reasoning.

3. Do these sample distributions provide enough evidence to draw conclusions about the heights of the populations from which the samples were drawn? Explain.

Problem 3.2 *continued*

D The dot plot below shows a distribution of heights for a sample of professional basketball players. Do you think this distribution shows a random sample of men or a random sample of women? Explain.

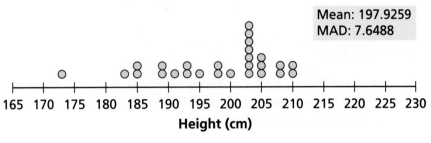

Heights of Mystery Players

Mean: 197.9259
MAD: 7.6488

Height (cm)

ACE Homework starts on page 69.

3.3 Five Chocolate Chips in Every Cookie

Using Sampling in a Simulation

Jeff and Hadiya work at the Custom Cookie Counter. Their advertising slogan is "Five giant chips in every cookie!"

One day, a customer complains that her cookie only has three chocolate chips. Jeff thinks she must have miscounted because he mixes 60 chips into the dough of each batch of a dozen cookies. Jeff and Hadiya examine a batch of cookies fresh from the oven. The picture at the right shows what they see.

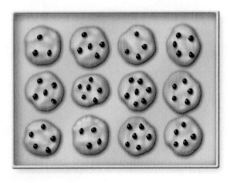

- How might you correct Jeff's reasoning about how many chocolate chips to add to each batch of cookie dough?

- What advice would you give to Jeff and Hadiya to help them solve this quality-control problem?

Hadiya wants to figure out how many chocolate chips they should add to each batch of dough. She wants to be fairly confident that each cookie will have five chips. She simulates the situation by using random sampling. When Hadiya **simulates** the quality-control problem, she runs an experiment that models the relevant characteristics of the cookie-dough problem.

Hadiya says, "Think of a batch of dough as 12 cookies packed in a bowl. Each chip that we add to the dough lands in one cookie. There is an equally likely chance that a chip will land in any one of the 12 cookies. We can simulate the situation."

Hadiya's Simulation

- Select integers from 1 to 12 at random to assign chocolate chips to cookies. A "1" means a chip is included in Cookie 1. A "2" means a chip is included in Cookie 2, and so on.

- Keep a tally of where the chips land. Stop when each cookie includes at least five chips.

- The total number of tallied chips will be an estimate of the number of chips needed for each batch.

Jeff extends Hadiya's idea. He says, "Each time we simulate the situation, we might get a different number of chips. For some simulations, some cookies might be loaded with chips before each cookie gets five chips. We need to repeat the experiment enough times to find a typical result."

- What is the typical number of chips needed to have at least five chips in each cookie?

Problem 3.3

A **1.** For each cookie, 1 to 12, what is the theoretical probability of a chip being assigned to that cookie?

   2. Describe a method that you can use to give each chip a cookie number. Explain why your method makes it equally likely for each cookie to be assigned a chip.

   3. Conduct the simulation Hadiya described. Record your results in a table such as the one below.

Cookie Simulation

Cookie Number	1	2	3	4	5	6	7	8	9	10	11	12
Number of Chips in the Cookie	■	■	■	■	■	■	■	■	■	■	■	■

B Find the total number of chips in your simulated batch of cookie dough.

C Ask each group in your class for the total number of chips in their simulated batches of cookie dough.

   1. Make a *histogram* of the class data.

   2. Describe your histogram. Explain how you chose the interval size. What does the histogram tell you about the results of the simulations?

   3. Make a box-and-whisker plot of the class data.

   4. Describe your box plot. What does the box plot tell you about the results of the simulations?

   5. Compute the mean and the median of the class data. Compare the mean and the median. What do you notice?

D Jeff and Hadiya want to be sure that most of the cookies they make will have at least five chips. They do not want to waste money, however, by mixing in too many chips. How many chips do you predict they need to use in each batch? Use your answers to Question C to explain your reasoning.

continued on the next page >

Problem **3.3** *continued*

E 1. As a class, discuss your answers to Question D. Choose a number to suggest to Jeff and Hadiya that the whole class agrees on.

2. Use the number of chips your class agreed on.

- As a class, conduct 30 simulations to distribute the recommended number of chips among 12 cookies.

- For each simulation, record whether each of the 12 cookies has at least five chips.

- Organize your information in a table such as the one below.

Trials for Recommended Number of Chips

Simulation Trial Number	Does Each Cookie Have at Least Five Chips?
1	▪
2	▪
3	▪
4	▪
⋮	▪
30	▪

3. What percent of the simulations resulted in at least five chips per cookie?

4. Make a final recommendation. How many chips should Jeff and Hadiya put in each batch? Use your simulation results to justify your choice.

5. Suggest a new advertising slogan for Jeff and Hadiya that might promote their cookies in a more accurate way.

 Homework starts on page 69.

3.4 Estimating a Deer Population
Using Samples to Estimate the Size of a Population

Scientists and environmentalists estimate populations of various animals in particular habitats.

- How can you estimate the deer population of a town, state, or region?

The **capture–tag–recapture method** is one way to estimate a deer population. Biologists capture a sample of deer in a specific area, tag the deer, and then release them. Later, they capture another sample of deer. They count the number of deer with tags and compare that number to the number of deer in the sample. Then, they use their comparison to estimate the number of deer in the area.

You can simulate the capture–tag–recapture method using beans. Think of each bean in a container as a deer. Your job is to estimate the total number of beans without counting them all.

How to Simulate the Capture–Tag–Recapture Method

Capture–Tag

- Remove 100 beans from the container. Mark them with a pen or marker.

- Put the beans back in the container. Gently shake the container to mix the marked and unmarked beans.

Recapture

- Without examining the beans, scoop out a sample from the container. Record the number of marked beans and the number of beans in the sample.

- Return the sample of beans to the container. Mix the beans together again.

- How does the sample of beans you recaptured help you determine how many beans are in the population?

When biologists use the capture–tag–recapture method, they do not collect samples of specific sizes. In this Problem, however, you will collect samples of specific sizes so that you can compare your answers with your classmates' answers.

Problem 3.4

Work with your group to simulate the capture–tag–recapture method.

A 1. Take a sample of 25 beans. Record the number of marked beans and the number of unmarked beans in a table such as the one below. Use the data to estimate the total number of beans in the container.

Capture–Tag–Recapture Sampling Data

Sample Size	Number of Marked Beans	Number of Unmarked Beans	Estimate of Total Number of Beans
25	▦	▦	▦
50	▦	▦	▦
75	▦	▦	▦
100	▦	▦	▦
125	▦	▦	▦
150	▦	▦	▦

2. Follow the steps you used in part (1) with samples of 50 beans, 75 beans, 100 beans, 125 beans, and 150 beans. Record your data.

3. Describe the strategy you used to estimate the total number of beans in the container.

B Explain why this experiment can be considered a simulation.

C Use the table from Question A. Make a final estimate for the number of total beans in the container. Explain your reasoning.

D Ask each group in your class for their estimates of total number of beans in the container for each sample size.

1. For each sample size, draw a line plot of the data you collected from your class.

2. Explain how the line plots you drew in part (1) might change your final estimate for the total number of beans in the container.

E Use what you have learned from this experiment. How do you think biologists count deer populations?

A C E Homework starts on page 69.

Applications

1. A zookeeper has tracked the weights of many chimpanzees over the years. The box plots below show the weights of two samples of chimpanzees. The top box plot shows a sample of 8-year-old chimpanzees. The bottom box plot shows a sample of 10-year-old chimpanzees.

8-Year-Old Chimpanzees

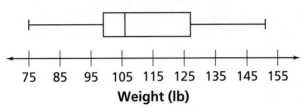

Weight (lb)

10-Year-Old Chimpanzees

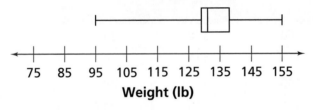

Weight (lb)

The zoo acquired some chimpanzees from a nearby zoo that was closing. They received a cage of 8-year-old chimpanzees and a cage of 10-year-old chimpanzees. The zoo forgot, however, to keep track of the cages. They weighed the chimpanzees in one cage and graphed the data.

Mystery Chimpanzees

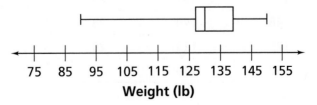

Weight (lb)

How old are the chimpanzees shown in the distribution above? Explain your reasoning.

2. a. Use the arrowhead tables from Problem 3.1. The tables include the neck widths of the arrowheads from two unknown sites and four known sites. For each of the six sites, calculate the five-number summaries of the neck-width data.

neck width

b. Make a box-and-whisker plot of the neck-width data for each site. You can use the same number line to plot all the box plots.

c. During which time periods do you think Sites I and II were settled? Use your answers to parts (a) and (b) to justify your response.

A sample of students measured their heights, arm spans, and foot lengths. Use the table below for Exercises 3–6.

Student Measurement Data

Gender	Height (cm)	Arm Span (cm)	Foot Length (cm)
F	160	158	25
M	111	113	15
F	160	160	23
F	152	155	23.5
F	146	144	24
F	157	156	24
M	136	135	21
F	143	142	23
M	147	145	20
M	133	133	20
F	153	151	25
M	148	149	23
M	125	123	20
F	150	149	20

3. a. Make a line plot displaying the foot lengths of the female students.

b. What is the mean of the data? The MAD?

c. On your line plot, mark the locations of one MAD and two MADs less than and greater than the mean.

4. a. Make a line plot displaying the foot lengths of the male students.

  b. What is the mean of the data? The MAD?

  c. On your line plot, mark the locations of one MAD and two MADs less than and greater than the mean.

5. Use your answers to Exercises 3 and 4. Mark the mean male foot length on the line plot of female foot lengths. Is the mean male foot length an unexpected data value for the female line plot? Explain.

6. Use your answers to Exercises 3 and 4. Mark the mean female foot length on the line plot of male foot lengths. Is the mean female foot length an unexpected data value for the male line plot? Explain.

7. The line plots below display the name lengths of a sample of 30 U.S. students and a sample of 30 Chinese students.

Keron and Ethan notice that U.S. names are longer than Chinese names for these samples. Keron thinks this is due to naturally occurring variability. Ethan thinks the differences are too great to be explained only by naturally occurring variability. Do you agree with Keron or with Ethan? Explain.

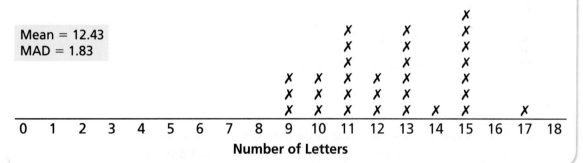

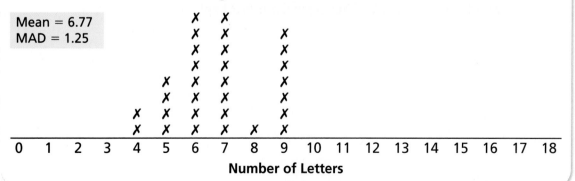

Keisha opens a bag containing 60 chocolate chip cookies. She selects a sample of 20 cookies and counts the chips in each cookie. For Exercises 8 and 9, use Keisha's data below.

Cookie Sample

Cookie Number	Number of Chips
1	6
2	8
3	8
4	11
5	7
6	6
7	6
8	7
9	11
10	7

Cookie Number	Number of Chips
11	8
12	7
13	9
14	9
15	8
16	6
17	8
18	10
19	10
20	8

8. Estimate the number of total chips in the bag. Explain your answer.

9. Copy and complete each statement with the most appropriate fraction: $\frac{1}{4}$, $\frac{1}{6}$, or $\frac{1}{2}$.

More than ▇ of the cookies have at least 8 chips.

More than ▇ of the cookies have at least 9 chips.

More than ▇ of the cookies have at least 10 chips.

10. **a.** A baker makes raisin muffins in batches of four dozen muffins. She pours a box of raisins into each batch. How could you use a sample of muffins to estimate the number of raisins in a box?

b. Suppose there are 1,000 raisins in each box. How many raisins would you expect to find in a typical muffin? Explain.

11. Yung-nan wants to estimate the number of beans in a large jar. She takes out 150 beans and marks each with a red dot. She returns the beans to the jar and mixes them with the unmarked beans. She then takes four samples from the jar. The table shows Yung-nan's data.

Bean Samples

Sample	Total Number of Beans	Number of Beans With Red Dots
1	25	3
2	150	23
3	75	15
4	250	25

a. For each sample, find the relative frequency of total beans that are marked with red dots.

b. Which sample has the greatest percent of marked beans? Use this sample to estimate the number of beans in the jar. Be sure to show your work.

c. Which sample has the least percent of marked beans? Use this sample to estimate the number of beans in the jar. Show your work.

d. Diya used the shaded bars below to make an estimate from Sample 3. Explain what the bars show and how they can be used to estimate the number of beans in the whole jar.

Sample 3

Number of beans in sample: 75

15, or 20% marked				

Whole Jar

Number of beans in jar: ?

150, or 20% marked				

e. Use your answers to parts (a)–(d). What is your best guess for the total number of beans in the jar? Explain your reasoning.

12. Salome is a biologist who studies the albatross, a type of bird. She lives on an island in the Pacific Ocean. Two summers ago, Salome's team trapped 20 albatrosses. They tagged and released them. This past summer, Salome's team trapped 50 albatrosses. They found that two of the albatrosses were tagged.

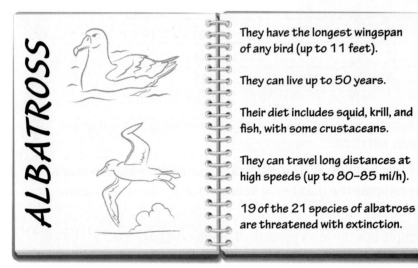

ALBATROSS

They have the longest wingspan of any bird (up to 11 feet).

They can live up to 50 years.

Their diet includes squid, krill, and fish, with some crustaceans.

They can travel long distances at high speeds (up to 80–85 mi/h).

19 of the 21 species of albatross are threatened with extinction.

a. Use Salome's findings. Estimate the number of albatrosses on the island. Explain how you made your estimate.

b. How confident are you that your estimate is accurate? Explain your answer.

c. Describe how Salome's team might use the capture–tag–recapture method to track how much the albatross population changes over time.

13. After independently testing many samples, an electric company determines that approximately 2 of every 1,000 light bulbs on the market are defective. Suppose Americans buy over one billion light bulbs each year. Estimate how many of these bulbs are defective.

14. **Multiple Choice** After testing many samples, a milk shipper determines that approximately 3 in every 100 milk cartons leak. The company ships 200,000 cartons of milk every week. About how many of these cartons leak?

    A. 3   **B.** 600   **C.** 2,000   **D.** 6,000

Connections

Graphs tell stories. Suppose you are a news reporter. For Exercises 15 and 16, use the graphs to write a short news paragraph that tells the story portrayed.

15.

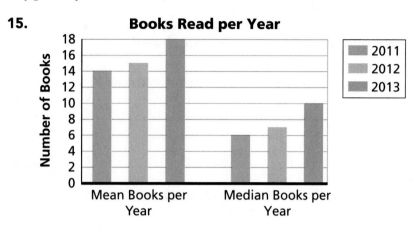

16.

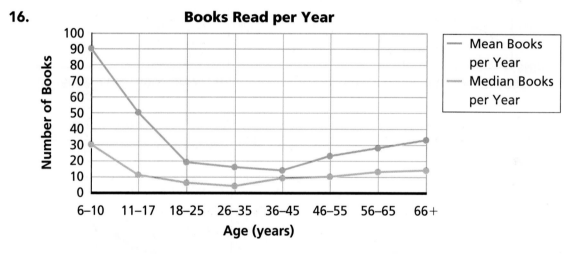

17. Multiple Choice The circle graph shows data for 1,585 students. About how many students are represented by the purple sector?

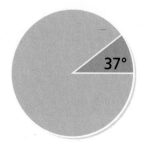

F. 40   **G.** 160   **H.** 590   **J.** 58,650

18. Sometimes graphs can be misleading. The graphs below all display the same data about the percent of paper and paperboard recovered from 2001 to 2012.

   a. Which graph do you think gives the clearest picture of the data pattern? Explain your reasoning.

   b. Why are the other graphs misleading?

**Percent of Recovered Paper and Paperboard
(2001–2012)**

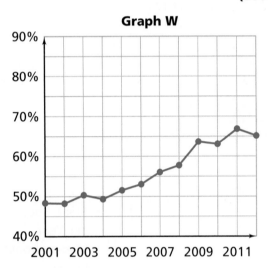

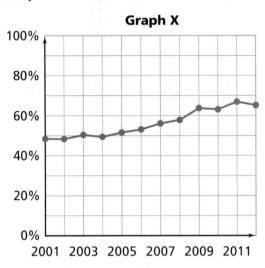

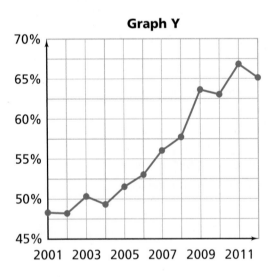

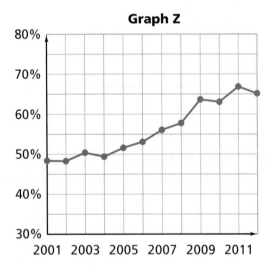

For Exercises 19–23, evaluate each survey described. Use the questions below to help you with your evaluation.

- **What is the goal of the survey?**
- **What population is being studied?**
- **How is the sample chosen?**
- **How are the data analyzed and reported?**
- **Does the analysis support the conclusions?**

19. A television manufacturer wants to design a remote control. Representatives for the company call 1,000 homes with televisions. They find that remote-control users sit an average of 3 meters from their televisions. Based on this finding, the company designs the remote control to work well at distances of 2.5 meters to 3.5 meters from a television.

20. A light bulb manufacturer wants to know the "defect rate" for its product. The manager takes 10 boxes of light bulbs from the assembly line and tests them. Each box contains 50 light bulbs. The manager finds that 5 bulbs are defective. He concludes that production quality is acceptable.

21. A nutritionist wants to know how many Calories in a typical U.S. teenager's diet are from fat. She asks Health teachers in Dallas, Texas to have their students record what they eat during one day. The nutritionist analyzes the records. The median intake is 500 Calories from fat per day, which is the recommended daily allowance. She concludes that Calories from fat are not a problem in the diets of teenagers.

22. A cookie maker claims that there are over 1,000 chocolate chips in a bag of its cookies. A consumer calls the company and asks how it knows this. A spokesperson says the company chooses a sample of bags of cookies. It soaks each bag in cold water to remove everything but the chips. Then the company weighs the chips that remain. In each case, the chips weigh more than a bag of 1,000 chocolate chips.

23. In the cafeteria line, Sam wrinkles his nose when he sees salami subs. The cook asks what he would prefer. Sam replies, "I like bologna better." The cook surveys the next ten students. Seven students say they prefer bologna over salami. The cook decides to serve bologna subs instead of salami subs in the future.

For Exercises 24–28, use the box plot below. Tell whether each statement is *true* or *false*. Explain.

Social Studies Test Scores

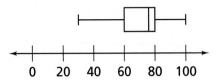

24. The class median is less than 80.

25. Half the class scored between 60 and 80.

26. At least one student earned a score of 100.

27. The class mean is probably less than the median.

28. If there are 30 students in the class, at least 10 scored above 80.

Extensions

29. Use a simulation to help you answer this question:

If you select five students at random from your class, what is the probability that at least two will have the same birth month?

a. Design a simulation to model this situation. Tell which month each simulation outcome represents.

b. Use your birth-month simulation to generate at least 25 samples of five people each. Use your results to estimate the probability that at least two people in a group of five will have the same birth month.

c. Explain how you could revise your simulation to explore this question:

What are the chances that at least two students in a class of 25 have the same birthday?

30. The percents of pushpin colors a company produces are on the bulletin board. A school secretary opens a large bag of pushpins. She puts the pins into boxes to distribute to teachers. She puts 50 pins in each box.

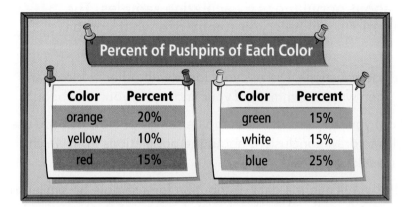

Percent of Pushpins of Each Color

Color	Percent
orange	20%
yellow	10%
red	15%

Color	Percent
green	15%
white	15%
blue	25%

a. How many pushpins of each color would you expect to be in a teacher's box?

b. How might the number of pushpins of each color vary across the boxes?

c. You can simulate filling the boxes by generating random integers from 1 to 20. Which numbers would you use to represent each color? How many numbers do you need to generate at random to simulate filling one box?

d. Carry out the simulation described in part (c) three times. Compare the distributions of colors in your simulated samples with the expected distribution from part (a).

e. Suppose the secretary selects a random sample of 1,000 pushpins from the bag. How closely would you expect the percents of each color in her sample to match the percents in the table?

In this Investigation, you developed strategies to draw conclusions about populations by analyzing samples. The following questions will help you summarize what you have learned.

Think about these questions. Discuss your ideas with other students and your teacher. Then write a summary of your findings in your notebook.

1. a. **How** can you use statistics to compare samples? **How** can you use samples to draw conclusions about the populations from which they are selected?

    b. **In what ways** might a data distribution for a sample be similar to or different from the data distribution for the entire population?

2. a. **How** can you use box plots, medians, and IQRs to compare samples? Give an example.

    b. **How** can you use means and MADs to compare samples? Give an example.

    c. **How** can you use statistics to decide whether differences between samples are expected due to natural variability or reflect measurable differences in underlying populations?

3. a. **How** can you use simulations to generate samples?

    b. **How** can you use data from a capture–tag–recapture simulation to estimate the actual size of a population?

4. The process of statistical investigation involves posing questions, collecting and analyzing data, and making interpretations to answer the original questions. Choose a Problem from this Investigation. **Explain** how you used the process of statistical investigation to solve the Problem.

Common Core Mathematical Practices

As you worked on the Problems in this Investigation, you used prior knowledge to make sense of them. You also applied Mathematical Practices to solve the Problems. Think back over your work, the ways you thought about the Problems, and how you used Mathematical Practices.

Shawna described her thoughts in the following way:

In Problem 3.1, I compared arrowhead lengths. I used the mean, median, range, and MAD for each site.

The mean arrowhead length for Site I (39.6 mm) is greater than the mean length for Site II (23.6 mm). The mean length for Site I is between the means for Laddie Creek/Dead Indian Creek (35 mm) and Kobold/Buffalo Creek (45.8 mm). These relationships are similar for the median values, too. Site I was probably settled between 4000 B.C. and A.D. 500.

The data for Site II (mean of 23.6 mm, median of 24 mm) is similar to the Big Goose Creek (mean of 25.3 mm, median of 25.5 mm) and Wortham Shelter data (mean of 26.3 mm, median of 26 mm). Site II must have been settled between A.D. 500 and A.D. 1600.

The minimum data values, maximum data values, and IQRs of all the sites also supported my ideas.

Common Core Standards for Mathematical Practice
MP2 Reason abstractly and quantitatively.

 • What other Mathematical Practices can you identify in Shawna's reasoning?

• Describe a Mathematical Practice that you and your classmates used to solve a different Problem in this Investigation.

In this Unit, you learned about sampling data. You used samples to draw conclusions about the populations from which they were taken. You learned how to:

- Analyze and compare sets of data by using measures of center and measures of spread

- Select representative samples by using random sampling techniques

- Collect, organize, and display sample data

- Use your analyses of the samples to draw conclusions about populations

Use Your Understanding of Statistical Reasoning

1. Scientists often study the health of a habitat by gathering data about the number of animals that live there. Suppose you use the capture–tag–recapture method to find out how many butterflies live in a particular field.

   a. Suppose you capture and mark 20 butterflies and then release them. You return to the field and catch 10 butterflies. Only one butterfly is marked. Estimate the size of the population of butterflies in the field. Explain your reasoning.

   b. Suppose you return to the same field on a different day and catch 10 butterflies. Nine butterflies are marked. With this new information, estimate the size of the population of butterflies in the field. Explain.

   c. Suppose you return to the same field on a different day and capture and mark 80 additional butterflies. You then release them. You return to the field and catch 50 butterflies. Twenty-five are marked. Estimate the size of the population of butterflies in the field.

   d. For each part (a)–(c), how might you change your estimate to make sure that it is close to the actual number of butterflies in the field?

2. Glove makers are interested in the lengths and widths of their customers' hands. They look for patterns so they can make gloves that will fit most people. Each data value in the dot plots on the next page represents the mean of a sample of hand lengths.

- Two dot plots display data collected from 100 samples of males.

- Two dot plots display data collected from 100 samples of females.

- Two dot plots (one male and one female) show data from 100 samples of size 10.

- Two dot plots (one male and one female) show data from 100 samples of size 30.

- Assume that, on average, men's hands are longer than women's.

a. Which two distributions show data collected from males? Which two distributions show data collected from females? Explain your reasoning.

b. Look at the distributions of male data. Which distribution shows means from 100 samples of 10 males each? From 100 samples of 30 males each? Justify your reasoning.

c. Look at the distributions of female data. Which distribution shows means from 100 samples of 10 females each? From 100 samples of 30 females each? Justify your reasoning.

d. Compare the distribution of data collected from 100 samples of 30 males each with the distribution of data collected from 100 samples of 30 females each. How are the distributions alike? How are they different?

e. The MAD for the distribution of data collected from 100 samples of 30 males each is 0.072 centimeter. The MAD for the distribution of data collected from 100 samples of 30 females each is 0.077 centimeter.

How can you use this new information to support your answer to part (d)? What other comparisons can you now make?

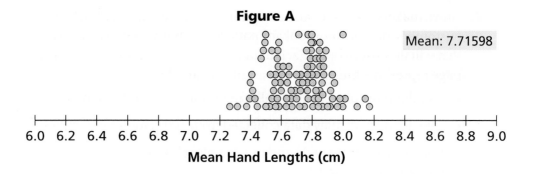

Figure A

Mean: 7.71598

Mean Hand Lengths (cm)

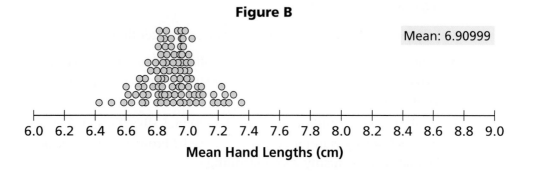

Figure B

Mean: 6.90999

Mean Hand Lengths (cm)

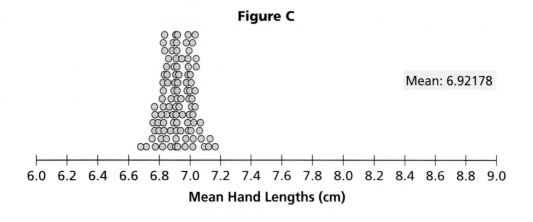

Figure C

Mean: 6.92178

Mean Hand Lengths (cm)

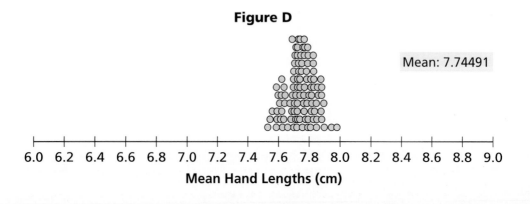

Figure D

Mean: 7.74491

Mean Hand Lengths (cm)

3. Below are two box plots. One box plot is constructed from the data collected from 100 samples of 30 males each from Exercise 2. The other is constructed from the data collected from 100 samples of 30 females each from Exercise 2.

Figure E

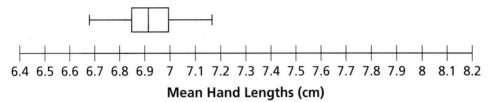

Mean Hand Lengths (cm)

Figure F

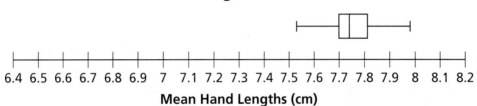

Mean Hand Lengths (cm)

 a. Which box plot shows data for males? For females? Explain.

 b. Identify the IQR from each box plot. Do these IQRs support your answers for Exercise 2, parts (d) and (e)? Explain.

 c. What other comparisons can you make using the box plots?

Explain Your Reasoning

When you choose samples, compare data sets, and use statistics to draw conclusions about populations, you should be able to justify your reasoning.

 4. When you report the mean, what related measure of spread can you report? What does this measure tell you about the data distribution?

 5. When you report the median, what related measure of spread can you report? What does this measure tell you about the data distribution?

 6. Describe three kinds of sampling methods that are not random sampling. Identify each method's strengths and weaknesses. Give an example of each kind of method.

 7. Give an example of a random sampling technique.

 8. When should you use sampled data to study a population?

B **bar graph** A graphical representation of a table of data in which the height or length of each bar indicates its frequency. The bars are separated from each other to highlight that the data are discrete or "counted" data. In a vertical bar graph, the horizontal axis shows the values or categories, and the vertical axis shows the frequency for each of the values or categories. In a horizontal bar graph, the vertical axis shows the values or categories, and the horizontal axis shows the frequencies.

gráfica de barras Representación gráfica de una tabla de datos en la que la altura o la longitud de cada barra indica su frecuencia. Las barras están separadas entre sí para subrayar que los datos son discretos o "contados". En una gráfica de barras vertical, el eje horizontal representa los valores o categorías y el eje vertical representa la frecuencia de cada uno de los valores o categorías. En una gráfica de barras horizontal, el eje vertical representa los valores o categorías y el eje horizontal representa las frecuencias.

Vertical Bar Graph

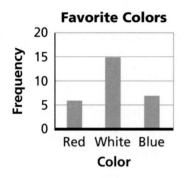

Horizontal Bar Graph

Gráfica de barras vertical

Gráfica de barras horizontal

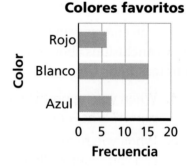

box-and-whisker plot, or box plot A display that shows the distribution of values in a data set separated into four equal-size groups. A box plot is constructed from a five-number summary of the data.

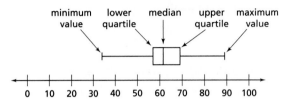

gráfica de caja y bigotes o diagrama de caja Una representación que muestra la distribución de los valores de un conjunto de datos separados en cuatro grupos de igual tamaño. Un diagrama de caja se construye a partir de un resumen de cinco números de los datos.

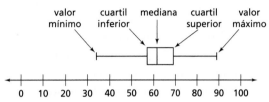

C capture–tag–recapture method A sampling method used to estimate the size of a wildlife population. When using this method, scientists take a sample of animals, mark them in some way, then release them back into their habitat. Later, they capture another sample and count how many animals in that sample are marked. They use these data to estimate the population size.

método de captura-marcaje y recaptura Un método de muestreo que se usa para estimar el tamaño de una población de animales silvestres. Al usar este método, los científicos toman una muestra de los animales, los marcan de alguna manera y luego los vuelven a liberar en su hábitat. Más tarde, capturan otra muestra y cuentan cuántos animales de esa muestra están marcados. Usan estos datos para estimar el tamaño de la población.

categorical data Non-numerical data sets are categorical. For example, the responses to "What month were you born?" are categorical data. Frequency counts can be made of the values for a given category. The table below shows examples of categories and their possible values.

Category	Possible Values
Month people are born	January, February, March
Favorite color to wear	magenta, blue, yellow
Kinds of pets people have	cats, dogs, fish, horses

datos categóricos Los conjuntos de datos no numéricos son categóricos. Por ejemplo, las respuestas a "¿En qué mes naciste?" son datos categóricos. Los conteos de frecuencia se pueden hacer a partir de los valores de una categoría dada. La siguiente tabla muestra ejemplos de categorías y sus posibles valores.

Categoría	Valores posibles
Mes de nacimiento de las personas	enero, febrero, marzo
Color preferido para vestir	magenta, azul, amarillo
Tipos de mascotas que tienen las personas	gatos, perros, peces, caballos

census Data collected from every individual in a population.

censo Los datos recopilados de todos los individuos de una población.

convenience sampling Choosing a sample because it is convenient. For example, if you ask all the students on your bus how long it takes them to get to school and then claim that these data are representative of the entire school population, you are surveying a convenience sample.

muestreo de conveniencia Una muestra seleccionada porque es conveniente. Por ejemplo, si les preguntas a todos los estudiantes que van en el autobús cuánto tiempo tardan en llegar a la escuela y luego afirmas que esos datos son representativos de toda la población escolar, estás aplicando un muestreo de conveniencia.

- -

D **describe** Academic Vocabulary
To explain or tell in detail. A written description can contain facts and other information needed to communicate your answer. A diagram or a graph may also be included.

related terms *express, explain, illustrate*

sample The band members want to conduct a survey. Describe a plan that uses systematic sampling.

> The band members can randomly select a starting time and then survey every sixth student who enters the school. This gives the band members a methodical way of collecting data.

describir Vocabulario académico
Explicar o decir con detalle. Una descripción escrita puede contener datos y otro tipo de información necesaria para comunicar tu respuesta. También puede incluir un diagrama o una gráfica.

términos relacionados *expresar, explicar, ilustrar*

ejemplo Los integrantes de la banda quieren hacer una encuesta. Describe un plan que use el muestreo sistemático.

> Los integrantes de la banda pueden seleccionar al azar un tiempo de inicio y luego aplicar la encuesta a cada sexto estudiante que entre a la escuela. Esto da a los integrantes de la banda una manera metódica de recopilar datos.

distribution The entire set of collected data values, organized to show their frequency of occurrence. A distribution can be described using summary statistics and/or by referring to its shape.

distribución Todo el conjunto de valores de datos recopilados, organizados para mostrar su frecuencia de incidencia. Una distribución se puede describir usando la estadística sumaria y/o haciendo referencia a su forma.

E **estimate** Academic Vocabulary
To find an approximate answer that is relatively close to an exact amount.

related terms *approximate, guess*

sample A cup manufacturer knows that approximately 4 out of every 2,000 cups are defective. Estimate how many of 10,000 cups bought by a restaurant will be defective.

I can write 4 out of 2,000 as a percent.
$$\frac{4}{2,000} = 0.002 = 0.2\%$$
Then I can multiply 10,000 by 0.2% to estimate the number of defective cups bought by the restaurant chain.
$0.002 \times 10,000 = 20$
About 20 of the cups are defective.
I can also use a proportion.
$$\frac{4}{2,000} = \frac{x}{10,000}$$
$2,000x = 40,000$
$x = 20$

hacer una estimación Vocabulario académico
Hallar una respuesta aproximada que esté relativamente cerca de una cantidad exacta.

términos relacionados *aproximar, suponer*

ejemplo Un fabricante de tazas sabe que aproximadamente 4 de cada 2,000 tazas son defectuosas. Estima cuántas de 10,000 tazas compradas por un restaurante son defectuosas.

Puedo escribir 4 de 2,000 como un porcentaje. $\frac{4}{2,000} = 0.002 = 0.2\%$
Luego, puedo multiplicar 10,000 por 0.2% para estimar el número de tazas defectuosas compradas por el restaurante.
$0.002 \times 10,000 = 20$
Alrededor de 20 de las tazas están defectuosas.
También puedo usar una proporción.
$$\frac{4}{2,000} = \frac{x}{10,000}$$
$2,000x = 40,000$
$x = 20$

expect Academic Vocabulary
To use theoretical or experimental data to anticipate a certain outcome.

related terms *anticipate, predict*

sample A cook makes trail mix in 2-pound batches. She puts a bag of almonds into each batch. There are about 120 almonds in each bag. Explain how many almonds you would expect to find in $\frac{1}{2}$ pound of trail mix.

If I divide 2 pounds of trail mix into half-pound parts, I will have 4 parts. Since the cook puts 120 almonds into each batch, divide 120 by 4 to determine the expected number of almonds in one-half pound. I can expect to find 30 almonds in one-half pound of trail mix because 120 ÷ 4 = 30.

esperar Vocabulario académico
Usar datos teóricos o experimentales para anticipar un resultado determinado.

términos relacionados *anticipar, predecir*

ejemplo Una cocinera prepara una mezcla de nueces y frutas secas en recetas de 2 libras. Pone una bolsa de almendras en cada receta. Hay aproximadamente 120 almendras en cada bolsa. Explica cuántas almendras esperarías hallar en media libra de mezcla de nueces y frutas secas.

Si divido 2 libras de mezcla de nueces y frutas secas en partes de media libra, tendré 4 partes. Dado que la cocinera pone 120 almendras en cada receta, divido 120 por 4 para determinar el número esperado de almendras en media libra. Puedo esperar hallar 30 almendras en media libra de mezcla de nueces y frutas secas, porque 120 ÷ 4 = 30.

explain Academic Vocabulary
To give facts and details that make an idea easier to understand. Explaining can involve a written summary supported by a diagram, chart, table, or a combination of these.

related terms *analyze, clarify, describe, justify, tell*

sample Explain why the line graph is misleading.

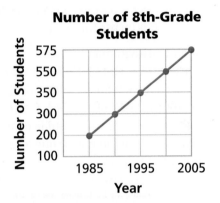

Number of 8th-Grade Students

The vertical axis of the graph does not start with zero and does not increase by the same amount for each interval. This causes the data to appear to increase at a constant rate, but it is increasing at different rates. Therefore, the graph is misleading.

explicar Vocabulario académico
Dar datos y detalles que hacen que una idea sea más fácil de comprender. Explicar puede incluir un resumen escrito apoyado por un diagrama, una gráfica, una tabla o una combinación de estos.

términos relacionados *analizar, aclarar, describir, justificar, decir*

ejemplo Explica por qué la gráfica lineal es engañosa.

Número de estudiantes del grado 8

El eje vertical de la gráfica no empieza en cero y no aumenta en la misma cantidad en cada intervalo. Esto hace que los datos parezcan aumentar en una tasa constante, pero están aumentando en diferentes tasas. Por tanto, la gráfica es engañosa.

- -

F **five-number summary** The minimum value, lower quartile, median, upper quartile, and maximum value for a data set. These five values give a summary of the shape of the distribution and are used to make box plots. The five-number summary is noted on the box plot below.

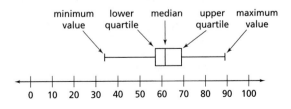

resumen de cinco números El valor mínimo, el cuartil inferior, la mediana, el cuartil superior y el valor máximo de un conjunto de datos. Estos cinco valores dan un resumen de la forma de una distribución y se usan para construir diagramas de caja. El resumen de cinco números se observa en el siguiente diagrama de caja.

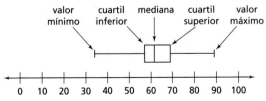

frequency The number of times a given data value occurs in a data set.

frecuencia El número de veces que un valor de datos dado se produce en un conjunto de datos.

histogram A display that shows the distribution of numeric data. The range of data values, divided into intervals, is displayed on the horizontal axis. The vertical axis shows the frequency in numbers or in percents. The height of the bar over each interval indicates the count or percent of data values in that interval.

The histogram below shows quality ratings for certain brands of peanut butter. The height of the bar over the interval from 20 to 30 is 4. This indicates that four brands of peanut butter have quality ratings greater than or equal to 20 and less than 30.

histograma Una representación que muestra la distribución de datos numéricos. El rango de valores de datos, dividido en intervalos, se representa en el eje horizontal. El eje vertical muestra la frecuencia en números o en porcentajes. La altura de la barra sobre cada intervalo indica el conteo o porcentaje de valores de datos en ese intervalo.

El siguiente histograma representa la calificación de la calidad de ciertas marcas de mantequilla de maní. La altura de la barra sobre el intervalo de 20 a 30 es 4. Esto indica que cuatro marcas de mantequilla de maní tienen una calificación mayor que o igual a 20 y menor que 30.

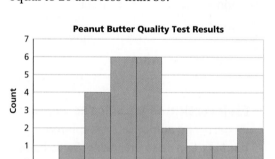

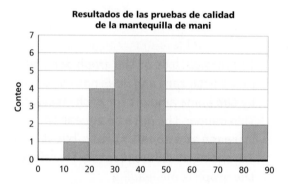

interquartile range (IQR) The difference of the values of the upper quartile (Q3) and the lower quartile (Q1). In the box-and-whisker plot below, the upper quartile is 69, and the lower quartile is 58. The IQR is the difference 69 – 58, or 11.

$$IQR = 69 - 58 = 11$$

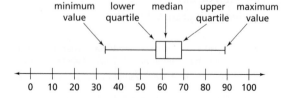

rango entre cuartiles (REC) La diferencia de los valores del cuartil superior (C3) y el cuartil inferior (C1). En el siguiente diagrama de caja y bigotes, el cuartil superior es 69 y el cuartil inferior es 58. El REC es la diferencia de 69 a 58, u 11.

$$REC = 69 - 58 = 11$$

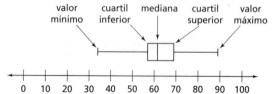

L **line plot** A way to organize data along a number line where the ✗s (or other symbols) above a number represent how often each value occurs in a data set. A line plot made with dots is sometimes referred to as a dot plot.

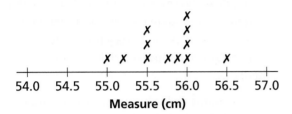

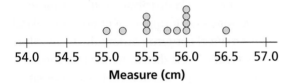

diagrama de puntos Una manera de organizar los datos a lo largo de una recta numérica donde las ✗ (u otros símbolos) colocadas encima de un número representan la frecuencia con que se menciona cada valor. Un diagrama de puntos hecho con puntos algunas veces se conoce como gráfica de puntos.

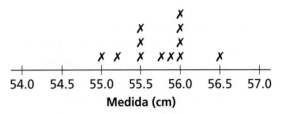

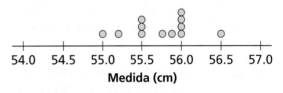

M **mean** The value found when all the data are combined and then redistributed evenly.

For example, the total number of siblings for the data in the line plot below is 56. If all 19 students had the same number of siblings, they would each have about 3 siblings.

Differences from the mean "balance out" so that the sum of differences below and above the mean equal 0. The mean of a set of data is the sum of the values divided by the number of values in the set.

Number of Siblings Students Have

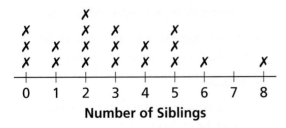

media El valor que se halla cuando todos los datos se combinan y luego se redistribuyen de manera uniforme.

Por ejemplo, el número total de hermanos y hermanas en los datos del siguiente diagrama es 56. Si los 19 estudiantes tuvieran la misma cantidad de hermanos y hermanas, cada uno tendría aproximadamente 3 hermanos o hermanas.

Las diferencias de la media se "equilibran" de manera que la suma de las diferencias por encima y por debajo de la media sea igual a 0. La media de un conjunto de datos es la suma de los valores dividida por el número de valores en el conjunto.

Número de hermanos y hermanas que tienen los estudiantes

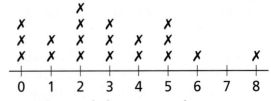

mean absolute deviation (MAD) The average distance of all of the data values in a data set from the mean of the distribution.

median The number that marks the midpoint of an ordered set of data. At least half of the values lie at or above the median, and at least half lie at or below the median.

For the sibling data (0, 0, 0, 1, 1, 2, 2, 2, 2, 3, 3, 3, 4, 4, 5, 5, 5, 6, 8), the median of the distribution of siblings is 3 because the tenth (middle) value in the ordered set of 19 values is 3. When a distribution contains an even number of data values, the median is computed by finding the average of the two middle data values in an ordered list of the data values.

For example, the median of 1, 3, 7, 8, 25, and 30 is 7.5 because the data values 7 and 8 are third and fourth in the list of six data values.

mode The value that appears most frequently in a set of data. In the data set 2, 2, 2, 2, 3, 3, 7, 7, 8, 9, 10, 11, the mode is 2.

N **numerical data** Values that are numbers such as counts, measurements, and ratings. Here are some examples.

- Number of children in families
- Pulse rates (number of heart beats per minute)
- Heights
- Amounts of time people spend reading in one day
- Ratings such as: on a scale of 1 to 5 with 1 as "low interest," how would you rate your interest in participating in the school's field day?

desviación absoluta media (DAM) La distancia media de todos los valores de datos en un conjunto de datos a partir de la media de la distribución.

mediana El número que marca el punto medio de un conjunto ordenado de datos. Por lo menos la mitad de los datos se encuentran en o encima de la mediana y por lo menos la mitad se encuentran en o debajo de la mediana.

Para los datos de los hermanos y hermanas (0, 0, 0, 1, 1, 2, 2, 2, 2, 3, 3, 3, 4, 4, 5, 5, 5, 6, 8), la mediana de la distribución de hermanos y hermanas es 3 porque el décimo valor (el del medio) en el conjunto ordenado de 19 valores es 3. Cuando una distribución contiene un número par de valores de datos, la mediana se calcula hallando el promedio de los dos valores de datos del medio en una lista ordenada de los valores de datos.

Por ejemplo, la mediana de 1, 3, 7, 8, 25 y 30 es 7.5, porque los valores de datos 7 y 8 son tercero y cuarto en la lista de seis valores de datos.

moda El valor que aparece con mayor frecuencia en un conjunto de datos. En el conjunto de datos 2, 2, 2, 2, 3, 3, 7, 7, 8, 9, 10, 11, la moda es 2.

datos numéricos Valores que son números como conteos, mediciones y calificaciones. Los siguientes son algunos ejemplos.

- Número de hijos e hijas en las familias
- Pulsaciones por minuto (número de latidos del corazón por minuto)
- Alturas
- Cantidades de tiempo que las personas pasan leyendo en un día
- Calificaciones como: en una escala de 1 a 5, en la que 1 representa "poco interés", ¿cómo calificarías tu interés por participar en el día de maniobras de tu escuela?

outlier A value that lies far from the "center" of a distribution and is not like other values. *Outlier* is a relative term, but it indicates a data point that is much higher or much lower than the values that could be normally expected for the distribution.

To identify an outlier in a distribution represented by a box plot, measure the distance between Q3 and any suspected outliers at the top of the range of data values; if this distance is more than $1.5 \times$ IQR, then the data value is an outlier. Likewise, if the distance between any data value at the low end of the range of values and Q1 is more than $1.5 \times$ IQR, then the data value is an outlier.

valor extremo Un valor que se encuentra lejos del "centro" de una distribución y no es como los demás valores. El *valor extremo* es un término relativo, pero indica un dato que es mucho más alto o mucho más bajo que los valores que se podrían esperar normalmente para la distribución.

Para identificar un valor extremo en una distribución representada por un diagrama de caja, se mide la distancia entre C3 y cualquier valor que se sospeche es extremo en la parte superior del rango de los valores de datos; si esta distancia es mayor que $1.5 \times$ REC, entonces el valor de datos es un valor extremo. Del mismo modo, si la distancia entre cualquier valor de datos en la parte inferior del rango de valores y C1 es mayor que $1.5 \times$ REC, entonces el valor de datos es un valor extremo.

P

population The entire collection of people or objects you are studying.

población El grupo completo de las personas o los objetos que se están estudiando.

Q

quartile One of three points that divide a data set into four equal groups. The second quartile, Q2, is the median of the data set. The first quartile, Q1, is the median of the lower half of the data set. The third quartile, Q3, is the median of the upper half of the data set.

cuartil Uno de los tres puntos que dividen un conjunto de datos en cuatro grupos iguales. El segundo cuartil, C2, es la mediana del conjunto de datos. El primer cuartil, C1, es la mediana de la mitad inferior del conjunto de datos. El tercer cuartil, C3, es la mediana de la mitad superior del conjunto de datos.

R

random sampling Choosing a sample in a way that gives every member of a population an equally likely chance of being selected.

muestreo aleatorio Elegir una muestra de manera que todo miembro de una población tenga la misma probabilidad de ser seleccionado.

range The difference of the maximum value and the minimum value in a distribution. If you know the range of the data is 12 grams of sugar per serving, you know that the difference between the minimum and maximum values is 12 grams. For example, in the distribution 2, 2, 2, 2, 3, 3, 7, 7, 8, 9, 10, 11, the range of the data set is 9, because $11 - 2 = 9$.

rango La diferencia del valor máximo y el valor mínimo en una distribución. Si se sabe que el rango de los datos es 12 gramos de azúcar por porción, entonces se sabe que la diferencia entre el valor mínimo y el máximo es 12 gramos. Por ejemplo, en la distribución 2, 2, 2, 2, 3, 3, 7, 7, 8, 9, 10, 11, el rango del conjunto de datos es 9, porque $11 - 2 = 9$.

relative frequency The ratio of the number of desired results to the total number of trials. Written as a percent, relative frequencies help you compare samples of different sizes.

frecuencia relativa La razón del número de resultados deseados al número total de pruebas. Escritas como porcentajes, las frecuencias relativas ayudan a comparar muestras de diferentes tamaños.

representative sample A sample whose characteristics accurately reflect those of the larger population from which the sample was selected.

muestra representativa Una muestra cuyas características reflejan con exactitud las características de la población más grande de la que se seleccionó la muestra.

S **sample** A group of people or objects selected from a population.

muestra Un grupo de personas u objetos seleccionados de una población.

sampling distribution The distribution of the means (or medians) from a set of same-size samples, each selected randomly from the same population.

distribución muestral Distribución de las medias (o medianas) de un conjunto de muestras del mismo tamaño, seleccionadas al azar de la misma población.

sampling plan A detailed strategy for selecting a sample from a population, including what data will be collected, in what manner, and by whom.

plan de muestreo Una estrategia detallada para seleccionar la muestra de una población, incluyendo los datos que se recopilarán, de qué manera y por quién.

simulate To run an experiment modeling the relevant characteristics of a real-world situation for use in studying the behavior of the real-world situation.

simular Llevar a cabo un experimento representando las características relevantes de una situación de la vida diaria para usarlas en el estudio del comportamiento de esa situación.

systematic sampling Choosing a sample in a methodical way. For example, if you survey every tenth person on an alphabetical list of names, you are surveying a systematic sample.

muestreo sistemático Una muestra seleccionada de una manera metódica. Por ejemplo, si se encuesta a cada décima persona de una lista de nombres en orden alfabético, se estaría aplicando el muestreo sistemático.

V **voluntary-response (or self-selected) sampling** A sample that selects itself. For example, if you put an ad in the school paper asking for volunteers to take a survey, the students who respond will be a voluntary-response sample.

muestra de respuesta voluntaria (o autoseleccionada) Una muestra que se selecciona a sí misma. Por ejemplo, si se pone un anuncio en el periódico escolar pidiendo voluntarios para participar en una encuesta, los estudiantes que respondan serán una muestra de respuesta voluntaria.

Index

Index

Acknowledgments

Cover Design

Three Communication Design, Chicago

Text

American Forest and Paper Association

076 Data from the **"Paper & Paperboard Recovery"** from WWW.PAPERRECYCLES.ORG

George C. Knight

057 From **"Site 1 and Site 2 Arrowhead Sizes"** by George C. Knight and James D. Keyser from PLAINS ANTHROPOLOGIST VOLUME 28, NUMBER 101, 1983. Reprinted by permission of the author.

058 From **"A Mathematical Technique for Dating Projectile Points Common to the Northwestern Plains (Big Goose Creek Arrowheads)"** by George C. Knight and James D. Keyser from PLAINS ANTHROPOLOGIST VOLUME 28, NUMBER 101, 1983. Reprinted by permission of the author.

058 From **"A Mathematical Technique for Dating Projectile Points Common to the Northwestern Plains (Wortham Shelter Arrowheads)"** by George C. Knight and James D. Keyser from PLAINS ANTHROPOLOGIST VOLUME 28, NUMBER 101, 1983. Reprinted by permission of the author.

059 From **"A Mathematical Technique for Dating Projectile Points Common to the Northwestern Plains (Kobold/Buffalo Creek Arrowheads)"** by George C. Knight and James D. Keyser from PLAINS ANTHROPOLOGIST VOLUME 28, NUMBER 101, 1983. Reprinted by permission of the author.

059 From **"A Mathematical Technique for Dating Projectile Points Common to the Northwestern Plains (Laddie Creek/Dead Indian Creek Arrowheads)"** by George C. Knight and James D. Keyser from PLAINS ANTHROPOLOGIST VOLUME 28, NUMBER 101, 1983. Reprinted by permission of the author.

Duane Marden

016 "Roller Coaster Census Report" by Duane Marden from WWW.RCDB.COM/CENSUS.HTM

National Geographic Stock

026 "Survey 2000: Census Information" from WWW.NATIONALGEOGRAPHIC.COM. Used by permission of NGS/National Geographic Stock.

Pew Research Center

034 Data on teen text messaging and teen cell phone ownership from the Pew Research Center from WWW.PEWRESEARCH.ORG

Photographs

Photo locators denoted as follows: Top (T), Center (C), Bottom (B), Left (L), Right (R), Background (Bkgd)

002 (TR) AndreAnita/Shutterstock , (BR) David R. Frazier Photolibrary, Inc./Alamy; **003** Fritz Polking/The Image Works; **070** Hemera Technologies/Alamy; **074** AndreAnita/Shutterstock; **016** (BL) David R. Frazier Photolibrary, Inc./Alamy, (BR) David Kleyn/Alamy; **034** (BL) iStockphoto/Thinkstock, (BCL) Milosluz/Fotolia, (BCR) Marco Desscouleurs/Fotolia, (CR) SP-PIC/Fotolia; **056** Alberto Paredes/Alamy; **057** Hemera Technologies/Alamy.